# Phonological Theory: *The Essential Readings*

In memory of
James D. McCawley
1938–1999

# Phonological Theory

*The Essential Readings*

## John A. Goldsmith

University of Chicago

BLACKWELL *Publishers*

First published 1999

2 4 6 8 10 9 7 5 3 1

Blackwell Publishers Inc.
350 Main Street
Malden, Massachusetts 02148
USA

Blackwell Publishers Ltd
108 Cowley Road
Oxford OX4 1JF
UK

*Library of Congress Cataloging-in-Publication Data*

Phonological theory: the essential readings / [edited by] John A. Goldsmith.
p.    cm.
Includes bibliographical references and index.
ISBN 0–631–20469–5 (hardbound: alk. paper). — ISBN 0–631–20470–9
(pbk.: alk. paper)
1. Grammar, Comparative and general—Phonology. I. Goldsmith, John A.
P217.P486   1999
414—dc21                                                                98–54654
CIP

*British Library Cataloguing in Publication Data*

A CIP catalogue record for this book is available from the British Library.

Typeset in 10½ on 12½ pt Ehrhardt
by Graphicraft Limited, Hong Kong
Printed in Great Britain by TJ International Ltd, Padstow, Cornwall

This book is printed on acid-free paper.

# Contents

# Acknowledgments

The publisher and editor wish to thank the following for permission to reprint copyright material in this book:

Michael K. Brame for "The Cycle in Phonology: Stress in Palestinian, Maltese, and Spanish," in *Linguistic Inquiry*, 5/1 (Winter 1974), © 1974 by Michael K. Brame.

Cambridge University Press for selections from "Syllables," by E. C. Fudge, from *Journal of Linguistics*, 5 (1969); for selections from "The Geometry of Phonological Features," by G. N. Clements, in *Phonology*, 2 (1985).

N. Chomsky, M. Halle, and MIT Press for "Phonetic and Phonological Representation," in *The Sound Pattern of English* (Harper & Row, 1968).

Mouton de Gruyter for selections from "From Cyclic Phonology to Lexical Phonology," by Paul Kiparsky, in *The Structure of Phonological Representations*, vol. 1, ed. H. van der Hulst and N. Smith (Dordrecht: Foris Publications).

John Goldsmith for selections from "An Overview of Autosegmental Phonology," in *Linguistic Analysis*, 2/1 (1976), © American Elsevier Publishing Company, Inc., 1976.

Bruce Hayes and the Linguistic Society of America for selections from "Inalterability in CV Phonology," in *Language*, 62/2 (1986).

John McCarthy and Alan S. Prince for selections from "Prosodic Morphology," in *Rutgers Center for Cognitive Science Technical Report*, 32 (1996).

John McCarthy, Alan S. Prince, and Kluwer Academic Publishers for selections from "Generalized Alignment," in *Yearbook of Morphology* (1993), ed. Geert Booij and Jaap van Marle, © 1993 Kluwer Academic Publishers.

James D. McCawley for "On the Role of Notation in Generative Phonology," in *Adverbs, Vowels, and Other Objects of Wonder* (University of Chicago Press, 1979).

MIT Press for selections from *CV Phonology: A Generative Theory of the Syllable*, by G. N. Clements and S. J. Keyser (1983); for "Phonology with Tiers," by Alan S. Prince, in *Language Sound Structure*, ed. M. Aronoff and R. Oehrle (1984).

MIT Press Journals for selections from "Compensatory Lengthening in Moraic Phonology," by Bruce Hayes, in *Linguistic Inquiry*, 20/2 (Spring 1989), © 1989 by The Massachusetts Institute of Technology; for selections from "Relating to the Grid," by Alan S. Prince, in *Linguistic Inquiry*, 14/1 (Winter 1983), © 1983 by The Massachusetts Institute of Technology; for selections from "Extrametricality and English Stress," by Bruce Hayes, in *Linguistic Inquiry*, 13/2 (Spring 1982), © 1982 by The Massachusetts Institute of Technology; for selections from "A Prosodic Theory of Nonconcatenative Morphology," by John J. McCarthy, in *Linguistic Inquiry*, 12/3 (Summer 1981), ©

1981 by The Massachusetts Institute of Technology; for selections from "On Stress and Linguistic Rhythm," by Mark Liberman and Alan Prince, in *Linguistic Inquiry*, 8/2 (Spring 1977), © 1977 by The Massachusetts Institute of Technology.

David Odden and the Linguistic Society of America for selections from "On the Role of the Obligatory Contour Principle," in *Language*, 62/2 (1986).

Kenneth L. Pike, Eunice Victoria Pike, and the University of Chicago Press for selections from "Immediate Constituents of Mazateco Syllables," in *International Journal of American Linguistics*, 13 (1947).

Alan H. Sommerstein and Cambridge University Press for selections from "On Phonotactically Motivated Rules," in *Journal of Linguistics*, 10 (1974).

Elizabeth O. Selkirk and Mouton de Gruyter for selections from "The Syllable," from *The Structure of Phonological Representations*, vol. 2, ed. H. van der Hulst and N. Smith (Dordrecht: Foris Publications).

University of Chicago Press for selections from "Harmonic Phonology," by John Goldsmith, in *The Last Phonological Rule: Reflections on Constraints and Derivations*, ed. John Goldsmith (1993).

Every effort has been made to obtain permission from all copyright holders, but in some cases this has not proved possible at the time of going to press. Blackwell therefore wish to thank those authors whose work is included without full acknowledgment, and would be pleased to rectify any omissions brought to their attention at the earliest opportunity.

# Introduction

## John Goldsmith

## 1  Preface

This collection of papers is not *all* you need to have read from the phonological literature over the past 30 years to be a phonologist – certainly not – but it contains a sizable part of the literature from that period which is essential to understanding why phonological theory is where it is today. These are not papers selected simply for their historical interest, for if historical significance had been the major criterion for selection, the reader would have found here many more papers that explored issues that once seemed important but which in the end turned out to be dead ends. These papers are rather of relevance and interest today – despite, in the case of many of them, their age. Virtually all of them are available only in xeroxed form to most people who have entered the field in the last few years.

There is another fact about these papers which I came to appreciate upon gathering them together: there is not one of them which does not shine brightly in comparison to the way that they have been summarized and handed down in secondary sources – especially in textbooks. An intellectual pleasure awaits the student or scholar who understands in rough outline the concepts explored in the pages ahead, because the descriptions that will be found here are reports from early and original explorers, not travel guides written for vacation travelers. Using this book as a supplement to a text-book in a basic course on phonological theory, or as the course book in a more advanced course, should make a splendid read for students and teacher alike. Readers who wish to find more details about current positions in phonological theory are encouraged to refer to *The Handbook of Phonological Theory* (Goldsmith 1995).

Martin Joos published a collection of papers four decades ago that brought together the major papers of American studies on phonemic analysis (Joos 1957). That book is still an important source book for scholars who wish to understand this era in phonological theory, and in abridged form, Joos's book has recently reappeared on the market. Some years later, a collection of papers with a more catholic point of view was published (Makkai 1972), covering not only American structuralism, but some early generative papers, as well as a number of European perspectives.

The present volume deals exclusively with the most influential themes in mainstream American phonological theory – though that description should not hide the fact that this tradition is now vigorously pursued on several other continents. In certain respects, it has its roots in, and has grown out of, the generative phonology of Chomsky and

Halle (1968, known widely as *SPE*). I will refer to the tradition inspired immediately by *SPE* as *classical generative phonology*, but the subsequent tradition that has in a sense carried the baton since the mid-1970s has no good name, though from time to time labels such as "nonlinear phonology" or "post-*SPE* phonology" have been tried out. Perhaps "post-generative phonology" is as good a title as can be invented, though the term leaves open just what the relationship is between generative and post-generative phonology. It is also true that this post-generative tradition has incorporated insights and analyses from earlier approaches and from competing approaches. For example, Firthian (also known as *prosodic*) analysis is the best-known phonological theory developed in England, and a good case can be made that its insights directly contributed to the birth of autosegmental phonology.[1] But while cross-tradition fertilization happens occasionally, it is within the tradition that is covered in this book that the greatest amount of exploration and the highest level of simple energy is found. I have included a brief excerpt from *The Sound Pattern of English*, in which the authors summarize the most important of the positions defended in that book.

Deciding what papers to include – and then what *portions* of these papers, for very few papers appear in their full, uncut entirety – has been a challenge, much like packing a single suitcase with everything one will need for six months. Initially I considered all the papers I had ever assigned as reading in a phonology course and all the papers cited in Blackwell's *Handbook of Phonological Theory* (1995), and I asked a number of professional colleagues for their suggestions. Our doctoral students at the University of Chicago often prepare excellent lists of papers on which they expect to be tested, but all these cases involve lists of 5,000 pages, or more, of published work in phonology. How, then, to pare down from there to achieve a book under 500 pages in length?

Many of the finest papers in phonological theory do not directly address phonological theory *per se*, but rather develop original analyses of data from particular languages. In many cases, these analyses have been so impressive that they immediately signaled other linguists, who in turn looked to see if the languages they knew could be more insightfully analyzed along the lines of such ideas.[2] It could be argued that these exemplars of insightful analysis constitute the most important way in which theory is modified and improved and is passed on from one scholar to another; indeed, *this* is the core sense of the term *paradigm* in the first edition of Thomas Kuhn's extraordinarily influential *The Structure of Scientific Revolutions* (1962). But most papers of this sort were simply too long for the present collection. Phonological theory attempts to distill the insights of such papers into compact statements, and it was to such papers that I have attempted to restrict myself. Minor infractions of this rule will be found here, nonetheless, where space limitations permitted, such as Brame's cyclic analysis of Arabic stress and McCarthy's analysis of Arabic consonantism. But as a principle, I applied it: the presumption that papers which primarily presented analyses of particular languages were to be excluded. Perhaps someday a companion volume including those papers can be published.

Another criterion came into play, one that I have already alluded to. I have selected only papers that are directly relevant to issues of concern today. There is little discussion to be found, for example, of rule ordering, despite the fact that this was a major focus of interest in phonological theory during the heyday of generative phonology, the late 1960s and early 1970s. That issue is no longer one of direct interest to phonologists, though much that came to light in those discussions still merits our attention today. But we have libraries for a reason, and the present book is not intended to make libraries less important places to spend one's time.

On the other hand, this book is not just another collection of papers on current phonological theory, or even a comprehensive view of the theory, such as is offered by *The Handbook of Phonological Theory* (Goldsmith 1995). I hesitated before including items that were too easily accessible.

## 2   The Theoretical Framework

The papers that follow represent a homogeneous theoretical tradition, I would say – but homogeneous, one might well ask, compared to what? What is the yardstick for measurement? Let us initially think of classical generative phonology and post-generative phonology as forming a single point of view, one which we may contrast with what preceded it; we can return below to the themes that separated the classical generative model from those that appear more prominently in this collection.

One way to detect the common core of agreement that unites classical generative and post-generative phonology is to look at the literature in phonological theory a decade or so before the appearance of *The Sound Pattern of English* in 1968. An excellent state-ment of the vision of that period is Charles Hockett's *A Manual of Phonology* (1955), and I have briefly discussed in Goldsmith 1990 some of the ways in which it adum-brated contemporary work on feature geometry and autosegmental phonology. But for all that it points ahead to ideas later developed, there are a number of ways in which it stands apart from the approach that is found uniformly in the next generation's style of phonology: for example, the excitement about the prospect of using probability and information theory to bring linguistics into the modern era; the importance (I might even say, the *fascination*) of displaying inventories of various items in different lan-guages (an echoing of that same fascination in Troubetzkoy's *Grundzüge* (1939)); and a theoretical concern within phonological theory for the status of speakers' judgments.[3] None of these seems to play an important role in the phonological theory developed in the present papers.

To be sure, Hockett's themes develop organically out of the structuralist tradition which dominated American linguistics in the decades preceding the publication of his *Manual*. As Durand and Laks (1996) have observed recently, it would be no exaggera-tion to say that during the structuralist era, the unity of the entirety of linguistics, not just of phonological theory, was maintained by the perception that *the analysis of speech sounds in a language into a structure of phonemes was the most important contribution of modern linguistics, and it was what linguists did best.* Workers in the discipline felt that when linguistics was ready to advance from the treatment of sounds to the treatment of word structure, it would be by extending phonemic analysis to morphology, and when it was ready to advance to sentence structure, it would be by extending phonemic analysis to syntax.

That vision is not shared in the generative and post-generative work contained in this book.[4] Phonemic analysis is dismissed for three sorts of reasons: first, the grouping of sounds on grounds that are purely phonetic is simply presumed and taken for granted (one might say that from a structuralist's point of view, the real work carried out now is morphophonological); second, as in Firthian linguistics, if a phonological problem arises that is interesting, and if we find it mixes contrastive and noncontrastive aspects of language, we proceed with a generative analysis nonetheless (that was the point of Halle's celebrated argument against the phonemic level) – the concern about mixing contrastive and noncontrastive elements of the phonological is simply not a serious one; and third, the shift to a cognitive paradigm – from a passive, Humean view of mental life to an active, Kantian view – made adherence to strict phonemics seem pointless. Let's consider these points in turn briefly.

Many structuralist observers of generative phonology remarked early on that the research done in generative phonology had a counterpart in structuralist analysis, but there it was called *morphophonology*, and it was held to be distinct from phonology in a strict sense. Both structuralist and generativists were interested in accounting for phonological differences that might be found in the inflectional paradigm of a verb, for example; but if the modifications in the phonological form of the stems (for example) were not the results of rules that held uniformly throughout the language, the structuralist would deem the analysis to be part of morphophonology rather than phonology. Generative phonology, more often than not, adopted sets of data of this sort as its prototypical target of analysis and called it phonological. Those parts of the phonology that were subphonemic, or allophonic, were frequently not discussed, and in any event, it was typically the case that phonetic variation that was truly allophonic would shed little light on anything of immediate concern to generative phonology (with the possible exception of the question of the nature of phonological features).

There was a second exception as well: generative as well as post-generative phonologists shared with Firthian analysts the view that it was, and still is, their right to deal with *all* phonological changes – alternations in a broad sense – even if that means combining contrastive ("morphophonemic") and noncontrastive ("allophonic") differences in a single analysis. This freedom has been challenged to some degree by the tenets of lexical phonology (see chapter 3), but it is important to note that it was this freedom of analysis that was demanded by Morris Halle's influential critique of phonemic analysis. In more contemporary terms, it is perfectly reasonable to explain surface generalizations on the basis of phonological material not present on the surface, a move which utterly conflates contrastive and allophonic differences. For example, in most languages – even in English – a High tone is lower in pitch than a preceding High tone if a Low tone intervenes. In many tone languages, a High tone may be shifted lower in pitch than an *immediately* preceding High tone, an effect called "downstep," and most cases of downstep are today analyzed as being the result of a floating Low tone – combined with the belief that the High tone whose pitch is lowered will undergo those lowering effects regardless of whether the effects are "contrastive" (in the case where the Low tone is covert = downstep) or "allophonic" (in the case where the Low tone is overtly realized = downdrift). Indeed, this perspective is so deeply embedded in generative and post-generative phonology that the normal way to argue for an *abstract* phonological analysis is to show that there is "independent," surface-motivated evidence for each rule in the analysis.[5]

But from a wider perspective, the most important reason that post-structuralist phonology no longer shares the belief that there is a gulf between allophonic and contrastive differences derives from the shift in the conception of mind, a shift that has been felt throughout the human sciences. There has always been a tension between two ways of understanding linguistics: on one view, the goal of linguistics is a systematic analysis of linguistic data, and the principles governing how those data are obtained and analyzed are parallel to the ways in which data are analyzed in other sciences. Language, on this view (which was dominant in the first part of this century), has a structure that can be explored independently of any efforts to figure out what particular speakers may do or think; this perspective is particularly attractive if one has relatively little confidence in our ability to peer, in any serious sense, into speakers' heads. On the other view of linguistics (a view that has come to be relatively dominant in the past several decades), the goal of linguistics is to model what it is that goes on inside a speaker's head, and data regarding language use are employed in relatively indirect ways in reaching this goal. It is probably fair to observe that most linguists hold to both views most of the time, hoping that in the long run the two perspectives will not prove to be inconsistent one with the other. Structuralist phonology was built upon a model of perception in which language learning (or at least the phonological part of language learning) meant tuning one's nervous system so that it would respond to some differences and *not* respond to other differences: tuning in to the categories of perception. The pendulum has shifted radically to the opposite, activist extreme, the view that the mind effortlessly creates a range of possible percepts and categories, and that a person's subjective perception is based on an unconscious selection of the percept that best matches the sensory input. On such a view, listening is a complex form of generation! – and once again, there is no gain from (and indeed, much lost by) separating contrastive and allophonic effects.

Thus a considerable sea-change occurred in the passage from structuralist to generative and post-generative phonology. And in the post-*SPE* papers contained in this book, other issues are joined which separate them from the period of classical generative phonology, most notably the question as to the correct geometrical representations for phonological theory and what kind of active principles should determine the relationship between underlying form and surface form. Most of the contributions in this volume address the question of geometrical representation directly, in the pursuit of autosegmental structure, metrical structure, and syllable structure. At the same time, a considerable effort is made to integrate into phonological theory the insights from other phonological traditions, and to find a place for all the major themes of phonological scholarship in this century.

## 3   The Selections

The first item is a short selection from Chomsky and Halle's *The Sound Pattern of English*, the massive, encyclopedic work whose assumptions and points of view influence in one fashion or other most of the papers in the book. The unprepared reader may be put off (or even alarmed!) by this brief passage: it is not simple to read, and it assumes that the reader has a basic familiarity with classical generative phonology – but it has the virtue of quickly getting down to brass tacks.

In the few pages reprinted here, Chomsky and Halle summarize many of the important principles that lie behind their work. A phonological representation is composed of a sequence of units, each of which specifies the values for a universally fixed set of features (and these values can only be + and −). The phonological representation is the concatenation of the underlying representations of various morphemes in the language. The underlying representation of each individual morpheme is not a surface representation: our long-term representation of an item, so to speak, is not merely a dimmed memory of a sound once heard, for three reasons: postulating that we remember *all* the phonetic renditions of a morpheme is implausible; postulating that we remember just *one* phonetic rendition forces us to make a unjustifiably arbitrary choice among the set of phonetic renditions; and, finally, phonological generalizations often require access to information that is not present in the surface representation.[6] The *phonetic features* that describe (in a continuous, not a binary, fashion) the ways sounds are realized are the same set of features used to mark contrasts at an underlying level, though only two values may play a role in underlying representation (+ and −, as the values are traditionally called). There will thus be discrepancies between the underlying and the surface representations in the descriptions of *all* languages; and we will choose as our best description of English (or French, Turkish, etc.) that description which most compactly describes the realizations of *all* of the words of the language.

Of course, linguists will want to work on more languages than one, and the linguistic theory that they employ must be the *same* across languages – if not, it does not make any sense to postulate that the most compact description of a language is the best one, since it is not hard to handcraft a theory in order to make a particular analysis look compact. But suppose we choose a half-dozen unrelated languages as our test-bed (or some other number of languages that is not too small). If we have two or more competitors among theories, then we must do the following to choose among them: for each theory, we must find the *best* analysis of each of the languages permitted by the theory. Then the best theory (and the one that we, as rational scientists, should accept) is the one for which the sum total of the "complexity" or *length* of the grammars is the least (that is, for which the summed "value" of the grammars is the greatest).[7]

The complexity of the phonological grammars will be in the first instance *increased* by the inclusion of phonological rules, but that "cost" will be offset by the total decrease in complexity which those rules permit, either in reducing the number of feature specifications underlyingly, or simply in the total *count* of underlying representations. Indeed, it may fairly be said that the governing watchword of classical generative phonology is: *Minimize allomorphy!* That is, if it is at all possible, postulate a single phonological representation underlyingly for each morpheme, and account for all other phonetic variation by means of phonological rules.

It remains only for us to discuss the crucial notion of *notational conventions* in Chomsky and Halle's view of phonological theory, a notion that is taken up again in detail in McCawley's paper (chapter 2). Let us imagine Phonological Theory in this way: it is a large computer that has been mass-produced so that every child is given one at birth. It mimics what children are doing inside their heads. It has a microphone for its input and various sophisticated devices to produce sounds as its output. It contains digital signal processing chips set up in such a way that at the level of sound production and of signal input the various features take on a large range of values. But through some fabulous design feature, Phonological Theory is able to compress the complexities of the language it is learning to a small number of binary features, and after a minimal amount of training, it can produce compact representations of utterances in binary format and can also generate an utterance in real time, given a representation in binary format.

At first, it keeps track of all the utterances it is exposed to. Soon, however, memory limitations get in the way, and it becomes necessary to economize. The engineers responsible for this Phonological Theory have designed it so that very detailed rules will emerge automatically which relate allomorphs (that is, variant pronunciations of a given morpheme) or permit the system to eliminate feature information from long-term storage. This rule component eases the memory bottleneck for a while. It quickly turned out, however, that these *rules*, in turn, could become too numerous and hence a drag on memory and computational resources. Hence an even *higher* level of organization has been designed by a smaller group of engineers, one that can summarize (or "compress") large sets of rules into simpler generalizations that are called *rule schemas* (or *rule schemata*), after which the rules themselves can be eliminated from long-term memory. It is the set of *abbreviatory conventions* which describe in detail how the rule schemas arise as abbreviated statements of sets of rules. It is these rule schemas that are the so-called rules of classical generative phonology, and it is the work of this second group that constituted the real work of phonological theorists, on the *SPE* account.

James McCawley's "On the Role of Notation in Generative Phonology" (chapter 2) discusses a range of questions in detail, including the notion of abbreviatory conventions in generative phonology, arguing that in some respects the rule schemas of *SPE* are both fundamental and real, more so than the rules that they are supposed to abbreviate. McCawley also adumbrates certain characteristics of feature geometry (see chapter 11 below), such as the commitment to viewing each phonological rule as producing *one* change, even if this means that one segment assimilates to another with respect to two features: somehow it should be possible (as we will see eventually that it is) that assimilations involving certain classes of phonological features constitute single phonological operations.

"From Cyclic Phonology to Lexical Phonology," by Paul Kiparsky (chapter 3), has been excerpted from a longer paper (Kiparsky 1982). The framework developed there has something to say about a large number of classic questions in phonology, but none more centrally than the objection to generative phonology to the effect it had erred in its decision to allow large numbers of irregular phonological patterns to be viewed as regular, automatic phonological rules. Phonologists no longer require phonological rules to be statable in terms of segments present on the surface; but they do expect them to work by and large automatically, which means that they should not be explicitly marked to apply to specific morphemes. Lexical phonology undertook to show that if we think of the morphology as successively introducing morphemes throughout the phonological derivation, the form of phonological rules could be simplified, and many rules could be written in a form that allowed them to apply automatically.

Kiparsky's paper integrated a large number of theoretical proposals by a number of linguists during the 1970s and brought back into the consciousness of phonologists the distinction that in an earlier era would have been called the distinction between morphophonemic and phonetic rules and would henceforth be called the distinction between lexical and post-lexical rules. No influence on Kiparsky's lexical phonology was greater than that of David Stampe's natural phonology (Stampe 1972), developed in the late 1960s at the University of Chicago, a framework that highlighted the difference between *phonological rules*, which could in principle be overridden within a language, and *processes*, which could not – corresponding roughly to lexical and post-lexical rules in the later terms of lexical phonology, and also corresponding in a rough way to morphophonemic and allophonic rules, respectively.

Now, in the context of structuralist phonology, rules of allophony typically determine the particular phone that will be used to realize a phoneme, given the sounds that appear on either side, and it is of no concern whether those sounds are in the same morpheme or in a neighboring morpheme. On the other hand, a morphophonemic rule is much more likely to find its domain of application limited to the edge of a morpheme, as when /k/ is replaced by /s/ in the alternation *politi[k]/politi[s]ize*, a change known traditionally as *velar softening*. Morphophonemic rules *sometimes* occur far from the edge of a morpheme, but more often than not they do not; rules of allophony, on the other hand, apply in a fashion quite heedless of the location of any morpheme boundaries. But the alternation of /k/ with /s/ occurs *only* when a suffix immediately follows – and even then, only with certain suffixes (*take*, for example, does not see its /k/ change when the suffix *-ing* is added).

These observations are of significance when we reflect on the fact noted above that lexical phonology is a major effort to defend the notion that phonology applies in an automatic fashion. "Automatic" here means that rules themselves bear no explicit marking to show what affixes trigger it. Kiparsky's initial proposal was that rule application be divided into *lexical* and *post-lexical* application and that (as a first approximation) lexical application be limited to those cases where the application in question involved material that was *derived* – that is, was different from what appeared in the underlying representation. This had the result that in the vast majority of cases where it might appear that a lexical rule's conditions had been satisfied inside a morpheme (such as in the case of velar softening alluded to above – a /k/ appearing before an /i/ inside a morpheme such as *king*), the rule would correctly not apply. Rules of the post-lexical phonology, however, were not limited in this way; only lexical rules were constrained to apply in *derived contexts*. Mascaró (1976) had argued that the rules that were so constrained were the set of *cyclic* phonological rules, and Kiparsky adopted and developed this point of view, proposing (in the earliest model of lexical phonology) that all lexical rules were necessarily *cyclic* as well.

During the period in which these ideas were developing – roughly the 1970s – the cycle was a notion that was more at home in syntax than it was in phonology. Chomsky had proposed the cycle in syntax (Chomsky 1965), pursuing an earlier observation by Fillmore (1963). Ross's extremely influential dissertation (1967) attempted to develop a theoretical explanation for a range of differences between the properties of various syntactic rules in a large number of languages, and linguists such as Ross, George Lakoff, Paul Postal, and David Perlmutter soon argued that deeper explanations of the differences between rule types could be obtained by distinguishing between those rules which were cyclic and those which were post-cyclic. Roughly speaking, prototypical cyclic rules were those which modified the grammatical relation of a noun phrase to other lexical elements, principally to verbs, such as in the case of passive formations, while post-lexical rules involved such "long-distance" constructions as question formation and relative-clause formation. Much controversy raged during the 1970s as those following Chomsky (1973) tried to show that there were no systematic differences to be explained by such a theoretical distinction, while others pursued and deepened the role of the contrast between cyclic and post-cyclic rules. Thus, while the notion of cyclic rule application in phonology had its roots in developments in syntax, by the end of the 1970s it had very much taken on a life of its own.

As we have seen, developments in lexical phonology in the 1980s defended the notion that building the cyclic/non-cyclic distinction into the theory in a fundamental way was an important way to deepen our understanding of phonological systems. But various conceptions of the cycle and alternative ways to understand the phonological effects dealt with in this way continue to play significant roles in the ongoing development of phonological theory.

Michael Brame's "The Cycle in Phonology" (chapter 4) contains arguments that are replayed with little change today. Brame's study focused on an understanding of cyclicity different from that developed in lexical phonology (see Cole 1995 for a general discussion). It is helpful to bear in mind that two different notions have been associated with the term *cyclic*. In one case (associated with the contrast discussed in *SPE* between the words *condensation* and *compensation*), the phonology of a morphologically complex word is explained by virtue of its relation to the phonology of its morphological base – that is, the word from which it is formed by affixation. If *condensation* has more stress on its second syllable than *compensation* does, this could be argued to be the result of the stress pattern assigned to the second syllable of *condense*, given that the base of *compensation* (which is *compensate*) has no stress on its second syllable. Cyclicity in this sense means that phonological effects on a complex word appear which are motivated for a subpart of the word, and which would have appeared (so to speak) on the subpart if that word appeared as a free-standing word. This conception of cyclicity is quite different from the type of cyclicity discussed in connection with the preceding paper (chapter 3).

Sommerstein's "On Phonotactically Motivated Rules" (chapter 5) was an early discussion of weaknesses of a derivational approach that appears very prescient today. He argued that generalizations regarding surface patterns in Latin phonology are important phonologically, but missed in two ways by classical generative treatments: surface generalizations may emerge from the effects of two or more rules (and hence be a generalization larger in scope than a single rule, a possibility for which there is no provision in classical generative phonology), and it may be the case that generative rules can be significantly simplified if we think of them as being triggered by the need to satisfy some positive surface condition. (Classical generative rules of the form $A \rightarrow B \: / \: C \_\_ D$ which actually change a feature-value can often be understood as being related to a surface constraint against *CAD, but it is not quite as straightforward to rethink a classical generative rule whose effect is to satisfy a positive constraint.)

In the excerpts from my paper "Harmonic Phonology" presented here (chapter 6), I review two fundamental issues: (1) the relationship between the notion of derivation and of levels in phonology, and (2) the notion of "harmonic rule application." The central idea is to move past thinking of constraints as absolute conditions or filters and to think of them rather as graded means of understanding how well, or poorly, a given representation is built. (We will see some of the origins of this notion in chapter 8 below) In particular, the notion of harmonic rule application presumes that we can speak of the relative well-formedness of any two representations;[8] for a rule to apply in a harmonic fashion means that it applies just in case its output is better formed than its input. The term *harmonic* is an allusion to "harmony theory,"[9] a machine-learning approach which quite remarkably computes a fully explicit well-formedness measure when simply presented with a sample of data.

"Generalized Alignment," by John McCarthy and Alan Prince (chapter 7), is an early exploration in the framework of Optimality Theory (OT). Part of its goal is to review a number of familiar typological patterns – of stress systems, for example – which have been treated in other frameworks, and to illustrate how OT's mechanisms allow for a simple statement of these patterns. The core of OT, as presented here, is a hierarchy of surface constraints ranked in an absolute way, in the sense that to compare the relative well-formedness of two representations, one need merely look at the highest-ranked constraint for which the two representations score differently: the one which better satisfies that constraint *is* better-formed, regardless of how poorly it fares with respect to any or all of the constraints ranked lower.

In the version of OT presented in this paper, the discrepancies (or "distance," we might also say) between the underlying and the surface form is formally analyzed by using a set of constraints on the surface representation, and by appending a formal tag, so to speak, on all features where there is a difference between its specification on the surface and its specification underlyingly. Each feature on the surface that has been "inserted" (that is, which is not present at the underlying representation) and each one that has been deleted (that is, one for which a phonetically null "trace" of the superficially absent segment appears in the surface form) are given additional markings showing that they have been inserted or deleted. Constraints on the costs of such formal devices allow one to use the constraint hierarchy to indicate when deletion and insertion will be employed in a language's phonology.

In more recent work in OT, "faithfulness" constraints have explicitly put conditions on what discrepancies may appear between representations at distinct levels (such as underlying and surface levels) and have analyzed these conditions as constraints which appear in the general ranking of constraints within the language.[10]

My paper "An Overview of Autosegmental Phonology" (chapter 8) proposed a new perspective on a number of problems in phonology, one of which focused on the geometrical properties of representations. As the paper illustrates, much of the early work along these lines involved studies of tone languages, especially African tone languages. I worked primarily on the tonal system of Igbo, a Niger–Congo language of Nigeria, and the intonational system of English, both discussed in this selection. There was a significant literature on African tonal systems created through the late 1970s and 1980s following up on the African side, and Janet Pierrehumbert developed in her (1980) dissertation a rich theory of English intonation based on the discussion in this paper and in Liberman (1975).

From a theoretical point of view, two major points were made here: first, that the simplicity of an analysis (hence, its general desirability[11]) is much more transparent and straightforward when we utilize tier-based autosegmental representations; and second, that a significant part of the dynamic of the work of phonological analysis could be handled by what I called "the well-formedness condition" (WFC), which could add or delete association lines, yet was not a rule *per se*. The well-formedness condition would add or delete association lines if the effect of that change was to improve the well-formedness of the resulting (surface) representation – the origin of the notion of harmonic rule application, discussed above (chapter 6).

John McCarthy's "A Prosodic Theory of Nonconcatenative Morphology" (chapter 9) established the importance of Semitic studies for mainstream phonological theory in the 1980s and 1990s. In a number of patterns in Semitic languages, vowels and consonants in the same word correspond to independent morphemes, and grammatical categories are realized by modifications of the syllable (or, more generally, prosodic) structure of a word. Now, there are several ways of expressing what McCarthy accomplished in this paper. From one perspective, he provided a fashion of reconceptualizing what had seemed like a very exotic pattern in Semitic languages, using autosegmental structure. From another perspective – and one that would be the seed leading to prosodic morphology (see below) – McCarthy showed that much of the complexity of the *morphology* employed the full mechanisms of *phonology* as it is played out. In most discussions of the interaction of morphology and phonology, the emphasis has been on the effects of morphological structure on phonology; now the tables have been turned, and we can begin to speak of a reconsideration of morphology in the light of what we know of phonology. We will return to this in chapter 13 below.

G. N. Clements and S. J. Keyser's *CV phonology*, excerpted here (chapter 10), makes a strong case for extending autosegmental structure to the familiar turf of segmental phonology – that is, the phonology of vowels and consonants. They argue that most of the behavior of tones that motivated autosegmental representation find their counterparts in segmental behavior, if one looks carefully, and they argue that it is equally important to organize phonological segments and information into syllables.

G. N. Clements's "The Geometry of Phonological Features" (chapter 11), along with work by K. P. Mohanan, Joan Mascaró, and Elizabeth Sagey, stimulated a good deal of work that developed a universal organization of phonological features. On this model, each feature is represented on a distinct autosegmental tier, and the features are themselves organized hierarchically in a tree structure. Nonterminal nodes in such a tree dominate entire sets of features and reside on higher-level autosegmental tiers; these are called *class nodes*. The addition of association lines linking class nodes on one segment to a still higher class node on a neighboring segment is the formal expression of the simultaneous assimilation of several features (all the features dominated by that class node); by limiting assimilation rules to such processes, phonologists have been able to develop a constrained and predictive theory of possible assimilation rules.

Bruce Hayes's "Inalterability in CV Phonology" (chapter 12), along with a paper that appeared at the same time by Schein and Steriade (1986), constituted the first in-depth study of an abstract phonological problem in the context of a *non*-prosodic system using the autosegmental model developed by McCarthy (see chapter 9). Geminate segments (also called *long* consonants or vowels) often fail to undergo rules that we would otherwise expect them to be subject to. Why is this? Hayes's paper explores a wide range of rules and proposes an answer to the more general question.

"Prosodic Morphology (1986)," by John McCarthy and Alan Prince (chapter 13), is excerpted from a long paper that was widely circulated in the late 1980s but never published. From its authors' point of view, it has been superseded by a book-length study with a similar title (*Prosodic Morphology I: Constraint Interaction and Satisfaction*) dating from 1993, covering similar material from the perspective of optimality theory. The manuscript treated for the first time in an extended discussion a range of topics which were equally phonological and morphological, such as reduplication and the role of syllable weight in reduplication, templatic morphology of the famous Semitic sort, infixation, and word minimality (the notion that phonological rules are sensitive to the need for words not to be too short). The authors have recently reviewed this manuscript and added a number of comments and references dealing with additional work of theirs and others that bears on the proposals made in the 1986 manuscript.

David Odden's "On the Role of the Obligatory Contour Principle in Phonological Theory" (chapter 14) addresses an important issue in autosegmental analysis. Autosegmental representation emphasizes the important role that is played in phonology by *multiple association*: a single segment – a High tone, for example, or a consonant – can be linked to two positions, creating a sequence of two vowels on a high pitch, or a geminate consonant. But, one might wonder, what about the possibility of *two* High tones in the same position: if we *hear* someone say *múntú* with a High on both syllables, should we analyze it as a single High tone linked to both syllables or as two High tones, one on each syllable? Or do we have the freedom to decide on some other grounds how to analyze it? We might even ask: Is the fact that the theory apparently gives us the freedom to analyze an utterance in several ways of concern to us?

In Goldsmith 1976, I formulated and considered within an autosegmental context a principle dubbed the "Obligatory Contour Principle," one which would have as its effect to unambiguously choose multiple association rather than repetition of an autosegment; but I there argued against the validity of this position.[12] Odden takes this issue up again, and develops a nuanced analysis of the problem against the background analysis of data from several languages. In the years since, the issue has been engaged several times in different contexts,[13] and it remains an open one today.

Alan Prince's "Phonology with Tiers" (chapter 15) is notable for several features, including the observation at the end that many languages permit a striking kind of syllable structure, one where a coda obstruent is permitted only if that obstruent is the first part of a geminate consonant. This important observation has been developed by a number of linguists and has had rich consequences.

"Immediate Constituents of Mazateco Syllables" by Kenneth and Eunice Pike (chapter 16) is the oldest paper in this collection, and it is an article remarkably ahead of its time. One important point to take away from reading it is that it is consciously framed as an argument that the theory of constituent structure in syntactic analysis can be profitably transferred to the study of syllable structure.[14] Its explicit focus on structure and the careful arguments, such as that based on the relationship between tone assignment and syllable structure, put it squarely on a par by any generation's standards with the later highly influential papers by Fudge, Selkirk, Clements and Keyser, and others. Kenneth Pike has observed[15] that the critical observation in arriving at this picture was the difference that he observed between Mixtec and Mazatec: in Mixtec, timing was sensitive to individual vowels (and tones), while in Mazatec, no such sensitivity was found; what was critical was to think in terms of large groupings, what amounted to the syllable. It should be noted that Kenneth Pike's work and that of his collaborators in the years since this paper have developed ideas regarding structure in phonology that have had a significant impact on how phonological structure is best viewed.

Elisabeth Selkirk's "The Syllable" (chapter 17) offered a detailed study of syllabi-fication in English, arguing that the syllable was necessary for the most general and explanatory statement of phonotactics and productive rules in English phonology, and that phonological structure was equally necessary *below* the level of the syllable and *above* that level as well, a view that has been explored for a range of languages in the years since.

"Compensatory Lengthening in Moraic Phonology," by Bruce Hayes (chapter 18) addresses the issue of vowel length in a nonlinear framework. Clements and Keyser (chapter 10 above) proposed distinguishing representationally between membership in the onset (a status which allows segments to contribute little or nothing to prosody) and membership in the coda of a syllable. Hyman (1985) extended this notion, suggesting that the traditional notion of weight (Newman 1972) and moraicity could best be understood in terms of an autosegment-like unit (to be called a mora, $\mu$) which would associate with material in the rhyme but not the material in the onset. Languages that draw a distinction between light and heavy syllables do this by endowing those we call "heavy" with two $\mu$'s, and those we call "light" with one $\mu$. The present paper by Hayes was influential in establishing this perspective as an important one, by surveying a wide range of cases of compensatory lengthening and showing that many of the cases of what had seemed like strange behavior could be accounted for under this representa-tional proposal for the treatment of moras.

Erik Fudge's "Syllables" (chapter 19), notably published in the *Journal of Linguistics*, journal of the Linguistics Association of Great Britain, made the point succinctly and with muted rhetorical flourish that the syllable must remain an important element in the inventory of theoretical concepts in phonology, and this at a moment when the point of view presented in the recently published *Sound Pattern of English* – the view that the syllable was an otiose construct and unnecessary – held considerable sway.

The excerpt included here from "On Stress and Linguistic Rhythm," by Liberman and Prince (chapter 20), is only a brief part of this lengthy paper, which deals both with the English stress system and with stress systems more generally. It presents a consider-able break with the theoretical model for English prosody presented ten years earlier in *SPE*, and the newer model, known as *metrical phonology*, was adopted by phonologists in short order. At the heart of the proposal was the notion that prosodic systems of the sort found in English were based on the prosodic constituency of an utterance and the principles that give rise to that constituency, and on the *relative* prominence of sister constituents in the utterance. These notions were quite different in kind from the feature-based tools provided by classical generative phonology, and though there was no direct connection linking the tools of autosegmental phonology and those of metrical phono-logy, it was evident that both perspectives focused on global representational issues, as opposed to featural or derivational issues, and a natural alliance was formed between these theoretical innovations.

Alan Prince's "Relating to the Grid" (chapter 21) was extremely influential in its call to reconsider what is essential and what is not in the view of metrical structure developed in earlier work on metrical phonology. Prince argued that the notion of stress clash is very important, and that too much concern with metrical constituency can be a problem for the theory if it comes at the expense of being able to focus on stress clash between adjacent syllables. He argued that the theory ought to have a simple and direct way of assigning prominence on the leftmost or rightmost element of a domain, a generalization more fundamental than one based on constituency.

Bruce Hayes's "Extrametricality and English Stress" (chapter 22) adopted the notion of an *extrametrical* constituent from Liberman and Prince (chapter 20) and showed that it is essential to the goal of developing an elegant and coherent theory of prosody that is applicable to a wide range of natural languages. In this excerpt, Hayes discusses related issues in English, Arabic, Latin, and Hopi.

## 4   A final comment to the reader

As I have noted, very few of the papers included here are reproduced in their entirety, due to my desire to include as many papers as possible in this collection. I have indicated the places where material has been left out with the standard ellipsis [ . . . ]. I have removed notes that are irrelevant to the present reprinting and have renumbered the remaining notes; but I have left numberings of headings and examples as in the originals, so in some cases successive headings and examples have gaps in the numbering. To the extent possible, I have corrected errors or anachronisms in the bibliographies of the original papers.

## Notes

The author would like to thank Bernard Laks and Richard Janda for useful discussions of these issues.

1   I myself have explored this issue in Goldsmith 1992; see also Ogden and Local 1994 for a reply, and a rejoinder in Goldsmith 1994.
2   The best-known reader on prosodic analysis (Palmer 1970) is essentially a collection of such paradigmatic papers, models of Firthian analysis.
3   Phonological theory has not yet integrated probability and information theory into its models, but the last word on the subject may well not have been heard. Andras Kornai has argued in a number of places (including Kornai 1996) that turning a deaf ear to probabilities is a very risky move. The fact of the matter is that modern science has always had a heavily instrumental bias, and if one attempts to learn from history, it is clear that success in science has virtually always gone hand in hand with prediction and, more generally, with increased control. Exceptions like astronomy are arguably more apparent than real, and Kornai argues that it should be a matter of concern that the critical step taken in the late 1980s that made speech recognition a workable technology was the development of hidden Markov models, a system that exploits observed probabilities from a training corpus and that avoids the trap of combinatorial explosion as it hypothesizes the words that were pronounced by exploiting the fact that it is internally a finite-state device: it retains at any moment only a finite number of guesses as to the identity of the segments uttered, as it scans from left to right. Considerations of this sort play no role at all in current phonological theory.
4   It should be noted that such a vision was worked out in the tagmemic tradition by Kenneth Pike.
5   It is worth bearing in mind that the shift from problems of "allophony" to a combination of "allophony" and "morphophonology," with an emphasis on "morphophonology," did not mean that the problems of allophony were either solved or easy. It remains today an unsolved problem how to pass explicitly from a complete phonetic description of an utterance in a language to a segmental description of any sort, whether phonemic or generative (or anything else). This is the problem of automatic speech recognition.

6   Naturally, these points require considerably more discussion than these brief remarks suggest.
7   See n. 10 for further discussion.
8   More generally, of the best-formed representation among a set of representations.
9   Smolensky 1986; see also related work on Boltzmann machines or Markov networks; an overview is given in Baldi and Brunak 1998.
10  We can rephrase this insight in another fashion that is independent of OT's commitment to strict hierarchical ranking of constraints. One can compute a notion of *how well* two representations line up as pairs (underlying representation, surface representation), focusing not on whether these two representations are well-formed at their respective levels, but on the discrepancies and the identities between the two representations. Applying this notion to harmonic phonology (see chapter 6), the best surface representation SR for a given underlying representation $UR_0$ would be the $SR_i$ for which the following quantity is a maximum: the well-formedness of $SR_i$ − distance $(UR, SR_i)$ (finding, that is, an optimal trade-off between the well-formedness of the surface form and the divergence between the surface and the underlying form).
11  While this is not the place to go fully into the question of the role of simplicity arguments in phonology and in linguistics more generally, we can make some basic observations that are relevant. Humans are generally convinced by a theory packaged together with a set of observations if three conditions hold: the theory is (in some a priori or abstract sense) simple and elegant; if the theory can be shown to explicitly predict that the observations are likely to occur; and if the observations are unexpected and surprising. There is in fact a large, flourishing discipline that studies this mathematically and computationally called *Bayesian decision theory* (it is described in many places; one accessible source is Ballard 1997). One outgrowth of this perspective is the *minimum description length* framework (Rissanen 1989; see also Ballard 1997 or, for the more adventurous, Li and Vitanyi 1993), which explores the notion of a theory being in some a priori or abstract sense simple and elegant, arguing that the number of symbols in the most compact representation of the theory is a good measure of its simplicity. There are important developments in these areas, which remain to be taken up by linguists.
12  Leben (1973) proposed something of a different sort in his analysis of Mende, where he suggests that two distinct tones (i.e., tones from different morphemes inside a single word) would be merged or conflated before the application of the rule mapping tones to syllables. Detailed studies of Bantu languages in the 1970s established that this is not correct (see, e.g., Clements' 1984 treatment of Kikuyu, where sequences of two or three Highs or Lows are frequently encountered).
13  McCarthy 1986, Yip 1988, Goldsmith 1990, and a number of works within the context of optimality theory.
14  A number of times in the early 1980s it was said in print that one of the advantages of the constituent theory of syllable structure was that it brought us to the remarkable conclusion that the structure of phonology and the structure of syntax were much more similar than we had thought. The irony, of course, is that this was by design (thanks to the Pikes) and not a *post hoc* discovery.
15  In correspondence with this writer.

# References

Baldi, Pierre and Søren Brunak. 1998. *Bioinformatics: The Machine Learning Approach*. Cambridge, Mass.: MIT Press.

Ballard, Dana. 1997. *An Introduction to Natural Computation*. Cambridge, Mass.: MIT Press.

Chomsky, Noam. 1965. *Aspects of the Theory of Syntax*. Cambridge Mass.: MIT Press.

Chomsky, Noam. 1973. Conditions on transformations. In Stephen Anderson and Paul Kiparsky (eds), *A Festschrift for Morris Halle*, New York: Holt, Rinehart and Winston, 232–86.

Chomsky, Noam and Morris Halle. 1968. *The Sound Pattern of English*. New York: Harper and Row. Repr. Cambridge, Mass.: MIT Press.

Clements, G. N. 1984. Principles of tone association in Kikuyu. In G. N. Clements and J. Goldsmith (eds), *Autosegmental Studies in Bantu Tone*, Dordrecht: Foris Publications, 281–339.

Cole, Jennifer. 1995. The cycle in phonology. In Goldsmith 1995, 70–113.

Durand, Jacques and Bernard Laks (eds) 1996. *Current Trends in Phonology: Models and Methods.* CNRS, ESRI, University of Aix-Marseille, University of Manchester, University of Oslo, Paris X.

Durand, Jacques and Bernard Laks. 1996. Introduction. In Durand and Laks 1996.

Fillmore, Charles. 1963. The position of embedding transformations in a grammar. *Word* 19: 208–31.

Goldsmith, John. 1976. Autosegmental Phonology. Ph.D. dissertation, MIT.

Goldsmith, John. 1990. *Autosegmental and Metrical Phonology*. Oxford: Basil Blackwell.

Goldsmith, John. 1992. A note on the genealogy of research traditions in modern phonology. *Journal of Linguistics* 28: 149–63.

Goldsmith, John. 1994. Disentangling autosegments: a response. *Journal of Linguistics* 30: 499–507.

Goldsmith, John (ed.). 1995. *The Handbook of Phonological Theory*. Oxford: Basil Blackwell.

Hockett, Charles. 1955. *A Manual of Phonology*. Indiana University Publications in Anthropology and Linguistics. Memoir 11 of IJAL = IJAL vol. 21, no. 4, pt 1.

Hyman, Larry. 1985. *A Theory of Phonological Weight*. Dordrecht: Foris Publications.

Joos, Martin. 1957. *Readings in Linguistics*. Washington: ACLS. Repr. Chicago: University of Chicago Press.

Kiparsky, Paul. 1982. From cyclic phonology to lexical phonology. In H. van der Hulst and N. Smith (eds), *The Structure of Phonological Representations*, vol. 1, Dordrecht: Foris Publications, 131–75.

Kornai, Andras. 1996. Analytic models in phonology. In Durand and Laks 1996, 395–417.

Kuhn, Thomas. 1962. *The Structure of Scientific Revolutions*. Chicago: University of Chicago Press.

Leben, Will. 1973. Suprasegmental Phonology. Ph.D. dissertation, MIT.

Li, Ming, and Paul Vitanyi. 1993. *An Introduction to Kolmogorov Complexity and Its Applications.* Texts and Monographs in Computer Science. New York: Springer-Verlag.

Liberman, Mark. 1975. The Intonational System of English. Ph.D. dissertation, MIT.

Makkai, Valerie Becker (ed.). 1972. *Phonological Theory: Evolution and Current Practice.* New York: Holt, Rinehart and Winston.

Mascaró, Joan. 1976. Catalan Phonology and the Phonological Cycle. Ph.D. dissertation, MIT.

McCarthy, John. 1986. OCP effects: gemination and antigemination. *Linguistic Inquiry* 17: 207–99.

McCarthy, John and Alan Prince. 1993. Prosodic Morphology I: Constraint Interaction and Satisfaction. Unpublished MS, University of Massachusetts and Rutgers University.

Newman, Paul. 1972. Syllable weight as a phonological variable. *Studies in African Linguistics* 3: 301–23.

Ogden, R. A. and J. K. Local. 1994. Disentangling autosegments from prosodies: a note on the misrepresentation of a research tradition in phonology. *Journal of Linguistics* 30: 477–98.

Palmer, F. R. 1970. *Prosodic Analysis*. Oxford: Oxford University Press.

Pierrehumbert, Janet. 1980. The Phonetics and Phonology of English Intonation. Ph.D. dissertation, MIT.

Rissanen, J. 1989. *Stochastic Complexity in Statistical Inquiry*. Singapore and River Edge, N.J.: World Scientific.

Ross, John R. 1967. Constraints on Variables in Syntax. Ph.D. dissertation, MIT.

Schein, Barry and Donca Steriade. 1986. On geminates. *Linguistic Inquiry* 17: 691–744.

Smolensky, Paul. 1986. Information processing in dynamic systems foundations of harmony theory. In David Rumelhart, James McClelland, and the PDP Research Group (eds), *Parallel Distributed Processing: Explorations in the Microstructure of Cognition*, Cambridge Mass.: MIT Press, 194–281.

Stampe, David. 1972. A Dissertation on Natural Phonology. Ph.D. dissertation, University of Chicago.

Troubetzkoy, N. 1939. *Grundzüge der Phonologie*. Trans. as Trubetzkoy, *Principles of Phonology*, Berkeley: University of California Press, 1969.

Yip, Moira. 1988. The Obligatory Contour Principle and phonological rules: a loss of identity. *Linguistic Inquiry* 19: 65–100.

# 1

# From *The Sound Pattern of English*: Phonetic and Phonological Representation (1968)

## Noam Chomsky and Morris Halle

. . . [T]he phonetic transcription is related by the rules of the phonological component to a string of formatives with labeled bracketing which represents the surface syntactic structure of the sentence. We will now examine in some detail the manner in which these formatives are represented in a linguistic description. Many of the formatives are lexical items, the "roots" or "stems" of traditional grammar. A grammar must include a list of these items, for part of a speaker's knowledge of his language consists of knowing the lexical items of the language. It is by virtue of this knowledge that the native speaker is able to distinguish an utterance in normal English from an utterance such as Carnap's "Pirots karulized elatically" or from Carroll's jabberwocky, which conform to all rules of English but are made up of items that happen not to be included in the lexicon of the language.

The representations of the individual items in the lexicon must incorporate the knowledge which makes it possible for the speaker to utilize each lexical item in grammatically correct sentences. This includes certain syntactic information which the speaker must have. For example, he must know that a particular item is a noun and that it belongs to a large number of intersecting categories such as "animate" or "inanimate," "human" or "nonhuman," "feminine" or "masculine." Since the only question of interest here is whether or not a given item belongs to the category in question, it is natural to represent this information by means of a binary notation: *cow*, for example, would be specified as [+animate, −human, +feminine]. In addition to these syntactic features, each lexical entry must contain specified features which determine the phonetic form of the item in all contexts. We shall call these the "phonological features." The phonological features cannot be chosen arbitrarily, for the phonological component would then have to include a huge number of ad hoc rules of the type

$$[+A, -B, -C, +D] \rightarrow [\text{hʌt}]$$
$$[-A, -B, -C, +D] \rightarrow [\text{rʌt}]$$
$$[-A, +B, -C, +D] \rightarrow [\text{əlíps}]$$

Moreover, if we represented lexical items by means of an arbitrary feature notation, we would be effectively prevented from expressing in the grammar the crucial fact that items which have similar phonetic shapes are subject to many of the same rules.

We might consider overcoming these difficulties by representing each lexical item in its phonetic representation. However, this solution is not open to us either, for a lexical item frequently has several phonetic shapes, depending on the context in which the item appears. If we chose to represent each lexical item by the set of its phonetic representations, we would be treating all phonetic variations as exceptions and would, in principle, be unable to express within our grammar the phonetic regularities and general phonological processes that determine phonetic form. If, on the other hand, we chose to allow only a single phonetic representation for each item, then we would have to provide some rationale for our selection. Furthermore, it is easily shown that many of the most general and deep-seated phonological processes cannot be formulated as rules that directly relate phonetic representations; rather, these processes presuppose underlying abstract forms.

We therefore can represent lexical items neither in phonetic transcription nor in an arbitrary notation totally unrelated to the elements of the phonetic transcription. What is needed is a representation that falls between these two extremes. Accordingly we propose that each item in the lexicon be represented as a two-dimensional matrix in which the columns stand for the successive units and the rows are labeled by the names of the individual phonetic features. We specifically allow the rules of the grammar to alter the matrix, by deleting or adding columns (units), by changing the specifications assigned to particular rows (features) in particular columns, or by interchanging the positions of columns. Consequently, the matrix that constitutes the phonetic transcription may differ quite radically from the representation that appeared in the lexicon. There is, however, a cost attached to such alterations, for they require the postulation of rules in the phonological component. Such rules are unnecessary in cases where the lexical representation can be accepted as the phonetic representation. In general, the more abstract the lexical representation, the greater will be the number and complexity of the phonological rules required to map it into a phonetic transcription. We therefore postulate abstract lexical entries only where this cost is more than compensated for by greater overall simplification – for example, in cases where the combination of abstract lexical entries and a set of rules permits the formulation of phonological processes of great generality that would otherwise be inexpressible.

Thus, lexical representations and a system of phonological rules are chosen in such a way as to maximize a certain property that we may call the "value" of the grammar, a property that is sometimes called "simplicity." As has been emphasized repeatedly in the literature, the concept of "simplicity" or "value" is an empirical one. There is some correct answer to the question of how lexical items are represented and what the phonological rules are. A particular notion of "value" or "simplicity" will lead to an assumption about lexical items and phonological rules which is either right or wrong, and therefore the validity of the notion must be determined on empirical grounds, exactly as in the case of every other concept of linguistic theory. It may be difficult to obtain crucial empirical evidence bearing on proposed definitions of "simplicity," but this cannot obscure the fact that it is an empirical concept that is involved, and that one can no more employ a priori arguments in determining how "value" should be defined than in determining how to define "set of distinctive features" or "grammatical transformation" or any other concept of linguistic theory.

A specific proposal as to the definition of "value" will make certain assumptions as to what constitutes a linguistically significant generalization, as to what constitutes a "regularity" of the sort that a child will use as a way of organizing the data he is confronted with in the course of language acquisition. The child is presented with certain data; he arrives at a specific grammar, with a specific representation of lexical items and a certain system of phonological rules. The relation between data and grammar is, we naturally assume, language-independent: there is no basis for supposing that individuals differ genetically in their ability to learn one rather than another natural language. Consequently, the relationship is determined by a principle of universal grammar. Specifically, the definition of "value" or "simplicity" must be part of universal grammar, and a specific proposal will be right or wrong as it does or does not play its part in accounting for the actually existing relation between data and grammar.

Summarizing, we postulate a set of lexical matrices and a system of phonological rules which jointly maximize value, in some sense which will be defined. Phonological representation in terms of lexical matrices (as modified through readjustment rules) is abstract in the sense that the phonological representation is not necessarily a submatrix of the phonetic representation. We do not, in other words, impose the conditions of linearity and invariance (see Chomsky, 1964) on the relation between phonological and phonetic representation. The indirectness of this relation must be purchased at the cost of adding rules to the grammar. Given a definition of "value," we can therefore say that the facts of pronunciation induce the representation of items in the lexicon.

Notice that the phonetic features appear in lexical entries as abstract classificatory markers with a status rather similar to that of the classificatory features that assign formatives to such categories as "noun," "verb," "transitive." Like the latter, the phonological features indicate whether or not a given lexical item belongs to a given category. In the case of the phonological matrices, these categories have the meaning "begins with a voiced stop," "contains a vowel," "ends with a strident nonback obstruent," and so on. In view of the fact that phonological features are classificatory devices, they are binary, as are all other classificatory features in the lexicon, for the natural way of indicating whether or not an item belongs to a particular category is by means of binary features. This does not mean that the phonetic features into which the phonological features are mapped must also be binary. In fact, the phonetic features are physical scales and may thus assume numerous coefficients, as determined by the rules of the phonological component. However, this fact clearly has no bearing on the binary structure of the phonological features, which, as noted, are abstract but not arbitrary categorial markers.[1]

As already noted, the phonetic representation can be thought of formally as a two-dimensional matrix in which the columns stand for consecutive units and the rows stand for individual phonetic features. The phonetic features can be characterized as physical scales describing independently controllable aspects of the speech event, such as vocalicness, nasality, voicing, glottalization. There are, therefore, as many phonetic features as there are aspects under partially independent control. It is in this sense that the totality of phonetic features can be said to represent the speech-producing capabilities of the human vocal apparatus. We shall say that the phonetic representations of two units are distinct if they differ in the coefficient assigned to at least one feature; phonetic representations of sequences of units are distinct if they contain distinct units or if they differ in the number or order of units.

At the level of phonetic representation, utterances are comparable across languages; it thus makes sense to ask whether the phonetic representation of an utterance of language $L_1$ is distinct from a phonetic representation of an utterance of a different language $L_2$. For example, an utterance containing an apical dental stop must have a different phonetic representation from an utterance that is identical except for containing a laminal dental stop in place of the apical dental stop. The representation must differ, since the distinction is determined in part by language-specific rules; it is not a case of universal free variation. An interesting example of cross-language contrasts that require a special phonetic feature is provided by the labiovelar consonants found in many African languages. In some languages, such as Yoruba, these consonants are produced with a special clicklike suction, whereas in other languages, such as Late, they are produced without this suction (Ladefoged, 1964, p. 9). Since clicklike suction is clearly an independently controllable aspect of the speech event, the data just cited establish suction as a separate phonetic feature, regardless of the fact that apparently in no language are there contrasting pairs of utterances that differ solely in this feature.

The situation is not always straightforward, however. Since phonetic features are scales which may in principle assume numerous discrete coefficients, the question may arise, under certain circumstances, whether a certain phonetic contrast is to be represented by means of a new phonetic feature or by increasing the number of coefficients that some already extant phonetic feature may be allowed to assume. The latter solution may appear especially attractive in cases where a slight redefinition of some phonetic feature would readily accommodate the proposed solution.

To summarize, the features have a phonetic function and a classificatory function. In their phonetic function, they are scales that admit a fixed number of values, and they relate to independently controllable aspects of the speech event or independent elements of perceptual representation. In their classificatory function they admit only two coefficients, and they fall together with other categories that specify the idiosyncratic properties of lexical items. The only condition that we have so far imposed on the features in their lexical, classificatory function is that lexical representations be chosen in such a way as to maximize the "value" of the lexicon and grammar, where the notion "value" is still to be defined precisely, though its general properties are clear. Apart from this, the representation of a lexical item as a feature complex may be perfectly abstract.

In a later discussion (see chapter 9 [of *Sound Pattern of English*]), we will consider significantly heavier conditions on lexical representation. There we will turn to the question of "plausible phonological rules" and, more generally, to ways in which a particular feature may or may not function in the lexicon and in the phonology. These considerations will differentiate features from one another with respect to the role that they can play in the system of rules and in lexical representation. At that point in the development of our theory, considerations beyond maximization of value will enter into the determination of lexical representations.

## Note

1  Failure to differentiate sharply between abstract phonological features and concrete phonetic scales has been one of the main reasons for the protracted and essentially fruitless debate concerning the binary character of the Jakobsonian distinctive features.

## References

Chomsky, Noam. 1964. *Current Issues in Linguistic Theory*. The Hague: Mouton.
Ladefoged, Peter. 1964. *A Phonetic Study of West African Languages*. West African Language Monographs, 1. Cambridge: Cambridge University Press.

# 2

# On the Role of Notation in Generative Phonology (1973)

## James D. McCawley

This paper is concerned with the kinds of arguments that can be given for or against notational systems in phonology. Such arguments as have been given are of three types: those relating to evaluation measures, those relating to 'insufficient power', and those relating to 'excessive power'. The classic argument relating to evaluation measures is that given by Morris Halle (1964: 337) for a feature notation rather than an alphabetic notation in phonology. Halle points out that an evaluation measure which counts feature specifications in rules written in a feature notation evaluates a rule that fronts [a] to [æ] before all front vowels as less costly than a rule that fronts [a] to [æ] before [i] and evaluates the latter rule as in turn less costly than a rule which fronts [a] to [æ] before [i, p, z] (see table 2.1). Halle claims that this is in fact the correct ordering of the 'complexity' of the rules and that there is no apparent way in which to set up an evaluation measure based on alphabetic symbols which would yield this ordering: "It is, of course, conceivable that a simplicity criterion may be formulated that yields the proper results even when segments are represented as indivisible entities. The burden of proof, however, is clearly on those who reject the view that segments are complexes of distinctive features."

An important unstated step of this argument is Halle's rejection of the alternative proposal that both rules and 'items' are represented in an alphabetic notation but the evaluation of rules is done by translating them into a feature format and counting the feature specifications in the translation. Halle rightly rejects that proposal on (I gather) the grounds that the alphabetic symbols which it involves are completely dispensable: that at the one place where he has shown it to matter whether one has a feature representation or an alphabetic notation, the feature representation is necessary. To read more into Halle's remarks than he actually says, Halle is rejecting the free use of 'secondary concepts' defined in terms of 'primary concepts': while one could take either 'feature' or 'atomic segment' as basic and define the other in terms of it, a symbol defined in terms of the 'basic' symbols is for Halle an "unofficial circumlocution . . . lacking all systematic import" (p. 336). He evidently regards his notational system not merely as a device for expressing what happens in a language but as a hypothesis as to what entities are present in linguistic competence. It is this exclusion of 'secondary concepts' from the theory which makes Halle's argument for a feature representation in rules also an argument for a feature representation for 'items'.

Table 2.1

| *Effect of the rule* | *Formulation of the rule according to notation of Chomsky and Halle 1968* |
| --- | --- |
| *a* becomes *æ* before *i, e, æ* | $\begin{bmatrix} +\text{syll} \\ +\text{low} \end{bmatrix} \rightarrow [-\text{back}]/ \underline{\quad} \begin{bmatrix} +\text{syll} \\ -\text{back} \end{bmatrix}$ |
| *a* becomes *æ* before *i* | $\begin{bmatrix} +\text{syll} \\ +\text{low} \end{bmatrix} \rightarrow [-\text{back}]/ \underline{\quad} \begin{bmatrix} +\text{syll} \\ -\text{back} \\ +\text{high} \end{bmatrix}$ |
| *a* becomes *æ* before *i, p, z* | $\begin{bmatrix} +\text{syll} \\ +\text{low} \end{bmatrix} \rightarrow [-\text{back}]/ \underline{\quad} \left\{ \begin{bmatrix} +\text{syll} \\ -\text{back} \\ +\text{high} \end{bmatrix} \begin{bmatrix} +\text{obst} \\ -\text{cont} \\ -\text{voice} \\ +\text{anterior} \\ -\text{coronal} \end{bmatrix} \begin{bmatrix} +\text{obs} \\ +\text{cont} \\ +\text{voice} \\ +\text{anterior} \\ -\text{coronal} \\ +\text{strident} \end{bmatrix} \right\}$ |

It is not the case that Chomsky and Halle exclude 'secondary concepts' entirely; but I will argue that the 'secondary concepts' which they do admit are either not secondary or not justified. Their conception of 'evaluation measure' involves a number of notational devices which they refer to as 'abbreviatory conventions' and which they treat as defining a 'rule' in an expanded notation as a sequence of rules in a more restricted notation. I maintain that with one exception, these so-called abbreviatory conventions are not abbreviatory; that is, that they do not really 'define' a composite rule as a sequence of other rules, and that the one 'abbreviatory convention' which is truly abbreviatory, namely, curly brackets, is wrong in the sense that when combined with an adequate system of phonological features the only instances in which it would be applicable are instances of consecutive rules in a grammar which have purely accidental similarities and which can in no sense be said to act as a unit.[1]

However, I wish first to say something about the other type of argument that has been used in choosing between notational systems, namely, arguments relating to 'excessive' or 'insufficient' power. Arguments based on 'insufficient power' often crucially involve the notion of 'significant generalization'. Assuming that a feature system allows one to distinguish among all the segment types that are involved in phonological derivations in a language,[2] the effect of almost any[3] putative phonological rule can be brought about by simply listing its inputs and outputs, expressed in the given feature system, and putting arrows in between. However, in that case, one has not written a rule but a sequence of rules. If it can be established that there is a single phenomenon here rather than several disparate phenomena (evidence that there is a single phenomenon rather than several would include, for example, evidence that in language acquisition or aphasia the various effects of the putative rule are acquired together or lost together, evidence that in language change the whole rule is modified or generalized rather than just special cases of it, or evidence that dialects differ by the ordering of the putative rule with respect to other rules but do not differ by the ordering of the special cases which the 'list' alluded to above would distinguish), then it is correct to argue that a grammar must have a single rule to cover the various special cases and that a notational system which does not make it possible to formulate such a single rule is inadequate on grounds of 'insufficient power'. As an example, consider the argument which I have offered (1967) against the Jakobsonian feature 'diffuse' on the grounds of both excessive and insufficient power. High vowels and alveolar, dental, and labial consonants are [+diffuse] and velar and palatal consonants and mid and low vowels are [−diffuse]. I argued that no language has rules in which diffuse vowels and diffuse consonants are treated alike (although Jakobson's feature system would allow the formulation of such rules, so that it has 'excessive power'), whereas there are a number of rules (e.g., the Sanskrit retroflexion of [s] before [i, u, r, k]) which treat 'diffuse vowels' and 'non diffuse consonants' alike (although the Jakobsonian feature system does not group them together and thus has 'insufficient power').

Arguments on the grounds of 'excessive power' crucially involve the notion of 'possible rule', which in turn crucially involves the notion of 'significant generalization'. One who takes 'excessive power' arguments seriously has as his goal characterizing 'phonological rule' so as to include all and only the phonological rules that the phenomena of a natural language could demand, and the mere fact that a certain putative rule would give correct answers if incorporated in a grammar of some language does not justify calling it a 'possible rule'. For example, the fact that the shortening of vowels in my dialect could be described by three rules, one which shortens vowels before (oral) stops, one which shortens vowels before nasals, and one which shortens vowels before [l], does not mean that those three rules must be included in the set of possible rules: here there is a single rule that shortens vowels before segments with closure, and the fact that the three rules mentioned could duplicate the effect of that single rule does not justify admitting them as 'possible rules'. An example of an 'excessive power' argument to which I will return below has to do with Chomsky and Halle's use of numerical subscripts (meaning 'that number or more') in rules like the following:

(1a)   Penultimate stress: $[+syll] \rightarrow [1\ stress]/\text{———}[-syll]_0[+syll][-syll]_0\#$.

Chomsky and Halle's conception of numerical subscripts as an 'abbreviatory convention' abbreviating a (potentially infinite) set of rules, each of which calls for a specific number of segments of the type in question (e.g., one rule is 'vowel is stressed before zero consonants plus one vowel plus zero consonants plus word boundary', another is 'vowel is stressed before one consonant plus one vowel plus zero consonants plus word boundary', another is 'vowel is stressed before three consonants plus one vowel plus two consonants plus word boundary', etc.), forces one to include among rules supposedly abbreviated by the numerical subscripts rules which in fact are not possible: for example, no language could have a stress placement rule which applied *only* to words ending in a vowel plus three consonants plus a vowel plus two consonants. The statement that a rule is impossible crucially involves the notion of 'significant generalization': while there are hundreds of languages in which all words ending in vowel plus three consonants plus vowel plus two consonants have penultimate stress, the placement of stress in those languages always goes under some generalization such as that the penultimate syllable is stressed (regardless of how many consonants or vowels each syllable contains) or that stress is put two moras before the last syllable (as in Latin).

I now return to the status of the so-called abbreviatory conventions of Chomsky and Halle (1968). Regarding curly brackets, which Chomsky and Halle use to combine into a single rule consecutive rules which are partially identical, I maintain that all cases where linguists have used this device fall into the following categories: (1) one of the rules supposedly abbreviated gives wrong outputs (e.g., the second environment of Chomsky and Halle's vowel shift rule, which is supposed to account for height alternations in strong verbs, gives the right alternation in verbs with an underlying high or low vowel but not in verbs with an underlying mid vowel);[4] (2) the convention is not applicable, since (contrary to the claim of their author) the rules are not consecutive in the grammar (e.g., the lowering of [u] to [ʌ], which Chomsky and Halle make the third environment of the vowel shift rule, is not adjacent to vowel shift in the rule ordering, since the rule which laxes the vowel of *says*, *said*, and *does* must apply after vowel shift and before [u] into [ʌ]; (3) the rule presupposes something incorrect which, if corrected, would eliminate the occasion for using curly brackets (e.g., many rules in Chomsky and Halle 1968 and earlier works involve {+cons, −voc}; the feature system which those rules presuppose must for various reasons be rejected in favor of one containing the feature of 'syllabicity', and the rules should all have [−syll] in place of the material in the curly brackets); and (4) the curly brackets are applied to consecutive rules which only accidentally have identical parts and which in no way act as a unit. I thus propose abolishing curly brackets from linguistics as serving no function other than the pernicious one of making it easy for the linguist to ignore defects in his analysis.[5]

The remaining abbreviatory conventions used by Chomsky and Halle are: 'variable coefficients', which mark sameness or difference between feature coefficients, for example,

(2)   Progressive voicing assimilation: $[-\text{syll}] \rightarrow [\alpha\text{voice}] \Bigg/ \begin{bmatrix} -\text{syll} \\ \alpha\text{voice} \end{bmatrix}$ ——— ;

numerical subscripts (described above); and parentheses, which Chomsky and Halle use to indicate what might best be called 'semiobligatory material'; for example, I said that the Latin stress rule (following Jakobson) inserts stress two moras before the last syllable; but a Latin word which contains only one mora before the last syllable gets stressed one mora before the last syllable (e.g., *ibō*), and a monosyllable gets stressed on its single syllable (e.g., *res*), so that the rule should put stress on a mora which is followed by a mora (if one is available) followed by a syllable (if one is available) followed by word boundary:

(3a)   Latin stress: Insert [1 stress]/ <u>mora</u> (mora) (syll)#

(I am prepared to argue that it must be possible to state rules in terms of such units as syllables and moras as well as segments, but do not choose to go into that question here.) Similarly, the penultimate stress rule, if formulated in terms of segments rather than syllables would have to be

(3b)  penultimate stress: $[+\text{syll}] \rightarrow [1\text{ stress}]/\text{———}([-\text{syll}]_0[+\text{syll}])[-\text{syll}]_0\#$

so as to cover monosyllables also. Chomsky and Halle treat all three of these devices as abbreviating sequences of rules: in the first case, two rules of which one has a '+' in place of the variable and the other a '−'; in the second case, an infinite set of rules, one calling for $n$ segments, where $n$ is the subscript, one calling for $n + 1$ segments, one calling for $n + 2$, and so on; and in the third case, two rules, one calling for the parenthesized material and one not calling for it. There are two main reasons for withholding the term 'abbreviatory' from these notational devices. First, the rules they supposedly abbreviate are often not 'possible rules'. For Chomsky and Halle, the nasal assimilation rule

(4)  nasal assimilation: $[+\text{nasal}] \rightarrow \begin{bmatrix} \alpha\text{anterior} \\ \beta\text{coronal} \end{bmatrix} / \text{———} \begin{bmatrix} -\text{syll} \\ \alpha\text{anterior} \\ \beta\text{coronal} \end{bmatrix}$

is an abbreviation for four rules, each assimilating nasals to a specific place of articulation. However, not all of those four rules are possible; for example, no language has a rule assimilating nasals to the place of articulation of labials and only labials. An example of an impossible rule included in what is supposedly abbreviated by the subscript convention was given above. And I conjecture that a rule assigning stress to the second mora before the last syllable and only there (thus leaving the possibility for another rule to assign final stress to two-syllable words whose first syllable has only one mora) is not a possible rule either. Second, as Chomsky and Halle point out, the sets of rules supposedly abbreviated by these devices do not stand in the same kind of ordering relations that rules normally do. Whereas rules normally are 'conjunctively ordered', so that the output of one rule is the input to the next rule, Chomsky and Halle must say that the rules 'abbreviated' by these devices are 'disjunctively ordered' with respect to each other, that is, if one of the rules applies, then the others are inapplicable. This interpretation is necessary, since if the two rules which Chomsky and Halle say are abbreviated by rule (4) were 'conjunctively ordered', any word of at least two syllables in length would receive two stresses: one from the one rule and one from the other.

I thus conclude that the types of rules which Chomsky and Halle express using the above devices are in fact not definable in terms of the other devices of the theory (+ and − feature specifications and [conjunctive] rule ordering) and that, assuming that the kinds of rules which Chomsky and Halle express using those three devices are in fact necessary in phonology, phonological theory must have more 'first order concepts' relating to rules than Chomsky and Halle proposed. For representing items, it suffices to specify what segment follows what segment and which value (+ or −) each segment has for each feature. Rules may call for one segment to follow another or to be + or −

for a certain feature, but they may equally well call for one segment to be the closest segment of a given type before or after a given segment (e.g., the penultimate stress rule calls for the last vowel before a word boundary and for the last vowel before that vowel) and may call for one segment to agree (or disagree) with another on a certain feature. I propose the following notation for rules as something which at least makes clear the primitive notions involved:

(5)   nasal assimilation:  If 1 impr 2                                 (impr = 'immediately
                                    syll (1) = −                          precedes')
                                    nasal (1) = +
                                    syll (2) = −
                                    Then coron (1) → coron (2)   (i.e., the coronality specifica-
                                                                          tion of 1 becomes whatever the
                                                                          coronality specification of 2 has
                                                                          been)

                                    anterior (1) → anterior (2)

(6a)  penultimate stress:  If seg (1) = −                         (i.e., 1 is a non-segment, i.e.,
                                    2 is last [+syll] before 1        a boundary)
                                    3 is last [+syll] before 2
                                    then stress (3) → 1.

'Excessive power' arguments are arguments that a notational system is wrong because it allows one to express impossible rules. One can reasonably ask whether it makes sense to demand that a notational system be solely responsible for distinguishing between possible rules and impossible rules. Such a demand of course unheard of outside of linguistics – no mathematician criticizes a notation on the ground that it allows one to write the sentence $2 + 2 = 59$. The following extremely interesting suggestion by Quine (discussion at a conference in Palo Alto, August 1969[6]) was intended as a *reductio ad absurdum* of the position that one should expect a notational system to do all the work of separating the 'possible' from the 'impossible'. Quine points out that one could give an 'excessible power' argument against the traditional notations of symbolic logic and in favor of the following notation, which allows the formulation of fewer contradictions.[7] Suppose that *and*, *or*, *all*, and *some* are represented by the symbols ∧, ∨, ⋀, ⋁ (which are the symbols used anyway by many logicians), predicates are represented by symbols which do not look the same when turned upside down (e.g., *p*, *q*, *f*, *g*), individuals are represented by symbols which look the same when turned upside down (e.g., ×, o), and the negation of a formula represented by writing each of its symbols upside down, for example, the negation of ⋀ × (*f* × ∨ *g* ×) would be ⋁ × (*ʃ* × ∧ *ẞ* ×). The formulas which are contradictory by virtue of the law of double negation or de Morgan's laws cannot even be stated. Moreover, it is unnecessary to state either of those two principles as postulates: no law of double negation is needed, since inverting a symbol twice restores it to its original form, and de Morgan's laws (which say that the negation of a conjunction is equivalent to the disjunction of the negations of the terms, and the negation of a disjunction is equivalent to the conjunction of the negations of the terms) would be unnecessary, since negating a conjunction would involve turning the symbol for *and* into the symbol for *or* and the symbols for the conjuncts into the symbols for their negations.

Of course, Quine's proposed notation does not make the law of double negation and de Morgan's laws unnecessary: it merely shifts them from postulates which one expresses in the notational system to postulates which one assumes in accepting the notational system (or rather, consequences of such postulates). The relation as described by Quine relies heavily on the typeface used: typefaces differ as to whether *x*, *o*, *D*, and *B* are changed into something different by turning them upside down. In using the notation system, one assumes that every symbol has an 'inverse', that 'inverse' is a 'symmetric relation', and that the symbols divide into two types: those which are their own inverses (individual constants and variables) and those which are distinct from their inverses (predicates, conjunctions, and quantifiers). If the negation of a formula is defined as the formula obtained from it by replacing each of its symbols by its inverse, the law of double negation and de Morgan's laws become theorems deducible from the assumptions just listed.

The point of the above example is that in any notational system, certain typographical characteristics of the formulas are treated as 'significant' and others not. Specifying what characteristics are significant amounts to giving postulates which are really postulates not about the notational system but about the entities in the description of which the notational system is employed. A choice between two notational systems is really a choice between two alternatives for what entities are to be hypothesized and what properties are to be postulated of them. A postulate for which it is possible to set up a notational system that exactly 'fits' that postulate should not thereby be accorded any special status. This has the unhappy consequence of making it much less clear than it previously seemed how to choose between alternatives, since there is no obvious criterion for choosing between alternative postulate systems that are 'deductively equivalent'. The only criterion I can think of that will ever go beyond esthetic reactions in the viscera is the criterion that a system of postulates must be wrong if it lists separate cases that clearly belong under a generalization. I conclude that an 'excessive power' argument, if taken literally, is as nonsensical as Quine suggested but in many cases can be replaced by an argument about alternative postulates which some sense can be made of.

Having, I hope, clarified the status of 'excessive power' arguments, let me turn to one in particular which I have recently given, an argument against the position generally accepted by generative phonologists that all phonological features are binary and in favor of the position that at least vowel height and pitch should be represented by single nonbinary features rather than by combinations of binary features (e.g., that high, mid, and low vowels be represented as [2 high], [1 high], and [0 high] rather than as $\left( \begin{bmatrix} +\text{high} \\ -\text{low} \end{bmatrix}, \begin{bmatrix} -\text{high} \\ -\text{low} \end{bmatrix}, \begin{bmatrix} -\text{high} \\ +\text{low} \end{bmatrix} \right)$.

Several examples exist of phonological rules which raise low and mid vowels to mid and high, respectively, or which lower high and mid vowels to mid and low, respectively; as examples of the former I can cite the vowel shift rule in English (see McCawley 1974 for justifications of this version of vowel shift and criticism of Chomsky and Halle's) and the rule in Eastern Finnish dialects which converts *ee, öö, oo, ää, aa* into *ie, üö, uo, eä, oa*, respectively; as an example of the latter, I can cite a rule in a southern

Lappish dialect (Ove Lorentz, personal communication) which lowers the second element of long high and mid vowels, so that *ii, üü, uu, ee, oo* become *ie, üö, uo, eä, oa*. To express such a rule using exclusively binary features (e.g., Chomsky and Halle 1968 feature system), it is necessary that the rule involve a change of two features and a variable which connects a feature in the 'structural change' to a different feature in the 'structural description':

(6b)   part of English vowel shift: $\begin{bmatrix} +\text{syll} \\ -\text{high} \\ \alpha\text{low} \\ +\text{tense} \end{bmatrix} \rightarrow \begin{bmatrix} -\alpha\text{high} \\ -\text{low} \end{bmatrix}$

However, the only well-founded rules that are of the form

(7)   $\begin{bmatrix} \alpha F \\ -G \end{bmatrix} \rightarrow \begin{bmatrix} -\alpha G \\ -F \end{bmatrix}$

are rules in which $F$ and $G$ are binary features used to split up a domain such as vowel height or pitch height[8] which the alternative under consideration would represent in terms of a nonbinary feature which could be incremented in a phonological rule, for example,

(8)   vowel shift revised: $\begin{bmatrix} +\text{syll} \\ n < 3 \text{ high} \\ +\text{tense} \end{bmatrix} \rightarrow [n + 1 \text{ high}]$

   The binary proposal thus requires a notion of 'possible rule' in which symbol combinations are allowed that in fact do not correspond to possible phenomena of real languages, for example, a rule of the form (7) in which $F$ was 'low' and $G$ 'rounded', which would have the effect of rounding *i* and *e* to *ü* and *ö* while raising *æ* and *a* to *e* and ʌ. To translate the above from a nonsensical argument about notation into a possibly meaningful argument about alternative sets of postulates, the choice is between a set of postulates like the following:

(9)   Every feature has the two values + and −.
   Each line in the 'then'-part of a rule has one of the forms

   $F(n) \rightarrow +$
   $F(n) \rightarrow -$
   $F(n) \rightarrow G(m)$
   $F(n) \rightarrow -G(m)$, where $F$ and $G$ are features.

   If a rule has an 'if'-part containing $F(n) = -$ and a 'then'-part containing $F(n) \rightarrow -G(n)$ and $G(n) \rightarrow -$, then $F$ and $G$ are either high and low (tongue position) or high pitch and low pitch.

And a set of postulates like the following:

(10)   (Tongue) height and pitch have the values 0, 1, 2, and all other features have the
       values 0 and 1.[9]
       Each line in the 'then'-part of a rule has one of the forms

       $F(n) \rightarrow a$, where $F$ is a feature and $a$ is a value of $F$
       $F(n) \rightarrow F(n) + 1$
       $F(n) \rightarrow F(n) - 1$
       $F(n) \rightarrow G(m)$, where $F$ and $G$ are two features with the same set of values
       $F(n) \rightarrow -G(m)$, where $F$ and $G$ are both 'binary' features.

       A rule cannot have an 'if'-part containing $F(n) = 0$ and a 'then'-part containing
       $F(n) \rightarrow -G(n)$ and $G(n) \rightarrow 0$.

Or at least, that would be choice if the last line in (9) or (10) was to be the extent of
restrictions on the use of 'variables' in rules. But these restrictions are clearly insufficient to characterize the set of possible rules, since they do not exclude such impossible
rules as [$\alpha$high] $\rightarrow$ [$\alpha$nasal] (which would make velar consonants and high vowels
nasal and make everything else nonnasal). It will not do simply to exclude rules in
which a 'variable' links two different features, since there are fairly clear cases (at least,
among redundancy rules) of rules that make rounding agree with backness (back vowels
become rounded and front vowels unrounded) or make voicing disagree with obstruence
(obstruents become voiceless and sonorants voiced). Rather than all rules of a certain
format being possible, it appears that there are only a small number of pairs of features
that may be linked by such a rule. If this is so, then a set of postulates correctly characterizing the set of possible rules would presumably have to have a postulate that simply
listed the formulas of the type $F(n) \rightarrow (-) G(n)$ that could appear in the 'then'-part
of a rule. The postulate for the binary proposal would involve a longer list than the
corresponding postulate for the nonbinary proposal, and the former list would also have
to have a qualification that when the 'then'-part contained high($n$) $\rightarrow$ low($n$), the
'if'-part would have to contain high($n$) $= -$ and the 'then'-part would have to contain
low($n$) $\rightarrow -$ (and a similar condition on a rule that lowered tongue height or a rule that
raised or lowered pitch height).
    This leaves the postulates for the binary proposal looking somewhat messier than those
for the nonbinary proposal. More importantly, it can reasonably be argued that the side
conditions mentioned two sentences back are not randomly distributed among the rules
in question but go only with those pairs of features which divide up some multivalued
domain, that is, the binary proposal necessarily involves postulates which miss a valid
generalization as to why some rules but not others are possible. While this is something of an argument, it does not give a really crushing case one way or the other. What
would give a really crushing case for the nonbinary proposal would be to show some
major restriction on rules which could be imposed under the nonbinary proposal but
not under the binary proposal. Since the binary proposal requires rules which make two
changes (see (6)) where the corresponding rule under the nonbinary proposal would
make only one change (see (8)), the case for the nonbinary proposal would be really

clear if it could be shown that it allowed all rules to be 'one-change' rules.[10] There are some obvious objections to raise to a proposal that all rules are 'one-change' rules; note, for example, the extremely common nasal assimilation rule cited earlier (which makes the nasal agree in both coronality and anteriority with the following segment; here a rule making only one of the two changes would not be possible, its effects being to turn [ŋ] into [m] before [t], and [n] into [ñ] before [k]) and 'compensatory lengthening' rules, which simultaneously lengthen the vowel on one side of a consonant and shorten or delete the vowel on the other side of it.

It is in fact possible to treat these rules as 'one-change' rules, though doing so involves two important additions to phonological theory, which, however, I maintain are necessary anyway. The first is the principle that rules may have 'side effects' beyond the change that the rule specifically mentions; specifically, any additional changes are made that are necessary in order that the output of the rule contain only possible combinations of features; for example (see McCawley 1967), the rule in Korean that makes all syllable-final consonants unreleased has the side effect of giving them a closure, since only a segment with a closure can be unreleased, and also has the side effect of making them unaspirated, since only a released segment can be aspirated. The second addition to phonological theory is the recognition of the distinction between 'states' and 'events' and the recognition of rules whose effect is to change the timing of an event. For example, it is necessary to distinguish between 'closure', the state of there being a total occlusion, and 'closure', the event of an active articulator entering into an occlusion with a passive articulator. In the case of the nasal assimilation rule, the rule can be stated as the shift of the closure event (or more generally, the 'onset') of the second consonant to the beginning of the preceding segment. The fact that the first segment acquires the coronality and anteriority of the second can be said to be a 'site effect': a segment which begins with a certain closure event must have the place-of-articulation features of that closure. Similarly, many cases of 'compensatory lengthening' are the delay by one segment of the onset of a consonant, and the rule found in many Bantu languages whereby a nasal prefix is realized as prenasalization of the following consonant plus lengthening of the preceding vowel (e.g., . . . a N-la . . . → . . . a· ⁿda . . . ) is a postponement by one segment of the onset of the nasal (including the lowering of the velum). If stated in feature notation without the aid of the two theoretical innovations referred to above, these rules would involve wholesale changing of features – note that the Bantu rule would involve simultaneous changes in three segments. A theory of 'possible rules' must characterize which wholesale changes of features are possible; the theory that I am proposing here says that wholesale changes of features only arise as side effects of atomic changes, where the atomic changes include anticipation or postponement of phonological events. Obviously, what I have presented falls far short of a complete demonstration that phonological rules can be restricted to making a single change (which may then have predictable side effects); however, I think it has disposed of the most formidable objections that might be presented against that conclusion. The conclusion, if established, would then provide strong evidence that the binary treatment of vowel height was wrong, since it would require two-change rules, and that vowel heights should be represented in terms of a single nonbinary feature. It should be noted, incidentally, that within the approach that I am taking here, the behavior of Bantu prefixes has a bearing on how one is to formulate the English vowel shift rule.

The main moral that I want to draw from the above discussion is that except for arguments relating to evaluation measures, which in my opinion can never be put on a sound footing, all arguments about the correctness of a system of phonological description revolve about the notion often called 'linguistically significant generalization' and perhaps better called 'unitary linguistic phenomenon'. I mentioned earlier several kinds of evidence that can be offered (but rarely are) for concluding that there is or is not a single 'piece of linguistic competence' reflected in a set of facts. Much of my argument is weak because of lack of such evidence, especially for the language universals that I have stated. However, I would at least claim that these statements are not incorrigible, whereas such statements as Halle's assertion about the relative complexity of the rules of table 2.1 probably *is* incorrigible. The notion of 'linguistically significant generalization' is much more pervasive in recent transformational linguistics than an examination of the available literature would suggest. It deserves much more attention than the completely barren notion of 'evaluation measure', which, regrettably, a tremendous fuss is made over in most of the works that students are given to read in courses on transformational grammar.

## Notes

1   In one respect I would now weaken this statement. There are cases in which it is plausible to conjecture that a child acquires phonological alternations by first observing that strange things happen in a certain context and later learning the details of what it is that happens in that context, without necessarily learning a single generalization that will cover all of the things that happen. I suspect that this is the case with Finnish consonant gradation, for example, and that attempts to give a uniform gradation rule (e.g., a rule that voices a stop at the beginning of a non-initial short closed syllable, with subsequent rules deleting, spirantizing, or assimilating the resulting voiced stop under various conditions) are misguided. While I thus now find plausible a treatment of consonant gradation that would be formalizable using curly brackets, the curly brackets would not serve the function of 'abbreviation': if my conjecture about the acquisition of consonant gradation is correct, the child would never have the rules that are supposedly abbreviated by the curly brackets, since he would have 'learned the curly brackets' (i.e., internalized a rule that allows for a list of disparate subcases) before he learned what was to go inside the curly brackets.

2   Of course, many 'insufficient power' arguments have been arguments that this condition was not met by a certain feature system and that therefore a different system was necessary (e.g., McCawley 1967, Chomsky and Halle 1968, Postal 1968).

3   This qualification is necessary because of putative phonological rules that would exchange segment types, e.g., Chomsky and Halle's (1968) proposed rule that makes tense high vowels mid and tense mid vowels high. I have argued (McCawley 1974) against the supposed examples of rules of that type but do not wish to exclude them from the present discussion.

Here and in the next sentence of the text, I have gratuitously assumed that rules must apply sequentially.

4   I give detailed justification of this claim and the next one in McCawley 1974.

5   This function is not as pernicious as I made it sound here: to get anything done, you *have to* ignore some defects in your analysis, at least until you have enough hindsight to be able to judge what would be an improvement. What is pernicious about Chomsky and Halle's policy on curly brackets is that it gave a major role in a linguistic theory to something that should have been only a temporary makeshift. Perhaps this is what is liable to happen to you if your office is in a building that was erected in 1942 as a temporary structure.

6   The conference referred to here is the one that gave rise to Davidson and Harman 1972.

7   For the purposes of this discussion I assume that this notation is being used as a language for formulating propositions of some science, so that all contradictions would be wrong. The fact that certain contradictions cannot be formulated in this notation is actually a defect of it if it is being used not to state propositions about the world but to represent the meaning of sentences. Contradictory sentences can be perfectly grammatical and meaningful, and a linguist must be able to describe their meanings.

Quine's notation does not so much make contradictions unstateable as it makes tautologies unstateable. The only unstateable contradictions are indeed the negations of unstateable tautologies.

8   There is a well-known counterexample to this sweeping claim: the weakening of stops in Danish, which can plausibly be formulated as

$$\begin{bmatrix} -\text{cont} \\ \alpha\,\text{voice} \end{bmatrix} \rightarrow \begin{bmatrix} +\text{voice} \\ \alpha\,\text{cont} \end{bmatrix}$$

9   I have chosen 0 and 1 rather than + and − to avoid making the difference between binary and ternary features appear greater than it is. A much more satisfactory treatment of nonbinary features than is given here is found in unpublished work by Martin Minow.

10  I am embarrassed to acknowledge having suggested that this putative universal could provide "a really crushing case" for anything. Here, as earlier in "English as a VSO language" (1970) where I also based an argument on the possibility of enforcing this universal, I was following the prevalent custom of constructing cheap arguments by presenting one's favourite conclusions as part of the ongoing war on excessive power. In fact, many of the universals that linguists have proposed in doing their bit in the war effort are propositions that I find it hard to imagine a sane linguist wanting to be universal, e.g., the often proposed constraint against quantifiers in the formulation of rules (which would exclude conditions like 'where X contains no V'). That constraint excludes rules that pick out the first or last occurrence of something in a domain, which is a bizarre thing to want to exclude, in that virtually all perception and cognition involves searches through structured domains (Miller and Johnson-Laird 1976). To adopt that constraint is to say that language is impoverished in comparison with most cognitive domains. The 'one-change' universal is not as bizarre as this, but it does not have much plausibility: if 'changes' correspond in any sense to things that speakers or hearers do in using language, what could possibly prevent one from doing two such things together? The other arguments for nonbinary vowel height are really much better arguments.

# References

Chomsky, Noam A. and Morris Halle. 1968. *The Sound Pattern of English*. New York: Harper and Row.

Davidson, Donald and Gilbert Harman. 1972. *Semantics of Natural Language*. Dordrecht: Reidel.

Halle, Morris. 1964. Phonology in generative grammar. In Jerry A. Fodor, and Jerrold J. Katz (eds), *The Structure of Language*, Englewood Cliffs, N.J.: Prentice-Hall, 324–33.

McCawley, James D. 1967. Le rôle d'un système de traits phonologiques dans une théorie du language. *Languages* 8: 112–23. Repr. in English in V. Makkai (ed.), *Phonological Theory* (New York: Holt, Rinehart and Winston, 1972), 322–8, as well as in James McCawley, *Adverbs, Vowels, and Other Objects of Wonder* (Chicago: University of Chicago Press, 1979), 20–9.

McCawley, James D. 1970. English as a VSO language. *Language* 46: 286–99.

McCawley, James D. 1974. Review of Chomsky and Halle 1968. *International Journal of American Linguistics* 40: 58–88.

Miller, George and Philip Johnson-Laird. 1976. *Language and Perception*. Cambridge, Mass.: Harvard University, Belknap Press.

Postal, Paul. 1968. *Aspects of Phonological Theory*. New York: Harper and Row.

# 3

# From Cyclic Phonology to
# Lexical Phonology (1982)

## Paul Kiparsky

The approach to word structure that I shall explore here represents a convergence of several originally independent strands of research. One is the emerging theory of morphology and the lexicon (e.g. Aronoff 1976), and more particularly the idea of a level-ordered morphology elaborated by D. Siegel (1974, 1977), M. Allen (1978), and others. Another centers around the problem of constraining lexical representations and phonological rules, beginning with various versions of the Alternation Condition (Kiparsky 1968, 1973a) and continuing with the conception of Cyclic Phonology first proposed by Mascaró (1976) and subsequently pursued in a number of studies of the phonologies of particular languages (most extensively Rubach 1981). I shall also be drawing on aspects of the recent metrical theory of stress (Liberman and Prince 1977, Hayes 1981) and syllable structure. When these ideas are put together, and developed in a certain direction, they explain a series of properties of phonological rules and their relation to morphology and the lexicon that have so far appeared as unexplained generalizations, or in some cases even defied coherent formulation or escaped notice altogether.

The basic insight of level-ordered morphology is that the derivational and inflectional processes of a language can be organized in a series of levels. Each level is associated with a set of phonological rules for which it defines the domain of application. The ordering of levels moreover defines the possible ordering of morphological processes in word formation. Following a proposal of Pesetsky (MS) let us assume that the output of each word-formation process is submitted within the lexicon itself to the phonological rules of its level. This establishes a basic division among phonological rules into those which are assigned to one or more levels in the lexicon, and those which operate after words have been combined into sentences in the syntax. The former, the rules of *lexical phonology*, are intrinsically cyclic because they reapply after each step of word formation at their morphological level. The latter, the rules of *postlexical phonology*, are intrinsically noncyclic. The lexicon is accordingly structured in the following way:

(1)

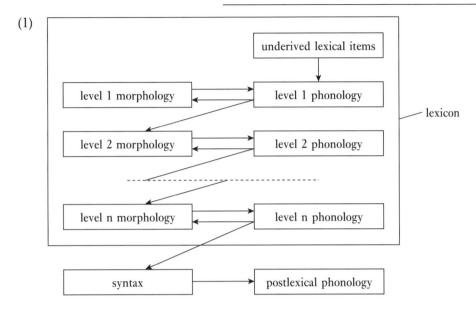

The output of the right-hand boxes collectively constitutes the set of lexical items of the language. The point that the result of every layer of derivation is itself a lexical item will have important consequences later on.

Models of this type have also been investigated by Strauss (1979a), Booij (1981), Pulleyblank (MS [see now Pulleyblank 1986]), and especially by Harris (1983) for Spanish and Mohanan (1981) for Malayalam, the latter also with extensive theoretical justification of the framework.

For concreteness I add a tentative sketch of how the English lexicon might be organized. It draws on previous explorations of English morphology by Siegel (1974), Allen (1978), Selkirk (1981), and Williams (1981), but differs in some respects from each.

Of the three levels in (2), the first level comprises the affixes which have usually been associated with the +boundary. They correspond to the "primary suffixes" of traditional descriptions such as that of Sanskrit by Whitney (1889). This level includes derivational suffixes such as *-al, -ous, -ity, -th*, and inflectional suffixes such as those in *kept, met, hidden, children, addenda, indices, foci* as well as "ablaut," "umlaut," and other stem-changing morphology as in *teethe, bleed, bathe, teeth, lice*. To the second level we assign # boundary ("secondary") derivation and compounding. Such derivational suffixes as *-hood, -ness, -er, -ism, -ist* belong here. The third level takes care of the remaining "regular" inflection (*leaped, pleated, books*, etc.).

Although the division between level 1 and level 2 affixes coincides entirely with the familiar distinction between the "+boundary" and the "# boundary" affixes, we shall see that it in fact has deeper roots in the morphological system. In what follows I will first motivate (2) on morphological grounds and then proceed to develop some of its consequences on the phonological side.

(2)

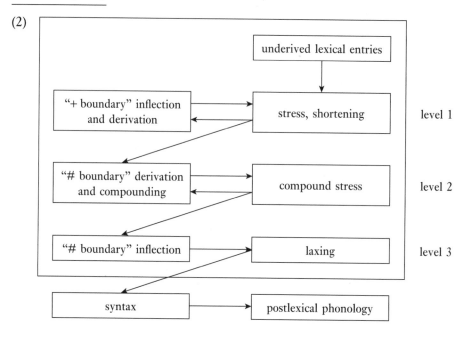

First let us introduce a specific format for morphological rules in the grammar. Following Lieber (1980) I shall distinguish two basic classes of word-formation processes, compounding and affixation, and assume that all word formation is endocentric. By this I mean that the category of a derived word is always non-distinct from the category of its head, in English usually the rightmost constituent (cf. Williams 1981).[1] The categories in question include not only lexical categories but also features like Transitive, Agent, etc. In any approach to morphology it is necessary to provide certain kinds of information for any given affix: to what sorts of things the affix may be added, whether it is prefixed or suffixed, and what are the properties of the resulting form. Lieber proposes that this information is encoded in the lexical entry of the affix itself by means of a subcategorization frame and an inherent categorial specification which percolates upward from an affix to the constructions whose head it is. For our purposes it will be convenient to construe these subcategorizations and inherent feature specifications of affixes as so many contextual restrictions on the rules which insert them. Affixes will then not be lexical entries, and they will have no lexical features either inherently or by percolation. Each affix A is introduced by a rule of the form

(3)  Insert A in env. $[Y\_\_\_Z]_X$

where Y,Z corresponds to the "subcategorization frame" of A, and X corresponds to its inherent categorial specification in Lieber's format.

Consider first inflection. To illustrate, let the noun *ox* have been inserted in [   ]$_{Noun, +Plural}$. A morphological rule at level 1 then obligatorily inserts the suffix *-en* after it:

(4)  Insert /en/ in env. $[ox \_\_\_\_]_{Noun, +Plural}$

The noun *boy* is not subject to (4), but if [+Plural] it undergoes rule (5) at level 3:

(5)   Insert /z/ in env. $[X\_\_\_]_{Noun, +Plural}$

The morphological processes at different levels are related in certain characteristic ways which recur from language to language.

(1)   One phenomenon to be accounted for is the "blocking" effect, which has been discussed for derivational morphology by Paul (1896), Esau (1973), Aronoff (1976), Clark and Clark (1979), Toman (1980), and shows up still more clearly in inflection. Words which are inflected at level 1, for example, usually do not receive the general suffixes at level 3. There is no *\*foots*, *\*oxes* alongside *feet*, *oxen*, and no *\*keeped*, *\*meeted* alongside *kept*, *met*. We shall, however, have to explain not only why such is the normal case, but also how it is possible for occasional doublets to exist, e.g. *kneeled/knelt*, *dreamed/dreamt*, *crocuses/croci*, *indexes/indices*. In derivational morphology doublets are actually quite common, to the point that blocking there can hardly be considered more than a general tendency.

The blocking phenomenon follows from obligatoriness of morphological rules. For example, *ox*, if [+Plural], must undergo (4), and so there is no way to derive *\*oxes* by the later rule (5). Failure of blocking, resulting in doublets like *crocuses/croci* and *dreamed/dreamt* – which we can take to be the marked case – is obtained by making the special rule optional for those words.

To get the blocking effect for derivational affixes, we treat them also as inserted in the context of the appropriate morphological categories. We shall suppose that lexical items are freely inserted into categorial frames [    ]$_X$, where X is a bundle of features. We illustrate with the derivation of deverbal agent nouns. A restricted set of verbs allow nouns to be made at level 1 by such suffixes as *-ant* or zero derivation (which I take to be a phonologically empty suffix). These suffixes are inserted at level 1 by such rules as (6):

(6)   Insert /Ø/ in env. $[V_n\_\_\_]_{Noun, +Agent}$
      where $V_n$ = *guide, bore, gossip* . . .

So from $[[guide]_V]_{N, +Agent}$ we derive the noun $[[guide]_V Ø]_{N, +Agent}$, which is well-formed because it is endocentric. If V is not in $V_n$, (6) cannot apply, and the resulting structure is filtered out because it is not endocentric. The interesting generalization is that verbs subject to one of these level 1 rules tend not to get the otherwise productive *-er* suffix added by the corresponding rule (7) at level 2:

(7)   Insert *er* in env. $[V\_\_\_]_{Noun, +Agent}$

(8)   spy$_N$          :   *\*spier*
      inhabitant    :   *\*inhabiter*

And when both do exist, the *-er* noun is mostly restricted to meanings not covered by the level 1 noun:

(9)  cook (person)    :   cooker (device)
     drill (device)    :   driller (person)
     divide (dividing line, ridge, etc.)   :   divider (person, device)
     stimulant, expectorant (substances)   :   stimulator, expectorator (devices, persons)
     defendant (of self, in court)   :   defender

If we formulate the appropriate verb-particular meaning conditions on the insertion of level 1 affixes, the distribution and meaning or -er can be left basically unrestricted; it will simply appear whenever not pre-empted by some level 1 agent suffix.

(2)   An absolute constraint, on the other hand, seems to be that a blocking process can only be located at the same level or at an earlier level than the process it blocks. We do not find, for example, cases where word-specific affixes are ordered (on phonological or independent morphological grounds) *after* the general affix for that category. An adequate theory of morphology must exclude in principle, for example, a language in which the English facts are reversed and it is the level 3 inflections which occur only with specially designated words.

   Given the above format for morphology, this simply follows from the ordering of levels. It is impossible for a process to block a process that precedes it because blocking is pre-emption by prior application.

(3)   From this it follows in turn that among processes in a blocking relationship, those with restricted applicability have to be ordered before those with general applicability. This explains why processes at later levels are also typically more productive than functionally related processes at earlier levels.

(4)   Derivational processes at later levels are semantically more uniform than those at earlier levels, where various specialized uses are prone to develop. As before, the point generalizes from derivation to inflection, cf. the semantic differentiation *brothers/brethren*. The greater semantic coherence of the general word-formation processes which are ordered at later levels is a consequence of their productivity (as suggested by Aronoff 1976: 45). The fact that they do not require word-by-word specification but apply across the board to a whole category (subject to blocking as discussed above) means that there is no foothold for imposing word-specific semantic conditions on them either. In other words, imposing an additional word-particular semantic restriction adds a relatively small increment of complexity to an early (level 1) process because the words it applies to must be listed anyway, but it adds a large increment of complexity to a late process because its context can otherwise be given categorially.

(5)   Lexical items which are *inherent* bearers of some morphological feature do not receive the morpheme that marks that feature. E.g. inherently plural nouns like *cattle* and *people* do not receive a plural ending. Here we shall invoke the Elsewhere Condition (which will play an important role in a quite different aspect of our theory to be discussed below). The formulation in (10) modifies slightly an earlier version proposed in Kiparsky (1973b), cf. Koutsoudas, Sanders and Noll (1974).[2]

(10)   Rules A,B in the same component apply disjunctively to a form $\phi$ if and only if
   (i)   The structural description of A (the special rule) properly includes the structural description of B (the general rule)
   (ii)   The result of applying A to $\phi$ is distinct from the result of applying B to $\phi$
   In that case, A is applied first, and if it takes effect, then B is not applied.

Consider now a *plurale tantum* like *people*. Assume its lexical entry is inherently marked [+Plural]. We would like (10) to block such inherent plurals from being pluralized by rule (5). Suppose then we construe each lexical entry L as a rule, namely the identity rule L, whose structural description and structural change are both = L. Then the rule corresponding to the lexical entry [people]$_{+Noun, +Plural}$ is disjunctive with (5) by virtue of (10). That is, the structural description of the lexical identity rule (namely [people]$_{+Noun, +Plural}$) properly includes the structural description of the general plural rule (namely [X__]$_{+Noun, +Plural}$) and their outputs are distinct (namely, *people* and *people* + z, respectively). Therefore the special rule, the lexical identity rule, sets aside the general plural rule.

(6)   Related to the preceding is the exclusion of stacked affixes having the same function. For example, having derived *oxen* at level 1 we cannot add another plural suffix at level 3 to get *\*oxens*. Nothing in (2) precludes this possibility *per se*. However, it now follows as in the preceding case given our assumption that the output of each stage of word formation (with the rules of lexical phonology applied to it) is itself a lexical entry. The lexical entry [oxen]$_{+Noun, +Plural}$ derived at level 1 is then not liable to receive a plural suffix at level 3 for precisely the same reason as the underived lexical entry [people]$_{+Noun, +Plural}$ is not liable to receive it.
   The organization of morphological rules depicted in (2) derives inflection at two levels. This predicts that irregular inflection, derived at level 1, should be available to derivational processes at level 2, while regular inflection, derived at level 3, should not. This is confirmed by the occasional appearance of level 1 plurals inside ordinary noun compounds:

(11)   (a)   teeth marks          (b)   *claws marks
             lice-infested                *rats-infested

Secondly, consider *pluralia tantum* with plural morphology, such as *alms*, *odds*. These nouns must be marked as inherently [+Plural] in the lexicon. The theory consequently does not allow them to be entered as underlying /alm/, /odd/ because (10) prohibits the plural affix to be added to them by (5). Therefore the underlying form must be *alms*, *odds*, etc., which should also show up inside compounds, but this time *obligatorily*. This again appears to be correct:[3]

(12)   almsgiving                  *almgiving
       oddsmaker                   *oddmaker
       painstaking                 *paintaking
       Humanities Department       *Humanity Department
       clothesbrush                *clothbrush
       arms race                   *arm race

The only other cases where plurals systematically appear inside compounds in English can (and in most cases must anyway for other reasons) be analyzed as involving phrases embedded in compounds. We must assume some limited recursion from phrase-level syntax back into morphology anyway. The occurrence of level 3 plurals in these cases is predicted:

(13) (a)   a heads-up play, a hands-off policy, a hands-down victory, hands-on training
     (b)   (daddy) long-legs, (Judy) blue-eyes[4]
     (c)   excess profits tax, the save-the-whales campaign, the Model Cities program

In the same way as (11), we predict the formation of *withstood, understood,* and similar verb compounds with level 1 inflection on their second members. Since these inflections are formed at level 1, they are available for word formation at level 2. Moreover, the theory predicts not only that they can but that they *must* appear in past tenses of such compounds. The tensed output of level 2 is $[\text{withstand}]_{+\text{Verb}, -\text{Past}}$ and $[\text{withstood}]_{+\text{Verb}, +\text{Past}}$, neither of which can receive the level 3 past ending *-ed*, the former because of feature conflict, and the latter by virtue of (10) as shown above.

The prediction is particularly interesting in view of the opposite outcome in cases like *grandstanded* (*\*grandstood*). This too follows because of the intrinsic ordering of compounding and level 1 inflection imposed by (2). The derivation proceeds as shown in (14):

(14)  level 1:   $\text{stand}_V$              $\rightarrow \text{stand}_N$
      level 2:   $\text{grand}_A + \text{stand}_N \rightarrow \text{grandstand}_N$
                 $\text{grandstand}_N$       $\rightarrow \text{grandstand}_V$
      level 3:   $\text{grandstand}_V$        $\rightarrow \text{grandstanded}$

Nouns can only be formed from untensed verbs, because tense must agree with a nominative subject (cf. Kiparsky and Kiparsky 1971: 356–7) and nouns do not have nominative subjects. Only when the verb is derived from the compound noun at level 2 can tense be assigned; at that point level 1 inflection is no longer accessible, and only the regular inflectional suffixes can be assigned.

More generally, we are now in a position to explain why exocentric (*bahuvrihi*) compounds are characteristically inflected at level 3 even if their second members are by themselves inflected at level 1, whereas endocentric compounds retain the inflection that their second member has by itself. Consider e.g. *milk teeth* (endocentric) vs. *sabertooths* 'sabertooth tigers' (exocentric). As in the verb compound just discussed, endocentric noun compounds are formed at level 2 by combining words, including words derived at level 1 such as *teeth*. Exocentric compounds, however, must on our assumptions be assigned zero-derivational suffixes since they otherwise would share the properties of their heads, i.e. be endocentric. But as noted in n. 3, derivational suffixes cannot be added to derived plurals. Therefore exocentric compounds come out of level 2 with exclusively singular morphology and can receive plural endings only at level 3 where they are adjoined to the whole compound.

The model of lexical phonology directly predict the correlation between "boundary strength" and affix order which was observed for English by Siegel (1974), and is apparently a general property of languages. The generalization is that affixes of level n are not added to stems which already contain affixes of level n + 1. For example, consider the two negative prefixes *in-* and *non-*. *In-* assimilates to a following consonant (Singh 1981) but *non-* does not. In standard generative phonology this is dealt with by assigning them + and # boundaries respectively and restricting assimilation to apply across + only:

(15)   in + legible   →   illegible
       non # legible  ↛   *nollegible

This phonological difference between *non-* and *in-* is related to the fact that *non-* can be prefixed to a word with *in-* but *in-* cannot be prefixed to a word with *non-*:

(16)   nonillegible
       *innonlegible

In the present theory both the phonology and the ordering of the two prefixes follows from putting *in-* and the assimilation rule on level 1 and *non-* on level 2. No boundary is then needed to block the assimilation of *non-*. In this way, boundary symbols such as + and # can be entirely eliminated from phonological representations. The requisite information is carried by the appropriate ordering of levels and the morphological bracketing of the string, cf. Strauss (1979a), Mohanan (1981).

The cyclic application of phonological rules has generally been assumed to be subject to the convention that internal brackets are erased at the end of a cycle (Chomsky and Halle 1968: 20). We shall assume here the weaker version (17), equivalent to the "Opacity Condition" of Mohanan (1981).

(17)   Bracketing Erasure:
       Internal brackets are erased at the end of a level

Hence the use of even the limited boundary information encoded in the morphological bracketing is restricted to the level at which the morphology itself is assigned. Moreover, morphological rules also do not have access to internal morphological structure of earlier levels. Pesetsky (MS) and Allen (1978) have suggested more restrictive conditions, but these appear to be difficult to maintain in view of the English example [discussed in the original paper], the Malayalam cases cited in Mohanan (1981), and the extensive material discussed, from a different point of view, in Carstairs (1981).

In addition to giving a more restrictive theory of morphological junctures, lexical phonology makes it possible to deal with phenomena where boundary symbols fail. A well-known problem for cyclic assignment of word stress in English arises in zero derivation.[5] When nouns are formed from verbs, they shift to the nominal stress pattern (18a), but when verbs are formed from nouns, they do not shift as expected to the verbal stress pattern (18b):

(18)   (a)   tormént$_V$ → tórmènt$_N$
       (b)   páttern$_N$ → *pattérn$_V$ (cf. *cavórt*, *usúrp*)

This difference in stress behavior is directly accounted for by forming nouns from verbs at level 1 and verbs from nouns at level 2, where they escape the level 1 rules of word stress. This correlates in the first instance with the productivity difference that we expect between level 1 and level 2 derivational process. N to V derivation enjoys great productivity in English (Clark and Clark 1979), while V to N derivation is comparatively restricted in scope. As a broad generalization it can be said that verbs are freely zero-derived from nouns whenever not blocked by a synonymous formation at level 1, such as *systematize* (*\*to system*), while nouns are zero-derived from verbs in special cases which themselves block the productive agent and action suffixes as level 2 such as *-er* (rule 7) and *-ing*. [ . . . ]

This organization of the lexicon, in conjunction with the proposals developed earlier, has further consequences on the phonological side. It embodies the claim that all and only lexical categories are cyclic domains. The prediction is that there should be no cyclic rule application above the word level. Up to recently this consequence would by itself have sufficed to wreck the theory in view of the fact that sentence stress was one of the cast-iron arguments for cyclicity. However, Rischel (1964, 1972) and Liberman and Prince (1977) have pointed out that metrical theory eliminates the need for cyclic assignment of sentence stress. In that framework the Nuclear Stress rule, which assigns prominence to the right branch of a phrasal constituent, can apply in any order or simultaneously to all constituents in the sentence. As far as I know, there are *no* rules which have to apply cyclically from the innermost phrasal constituents out and the theory of lexical phonology predicts that.

There are, however, cases where rules of word phonology seem to apply once at the lowest level of phrase syntax. I have argued (Kiparsky 1979) that the English Rhythm rule applies both below and above the word level, in cases like *expéct ~ èxpectátion* and *abstráct ~ ábstràct árt* respectively. These applications take place at different stages in the derivation because the destressing of metrically weak initial syllables must crucially intervene between them. A somewhat similar situation has been found in the tonology of Ewe by Clements (1977: 119). In neither case is there evidence of cyclic iteration within the syntax itself: each rule applies once at the phrasal level and does not need to reapply cyclically on successively higher syntactic constituents.

The most straightforward assumption is that these rules belong to both the lexical and postlexical system. However, it is surely significant that they concern what may be called phrase phonology rather than full-fledged sentence phonology. Both rules are subject to a constraint which blocks their application to verbs followed by object Noun Phrases (*màintáin órder ↛ \*máintàin órder*; for Ewe cf. Clements 1977: 122ff). Both rules have lexical exceptions (e.g. *profóund trúth ↛ \*prófòund trúth*; cf. again Clements 1977: 137). So one conclusion that could be drawn from this is that the lowest level of phrase structure can in some way be fed back into the lexicon. Quite apart from phonological considerations this would be suggested by the fact that phrasal combinations at this level are subject to selectional restrictions and liable to get fixed as idioms and formulas. We already noted above that they can be inputs to word-formation rules, e.g. *American history teacher, to stonewall, a hands-off policy*. A specific example of lexicalization is that *ábstràct* has for many people acquired inherently the specialized technical sense it bears in the phrase *ábstràct árt*, denoting a specific type or school of art.[6] These speakers make a difference between the sentences

(29)   (a)   This art is ábstràct (not representational)
       (b)   This art is abstráct (not concrete)

In the light of such facts, the nature of phrase phonology and its relation to word phonology and sentence phonology deserves deeper investigation.

As for a lower bound on cyclicity, there is some evidence that nonlexical categories are not cyclic domains. A quite compelling case has been made by J. Harris (1983) for Spanish on the basis of a study of stress and syllable structure. One of his examples is summarized in (30).

(30)

|  |  | $desden + es$ | 'disdains' | (noun plural) |
|  |  | $desde\tilde{n} + es$ | 'you disdain' | (2. sg. subj.) |

$[desde\tilde{n}]_N\ es]_N$  $\quad\quad$  $[[desde\tilde{n} + a]_V\ e + s]_N$

| I | Syllabification | [ $\sigma$ ] | [ $\sigma$ ] |
|  | $\tilde{n} \to n$ in coda | n | (inapplicable) |
| II | Truncation | [——] | Ø |
|  | Syllabification | nes | ñes |
|  |  | $\sigma$ | $\sigma$ |

The point concerns the application of a cyclic rule which depalatalizes $\tilde{n}$ to $n$ in the coda of a syllable. The contrast between the noun plural $desden + es$ and the subjunctive verb from $desde\tilde{n} + es$ arises because the underlying palatalized $\tilde{n}$ is syllable-final in the noun stem /desdeñ/ but syllable-initial in the verb stem /desdeñ + a/. These respective stems constitute the first cyclic domains, and the nasal depalatalization finds its correct syllable environment there, not at the root or word level. Harris demonstrates that the cyclic domains required for both stress and syllabification in Spanish are exactly the lexical categories.

A general condition to this effect was proposed already by Brame (1974) [ch. 4 below] on the basis of Arabic and English data. He noted the Palestinian Arabic contrast *fhímna* 'we understood' vs. *fihímna* 'he understood us', with the same morphemes except that *na* is an ending in the first form and a clitic in the second. As he pointed out, the data can be explained by assuming that the rule syncopating unstressed vowels is ordered cyclically after the rule assigning penult stress on the assumption that the bare verb root is not a cyclic domain:

(31)

|  |  | $[fihim + na]_V$ | $[[fihim + Ø]_V + na]_V$ |
|  | I Stress | $[fihím + na]$ | $[fíhim\ \ ]$ |
|  | Syncope | fhím + na | — |
|  | II Stress | — | $[fíhím + na\ \ ]_V$ |
|  | Syncope | — | — |

Brame proposed that (1) cycled substrings must occur as independent words, and (2) all and only rules mentioning brackets are cyclic. The first condition taken literally is actually too strong because stems, which must be lexically categorized as N, V, or A and which do constitute cyclic domains, are not necessarily capable of occurring as independent words in inflectional languages, where they may require an obligatory case ending. Moreover, in many languages word formation must to all appearances be taken back to roots which in themselves are not necessarily members of any lexical category. If this is true, then it is necessary to stipulate that lexical rules apply only in domains delimited as lexical categories [     ]$_{N,A,V}$.

Perhaps the most significant consequences that the theory has for phonology have to do with the nature of lexical representations. Here it promises to resolve the long-standing issues that have been discussed in terms of constraints on abstractness, the Strict Cycle Condition, morpheme structure rules, and other notions. We shall summarize the problems in historical perspective and then show how they may be approached from the perspective of lexical phonology.

The theory worked out in Chomsky and Halle (1968) claims that underlying representations are chosen so as to give the simplest total grammar, where the grammar includes both lexicon and rules. The effect is to guarantee that lexical representations will be at *least* as abstract as the classical phonemic level. But they will be more abstract whenever, and to whatever extent, the simplicity of the system requires it. The simplicity of the system may require more abstract representations for several kinds of reasons. The most important kind of reason for setting up an abstract representation of a morpheme is systematically governed variation in its phonological shape. Underlying representations are set up in such a way as to permit such regular variation to be characterized by the simplest and therefore most general rules possible. Let us illustrate the point with an example from English phonology. The [s] in *dissonant* is to be derived by a degemination rule from /s + s/, on the strength of its component morphemes, which elsewhere appear as /dis/ (cf. *disreputable*, *discourteous*) and /sɔn + ænt/ (cf. *sonant*, *consonant*). Moreover, this representation directly explains why the word does not undergo the voicing rule to which single *s* is normally subject in that environment (cf. *resonant*). Similarly, the [s] in *criticize* is derived from /k/ by a "Velar Softening" rule, which applies throughout the derivational ("Romance") vocabulary of English, and accounts here for the regular relationship between *criticize*, *criticism* and *critic*, *critical*. This does *not* imply that the speaker or hearer need in any way mentally "derive" the words he says or hears by means of such rules as Velar Softening. What it *does* mean is that the alternations they govern belong to the regular phonological pattern of English, while for example a hypothetical *k ~ s* alternation in the reverse context, such as *criti[k]ize ~ *criti[s]al*, would be irregular. The claim made is that someone who knows English implicitly knows that pattern, and will under appropriate circumstances recognize the difference between regular and irregular alternations, though he may not be able, even after reflection, to verbalize the rules that underlie it.

The system that is set up in order to account for phonological alternations may then in turn permit further abstraction in the underlying representations of non-alternating forms as well. Often it may be positively required by the evaluation measure that selects the simplest grammar. "Abstractness" in this sense cannot be criticized on any legitimate a priori grounds; in the absence of further evidence it would indeed be demanded by sound scientific method. There is, however, evidence which shows that at precisely this point the theory induces a characteristic type of wrong analysis. Identifying and correcting the source of error in the theory was the focus of the so-called abstractness controversy resulting in various versions of "concrete" phonology and more recently cyclic phonology.

Perhaps the most familiar English example of a rule which causes difficulties of the sort which are at issue here is Trisyllabic Shortening (or Trisyllabic Laxing). This rule shortens a vowel if followed by at least two more vowels, of which the first is unstressed:

(32)   V → [−long] / ___ C$_o$ V$_i$ C$_o$ V$_j$   where V$_i$ is not metrically strong.

It applies, for example, to shorten the long vowels in the initial syllables of

(33)   opacity, declarative, tabulate

(cf. *opaque, declare, table*). The rule has to be assigned to level 1 on the evidence of words like

(34)   mightily, bravery, weariness

Clearly all morphologically simple words such as

(35)   ivory, nightingale, stevedore, Goolagong, Averell, Oedipus, Oberon

must somehow be exempted from undergoing it. Standard generative phonology forces their phonological representatives to be adjusted, if possible, in such a way that the structural description of the rule is not met. For *ivory* it is possible to postulate a final /y/, which will become *i* by an independently needed rule of English phonology. For *nightingale*, Chomsky and Halle (1968: 234) rather less persuasively suggest underlying /nixtVngæl/, with *ix* → *ī* → *ay* by rules they claim are required on other grounds. The reason this is ultimately unilluminating is that in the bulk of the cases – *stevedore* and so forth – the failure of Trisyllabic Shortening cannot be explained away by changing the underlying form anyway.

Along with the problem that many ordinary words have no regular derivation in the grammar, there is the complementary problem that words like

(36)   alibi, sycamore, camera, pelican, enemy, Amazon, Pamela, calendar

have *two* possible derivations, while only one is ever needed. They could be derived at face value from an underlying representation with a short vowel in the first syllable. But they could also be assigned a *long* vowel in the first syllable and taken for a "free ride" on the Trisyllabic Shortening rule.

Let us now look at some possible solutions to these problems.

A primitive attempt at solving this problem was the so-called Alternation Condition. In its strong version, it went as follows (Kiparsky 1968, sec. 1):

(37)   Obligatory neutralization rules cannot apply to all occurrences of a morpheme.

The general effect is to limit the "abstractness" of underlying representations to cases motivated by phonological alternations. With regard to our particular example, the Alternation Condition does two things. It resolves the indeterminacy in the underlying representation of (36) by fixing the vowels of the first syllables as short. And it prohibits the possibility of dealing with (35) by such phonological devices as postulating /x/ in *nightingale* and nonsyllabic /y/ in *ivory*. Nevertheless, the Alternation Condition as stated in (37) is unquestionably inadequate. Without attempting to do justice to the complex discussion that broke out around it,[7] let us summarize what are perhaps its most damaging flaws.

(1)   The Alternation Condition is not interpretable as a formal condition on grammars. In order to check whether it is satisfied in a given grammar, it would be necessary to inspect every derivation of that grammar. The only sense that can be made out of it is as a strategy of language acquisition which says that a learner analyzes a form "at face value" unless he has encountered variants of it which justify a more remote underlying representation.

(2)   The Alternation Condition leaves the theory with an inherent redundancy. For example, it says that words like (36) cannot be derived from underlying representations with long vowels in the first syllable. That fact ought to be of one piece with the fact that words like (35) do not undergo Trisyllabic Shortening. Yet we shall still either have to mark the latter as exceptions to the rule, or else restate its environment so that it applies only across morpheme boundaries. This is redundant because the theory already tells us, by the Alternation Condition, that these words *could not* be subject to Trisyllabic Shortening. The problem is that the constraint on underlying representations leads to a predictable restriction on the application of rules which cannot, in this formulation, be expressed systematically in the grammar.

(3)   The Alternation Condition is too weak in that it imposes no restrictions whatever on possible patterns of alternation. It appears that a certain type of rule, of which Trisyllabic Shortening is an example, could not apply morpheme-internally as in (35), (36), even if alternations did exist. To see what is at stake, consider the condition on Trisyllabic Shortening that the following vowel must be unstressed. It correctly blocks the rule from shortening the first vowel in such words as (38), (39):

(38)   quōtátion
       flōtátion
       gȳrátion
       cītátion
       mīgrátion

(39)   fīnálity
       vītálity
       glōbálity
       tōnálity
       tītánic

What does not exist, and arguably could not exist, is a pattern illustrated by the hypothetical cases in (40), where we would have to allow morpheme-internal application of Trisyllabic Shortening, on the strength of the long vowel that shows up in the derivative, where Trisyllabic Shortening is bled by stress.

(40)  órigin    :  * ōríginal    (ŏríginal)
      sýnonym  :  * sȳnónymous  (sўnónymous)

The Alternation Condition is incapable of predicting that such cases do not exist.[8]

(4)  On the other hand, the Alternation Condition is too strong in that it excludes analyses which are well motivated on internal grounds. That is, it cannot be maintained without unacceptable loss of generalization. It is this failing which attracted the most discussion in the controversy over the Alternation Condition.

For example, while no one will miss the putative /x/ in *nightingale*, a final /y/ is rather well motivated by the system of English word stress. Words ending in *-ory* and *-ary*, as well as words like *galaxy*, *industry*, systematically behave as if the final vowel was really a consonant, with respect to several of the stress rules (Chomsky and Halle 1968: 130; Liberman and Prince 1977; Hayes 1981: ch. 5). The same final /y/ accounts for the failure of Trisyllabic Shortening in derived words like *vacancy*, *piracy*, *agency*, *secrecy*, where the rule would otherwise be expected to apply (Rubach 1981). Also the only exception to the generalization noted above that *-al* is added after stressed syllables is *burial*; which can be resolved by taking the final *-y* as nonsyllabic. But the required rule

(41)  y → i / ___ #

is an obligatory neutralization rule, since *i* is a phoneme of English, and so cannot apply in the proposed cases consistent with the Alternation Condition.

   An alternative approach is to deny the phonological character of rules such as Trisyllabic Shortening. It is commonly said that rules of this type are to be considered as "morphological" or "morphologized." This claim may actually mean a number of things, since there are several possible ways of treating morphologically conditioned rules in the phonology. But on any of the possible construals, the properties of the rule seem to be obscured rather than explained by the proposal. Let us consider three versions in turn.

   The first version would be to simply add to the phonological environment of (32) a morphological environment consisting of the list of formatives before which the shortening process can take place, e.g.:

(42)  -ous     :  ōmen      ~  ominous
      -ate     :  pōllen    ~  pollinate
      -ar      :  līne      ~  linear
      -al      :  nātion    ~  national
      -ty      :  pēnal     ~  penalty
      -ison    :  compāre   ~  comparison
      -(it)ive :  compēte   ~  competitive
      -(i)fy   :  vīle      ~  vilify
      -ent     :  rēfer     ~  referent

This list is, however, redundant. The suffixes which have to be included in it are simply *all* "+boundary" suffixes which can cause the phonological conditions of Trisyllabic Shortening to be met. The only suffixes of that class that may be omitted are those which happen never to occur in the appropriate phonological circumstances, for example deverbal -*al*, which is only added to end-stressed words (*arrival, arousal, betrayal*). The correct generalization is that all and only suffixes of the +boundary class may trigger Trisyllabic Shortening in the environment of (32).

A second morphologized version of (32) would omit the phonological conditions entirely and state the rule simply as triggered by the suffixes of (42). It is open to the same objection as the first version and has to be rejected for that reason alone. Moreover, it misses the further generalization embodied in the *phonological* environment of the rule and therefore enormously adds to the *lexical* arbitrariness of the rule in such cases as:

(43)   ŏmin + ous          vs.   hēīn + ous
      pŏllin + ate         vs.   vāc + ate
      lĭne + ar            vs.   sōl + ar
      nătion + al          vs.   fōc + al
      compĕt + it + ive    vs.   invās + ive
      prepăr + at + ory    vs.   advīs + ory
      prĕfer + ence        vs.   clēār + ance
      rĕfer + ent          vs.   sōn + ant

The third version is that morphophonemic processes are integral parts of morphological operations. This is the most unfortunate treatment of all because it denies that there is a single process involved, and claims that there are as many "Trisyllabic Shortening" rules as there are suffixes that can trigger the shortening process. Since the shortening is stated separately in connection with each affixation process, there is no way in this theory to distinguish between English and a hypothetical language in which each suffix triggers its own arbitrary set of changes in the stem. It even becomes impossible to relate irregular derivations to regular ones. It seems correct to say that *obēsity* and *oblīquity* are formed from *obese, oblique*, by the same morphological process as *obscĕnity* from *obscēne* but are exceptions to Trisyllabic Shortening and Vowel Shift, respectively. But if Trisyllabic Shortening and Vowel Shift are integral parts of that morphological process, then it is necessary to say that the three derived words are formed by three *different* morphological processes.

Not only is the central regularity underlying a rule such as Trisyllabic Shortening obscured by combining it with the various suffixation processes; the very patterning of exceptions is lost sight of. For example, the morpheme /nōt/ (*note*) is an exception to Trisyllabic Shortening: cf. *denōt + ative* (vs. *compăr + ative*), *nōt + ify* (vs. *cŏd + ify*). On the proposal under consideration it would have to be considered as subject to as many exceptional, otherwise unmotivated morphological operations as happen to give rise to the conditions that ordinarily trigger Trisyllabic Shortening.[9]

The germ of truth in the morphologization idea is that instead of stating a constraint on underlying representations directly, it should be made derivative of a primary constraint on the operation of phonological rules, which limits certain rules to "derived" inputs. If we can state a principle that prohibits Trisyllabic Shortening from operating in underived cases like (35), then the desired underlying representations are at the same time automatically enforced because no others will yield the correct output in conformity with the principle.

The search for a constraint on the application of rules, moreover, makes more sense in the theoretical framework of generative grammar, and it is the strategy by which the most interesting discoveries of theoretical linguistics have been achieved.

We can approach the problem by introducing a notion of *derived environment*.

Def.: An environment E is *derived* with respect to a rule R if E satisfies the structural description of R crucially by virtue of a combination of morphemes or the application of a rule.

We can then reformulate the Alternation Condition as restricting the corresponding class of rules as follows:

(44)   *Revised Alternation Condition (RAC)*
       Obligatory neutralization rules apply only in derived environments.

That is, an obligatory neutralization rule can apply only if the input involves crucially a sequence which arises in morpheme combinations or through the earlier application of a phonological rule. Otherwise, that is, if the environment is met already in the underlying representation of a single morpheme, the process cannot apply. Requiring that a neutralization process apply only in derived environments guarantees in particular that neutralization will always be contextual (as opposed to absolute).

The RAC, then, does double duty as a constraint on the abstractness of underlying representations and as a principle of rule application allowing us to explain a class of cases which are unstatable in the older theory.

While the Revised Alternation Condition is a substantial improvement, it still retains some of the weaknesses discussed above. In the first place, it is still not a formal condition of the desired sort because the property of being a "neutralization rule" is not determinable from inspection of the grammar. Once again it is in principle necessary to check all the derivations in order to see whether the condition is satisfied. Secondly, there remain problems of empirical adequacy. An example of a loss of generalization entailed by the Revised Alternation Condition in English phonology can be seen in the regularities governed by the Velar Softening rule. This rule, which can be formulated as

$$(45) \quad k \rightarrow s \, / \underline{\quad} \begin{bmatrix} -\text{back} \\ -\text{low} \end{bmatrix}$$

(perhaps via an intermediate $c$ as in Chomsky and Halle 1968) is an obligatory neutralization rule, since $s$ is phonemic in English. Because of *critic* ~ *criticize* and similar alternations, (45) must be in the phonology of English in any case. Prohibiting its application in non-derived cases like *conceive, proceed, recite* has several unfortunate consequences. In the first place, the explanation for the distribution of $s$, $z$, and $k$ in those stems is lost. We find one set of cases where the root initial consonant is *z* intervocalically and *s* elsewhere, and another set of cases where the root-initial consonant is *s* if a nonlow front vowel follows and *k* elsewhere:

(46)  /s/  :  re[z]ist      con[s]ist
      /s/  :  re[z]ort      con[s]ort

      /k/  :  re[s]eive     con[s]eive
      /k/  :  re[k]ord      con[k]ord

The problem is explained by assuming underlying /s/ and /k/ respectively. The independently motivated rules of Velar Softening and intervocalic voicing of s, applied in that order, account for the observed surface reflexes of /k/ and /s/. The Revised Alternation Condition loses the generalization that /z/ does not appear in roots and sets up a set of exceptions to the intervocalic voicing rule (*receive*). Furthermore, the *k* in the prefix of *accede*, *succeed*, *accept* (pronounced with [ . . . ks . . . ]), should be attributed to the assimilation rule that operates transparently in *afford*, *support*, *account*, etc., but this cannot be done if the non-alternating initial *s* has to be set up as underlying /s/ as required by the Revised Alternation Condition. Thus many of the convincing aspects of the analysis by Chomsky and Halle (1968) would have to be abandoned along with the less compelling ones.

   A major step forward, which puts the whole problem into an entirely new light, was made by Joan Mascaró in his dissertation of (1976). Mascaró proposed that the class of rules which exhibits the "derived-environment-only" behavior is the class of cyclic rules, and that this behavior follows from the definition of "proper application of a cyclic rule." With some simplification, his proposal was:

(47)  *Strict Cycle Condition* (SCC):
      (a)  Cyclic rules apply only to derived representations.
      (b)  Def.: A representation $\phi$ is *derived* w.r.t. rule R in cycle j iff $\phi$ meets the structural analysis of R by virtue of a combination of morphemes introduced in cycle j or the application of a phonological rule in cycle j.

The correct mode of application for Trisyllabic Shortening is thus obtained by setting it up as a cyclic rule, and the previously problematic Velar Softening rule has different properties by virtue of being a postcyclic rule.

   The most important consequence of the Strict Cycle Condition is that there should be a relationship between the way a rule is *ordered* and the way it *applies*: cyclic ordering should correlate with the restriction to derived environments, and postcyclic ordering should correlate with across-the-board application. Naturally, while the evidence from ordering and from application to non-derived forms should in principle coincide, we should not expect to find *both* kinds of evidence for *all* rules. There should, however, be no conflict between the two criteria, and one would hope to find some nontrivial convergence between them. The recent study of Polish phonology by Rubach (1981) is devoted to exploring precisely this hypothesis in a rich body of material. His findings confirm it in rather striking ways. [ . . . ]

There are also some empirical problems with the theory. For one thing, cyclic rules are known which do not show the expected "strict cyclic" properties, in that they must apply to non-derived environments on the first cycle. We have encountered one such example in the Spanish syllabification rule (see (30)). A notorious case is stress in English. Although a metrical treatment eliminates the need for cyclic assignment of sentence stress, it remains true that lexical stress must be assigned cyclically (Kiparsky 1979, Hayes 1981). And it is evidently assigned by exactly the same rules to non-derived stems as to derived stems. That is, the antepenult stress in *Menómini* is an instance of the same regularity as the antepenult stress in *synónym* + *y*. The formulation of (47) incorrectly entails that this cannot be the case.

A second question that the Strict Cycle Condition leaves unanswered harks back to the original "abstractness" issue. One of the basic observations that the Alternation Condition set out to explain was the tendency for non-derived outputs of obligatory neutralization rules to get lexicalized. Mascaró suggested that this class of rules is necessarily cyclic, but this is evidently untenable for the reasons already discussed in connection with the Revised Alternation Condition. The weaker formulation that obligatory neutralization rules are cyclic in the so-called unmarked case is at the very least ad hoc. And finally, if nothing at all is said beyond (47), the theory is simply left with two classes of rules, cyclic and noncyclic, and does not have the leverage required to account for the observed drift into the lexicon. The problem, then, is to develop a theory capable of explaining why, in case after case, obligatory absolute neutralization rules bequeathed to a language by sound changes that merge segments are reanalyzed out of it, and non-derived outputs of obligatory contextual neutralization rules are lexicalized, so that the actual phonologies of languages are practically always more concrete than history would make one expect.

A third question concerns the relation between the morpheme structure of a language and its cyclic rules. Typically, the output of the cyclic rules (again excluding metrical rules) has the same form as do underlying representations, both as regards the segment inventory and the possible combinations of segments. In other words, cyclic phonology is structure-preserving. The theory as it now stands does not explain why it should be so. Moreover, it saddles grammar with a characteristic redundancy, where phonological rules recapitulate the unmarked structure of morphemes. For example, the theory cannot relate the existence of the (cyclic) Trisyllabic Shortening rule (32) to the fact that non-derived words that violate it, such as (35), are nevertheless much rarer than non-derived words that conform to it, such as (36). In the theory of Chomsky and Halle (1968) the former are outright exceptions, in cyclic phonology they are entirely on a par with the latter and fully as regular; the truth would rather seem to be that morpheme-internal $\bar{V}CVCV$ sequences are "marked" relative to $\breve{V}CVCV$ within English phonology.

In sum, the class of cyclic rules seems to be distinguished from the class of postcyclic rules by a syndrome of properties which define a special mode of rule application, and which have no apparent intrinsic connection either with each other or with rule ordering. Why are cyclic rules structure-preserving? Why do cyclic rules characterize unmarked morpheme structure? Why do obligatory neutralization rules tend to become cyclic? Why do *metrical* cyclic rules seem to work differently? And more generally, why do these properties go together, and what do they have to do with cyclicity?

The answers to these questions are actually already at hand. The Strict Cycle Condition does not have to be stipulated in the theory. A version of it is deducible from the Elsewhere Condition. The version so deduced, unlike the original version, directly predicts the apparently deviant behavior of cyclic metrical rules as well as the relationship we noted between cyclic phonology and the lexicon.

The basic point is that the blocking of cyclic rules in non-derived environments effected by the Strict Cycle Conditions follows from the Elsewhere Condition under the assumption, already justified on morphological grounds above, that every lexical entry constitutes an identity rule whose structural description is the same as its structural change. For example, we shall then have the two rules

(60)   (a)   /nītVngæl/
       (b)   Trisyllabic Shortening (32)

The structural description of (60a) properly includes (60b), i.e. (60a) defines a subset of the contexts of (60b). The outputs of (60a) and (60b) are distinct, with (60a) specifying a long vowel in a position where (60b) specifies a short vowel. So the Elsewhere Condition is applicable and says that only rule (60a) is applied to the string /nītVngæl/, which gives us the desired result that the word is not subject to the Trisyllabic Shortening rule. The rule is, however, free to apply to derived inputs such as [[sæ n]$_A$iti]$_N$, because they do not constitute lexical entries.

(61)       [[sæn]$_A$iti]$_N$       [nītVngæl]$_N$
    I   [ – ]              (blocked by E.C.)
    II  [[sæn]$_A$iti]$_N$
           *sanity*            *nightingale*

We not only derive the special case of blocking on the first cycle, but the full effect of the Strict Cycle Condition, which blocks rules on any cycle n from applying to inputs which are not derived (in the sense of (47b)) on cycle n. This is by virtue of the principle, which we also saw to be necessary on independent morphological grounds above, that the output of every layer of derivation, such as [sæniti], is itself a lexical entry, and thereby an identity rule which enters into a disjunctive relation with other lexical rules such as Trisyllabic Shortening by the Elsewhere Condition in exactly the same way as underived lexical entries do.

Finally, the reason postlexical rules such as Prevocalic Lengthening are free to apply to non-derived inputs is that being in a different component they cannot be linked disjunctively to a rule in the lexicon by the Elsewhere Condition.

The version of strict cyclicity that we arrive at in this way, however, differs crucially from (47) in that it blocks conjunctive application only when the outputs are *distinct*. That has been the case in the examples considered so far, but it is not the case in a large class of other cases, most obviously in rules that assign metrical structure to strings not already bearing metrical structure. Consider the lexical entry *parent* and the rule of
$\wedge$
English word stress that assigns it the stress pattern SW. We have two rules whose respective outputs when applied to the string *parent* are *parent* itself (the identity rule)

and *parent* (the stress rule). These outputs are not distinct in that they do not have contradictory feature specifications or contradictory metrical structure. Rather, one has a specified metrical structure where the other is unspecified as to metrical structure. The outputs not being distinct, clause (ii) of the Elsewhere Condition is not met, and both rules accordingly apply, which means that stress is free to apply on the first cycle. In the same way, syllable structure in Spanish is assigned on the first cycle by rules with the effect of (62b) (among others) because condition (ii) of (10) is not met and (62a, b) therefore apply conjunctively.

(62)   (a)   desdeñ

(b)   VC → VC

We also correctly predict that cyclically derived phonological properties can trigger subsequent rules on the same cycle. Thereby even feature-changing rules can apply on the first cycle if they are fed by cyclic rules. This is illustrated in the Spanish example we cited from Harris, where the cyclically assigned syllable-final status of *n* causes depalatalization:

(63)   (a)   desdeñ

(b)   Vñ → Vn

Here (10) is not met, and the rules therefore apply conjunctively. Hence we have the correct derivation *desdeñ* (62a = 63a) → *desdeñ* (62b) → *desden* (63b), all in the first cycle.

A further corollary is that rules which assign metrical structure *will* be blocked on the first cycle to the extent that the input is metrically structured already in the lexicon. In Spanish, cases like *huir* (two syllables), *oiremos* (four) can be simply marked so in the lexicon (as suggested by Harris), and the syllabification rules will not apply.

These assumptions afford a series of major simplifications in Hayes's theory of English word stress. Hayes introduces two basic rules of stress assignment (foot formation): the English Stress rule (ESR) and Strong Retraction rule (SRR). The ESR applies at the right edge of the word, assigning maximally binary feet labeled S W, where W may not be a heavy syllable (not counting "extrametrical" material). The SRR applies iteratively from right to left, also assigning maximally binary feet labeled S W, but without restrictions as to syllable weight. As proposed by Selkirk (1980), stress is not a feature but the property of being the strong or only syllable of a foot. Thus, we have such derivations as (64), where parentheses denote extrametricality:

(64)

(a)   hamamelidanthemum → (ESR) hamamelidanthe (mum) → (SRR) hamamelidanthemum

(b)   Tīconderōga → Tīconderō (ga) → Tīconderōga

[ ... ]

A priori the elimination of a special category of "morpheme structure rules" is welcome because the status of these putative rules has almost from the beginning of generative phonology been beset with problems. Kenstowicz and Kisseberth (1977) identify four of them:

1   Condition or rule: are MSRs to be construed as rules that fill in predictable feature specifications left blank in the matrices entered in the lexicon, or are they to be construed as static well-formedness conditions that check the acceptability of fully specified lexical entries?
2   The duplication problem: why are regularities expressed by morpheme structure rules often recapitulated by phonological rules proper, applying to derived forms?
3   The domain problem: on what sorts of entities are lexical constraints defined – morphemes, stems, or finished words?
4   The level problem: to what stage of derivation are lexical constraints applicable – underlying representations, the phonetic output, or some intermediate level?

In the approach proposed here, the answers to these questions must run as follows:

1   Predictable feature specifications are left unspecified in lexical entries and are filled in by the system of universal and language-particular rules of lexical phonology.
2   There is no duplication problem because the rules that apply to non-derived forms in a blank-filling function, governing the structure of primitive lexical entries, are the same lexical rules that apply after the first cycle in a feature-changing function, governing the structure of derived lexical forms.
3   The domains on which lexical constraints are defined are *lexical categories*, i.e. the cyclic constituents N, A, V. Lexical constraints are therefore only indirectly pertinent to morphemes (roots, affixes, etc.).
4   Lexical constraints are applicable in lexical (cyclic) phonology as determined by the ordering of the relevant rules. Thus they are not necessarily true either of underlying representations or of the phonetic output. In particular, the application of postlexical rules may totally obscure the canonical structure of lexical items.

From our point of view, "duplication" between morpheme structure rules and rules of lexical phonology, far from being a problem, is actually the predicted normal case. We do not allow rules whose domain is defined as the morpheme; minimally they must belong to level 1 and apply also to such derived forms as meet their structural description. This does not mean that all rules will actually exhibit duplication. It can very well happen that the environment of a level 1 rule occurs only in underived lexical items or only in forms derived at level 1; what is predicted is that *if* it occurs in both, then the rule will indeed apply to both.

It is of course still necessary to make some distinction between those lexical rules which govern the structure of underived lexical items merely in the unmarked case and those which govern it absolutely. That is, when are lexical rules contradicted by inherent feature specifications in lexical items and when are they not? Even in its present skeletal form our theory makes an interesting prediction on this score. Namely, lexical rules which apply in non-derived environments should all be potentially "cancelable" on the first cycle, while lexical rules which apply in derived environments on the first cycle should not be cancelable. The only way a lexical rule can come to be applicable on the first cycle in a derived environment is for it to be fed there by a previously applying lexical rule (which by what we have said must either have applied in a non-feature-changing way or itself have been fed by an earlier rule). The obvious examples are segmental rules that apply within metrical domains such as stress feet or syllables themselves assigned by earlier lexical rules. We had such a case in the Spanish depalatalization rule (63b), which applies within a syllable structure created earlier on the same cycle. So it follows that we cannot keep a syllable-final ñ in Spanish simply by marking it as /ñ/ in the lexicon. And in fact, it appears that this is never necessary.

If we are to allow unspecified feature values in the lexicon, then it becomes incumbent upon us to answer the well-known objections of Stanley (1967) against that procedure. We shall do this by stipulating that no feature can appear marked both + and − in the same environment in the lexicon.

For our starting point we revert to the natural assumption of early generative phonology that phonological features are unspecified in underlying representations if their value can be assigned by a rule. The theory of grammar will provide a set of universal redundancy rules functionally analogous to the markedness principles of Chomsky and Halle (1968), but formally identical to ordinary phonological rules. In particular, assume that for every feature F there is minimally a rule

(72)   [     ] → [αF]

where $\alpha$ (+ or −) is the "unmarked" value. In addition, other rules may be applicable in specific syntagmatic or paradigmatic contexts. For example, for voicing we may have the rules

(73)   (a)   [     ] → [+voiced]
        (b)   [+obstr] → [−voiced]

putting the unmarked value as [−voiced] for obstruents and [+voiced] elsewhere. We now say that voiceless obstruents and voiced sonorants are represented as [0 voiced], that is, unspecified for voicing, and that their respective specifications for voicing are filled in by the application of rule (73). This much is quite in the spirit of traditional markedness theory.

Suppose further that the lexical phonological rules of a language apply to lexical entries together with universal rules such as (73), as part of the system of lexical redundancy rules. For example, the English lexical rule of regressive voicing assimilation applies on the first cycle as a lexical redundancy rule that assigns [αvoiced] as the normal value to obstruents in the context [αvoiced]. This again means that obstruents in that context are [0 voiced] in lexical entries of English.

We thus obtain a hierarchy of successively more specific rules, all but the first rule (73a) applying in domains included in more general rules and superseding them in the shared domain. The portion of the hierarchy that we have seen so far is shown together in (74):

(74)　(a)　[　　]　→ [+voiced]
　　　(b)　[+obstr]　→ [−voiced]
　　　(c)　$\begin{bmatrix} +\text{obstr} \\ \alpha\text{voiced} \end{bmatrix}$ → [αvoiced] / __ $\begin{bmatrix} +\text{obstr} \\ \alpha\text{voiced} \end{bmatrix}$

The disjunctive ordering among such sets of rules comes by the Elsewhere Condition.

Clearly, lexical redundancy rules must not be allowed to change lexically specified features. For example, rule (74b) only "fills blanks," and does not apply to segments inherently specified as [+voiced], such as /z/. This does not have to be specially stipulated in the theory, but falls out directly from (10) if we construe each lexical item L as a rule as proposed above. Suppose we have the English words *sip* and *zip*. We then have the rules (75a–c), where (a) and (b) are disjunctive by (10), but (a) and (c) are not disjunctive because their outputs are not distinct (condition (ii) of (10) is not met).

(75)　(a)　[+obstr]　→　[−voiced]

　　　(b)　$\begin{bmatrix} +\text{obstr} \\ +\text{cor} \\ \text{etc.} \\ +\text{voiced} \end{bmatrix}$　*ip* (disjunctive with (a))

　　　(c)　$\begin{bmatrix} +\text{obstr} \\ +\text{cor} \\ \text{etc.} \\ 0 \text{ voiced} \end{bmatrix}$　*ip* (conjunctive with (a))

In exactly the same way, the /b/ of *absent*, lexically specified as [−voiced], does not undergo the voicing assimilation (74c), while the unspecified /b/ of *abdomen* does. Thus the lexical entries themselves are the end points of the above-mentioned hierarchies of successively more specific rules:

(76)                (74a)
                      |
                   (74b)

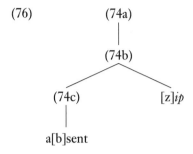

         (74c)            [z]*ip*
           |
       a[b]sent

It follows that in every context C, only two lexical specifications will be possible for any feature F, viz. [0F] and [$\alpha$F], where [$\alpha$F] is the unpredictable value. Therefore we escape Stanley's (1967) objection that allowing unspecified features in the lexicon amounts to introducing a three-valued feature system.

Not every context allows both possible feature specifications. If only one specification of F occurs in some context C′, i.e. if some branch of the hierarchy for F does not terminate in any lexical items but in the rule for C′ itself, then we shall say that F is *non-distinctive* in C′. Its lexical specification in C′ is then necessarily [0F].

We still have an IOU to pay off to the abstractness issue. Although we have been able to derive the "cyclic syndrome," including the properties associated with the Strict Cycle Condition, from independently motivated principles governing the lexicon, we have as yet no explanation for why rules should become lexical in the first place. After all, sound changes enter a language as postlexical rules, and there is no a priori reason why they should in time tend to graduate to lexical status, with concomitant reanalysis of their synchronically non-derived outputs. More particularly, as was made explicit in several formulations of the Alternation Condition and the Strict Cycle Condition, obligatory neutralization rules have a special affinity for the cycle/lexicon which still needs to be accounted for.

To begin with this last question, the answer is evidently that obligatory neutralization rules are precisely those rules whose outputs are potentially subject to lexicalization without complicating the grammar. Why neutralization rules? They are rules which merge one set of representations with another:

(77)   A                B

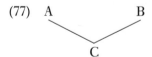

         C

where possibly C = A or B. So in this case C derived from A has by definition another possible source in the lexicon, namely B or whatever is the source of B. The lexicalization of the output of a non-neutralization rule (say, aspiration in English) requires adding some redundant category to underlying representations, which, other things being equal, will be rejected on grounds of simplicity. And why just *obligatory* neutralization rules? If the output of an *optional* rule is lexicalized, then its relationship to the other variant cannot be accounted for by the rule. This will again be rejected on grounds of simplicity. Imagine, for example, that the Trisyllabic Shortening rule in English was postlexical and optional. Then obviously the shortened variant of *nightingale* would not be lexicalized because it could not then be related to the variant with a long vowel. So if a postlexical rule is non-neutralizing or optional, simplicity considerations will generally require that it continue to apply to non-derived forms, and the Elsewhere Condition then entails that it remain in the postlexical component.

This does *not* mean that there could not be non-neutralizing rules or optional rules in the cyclic phonology. Such cases have certainly been documented in the literature. All that is predicted is that postlexical rules can shift into the lexicon without either overt changes in their non-derived inputs or loss of generality only if they are obligatory non-neutralization rules.

Assuming this account of why it is obligatory non-neutralization rules that may become lexical, we now come to the question why the rules that may become lexical so readily do so. To postulate a principle that the "unmarked" status of a rule is lexical is no more than a restatement of the observation that we wish to explain. Assume instead that the language learner is guided by a principle that selects the simplest available derivation, the criterion of derivational simplicity being length. By "available" I mean "allowed by the evaluation measure." This means that derivational simplicity is strictly subordinated to grammatical simplicity, and only comes into play when the evaluation measure is indeterminate as between alternative grammars. The principle that the shortest derivations are preferred is related to Zwicky's (1970) "No Free Ride" Principle and more distantly to Postal's Naturalness Condition, which is formulated as a condition of adequacy on phonological theories, rather than as a principle for selecting between alternative descriptions within a theory. The idea was actually implicit in some generative treatments of analogical leveling, e.g. the discussion of the loss of final devoicing in Swiss dialects in Kiparsky (1968). We shall call it the Derivational Simplicity Criterion (DSC) and formulate it as follows:

(78)   *Derivational Simplicity Criterion* (DSC)
       Among alternative maximally simple grammars select that which has the shortest derivations.

The favored status of lexical phonological rules is derivable from the DSC because putting a rule into the lexical phonology always enables non-derived forms to be derived from the shallowest source, in satisfaction of (78). As a schematic example, consider how Trisyllabic Shortening might have become a lexical rule. Suppose that at a certain period there arose surface exceptions to it such as *nightingale*, from degenerate compounds, vowel lengthening, and other sources. Faced with data such as *nightingale*, two analyses are available to the learner. The first possibility is to take the word "at face value," and set up /nītVngæl/, with an underlying long vowel. The second, assuming for the sake of the example that an /x/ deleted with compensatory lengthening can still be motivated for this stage of English, is the more abstract /nixtVngæl/. These two alternatives commit the learner to different assumptions about the phonological rules as well. Underlying /nītVngæl/ entails that Trisyllabic Shortening is lexical. Underlying /nixtVngæl/ entails that the rule deleting /x/ is postlexical. But the DSC fixes the underlying form as /nītVngæl/, in turn forcing Trisyllabic Shortening into the lexical phonology. Such restructuring erodes the support for the /x/-deletion rule and eventually brings about its demise.

To summarize, we have arrived at the conclusion that what is right about the Strict Cycle Condition is derivable from the Elsewhere Condition on the assumption that word phonology is integrated with the morphology in the lexicon. The resulting theory can be considered an advance from both the conceptual and the empirical point of view. Conceptually, it achieves a greater explanatory depth in that various principles that had to be stipulated previously are now derived from the interaction of more elementary principles. Empirically, it marks a step towards overcoming the tension between two goals, each legitimate in themselves but so far curiously difficult to reconcile with each other in generative phonology: maximal generality and elegance of descriptions on the one hand, and maximal realism, naturalness, etc. on the other. It no longer seems necessary to make compromises in one in order to achieve the other.

The notable feature of this theory when compared to earlier approaches to the same problems in generative phonology, as well as to current trends in syntax, is that the main explanatory burden is carried by simplicity and the structure of the grammar itself, as opposed to conditions on rules or representations. The only condition we required was the essentially trivial Elsewhere Condition, which may very well be reducible to a more general cognitive principle.

## Notes

This research was supported in part by a grant from the National Institute of Mental Health (grant Number 89283).

1   Marchand (1969: 228) accurately points out that ". . . a prefix is the determinant of a syntagma whereas a suffix is the determinatum." "A prefixal derivative joins the category the unprefixed word belongs to. In a suffixal derivative, however, the suffix is the grammatically and semantically dominant element. In combinations such as *father-hood*, *father-ly*, the word *father* merely determines what is essentially a '-hood' or '-ly' respectively." He further observes that the order of determinant and determinatum (modifier and head) is reversed in "combinations based on the underlying theme of appreciation": diminutives and hypocoristics (*booklet*, *daddy*), approximatives (*yellowish*), frequentatives (*crackle*).

2   The formulation of (10) is generalized from that of Kiparsky (1973a) in that it need specify only that the structural changes effected by the rules be incompatible (condition ii). The earlier version had to apply also to cases where the structural changes are identical. But, as pointed out by Howard (1975), the case where the changes are identical was only necessary for stress rules. For example, the two rules collapsed in the schema

$$V \rightarrow \acute{V} / \underline{\quad} C_o(V\ C_o)\ \#$$

must apply disjunctively so that a stress is assigned to the final syllable only if there is no penult (i.e. in monsyllables). However, if we adopt metrical phonology, the stress patterns

are distinct if we construe distinctness for metrical structure in the obvious way as incompatibility of labeling or bracketing. And in any case, the metrical version of the rule simply assigns a maximally binary foot to the right edge of a word, and so does not properly constitute a schema abbreviating two rules. We therefore need only specify distinctness of outputs as in (ii) of (10).

3   The model predicts that level 1 plurals should be inputs not only to compounding, but also to level 2 affixation. This possibility is to my knowledge not realized. We therefore require an ad hoc constraint that blocks it. Interestingly, this constraint does *not* apply to *inherent* plurals, cf. *to people, to dice, dicey, sudsy, woodsy*.

Another point is that nouns which denote things that are classified as coming in pairs, e.g. (*a pair of* ) *trousers*, systematically deviate from the pattern of (12) in that they do not require plural endings in compounds:

trouser pockets      (trousers)
scissor tail         (scissors)
spectacle case       (spectacles)
pincer movement      (pincers)

They must therefore be considered as morphologically derived plurals, however this is to be done. This is independently required because the stems *trouser* etc. that we are forced to set up in the lexicon are indeed *not* bound to the plural morpheme, for they show up also in derivatives like *trousered, bespectacled, to scissor.*

4   These examples were called to my attention by Nigel Fabb.

5   For discussion of zero derivation see Marchand (1969), Rardin (1975), Allen (1978: 271ff), Clark and Clark (1979), as well as the criticism by Lieber (1980: ch. 3) and Carlson and Roeper (1980).

6   I owe this observation to Richard Oehrle.

7   See e.g. Kenstowicz and Kisseberth (1977: ch. 1) for a review of the issue.

8   The pronunciations cited here and below follow the norm given by *Webster's Dictionary* (third edition). It should be noted that many speakers show some variation in quantity in initial open syllables, apparently involving both shortening of long vowels (*tonálity* → *tŏnálity*) and lengthening of short vowels (*prŏgress* → *prógress, pŏlíce* → *pōlíce, rĕsídual* → *rēsídual*).

9   Taken literally, this is what Linell (1979) must be advocating when he says that "phonotactic rules" and "morphophonological rules proper" are not "separate rules" but "aspects of certain morphological operations" (pp. 131, 142). For example (p. 133), Trisyllabic Shortening and Vowel Shift are both considered by him as a part of the morphological operation by which the suffix *-ity* is added to adjectives (and, presumably, of the many other morphological operations that can cause the relevant alternations to come into play). Similarly, epenthesis of [I] between sibilants and devoicing of *z* after voiceless obstruents are considered by him part of plural suffixation (and, presumably, duplicates of these rules are part of genitive and 3 sg. suffixation as well as applying somehow to the reduced forms of *is* and *has*.

## References

Allen, Margaret Reece. 1978. Morphological Investigations. Ph.D. dissertation, University of Connecticut.

Aronoff, Mark. 1976. *Word Formation in Generative Grammar*. Linguistic Inquiry Monograph, 1. Cambridge, Mass.: MIT Press.

Booij, Geert. 1981. Rule Ordering, Rule Application, and the Organization of Grammars. In W. Dressler (ed.), *Phonologica 1980*, Proceedings of the 4th International Phonology Meeting.

Brame, Michael. 1974. The Cycle in Phonology: Stress in Palestinian, Maltese, and Spanish. *Linguistic Inquiry* 5: 39–60.

Carlson, Greg and Thomas Roeper. 1980. Morphology and Subcategorization: Case and the Unmarked Complex Verb. In Teun Hoekstra, H. van der Hulst, and M. Moortgat (eds), *Lexical Grammar*, Dordrecht: Foris, 49–71.

Carstairs, Andrew. 1981. Constraints on Allomorphy in Inflexion. Ph.D. dissertation, University of London.

Chomsky, Noam and Morris Halle. 1968. *The Sound Pattern of English*. New York: Harper and Row.

Clark, E. and H. Clark. 1979. When Nouns Surface as Verbs. *Language* 55: 767–811.

Clements, George N. 1977. Tone and Syntax in Ewe. In *Harvard Studies in Phonology*, vol. 1, ed. G. N. Clements, pp. 75–186.

Esau, Helmut. 1973. *Nominalization and Complementation in Modern German*. Amsterdam/London: North Holland.

Harris, James. 1983. *Syllable Structure and Stress in Spanish: A Nonlinear Analysis*. Cambridge, Mass.: MIT Press.

Hayes, Bruce. 1981. *A Metrical Theory of Stress Rules*. Bloomington: Indiana University Linguistics Club.

Howard, Irwin. 1975. Can the "Elsewhere Condition" Get Anywhere? *Language* 51: 109–27.

Kenstowicz, Michael and Charles Kisseberth. 1977. *Topics in Phonological Theory*. New York: Academic Press.

Kiparsky, Paul. 1968 = 1973. How Abstract is Phonology? Indiana University Linguistics Club. In O. Fujimura (ed.), *Three Dimensions in Linguistic Theory*, Tokyo: TEC, 1973.

Kiparsky, Paul. 1973a. Abstractness, Opacity, and Global Rules. In *Three Dimensions of Linguistic Theory*, ed. O. Fujimura. Tokyo: Taikusha.

Kiparsky, Paul. 1973b. Elsewhere in Phonology. In S. Anderson and P. Kiparsky (eds), *A Festschrift for Morris Halle*, New York: Holt Rinehart and Winston, 93–106.

Kiparsky, Paul. 1979. Metrical Structure Assignment is Cyclic. *Linguistic Inquiry* 10: 421–42.

Kiparsky, Paul and Carol Kiparsky. 1971. Fact. In D. D. Steinberg and Leon A. Jakobovits (eds), *Semantics*, Cambridge: Cambridge University Press.

Koutsoudas, G. Sanders, and C. Noll. 1974. On the Application of Phonological Rules. *Language* 50: 1–28.

Liberman, Mark and Alan Prince. 1977. On Stress and Linguistic Rhythm. *Linguistic Inquiry* 8: 249–336.

Lieber, Rochelle. 1980. On the Organization of the Lexicon. Ph.D. dissertation, MIT.

Linell, P. 1979. *Psychological Reality in Phonology*. Cambridge: Cambridge University Press.

Marchand, Hans. 1969. *The Categories and Types of Present-Day English Word-Formation*. Munich: C. H. Beck.

Mascaró, Joan. 1976. Catalan Phonology and the Phonological Cycle. Ph.D. dissertation, MIT. Repr. by the Indiana University Linguistics Club.

Mohanan, K. P. 1981. Lexical Phonology. Ph.D. dissertation, MIT.

Paul, Hermann. 1896. Über die Aufgaben der Wortbildungslehre. In Sitzungsberichte der königl. bayer. Akademie der Wissenschaften, philosophisch-philologische und historische Classe, Munich, 692–713.

Pesetsky, David. MS. Russian morphology and lexical theory. MIT.

Pulleyblank, Douglas. MS. Tone in Tiv. MIT.

[Pulleyblank, Douglas. 1983. Tiv and the Association Conventions. In *Proceedings of ALNE 13/NELS 13*, Amherst: GLSA, 211–28.]

[Pulleyblank, Douglas. 1986. *Tone in Lexical Phonology*. Dordrecht: D. Reidel.]

Rardin, Robert. 1975. Studies in Derivational Morphology. Ph.D. dissertation, MIT.

Rischel, Jørgen. 1964. Stress, Juncture, and Syllabification in Phonemic Description. In *Proceedings of the IXth International Congress of Linguists*, 85–93.

Rischel, Jørgen. 1972. Compound Stress in Danish without a Cycle. ARIPUC 6, University of Copenhagen.

Rubach, Jerzy. 1981. *Cyclic Phonology and Palatalization in Polish and English*. Warsaw: Wydawnictwa Uniwersytetu Warszawskiego.

Selkirk, Elisabeth. 1981. English Compounding and the Theory of Word Structure. In M. Moortgat, H. van der Hulst, and T. Hoekstra (eds), *The Scope of Lexical Rules*, Dordrecht: Foris, 229–78. Also in her *Phonology and Syntax: The Relation between Sound and Structure*, Cambridge, Mass.: MIT Press, 1984.

Selkirk, Elisabeth. 1980. The Role of Prosodic Categories in English World Stress. *Linguistic Inquiry* 11: 563–605.

Siegel, Dorothy. 1974. Topics in English Morphology. Ph.D dissertation, MIT.

Siegel, Dorothy. 1977. The Adjacency Condition and the Theory of Morphology. In *Proceedings of the Eighth Annual Meeting of the North East Linguistic Society*, Amherst, Mass.

Singh, Rajendra. 1981. The English Negative Prefix *in-*. *Montreal Working Papers in Linguistics* 17: 139–43.

Stanley, Richard. 1967. Redundancy Rules in Phonology. *Language* 43: 393–436.

Strauss, Steven. 1979a. Against Boundary Distinctions in English Morphology. *Linguistic Analysis* 5: 387–419.

Strauss, Steven. 1979b. Stress Assignment as Morphological Adjustment in English. Paper presented at the Linguistic Society of America Winter Meeting, Los Angeles.

Toman, Jindrich. 1980. Wortsyntax. Ph.D. dissertation, University of Cologne.

Whitney, W. D. 1889. *Sanskrit Grammar.*[2] Cambridge, Mass.: Harvard University Press.

Williams, Edwin. 1981. On the Notions "Lexically Related" and "Head of a Word". *Linguistic Inquiry* 12: 245–74.

Zwicky, Arnold. 1970. The Free-Ride Principle and Two Rules of Complete Assimilation in English. *Papers from the Sixth Regional Meeting, Chicago Linguistic Society*, Chicago, Illinois.

# 4

# The Cycle in Phonology: Stress in Palestinian, Maltese, and Spanish (1974)

## Michael K. Brame

In this article I will adduce evidence supporting the hypothesis that stress rules apply cyclically in natural languages. A survey of some phonological alternations in Palestinian Arabic, Maltese, and Spanish leads to the postulation of an ordered set of phonological rules for each language. Further examples give rise to a series of dilemmas, and the cycle proves to be an efficient technique for their solution and for the expression of a generalization that cuts across languages.

In section 1 the Palestinian data are explored, a set of rules is motivated, and an apparent contradiction is averted by appealing to the cycle. In section 2, a set of facts similar to those of Palestinian are investigated, and a similar result is obtained. In section 3 some facts of Spanish are laid bare, and the program repeats itself. Section 4 poses and seeks to answer a question concerning alternatives to cyclic analyses. New hypotheses for constraining the cycle are hazarded in section 5, which concludes the paper.

## 1  Palestinian Arabic

The following examples can be utilized to motivate the rule that assigns stress in Palestinian Arabic.

(1)  kátab 'he wrote'       ʔíbil 'he accepted'     fíhim 'he understood'
      kátabit 'she wrote'     ʔíblit 'she accepted'   fíhmit 'she understood'
      katábna 'we wrote'      ʔbílna 'we accepted'    fhímna 'we understood'

The stem underlying the verb 'to write' in the above paradigm is *katab*, with suffixes -ɸ 'he', *-it* 'she', and *-na* 'we'. The CVCVC shape of the underlying stem of 'to write' can be generalized to the verbs 'to accept' and 'to understand'. Assume underlying *ʔibil* and *fihim* and further assume that the vowel bears stress in every case as it does in (1). We thus obtain the following more abstract representations.

(2)  kátab      ʔíbil     fíhim
      kátabit    ʔíbilit   fíhimit
      katábna    ʔibílna   fihímna

The phonetic representations of (1) may now be obtained from the more abstract representations of (2) by applying the following rule of Syncope.

(3)  *Syncope*
$$\breve{\imath} \to \phi \;/\; \underline{\quad} \; CV$$

This rule drops unstressed *i* before consonant–vowel sequences. It can be generalized to apply to all high vowels, but only *i* will be of immediate concern. Syncope will derive *ʔiblit* and *fihmit* from *ʔibilit* and *fihimit*, *ʔbílna* and *fhimna* from *ʔibilna* and *fihimna*; but it will not affect *ʔibil* and *fihim*, due to the condition that *i* be unstressed.

Given the foregoing analysis, it is easy to see that stress can be assigned in a straightforward manner by the following rule.

(4)  *Stress Assignment*
$$V \to [1 \text{ stress}] \;/\; \underline{\quad} \; C_0((VC)VC_0^1)]$$

This rule abbreviates three disjunctively ordered subcases, which are displayed in (5).

(5)   (i)   $V \to [1 \text{ stress}] \;/\; \underline{\quad} \; C_0 VCVC_0^1]$
      (ii)  $V \to [1 \text{ stress}] \;/\; \underline{\quad} \; C_0 VC_0^1]$
      (iii) $V \to [1 \text{ stress}] \;/\; \underline{\quad} \; C_0]$

The rule of Stress Assignment, along with Syncope, provides for the following representative derivations of the examples listed in (1).

(6)  fihim    katab    fihim + it    katab + it

|       |       | fíhim + it | kátab + it | Stress Assignment (i) |
| fíhim | kátab |            |            | Stress Assignment (ii) |
|       |       | fíhm + it  |            | Syncope |
| fíhim | kátab | fíhmit     | kátabit    | |

fihim + na    katab + na

|           |          | Stress Assignment (i) |
| fihím + na | katáb + na | Stress Assignment (ii) |
| fhím + na  |          | Syncope |
| fhímna    | katábna  | |

Case (iii) of Stress Assignment applies to a large class of monosyllables in Palestinian, e.g. *sádd* 'dam', *ḥúbb* 'love', *sítt* 'lady', and many others. Case (iii) applies to an even larger class of inflected verb forms, which has purposely been omitted in (1). This class will be introduced directly.

Stress Assignment predicts the correct stress for a large majority of the forms of Palestinian. There are several classes of forms, however, that appear to be counterexamples to the rule postulated above. Consider the contrast in stress that exists between the examples presented below in column I and those recorded under column II.

(7)  
               I                        II

(a)   kátabit 'she wrote'     katábit 'I wrote'  
      ṭálabit 'she ordered'   ṭalábit 'I ordered'

(b)   ʔbílna 'we accepted'   ʔábilna 'before us'  
      šríbna 'we drank'     ḥíbirna 'our ink'  
      malíkna 'our king'    mílihna 'our salt'

(c)   ʔíbil 'he accepted'    ʔábil 'before'  
      šírib 'he drank'      ḥíbir 'ink'  
      málik 'king'        mílih 'salt'

How can the two classes be reconciled? In particular, how can the stress difference between *kátabit* and *katábit* be predicted? Or that between *ʔbílna* versus *ʔábilna*? Since *ʔbílna* derives from underlying *ʔibil + na*, which is of the same *CVCVC + na* canonical shape as *ʔábilna*, there seems to be no basis for predicting the stress difference. Nevertheless, there is a satisfying resolution of this dilemma, a phonological solution which salvages the above analysis *in toto*. This solution becomes more transparent upon the observation that with the exception of geminates, there are no word-final consonant clusters in Palestinian. This suggests a general rule that serves to break up underlying word-final clusters. Also absent from Palestinian are triconsonantal clusters, again suggesting a phonological rule that serves to ensure their nonoccurrence. The two processes can be viewed as a single rule, which is stated as (8).

(8)  *Epenthesis*

$$\phi \rightarrow i \; / \; C \underline{\hspace{1.5em}} C \begin{Bmatrix} \# \\ C \end{Bmatrix}$$

To ensure that Epenthesis does not apply to the identical consonant sequences of *sadd*, *ḥubb*, *sitt*, etc. mentioned above, either of two things could be done. We could associate with Epenthesis a condition excluding the possibility that the left and right consonants straddling the dash of (8) be identical. Or we could assume a general rule of gemination, a rule turning two identical consonants to a single geminate or long consonant. If this rule were made to apply before Epenthesis, there would be no need to tag Epenthesis with a special condition. The latter possibility will be adopted here, although neither choice affects the principal point of this section.

    The existence of Epenthesis explains the nonoccurrence of certain clusters in phonetic representations. But there is a more cogent motivation for this rule: its existence affords us an explanation for the contrast seen in the paradigms of (7). The following forms will underlie those of (7).

(9)  
            I           II

(a)   katab + it     katab + t  
      ṭalab + it     ṭalab + t

(b)   ʔibil + na     ʔabl + na  
      širib + na     ḥibr + na  
      maliḳ + na    milḥ + na

(c)   ʔibil         ʔabl  
      širib        ḥibr  
      malik       milḥ

Epenthesis will be ordered after Stress Assignment, and all the correct phonetic representations will fall out as a natural consequence of our analysis. Representative derivations are displayed in (10).

(10)

| katab + it | katab + t | ʔibil + na | ʔabl + na | ʔabl | |
|---|---|---|---|---|---|
| kátab + it | katáb + t | ʔibíl + na | ʔábl + na | ʔábl | Stress Assignment |
| ———— | ———— | ʔbíl + na | ———— | —— | Syncope |
| ———— | katáb + it | ———— | ʔábil + na | ʔábil | Epenthesis |
| kátabit | katábit | ʔbílna | ʔábilna | ʔábil | |

Forms such as underlying *katab + t* and *ṭalab + t* are assigned stress by case (iii) of Stress Assignment. We should also expect to find underlying *ʔibil + t* and *fihim + t* for the first person singular of the stems *ʔibil* and *fihim*. The correct phonetic representations are *ʔbílit* 'I accepted' and *fhímit* 'I understood'. This is correctly predicted by the set of rules at our disposal.

(11)

| ʔibil + t | fihim + t | |
|---|---|---|
| ʔibíl + t | fihím + t | Stress Assignment |
| ʔbíl + t | fhím + t | Syncope |
| ʔbíl + it | fhím + it | Epenthesis |
| ʔbílit | fhímit | |

Yet another problem arises in connection with the following examples.

(12)

|  | I | II |
|---|---|---|
| (a) | ṭalábna 'we ordered' | ṭalábna 'he ordered us' |
| | ṭalábtu 'you (pl) ordered' | ṭalábkum 'he ordered you (pl)' |
| | ʔaṭáʔna 'we cut' | ʔaṭáʔna 'he cut us' |
| | ʔaṭáʔitu 'you (pl) cut' | ʔaṭáʔkum 'he cut you (pl)' |
| (b) | fhímna 'we understood' | fihímna 'he understood us' |
| | fhímtu 'you (pl) understood' | fihímkum 'he understood you (pl)' |
| | smíʔna 'we heard' | simíʔna 'he heard us' |
| | smíʔtu 'you (pl) heard' | simíʔkum 'he heard you (pl)' |

Verbs having low stem vowels exhibit no contrast in syllabic structure when the subject markers -*na* and -*tu* and the object markers -*na* and -*kum* are suffixed. The (b) verbs, however, do exhibit such a contrast. The problem is that *fhímna* and *smíʔna* derive from the more abstract *fihim + na* and *simiʔ + na*, which appear to be identical to the underlying representations of the column (b)II forms. Why is it that the underlying initial *i* of *fihim + na* and *simiʔ + na* drops to give rise to the column (b)I examples, but the initial *i* does not elide from the underlying *fihim + na* and *simiʔ + na* representing the column (b)II examples? Before answering this question, another class of noneliding forms will be recorded under column II of the following display.

(13)  I                                    II
      fíhim 'he understood'                ma fihímiš 'he did not understand'
      ʔíbil 'he accepted'                  ma ʔibíliš 'he did not accept'
      símiʕ 'he heard'                     ma simíʕiš 'he did not hear'
      šírib 'he drank'                     ma širíbiš 'he did not drink'

Here we see that when the negative particle -š is suffixed, the initial *i* does not drop, just as with the column (b)II examples of (12).

The explanation for the facts adduced in (12) and (13) becomes clear once we reflect on the nature of the suffixes involved. All verbs in Palestinian require the presence of a subject pronoun (although -ϕ in the third person masculine singular), but not all verbs require the presence of object pronouns or the negative particle -š. Thus, the subject pronouns are much more intrinsically bound to the stem. On the other hand, the encliticization of object pronouns and the incorporation of negative particles are the kinds of operations we frequently encounter in the syntax of natural languages. Thus, there seems to be a legitimate basis for assuming a difference in hierarchical structure between ʔaṭáʕna 'we cut', with a subject pronoun, and ʔaṭáʕna 'he cut us', with an object pronoun. This distinction can be made explicit by positing a labeled bracketing of the form [ʔaṭaʕ + na] for the former example, and a labeled bracketing of the form [[ʔaṭaʕ]na] for the latter. Analogous to the latter will be [[ʔaṭaʕ]š] with the negative particle -š. Translating this distinction to stems such as *fihim*, we get [fihim + na] with subject pronoun suffix versus [[fihim]na] with object pronoun suffix and [[fihim]š] with the negative particle. This distinction, together with one further assumption, yields an explanation for why the initial vowel drops from the column I examples of (12b), but not from the column II examples of (12b) and of (13b). The further assumption is that Stress Assignment applies in a cyclic fashion. Sample derivations follow.

(14)  [fihim + na]   [[fihim]na]   [[fihim]š]
                                              *First Cycle*

           1              1              1
      fihim + na       fihim         fihim        Stress Assignment

                                              *Second Cycle*

           1            2 1            2 1
      fihim + na       fihim + na    fihim + š    Stress Assignment

           1
      fhim + na       _____    _____    Syncope

                                      2 1
                                    fihim + iš    Epenthesis

           1            2 1            2 1
      fhimna          fihimna        fihimiš

The idea behind this analysis is precisely this: just where the rule of Stress Assignment would assign primary stress if no object pronoun suffix or negative particle were present is just where the initial *i* of the puzzling examples adduced in (12) and (13) do not elide.

Before closing this section, two minor points should be mentioned. First, it is possible to allow Syncope to apply cyclically in (14), but I see no proof that it must apply cyclically, and therefore I am assuming that it is a word-level rule. Second, if the secondary or reduced stress generated in (14) is not actually present in phonetic representations, it may be eliminated by postulating an additional rule. The same is true of the analyses in sections 2 and 3, and nothing further will be said concerning this point.

## 2   Maltese

Although Maltese and Palestinian are not mutually intelligible, both languages have developed from a common source. The reader will therefore detect a similarity between the Maltese data to follow and the Palestinian examples discussed in section 1. As illustrated in the following paradigms, the stress patterns are strikingly similar to those of Palestinian.

(15)   ḥátaf 'he grabbed'        bézaʔ 'he spit'
       ḥátfet 'she grabbed'      bézʔet 'she spit'
       ḥtáft 'I grabbed'         bzáʔt 'I spit'

If *ḥataf* and *bezaʔ* are adopted as the stems underlying the preceding examples, together with -$\phi$ 'he', -*et* 'she', and -*t* 'I', it is possible to give a plausible analysis by recourse to three rules. First, a rule of Syncope is needed to account for the absence of stem vowels in four of the above examples. This rule of Syncope, it will be noticed, is more general than that required for Palestinian.

(16)   *Syncope*
       $\check{V} \rightarrow \phi$ / ___ CV

This rule has the effect of dropping all unstressed vowels appearing before a consonant–vowel sequence. The forms listed in (15) can be derived by means of Syncope from the more abstract *ḥataf*, *ḥataf* + *et*, *ḥataf* + *t*, *bezaʔ*, *bezaʔ* + *et*, and *bezaʔ* + *t*. But now, as with Palestinian, stress is predictable according to the following rule of Stress Assignment.

(17)   *Stress Assignment*
       $V \rightarrow [1 \text{ stress}]$ / ___ $C_0((VC)VC_0^1)]$

Stress Assignment in Maltese is stated in a format identical to that of Palestinian, cf. (4). It also abbreviates three disjunctively ordered subcases, which are given for convenience as (18).

(18)   (i)    $V \rightarrow [1 \text{ stress}]$ / ___ $C_0VCVC_0^1]$
       (ii)   $V \rightarrow [1 \text{ stress}]$ / ___ $C_0VC_0^1]$
       (iii)  $V \rightarrow [1 \text{ stress}]$ / ___ $C_0]$

The phonetic representations of (15) can now be generated from underlying stressless phonological representations. Representative derivations follow in which all three subcases of (17) are utilized.

(19)

| ḥataf | ḥataf + et | ḥataf + t | bezaʔ | |
|---|---|---|---|---|
| ___ | ḥátaf + et | _____ | ___ | Stress Assignment (i) |
| ḥátaf | _____ | | bézaʔ | Stress Assignment (ii) |
| ___ | _____ | ḥatáf + t | ___ | Stress Assignment (iii) |
| ___ | ḥátf + et | ḥtáf + t | ___ | Syncope |
| ḥátaf | ḥátfet | ḥtáft | bézaʔ | |

| bezaʔ + et | bezaʔ + t | |
|---|---|---|
| bézaʔ + et | _____ | Stress Assignment (i) |
| _____ | _____ | Stress Assignment (ii) |
| _____ | bezáʔ + t | Stress Assignment (iii) |
| bézʔ + et | bzáʔ + t | Syncope |
| bézʔet | bzáʔt | |

Case (i) of (18) exhibits the longest environment and thus is the first subcase of (17) to be invoked. By this case, *ḥataf + et* and *bezaʔ + et* are correctly stressed, the medial vowel being dropped by Syncope. Case (ii) correctly stresses *ḥataf* and *bezaʔ*. Case (ii) does not apply to *ḥátaf + et* and *bézaʔ + et*, even though the environmental conditions are fulfilled. This follows from the principle of disjunctive ordering associated with parentheses notation (cf. Chomsky 1967 and Chomsky and Halle 1968). Case (iii) assigns stress to underlying *ḥataf + t* and *bezaʔ + t*, and Syncope follows. For the reason given above, case (iii) does not apply to the other forms. In this way, all the desired phonetic representations are generated; the stems and suffixes are generalized for all forms at the abstract phonological level.

There is a further rule involved in the derivation of *ḥátfet* and *bézʔet*, which can be motivated on the basis of the following paradigms.

(20)   kínes 'he swept'       zífin 'he danced'
          kínset 'she swept'     zífnet 'she danced'
          kníst 'I swept'         zfínt 'I danced'

At first glance, the underlying stems for these forms appear to be *kines* and *zifen*, with *e* as the second vowel of the stem. However, this vowel alternates with *i* in *kníst* and *zfínt*. If the latter were derived from underlying *kines + t* and *zifen + t*, a rule turning *e* to *i* under stress would be needed. But *e* shows up under stress elsewhere, e.g. *bézaʔ*, *bézʔet*, etc. The alternative is to assume an underlying *i*, viz. *kinis + t* and *zifin + t*, together with a rule of Vowel Reduction, stated below as (21).

(21)   *Vowel Reduction*
          ĭ → e / ___ C₀#

Vowel Reduction, like Syncope, is ordered after Stress Assignment, giving rise to derivations such as the following.

(22)

| kinis + t | kinis | zifin + t | zifin | |
|---|---|---|---|---|
| kinís + t | kínis | zifín + t | zífin | Stress Assignment |
| knís + t | ____ | zfín + t | ____ | Syncope |
| _____ | kínes | _____ | zífen | Vowel Reduction |
| kníst | kínes | zfínt | zífen | |

The existence of Vowel Reduction suggests that the feminine ending *-et* of *ḥátfet*, *bézʔet*, *kínset*, and *zífnet* may in fact derive from the more abstract *-it*. If so, Vowel Reduction would correctly derive *-et*, since this suffix is unstressed in the aforementioned examples. The test is to find forms in which the third person feminine singular suffix shows up with stress. If *-et* derives from *-it* via Vowel Reduction, such forms would be expected to exhibit *-it*. The requisite forms are abundant. They include *ḥatfítkom* 'she grabbed you (pl)', *bezʔítlek* 'she spit to you (sg)', *ma ḥatfitkómš* 'she did not grab you (pl)', and *ma bezʔitlíkš* 'she did not spit to you (sg)', in which the feminine suffix shows up as *-it*. (Also note the *-ek* ~ *-ik* alternation for 'you (sg)'.) The correct derivations for *ḥátfet* and *bézʔet*, along with those required for *kínset* and *zífnet*, are given below.

(23)

| ḥataf + it | bezaʔ + it | kinis + it | zifin + it | |
|---|---|---|---|---|
| ḥátaf + it | béźaʔ + it | kínis + it | zífin + it | Stress Assignment |
| ḥátf + it | bézʔ + it | kíns + it | zífn + it | Syncope |
| ḥátf + et | bézʔ + et | kíns + et | zífn + et | Vowel Reduction |
| ḥátfet | bézʔet | kínset | zífnet | |

Let us now turn to the rule that will figure crucially in the main argument of this section. The examples that motivate this rule, some of which are displayed in (24), are drawn from the imperfective conjugation of Maltese.

(24)

| I | II |
|---|---|
| níkteb 'I write' | níktbu 'I write it' |
| tíkteb 'you write' | tíktbu 'you write it' |
| níkšef 'I uncover' | níkšfu 'I uncover it' |
| tíkšef 'you uncover' | tíkšfu 'you uncover it' |
| nízbor 'I prune' | nízbru 'I prune it' |
| tízbor 'you prune' | tízbru 'you prune it' |
| nízboḥ 'I paint' | nízbḥu 'I paint it' |
| tízboḥ 'you paint' | tízbḥu 'you paint it' |

The prefixes marking the first and second persons appear to be *ni-* and *ti-*. The object marker is clearly *-u*, and the underlying stems can be taken to be of the shape CCVC. The examples listed under column I exhibit stem vowels *e* and *o*. This *e* actually derives from the more abstract *i* by Vowel Reduction, as proved by alternations such as *ma niktíbš* 'I do not write' and *niktíblek* 'I write to you (sg)'. The column II examples of (24) may therefore be derived from underlying CV + CCVC + V sequences. Sample derivations follow.

(25)   ni + ktib + u   ni + zbor + u
       ní + ktib + u   ní + zbor + u   Stress Assignment
       ní + ktb + u    ní + zbr + u    Syncope
       níktbu          nízbru

The following examples should now be compared with those listed in (24).

(26)            I                          II
       nítlef 'I lose'            nitílfu 'I lose it'
                                  nitílfek 'I lose you (sg)'
       títlef 'you lose'          titílfu 'you lose it'
                                  titílfek 'you lose it'
       níšrob 'I drink'           nišórbu 'I drink it'
       tíšrob 'you drink'         tišórbu 'you drink it'

The forms listed under column I are analogous to those of (24I) and present no problem. The forms listed under column II, however, differ considerably from those of (24II). Given the (26I) forms and the underlying suffixes *-u* 'it' and *-ik* 'you (sg)', we conclude that the column II examples of (26) should derive from underlying *ni + tlif + u, ni + tlif + ik, ti + tlif + u, ti + tlif + ik, ni + šrob + u*, and *ti + šrob + u*, with canonical shapes completely analogous to the underlying representations of the (24II) examples. Stress should be assigned to the initial syllable of these underlying representations by case (i) of Stress Assignment. But then Syncope should follow, dropping the stem vowel, which cannot be recovered due to the fact that some stem vowels are *i* and others *o*. The fact that the stem vowel actually shows up in phonetic representations after the initial stem consonant suggests that a rule of metathesis has applied before Syncope has the opportunity to eliminate the stem vowel. What distinguishes the class of metathesizing stems of (26) from the nonmetathesizing stems of (24) is the appearance of the liquids *r* and *l* as the medial root consonant of the stem. The nasals *m* and *n* and the laryngeal *ʕ* also participate in the metathesizing process (cf. Brame 1972b). If the class *r, l, m, n,* and *ʕ* is informally denoted by *R*, the rule of metathesis can be formulated as follows.

(27)   *Metathesis*
       CRVCV → CVRCV

Above, it was noted that Metathesis must precede Syncope, for otherwise the stem vowel would be forever lost. Note that Metathesis must also precede Stress Assignment, since stress falls on the strong cluster created by Metathesis. Let us now consider the fruit these hypotheses bear.

(28)   ni + tlif + ik   ni + šrob + u
       ni + tilf + ik   ni + šorb + u   Metathesis
       ni + tílf + ik   ni + šórb + u   Stress Assignment
       n + tílf + ik    n + šórb + u    Syncope
       n + tílf + ek    _____     Vowel Reduction
       *ntílfek         *nšórbu

We see that Metathesis creates an environment for the subsequent application of Syncope. Thus, Syncope drops the prefixal vowel, which yields incorrect results. It would appear, then, that Syncope must precede Metathesis so that the prefixal *i* will not elide. Yet if Syncope precedes Metathesis, the stem vowel will drop, giving *\*nítlfu*, *\*nítlfek*, *\*títlfu*, *\*títlfek*, *\*nišrbu*, *\*nišrbek*, *\*tišrbu*, and *\*tišrbek*. To solve the latter problem we want Metathesis to precede Syncope, thus bleeding it; but this in turn creates a new problem, since it gives rise to a new environment for Syncope, thereby feeding it and resulting in the loss of the prefixal vowel. But consider the following important fact: the prefixal vowel is just that vowel that would be stressed if Stress Assignment preceded Metathesis, and if the prefixal vowel were stressed, it would never be susceptible to elision by Syncope; further, it is the object pronoun suffix which in a sense triggers Metathesis, which in turn accounts for the rightward placement of stress due to the creation of a strong cluster. From here it is easily seen that the ordering paradox finds a natural solution in terms of a cyclic analysis of the stress-assigning process. This analysis is summarized in the following derivations.

(29)   [[ni + tlif] + ik]   [[ni + šrob] + u]

|  |  |  |
|---|---|---|
| | | *First Cycle* |
| nɪ + tlif | nɪ + šrob | Stress Assignment |
| | | *Second Cycle* |
| nɪ + tilf + ik | nɪ + šorb + u | Metathesis |
| nɪ + tɪlf + ik | nɪ + šorb + u | Stress Assignment |
| | | Syncope |
| nɪ + tɪlf + ek | | Vowel Reduction |
| nɪtɪlfek | nɪšorbu | |

By assuming that Metathesis precedes Stress Assignment (and hence Syncope), but that only Stress Assignment is a cyclic rule, the correct phonetic representations can be generated. As in Palestinian, subject pronouns must co-occur with the verb stem and are consequently more intimately correlated with the stem. On the other hand, object pronouns are less closely associated with verbal stems, and it therefore seems natural to capture this difference by means of a difference in bracketing. This is precisely the kind of bracketing we need to effect a reapplication of Stress Assignment. First cycle stress thereby inhibits Syncope from later affecting the prefixal vowel. Maltese is therefore a second example illustrating the explanatory value of the transformational cycle.

## 3   Spanish

There are three classes of verbs in Spanish. These classes are represented by the following present tense forms.

Stress falls on the penultimate syllable of the adverbs as predicted by Stress Assignment. The segmentation of the adverbs is straightforward: *resign + a + d + a + mente*, *cumpl + i + d + a + mente*, etc. By analogy to these forms, one expects to encounter adverbs corresponding to second conjugation infinitives. Thus, given verbs such as *conocer*, *extender*, and *deber*, one expects to find corresponding adverbs *conocedamente*, *extendedamente*, and *debedamente*. The actual occurring forms are listed below.

(36)          *Adverbs*                          *Infinitives*
        conoc*i*daménte 'knowingly'       conoc*er* 'to know'
        extend*i*daménte 'extendedly'     extend*er* 'to extend'
        deb*i*daménte 'justly'            deb*er* 'to owe'

Where we expect to encounter the *e* theme vowel of the second conjugation in the adverbs, *i* actually occurs. This *i*, however, bears no primary stress, and unstressed *e* does not change to *i* in any analogous environment.

The explanation for the phonetic *i* of these adverbs follows the pattern of that given for the Palestinian and Maltese data. It is no coincidence that *conocída*, *extendída*, and *debída* actually appear in Spanish as phonetic representations and that as such stress falls on the theme vowel *i*, which is raised from *e* precisely because it is stressed. Thus, there is a natural bracketing that can be associated with the adverbs of (35) and (36). Moreover, this bracketing can be utilized to explain the occurrence of *i* in (36), provided of course that Stress Assignment is a cyclic rule of Spanish. Representative derivations follow.

(37)   [[conoc + e + d + a] + mente]
                                              *First Cycle*

              $\overset{1}{\text{conoc + e}}$ + d + a          Stress Assignment

                                              *Second Cycle*

         $\text{conoc} + \overset{2}{\text{e}} + \text{d} + \text{a} + \overset{1}{\text{mente}}$          Stress Assignment
         $\text{conoc} + \overset{2}{\text{i}} + \text{d} + \text{a} + \overset{1}{\text{mente}}$          Raising

The rule of Raising, like the rule of Syncope in Palestinian, could be assumed to apply cyclically. We have no evidence that Raising must apply cyclically, so we assume that Raising is a word-level rule. Stress Assignment in Spanish, however, must apply cyclically. Spanish is therefore yet a third language supporting the principle of the transformational cycle.

## 4   An Alternative to Cyclic Stress Assignment?

As an alternative to the cyclic analysis of the Spanish data, we might formulate a rule of secondary (or tertiary) stress placement and require this new rule to follow the main stress rule of Spanish.

(38)   *Stress Adjustment*

$$V \rightarrow \overset{2}{V} / \underline{\quad} C_0 V C_0 \overset{1}{V}$$

If Stress Adjustment is ordered before Raising in Spanish, there would apparently be no need for a cyclic analysis of stress, since the correct phonetic representations would be generated from the correct underlying representations.

(39)   conoc + e + d + a + mente

| | |
|---|---|
| conoc + e + d + a + $\overset{1}{\text{mente}}$ | Stress Assignment |
| conoc + $\overset{2}{\text{e}}$ + d + a + $\overset{1}{\text{mente}}$ | Stress Adjustment |
| conoc + $\overset{2}{\text{i}}$ + d + a + $\overset{1}{\text{mente}}$ | Raising |
| $\overset{2}{\text{conoc}}\overset{1}{\text{idamente}}$ | |

As an alternative to the cyclic analysis of the Maltese data, we might also attempt to formulate a rule assigning a subordinate stress.

(40)   *Stress Adjustment*

$$V \rightarrow \overset{2}{V} / \underline{\quad} C\overset{1}{V}RCV$$

If Stress Adjustment (40) were ordered before Syncope (16) in Maltese, the following derivation would account for forms such as those listed in (26II).

(41)   ni + šrob + u

| | |
|---|---|
| ni + šorb + u | Metathesis (27) |
| ni + $\overset{1}{\text{šorb}}$ + u | Stress Assignment (17) |
| $\overset{2}{\text{ni}}$ + $\overset{1}{\text{šorb}}$ + u | Stress Adjustment (40) |
| $\underline{\qquad\qquad}$ | Syncope (16) |
| $\overset{2}{\text{ni}}\overset{1}{\text{šorbu}}$ | |

Since the appearance of *The Sound Pattern of English* (Chomsky and Halle 1968), some linguists have reacted against the cycle in phonology. For example, Ross (MS) argues for a noncyclic approach to English word stress, and, though largely an oral tradition, others have voiced objections to the phonological cycle (cf. Hoard 1971). Apparently the dissatisfaction with the cycle is due in part to a feeling that the bracketings adopted in *The Sound Pattern of English* are to some extent artificial and contrived. If this claim is granted, it would not seem to follow that cyclic stress assignment should be abandoned. Consider the implications for the examples discussed above. By eliminating the cycle in favor of auxiliary rules of stress adjustment, we must postulate two unrelated stress adjustment rules for Spanish and Maltese. Thus, under a noncyclic approach to stress assignment, the fact that the *i* of Maltese *nišórbu* does not elide by Syncope (16) and the fact that the *i* of *conocidaménte* is raised from *e* in Spanish become two unrelated facts. It is precisely this ill consequence that cyclic stress avoids, since the problems that arise in connection with Raising in Spanish and Syncope in Maltese can be reduced to a single universal explanation embodied in the cyclic hypothesis. This hypothesis explains the troublesome facts of Maltese, Spanish, and Palestinian Arabic. The same facts are not explained, but described, within a noncyclic framework of the type illustrated above.

A noncyclic approach to stress in Maltese and Spanish reduces other facts to the status of accidents. For example, it is accidental that Maltese Stress Adjustment should precede Syncope in derivation (41) and that Spanish Stress Adjustment should precede Raising in (39). This accidental property of the noncyclic approaches is not found in the cyclic approach. Cyclic stress relates what is dismissed as accidental in (39) and (41), since Stress Adjustment is not needed in the cyclic approaches and Stress Assignment is required to precede Syncope in Maltese and Raising in Spanish in both the cyclic and noncyclic approaches.

The argument for the cycle in Palestinian Arabic is even more powerful, for, due to the identity of the subject pronoun suffix -na 'we', with the object pronoun suffix -na 'us', recourse to a purely phonological rule of stress adjustment is not possible.

In conclusion, it seems to me that there are two factors that influence recent tendencies to abandon the cycle in phonology. First, there appears to be the mistaken and perverse idea that the theory would be more general without this one extra device. This reasoning is questionable and otiose; whereas abandoning the cycle in a single language may appear to yield a more general theory with less theoretical machinery, whatever appeal may have existed completely evaporates when the elimination of the cycle is viewed in the context of several languages or of language in general, as Chomsky and Halle intended. In other words, the principle of the cycle is a universal, which reduces what may appear to be disparate facts from differing languages to a single fact and thereby offers an explanation for these facts. In this view, the child acquiring Maltese or Spanish need not consider the noncyclic language-specific analyses embodied in (39) and (41). Rather, the universal cyclic principle forms the basis which facilitates the acquisition of Maltese and Spanish, thereby significantly limiting the hypotheses that need be made in the acquisition process. Similar arguments can be made in support of deep structure, ordering, and other devices of generative grammar that have come under attack on vague grounds of simplicity and generality.

A second, and more serious, factor responsible for the intellectual discomfort with the phonological cycle derives from a justified concern for the unmotivated use of labeled brackets. It is this issue to which attention is directed in the following section. With regard to this point, it appears that there is a fundamental confusion over what is at issue, the status of the cycle or the status of natural bracketings. I agree there is need for constraining the use of labeled brackets, but I fail to see how it follows from this that the phonological cycle should be abandoned.

## 5   Constraints on Natural Bracketings and Constraints on the Cycle in Phonology

The question of whether other than stress-assigning rules can apply in a cyclic fashion is still very much open. Some speculative evidence for non-stress-assigning cyclic rules is given in Brame (1972c). In spite of the examples presented in that paper, the most convincing of cyclic phonological rules appear to me to be those involved in assigning primary stress. This fact is itself in need of explanation, and I venture a conjecture below. However, I will be primarily concerned in this section with advancing a proposal for constraining natural bracketings. Since the phonological cycle is dependent on bracketings, a consequence of my constraint will be a delimitation of where rules can be expected to cycle. In other words, my proposal will serve as an indirect means of constraining the cycle in phonology.

The constraint I intend to offer is grounded in the examples presented in sections 1, 2, and 3 above but may in the long run prove to be too strong. What stands out about each of the earlier examples of cyclic application of stress is the fact that the string constituting the first cycle itself shows up elsewhere as an independent phonetic word sequence. Thus, the string of the inner cycle of [[fihim] + na] of Palestinian Arabic has an independent status as the word *fíhim* 'he understood'; the string constituting the inner cycle of Maltese [[ni + šrob] + u] shows up as the independent word sequence *níšrob* 'I drink'; and finally, the string constituting the inner cycle of Spanish [[conoc + e + d + a] + mente] shows up as an independent word of Spanish, viz. *conocída* 'known'. There are additional examples illustrating this point for Spanish.

(42)　　　　*Adverbs*　　　　　　　*Infinitives*
　　　aborreciblemēnte 'hatefully'　　aborrecer 'to hate'
　　　creiblemēnte 'credibly'　　　　creer 'to believe'
　　　invenciblemēnte 'invincibly'　　vencer 'to conquer'
　　　placiblemēnte 'agreeably'　　　placer 'to please'

The fact that the infinitives are second conjugation forms, i.e. they bear the theme vowel *e*, proves that the *i* of the adverbs derives from *e* by Raising. Again a cyclic approach to stress in Spanish will correctly predict this outcome in terms of derivations analogous to (37). A representative derivation is given as (43).

(43)   [[aborrec + e + ble] + mente]

　　　　　　　　　　　　　　　　*First Cycle*

　　　　　　　　1
　　　aborrec + e + ble　　　　　Stress Assignment

　　　　　　　　　　　　　　　　*Second Cycle*

　　　　　　　　2　　　　1
　　　aborrec + e + ble + mente　　Stress Assignment
　　　　　　　　2　　　1
　　　aborrec + i + ble + mente　　Raising

Of significance for this section is the fact that, like the other examples cited above in Palestinian, Maltese, and Spanish, the strings of the innermost cycles of the adverbs of (42) have an independent status as word sequences of Spanish.

(44)　　　*Adjectives*
　　　aborrecíble 'hateful'
　　　creíble 'credible'
　　　invencíble 'invincible'
　　　placíble 'agreeable'

To clarify the point being made, the data may be summarized in the following table.

| Cycles | Word Sequences |
|---|---|
| Palestinian: [[fihim] + na] | fíhim 'he understood' |
| | fihímna 'he understood us' |
| [fihim + na] | fhímna 'we understood' |
| [[fihim] + š] | fíhim 'he understood' |
| | fihímiš 'he did not understand' |
| Maltese: [[ni + šrob] + u] | nîšrob 'I drink' |
| | nišróbu 'I drink it' |
| Spanish: [[conoc + e + d + a] + mente] | conocída 'known' |
| | conocidaménte 'knowingly' |
| [[aborrec + e + ble] + mente] | aborrecíble 'hateful' |
| | aborreciblemênte 'hatefully' |

The following definition will serve to express the relation alluded to in the preceding discussion.

*Definition*
Two strings in phonological representations are said to be *equipotent* if they are identical and at least one of the two is not represented as a proper substring in phonetic representations.

On the basis of the foregoing examples, I propose the following constraints on natural bracketings.

*Natural Bracketing Hypothesis*
For a substring $\psi$ to be bracketed, it must be equipotent to a string $\sigma$.

All of the cyclic arguments given earlier are alike in that stress is utilized to crucially affect a later rule which mentions stress. Thus, stress is utilized in Palestinian and Maltese to inhibit Syncope, which applies only to unstressed vowels. In Spanish, stress is utilized to bring about a later application of Raising, which requires stress to be present. In any language, a potential situation exists in which a stress-assigning rule can be proved to be cyclic provided the language possesses a second rule mentioning stress. In English there is a rule of *h*-elision, or psilosis, which mentions stress. This rule drops *h* when *h* is followed by a stressless vowel. In English we therefore have a situation in which the English stress-assigning rule can potentially be proved to be cyclic. In my dialect, a crucial distinction is made between *Prohibition*, pronounced [proəbíšən] without *h*, as in *the days of Prohibition*, and *prohibition* with verbal force, pronounced [prohibíšən] with *h*, as in *the prohibition of X by Y*. Although the latter is not particularly elegant English, most speakers agree that *prohibition* with verbal force admits the presence of *h*, while *Prohibition* as in *the days of Prohibition* does not admit the presence of *h*. The explanation for this difference is again cyclic stress assignment. What could be more natural than the assumption that *prohibition* with verbal force requires a bracketing labeled *V*, viz. [[prohibit]$_V$ + ion]$_N$ as opposed to the totally nounlike *Prohibition* with no inner cycle? Such an assumption, along with cyclic stress assignment in English, explains why *h* does not elide. The innermost cycle will be stressed *prohibit*, just like the true verb, and the traces of this stress will inhibit psilosis from dropping the *h*. A similar explanation is given by Chomsky and Halle for why the *a* of *elasticity* does not reduce to *ə* by Vowel Reduction, a rule which mentions stress, as opposed to the *e* of *compensation* which does reduce. Because *elastic* is cycled, with the effect that stress is placed on *a*, reduction is prevented. No inner cycle exists in the case of *compensation*, however. Hence the *e* never bears stress and consequently reduces. Examples such as *prohibition* and *elasticity* in English, which require inner cycles, satisfy the Natural Bracketing Hypothesis, since *prohibit* and *elastic* are independent word sequences of English. The Natural Bracketing Hypothesis, however, rules out analyses such as [[ortho[dox]]y] and [[aristo[crat]]y], which are proposed in *The Sound Pattern of English*, while allowing for much else in that work. If correct, the Natural Bracketing Hypothesis suggests that -*dox*- and -*crat*- bear lexical [1 stress]. Halle and Keyser (1971) have made use of lexical stress with respect to other classes of English vocabulary. The Natural Bracketing Hypothesis thus forces more material into the lexicon and thereby makes a claim as to what are true generalizations and what idiosyncratic facts.

The domain of cyclic rules is determined by the bracketing that particular phonological representations exhibit. Thus, it is a necessary condition that substrings be equipotent to identical strings in order to qualify for cyclehood, but this condition is not sufficient. In other words, if a substring is equipotent to an identical string, this does not imply that the substring must be bracketed. For example, although *fihim* shows up as an independent word, this does not imply that *fihim* 'he understood' constitutes a cycle for the deep representations of both *fhimna* 'we understood' and *fihimna* 'he understood us'. A strengthening of our hypothesis so as to rule out *fihim* as a potential cycle for *fhimna*, as opposed to *fihimna*, which requires an inner cycle, is desirable. The latter form is equipotent to *fihim* 'he understood', and the meaning of *fihimna* is a compositional function of the meaning of *fihim* 'he understood' and -*na* 'us'. Not so with *fhimna* 'we understood', which does not include 'he understood' as a component of its meaning. These observations suggest the following revised constraint on natural bracketings.

*Strong Natural Bracketing Hypothesis*
For a substring $\psi$ of a string $\phi$ to be bracketed, $\psi$ must be equipotent to a string $\sigma$, and the meaning of $\phi$ must be a compositional function of the meaning of $\sigma$ and $\phi - \psi$ ($\phi$ minus $\psi$).

It is clear that the Strong Natural Bracketing Hypothesis takes us into the realm of semantics and, for one thing, requires the meaning of the adverbs of Spanish to include the meaning of the past participles or adjectives. Such questions have not been investigated, but I suspect there may be adverbs in Spanish with idiosyncratic meanings, unrelated to the corresponding adverbs or adjectives. We must ask if such examples, should they be brought forward, refute the Strong Natural Bracketing Hypothesis or whether such forms are in fact to be considered underived, i.e. to be represented without an inner cycle. Still another question concerning the Strong Natural Bracketing Hypothesis arises in conjunction with certain plural verb forms in Maltese. Although

*-u* serves as an object pronoun in Maltese, it is homophonous with the plural subject marker *-u*. When the latter is suffixed to imperfective stems, we get metathesis and nonelision of the prefixal vowel, cf. *nišórbu* 'we drink', *titílfu* 'you (pl) lose'. Clearly we should welcome an explanation for the latter forms analogous to that of section 2. But if we opt for [[ni + šrob] + u] and [[ti + tlif] + u], to what extent can we claim that 'we drink' and 'you (pl) lose' are compositional functions of 'I drink' plus 'plural' and 'you (sg) lose' and 'plural'? For these reasons, the Strong Natural Bracketing Hypothesis may be too strong; yet the principle is of sufficient interest to bear in mind.

The Natural Bracketing Hypothesis admits the possibility that some segmental rules may be cyclic. While it allows for the first example discussed in Brame (1972c), it disallows the second example brought forward in that work. The Natural Bracketing Hypothesis could in fact be sufficiently weakened so as to cover both examples. This could be accomplished by stating the principle as a constraint on stress-assigning rules (of the type illustrated in Palestinian, Maltese, and Spanish), rather than as a condition on bracketing.

### Natural Cycle Hypothesis
For a substring $\psi$ to be cycled by a stress rule, it must be equipotent to a string $\sigma$.

A corresponding strong version of this principle could be formulated to replace the Strong Natural Bracketing Hypothesis. Due to the almost total lack of detailed phonological analyses of more than a few languages, it is at present difficult to decide between the alternative hypotheses. However, I tend to favor the Natural Bracketing Hypothesis. Since cyclic rules are dependent on bracketing, it seems natural to constrain the cycle by placing constraints on where brackets can occur. This raises the question, mentioned at the outset, of why stress-assigning rules are typically those that can most convincingly be demonstrated to be cyclic. My answer to this question is implicit in the following universal principle which I conjecture.

### Principle of Cyclicity
All and only the rules mentioning brackets apply cyclically.

This hypothesis supersedes an earlier conjecture made in Brame (1972c). Like all other hypothetical linguistic universals, it must be tested against detailed phonological analyses. Since it is typically stress-assigning rules that mention brackets in their formal statement, the Principle of Cyclicity correctly predicts that stress-assigning rules are the ones that are typically cyclic. However, the Principle of Cyclicity does not rule out the possibility that some segmental rules must be formulated with brackets. In the event of the latter, the prediction is that these segmental rules apply cyclically. In Kaye (1971) some evidence is given to show that nasalization applies cyclically in Desano. Although Kaye's formulation of this rule in the main body of his article violates the Principle of Cyclicity, he does provide an alternative formulation of his cyclic rule in footnote 15 of the article which satisfies the Principle of Cyclicity. Arguments are offered in Kisseberth (1972) in support of several cyclic segmental rules of Klamath. Unfortunately those rules, with one exception, are not explicitly stated; an explicit formulation of rules is particularly crucial to a proper evaluation of the Principle of Cyclicity. Kean (1971) accepts Kisseberth's argument that some segmental rules must apply cyclically in Klamath, while rejecting some of the details of his analysis. It is interesting to note that Kean does explicitly state the relevant segmental rules of Klamath. (Kean points out that Kisseberth's cycle violates the Principle of Strict Cyclicity, outlined in Kean (MS), shows that this is a consequence of Kisseberth's global rule, and proceeds to reanalyze Klamath without recourse to global rules.) If Kean's analysis is correct, it is one consistent with the Principle of Cyclicity, since her relevant segmental rules are formulated with brackets. On the other hand, White (1972) has given a detailed analysis of Klamath in which the cycle is not invoked. Turning now to English phonology, it should be noted that all rules formulated with brackets by Chomsky and Halle in *The Sound Pattern of English* are cyclic rules. And all cyclic rules of *The Sound Pattern of English*, with one exception, are formulated with brackets. (The exception is a segmental rule which can conceivably be reformulated.) In the standard theory of generative phonology, as in *The Sound Pattern of English*, cyclic rules are marked ad hoc to distinguish them from noncyclic rules. The Principle of Cyclicity obviates the necessity for such special marks and resolves the issue in what I suspect is a natural fashion.

## Notes

Some of the material included in this article can be found in Brame (1973). For additional material on Palestinian Arabic, see Brame (1971) and Abdo (1969), the latter treating a different dialect. For additional material on Maltese, see Brame (1972b). A detailed treatment of Spanish can be found in Harris (1969), and a somewhat different approach to Spanish is given in Brame and Bordelois (1971, 1973). I have assumed throughout this paper a principle of stress subordination explicit in Chomsky and Halle (1968: 64): "The rules that determine stress contours are, for the most part, rules that assign primary stress in certain positions, at the same time weakening the stresses in all other positions by one." Since writing this article, I have had the opportunity of seeing Halle (1973), in which this principle is restricted. Adopting Halle's new proposal for stress subordination does not alter the results obtained here. It would be a simple and routine matter to translate the rules and derivations of this paper into the new system.

I am indebted to Joan Bresnan for important criticism of this paper, which led to significant revisions. I also wish to thank Noam Chomsky and Morris Halle for helpful comments. C. L. Baker and Joe Emonds read an earlier abbreviated version of this article and I benefited from their remarks. None of the aforementioned linguists necessarily agrees with my analyses or conclusions.

## References

Abdo, D. 1969. *On Stress and Arabic Phonology*. Khayats, Beirut.

Anderson, S. and P. Kiparsky (eds). 1973. *A Festschrift for Morris Halle*. Holt, Rinehart, and Winston, New York.

Brame, M. K. 1970. Arabic Phonology, unpublished Ph.D. dissertation, MIT, Cambridge, Mass.

Brame, M. K. 1971. Stress in Arabic and Generative Phonology. *Foundations of Language* 7, 556–91.

Brame, M. K. (ed.). 1972a. *Contributions to Generative Phonology*. University of Texas Press, Austin.

Brame, M. K. 1972b. On the Abstractness of Phonology: Maltese ʕ. In Brame (1972a).

Brame, M. K. 1972c. The Segmental Cycle. In Brame (1972a).

Brame, M. K. 1973. Stress Assignment in Two Arabic Dialects. In Anderson and Kiparsky (1973).

Brame, M. K. and I. Bordelois. 1971. Some Controversial Questions in Spanish Phonology. *Linguistic Inquiry* 2: 282–98.

Brame, M. K. and I. Bordelois. 1973. Vocalic Alternations in Spanish. *Linguistic Inquiry* 4, 111–68.

Chomsky, N. 1967. Some General Properties of Phonological Rules. *Language* 43, 102–28.

Chomsky, N. and M. Halle. 1968. *The Sound Pattern of English*, Harper and Row, New York.

Halle, M. 1973. Stress Rules in English: A New Version. *Linguistic Inquiry* 4, 451–64.

Halle, M. and S. J. Keyser. 1971. *English Stress: Its Form, Its Growth, and Its Role in Verse*, Harper and Row, New York.

Harris, J. W. 1969. *Spanish Phonology*, MIT Press, Cambridge, Mass.

Hoard, J. E. 1971. The New Phonological Paradigm. Review of *The Sound Pattern of English*, *Glossa* 5, 222–68.

Kaye, J. D. 1971. Nasal Harmony in Desano. *Linguistic Inquiry* 2, 37–56.

Kean, M.-L. 1971. A Reply to Kisseberth's "Cyclic Rules in Klamath Phonology". Unpublished mimeograph, MIT, Cambridge, Mass.

Kean, M.-L. MS. The Strict Cycle in Phonology. Unpublished MS.

Kisseberth, C. W. 1972. Cyclical Rules in Klamath Phonology. *Linguistic Inquiry* 3, 3–33.

Ross, J. R. MS. A Reanalysis of English Word Stress: Part II.

White, R. B. D. 1972. *Klamath Phonology*, Ph.D. dissertation, University of Washington, Seattle (reproduced as vol. 12 of *University of Washington Studies in Linguistics and Language Learning* (1973)).

# 5

# On Phonotactically Motivated Rules (1974)

## Alan H. Sommerstein

The main thesis of this paper is that the grammars of natural languages contain an exhaustive set of conditions on the output of the phonological rules – in fact, a surface phonotactics. I shall show that, contrary to what is usually assumed in generative phonology, a surface phonotactics is not redundant in a generative grammar if the grammar is indeed intended as 'a theory of linguistic competence' (Chomsky 1965: 3), and that if any set of rules in the phonological section of the grammar is redundant it is the morphophonotactic rules, better known as morpheme structure conditions.[1] I shall propose a format for the statement of rules (including so-called conspiracies) which are 'motivated' by the phonotactics in the sense of Matthews (1972: 219–20). Finally, I shall present a set of phonotactic rules for consonant clusters in Latin, and show how the statement of certain rules of Latin phonology can be simplified by taking their phonotactic motivation into account.

It is established generative phonological theory that the inclusion in the grammar of a surface phonotactics is not necessary and indeed not even possible. In brief, the arguments advanced for this position are as follows. It is contended that a surface phonotactics is not NECESSARY because 'every fact which [it] describes is accounted for ... by the morpheme internal restrictions on morphophoneme combinations and the morphophonemic rules which must exist in any event' (Postal 1968: 214). And a surface phonotactics is not POSSIBLE, it is argued, because it would have to be stated at the autonomous phonemic level, and generative phonology does not recognize any such level.

Neither of these arguments is valid. The second in particular is completely undermined if the suggestion of Schane (1971) is correct that generative phonology must, for reasons quite unconnected with phonotactics, provide some kind of 'representation of relevant surface contrasts'; but even on the more usual view that a generative phonology contains nothing corresponding to a level of autonomous phonemics, it still does not follow that a surface phonotactics is impossible. For the autonomous phonemic level is not the only one at which a surface phonotactics could be stated. For example, it is basic to generative phonology that the output of the phonological rules is a discrete, segmented phonetic representation. There is no reason why a set of tactic rules could not be stated over this representation. It is true that at the level of phonetic output, features are multi-valued rather than binary, and the tactic rules might, therefore, have to be made unnecessarily complex; but there is an alternative which still does not require the postulation of an autonomous phonemic level.

Postal (1968: 65–70) points out that generally speaking (though there are exceptions) languages do not have language-particular phonological rules assigning feature values more finely graded than + and −. He suggests that 'when the independently motivated rules of a particular phonology terminate with + and − values for particular features', a set of semi-universal DETAIL RULES are applied to convert from binary (categorial) to $n$-ary (phonetic) feature values. He speculates that the input of a detail rule may be determined by its output, i.e. that for every feature F, the outputs of possible detail rules whose input is [+F] and the outputs of possible detail rules whose input is [−F] are disjoint.

If Postal is correct in this, then we can define a level of representation which is a state in all phonological derivations in all languages, having the properties that the only rules still to apply are detail rules and that the last rule to have applied was not a detail rule. The representations at this level will be, as it were, a black and white picture of the phonetic representations; all values of a feature weaker than a certain universal standard (fixed separately for each feature) will be replaced by −, and all stronger values by +, except in the case of those features (such as stress in English) for which values more detailed that + and − are assigned by language-specific rules. This level I call the CATEGORIAL PHONETIC level, and it is eminently suitable for the stating of a set of surface phonotactic rules. It is, in fact, not too dissimilar from the output of the rule systems actually presented (as distinct from those stated to be theoretically required) in many generative phonological studies.[2]

Having shown that a surface phonotactics is possible, I must now show that it is necessary. Postal's argument (1968: 208–16) that it is not necessary in fact shows only that IF a generative grammar already contains a set of rules defining the possible combinations of (systematic) phonemes in morphemes and of morphemes in words, it automatically determines the possible combinations of elements in words at the phonetic and all intermediate levels. But Postal does not establish the all-important premise that a grammar must contain 'a set of "morphophonotactic" rules or their equivalent'; this premise appears to rest on an assumption, not made fully explicit, that if a level of representation is linguistically significant it MUST have 'its own partially independent principles of combination' (Postal 1968: 213). But this assumption is inconsistent with Postal's argument; for it entails that if, as Postal (in common with all generative phonologists) believes, the phonetic level is 'significant', then that level must have 'its own partially independent principles of combination', i.e. a surface phonotactics.

In current generative phonology, tactic rules occupy a peculiar position. Since Stanley (1967), morpheme structure rules or conditions have played no role in the phonological interpretation of surface structures; if such rules or conditions are to be justified at all, it must be for other reasons. I have argued elsewhere (Sommerstein 1973: 110) that the justification for tactic rules of some kind in phonology is that native speakers can tell the difference between forms that on the evidence of their phonological shape 'belong' in their language (even though the forms may not actually appear in the lexicon) and forms that do not; in the time-honoured illustration, between *blick and *bnick. But while this ability makes it necessary, in order to account fully for the native speaker's linguistic competence, to have rules stating the possible combinations of phonological elements at some level, this argument says nothing about WHICH level these rules must be stated at.

Under what circumstances, after all, is this aspect of a native speaker's linguistic competence called into use? Only when he hears a word that does not already belong to his vocabulary. Now either the word is such that from his prior knowledge he can deduce its morphemic composition, or it is not. If it is – an example would be *ophthalmoscope*, for a speaker whose vocabulary included *ophthalmic* on the one hand, and *telescope*, *microscope*, etc., on the other – he would judge the well-formedness of the word according to the principles of combination of morphemes in words, not of phonemes in morphemes. Only if the word is morphemically simple or if its composition is opaque would principles about possible combinations of phonological elements come into play. But how can we suppose that at this stage, at first acquaintance with a word whose internal structure, if any, is *ex hypothesi* unknown, an underlying representation could in every case be deduced? This could only be so if underlying representations satisfied a biuniqueness condition, which we know they do not. It follows that judgments about whether a previously unknown form 'belongs' in the language must be made on the basis of a surface or near-surface representation.

Therefore, if it is accepted that the ability to tell which forms 'belong' in one's language is a part of one's linguistic competence, something like a surface phonotactics is necessary, and a set of morpheme structure rules is not.

Having now a surface phonotactics in our grammar in any case, we note that certain phonological rules are in whole or in part duplicates of certain phonotactic rules. For example, there may be a phonotactic rule requiring obstruent clusters to consist of all voiced or all unvoiced obstruents, and also a rule of the phonology (a 'P-rule') assimilating an obstruent in voice to a following obstruent. Can we avoid this repetition?

Suppose that in the spirit of Matthews (1972) we define a class of PHONOTACTICALLY MOTIVATED P-rules, as follows:

(1)   A P-rule R is positively motivated[3] with respect to a phonotactic constraint C just in case the input to R contains a matrix or matrices violating C AND the set of violations of C found in the output of R is null or is a proper subset of the set of such violations in the input to R.

As Matthews says, in such a situation it makes more sense to claim that R is explained by C than to claim that C is explained by R. Is there, then, any way in which we can express, in our formal statement of R, that it is explained by C?

One possibility is to regard phonotactically motivated rules not (like ordinary P-rules) as instructions to do something to an input of a certain form, but as instructions to remove certain violations of a phonotactic constraint. This in turn gives us a new kind of principle for grouping rules into schemata. We need not confine ourselves to grouping rules that operate on similar inputs, or make similar changes to their inputs, such that the similarities can be captured by our notational conventions. We can group RULES THAT REMOVE VIOLATIONS OF THE SAME PHONOTACTIC CONSTRAINT. Such rules all achieve similar ends by possibly different means: they constitute, in fact, a CONSPIRACY in the sense made familiar by Kisseberth (1970).

A phonotactically motivated rule or conspiracy may be stated as a P-rule or set of P-rules in the ordinary form, but with the addition of a reference to the motivating phonotactic constraint. The manner of application of such a schema may be illustrated by a simple hypothetical example.

Suppose a language in which all words end phonetically in a vowel, but morpho-phonemically some end in consonants; and suppose that in a standard generative phono-logical analysis, this language would have a rule deleting word-final voiceless consonants and a rule inserting a schwa vowel after word-final voiced consonants. We might express these facts in the following way. The phonotactics of the language would include a con-straint excluding word-final consonants, which could be formulated in the manner of Stanley (1967) as a 'negative condition':

(2)   * C #

And the relevant phonological rules might be stated thus:

(3)   FINAL CONSONANT CONSPIRACY (motivated by (2))
      (a)   [−voice] → ø
      (b)   ø → ə
      (c)   (3a) has preference over (3b)[4]

The conspiracy (3) is applied in accordance with the following convention:

(4)   A rule, or subcase of a conspiracy, positively motivated by phonotactic constraint C does not apply unless its application will remove or alleviate a violation or violations of C.

In a moment we shall have to define the term 'alleviate' in (4); but it is not relevant to the conspiracy (3). The effect of (4) on (3) is twofold. First, it is not necessary to state, as part of the structural description of (3), that it is limited to the position before word boundary; for in no other position can the application of either (3a) or (3b) remove a violation of (2). For the same reason it is not necessary to stipulate that (3b) does not apply where the insertion site is preceded by a vowel. Secondly, (4) ensures that once one or more applications of a given rule or conspiracy have removed all violations of the motivating constraint, that rule or conspiracy ceases to be applicable (though, unless prevented by ordering constraints, it may reapply if subsequent applications of other rules introduce fresh violations of the motivating constraint).

In the absence of a theory of phonotactic motivation, (3) would have had to be replaced by two separate rules:

(5)   [−voice] → ø /——#

(6)      ø    → ə /C——#

It would have been possible to collapse (5) and (6), since they share part of their environment; but it would not have been possible to show their relationship to (2).

The words 'or alleviate' in (4) were included to allow for the possibility that multiple applications of a rule or subrule, or the application of several subrules, may be needed before a phonotactic violation is finally removed. If we are to define 'alleviate', we need some measure of the grossness of a phonotactic violation. Chomsky and Halle's measure

(1968: 416–17) of 'distance from the lexicon', or some modification thereof, suggests itself; but such a measure would not be suitable for dealing with the kind of rule here under consideration. Chomsky and Halle's measure has to do with the relationship of a form to ALL the phonotactic (actually morphophonotactic) constraints, and we are interested in the relationship of a form to an individual constraint. Rather, we look for the minimal structural change necessary to remove any violation present, assigning for this purpose a 'cost' to structural changes according to the same measure that we use to evaluate phonological rules generally. Then we define:

(7)   The DEGREE OF VIOLATION $V_{M,C}$ to which a matrix M violates a phonotactic constraint C is equal to the cost of the minimal structural change necessary to turn M into a matrix satisfying C.

(8)   The application to a matrix M of operation A ALLEVIATES a violation in M of phonotactic constraint C just in case the output M′ of such application is such that

$$0 < V_{M'C} < V_{M,JC}$$

It will now be fairly clear how an evaluation measure may be able to take account of the greater naturalness of a conspiracy like (3) compared with a pair of phonotactically unmotivated rules like (5, 6). We can in effect say that, since the constraint motivating the conspiracy is going to have to be stated in the phonotactics in any event, it does not need to be taken into account when determining the cost of the conspiracy itself, and similarly with a single phonotactically motivated rule. Probably, however, a small, fixed cost should be assigned to the reference that the motivated rule must make to the motivating constraint; this will ensure that a pair of rules motivated by the same phonotactic constraint (hence forming a conspiracy) will be preferred by the evaluation measure to a pair of rules identical to the first pair except that they are motivated each by a different phonotactic constraint.

So far we have allowed only for what we have termed positively motivated rules – that is, rules which apply only when they help to remove phonotactic violations. Kisseberth (1970), however, has also drawn attention to cases of the converse type, in which an otherwise general rule fails to apply just in case its application would create (or perhaps intensify) a phonotactic violation, and has redefined 'obligatory rule' accordingly (Kisseberth 1970: 304). I term rules of this type 'negatively motivated'; their application will be controlled by a convention complementary to (4), incorporating the restriction mentioned in the last sentence. In this article, however, I shall exemplify only the less-discussed positively motivated rules. [ . . . ]

I have sought to formalize the notion of phonotactic motivation of phonological rules, and to establish two basic dichotomies among phonotactically motivated rules: one, between POSITIVELY MOTIVATED rules which apply only when they can 'help' the phonotactics and NEGATIVELY MOTIVATED rules which apply whenever they do not 'hinder' the phonotactics; the other, between PARTICULARLY MOTIVATED rules which are motivated by one or more individual phonotactic constraints and GENERALLY MOTIVATED rules whose motivation comes from the phonotactics as a whole. The resulting new conventions for the statement of rules will eliminate a great deal of repetition both between different subcomponents of the phonology and between different phonological rules, and will distinguish clearly between the phonotactic 'target' at which a phonological rule aims and the means it employs to ensure that the target is hit.

One further remark. Kiparsky (1971) has defined a notion of TRANSPARENCY of a phonological rule, and has noted a tendency for rules to change their order, in the course of linguistic history, in such a way as to maximize transparency. A rule is transparent just in case it constitutes a true generalization about the final output of the phonology – equivalently, just in case there is no form in the final output to which the rule could apply non-vacuously.

Now every positively phonotactically motivated rule (PPM-rule) is transparent in this sense. For every application of a PPM-rule, by convention (4), removes or alleviates a phonotactic violation; therefore every input to such an application is phonotactically deviant; therefore no form can both appear in categorial phonetic representation and be input to a non-vacuous application of a PPM-rule; therefore all PPM-rules are transparent, Q.E.D. Conversely, it can be proved that corresponding to any transparent rule R a true phonotactic constraint C can be stated, such that all inputs to non-vacuous applications of R violate C and at least some outputs of such applications satisfy C, while the remaining outputs, if any, require less alteration to make them satisfy C than they did before the application of R; in other words, that R is a PPM-rule. In short, transparency and positive phonotactic motivation are one and the same thing, and we can, if we wish, give Kiparsky's principle in the form:

(59)  P-rules tend towards that ordering which maximizes positive phonotactic motivation.

This evidence from linguistic change is valuable confirmation of the thesis of this paper that a PPM-rule is more natural than a rule with the same effect but without the phonotactic motivation; and conversely, the theory of phonotactic motivation, proposed on independent grounds, supports Kiparsky's principle by showing it to be a special case of the general principle (Kiparsky 1968) that phonological change other than by rule addition proceeds in the direction of decreasing markedness or increasing naturalness.

## Notes

The help of F. W. Householder and P. H. Matthews, who kindly read and commented on an earlier version of this paper, is gratefully acknowledged. All remaining errors are of course my own.

1   In earlier work (Sommerstein 1973: 110–11) I argued that morpheme structure conditions or their equivalent were needed in a generative phonology. This argument depended on the tacit assumption, which I now see to be mistaken (cf. p. 85), that a surface phonotactics was not possible in a theory of phonology which did not recognize a significant level of autonomous phonemics.

2   Schane (1971) makes the point that such studies rarely give detail rules and their final outputs are often close to an autonomous phonemic representation. With the proposal to make phonotactic statements at the categorial phonetic level, cf. Krivnova and Kodzasov (1972: 118): 'All phonotactic regularities can be described in terms of systematic phones rather than in terms of autonomous phonemes.'

3   The import of 'positively' here is explained on p. 88.

4   'Preference' is one of two relations which are commonly confused under the name 'ordering'; it is concerned with the choice between the application of two rules both of whose structural descriptions are simultaneously satisfied by the same form – the preferred rule is applied first, even if its application prevents the non-preferred rule from applying by destroying its environment or the segment to which it would have applied.

# References

Allen, W. S. 1965. *Vox Latina*. Cambridge: Cambridge University Press.

Anderson, S. R. 1971. On the description of 'apicalized' consonants. *Linguistic Inquiry* 2, 103–7.

Chomsky, N. 1965. *Aspects of the Theory of Syntax*. Cambridge, Mass.: MIT Press.

Chomsky, N. and Halle, M. 1968. *The Sound Pattern of English*. New York: Harper & Row.

Kiparsky, P. 1968. Linguistic universals and linguistic change. In E. Bach and R. T. Harms (eds), *Universals in Linguistic Theory*, New York: Holt, Rinehart & Winston.

Kiparsky, P. 1971. Historical linguistics. In W. O. Dingwall (ed.), *A Survey of Linguistic Science*, University of Maryland: Linguistics Program.

Kisseberth, C. W. 1970. On the functional unity of phonological rules. *Linguistic Inquiry* 1, 291–306.

Krivnova, O. F. and Kodzasov, S. V. 1972. Review of Postal (1968). *Linguistics* 94, 111–27.

Matthews, P. H. 1972. *Inflectional Morphology*. Cambridge: Cambridge University Press.

Postal, P. M. 1968. *Aspects of Phonological Theory*. New York: Harper & Row.

Schane, S. A. 1971. The phoneme revisited. *Language* 47, 503–21.

Sommerstein, A. H. 1973. *The Sound Pattern of Ancient Greek*. Publications of the Philological Society. Oxford: Blackwell.

Stanley, R. 1967. Redundancy rules in phonology. *Language* 43, 393–436.

# 6

# Harmonic Phonology (1993)

## John Goldsmith

## 1  Introduction

This chapter is a discussion of several basic issues which I have been exploring recently.[1] All of them involve very simple questions, so simple that they will no doubt frequently run the risk of striking the reader as having been fully and satisfactorily treated in the past. I am convinced that this is not so, and can do no more than invite the reader to reconsider some of these questions with me. Among the issues I am concerned with are the matter of extrinsic rule ordering; the appropriateness in a derivation of intermediate stages which are not at a specifiable linguistic level; and, most importantly, the notion of the derivation as a sequential set of steps, as a part of a production system. [ . . . ]

Much of the material discussed here arose out of a critical analysis of lexical phonology,[2] which depends heavily on what appear to be thoroughgoing uses of an implausible metaphor[3] involving space and time: "First add an affix, then send that material through a set of rules which modifies the resultant form; then go to the next level, add another affix, and finally string all the words together, only after which do we reach a point where the postlexical rules get a chance to apply." The hope is implicit in such an account that the ungainly metaphors are present only for expository reasons; but as I attempted to extract the essence from the packaging, for my own purely pedagogical purposes, I slowly, and reluctantly, came to the conclusion that the operation left little behind. In short, and at the risk of oversimplifying, the essence of lexical phonology emerged as an implausible metaphor. But such a conclusion demands swift and positive action: lexical phonology has the good sense to make us confront important questions, and we must not lose sight of that. More than that, there are some important insights at the core of lexical phonology that seem to easily get lost – such as the thoroughgoing identity of morpheme-structure conditions and lexical phonological rules.

The phonological conclusion that the present paper aims toward is this: that all phonological rules which apply at a particular level have the explicit function of moving a representation as far as possible toward meeting the phonotactics of that level; that these rules, within a level, are not ordered; that rules which apply across levels do not necessarily have such properties, in general, but that these rules do not give rise to derivations (i.e., to derivations with intermediate stages); that the levels of a phonological account are few in number, and that their properties are largely independent of one another (*pace* suggestions of structure preservation); and, finally, stratificationalism: that greater attention to what defines well-formedness at a given level will lead to a far simpler overall grammar. The present paper is perhaps no more than a propaedeutic to a proper and full treatment.[4]

## 2   Representations, Levels, and Rules

All theories of phonology – and, more generally, of formal linguistics – can be usefully divided into theories of representations, of levels, and of rules. All three are potentially problematic notions, and the boundaries are on occasion difficult to define. But this tripartite division is nonetheless very useful, and worth the effort we expend on establishing it.

Of the three notions, that of representation is the most familiar at present. Most of the work in phonological theory in the post-*SPE* period – 1975–90, let us say, following the publication of *The Sound Pattern of English* (*SPE*; Chomsky and Halle 1968) – has been in this domain. Over the last 15 years, phonologists have taken it to be a matter of debate and exploration to find the most appropriate geometrical and algebraic models for representing phonological information. These explorations have included the development of autosegmental tiers and association lines, of metrical trees and grids, of feature geometries, of dependency relations among feature specifications, of "particulate" approaches to segmental structure (involving hypotheses regarding the atoms that compose vowels and consonants), and so on.

It is worth bearing in mind that current openness to such discussion has not been achieved effortlessly. The generally unchallenged assumption throughout American phonological thought had been that phonological representation was largely unproblematic and consisted, in particular, of sequences of segments. The dominance of this position was reinforced by its centrality to both Bloomfieldian thought and to that of *The Sound Pattern of English,* and the voices that were raised to question it had little impact on the global assumptions made by theoretical phonologists during this period. Much of this has changed now, to be sure, but the change has been a recent one. In the domain of rules and levels, the range of debated issues has been much less varied and much more restricted than in the domain of representations, but we may reasonably hope that this has been in large part a matter of focus of attention: as the field, in the last 15 years, has satisfactorily established for itself a class of adequate phonological models, it is now in a position to turn its attention to other, equally difficult matters whose consideration has largely, though by no means entirely, been put on hold during this period.

## 3   Levels

The notion of level is perhaps the single most important notion in modern linguistics, and there is a danger that our understanding of this notion may fade from our consciousness as various technical concerns vie for our professional attention: the case could be made that linguists' appreciation of this notion has diminished as a result of certain competing interests. There is a sense in which we[5] are all comfortable with the notion of levels in linguistic analysis; but I invite the reader to consider some basic questions once again.[6] Our first goal is to clarify the notion of level, and when we do so, we find, first, that it is best (and quite well) explicated in pregenerative writings; second, that generative grammar was originally conceived – no surprise! – as an answer to questions formulated within this clear and traditional understanding of the notion of level; and third, that the notion of a derivation has passed from being, at its origin, a possible approach to the problem of linguistic levels, to a view of linguistic analysis which stands in the way of a clear understanding of the notion of levels.[7]

Like all important ideas, that of linguistic levels is very simple: a linguistic level is a way of looking at – of describing – a linguistic expression. We may look at an expression from a syntactic perspective, and posit a syntactic level of representation; or from a morphological perspective, and posit a morphological level of representation; and so forth. In our usual linguistic way of thinking, there is an inherent ordering – or at least a relationship close to ordering – of these levels based on the relative size of the units that are established on each level of representation: if the units on the syntactic level (always, or typically) correspond to one or more units on the morphological level, then there may well seem to be an inherent ordering of these two levels, with one "above" the other; and, indeed, the term "level" might encourage such an addition to the concept. But this kind of ordering is not inherent in the notion of level.

Let us recall a simple example of how levels of analysis of an utterance may differ. A representation on the morphological level consists of units that are morphemes, and so as to be less misleading, it is often best not to spell a morpheme as, say, *dog* or [dɔg], but rather as $\mu_{122}$, for example, to emphasize that it has no internal segmental structure at that level. The analysis of an utterance such as *the dog barked* into morphophonemic elements, which may well include boundaries (if our theory countenances them) separating the morphemes, as in (1c), does not constitute a representation on the morphological level – it is an analysis on a phonological or morphophonological level, as evidenced precisely by the kind of units (here, phonological units) that constitute the representation.

(1)  (a)  The dog barked.                    (English orthography)
     (b)  [det: definite] [$\mu_{345}$] [Verb$_{533}$] [PAST]   (morphological level)
     (c)  ðə + dɔg + bark + d                 (morphophonemic level)

Levels, indeed, may be quite autonomous and independent of each other. The degree of autonomy of the various levels was a significant issue in the 1950s; Hockett (1961), for example, argued at length that the morphological level and the phonological (or, specifically, phonemic) level are autonomous and cannot be viewed as having places on a single linear hierarchy of levels. Pike's work generally addressed this question, in the context of a theory involving three hierarchies of distinct levels; see Pike 1972 and references therein. Of this literature, little seems to remain in linguists' collective memory beyond the specific phonological issues formulated by Chomsky (1964), and yet the issues remain of significance.

Generative phonology – and generative grammar, more generally – proposed a specific account of the relation among traditional linguistic levels, an account that centers around Chomsky's 1975 [1955] conception of a linguistic derivation. Certain pairs of levels were to be related to each other by means of derivations (specifically, the systematic phonemic and the systematic phonetic levels, as well as deep structure and surface structure); in other cases, the level itself was defined in terms of a derivation. In a sense, this last move turns the logic of analysis into levels on its head, in a way that deserves our close attention. The most striking example of this is found in *Aspects of the Theory of Syntax* (Chomsky 1965: 138), where the notion of deep structure is defined not simply as the result of lexical insertion into the output of the phrase structure rules, the picture we tend to remember; a further condition is set there on being a deep structure. A structure which is created by the phrase structure rules and to which the rules of lexical insertion successfully assign lexical elements is called a "generalized phrase-marker." A generalized phrase-marker is a deep structure only if, in addition, it is part of a derivation that includes a well-formed surface structure, where "well-formed" is defined to mean "not containing any appearances of the symbol #" – where "#" marks the edges of sentences that have not yet been integrated derivationally into the larger, matrix clause. Thus a surface structure that contains a "#" is no surface structure at all, and it was this oddity that Chomsky suggested we could exploit in order to mark as ungrammatical any derivation based on such monstrosities as [*I saw the boy* [*the dog bit the cat*]]. Such a structure would "surface" with a telltale "#" (that is, as *I saw the boy #the dog bit the cat#*); hence it would not technically be a surface structure, and – the point here – its underlying structure would not be a deep structure as technically defined. In this way, the notion of deep structure was defined derivationally and in a fashion involving cross-level relationship (an effect which we would later learn to call a derivational constraint), rather than purely in terms of local conditions on a given formal representation.

With the passage of time, and of a generation of linguists, the notion of derivation changed, in many linguists' perception, from being an account of the fundamental problem of levels in linguistics to being the essence itself of a linguistic analysis. No precise moment dates this transition, but the late 1960s saw the development of modes of speaking about syntax and about phonology that were heavily committed to a dynamic model of linguistic analysis, in terms of which one representation is successively changed into another in a sequence that in its entirety is the account of the expression in question.

In generative syntax, this view has been challenged successively by approaches such as GPSG and, to a somewhat lesser degree, LFG.[8] But the derivational view remains powerful and virtually without challenge in phonology (see, for example, Bromberger and Halle 1989). We must explore why.

There is a close relationship – and frequently a competition – between the notion of level and that of derivation. The Halle–Chomsky position that challenged the adequacy of the classical phonemic level left a void which the phonological derivation made straight to fill.

Traditional structuralist phonology allowed three quasi-phonological representations: a phonetic representation (PT), a phonemic representation (PM), and a morphophonemic representation (MP). Any expression in a language could be associated with a representation on these three levels, and an adequate grammar provided an account of the relationship between units on a given level (PT, PM, MP) and those on the other levels. Traditionally, the levels were hierarchized, with rules of allophony relating the phonemic and the phonetic levels, and automatic and nonautomatic rules of alternation relating the morphophonemic and the phonemic levels. If we indicate allophony rules, then, as

(PM, PT) rules – rules relating the PM and PT levels, though with no particular significance attributed to the order of these terms – and rules of phonemic alternation as (MP, PM) rules, then there is, quite evidently, an inherent ordering to rules of these two "components," as (2) illustrates.[9]

(2)  Morphophonemic        Phonemic              Phonetic
     Representation MP      Representation PM      Representation PT

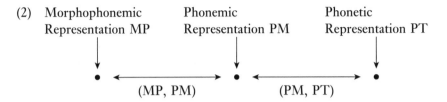

Thus the dismissal of a phonemic level, as argued by Halle and Chomsky, seemed to leave the picture in (2) in a seriously weakened position, with only two levels of representation, MP and PT, and thus only one set of principles relating these levels, as in (3).

(3)  Morphophonemic        Phonetic
     Representation MP      Representation PT

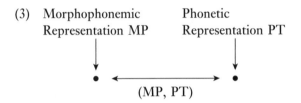

But the minimalistic organization offered by (3) is simply inadequate for the treatment of the phonology of any human language, as Chomsky and Halle were prepared to show. In case after case, it is necessary to have rule interaction, at the very least of the sort that (2) allows. Let us consider briefly a simple example from a recent analysis of Chukchi by Odden (1987), an example of a sort that could be multiplied *ad libitum*, to illustrate the kind of interaction that (3) does not permit, but which is very common in language. [ . . . ]

Inherent in the notion of level is the idea that there are specific generalizations that can, and perhaps must, be drawn concerning the representation of the expression on that level. For as we said earlier, a level is a way of representing, or describing, or analyzing, an utterance; many (perhaps a boundless number of) levels are thus conceivable, and the correct ones will be justified on the basis of the generalizations that can be stated at just those levels.

   Synthesizing, then, we may say that the logic of linguistic levels consists in the breaking down of the analysis into a number of distinct, autonomous representations, each with its own elements and its own generalizations (or tactics, or well-formedness conditions). To this we will add, presently, the notion that each level also contains complexity measures, in such a fashion that certain representations on a given level may be said to be more complex than others on the same level. We will then be in a position to propose that all the functions of derivations be replaced by two types of relations: rules that relate distinct levels, e.g. (MP, PM) rules, and rules that serve to decrease the complexity of representation on a single linguistic level. A grammar that consists of no other sort of rule will be called a *harmonic grammar*.

The notion of derivation in phonology has its origin both in historical linguistics and in the philosophy of mathematics. [ . . . ]

Neither the historical derivation nor the Post production system seem, upon mature reflection, likely to provide a sound basis for a practical and psychologically valid theory of phonology. Each had evolved with particular ends in mind: historical derivations, to treat a long-standing problem of regular Neogrammarian sound change, and production systems, to account for a formal theory of systems that possess a semantics in which truth must be preserved over the course of particular derivations – unlike anything, we hardly need add, in phonology.[10] I have emphasized the peculiar historicity of the current view of derivations for one simple reason: it is far too easy for us, in our present position, to think of derivations in phonology as arising somehow, ineluctably and logically, jointly out of the data and the task. It is, rather, in large measure a historical, or even biographical, matter that the theoreticians who have most influenced our current views on this (of whom the first and foremost is Chomsky) have offered us this particular view; others are equally congenial to the task.

What was lost in the generative emphasis on derivations, and thus equal emphasis upon rules, was the perception of the importance of levels, i.e., that language could be viewed as a whole system of interacting levels of representation.[11] Within recent years, the conception of language as an interaction of autonomous components, or modules, has indeed returned, but too frequently with the emphasis on the rules that function in each part, and the breaking up of the derivation into successive autonomous pieces.

Our central proposal is this: within the phonological part of a grammar, just as within the other components of the grammar, the acquisition of a language consists of the abstraction of a large number of well-formedness conditions – patterns, crudely put – on a small number of levels – three, a matter to which we shall return in detail. The proper definition of these language-particular and language-universal patterns will require all of the sophisticated phonological equipment at our disposal; with regard to matters of phonological representation, at least, this harmonic phonology will need all the mechanisms that recent phonological theory has offered. [ . . . ]

We may establish, then, for each level L, a set of intralevel (L,L) rules whose function is purely to allow the representation to achieve maximal satisfaction of L's well-formedness conditions; we may say that the representation at level L relaxes to a maximally well-formed state via the (L,L) rules, which function as transitions. A level consists of a vocabulary of items, a set of statements regulating how they may be put together, and – it is this third point that distinguishes our proposal from traditional theory – a measure of well-formedness.

From the point of view of traditional generative phonology, the rule applications within a level may be viewed as a mini-derivation, utilizing the (L,L) rules, but with the following caveats: (1) the (L,L) rules are not (that is, cannot be) ordered; (2) more generally, we will not expect that rules apply sequentially, though for the moment we may make the simplifying assumption that they do; (3) most importantly, intralevel (L,L) rules apply only if their effect is to shift the representation toward a better-formed state; putting the matter differently, the intralevel rules define what the allowable paths are that the representation may move through (or search) in its quest for a maximally relaxed (well-formed) state.

Even this model is unsatisfactorily derivationally oriented, and in some recent work, which we shall discuss in section 2.5 [not repr. here], we have succeeded, explicitly and computationally, in eliminating that aspect.[12] For present purposes, we will be satisfied with the conditions above. The difficulty in avoiding even these remnants of derivationalism lies in the question of how to compose two or more distinct phonological rules; without a more radical revision of the notion of a phonological representation, it is difficult, and perhaps impossible, to treat the effects of several rules without some remnants of derivationalism, which is to say, a linear sequence of distinct, identifiable representations.

We have seen that each level L consists of (1) a vocabulary permitting a linguistic description, (2) a set of relations expressing relative well-formedness, and (3) a set of intralevel (L,L) rules which express the paths that a representation may pass through to find maximal well-formedness. A representation of a given expression on a level L is thus, in general, not a single representation, but rather a pair of representations $(L_i, L_f)$ (that is, initial and final) where $L_f$ is the best-formed (with respect to L's phonotactics) representation accessible to $L_i$, given the (L,L) rules.

A grammar, however, consists of a set of perhaps as many as 10 or 15 separate levels, and generally there are specific principles limiting and defining representations on different levels; we will refer to these as *cross-level rules* (Goldsmith 1990 refers to them as interlevel rules; Sadock 1991 refers to them as interface principles). We propose, in particular, that there are three levels of phonological interest. (I will not carry out the exercise of illustrating the inadequacy of a system with only two levels; in light of the remarks just above concerning feeding within a single level, the example of feeding in Chukchi [omitted here] does not serve to establish the need for more than two levels, but bleeding and counterfeeding relations, also common in natural languages, do establish this; thus the proposal that there are three levels is, we may assume, the very minimal assumption that could even be considered.) These levels are:

- *M-level*, a morphophonemic level, the level at which morphemes are phonologically specified;
- *W-level*, the level at which expressions are structured into well-formed syllables and well-formed words, but with a minimum of redundant phonological information; and
- *P-level*, a level of broad phonetic description that is the interface with the peripheral articulatory and acoustic devices.

Of these, our greatest interest, as phonologists, will be with the W-level, which is where the bulk of the significant well-formedness conditions, or tactics, are stated.

There will thus be six types of phonological rules, in principle: three intralevel rule types: (M,M) rules, (W,W) rules, and (P,P) rules, and three cross-level rule types: (M,W) rules, (W,P) rules, and (M,P) rules (we should emphasize again that the order of the symbols is irrelevant; (M,W) rules could as well be called (W,M) rules, for example). This could be depicted as in (6). The traditional hierarchical conception of phonology amounts to a denial of the existence of (M,P) rules, in effect converting (6) to (7), whose form is hierarchical. For the present, we have no need for (M,P) rules, and may assume that such rules do not exist.

We add to the three proposed definitions of levels above, then, the assumption:

- Cross-level rules may or may not (i.e., need not) be harmonic.

(6)

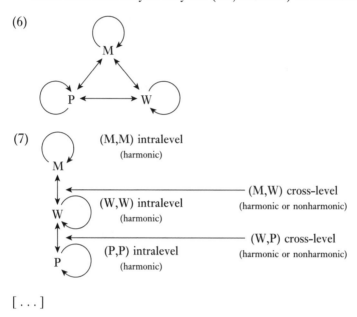

(7)

M   (M,M) intralevel
(harmonic)

(M,W) cross-level
(harmonic or nonharmonic)

W   (W,W) intralevel
(harmonic)

(W,P) cross-level
(harmonic or nonharmonic)

P   (P,P) intralevel
(harmonic)

[ . . . ]

## Conclusions

My purpose in this chapter has been to explore the consequences for phonological analysis of assuming a different kind of relationship between underlying and surface forms than that which has traditionally been posited. In the first half of this chapter, I have addressed the problem from the point of view of reasonably traditional conceptions of phonological representations, modifying in some measure the notion of rule application and offering a reconsideration of the traditional notion of level. In the latter part, I have reported on recent work that more radically changes the conception of phonological analysis by sharply reducing the conceptual distance between rules and representations and proposing specific means by which a phonological device can calculate its output in a dynamic fashion. This work, inspired in part by the computational tools of recent work in connectionism (Rumelhart and McClelland et al. 1986, and especially Smolensky 1986 and 1988), provides a radically new picture of the dynamic functioning that occurs within a phonological level.

If this direction of research is correct, then the picture of phonology that emerges is one in which our notions of phonological structure, including autosegmental, metrical, and prosodic components, will rearise as the scaffolding in a network of phonological elements whose well-formedness is calculated on the basis of an interaction of neighboring units. Such structures, with their concomitant calculation of maximal well-formedness, will be found on each of the three phonological levels (and, presumably, on other linguistic levels as well, including syntax and morphology), and cross-level rules will ensure proper registration across levels.

Virtually all of these final remarks are speculative at this point, to be sure, to some degree or other. What does come out clearly, however, is the need for serious reconsideration and reevaluation of the notions of level and derivation in current phonological theory, notions which were once well-motivated when placed against the conceptual backdrop of post-Bloomfieldian structuralist phonology, but which form no more than one team in the larger line-up of professional contenders.

## Notes

1 This chapter [only part of which has been reproduced here] has seen a number of versions circulated among colleagues over the past several years. It develops ideas that are discussed as well in Goldsmith (1989, 1990, in press a), and has been influenced by more linguists and nonlinguists than I could name. With regard to the notion of levels, I have been especially influenced by Charles Hockett and Noam Chomsky, as well as by J. R. Firth and Kenneth Pike; the reader will note the echoes of stratificational, prosodic, and tagmemic writing in some of the discussion herein. I have had a number of discussions with George Lakoff since 1987 on the notion of rule ordering and the challenges to intermediate representations. On the matter of harmonic rule application, the work by Singh and Sommerstein that I cite below deserves particular mention, as do in other ways lectures by John McCarthy at the 1987 Linguistic Institute at Stanford University. With regard to levels and harmonic application, various work on lexical phonology and phrase level phonology has been influential in that much of the work in these traditions seems to me to be quite wrongheaded; the present work aims to provide more attractive alternatives. On the importance of the notion of harmonic application in a larger cognitive perspective, I have been greatly encouraged by current work in connectionism, as discussed, for example, in Rumelhart and McClelland et al. 1986, and I have found especially helpful the work of Smolensky (1986 and elsewhere), whose work on harmony theory was at the origin of my choice of name of the present work.

I have as well been influenced by the work of Sydney Lamb and of Charles Hockett, I should note. I am greatly indebted to my colleagues and students at the University of Chicago, especially to Jerry Sadock, whose work on autolexical theory stands behind the present discussion, and to discussions with the students in our phonology seminars, including Anna Bosch, Diane Brentari, Gary Larson, Karen Peterson, and Caroline Wiltshire. Geoffrey Huck, Younghee Na, and Jessie Pinkham have made very helpful comments on earlier drafts of this paper. This material was presented at the University of Toronto and the University of California at Berkeley, and I am grateful to the linguists there for helpful comments as well.

This material is based upon work supported by the National Science Foundation under Grant No. BNS 9009678.

2 Goldsmith 1990: ch. 5. On lexical phonology, see particularly Kiparsky 1982, 1985.

3 Perhaps the phrase is tendentious. There are no methodological principles given to us a priori that would allow us to know when a theory's constructs have strayed too far from what can be translated into a psychologically accurate model.

4 To my surprise (and dismay), I have found that these preliminary observations are occasionally greeted with a certain hostility among my otherwise eminently judicious and sensible colleagues. I wish to explicitly avoid giving the impression either that I am rejecting all of contemporary phonological thought (that is the farthest thing from my mind) or that I am suggesting that my proposal here is without precedent in the recent literature. On the contrary, it is rather obvious, as I have tried to suggest here and in Goldsmith (1990: ch. 6), that the present proposal is a natural development of proposals that have been made over the past 20 years, and more, in some cases. I would emphasize that the central point of the present discussion is to encourage discussion, within the present context, of the relationship between derivations and levels.

A number of proposals in the current literature bear directly on the model discussed here. In certain respects, the "repair strategy" explorations of Singh (1987) and, following him, Paradis (1988), based explicitly on the proposals of Sommerstein (1974), are the closest, but in other respects their proposals are quite distinct (or perhaps "orthogonal" would be a better term) to the present discussion. Yip (1988) explores similar ideas. As I have noted, the work by Sydney Lamb, mentioned exceedingly rarely in the present literature despite its influence, is to be noted. Some work of Alan Prince, of John McCarthy, and of Junko Itô is highly relevant, though the list of work that is highly relevant would be hard to complete once it was started.

5   Throughout this section I use the vague pronoun "we" to refer to a common group of contemporary linguists. The reader may take the word to be used either inclusively or exclusively as the reader wishes; my intention is that it be inclusive.

6   A recent and thoughtful discussion of these notions is found in Ladusaw 1988.

7   For purposes of concreteness, I take Hockett's position in Hockett 1961 to epitomize the theoretical position that I refer to here as American structuralism. Chomsky 1975 [1955] offers a fine explanation of the notion of level:

> The development of a system of phonemic representation does not conclude the process of linguistic analysis. We also want to discover the morphemes, words, and phrases of the language, and to determine principles of sentence construction that could hardly be stated directly in terms of phonemes. Instead of giving a direct definition of these further notions within linguistic theory, we can continue to construct systems of representation for sentence tokens, calling these systems "linguistic levels." A sentence token can be represented as a sequence of phonemes; but it can also be represented as a sequence of morphemes, words, and phrases. Thus each sentence token will have associated with it a whole set of representations, each representation being its "spelling" in terms of elements of one linguistic level. (Pp. 98–9)

Perhaps better known is the following passage, on the opening page of Chomsky 1957:

> The central notion in linguistic theory is that of "linguistic level." A linguistic level, such as phonemics, morphology, phrase structure, is essentially a set of descriptive devices that are made available for the construction of grammars; it constitutes a certain method for representing utterances. (P. 11)

8   It goes beyond the scope of this paper to discuss the matter in detail, but the point may well be made that a major component in the lack of communication between the generative semanticists and the interpretive semanticists in the late 1960s derived from the use, by the generative semanticists, of the technical notion of derivation without a serious commitment to the view of syntactic analysis that lies behind its most natural use. Global rules (Lakoff 1969, 1970) seem like a formal abomination from the point of view of derivational syntactic analyses, though not from the point of view of a theory trying to link semantic and syntactic levels of analysis in as direct a fashion as possible – "direct" in the sense that an autonomous level of deep structure, distinct from semantic representation, was not included in the theory. This issue is discussed further in Huck and Goldsmith 1995.

9   A reviewer poses the question at his point as to whether we are to interpret the relation between levels as being achieved by rules acting simultaneously at each step, i.e., (MP, PM) and (PM, PT). The answer is yes, of course, though the structuralist would say that the word "simultaneously" is out of place. A relation is not something that *happens*; it is a state, we might say, not an event, and all cross-level relations are timeless states. If $2 + 6$ equals 8, and 8 equals $2 \times 4$, are we committed to saying that the two equalities are simultaneous when we write $2 + 6 = 8 = 2 \times 4$? In a word, no; to say they are true simultaneously would be misleading at best, a category mistake at worst.

10   András Kornai informs me that he has recently argued that such a position – developing a semantics, in effect, for phonology – has interesting consequences; I have not had the opportunity to study this work (Kornai 1991).

11   Chomsky 1975 [1955] provides a discussion of the introduction of representations that are motivated only by general simplicity of rule interactions (pp. 114–16 especially).

12    The present proposal leaves open a number of questions. If intralevel rules, for example, are unordered, is the claim not implicit that no cases will ever arise in which the order of application of two intralevel rules must be specified in a language-particular fashion? We will not, in fact, address that question, because we are trying to establish a rather different way of discussing phonological rules, adumbrated in the final section of this chapter [not repr. here]. The essence of the approach is that what we take to be phonological rules can best be formalized as something approaching a field of force in a large-dimensional phase space; these fields can be arithmetically summed, and the sum is what determines the effect that the phonological representation undergoes.

# References

Bromberger, Sylvain, and Morris Halle. 1989. Why phonology is different. *Linguistic Inquiry* 20: 51–70.

Chomsky, Noam. 1957. *Syntactic Structures*. The Hague: Mouton.

Chomsky, Noam. 1964. *Current Issues in Linguistic Theory*. The Hague: Mouton.

Chomsky, Noam. 1965. *Aspects of the Theory of Syntax*. Cambridge, Mass.: MIT Press.

Chomsky, Noam. 1975. *Logical Structure of Linguistic Theory*. New York: Plenum. Repr. Chicago: University of Chicago Press. Originally circulated, 1955.

Chomsky, Noam and Morris Halle. 1968. *The Sound Pattern of English*. New York: Harper and Row.

Goldsmith, John. 1990. *Autosegmental and Metrical Phonology*. Oxford and Cambridge, Mass.: Blackwell.

Hockett, Charles. 1961. Linguistic elements and their relations. *Language* 37: 29–53.

Huck, Geoffrey and John Goldsmith. 1995. *Ideology and Linguistic Theory*. New York: Routledge.

Kiparsky, Paul. 1982. Lexical phonology and morphology. In I. S. Yang (ed.), *Linguistics in the Morning Calm*, Seoul: Hanshin, 3–91.

Kiparsky, Paul. 1985. Some consequences of lexical phonology. *Phonology* 2: 85–138.

Kornai, András. 1991. Formal Phonology. Ph.D. dissertation, Stanford University.

Ladusaw, William. 1988. A proposed distinction between levels and strata. In S.-D. Kim (ed.), *Linguistics in the Morning Calm*, vol. 2. Seoul: Hanshin.

Lakoff, George. 1969. On derivational constraints. In *Papers from the Fifth Annual Regional Meeting of the Chicago Linguistics Society*, Chicago: Chicago Linguistics Society.

Lakoff, George. 1970. Global rules. *Language* 46: 627–39.

Odden, David. 1987. Dissimilation as deletion in Chukchi. In A. Miller and J. Power (eds), *Proceedings from ESCOL 3*, Columbus, Oh.: Ohio State University, 235–46.

Paradis, Carole. 1988. On constraints and repair strategies. *Linguistic Review*, 6: 71–97.

Rumelhart, David, James McClelland, and the PDP Group. 1986. *Parallel Distributed Processing: Explorations in the Microstructure of Cognition*. Cambridge, Mass.: MIT Press.

Sadock, Jerrold. 1991. *Autolexical Syntax*. Chicago: University of Chicago Press.

Singh, Rajendra. 1987. Well-formedness conditions and phonological theory. In Wolfgang Dressler et al. (eds), *Phonologica 1984*, London: Cambridge University Press, 273–85.

Smolensky, Paul. 1986. Information processing in dynamical systems: foundations of harmony theory. In Rumelhart et al. 1986, 194–281.

Smolensky, Paul. 1988. On the proper treatment of connectionism. *Behavioral and Brain Sciences* 11: 1–74.

Sommerstein, Alan. 1974. On phonotactically motivated rules. *Journal of Linguistics* 10: 71–94; part of which is repr. here as ch. 5.

Yip, Moira. 1988. The Obligatory Contour Principle and phonological rules: a loss of identity. *Linguistic Inquiry* 19: 65–100.

# 7

# Generalized Alignment (1993)

## John J. McCarthy and Alan S. Prince

## 1  Introduction

Overt or covert reference to the **edges** of constituents is a commonplace throughout phonology and morphology. Some examples include:

*   In English, Garawa, Indonesian and a number of other languages, the normal right-to-left alternation of stress is interrupted word-initially:

    (1)   Initial Secondary Stress in English
    (Tàta)ma(góuchee)       *Ta(tàma)(góuchee)
    (Lùxi)pa(lílla)          *Lu(xìpa)(lílla)

    As the foot-brackets ( ) indicate, the favored outcome is one in which the edge of the Prosodic Word coincides with the edge of a foot (cf. Liberman and Prince 1977: 276).
*   In Tagalog, the affix *-um-* falls as near as possible to the left edge of the stem, so long as it obeys the phonological requirement that its final consonant *m* not be syllabified as a coda:

    (2)   *-um-* Infixation in Tagalog
    u.ma.ral                            'teach'
    su.mu.lat            *um.su.lat      'write'
    gru.mad.wet          *um.grad.wet    'graduate'

*   In Ulwa, the affix *-ka-* 'his' falls immediately after the head foot of the word:

    (3)   *-ka-* Infixation in Ulwa
    (bás)ka                              'hair'
    (siwá)kanak                          'root'

    This affix is a suffix on the head foot, rather than on the word as a whole.

That is, the affix lies at the right edge of that foot.

These examples only hint at the generality of the phenomenon to be explored here, which extends to include all the various ways that constituents may be enjoined to share an edge in prosody and morphology.

Data like these have been given widely disparate treatments in the literature: directionality of foot-parsing, syllabic or segmental extrametricality, and prosodic circumscription.

Examination of a wider range of cases would reveal additional mechanisms claimed to depend crucially on the special status of constituent-edges: prosodic and morphological subcategorization, prosodic templates, and the cycle. These different ways in which constituent-edges figure in phonology and morphology would seem to make any effort at unification hopeless.

Here we propose that the diverse ways in which constituent-edges figure in morphological and phonological processes can be subsumed under a single family of well-formedness constraints, called *Generalized Alignment*.

(4)   Generalized Alignment
>      Align(Cat1, Edge1, Cat2, Edge2) =$_{\text{def}}$
>      ∀ Cat1 ∃ Cat2 such that Edge1 of Cat1 and Edge2 of Cat2 coincide.
>
>      Where
>      Cat1, Cat2 ∈ PCat ∪ GCat
>      Edge1, Edge2 ∈ {Right, Left}

PCat and GCat consist, respectively, of the sets of prosodic and grammatical (morphological or syntactic) categories provided by linguistic theory (see section 2 below for one proposal). Thus, a GA requirement demands that a designated edge of each prosodic or morphological constituent of type Cat1 coincide with a designated edge of some other prosodic or morphological constituent Cat2. (We return below at the end of section 2 to issues of formalization.)

For the examples cited above, for instance, the particular parametrization of GA is as follows:

(5)   Generalized Alignment, applied to (1)–(3)
>      (a)   English Stress
>            Align(PrWd, L, Ft, L)
>            This requirement is satisfied in [(*Tàta*)ma(*góuchee*)], since the left edge of the Prosodic Word coincides with the left edge of a foot. (See section 3 for the interaction of this type of constraint with others in the stress system.)
>      (b)   Tagalog *-um-*
>            Align([*um*]$_{\text{Af}}$, L, Stem, L)
>            This requirement is satisfied in |*umaral*, since the left edge of the affix *-um-* lies at the left edge of a stem. It is *minimally violated* (in a sense made precise below, section 4) in |*sumulat* or |*grumadwet*.
>      (c)   Ulwa *-ka-*
>            Align([*ka*]$_{\text{Af}}$, L, Ft′, R)
>            This requirement is satisfied in (*siwá*)|*-ka-nak*, from /siwanak + ka/, since the left edge of the affix |*ka* coincides with the right edge of the head foot, Ft′.

By virtue of statements like these, GA is able to express perhaps the full range of reference to edges in grammar. Taken together with X′-like restrictions on immediate domination and interpreted within the appropriate theory of constraint satisfaction, GA provides a mechanism for completely specifying a class of formal languages that, when substantive parameters are set, ought to be all-but-coextensive with possible human languages.

Because it is relatively abstract, and not tied to the particular details of a phonological or morphological sub-theory, GA has connections with more than a few other lines of analysis in the literature. The specific interpretation of GA as Align(GCat, PCat) has affinities with various approaches to phonological domains and apparent cyclic phenomena that involve simultaneous reference to prosodic and morphological structure: Liberman and Prince (1977: 256–61), Aronoff and Sridhar (1983), Booij and Rubach (1984), Poser (1985), Booij (1988), Inkelas (1989), Szpyra (1989: 178–229), Booij and Lieber (1993), Rubach and Booij (1990), Halle and Kenstowicz (1991: 479–81), Goldsmith (1990, 1991, 1992), Idsardi (1992), Cole (1992), Cole and Coleman (1992), Borowsky (1993), and Kisseberth (1994). By simultaneous reference to prosodic and morphological constituents, GA also converges with the notion of prosodic subcategorization in Broselow and McCarthy (1983: 53–60) and Inkelas (1989) and subsumes many aspects of prosodic circumscription in McCarthy and Prince (1990). With its focus on edges, GA further recalls the End Rule of Prince (1983) and subsequent developments, such as Mester's (1994) account of Latin pre-enclitic accent or, more abstractly, the treatment of boundary tones in Pierrehumbert and Beckman (1988: 126f). More specifically, we will see in section 3 below that it includes as special cases the family of constraints called 'edgemost' in Prince and Smolensky (1991a, b, 1992, 1993). Itô and Mester (1992) propose a constraint identical to (5a) for Japanese. On a related theme, Burzio (1992a, b) proposes a principle of Metrical Alignment, "which essentially requires that the [English foot] parsing be left-hand exhaustive," with obvious similarity to (5a).

Certain familiar morphology–prosody correspondence schemes amount to demanding a kind of alignment at both edges simultaneously. In this class are the 'Prosodic Constituent Formation' of Inkelas (1989: 53), concisely $[x]_m \rightarrow [x]_p$ (where $p$ represents a domain of phonological rule application, given formal constituent status in her theory) as well as the template-defining constraint format MCat = PCat, 'morphological category corresponds to phonological category' of McCarthy and Prince (1991a), where *PCat* represents a prosodic category of metrical structure. The crucial departure we advocate here is to allow separate control over the fate of each edge. We will see that conditions on left and right edges can indeed have very different grammatical status: cf. section 5 below. (Application of Alignment to prosodic-morphological templates is taken up in McCarthy and Prince 1993: section 7.)

In conception, therefore, GA is most directly connected with the edge-based theory of the syntax–phonology interface (Chen 1987; Clements 1978: 35; Hale and Selkirk 1987; Selkirk 1986; Selkirk and Tateishi 1988; Selkirk and Shen 1990). In this theory, the phonological representation of a sentence is constructed by rules that map the edges of syntactic constituents, such as the maximal projection of a lexical category, onto the corresponding edges of phonological constituents, such as the Phonological Word or Phonological Phrase. Cohn (1989) and Inkelas (1989) extend this model from syntactic to morphological constituents; for example, Cohn proposes a rule mapping the edge of the root onto the edge of a Phonological Word. In terms of the functional notation introduced in (4), the edge-based theory of sentence phonology reduces to Align(GCat, Edge1, PCat, Edge1), a mapping from the edges of grammatical categories onto the same edges of prosodic categories. Through GA, we extend this approach fully, so that opposite as well as corresponding edges can be aligned, and so that Align(PCat, GCat), Align(PCat, PCat), and Align(GCat, GCat) are also licit expressions. Furthermore, we extend it to all GCat's, morphological as well as syntactic, and to all PCat's, including the word-internal prosodic categories syllable and foot, and even features and subsegmental nodes.

One crucial aspect of the enterprise, without which this degree of abstraction would be impossible, is the idea that GA is embedded in a theory of constraints on the well-formedness of phonological and morphological representations, rather than a theory of rules or procedures for constructing representations. (This is a further respect in which GA is different from the edge-based theory of the syntax–phonology interface.[1]) Indeed, GA would fail utterly if it were cast in terms of operations rather than con-straints. In standard accounts, the operations subsumed by GA are extraordinarily diverse; consider how different the procedures are for building phonological structure from syntactic structure, for parsing words into feet, for prefixing an affix to a root, and for circumscribing the initial foot and suffixing to it. **As procedures**, these phenomena have nothing in common. The generality of Alignment is possible only in a system where it is imposed by constraints that evaluate the well-formedness of representations, without regard to the source of those representations.

A second crucial aspect of the enterprise, devolving from the first, is the idea that constraints on representation can be violated minimally, under specific conditions that compel violation. The case of Tagalog above is one example in which an Alignment constraint is minimally violated. For phonological reasons, the *m* of the affix -*um*- must not be syllabified as a coda. This phonological requirement takes precedence over Align([*um*]$_{Af}$, L, Stem, L), forcing misalignment of the affix-edge and stem-edge. But the departure from perfect Alignment is minimal, in the sense that the affix lies as near as possible to the designated edge, as can be seen by comparison of the actual forms with even more poorly aligned *sulumat* or *gradwumet*. Without the recourse of minimal violation, one would be forced to conclude that an analysis of Tagalog in terms of the constraint Align([*um*]$_{Af}$, L, Stem, L) is simply wrong, since this constraint is obviously unchallenged only in the occasional vowel-initial root like *aral*. GA, then, has a chance for success only if it is recognized that representational constraints need not be categorically true facts of a language.[2]

These two properties, which provide the foundation for GA, are the central claims of Optimality Theory (Prince and Smolensky 1991a, b, 1992, 1993). OT is a general approach to the role of well-formedness constraints in linguistic theory, embodied in the following principles:

(6) Principles of Optimality Theory[3]
    (a) Violability.
        Constraints are violable; but violation is minimal.
    (b) Ranking
        Constraints are **ranked** on a language-particular basis; the notion of min-imal violation is defined in terms of this ranking.
    (c) Inclusiveness
        The constraint hierarchy evaluates a set of candidate analyses that are admitted by very general considerations of structural well-formedness.

Within OT, the role of a grammar is to select the output form from among a very wide range of candidates, including at least all of the outputs that would be possible in any language whatsoever. Thus, language-particular rules or procedures for creating representations have no role at all in the theory, and the entire burden of accounting for the specific patterns of individual languages falls on the well-formedness constraints. These constraints are ranked in a language-particular hierarchy; any constraint is violated, minimally, if such violation leads to the satisfaction of a higher-ranking constraint.

In the remainder of this article, we will show some of the principal results of GA. The discussion opens in section 3 with an application of the alignment of prosodic categories to apparent directionality effects in stress systems. We then turn in section 4 and section 5 to alignment of morphological categories with one another and with prosodic categories. The subject of section 4 is infixation phenomena as a specific case of the alignment of affixes, and the material of section 5 is the alignment of prosodic categories at the edges of morphological ones, leading to a novel characterization of phenomena usually attributed to extrametricality, the cycle, or opacity of prosodic constituent-edges. Finally, section 6 [not repr. here] argues for constraints on the alignment of **different** edges of morphological and prosodic constituents, identifying them as a kind of prosodic subcategorization. The conclusion sums up the principal results. But first we must lay out some premises about the nature of prosodic and morphological constituency, and we must supply a more rigorous account of OT to serve as the basis for the analyses.

## 2   Substantive, Formal, and Technical Assumptions

Generalized Alignment *per se* is independent of any specific set of assumptions about prosodic and morphological constituency, except of course that there is **some** such constituency. The consequences we draw from GA will, however, rely on making claims about how some particular constituent aligns with another. To make any progress, then, we must first commit to a theory of prosodic and morphological constituency. Our results will be most secure, however, if we adhere to a minimally elaborated theory, so that they emerge from the judicious application of Alignment rather than from some dubious cleverness in the assignment of the constituents themselves.

In the realm of prosody, the Prosodic Hierarchy (7), evolved from that of Selkirk (1980a, b), is the simplest theory compatible with a very broad range of phenomena in the world's languages.

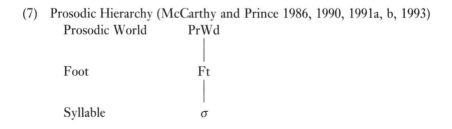

(7)   Prosodic Hierarchy (McCarthy and Prince 1986, 1990, 1991a, b, 1993)

Most phonological theories recognize an additional 'skeletal' level, subordinate to the syllable, consisting of moraic ($\mu$) or segmental (X) units (moraic: van der Hulst 1984; Hyman 1985; McCarthy and Prince 1986, 1988; Hayes 1989; Zec 1988; Itô 1989, etc.; segmental: McCarthy 1981; Steriade 1982; Clements and Keyser 1983; Levin 1985; Lowenstamm and Kaye 1986, etc.). We have not located any examples of Alignment constraints where PCat is a skeletal unit. This lacuna may be an accidental property of our sample. But it may reflect a deeper truth: the properties represented by the skeletal level – basically quantity and weight – are attributes of syllables and segments rather than constituents themselves (*cf.* Itô and Mester 1992). Whatever the explanation, the skeletal level is not treated further here (but see (37)–(38) below [not repr. here]).

The Prosodic Hierarchy expresses the domination relations among the prosodic con-stituents, but it does not express relations of immediate domination. Two departures from strict immediate domination are possible. First, because feet must be binary (Prince 1980; McCarthy and Prince 1986; Hayes 1991), single light syllables are normally unfooted and unfootable:

(8)   Unfooted Singleton Syllables
      [*po*(lice)]
      [(Tata)*ma*(gouchee)]

Following Itô and Mester (1992) (cf. McCarthy and Prince 1993: section A.2), we assume that syllables are optimally parsed by the foot, and that otherwise syllables are parsed directly by PrWd, as shown by the outer brackets '[ ]' in (8). Second, we assume that recursion of PrWd is possible, as in English (cf. Booij 1988: 137, McCarthy and Prince 1993: section A.1):

(9)   Recursion of PrWd
      [[light]$_{PrWd}$ [house]$_{PrWd}$]$_{PrWd}$
      [[help]$_{PrWd}$ less]$_{PrWd}$ ness]$_{PrWd}$

Recursion of the categories foot and syllable is impossible, however, not because of some special stipulation, but because the independently justified foot and syllable theories of Universal Grammar bar it (foot: McCarthy and Prince 1986, 1990, 1993; Hayes 1987, 1991; Kager 1989, 1992a, b, c, etc.; syllable: McCarthy and Prince 1988; Hayes 1989; Itô 1986, 1989, etc.). Through their various principles, foot theory and syllable theory license a very limited set of expansions of foot and syllable, and recur-sion is simply not among these options. There is no theory placing comparable limits on the expansion of PrWd, and indeed there could not be, if only because there is no upper bound on the length of a PrWd. In this way, phonological theory permits recursion of PrWd only.

In the realm of morphology, the available options are much broader, ranging from constituent-free process models all the way to richly articulated X' theories of word-syntax. If GA is to fly at all, we must assume **some** constituency, and if it is to be robust, we must not assume too much. (It is always easy to derive additional empirical results if more elaborated constituency turns out to be justified.) The hierarchy we assume is a traditional one, sufficient for present purposes:

(10)    Morphological Hierarchy
   MWd → Stem*
   Stem → Stem, Affix
   Stem → Root

The Morphological Hierarchy specifies constituency relations but not linear order of stem and affix. This move is essential in accounting for prosodic-morphological phenomena like the Tagalog infix *-um-* (2) or the Ulwa infix *-ka-* (3). In morphology that is prosody-governed, phonological constraints take precedence over morphological ones (McCarthy and Prince 1993: section 7); infixation shows that phonological constraints can determine even the linear order of morphemes and morpheme parts. Morphological structure represents a commitment only to the hierarchical organization of the constituent morphemes, not to linear ordering (cf. Sproat 1985: 80f) or continuity of the terminal string (cf. McCawley 1982; Scobbie 1991), so principles of phonology can affect linear order.

As noted above, an essential prerequisite to GA is Optimality Theory (Prince and Smolensky 1991a, b, 1992, 1993), with its emphasis on selection of optimal output forms by a system of ranked, violable constraints. OT shifts the explanatory burden of linguistic theory from input-based rewrite rules to output-based constraints. Instead of taking an underlying form and transforming it stepwise to its associated output, in OT it is necessary to allow for the specification of a large set of *candidate* outputs. The candidate set is evaluated by the system of constraints, which selects the actual output from the available candidates. Schematically, the grammar is like this:

(11)    An Optimality-Based Grammar, Schematically
   $\text{Gen}(\text{in}_i) = \{\text{cand}_1, \text{cand}_2, \ldots\}$
   $\text{Eval}(\{\text{cand}_1, \text{cand}_2, \ldots\}) \rightarrow \text{cand}_k$ (the output, given $\text{in}_i$)

The function Gen associates each input with a (possibly infinite) set of candidate analyses of that input. Gen involves, for example, deployment of many different prosodic parses or many different linear arrangements of morphemes. The function Eval is defined by the system of constraints, which assesses the various candidate output forms, ordering the candidates by how well they satisfy the constraint system of the language. Any candidate from $\text{Gen}(\text{in}_i)$ that best-satisfies the constraint system – a maximal element in the Eval ordering – is an output associated with the input $\text{in}_i$. Linguistic constraint systems typically associate just one output with a given input; therefore, we will usually write 'the output', even though it is possible in general for more than one form to best-satisfy a hierarchy.

The central analytical proposal of OT is that constraints are ranked in a hierarchy of relevance. Lower-ranked constraints can be violated in an optimal output form when such violation secures success on higher-ranked constraints. Universal Grammar specifies the set of constraints Con out of which grammars are constructed. Individual grammars are constructed by imposing a ranking on the entire universal constraint set Con, possibly with some setting of parameters and fixing of arguments within the constraints, such as the various arguments of Align. UG thus consists of Gen, Con, and definition of how a ranking of Con imposes evaluation on forms.

To best-satisfy a system of ranked well-formedness constraints means the following. Except for ties, the candidate that passes the highest-ranked constraint is the output form. A tie occurs either when more than one candidate passes the highest-ranked constraint or when all candidates fail the highest-ranked constraint. As we will see, ties of both kinds are common. (Constraint violation is therefore not necessarily the end of a candidate's chances: failure on a constraint can be fatal only when there are other competitors that pass it.) In case of ties, all surviving candidates are tested recursively against the rest of the hierarchy. Once a victor emerges, the remaining, lower-ranked constraints are irrelevant; whether the sole surviving candidate obeys them or not does not affect its grammaticality. Likewise, the evaluation of failed candidates by lower-ranked constraints is also irrelevant; no inferences about degree of deviation from grammaticality can be drawn from further inspection of the failed candidates.

The following example illustrates schematically how satisfaction of a constraint hierarchy proceeds. Assume a grammar consisting of two constraints, A and B. Like any grammar, this one functions to pair underlying forms with surface forms: $Eval(Gen(in_1))$ → $out_1$, $Eval(Gen(in_2))$ → $out_2$, and so on. Suppose that we have a certain underlying form $/in_k/$ which gives rise to a candidate set $\{k\text{-}cand_1, k\text{-}cand_2\}$ and that $k\text{-}cand_1$ is the actual output form.

If both A and B agree that one candidate passes and the other fails, then there is nothing to say. The optimal candidate – the output associated with $in_k$ – is just the one that meets both constraints, as in standard approaches to constraint satisfaction. If A and B **disagree**, however, we have a constraint conflict, represented by the following tableau:

(12)   Constraint Tableau, A ≫ B, $/in_k/$ → $k\text{-}cand_1$

| Candidates | | A | B |
|---|---|---|---|
| ☞ | k-cand$_1$ | | * |
| | k-cand$_2$ | *! | |

Here candidate $k\text{-}cand_1$ meets A but fails B; while $k\text{-}cand_2$ meets B but fails A. Because $k\text{-}cand_1$ is, by assumption, the actual output form, the grammar requires that constraint A **dominate** constraint B (A ≫ B), in the sense that, when A and B disagree on a candidate-pair, the decision between them is made by A alone. This tableau observes certain useful conventions: constraints are written in their domination order, violations are marked by '*', and **fatal** violations are also signalled by '!'. Shading emphasizes the **irrelevance** of a constraint to the fate of the candidate. A loser's cells are shaded after a fatal violation; the winner's, when there are no more competitors.

There are a variety of other ways that a pair of candidates can confront constraints. There is the tying configuration mentioned above: if both candidates fail a constraint equally, or succeed equally on it, then that constraint cannot contribute to a decision between them; the decision, if there is one, must be made elsewhere, by other constraints. It is entirely possible that no-decision configurations can arise for both A and B in the above example; then the 2-constraint hierarchy does not decide between the candidates considered. Situations like this arise relatively rarely with respect to *whole* hierarchies in the real world, because of the richness of the constraints in Con, but are seen quite commonly in subhierarchies, as we will see below.

A particularly interesting configuration arises when a constraint in the grammar admits of multiple or gradient violation. Suppose we are looking at a pair of candidates that tie on all constraints higher-ranked than C, and with C itself we have the following:

(13)   Multiple Violation

| Candidates | | . . . | C |
|---|---|---|---|
| ☞ | cand$_1$ | . . . | * |
| | cand$_2$ | . . . | *** |

In such a case, we say that cand$_1$ is the winner, because its accumulated violations of C are less than those of cand$_2$: C is violated **minimally**. Note that we are not counting the absolute number of violations; we are merely comparing more vs. less, a matter of ordering and not of quantity. Indeed, this case can be reduced to the first one by uniformly canceling out violations one-for-one in the C-column, a procedure whose validity is proved in Prince and Smolensky (1993: section 8). For further discussion and formalization see Prince and Smolensky (1993: section 2, section 5).

With these notions, we can compare any two forms *f* and *g* with respect to a constraint hierarchy or subhierarchy. If *f* fares better than *g*, we will say that *f* is more harmonic than *g* (with respect to the given hierarchy). If *f* and *g* fare equally, we will say that they are iso-harmonic. (The term 'harmony' is from Smolensky 1986.) Eval thus provides a Harmonic Ordering of Forms, along the lines just reviewed (Prince and Smolensky 1993: section 5). An output associated with a given input is the most harmonic member of the input's candidate set, a maximal element in the harmonic ordering; we will say that it is **optimal**. In order to avoid terminological and conceptual confusion we will strictly avoid terms like 'relative well-formedness' and 'better/worse-formed', preserving the categorical status of the term 'well-formed'. A form *f* is well-formed with respect to a grammar if it is chosen by the grammar as the output for some input: if it is an optimal member of some candidate set.

The candidate analyses are drawn from a broad range of possibilities, supplied by Gen. Three principles underlie the theory of Gen assumed here; the first two taken from Prince and Smolensky (1993):

(i)   **Freedom of Analysis**. Any amount of structure may be posited.
(ii)  **Containment**. No element may be literally removed from the input form. The input is thus contained in every candidate form.
(iii) **Consistency of Exponence**. No changes in the exponence of a phonologically specified morpheme are permitted.

True Freedom of Analysis means that Gen may supply candidates with syllabic, moraic, or other prosodic structure, with association lines, and with additional segmental material, ranging from empty nodes through fully specified vowels or consonants. Containment limits this freedom in one specific way: the input (the underlying representation) must be present in any licit candidate.

Freedom of Analysis is absolutely essential. Because of it, the basic principles of representational form supply a range of candidates so inclusive that no specific rules or repair strategies need be posited. There is, for example, no rule 'add syllable' (that is, a rule of epenthesis), because Gen already, as it were, adds syllables. The constraint hierarchy of a given language exerts control over the teeming space of possibilities.

The Containment property has been assumed in all Optimality-Theoretic analyses to date. (OT *per se* does not require it, but the effect is to make it possible to state all constraints on the output, without reference to the input–output relation.) It is similar but not identical to monotonicity in Categorial Phonology (Wheeler 1981; Bach and Wheeler 1981) or Declarative Phonology (Bird 1990; Scobbie 1992). Containment means, for example, that segmental deletion phenomena involve underparsing a segment of the input (e.g., ⟨k⟩*now/acknowledge*) rather than outright replacement of a segment by ∅. Respect for Containment entails, as indicated in (10), that infixal output candidates arise from inputs whose constituent morphemes are unspecified for linear order.

Consistency of Exponence, proposed in McCarthy and Prince (1993), is a specific hypothesis about the morphology–phonology relationship which is stronger than Containment. It means that the lexical specifications of a morpheme (segments, prosody, or whatever) can never be affected by Gen. In particular, epenthetic elements posited by Gen will have *no* morphological affiliation, even when they lie within or between strings with morphemic identity. Similarly, underparsing of segments – failure to endow them with syllable structure – will not change the make-up of a morpheme, though it will surely change how that morpheme is realized phonetically. Thus, any given morpheme's phonological exponents must be identical in underlying and surface form.[4]

As final preparation for the analytical arguments to follow, we comment briefly on the technical role of the term 'edge' in Alignment theory. The notion that we really need is relational, something like 'sharing an edge', rather than categorical, referring to edge *per se*. Two categories are aligned when they 'share an edge', and the Alignment constraint specifies the categories and which side of each is involved in 'sharing an edge'. To formalize this, we can use the notion of a *concatenative decomposition* of a string:

(14)   Dfn. Concatenative Decomposition
       A concatenative decomposition of a string S is a *sequence* of strings $\langle d_i \rangle_{j \leq i \leq k}$ such that $\widehat{d_j \ldots d_k} = S$.

The concatenative decompositions of a given string are numerous indeed, because any of the $d_i$ may correspond to the empty string $e$, which has the property that $s \widehat{\phantom{e}} e = e \widehat{\phantom{e}} s = s$, for any string s. Compare the role of 0 in addition: $3 + 0 = 0 + 3 = 0 + 3 + 0 = 3$. All these refer to the same number, but all are distinct as expressions. The notion 'concatenative decomposition' allows us to distinguish among the different ways of expressing a string as a sequence of binary concatenations. We can now define the notion of 'sharing an edge':

(15)   Dfn. Sharing an Edge

Let A, B be substrings of S. Let $\langle d_i \rangle_{1 \leq i \leq n}$ be a concatenative decomposition of S, such that for some subsequence $d_j, \ldots, d_k$ of $\langle d_i \rangle$, a subdecomposition, we have

$$\widehat{d_j} \ldots \widehat{d_k} = A$$

and for some subdecomposition $d_l, \ldots, d_m$ of $\langle d_i \rangle$ we have

$$\widehat{d_i} \ldots \widehat{d_m} = B.$$

If there is at least one such decomposition of S, such that $\{d_j, d_k\}\ \{d_l, d_m\} \neq \varnothing$, then we say that A and B *share an edge*.

To see how this works, consider the case of S = AB. Here substrings A and B share an edge because there is a decomposition of S as $\langle d_1, d_2, d_3 \rangle$ where $d_1 = A$, $d_2 = e$, and $d_3 = B$. Since $A = \widehat{d_1\, d_2}$ and $B = \widehat{d_2\, d_3}$, we have $d_2$ as the shared element of the decomposition. Consider now the case of S and A. Since $S = \widehat{d_1\, d_2\, d_3}$, we have $d_1$ as the element of the decomposition shared by S and A, and it follows that S and A also share an edge. This treatment shows that it is possible to develop a useful edge-predicate without a notion of edge as entity.[5]

At this point, it is straightforward to give a definition of GA. Let L be a function from decompositions to strings that returns the *first* element of a decomposition, and let R be a similar function that returns the last element. Then we have

(16)   Dfn. Align(Cat1, Edge1, Cat2, Edge2)

Let Edge1, Edge2 be either L or R. Let S be any string. Then, for any substring A of S that *is a* Cat1, there is substring B of S that *is a* Cat2, such that there is a decomposition D(A) of A and a decomposition D(B) of B, both subdecompositions of a decomposition D(S) of S, such that Edge1(D(A)) = Edge2(D(B)).

The interest of this construction is that the notion 'edge' does not appear as a referential term anywhere in it; the only notions deployed are those of constituency ('is a') and the ordinary predicates of string theory. In what follows we shall make free use of 'edge' as a term of convenience in various locations, and we shall make use of brackets and parentheses as handy notational tools to jog the eye and the imagination, but the actual theory deals only in strings of motivated elements and their motivated constituency.

## 3   Constraints on Prosodic Edges: Align(PCat, PCat)

The alignment of the edges of prosodic constituents provides the first example of GA that we will examine in depth. By demonstrating the role of Alignment constraints in prosody proper, it complements the cases of morphological and morphophonological Alignment discussed in subsequent sections. Thus, this evidence contributes to demonstrating the true generality of GA.

To simplify the exposition by limiting the profusion of candidates under consideration, we will assume that certain constraints are undominated and therefore (because Gen always happens to provide candidates that satisfy them) unviolated in the languages under discussion. These constraints, which are treated by Prince and Smolensky (1993: section 4) and McCarthy and Prince (1993: section A.2), include the following:

(17)   FT-BIN (Prince 1980; McCarthy and Prince 1986, 1991a, 1993)
      Feet must be binary under syllabic or moraic analysis.

Since our empirical focus will be limited to a rhythmically narrow range of systems, we note that the following holds of all admitted feet:

(18)   FOOT-FORM (TROCHAIC)
      $\text{Ft} \rightarrow \sigma_s \sigma_w$

This foot-type is familiar as the syllabic trochee, a quantity-insensitive foot, which makes no distinctions of syllable weight.[6] (For recent discussion see Hayes 1991, Kager 1992a, b, c). Another constraint assumed to hold quite generally is PARSE-SYLL:

(19)   PARSE-SYLL
      All $\sigma$ must be parsed by feet.

PARSE-SYLL is a familiar aspect of stress theory (e.g., Liberman and Prince 1977: 266, 294; Prince 1980: 535; Halle and Vergnaud 1987; Hayes 1987), corresponding broadly to the requirement that foot-parsing be "exhaustive" in rule-based metrical phonology.

We assume the dominance of FT-BIN over PARSE-SYLL, so that exhaustive footing cannot be achieved through the use of unit feet. This dominance relation is quite normal, and if universal, would entail that FT-BIN should be incorporated into Gen. (For relevant discussion, see e.g. McCarthy and Prince 1986, 1990; Hayes 1991; Kager 1993; Kiparsky 1982). We will also assume that the size and syllabic composition of the Prosodic Word is fixed for any given input form by superordinate principles of syllabification on the one hand and interface on the other, so it cannot vary among candidates derived from that form. In particular, we exclude from consideration candidates with epenthetic syllables and those with multiple PrWd's dividing up a single morphological word. For discussion of the syllabification principles, see Prince and Smolensky (1993: section 6); of the interface, see McCarthy and Prince (1993: section 4).

Given these strictures, the foot-parsing imposed on an even-parity input /$\sigma\sigma\sigma\sigma\sigma\sigma$/ is uniquely determined: [$(\sigma\sigma)(\sigma\sigma)(\sigma\sigma)$], where '[ . . . ]' indicates PrWd constituency and '( . . . )' indicates foot constituency. All syllables are parsed into feet, and all feet are binary: since all constraints are met, nothing can be more harmonic. For an odd-parity input of sufficient length, however, various possibilities are attested among the world's languages:

(20) Trochaic Stress Patterns, Schematically
  (a) L→R Pattern: Wankumara (McDonald and Wurm 1979: 5; Hayes 1991)
    [(óσ)(óσ)(óσ)σ]
  (b) R→L Pattern: Warao (Osborn 1966: 114–15; Hayes 1980, 1991)
    [σ(óσ)(óσ)(óσ)]
  (c) 'Initial Dactyl' – Initial Trochee + R→L: Garawa (Furby 1974; Hayes 1980, 1991)
    [(óσ)σ(óσ)(óσ)]
  (d) L→R + Final Trochee: Polish (Rubach and Booij 1985)
    [(óσ)(óσ)σ(óσ)]

Observe that PARSE-SYLL is violated, albeit minimally, in all these forms. The dominance of FT-BIN ensures this, as the following tableau illustrates:

(21) Necessity of PARSE-SYLL Violation in Odd-Length Strings

| Candidates | | FT-BIN | PARSE-SYLL |
|---|---|---|---|
| ☞ | (σσ)σ | | * |
| ☞ | σ(σσ) | | * |
| | (σσ)(σ) | *! | |
| | (σ)(σσ) | *! | |

The nonuniqueness of optimality highlights the fact that other principles must be at play to decide among the minimal violators.

The verbal descriptions of the various attested patterns of forced nonparsing are based on the classification in standard rule-based treatments (Prince 1976, 1983; Hayes 1980, 1991). In rule-based metrical theory, the L→R pattern (20a) and the R→L pattern (20b) are seen as evidence for a directional sweep of foot-parsing, first pairing up the leftmost (or rightmost) couple of syllables, then moving on to do the same to the remaining chunk of the word.[7]

This input-driven iterative foot-parse is impossible in OT, with its commitment to evaluating candidate output forms. It also runs afoul of the facts in (20c, d), in which pure directional iteration is compromised by a single trochee lying at the opposite end of the PrWd. (In rule-based metrical phonology, (20c, d) are accounted for by first laying down a single foot at one end, then iterating from the other.) Instead of iteration, GA supplies a set of output constraints that precisely control this interlinguistic variation.

We begin with the so-called initial dactyl stress pattern (20c), which illustrates all of the essential elements of this application of GA. Stress in Garawa respects the following generalization:

(22)   Stress in Garawa, Descriptively (Furby 1974; Hayes 1980, 1991)
     – Main stress falls on the initial syllable;
     – secondary stress falls on the penult;
     – tertiary stress falls on every other syllable preceding the penult (but not on
       the peninitial)

Attested PrWd's of Garawa are generously long, so the pattern is particularly easy to
see, as the following foot-parsings show:

(23)   Foot-Parsing in Garawa

| | | |
|---|---|---|
| $[(\acute{\sigma}\sigma)]$ | yámi | 'eye' |
| $[(\acute{\sigma}\sigma)\sigma]$ | púnja.*la* | 'white' |
| $[(\acute{\sigma}\sigma)(\grave{\sigma}\sigma)]$ | wátjim.pàŋu | 'armpit' |
| $[(\acute{\sigma}\sigma)\sigma(\grave{\sigma}\sigma)]$ | káma.*la*.řinji | 'wrist' |
| $[(\acute{\sigma}\sigma)(\grave{\sigma}\sigma)(\grave{\sigma}\sigma)]$ | yáka.lâka.làmpa | 'loose' |
| $[(\acute{\sigma}\sigma)\sigma(\grave{\sigma}\sigma)(\grave{\sigma}\sigma)]$ | ŋánki.*ři*.kîrim.pàyi | 'fought with boomerangs' |
| $[(\acute{\sigma}\sigma)(\grave{\sigma}\sigma)(\grave{\sigma}\sigma)(\grave{\sigma}\sigma)]$ | ŋámpa.lâŋin.mûkun.jìna | 'at our many' |
| $[(\acute{\sigma}\sigma)\sigma(\grave{\sigma}\sigma)(\grave{\sigma}\sigma)(\grave{\sigma}\sigma)]$ | náři.ŋ*in*.mûkkun.jîna.mìřa | 'at your own many' |
| $[(\acute{\sigma}\sigma)(\grave{\sigma}\sigma)(\grave{\sigma}\sigma)(\grave{\sigma}\sigma)(\grave{\sigma}\sigma)]$ | nímpa.lâŋin.mûku.nânji.mìřa | 'from your own two' |

Since the goal here is to account for the foot-parsing only, the degrees of stress will
be ignored.
   One observation is immediately apparent from (23): the first two syllables of the
PrWd are footed together, whatever the disposition of the rest of the word. This is
a typical Alignment effect, obtaining between the two prosodic categories foot and
PrWd:[8]

(24)   ALIGN-PRWD (Garawa)
      Align(PrWd, L, Ft, L)

That is, the left edge of each PrWd must match the left edge of some foot. This is a
matter of empirical, not logical, necessity, as shown by the comparison of competing
candidate parses for a trisyllabic or other odd-parity input (cf. (21)):

(25)   Application of ALIGN-PRWD

| | Align |
|---|---|
| ☞  $[(\sigma\sigma)\sigma]$ | √ |
| $[\sigma(\sigma\sigma)]$ | * |

In the first candidate, the left edge of PrWd does indeed coincide with the left edge
of a foot, satisfying Align(PrWd, L, Ft, L). In the second candidate, though, the left
PrWd-edge coincides with the left edge of a syllable, but not of a foot. Hence, the first
candidate is optimal. The same logic holds trivially for disyllables and can be extended
readily to polysyllables of indefinite length.

In the terms of Prince and Smolensky (1991a, b, 1992, 1993), such relations are established by a constraint EDGEMOST, defined by them as follows:

(26)   EDGEMOST($\varphi$;E;D)
       The item $\varphi$ is situated at edge E of domain D. (Prince and Smolensky 1993: 35)

It should be clear that this is rendered by the GA scheme ALIGN($\varphi$,E,D,E), where $\varphi$ is a daughter of D. In the case at hand, we have EDGEMOST(F;L;PrWd) as the correlate of ALIGN(PrWd, L, Ft, L). GA is more general in two respects: it does not restrict the hierarchical relation of Cat1 and Cat2; and it does not require sameness of the shared edge. Thus, GA subsumes EDGEMOST.

There is also an Alignment effect at the **right** edge of Garawa PrWd's. This is apparent from the odd-parity forms in (23) containing five or more syllables. Five-syllable words, for example, are parsed $(\sigma\sigma)\sigma(\sigma\sigma)$, with right Alignment, rather than *$(\sigma\sigma)(\sigma\sigma)\sigma$. This phenomenon also requires a constraint enforcing Alignment of foot and PrWd:

(27)   ALIGN-FT (Garawa)
         Align(Ft, R, PrWd, R)
           "Every foot stands in final position in the PrWd."

ALIGN-FT differs from ALIGN-PRWD in two respects. One is obvious: the edges, left or right, that must be aligned. The other much less so: the order of constituent arguments is reversed, Align(PrWd, Ft) at the left edge, Align(Ft, PrWd) at the right edge. This move is crucial, as we will show shortly, since it permits Alignment, within OT, to supplant both the non-iterative and the iterative operations of standard rule-based metrical phonology.

ALIGN-PRWD and ALIGN-FT are in conflict in trisyllables. In OT, constraint conflicts lead to constraint violations, and from the resolution of the conflict the ranking relation between the conflicting constraints can be determined. The following tableau presents an argument for ranking these two constraints:

(28)   ALIGN-PRWD $\gg$ ALIGN-FT, from /$\sigma\sigma\sigma$/

| Candidates | ALIGN-PRWD | ALIGN-FT |
|---|---|---|
| (a) ☞   $[(\acute{\sigma}\sigma)\sigma]$ | | * |
| (b)   $[\sigma(\acute{\sigma}\sigma)]$ | *! | |

The candidate (28b) violates ALIGN-PRWD, since the PrWd and the first foot do not commence together. It is, however, properly aligned on the right edge. In contrast, the candidate (28a) is well-aligned on the left and ill-aligned on the right. Thus, ALIGN-PRWD and ALIGN-FT are in conflict. Since (28a) is the actual output form, the conflict is resolved in favor of ALIGN-PRWD and at the expense of ALIGN-FT, proving that ALIGN-PRWD $\gg$ ALIGN-FT.

The optimal placement of a single foot in trisyllables is not the only circumstance when ALIGN-FT is violated. Recall the definition of GA from (4). Align(Cat1, ... , Cat2, ... ) quantifies **universally** over the edges of tokens of Cat1 and **existentially** over the edge of some Cat2. **Every** Cat1 must share an edge with **some** Cat2. The two Alignment constraints of Garawa, then, have the following sense when spelled out:

(29)   Alignment in Garawa
  (a) ALIGN-PRWD: Align(PrWd, L, Ft, L)
    Any [$_{\mathrm{PrWd}}$ is aligned with a ($_{\mathrm{Ft}}$.
  (b) ALIGN-FT: Align(Ft, R, PrWd, R)
    Any )$_{\mathrm{Ft}}$ is aligned with a ]$_{\mathrm{PrWd}}$.

ALIGN-PRWD is satisfied by any PrWd that begins crisply on a foot-edge – in fact, all the PrWd's of the language begin so, because, as was just shown, ALIGN-PRWD is undominated. But ALIGN-FT is violated by every foot that is not final in PrWd, so violations of it occur not only in trisyllables, but in all words of (23) containing more than one foot.

It might seem that a constraint that is violated so freely is of little use, but this is far from the truth. Pursuing an observation made to us by Robert Kirchner about EDGEMOST, we can see that ALIGN-FT is not a coarse sieve straining out non-final feet, but rather, through the Optimality-Theoretic imperative to violate constraints **minimally**, a fine mesh that subsumes the effects of directional iteration in rule-based theories. Prince and Smolensky propose that violation of EDGEMOST is gradient, with degree of violation measured by the distance of $\varphi$ from the designated edge. The examples discussed by Prince and Smolensky typically involve applying EDGEMOST to a unique element, like a single affix or the prosodic head of a word, but Kirchner notes that if EDGEMOST applies to every foot, then it will minimize the distance of each foot from a designated edge – exactly as in directional iteration of foot-building. GA leads directly to this result. Because ALIGN-FT quantifies universally over tokens of foot, all instances of foot in some PrWd must be evaluated for the goodness of their alignment with the PrWd's right edge. The pattern with minimal violation is optimal, where the minimally violating pattern is the one in which no right foot-edge could lie any closer to the right PrWd-edge.

Given our assumptions about preconditions on the candidates to be considered (PARSE-SYLL, FT-BIN, and so on), the following list includes all of the admissible parses of a heptasyllable:

(30)   Heptasyllabic Parses
  (a) [(óσ)(óσ)(óσ)σ]
  (b) [(óσ)(óσ)σ(óσ)σ]
  (c) ☞ [(óσ)σ(óσ)(óσ)]
  (d) [σ(óσ)(óσ)(óσ)]

The actual Garawa pattern is marked as optimal. Of these candidates, (30d) can be dismissed immediately, since it violates ALIGN-PRWD, an undominated constraint, as was shown above in (28). The remaining candidates differ in the disposition of

non-initial feet in a way that can be derived from ALIGN-FT. The table (31) categor-
izes each individual foot of the candidate forms for degree of violation of ALIGN-FT.

(31)   Comparison of Heptasyllabic Parses by ALIGN-FT

|  |  | Ft-1 | Ft-2 | Ft-3 |
|---|---|---|---|---|
| (a) | $[(\acute{\sigma}\sigma)_1(\acute{\sigma}\sigma)_2(\acute{\sigma}\sigma)_3\sigma]$ | $\sigma\sigma\sigma\sigma\sigma$ | $\sigma\sigma\sigma$! | $\sigma$! |
| (b) | $[(\acute{\sigma}\sigma)_1(\acute{\sigma}\sigma)_2\sigma(\acute{\sigma}\sigma)_3]$ | $\sigma\sigma\sigma\sigma\sigma$ | $\sigma\sigma\sigma$! | $\varnothing$ |
| (c) ☞ | $[(\acute{\sigma}\sigma)_1\sigma(\acute{\sigma}\sigma)_2(\acute{\sigma}\sigma)_3]$ | $\sigma\sigma\sigma\sigma\sigma$ | $\sigma\sigma$ | $\varnothing$ |

Violation of ALIGN-FT is gradient, not Boolean, so each foot is judged by the distance
of its right edge from the right edge of the PrWd. Degree of violation is indicated
graphically by the string of syllables separating the right edge of the foot under consideration from the right edge of the PrWd. The optimal candidate is the one whose
constituent feet violate ALIGN-FT the least. Comparison of the rightmost foot is
sufficient to eliminate the candidate (31a), whose last foot is non-final. Comparison of
the penultimate foot eliminates all candidates except (31c), which is the actual output.
In sum, ALIGN-FT quantifies over all the feet in a word, evaluating each for its
fitness. Observe that it is not necessary to distinguish the violations by the foot that is
responsible for them, as in table (31); aggregating the entire set of them gives the same
results. The foot-by-foot breakdown is shown for purposes of clarity only.

Consideration of a wider field of candidates than in (31) does not change the outcome.
As was already noted, the form (30d) violates dominant ALIGN-PRWD. Otherwise it
would be superior in terms of ALIGN-FT even to the actual output (31c), showing that
ALIGN-PRWD and ALIGN-FT conflict crucially in any odd-parity word, not just in
trisyllables like (28). Less complete parsings, such as $[(\acute{\sigma}\sigma)\sigma\sigma\sigma(\acute{\sigma}\sigma)]$, would also be superior
on grounds of ALIGN-FT to the actual output form, but these would contravene the
assumption that PARSE-SYLL is satisfied maximally in all legitimate candidates, subject only to dominant FT-BIN. Finally, it is logically possible to satisfy both constraints
fully with complex PrWd parses like $[[(\acute{\sigma}\sigma)][(\acute{\sigma}\sigma)][(\acute{\sigma}\sigma)]]$ or $[[[(\acute{\sigma}\sigma)](\acute{\sigma}\sigma)](\acute{\sigma}\sigma)]$, imposing
a multiple PrWd structure on a single stem, but this too contravenes one of the initial
assumptions introduced at the outset of the discussion.

We have shown, then, that Align(Ft, PrWd) subsumes the properties of directional
iteration of foot assignment in rule-based metrical phonology. Quantifying over all
instances of *foot* in a PrWd and evaluating each gradiently for alignment yields a system
in which each foot lies as close as possible to the designated PrWd-edge. In contrast,
Align(PrWd, Ft) quantifies universally over PrWd's, requiring only that there be **some**
foot which is left-aligned, not that **all** feet be left-aligned. If Align(X, Y) held of every
Y as well as every X, then all distinction would be lost between ALIGN-PRWD and
ALIGN-FT, and whichever was dominant would completely overrule the other, rendering the subordinate constraint inactive in the grammar. In the case of Garawa, there would
be no way to express the difference in status between right-edge and left-edge footing.
This result illustrates the need for a crucial asymmetry in the definition of GA (4):

universal quantification over the first constituent argument, existential quantification over the second.

A fundamental claim of OT is that languages differ principally in the ranking they impose on constraints. Permuting the ranking of these two senses of Align, combined with different parameters of the left or right edge, generates exactly the trochaic typology in (20):

(32)  Trochaic Stress Patterns, Analyzed
    (a)  L→R Pattern: [(óσ)(óσ)(óσ)σ]
        Align(Ft, L, PrWd, L) ≫ Align(PrWd, R, Ft, R)
    (b)  R→L Pattern: [σ(óσ)(óσ)(óσ)]
        Align(Ft, R, PrWd, R) ≫ Align(PrWd, L, Ft, L)
    (c)  'Initial Dactyl' – Initial Trochee + R→L: [(óσ)σ(óσ)(óσ)]
        Align(PrWd, L, Ft, L) ≫ Align(Ft, R, PrWd, R)
    (d)  L→R + Final Trochee: [(óσ)(óσ)σ(óσ)]
        Align(PrWd, R, Ft, R) ≫ Align(Ft, L, PrWd, L)

Patterns (32c) and (32d) are left/right mirror images of one another, the former exemplified by Garawa, which we have seen, and the latter by Polish.

In the patterns in (32a, b), the constraint Align(Ft, PrWd) is dominant. This constraint evaluates all feet, requiring that they lie as close as possible to the PrWd-edge. In contrast, Align(PrWd, Ft) looks at only a single foot, which should also lie near the PrWd-edge. Since Align(Ft, PrWd) applies to all feet, while Align(PrWd, Ft) applies to just one, the ranking Align(Ft, PrWd) ≫ Align(PrWd, Ft) renders the lower-ranking constraint invisible – it can have no observable effect on the well-formedness of representations, so the pure L→R or R→L pattern is obtained.

(33)  Align(Ft, R, PrWd, R) ≫ Align(PrWd, L, Ft, L) in Warao (20b)

| Candidates | Align(Ft, PrWd) | Align(PrWd, Ft) |
|---|---|---|
| (a) ☞ [σ(óσ)(óσ)] | Ft-1: σσ <br> – – – – – – – – – – <br> Ft-2: Ø | * |
| (b) [(óσ)σ(óσ)] | Ft-1: σσσ! <br> – – – – – – – – – – <br> Ft-2: Ø | |

The initial foot of (33b) is inferior, on grounds of ALIGN-FT, to the initial foot of (33a). Since the ALIGN-FT constraint is dominant, this inferiority is fatal, and so the lower-ranking ALIGN-PRWD constraint can have no effect.[9]

The typology can be extended further by permuting the ranking of Alignment with respect to the constraint PARSE-SYLL (19), which demands maximal parsing of syllables into feet, as in all the candidates examined thus far. If Align(Ft, R, PrWd, R) ≫ PARSE-SYLL, then the optimal candidate is [σσσσ(óσ)], with a single foot lying at the right edge:

(34)   Align(Ft, R, PrWd, R) ≫ PARSE-SYLL, Applied to /σσσσ/

| Candidates | Align(Ft, PrWd) | PARSE-SYLL |
|---|---|---|
| (a) ☞   [σσ(σ́σ)] | | * |
| (b)   [(σ́σ)(σ́σ)] | * ! | |

The penultimate foot of (34b) violates Align(Ft, R, PrWd, R). The degree of violation doesn't matter, since the other candidate (34a) is perfectly aligned, simply by virtue of positing only a single foot.[10] Thus, the pattern of 'non-iterative' foot-parsing can be obtained from a low ranking of PARSE-SYLL. [ . . . ]

# 5   Generalized Alignment and the Prosody–Morphology Interface

The interface constraints we have just examined are of the general form Align(GCat, Edge, PCat, Edge); they require that the edge of any instance of the morphological constituent GCat align with the corresponding edge of some prosodic constituent PCat. For example, ALIGN-ROOT (63 [not repr. here]) in Dakota requires that the left edge of the root coincide with the left edge of the PrWd, leading to an infixed locus for formal prefixes. But similar Alignment constraints on the morphology–prosody interface can have effects other than infixation when embedded in different systems of interacting constraints. In this section, we will show that Align(GCat, Edge, PCat, Edge) can have profound consequences for the prosody of a language in relation to its morphology. We will focus specifically on the following two constraints of this type:

(68)   ALIGN-LEFT
        Align(Stem, L, PrWd, L)

(69)   ALIGN-RIGHT
        Align(Stem, R, σ, R)

These constraints demand, respectively, that every stem begin at the left edge of a PrWd and that it end at the right edge of a syllable.[11] Phenomena variously attributable to the cycle, to domains of rule application, and to extrametricality can all be subsumed under this rubric, within OT.

Many of the consequences of ALIGN-LEFT and ALIGN-RIGHT for prosody and especially segmental phonology derive ultimately from a property of Gen dubbed Consistency of Exponence above in section 2 (see also McCarthy and Prince 1993: section 2). This condition places a fundamental limit on Gen's freedom to hypothesize output candidates: it cannot alter the grammatical analysis of the input. The input consists of various morphemes, root or affix, arranged into stems. The input also includes the lexical specifications of the phonological segments making up its constituent morphemes.

Gen takes this input and, respecting Containment, posits various candidate output forms. Under Consistency of Exponence, the affiliations of segments with particular morphemes cannot change in the output, nor can segments be added to or subtracted from a morpheme.

This is, however, not to say that all and only the segments of the input are actually pronounced; what is actually pronounced is determined by the prosody of the optimal output form. Epenthesis and deletion phenomena are simply special situations in prosodic parsing. For epenthesis, the syllable parse posits segmentally unfilled structural positions, which receive a default interpretation as some actual segment, such as *a* or *i*, *t* or *ʔ* (Selkirk 1981; Archangeli 1984; Itô 1986, 1989). For deletion, the syllable parse is incomplete, leaving some segments crucially unparsed, to be ignored in the subsequent interpretation (McCarthy 1979; Steriade 1982; Itô 1986, 1989). Unfilled structural positions in candidate output forms are indicated by □, and unparsed segments are bracketed with '⟨ ... ⟩'. Gen supplies output candidates with various combinations of unfilled and unparsed elements, and their distribution in actual languages is controlled by the following two fundamental constraints (Prince and Smolensky 1991a, b, 1992, 1993), which for present purposes can be stated like this:

(70)  PARSE
     ⟨α⟩ is prohibited.

(71)  FILL
     □ is prohibited.

The ranking of PARSE and FILL relative to each other and to the constraints on syllable well-formedness like ONSET and NO-CODA characterizes the basic syllabic typology of the world's languages (Prince and Smolensky 1993: section 6).[12]

With this much technical development in hand, we can see how two important Alignment effects come to affect the assignment of syllable structure. In Axininca Campa, an Arawakan language of Peru,[13] hiatus at /V + V/ juncture is prohibited. Potential hiatus leads to surface consonant epenthesis, shown by the element □ (interpreted as *t*) in (72).

(72)  Epenthetic Examples in Axininca Campa

| /i-N-koma-i/ | iŋ.ko.ma.□i | 'he will paddle' |
| /i-N-koma-aa-i/ | iŋ.ko.ma.□aa.□i | 'he will paddle again' |
| /i-N-koma-ako-i/ | iŋ.ko.ma.□a.ko.□i | 'he will paddle for' |
| /i-N-koma-ako-aa-i-ro/ | iŋ.ko.ma.□a.ko.□aa.□i.ro | 'he will paddle for it again' |
| /i.N-čʰik-i/ | iñ.čʰi.ki | 'he will cut' |
| /i.N-čʰik-aa-i/ | iñ.čʰi.kaa.□i | 'he will cut again' |
| /i.N-čʰik-ako-i/ | iñ.čʰi.ka.ko.□i | 'he will cut for' |
| /i.N-čʰik-ako-aa-i-ro/ | iñ-čʰi.ka.ko.□aa.□i.ro | 'he will cut for it again' |

The constraint implicated here is obviously ONSET. When morphemic combination brings together /V + V/, the heterosyllabic parse [V.V] produces an onsetless syllable. All such faithfully parsed candidates are sub-optimal; competing with them are

**unfaithful** candidate forms, which satisfy ONSET by positing FILL violation (that is, the empty consonant □ in (72)) or unparsed segments. Of these, PARSE violators – with phonetic loss of one or the other of the V's – are never found. Thus, PARSE is undominated and so unviolated. FILL-violation is the pattern seen in (72).

The appearance of □ satisfies the requirement that syllables have onsets. This means that ONSET dominates FILL in the constraint ranking, as the following tableau shows:

(73)   ONSET ≫ FILL, from /iN-koma-i/

| Candidates | | ONSET | FILL |
|---|---|---|---|
| ☞ | .iŋ.ko.ma.□i. | * | * |
| | .iŋ.ko.ma.i. | ** ! | |

The comparison between candidates here shows that FILL conflicts with ONSET. Since performance on ONSET is decisive, and FILL violation or satisfaction is irrelevant, we conclude that ONSET ≫ FILL.

Tableau (73) establishes the ranking of ONSET and FILL, but it is not a complete account of the optimality of candidates like *iŋ.ko.ma.□i*. Two problems remain. First, tableau (73) completely disregards the initial violation of ONSET in *iŋ.ko.ma.□i*; surely *□iŋ.ko.ma.□i.* should be more harmonic, since it contains no violations of ONSET at all. Second, because *ai* is a permissible diphthong of Axininca Campa, it is logically possible to parse /a + i/ as tautosyllabic, escaping the consequences of both FILL and ONSET, yielding *iŋ.ko.mai*. Given the constraints we have in hand, this output should beat FILL-violating *iŋ.ko.ma.□i*.

We record these two observations as follows:

(74)   Initial-V
       Axininca Campa has no word-initial epenthesis and freely tolerates initial onsetless syllables.

(75)   Non-coalescence of /V + V/
       Underlying /V – V/ sequences at stem-suffix juncture are never parsed as tautosyllabic; they always correspond to V.□V in the output.

The first observation bans epenthesis; the second requires it. Nevertheless, both observations devolve from conditions on GA, requiring coincidence of the edges of prosodic and morphological constituents.

We begin with the Initial-V phenomenon. Axininca surface structures are replete with vowel-initial words, in flagrant violation of ONSET. This mode of departure from strict ONSET obedience is common in other languages as well, so it is no mere fluke of Axininca Campa. As a bare-faced fact, this observation would seem to require parametrizing ONSET, to exclude PrWd-initial syllables from its purview:

(76) 'NO-HIATUS' (Hypothetical Constraint, Parametrizing ONSET)

$*[_\sigma$ V except word-initially.

The codicil is specifically crafted so that 'NO-HIATUS' cannot compel FILL-violation in initial position. This will eliminate initial epenthesis.

Parametrizing ONSET by adding 'NO-HIATUS' to the panoply of universal constraints is obviously unsatisfactory. It does not explain why just exactly word-initial position is special, and it compromises the claim of OT that languages differ principally in how they rank a fixed set of universal constraints. It would be far better to retain the original, simple version of ONSET, without parametrization via 'NO-HIATUS', as the only possibility permitted by phonological theory.

Another approach to the Initial-V phenomenon, this time a more familiar one, is to say that initial onsetless syllables are extrametrical, therefore outside the purview of ONSET. This is the tack taken by Spring (1990: 37–44) and Black (1991). It has both local and global problems. Within Axininca Campa grammar, there is no other good evidence that initial onsetless syllables are extrametrical, and there is much evidence, from word minimality, stress, allomorphy, and reduplication, showing that they are actually intrametrical (McCarthy and Prince 1993: section 6). We return to the broader issue of extrametricality below, in the discussion of example (97).

Rejecting these alternatives, we propose that the Initial-V phenomenon arises from the interaction of ONSET and ALIGN-LEFT (68), which says that the left edge of any stem must coincide with the left edge of a PrWd. ALIGN-LEFT is unviolated and therefore undominated in the constraint hierarchy of Axininca Campa. ONSET is violated when it conflicts with ALIGN-LEFT; therefore ONSET cannot dominate ALIGN-LEFT. This gives us ALIGN-LEFT ≫ ONSET. The effects on initial C-epenthesis are shown in (77), where the symbol '|' marks the relevant GCat-edge (here, $[_{Stem}$) and the PrWd-edge is shown by '[':

(77) Failure of Prothesis, from /i-N-koma-i/

| | Candidates | ALIGN-LEFT | ONSET | FILL |
|---|---|---|---|---|
| (a) | [. \| iŋ.ko.ma.i. | | ** ! | |
| (b) ☞ | [. \| iŋ.ko.ma.□i. | | * | * |
| (c) | [.□ \| iŋ.ko.ma.□i. | * ! | | ** |

The initial □ in the losing candidate (77c) shifts the PrWd-edge away from the stem-edge, causing misalignment of the leading edges of the PrWd and the stem. This means that all V-initial stems of Axininca must be parsed with an ONSET violation, to satisfy dominant ALIGN-LEFT. In contrast, both (77a) and (77b) are well-aligned, but the former contains multiple ONSET violations, in contravention of the Optimality-Theoretic imperative of minimal violation.

The application of ALIGN-LEFT in this example relies crucially on Consistency of Exponence, as explicated above. Specifically, the epenthetic element □ is part of the prosodic constituent PrWd, but it is not part of the stem, since 'stem' is a morphological notion, pertaining to the input, while an epenthetic segment is purely phonological, pertaining to the output only. Gen is denied the power to add elements like □ to a morpheme – indeed to add anything at all to a morpheme – so the segmental composition of root, affix, or stem is the same in the output as in the input. Thus, epenthetic elements have no morphological affiliation whatsoever. In this way, satisfaction of ALIGN-LEFT demands a faithful parse at the left edge of the stem, as in (77a, b); in (77c) the element □ at the left edge of PrWd, belonging to PrWd but not to stem, is sufficient to de-align the PrWd- and stem-edges.

An alternative to FILL-violation is PARSE-violation, leading to nonpronunciation of initial vowels. This alternative fares no better in the face of undominated ALIGN-LEFT, however, since an unparsed segment is still a part of the morpheme (and hence the stem) that sponsors it:

(78)   De-Alignment by Unparsed Initial Syllable
         * | ⟨iŋ⟩[koma□i

Underparsing can never bring a form into agreement with ALIGN-LEFT. For ALIGN-LEFT to be satisfied, the stem-initial segment, vowel or consonant, must occupy initial position in a PrWd. Consequently, an unparsed initial vowel, which occupies no position at all in any syllable, will de-align a stem.

Word-initial ONSET-violation could also be avoided by trans-junctural syllabification, parsing the final consonant of one word as the onset of the following word. Again, unviolated ALIGN-LEFT excludes this possibility, as the following schema shows:

(79)   De-Aligning Trans-Junctural Syllabification
         /matan iŋkomai/   →   * mata[.n | iŋkoma□i
                                * mata.n | iŋ[koma□i

The example is purely hypothetical, since Axininca Campa, with a strict constraint on possible codas (82), does not permit any word-final consonants whatsoever. Still, this effect of ALIGN-LEFT is real, and it is important in other languages discussed below.

In sum, ALIGN-LEFT explains why word-initial position should be an apparent exception to ONSET in terms of constraint interaction and the general theory of the prosody–morphology interface. Moreover, ALIGN-LEFT makes predictions beyond allowing initial onsetless syllables: it forbids all initial epenthesis – vocalic, consonantal, or syllabic – and forbids it for all stems, whether they begin with C or V. This broader prediction holds without exception, and it is equally important in the grammar of augmentation to bimoraicity (see below (89)). For purely empirical reasons, then, it's correct to reject NO-HIATUS and preserve the pristine constraint ONSET, abetted by ALIGN-LEFT.

The Axininca data in (72) also exhibit another phenomenon, Non-Coalescence of /V + V/. A further constraint is required, ALIGN-RIGHT (69). It must dominate FILL, because it compels FILL-violation. Observe how, in the following examples, epenthesis guarantees alignment of the end of the stem and the end of a syllable, whereas coalescence places the morphological stem-edge internal to a syllable:[14]

(80)  Stem-Syllable Alignment
    (a)   /iN-koma-i/         .iŋ.ko.ma. | □i.
                             *.iŋ.ko.ma | i.

    (b)   /iN-koma-ako-i/   .iŋ.ko.ma. | □a.ko. | □i.
                             *.iŋ.ko.ma | a.k.o | i.

Each suffix is assumed to create a new stem category recursively, and the right edge of each such stem lies at a syllable boundary, in accordance with ALIGN-RIGHT. It is crucial, of course, that ALIGN-RIGHT quantify universally over stems, but existentially over syllables, in accordance with the definition of GA in (4). Thus, ALIGN-RIGHT does not demand that every syllable-edge coincide with a stem-edge (which would say that roots and affixes must be monosyllabic).

As noted, ALIGN-RIGHT is ranked above FILL, forcing the appearance of empty structure even where a faithful, non-epenthetic parse would meet the purely phonological requirements on Axininca syllables. The following tableau makes this clear:

(81)  ALIGN-RIGHT ≫ FILL, from /iN-koma-i/

| Candidates | ALIGN-RIGHT | FILL |
|---|---|---|
| (a) ☞   .iŋ.ko.ma | .□i. |  | * |
| (b)   .iŋ.ko.ma | i. | * ! |  |

With this ranking, failure to meet ALIGN-RIGHT dooms the coalescent form.

These facts have been regarded previously as evidence of cyclic syllabification (Spring 1990: 52–3, 161–2; Black 1991: 205). The idea is that a syllable formed on one cycle is closed to the addition of further segments on later cycles. For example, in *iŋkoma□i*, the cyclic domain *iŋ.ko.ma* is fully syllabified as shown. When the suffix *i* is added on the next cycle, it cannot be joined to the syllable *ma*, which is now closed to the addition of further segments.

The cyclic analysis encounters various difficulties. For one thing, the failure of coalescence at morpheme juncture is the only evidence for cyclic rule application in the language.[15] For another, the specific details of the account are not compatible with any general theory of the cycle to be found in the literature. Steriade (1988: 309–10) has argued that closure is not true of cyclic syllabification (though she holds that it is true of cyclic foot assignment). Furthermore, Inkelas (1989: 59–66) and others have argued that bound roots are not cyclic domains. Axininca Campa verbal roots are bound (Payne 1981: 19), yet they would have to be cyclic domains, since they show closure just like affixes. Thus, cyclic syllabification in Axininca would be very much an isolated peculiarity, both within the language and within linguistic theory as a whole.

ALIGN-RIGHT is a dominated constraint, so it is violated elsewhere in the language. The circumstance where this is most obvious is /C + V/ juncture, as in /i-N-čʰik-i/ → *iñ.čʰi.ki* (72). The dominant constraint here is a 'coda condition', to use Itô's (1986) term, which bars *k* (and most other consonants) from syllable-final position. We state it informally here:

(82)   CODA-COND (Axininca Campa)

      A coda consonant can only be a nasal homorganic to following stop or affricate.

The following ranking argument establishes this result:

(83)   CODA-COND ≫ ALIGN-RIGHT, from /iñ-čʰik-i/

| Candidates | CODA-COND | ALIGN-RIGHT |
|---|---|---|
| (a) ☞       .iñ.čʰi.k ǀ i. | | * |
| (b)       .iñ.čʰik ǀ .□i. | * ! | |

The failed candidate in (83) is a FILL-violator too, but irrelevantly, since FILL is ranked below ALIGN-RIGHT, as (81) shows. Other possible candidate analyses fare no better than this:

(84)   Further Failures of ALIGN-RIGHT in /C + V/ Juncture

| Candidates | CODA-COND | ONSET | ALIGN-RIGHT | FILL |
|---|---|---|---|---|
| (a) ☞    .iñ.čʰi.k ǀ i. | | * | * | |
| (b)    .iñ.čʰik ǀ .□i. | * ! | * | | * |
| (c)    .iñ.čʰi.k ǀ □.i. | | ** ! | * | * |
| (d)    .iñ.čʰi.k ǀ □.□i. | | * | * | * ! * |
| (e)    .iñ.čʰik ǀ .i. | * ! | ** | | |

Under the ranking CODA-COND ≫ ALIGN-RIGHT, no amount of artifice can achieve satisfactory right Alignment in /C + V/ juncture.

In sum, ALIGN-RIGHT, crucially ranked below CODA-COND and above FILL, yields exactly the correct pattern of faithful versus epenthetic syllabic parsing at stem–suffix juncture. It is paralleled by the nearly symmetric constraint ALIGN-LEFT, which yields a very different phonological pattern: the possibility of initial onsetless syllables. This difference in the effects derived from the two Alignment constraints of Axininca Campa – ALIGN-RIGHT favors an epenthetic parse stem-finally, while ALIGN-LEFT favors a faithful one stem-initially – follows from a crucial difference in ranking. ALIGN-RIGHT pertains to the right edge of the syllable, and it is dominated by CODA-COND, which regulates the segments that can appear at the right edge of the syllable. ALIGN-LEFT pertains to the left edge of the PrWd, hence the left edge of the syllable, and it itself dominates ONSET, which regulates the segments that can appear at the left edge of the syllable. Because they interact differently with these other constraints, ALIGN-RIGHT and ALIGN-LEFT lead to these quite distinct effects on the surface. This is a frequently encountered situation in OT: similar constraints, when embedded in different ranking contexts, can lead to very different empirical results.

Both Alignment constraints also have significant consequences for the augmentation of sub-minimal roots in Axininca Campa. Under conditions explicated below (section 6 [not repr. here]), short roots /CV/ and /C/ are augmented to bimoraicity. In the current context, what we are concerned with is the form of augmentation, which depends on the shape of the input root:[16]

(85)  Augmentation of Sub-minimal Roots in Axininca Campa
   (a)   /CV/ Roots – Disyllabic Augmentation
        /na/      .na.□□.      (→ *nata*)      'carry on shoulder'
        /tʰo/     .tʰo.□□.     (→ *tʰota*)     'kiss, suck'

   (b)   /C/ Roots – Heavy Syllable Augmentation
        /p/       .p□□.        (→ *paː*)       'feed'

This pattern is entirely regular: /CV/ roots augment to a sequence of two light syllables, while /C/ roots augment to a single heavy syllable. Spring (1990) discovered this generalization, including the crucial evidence in (85b). She relates it, as we do, to the non-coalescence phenomenon, though under very different theoretical assumptions.

Consider first stems /CV/ like *na* 'carry'. There are three principal candidates to examine:

(86)  Augmentation of /CV/
   (a)   Monosyllabic:   *.na|□.      (→ *\*naː*)
   (b)   Disyllabic:     *.na|.□.     (→ *\*na.a*)
   (c)   Disyllabic:     .na|.□□.     (→ *nata*)

Only augmentation by a full CV syllable .□□, as in (86c), gives both proper alignment and syllabic well-formedness. The form (86b), though it is minimally augmented, obviously violates ONSET. The monosyllabic pattern (86a) is misaligned, because the stem (here identical to the root morpheme) ends amid the long vowel.[17] The following tableau certifies the argument:

(87)  Augmentation of /na/

| Candidates | ONSET | ALIGN-RIGHT | FILL |
|---|---|---|---|
| (a)      .na|□. |  | * ! | * |
| (b)      .na|.□. | * ! |  | * |
| (c) ☞   .na|.□□. |  |  | ** |

Axininca has long vowels elsewhere, so it can only be ALIGN-RIGHT that eliminates the possibility of minimal FILL-violation represented by *na*□. Just as in the analysis of /V + V/ juncture (81), dominant ALIGN-RIGHT forces violations of FILL that aren't justified on purely phonotactic grounds.

ALIGN-RIGHT alone has nothing to say about the **location** of the augmenting syllable. Equally satisfactory alignment is obtained whether epenthesis is initial or final:

(88)   Syllabic Augmentation Locational Possibilities
    (a)   .na|.□□.    (→ *nata*)
    (b)   .□□.na|.    (→ \**tana*)

But no epenthesis of any kind ever occurs at the beginning of words because of ALIGN-LEFT, which governs left edges. ALIGN-LEFT is unviolated and therefore undominated in the constraint hierarchy. Its effects on syllabic epenthesis are shown here, with the sign '|' used to mark the left edge of the stem and the bracket '[' used to mark the PrWd-edge:

(89)   Initial Alignment Dooms Initial Augmentation
    (a)   [|na.□□    (→ *nata*)
    (b)   [□□.|na.    (→ \**tana*)
    (c)   [□.|na.    (→ \**ana*)

These data confirm that ALIGN-LEFT, rather than NO-HIATUS, is responsible for the Initial-V phenomenon. Hiatus or onsetlessness is simply not an issue here, since the root /na/ forms an unimpeachable syllable.

ALIGN-RIGHT must also confront augmentation of monoconsonantal roots like /p/ 'feed'. For them, no analysis can simultaneously obtain both syllabic well-formedness and proper alignment. To see this, consider the following candidates, all of which achieve bimoraicity:

(90)   Augmentation of /p/
    (a)   End-aligned
            .□p|.    (→ \**ap*)
            .□□p|.    (→ \**tap*)
    (b)   End-misaligned
        (i)   .□.p|□.    (→ \**apa*)
            .□□.p|□.    (→ \**tapa*)
        (ii)  .p|□.□□    (→ *-ata*)
            .p|□□.    (→ *pa:*)

The only candidates with proper end alignment are in (90a). But they are doomed by violation of two undominated constraints, ALIGN-LEFT because of initial epenthesis and CODA-COND because of the coda *p*. Of the remaining candidates (90b), neither mono- nor disyllabic modes of epenthesis have any effect whatever on the fundamental misalignment. Initial epenthesis, as in (90bi) is impossible, of course. This leaves only (90bii) as viable candidates, both misaligned at the right edge of the root.

These remaining candidates in (90bii) tie by violating ALIGN-RIGHT. The matter then passes onto the next constraint in the hierarchy, FILL. Guided by the Optimality-Theoretic imperative of minimal violation, it selects the form making least use of empty structure: the monosyllable $p\square\square$, with only two □'s. This outcome is shown in (91):

(91)   Augmentation of /p/ 'feed'

| Candidates | CODA-COND | ALIGN-LEFT | ONSET | ALIGN-RIGHT | FILL |
|---|---|---|---|---|---|
| (a) ☞ [\|p\|□□. | | | | * | ** |
| (b) [\|p\|□.□□. | | | | * | ***! |
| (c) [\|p\|□.□. | | | *! | * | ** |
| (d) [□\|p\|. | *! | *! | * | | * |
| (e) [□□\|p\|. | *! | *! | | | ** |
| (f) [□.\|p\|□. | | *! | * | * | ** |
| (g) [□□.\|p\|□. | | *! | | * | *** |

There is no syllabically well-formed augmentation of the root /p/ that doesn't also violate ALIGN-RIGHT, because the segment $p$ must be parsed as an onset. Initial epenthesis is excluded by ALIGN-LEFT. The decision falls to FILL, at the bottom of the constraint hierarchy, which favors the minimally epenthetic $p\square\square$ over excessively empty $p\square.\square\square$.[18] [ . . . ]

# 7   Conclusion

In this article, a theory of categorial **alignment** has been developed. We have argued that violable constraints demanding the alignment of prosodic or morphological constituents underlie a wide range of linguistic phenomena. Because of their greater generality of formulation as well as their empirical superiority, they improve significantly upon the results obtained previously through diverse mechanisms like the phonological cycle, extrametricality, iterative foot-parsing, and prosodic circumscription. Many – perhaps all – of the various modes of reference to constituent-edges in grammar can be subsumed under a single schema, called here Generalized Alignment. The essential formal idea is to distinguish conditions on hierarchy (category X must/can contain category Y) from conditions on collocation; the collocational restrictions are handled by conditions on the sharing or alignment of specified edges of specified categories. This provides a formal means to define not only the admissible patterns within a single hierarchical (tree-structured) grouping, but also to define the relations between categories belonging to different hierarchies, when they partially share a terminal string (particularly the hierarchies of prosody and morphology).

Four principal types of descriptive results have been obtained here through application of GA:

- **Footing Patterns**. In prosody proper (section 3), the locus of foot-parsing within the Prosodic Word was analyzed by the constraints Align(PrWd, Ft) and Align(Ft, PrWd). The former requires a single foot left- or right-aligned within the PrWd; the latter, replacing foot iteration in standard metrical theory, requires that **any** foot lie as near to the designated edge of the PrWd as possible.
- **Infixability**. In morphology proper (section 4), a theory of infixation was developed from that of Prince and Smolensky (1991b, 1992, 1993) and McCarthy and Prince (1993), relying on the constraint Align(Affix, Stem), which characterizes ordinary prefixation or suffixation. This constraint on the alignment of one morphological category within another may be crucially dominated, and therefore violated, under the Prosodic-Morphological ranking schema P ≫ M. In attested cases of infixation, two types of crucially dominant P-constraints have been identified: purely prosodic constraints like ONSET and CODA, and constraints on the alignment of morphological constituents with prosodic ones, like Align(Root, PrWd) or the subcategorizational Align(Affix, Left, Foot, Right).
- **Prosody/Morphology Correspondence**. In the prosody–morphology interface (section 5), various phonological consequences of morphological constituent-edges were attributed to just two constraints on the alignment of morphological constituents with prosodic ones, Align(Stem, Left, PrWd, Left), and Align(Stem, Right, Syllable, Right). The phenomena subsumed under this rubric include prohibited or required epenthesis at stem-edge, asymmetries in trans-junctural syllabification, and final consonant 'extrametricality'.
- **Prosodic Subcategorization**. Again in the prosody–morphology interface (section 6 [not repr. here]), a complex pattern of the conditioning of augmentation follows from a subcategorizational alignment constraint, Align(Affix, Left, PrWd, Right).

The effects of Alignment, then, have been demonstrated in phonology, in morphology, and in their interaction.

Phenomena like these have received widely disparate treatment in previous work. The success of GA in unifying them is due in no small measure to the fact that all of these results were obtained with analyses embedded in OT. Two tenets of OT have played a central role throughout:

- Constraints are ranked in a hierarchy of domination, and constraints are violated when crucially dominated. Virtually none of the Alignment constraints discussed reflects a phonotactic truth in the language at hand, and surely none is an absolute requirement conspicuously true in every language. Even in individual languages, they hold only contingently, in circumstances where no dominant constraint compels violation.
- Constraints evaluate candidate output forms; they are indifferent to the process by which those candidates are generated. From a processual point of view, Alignment is expressed in incomprehensibly diverse ways. With processes out of the picture, as in OT, this diversity is not only tractable but expected, given the variety of ways in which Alignment can enter into crucial domination relations.

It is difficult to imagine how Alignment theory could be given a comparably general treatment without relying on these principles.

These, then, are the most significant empirical and theoretical claims argued here. Of course, an enterprise of this sort inevitably leads to predictions beyond the local problems addressed. It is obviously impossible to discuss them fully, but it is worthwhile to raise them as questions for future research.

GA predicts the existence of constraints of the form Align(PCat, GCat), where any instance of PCat must be aligned with the designated edge of GCat. Such constraints have several potential applications. With Align(Ft, Root) crucially dominated by PARSE-SYLL, the pattern obtained is directional foot-parsing, as in (31). Because this Alignment constraint mentions Root, rather than PrWd, it yields a quasi-cyclic pattern, in which the foot-parse is anchored on the root within the PrWd (cf. the case of Indonesian in Cohn and McCarthy 1994). If Align(Ft, Root) is undominated, hence unviolated, then any foot must be aligned on the root – thus, stress will fall on a syllable of the root and nowhere else.

Within OT, an important issue disclosed in the course of empirical investigation was that of determining the **mode of violation** which a constraint submits to. In many cases, ALIGN – like EDGEMOST before it – determines degree or multiplicity of violation in terms of distance from the designated edge. In section 5, however, we observed that in the application of ALIGN-RIGHT to Axininca augmentation, violation of the constraint must be observationally categorical (pass/fail) rather than gradient. We entertained the further refinement that in these cases violation was also gradient, but reckoned along a different dimension, counting substitution of a syllable-edge for a PrWd-edge as a violation superior to no alignment at all. This allows a uniform specification of the prosodic parameters in ALIGN-RIGHT and ALIGN-LEFT, with the differences in effect being attributed to constraint domination and minimal violation. The way is then opened for the theory of the prosody–morphology interface to be substantively strengthened. These proposals involve many open questions, empirical and theoretical, which invite further exploration.

Finally, we must ask whether the various constructs of familiar phonological theory that are partly supplanted by GA can be dispensed with entirely. Prince and Smolensky (1993: section 4) begin to address this question for extrametricality; McCarthy and Prince (1993: section 7) likewise approach the issue for prosodic circumscription. The question is largely answered in section 3 above and in McCarthy and Prince (1993: section A.2) for directional iteration of foot-parsing. Finally, alternatives to the cycle, addressed in section 5 above, have received much attention in the literature (see the references in section 2, among others). The emerging picture, then, is encouraging, though much remains to be done.

## Notes

We are grateful to Lee Bickmore, Juliette Blevins, Janet Pierrehumbert, Lisa Selkirk, and Paul Smolensky, among others, for discussion of this work and to Geert Booij, Abby Cohn, Sharon Inkelas, Chuck Kisseberth, and Orhan Orgun for comments on this paper. Financial support was provided to McCarthy by a fellowship from the John Simon Guggenheim Memorial Foundation and a Faculty Research Grant from the University of Massachusetts and to Prince by Rutgers University and the Rutgers University Center for Cognitive Science.

1   Selkirk (1993) proposes an Optimality-Theoretic development of the edge-based theory of the syntax–phonology interface.

2   The English constraint Align(PrWd, L, Ft, L) is also violated under various conditions, principally when main-stress falls on the peninitial syllable and the initial syllable is light, hence unfootable: *A(mán)da, po(líce), A(méri)ca.* See section 3 for discussion of related cases.

3   A fourth, Parallelism, is not considered here.

>   Parallelism
>   Best-satisfaction of the constraint hierarchy is computed over the whole hierarchy and the whole candidate set. There is no serial derivation.

See Prince and Smolensky (1993), McCarthy and Prince (1993) for discussion.

4   McCarthy and Prince (1993: section 5.2) recognize one further articulation of this condition: a morpheme that has no phonological specifications at all in the lexicon (such as is the case with reduplicative affixes) takes as its exponent whatever phonological elements are associated with it in the output. Such morphemes are therefore formally *un*specified, not specified as containing nothing; morphemic exponents must be, in the classical manner, nondistinct at input and output. Something similar to Consistency of Exponence was first mooted by Pyle (1972: 522), who noted that morphological boundary theory implausibly requires that epenthetic segments be assigned an arbitrary morphological affiliation.

5   In stress theory, Halle and Kenstowicz (1991) and Idsardi (1992) take a very different approach to establishing the coincidence of constituent edges. They propose to reify the constituent boundary-symbols; for example, in Diyari (cf. Poser 1989), where the left edge of each morpheme must coincide with the left edge of a foot, Halle and Kenstowicz propose a rule inserting a left foot-bracket symbol at the left edge of each morpheme. This reification of boundary-symbols is sharply at odds with other work which, beginning with Siegel (1974), Rotenberg (1978), and Selkirk (1980a), has rejected boundary-symbol theory elsewhere in phonology and morphology. It is essentially an artifact of commitment to the idea that phonological representations are literally *built* by rule, and indeed rules of string manipulation. The alternative is to view phonological representations like those of syntax: they conform to (a system of) constraints defined over constituency.

6   The constraints determining the headedness of feet can also be expressed in terms of GA. Trochaicity is Align(Ft, L, H(Ft), L), where H(Ft) = 'head of foot' = strongest syllable-daughter of F.

7   In contrast, there seems to be little or no evidence of directionality in iambic foot-parsing. McCarthy and Prince (1993: section A.2) show that specification of directionality in iambic foot-parsing is superfluous, given avoidance of final stress, NONFINALITY. In the current context, this result must mean that the Alignment constraints enforcing directionality of foot-parsing are always low-ranking relative to NONFINALITY.

8   For broadly similar approaches to phenomena of this sort, see Burzio (1992a, b), Idsardi (1992). An exact parallel is found in Itô and Mester (1992).

9   This masking of the more specific constraint when dominated by a more general one is an instance of Pāṇini's Theorem on Constraint Ranking (Prince and Smolensky 1993: section 5.3).

10  In cases like (34), where a viable candidate does not violate the gradient constraint at all, we do not bother to show the degree of violation for remaining candidates.

11  The asymmetry between PrWd-demanding ALIGN-LEFT and σ-demanding ALIGN-RIGHT is worthy of scrutiny. We return to this matter at the end of this section (p. 135 [not repr. here]), after exploring the empirical sense of the constraints as formulated.

12  FILL and PARSE are each representatives of families of constraints, where the specific instance of the constraint is determined by which node is taken as the focus of evaluation. PARSE demands that the node be properly mothered (PARSE-SEG, that segments be syllabified; PARSE-SYLL, that syllables be footed; and so on), and FILL demands that it dominate its proper child. FILL

militates against *empty* structure, and thus belongs to a family of constraints that militate against all kinds of structure, of which the most general is the virtually Manichean *STRUC: avoid structure altogether.

13   Axininca Campa is the subject of a comprehensive analysis by Payne (1981), from which most of our data come. (Some additional forms are taken from Spring (1990).) The discussion here is drawn from a near-complete Optimality-Theoretic account of Axininca Campa prosody and prosodic morphology in McCarthy and Prince (1993).

14   Yip (1983: 244–5) proposes that Axininca epenthesis is 'morphological' because it is limited to verb suffixation and because it breaks up syllables that would otherwise be permissible. The morphological condition is encoded by repeating an ALIGN-like restriction in the contexts of two separate epenthesis rules.

15   Another potential case, involving the phonology of the velar glide, is discussed in McCarthy and Prince (1993: section A.3).

16   To clarify the examples, we show the expected interpretation of the output phonological representations in parentheses.

17   This argument rests on the claim that the candidate (86a), phonetically realized as [na:], is misaligned. This is pre-theoretically reasonable, since the root /na/ 'carry on shoulder' contains a short vowel, contrasting minimally with /na:/ 'chew', and the extra mora comes from the phonology. The proposed explanation turns on the contrast between what is motivated lexically and what is motivated phonologically, which any theory will recognize in some way. One representational account of this is presented in McCarthy and Prince (1993: section 5), but others are no doubt possible.

18   What counts as less epenthesis will depend on precisely how FILL is formulated. But all reasonable formulations of FILL give the same result. If FILL measures empty positions without regard to their syllabic role, as reflected by the violation marks in (91), or if FILL reckons any incomplete syllable as a mark, then $p\square\square$ has fewer than $*p\square.\square\square$. If there are separate constraints 'FILL-Nucleus/Mora' and 'FILL-Onset', as in Prince and Smolensky (1991a, b, 1993), then $*p\square.\square\square$ but not $p\square\square$ will violate the latter. Finally, even if we modify our representational assumptions so that epenthetic elements are completely specified in the phonology, and then have FILL measure featural differences between input and output, it is still true that *aa* consists featurally of a single segment, but *ata* must contain the features of three segments. FILL, then, under any construal, limits augmentation of roots /C/ to a long vowel, because they are nonalignable.

There is, however, a somewhat subtle argument for the character of FILL, based again on augmentation of /CV/ roots. Consider the possibility of **medial** augmentation, here illustrated with the root /tʰo/, so that the contrast is phonetically apparent:

(a)   [tʰo.|$\square\square$.     ($\rightarrow$ *tʰota*)
(b)   [tʰ$\square$.$\square$o.|     ($\rightarrow$ **tʰato*)

Both candidates are properly aligned on both edges, so they tie on all relevant constraints. They also are treated equally by all methods of FILL evaluation except for the reckoning of incomplete syllables. In (b), two syllables are crucially incomplete, whereas in (a) all incompleteness has been confined to a single syllable. This suggests that at least one sense of FILL must assess whole syllables for empty structure they contain.

Alternatively, (b) may be disfavored because epenthesis introduces a discontinuity into the root (McCarthy and Prince 1993: section 4, p. 50n). If there is a cross-linguistic bias against medial epenthesis, especially in circumstances where there is a choice between medial and peripheral epenthesis, then an appropriate constraint legislating continuity can be devised. Whatever its ranking in Axininca Campa, this constraint would correctly select (a) over (b), since these two candidates tie on all other constraints. Kenstowicz (1993) finds additional evidence for such a constraint in the phonology of Chukchee.

# References

Archangeli, D. 1984. Underspecification in Yawelmani Phonology and Morphology. Ph.D. dissertation, MIT.

Aronoff, M. and S. N. Sridhar. 1983. Morphological Levels in English and Kannada; Or, Atarizing Reagan. In John Richardson et al. (eds), *Papers from the Parasession on the Interplay of Phonology, Morphology, and Syntax.* Chicago: Chicago Linguistic Society.

Bach, E. and D. Wheeler. 1981. Montague Phonology: A First Approximation. *University of Massachusetts Occasional Papers in Linguistics* 7, 27–45.

Bird, S. 1990. Constraint based Phonology. Ph.D. Dissertation, University of Edinburgh.

Black, H. 1991. The Phonology of the Velar Glide in Axininca Campa. *Phonology* 8, 183–217.

Booij, G. 1988. On the Relation between Lexical Phonology and Prosodic Phonology. In P. M. Bertinetto and M. Loporcaro (eds), *Certamen Phonologicum*, Torino: Sellier.

Booij, G. and R. Lieber. 1993. On the Simultaneity of Morphological and Prosodic Structure. In S. Hargus and E. Kaisse (eds), *Studies in Lexical Phonology*, San Diego: Academic Press, 23–44.

Booij, G. and J. Rubach. 1984. Morphological and Prosodic Domains in Lexical Phonology. *Phonology Yearbook* 1, 1–28.

Borowsky, T. 1993. On the Word Level. In S. Hargus and E. Kaisse (eds), *Studies in Lexical Phonology*, Phonetics and Phonology 4, San Diego: Academic Press, 199–234.

Broselow, E. and J. McCarthy. 1983. A Theory of Internal Reduplication. *Linguistic Review* 3, 25–88.

Burzio, L. 1992a. Metrical Consistency. Abstract of paper presented at DIMACS Workshop, Princeton University.

Burzio, L. 1992b. Principles of English Stress. MS, Johns Hopkins University.

Chen, Y. 1987. The Syntax of Xiamen Tone Sandhi. *Phonology Yearbook* 4, 109–50.

Clements, G. N. 1978. Tone and Syntax in Ewe. In D. J. Napoli (ed.), *Elements of Tone, Stress, and Intonation*, Georgetown: Georgetown University Press, 21–99.

Clements, G. N. and S. J. Keyser. 1983. *CV Phonology*. Cambridge, Mass.: MIT Press.

Cohn, A. 1989. Stress in Indonesian and Bracketing Paradoxes. *Natural Language and Linguistic Theory* 7, 167–216.

Cohn, A. and J. McCarthy. 1994. Alignment and Parallelism in Indonesian Phonology. MS, Cornell University and University of Massachusetts.

Cole, J. S. 1992. Eliminating Cyclicity as a Source of Complexity in Phonology. Cognitive Science Technical Report UIUC-BI-CS-92-03, Beckman Institute, University of Illinois, Urbana, Il.

Cole, J. S. and J. Coleman. 1992. Cyclic Phonology with Context-Free Grammars. Cognitive Science Technical Report UIUC-BI-CS-92-06. Beckman Institute, University of Illinois, Urbana, Il. [Appears in *Papers from the 28th Regional Meeting of the Chicago Linguistic Society*, Volume 2: *The Parasession: The Cycle in Linguistic Theory*, Chicago: Chicago Linguistic Society.]

Furby, C. 1974. Garawa Phonology. *Papers in Australian Linguistics* 7, 1–11.

Goldsmith, J. 1990. *Autosegmental and Metrical Phonology*. Oxford: Basil Blackwell.

Goldsmith, J. 1991. Phonology as an Intelligent System. In D. J. Napoli and J. Kegl (eds), *Bridges between Psychology and Linguistics*, Hillsdale, NJ: Lawrence Erlbaum Associates.

Goldsmith, J. 1992. Local Modelling in Phonology. In S. Davis (ed.), *Connectionism: Theory and Practice*, Oxford: Oxford University Press.

Hale, K. and E. Selkirk. 1987. Government and Tonal Phrasing in Papago. *Phonology Yearbook* 4, 151–83.

Halle, M. and M. Kenstowicz. 1991. The Free Element Condition and Cyclic versus Noncyclic Stress. *Linguistic Inquiry* 22, 457–501.

Halle, M. and J. R. Vergnaud. 1987. *An Essay on Stress*. Cambridge, Mass.: MIT Press.

Hayes, B. 1980. A Metrical Theory of Stress Rules. Ph.D. dissertation, MIT.

Hayes, B. 1987. A Revised Parametric Metrical Theory. In J. McDonough and B. Plunkett (eds), *Proceedings of NELS 17*, Graduate Linguistic Student Association, University of Massachusetts, Amherst.

Hayes, B. 1989. Compensatory Lengthening in Moraic Phonology. *Linguistic Inquiry* 20, 253–306.

Hayes, B. 1991. Metrical Stress Theory: Principles and Case Studies. MS, UCLA.

Hulst, H. van der. 1984. *Syllable Structure and Stress in Dutch*. Dordrecht: Foris.

Hyman, L. 1985. *A Theory of Phonological Weight*. Dordrecht: Foris.

Idsardi, W. 1992. The Computation of Prosody. Ph.D. dissertation, MIT.

Inkelas, S. 1989. Prosodic Constituency in the Lexicon. Ph.D. dissertation, Stanford University.

Itô, J. 1986. Syllable Theory in Prosodic Phonology. Ph.D. dissertation, University of Massachusetts, Amherst.

Itô, J. 1989. A Prosodic Theory of Epenthesis. *Natural Language and Linguistic Theory* 7, 217–60.

Itô, J. and R. A. Mester. 1992. Weak Layering and Word Binarity. MS, University of California, Santa Cruz.

Kager, R. 1989. *A Metrical Theory of Stress and Destressing in English and Dutch*. Dordrecht: Foris.

Kager, R. 1992a. Are There Any Truly Quantity-Insensitive Systems. Paper presented at BLS.

Kager, R. 1992b. Shapes of the Generalized Trochee. Paper presented at WCCFL XI.

Kager, R. 1992c. Alternatives to the Iambic-Trochaic Law. *Natural Language and Linguistic Theory* 11, 381–432.

Kager, R. 1993. Consequences of Catalexis. In H. van der Hulst and J. van de Weijer (eds), *Leiden in Last: HIL Phonology Papers I*, 269–98. The Hague: Holland Institute of Generative Linguistics.

Kenstowicz, M. 1993. Chukchee Epenthesis: A Constraints-Based Analysis. Class notes for 24.964, MIT, 29 March, 1993.

Kiparsky, P. 1982. Lexical Phonology and Morphology. In I. S. Yang (ed.), *Linguistics in the Morning Calm*, Seoul: Hanshin.

Kisseberth, C. to appear. On Domains. In J. S. Cole and C. Kisseberth (eds), *Perspectives in Phonology*, Stanford, Calif.: CSLI, 133–66.

Levin, J. 1985. A Metrical Theory of Syllabicity. Ph.D. dissertation, MIT.

Liberman, M. and A. Prince. 1977. On Stress and Linguistic Rhythm. *Linguistic Inquiry* 8, 249–336. Part of this paper is reproduced here as ch. 20.

Lowenstamm, J. and J. Kaye. 1986. Compensatory Lengthening in Tiberian Hebrew. In L. Wetzels and E. Sezer (eds), *Studies in Compensatory Lengthening*, Dordrecht: Foris.

McCarthy, J. 1979. Formal Problems in Semitic Phonology and Morphology. Ph.D. dissertation, MIT.

McCarthy, J. 1981. A Prosodic Theory of Nonconcatenative Morphology. *Linguistic Inquiry* 12, 373–418.

McCarthy, J. and A. Prince. 1986. Prosodic Morphology. MS, University of Massachusetts and Brandeis University.

McCarthy, J. and A. Prince. 1988. Quantitative Transfer in Reduplicative and Templatic Morphology. In Linguistic Society of Korea (ed.), *Linguistics in the Morning Calm 2*, Seoul: Hanshin, 3–35.

McCarthy, J. and A. Prince. 1990. Foot and Word in Prosodic Morphology: The Arabic Broken Plurals. *Natural Language and Linguistic Theory* 8, 209–82.

McCarthy, J. and A. Prince. 1991a. Prosodic Minimality. Lecture presented at University of Illinois Conference *The Organization of Phonology*.

McCarthy, J. and A. Prince. 1991b. Linguistics 240: Prosodic Morphology. Lectures and handouts from 1991 LSA Linguistic Institute Course, University of California, Santa Cruz.

McCarthy, J. and A. Prince. 1993. Prosodic Morphology I: Constraint Interaction and Satisfaction. MS, University of Massachusetts, Amherst, and Rutgers University.

McCawley, J. 1982. Parentheticals and Discontinuous Constituent Structure. *Linguistic Inquiry* 13, 91–106.

McDonald, M. and S. Wurm. 1979. *Basic Materials in Waŋkumara (Galali): Grammar, Sentences and Vocabulary*. Pacific Linguistics, Series B, no. 65. Canberra: Australian National University.

Mester, R. Armin. 1994. The Quantitative Trochee in Latin. *Natural Language and Linguistic Theory* 12: 1–61.

Osborn, H. 1966. Warao I: Phonology and Morphophonemics. *International Journal of American Linguistics* 32, 108–23.

Payne, D. 1981. *The Phonology and Morphology of Axininca Campa*. Arlington, Tex.: Summer Institute of Linguistics.

Pierrehumbert, J. and M. Beckman. 1988. *Japanese Tone Structure*. Cambridge, Mass.: MIT Press.

Poser, W. 1985. The Phonetics and Phonology of Tone and Intonation in Japanese, Ph.D. dissertation, MIT.

Poser, W. 1989. The Metrical Foot in Diyari. *Phonology* 6, 117–48.

Prince, A. 1976. "Applying" Stress. MS, University of Massachusetts, Amherst.

Prince, A. 1980. A Metrical Theory for Estonian Quantity. *Linguistic Inquiry* 11, 511–62.

Prince, A. 1983. Relating to the Grid. *Linguistic Inquiry* 14, 19–100. Repr. in part here as ch. 21.

Prince, A. and P. Smolensky. 1991a. Optimality. Paper given at Arizona Phonology Conference.

Prince, A. and P. Smolensky. 1991b. Notes on Connectionism and Harmony Theory in Linguistics. In *Technical Report CU-CS-533-91*, Department of Computer Science, University of Colorado, Boulder, Colo.

Prince, A. and P. Smolensky. 1992. Optimality: Constraint Interaction in Generative Grammar. Paper read at 12th West Coast Conference on Formal Linguistics, Los Angeles.

Prince, A. and P. Smolensky. 1993. Optimality Theory: Constraint Interaction in Generative Grammar. MS, Rutgers University, New Brunswick, and University of Colorado, Boulder.

Pyle, C. 1972. On Eliminating BM's. *CLS* 8.

Rotenberg, J. 1978. The Syntax of Phonology. Ph.D. dissertation, MIT.

Rubach, J. and G. Booij. 1985. A Grid Theory of Stress in Polish. *Lingua* 66, 281–319.

Rubach, J. and G. Booij. 1990. Edge of Constituent Effects in Polish. *Natural Language and Linguistic Theory* 7, 121–58.

Scobbie, J. 1991. Attribute–Value Phonology. Ph.D. dissertation, University of Edinburgh.

Scobbie, J. 1992. Towards Declarative Phonology. *Edinburgh Working Papers in Cognitive Science* 7, 1–26.

Selkirk, E. 1980a. Prosodic Domains in Phonology: Sanskrit Revisited. In M. Aronoff and M. L. Kean (eds), *Juncture*. Saratoga, Calif.: Anma Libri, 107–29.

Selkirk, E. 1980b. The Role of Prosodic Categories in English Word Stress. *Linguistic Inquiry* 11, 563–605.

Selkirk, E. 1981. Epenthesis and Degenerate Syllables in Cairene Arabic. In H. Borer and J. Aoun (eds), *Theoretical Issues in the Grammar of the Semitic Languages*, Cambridge, Mass.: MIT. (MIT Working Papers in Linguistics, Vol. 3)

Selkirk, E. 1986. On Derived Domains in Sentence Phonology. *Phonology Yearbook* 3, 371–405.

Selkirk, E. 1993. The Prosodic Structure of Functional Elements: Affixes, Clitics, and Words. Handout of talk presented at Signal to Syntax Conference, Brown University.

Selkirk, E. and K. Tateishi. 1988. Syntax and Phonological Phrasing in Japanese. In C. Georgopoulos and R. Ishihara (eds), *Studies in Honour of S.-Y. Kuroda*, Amsterdam: Reidel.

Selkirk, E. and T. Shen. 1990. Prosodic Domains in Shanghai Chinese. In S. Inkelas and D. Zec (eds), *The Phonology–Syntax Connection*, Chicago: University of Chicago Press, 313–37.

Siegel, D. 1974. Topics in English Morphology. Ph.D. dissertation, MIT.

Smolensky, P. 1986. Information Processing in Dynamical Systems: Foundations of Harmony Theory. In D. E. Rumelhart, J. L. McClelland, and the PDP Research Group (eds), *Parallel Distributed Processing: Explorations in the Microstructure of Cognition*. vol. 1: *Foundations*, Cambridge, Mass.: MIT Press/Bradford Books, 194–281.

Spring, C. 1990. Implications of Axininca Campa for Prosodic Morphology and Reduplication. Ph.D. dissertation, University of Arizona, Tucson.

Sproat, R. 1985. On Deriving the Lexicon. Ph.D. dissertation, MIT.

Steriade, D. 1982. Greek Prosodies and the Nature of Syllabification. Ph.D. dissertation, MIT.

Steriade, D. 1988. Greek Accent: A Case for Preserving Structure. *Linguistic Inquiry* 19, 271–314.

Szpyra, J. 1989. *The Phonology–Morphology Interface*. London: Routledge.

Wheeler, D. 1981. Aspects of a Categorial Theory of Phonology. Ph.D. dissertation, University of Massachusetts, Amherst.

Yip, M. 1983. Some Problems of Syllable Structure in Axininca Campa. In P. Sells and C. Jones (eds), *Proceedings of NELS 13*, Graduate Linguistic Student Association, University of Massachusetts, Amherst, 243–251.

Zec, D. 1988. Sonority Constraints on Prosodic Structure. Ph.D. dissertation, Stanford University.

# 8

# An Overview of Autosegmental Phonology (1976)

## John Goldsmith

The subject of linguistics being the relation between sound and meaning, we must ask what the nature and form of the phonetic and semantic levels are. For a generative linguistic system, this task begins with hypotheses about the type of formal representation that counts as a faithful rendering of the phonetic or the semantic aspects of a word, sentence, discourse, and so forth.

Autosegmental phonology is an attempt to provide a more adequate understanding of the phonetic side of the linguistic representation. Viewed in this light, this is a proposal at the same logical level as the proposal that a phonetic representation is a linear sequence of atomic units – call them segments; it is at the same level as the suggestion that these atomic units are cross-classified by distinctive features. Autosegmental phonology constitutes a particular claim, then, about the *geometry* of phonetic representations; it suggests that the phonetic representation is composed of a set of several simultaneous sequences of these segments, with certain elementary constraints on how the various levels of sequences can be interrelated or "associated."

To say that autosegmental phonology is a hypothesis about the geometry of phonetic, and ultimately phonological, representations is rather abstract at best. From a more down-to-earth vantage point, autosegmental phonology is a theory of how the various components of the articulatory apparatus, i.e., the tongue, the lips, the larynx, the velum, are coordinated. At the most superficial, observable level the linguistic signal is split up into a large number of separate information channels. Viewed from the production side, this consists of the specific commands to the larynx, the velum, the tongue, and so on, or perhaps the patterns which each channel then attempts to attain. At an "abstract" level, this information comes about from splitting up a more unified representation. Let us clarify this with an example. Suppose we utter the word "pin." As the orthography suggests, the linguistic representation of the word consists of three segments linearly ordered, as in (1).

(1)
$$
\begin{bmatrix} +\text{conson} \\ -\text{nasal} \\ +\text{labial} \\ -\text{coronal} \\ \vdots \end{bmatrix}
\begin{bmatrix} +\text{syllabic} \\ -\text{nasal} \\ -\text{labial} \\ -\text{coronal} \\ \vdots \end{bmatrix}
\begin{bmatrix} +\text{conson} \\ +\text{nasal} \\ -\text{labial} \\ +\text{coronal} \\ \vdots \end{bmatrix}
$$
$$\quad\; \text{'p'} \qquad\quad \text{'i'} \qquad\quad \text{'n'}$$

The production of this word, however, involves separate, though coordinated, activity by the velum, the lips, and so forth, expressed roughly in (2).

(2)   A Score for the Orchestration of *Pin*

> Lips:        . . . Close up . . . . open . . . . . . . . . . . . . . . .
> Tongue:    . . . High and front . . . . . . . . . touch the palate
> Velum:      . . . Raise . . . . . . . . . . lower . . . . . . . . . . . . . . . . . .

The standard assumption regarding the nature of phonological representations – that they look much like (1) – implies that the process of language acquisition includes the development of the ability to take a representation much like (2) and slice it vertically into columns, assigning the appropriate feature specifications to each column, ultimately deriving a representation like (1): P–I–N. In short, the normal assumption about phonological representations implies that in processing a signal, we learn to shift around slightly the horizontal alignment of the commands in (2). We "justify" it and patch it up so that it may be sliced up vertically into the phonologically, and hence psychologically, real segments. Let us call this assumption the "Absolute Slicing Hypothesis."

In the example we considered, saying *pin* as in (2), the process described above is essentially correct. The Absolute Slicing Hypothesis is then adequate to the level of detail we have considered in (2). Suppose, however, that we add to the orchestral score in (2) the activity of the larynx that gives rise to pitch. If we utter this word *pin* in isolation, and if we disregard the actual sluggishness of the vocal folds for the nonce, the syllable will be uttered at a rapidly falling pitch. For reasons that will be developed in section 1.2 and ref. 7 I will represent the Falling pitch as the sequence of a High pitch and a Low pitch. A more faithful orchestral score for *pin* would be (3).

(3)   A Revised Orchestral Score for *Pin*

> Lips:        . . . Close up . . . . open . . . . . . . . . . . . . . . . . . . . . . .
> Tongue:    . . . High and front . . . . . . . . . touch the palate
> Velum:      . . . Raise . . . . . . . . . . . . . . lower . . . . . . . . . . . . . .
> Larynx:     . . . High pitch . . . . . Low pitch . . . . . . . . . . . . . .

The assumption of the Absolute Slicing Hypothesis fails now, and this failure is in no sense a trivial one. The laryngeal pitch specifications are, we shall argue below (and in detail in [7]), not the result of specification of any of the segments in (1), the phonological representation. The falling pitch of this utterance is not part of the phonological segments in the same sense that the other commands are, as in (3) (those for the lips, the tongue, or the velum).

The speaker of English thus factors out the pitch, and does not attempt to include the pitch features in the huge musical score which is sliced up into the more abstract segments as in (1). In this sense, then, the Absolute Slicing Hypothesis fails; the slicing is not absolute or complete, but rather may exclude some parts of the linguistic signal.

This failure of the Absolute Slicing Hypothesis is nontrivial in two separate, important senses. First, it is only an accident about English that the laryngeal pitch features are excluded from the great slicing. Other languages may well include pitch as a part of the signal which is sliced up into successive segments. Conversely, a language may exclude some features from the great slicing that English happens to include. Guarani, as we shall see in section 5, happens to exclude the nasalization feature, while English includes it. Whether a particular channel of articulation is included cannot be specified universally once and for all.

The second sense in which the Absolute Slicing Hypothesis fails nontrivially will be the key to the successful formulation of its successor. The articulatory levels that are excluded – in the present example, pitch – are themselves susceptible to a slicing or segmentation. Thus, while the laryngeal pitch commands in (3) do not correspond to the standard phonological representation in (1), they do in fact correspond to a more abstract segmented level, as follows:

(4)  $\overset{*}{H}$ L     where H = High and L = Low

In the present example, of course, the empirical significance of the representation in (4), including the meaning of the star*, remains open for the present. The important point is, however: while a language may exclude an articulatory level from the great slicing that leads to the principal segmentation (corresponding to P–I–N in (1)), the excluded articulatory levels themselves form segmented domains, domains in which the segments are linearly ordered, and where the segments are cross-classified by feature-specifications. In general, the formal properties of the "phonological" representation, as in (1), will be mirrored on each level. Just as (1) corresponded to (2), then, the revised and now autosegmental representation given as (5) corresponds to (3), the more adequate orchestral score. And (5), we see, is a synthesis of (1) and (4). The precise significance of the "association lines" linking the tonological and the phonological levels will become clearer shortly.

(5)

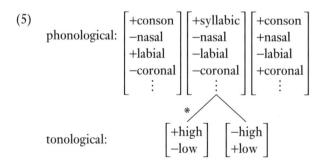

phonological:
$$\begin{bmatrix} +\text{conson} \\ -\text{nasal} \\ +\text{labial} \\ -\text{coronal} \\ \vdots \end{bmatrix} \begin{bmatrix} +\text{syllabic} \\ -\text{nasal} \\ -\text{labial} \\ -\text{coronal} \\ \vdots \end{bmatrix} \begin{bmatrix} +\text{conson} \\ +\text{nasal} \\ -\text{labial} \\ +\text{coronal} \\ \vdots \end{bmatrix}$$

tonological:
$$\begin{bmatrix} +\text{high} \\ -\text{low} \end{bmatrix} \begin{bmatrix} -\text{high} \\ +\text{low} \end{bmatrix}$$

To develop this idea, however, let us turn our attention from these rather general comments on the nature of phonological segmentation to some more pressing problems in generative phonology. A proposed theoretical revision must in general be shown to resolve a dilemma in the standard theory; we shall therefore proceed to several general types of phenomena that are all difficult or impossible to account for in the standard framework, which incorporates only one string of segments in a phonological representation. We shall show how each phenomenon of this type individually leads to the same solution, an autosegmental solution. In the course of doing so, we shall see that these phenomena in general, though not invariably, cluster together, as predicted by the autosegmental solution. We shall consider the following:

A. The existence of *contour-valued features*, such as rising or falling tones on vowels, or prenasalized stops, such as $^n$d, $^m$b, etc. Here the argument must be made that in some languages, short vowels[1] bear these dynamic or contour tones, and that furthermore such a contour tone is linguistically the concatenation of two level tones, rather than being an atomic unit itself. The existence of short vowels with contour tones has been argued for recently by a number of linguists, most forcefully by Leben [10]. No satisfactory alternative theoretical account has been given, however.

B. The phenomenon of *stability*. This is the tendency of a feature value to persist despite the erasure of the major segment (generally, vowel) which appeared to have borne that feature. Roughly we find in tone languages that when a tone-bearing vowel is deleted by a phonological rule, the accompanying tone does not also delete, but rather shows up elsewhere on a neighboring syllable.

C. *Melody levels* in the grammar. These are linguistically significant levels in the grammar which refer to just one or two features in the utterance. We have already seen a foreshadowing of this phenomenon in the discussion of the difference between the pitch features in English and the other features. If we view the musical scoring for the utterance *pin* as in (3), and many more like it, we will notice a difference in the different lines (or "voices," in the musical sense). Some, like the line of instructions to the velum legislating nasality, will appear rather uninteresting when viewed alone. No generalizations can be made by looking at nasalization alone in English. In other areas – such as the level of instructions for pitch – there are linguistic generalizations to be gained by restricting our attention to just those features. There are, thus, strictly pitch-feature regularities, which is not to deny that further insight is to be gained by observing how the pitch level is coordinated with the other levels, of course. However, the point is that certain subsequences of features *do* form linguistically significant melody levels, while others do not.

D. The heuristic notion of *floating tone*, which can be rigorously defended in autosegmental terms. The floating tone has served well in practical terms for linguists dealing with tone languages; it has, however, had a tainted reputation because of its apparent anomalous nature within the current theoretical framework.

E. Finally, we will consider some processes of automatic spreading of features, both to the left and right, over segments unspecified for those features. The accepted notation for phonological rules implicitly predicts that spreading should be simpler if it occurs only to the left or only to the right; we find, however, many cases of bidirectional spreading. When viewed from an autosegmental perspective, the reasons become clear.

This is, perhaps, an appropriate moment at which to point out some differences and similarities between autosegmental phonology and other treatments of what have been called suprasegmentals. Much of what is covered in this present analysis would be called suprasegmental by the criteria implicit in the literature. What is suggested by the term "suprasegmental"? Two things, I would submit, which are entirely different but which have been continually confused in the recent linguistic tradition.[2]

Calling tone "suprasegmental" immediately distinguishes it from the "segmental," correctly viewing pitch as different from and not part of the phonological segmentation as in (1), the segmentation into phonemes. But this first observation has led to the false assumption that "suprasegmentals" could not be segmental in their own right – the second, more fundamental, sense of "segmental," which is overlooked by the term "suprasegmental." If the "suprasegmental" of pitch does by itself form a sequence of tonal segments, then "suprasegmental" is a misleading label. A more accurate picture, we suggest, is parallel sequences of segments, none of which "depend" or "ride on" the others. Each is independent in its own right; hence the name, *auto*segmental level.

## 1   Contour Tones

Let us proceed to particular problems within the theory of phonology. Our first task is to make quite clear why having two tonal specifications on a single vowel is incontrovertibly in contradiction with the standard theory. I shall first sketch the argument heuristically, and then redo it in more technical language.

Suppose we analyze the tonal workings of a language and decide that where contour tones occur, they are really the concatenation of level tones.[3] That is, Rising tones are actually composed of the sequence Low tone and High tone; Falling tones are composed of High tone and Low tone. Suppose further that such contour tones occur on short vowels. We shall consider several actual examples shortly. A long vowel may be analyzed as a sequence of two short vowels, but a short vowel has no such analysis. How can we represent the contour tone of the short vowel?

Our conclusion will be simply that we cannot represent it if we stay within the assumptions of the standard theory. Let us assume, for purpose of exposition, that tone can be represented in terms of binary features[4] (although the assumption of the binary nature is not relevant at this point). Suppose, then, we try to represent *a* with a Falling tone, that is, *â* as in (6). This Falling tone, as we have said, is the combination of a High tone and a Low tone.

(6)

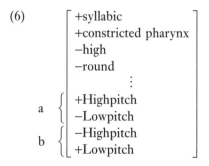

Now this clearly will not do. This curious segment (6) is both +Highpitch and −Highpitch; is both +Lowpitch and −Lowpitch. The features in the part labeled (a) seem to indicate a High tone; those in (b) seem to indicate a Low tone. But putting one on top of another does not order them, as we require. In particular, we must distinguish a Falling tone from a Rising tone; but to do so, a new and theoretically momentous set of conventions must be introduced in order to make *vertical* ordering of features within a segment play the role of left-to-right (temporal) ordering of segments elsewhere.

Or one could attempt an equally radical revision of the notion of segment with the introduction of a notation as in (7).

(7)
$$\begin{bmatrix} \text{+syllabic} \\ \text{+constricted pharynx} \\ -\text{high} \\ -\text{round} \\ \vdots \\ \begin{bmatrix} \text{+Highpitch} \\ {}_A-\text{Lowpitch}_A \end{bmatrix} \begin{bmatrix} -\text{Highpitch} \\ {}_B+\text{Lowpitch}_B \end{bmatrix} \end{bmatrix}$$

One has here, however, what is to all appearance a category error. The nontonal features have one relationship to the entire segment; they are, let us say, "features-of it." The tonal features are features of a subsegment (there are two subsegments here, A and B); and the subsegments bear some entirely other relationship to the entire segment: they "subcompose" it, let us say. Consequently, tonal features are "features-of a segment which subcomposes" the entire segment; in particular, the tonal features are no longer features-of the segment. Here, too, is a radical suggestion intended to make possible the representation of a contour tone.

Now these two attempts, the second of which is rather a commonplace in the literature, are not misguided; quite the contrary, even though both are wrong. They recognize that the existence of contour tones is a *problem* for the standard representation. Our task is to outline a third proposal, one which is conceptually simpler and which has a number of direct empirical consequences: autosegmental representation. First, let us review in more technical terms the argument that demonstrates the dilemma of the standard theory.

Segments are atomic elements ordered linearly left to right; this simple and elegant hypothesis is at the foundation of standard phonology. A feature-specification of a segment is, then, a property or an attribute of the segment. The property of being voiceless "belongs" to the first segment in *pin*, just as the property of being "front" belongs to the second segment. More technically, we would say that *pin* has a representation at the phonological level as in (8).

(8)    $S_{75}$  $S_{31}$  $S_{33}$

The subscripts indicate nothing but that these are primitive elements in the phonological vocabulary. We would further specify that there are various "feature-projection" maps – characteristic functions, in mathematicians' language – that tell us what the feature specifications for each segment are. For example, there is an $F_{voice}$ function which maps $S_{75}$ in the present example to − (minus). $F_{voice}(S_{75}) = -$. This says that the first segment in the representation of *pin* in (8) is voiceless.

Having made precise our notions of segment and feature-specification (following essentially Chomsky's *Logical Structure of Linguistic Theory*), it is clear that there is no way that a segment can be specified both + and − for some particular feature. In particular, no single segment can be both [+Highpitch] and [−Highpitch]; therefore no single segment can be High–Low in pitch, and therefore no single segment can be contour-toned unless there is a single feature which is "Falling" or "Rising," contrary to hypothesis. If a single segment were both +Highpitch and −Highpitch, then $F_{highpitch}$ would not be a function, again contrary to assumption, since it would be two-valued.

If we wished to resolve this formal conflict by saying that there were two separate characteristic functions associated with each phonological feature, one mapping to the specification + (plus) and the other to the specification − (minus), we would avoid the immediate contradiction, but lose the formal representation of the fact that the two values are values of the *same* feature; such an approach would clearly lead in the wrong direction.

The correct position to take is that the formalism demands that no segment may be doubly specified for a feature. If tones are features of the vowel segment, then there may be no Low–High sequence on a single vowel. Some other basic axiom must be abandoned.

The approach we will take toward a resolution of this problem is to deny that tonal features are features of the vowel in the case of the problematic contour tone. Rather, the tonal features are properties of another level; feature-specifications on the other level constitute segments, but their relation to the vowels with which they are associated is merely one of simultaneity in time. We represent this dynamic element by association lines. The Falling-toned *â*, then, is represented as in (9).

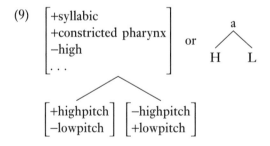

A more complex example, like the word *àkálă* would be represented as in (10).

(10)   a  k  a  l  a
       |  |  |  ╲
       L  H  L  H

Before proceeding with the development of this notation, let us turn to an example from a tone language.

## 1.1   Igbo

Our first example is from Uhuhu Igbo, as described in [8]. (These facts are discussed in much greater detail in chapter 2 of [6].) For the present we will content ourselves with finding a contour tone on a single segment, and showing that it is indeed the concatenation of two tones; we shall then see why the notation in (9) or (10) does more than describe these facts, but predicts and explains the intuitively clear sense of left-to-right order of tones that is revealed inside of contour tones by the tonological rules.

There is a simple tone rule that occurs in the "I Main" form. Throughout the Igbo language, the particular tone of the verb stem, suffixes, and prefixes is determined by the "form" of the clause. We may reserve our attention here to I Main form, in which the verb stem is Low-toned, in unexceptional cases. Consider, for example, a simple sentence in the I Main form where the subject is a pronoun:[5]

(11)   I Main form
    (a)  ọ́ cị̀  àkhwá    'He must carry some eggs' or
        he carry eggs      'He was carrying some eggs.'
    (b)  ó zà    úlò    'He must sweep the house.'
        he sweep house
    (c)  Ḿ cì   ánụ́    'I was carrying meat.'
        I   carry meat

We see that in the I Main form, the pronominal subjects are High in tone, and the verb stem is uniformly Low in tone. When the subject noun phrase (NP) ends in a Low tone, the tone pattern of the sentence is just what we would expect on the basis of the sentences in (11). The verb stem is Low; the subject bears its inherent (isolation) tones.

(12)   Ézè cị̀  àkhwá    'The chief was carrying eggs.'
      Chief carry eggs    Ézè 'chief' (HL)
      Ụ̀wà cị̀  àkhwá    'Uwa was carrying eggs.'
      Uwa carry eggs    Ụ̀wà (a name) (LL)

However, when the subject NP would normally (i.e., in isolation) end in a High tone, here it undergoes a slight tonal change. As we see in (14), the final H becomes a Falling tone.

(13)   Ékwê cị̀ àkhwá    'Ekwe was carrying eggs.'
                         Ékwé (a name) (HH)
      Àdhâ cị̀ àkhwá    'Adha was carrying eggs.'
                         Àdhá (a name) (LH)

What is happening is clear if we observe the tonal melody. In (13), the drop from the High on the last syllable of the subject NP to the Low of the verb stem is shifted leftward, or "anticipated" on the last syllable of the subject. Using the autosegmental notation, this change is represented as in (14), where the dotted line indicates that the association line was added. The process (15) separates the before and after stages; it says the same thing as (14) in more familiar but less perspicuous notation.

(14)

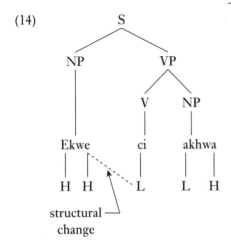

structural —
change

(15)   Ekwe cị akhwa      Ekwe cị akhwa

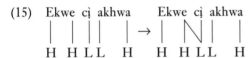

H  H L L   H    H  H L L   H

The point to observe is that the final syllable in *Ekwe* is associated with two tones – H and L – in the derived structures; this is what is identified as a contour tone.

Before proceeding to the behavior of the irregular verbs in the I Main form, let us see what this autosegmental notation has provided us with. By setting the tonal segments or tonemes off on a separate autosegmental level, we were forced to introduce "association lines" to coordinate the two levels in time. We hoped, thereby, to represent contour tones, which is *prima facie* a phenomenon purely internal to the vowel in question. The notation captures precisely, however, the fact that the tone associated with a vowel on the right – here, the verb stem – may associate with a vowel neighboring on the left, causing a change in the righthand side of the latter vowel. Thus we find processes like (16a), but not as in (16b), just as the notation predicts.

(16)   (a)   $\acute{V} \grave{V} \rightarrow \hat{V} \grave{V}$
       (b)   $\acute{V} \grave{V} \rightarrow \check{V} \grave{V}$

The difference between two such rules is intuitively plausible, and in fact borne out in empirical work in tone languages throughout the world. Process (16a) is in some sense a proper "assimilation"; (16b) is not. The representation in (14) makes clear what that sense is; alternative proposals, such as (6) or (7), do not.

Having called the tonal phenomenon in (13) an assimilation, and having characterized it as a "flop" rule as in (14), we have committed ourselves to a view with certain predictions. If the verb stem should be on a Mid tone, for whatever reason, then the falling tone of the subject's final syllable must fall to Mid, rather than to Low. This is in fact true, and is borne out in three separate cases, discussed in [6].

For example, a Low-toned suffix immediately following the stem causes the stem to raise to Mid, as in (17a). The pitch of the utterance is as drawn; the autosegmental representation is as in (17b).

(17)  (a)  H̃â dírì n'ọ́rụ̣          (b)  H̃â diri n'ọrụ

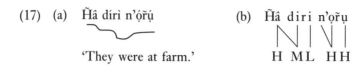

'They were at farm.'                    H  ML  H H

where the accent over *a* means "High vowel falling to a Mid which is level with the following vowel, which must be Mid." The reason for this complicated statement lies in the nature of Downstepping tonemes (the Mid here is one); these are discussed in section 3 below and in [6].

## 1.2    English

The next example is drawn from English, where the neutral intonation pattern is HL, with a star * over the H, indicating that the High tone is associated with the accented syllable.

Consider a polysyllabic word like *archipelago*. It has a tone pattern as in (18).

(18)  archipélago      archipélago

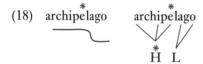

This is derived by linking the starred elements in either level. The Well-formedness Condition of autosegmental theory then comes into play and does the rest. Thus we start with a representation as in (19), with no linkage between the levels; then rule (20) comes into play, creating (21a). The Well-formedness Condition derives (21b) from (21a).

(19)  archipélago        (20)  V̊
         H̊ L                        ⋮
                                    T̊

In (20), as elsewhere, T stands for any arbitrary toneme, and V for any arbitrary vowel; a dotted association line indicates that the rule adds that line.

(21)  (a)  archipélago      (b)  archipélago

(22)  *Well-formedness Condition* (initial statement)
    (a)  All vowels are associated with at least one tone.
        All tones are associated with at least one vowel.
    (b)  Association lines do not cross.

Note that the Well-formedness Condition is in the indicative, not the imperative. A derivation containing a representation that violates it is not thereby marked as ill-formed; rather, the condition is interpreted so as to change the representation minimally by addition or deletion of association lines so as to meet the condition maximally. In the case at hand, (21a) is changed to (21b) minimally by addition of four association lines.

Holding aside one or two small points (cf. the discussion in [6]), the description just given accounts accurately for the assignment of neutral intonation to English words. So far no contour tones have been encountered, but that is because the accented syllable was not final in the example considered. If we consider a word like *balloon*, we get a structure as in (23), corrected to (24) by the Well-formedness Condition.

(23)   balloͦon        (24)   balloͦon

What the theory predicts about English is somewhat reminiscent of tone languages: nonfinal accent is realized as a High tone (as in (22)); final accent is realized as a Falling tone.

This conclusion is also true independent of the length of the final vowel; our search for contour tones on short vowels has led us to English with a clear example. Examples are provided in (25) (the reader will recall that were the final vowels in (25) long, they would undergo diphthongization and Vowel Shift).

(25)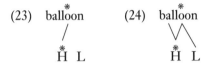

[ . . . ]

## 2   Stability

The second type of phenomenon we shall consider in motivating autosegmental representation is what I have named "stability."[6] In tone languages we find that when a vowel desyllabifies or is deleted by some phonological rule, the tone it bore does not disappear; rather, it shifts its location and shows up on some other vowel. The toneme or tone melody has a stability which is maintained independently of the other aspects of the signal, and thus is preserved despite modifications to the syllabic structure.

Reference to this type of phenomenon in the literature has generally been associated with the notion of "conspiracy" or derivational constraint: in this case, a derivational constraint or conspiracy to move around the tonal specifications from vowel to vowel in order to find on the surface the underlying tone melody. This is not to say that there are no tonal rules that delete or modify the tone melody: certainly there are such rules. But the normal case is where the tone melody survives the effects of phono-logical rules.

If the tone of a vowel is specified by its features, then the pitch of a vowel is just like any other of its characteristics, such as its tenseness or roundedness. If a phonological rule should delete that vowel, then its tonal specifications are deleted along with all other properties. For example, suppose we have a phonological rule deleting a vowel as in (32).

(32)   $V \rightarrow \emptyset / \underline{\quad} V$       V-Deletion

(A common Bantu rule; see e.g. [16: 78, rule (32)].) However, we need to save the tonal information of the deleted vowel, because it shows up on the surface. Looking at tone as a feature of the vowel, we could do this in one of two ways, both similar in intent.

*Solution 1.* We could posit a special "Tone Copy" rule which copies the tone of the to-be-deleted vowel onto its neighbor. We could do this, I should add, if we permit two tonal feature-specifications inside a single vowel segment, the position I have argued against in section 1. But in order to consider the logic of stability independently of that of "contour specifications," let us permit the latter for the moment to be expressed as in (33) below.

(33)   Tone Copy

$$
\begin{bmatrix} V \\ \alpha \text{ high} \\ \beta \text{ low} \end{bmatrix} \begin{bmatrix} V \\ \gamma \text{ high} \\ \delta \text{ low} \end{bmatrix} \rightarrow \begin{bmatrix} V \\ \alpha \text{ high} \\ \beta \text{ low} \end{bmatrix} \begin{bmatrix} \begin{bmatrix} \alpha \text{ high} \\ \beta \text{ low} \end{bmatrix} \begin{bmatrix} \gamma \text{ high} \\ \delta \text{ low} \end{bmatrix} \end{bmatrix}
$$

A typical derivation applying Tone Copy and V-Deletion would be as in (34).

(34)   ...à í...
       ...à ǐ...   Tone Copy
       ...   ǐ...   V-Deletion

*Solution 2.* Second, we could posit a general "derivational constraint" to apply to *all* tonal rules – this is, the approach Spa takes in his grammar of Enya, a Bantu language. He suggests, "when a segment carrying a High tone is deleted or becomes incapable of carrying a tone, the High tone is transferred to the nearest syllabic segment . . . [This constraint] applies each time any rule meets its structural description" [16: 139]. In fact, the correct statement of his derivational constraint should apply to preserve equally both High and Low tones. This modification both simplifies his phonological system and generalizes the derivational constraint.

Solution 2 is explicitly global, and therefore suspect within received generative theory: a theory countenancing global rules approaches vacuity. This solution introduces a general global condition on vowel-affecting rules, and while this seems like an improvement, in that it is a generalization, it is nonetheless worse theoretically because we now permit not only global rules, but a whole new kind of object which is global and applies any-where in the course of a derivation, outside the set of ordered rules. Only solution 1 holds promise, and yet what we find in actual work is that for every case of vowel-deletion or desyllabification, we must set up another case of tone-copying, and thus we have missed a generalization. But the generalization is precisely solution 2, the general derivational constraint. A paradoxical situation: to effect a satisfactory linguistic solu-tion, we need to state a generalization; but inclusion of this generalization within the standard theory amounts to a serious weakening of the theory of phonology. We have reached a crisis point.

We might note that even if we did include the derivational constraint, in the belief that constraining a theory must always take a back seat to stating a generalization, three important questions would be left unanswered: First, why are tonal features copied, but not the other features? What makes them special? Second, what is meant by a representation with two feature-specifications inside a single vowel (the issue pursued in section 1)? Is there a connection between the fact that there can be contour tones and the phenomenon of stability – apparently so different? Third, and most telling, the "conspiracy" to preserve tonal melodies extends past a derivational constraint that whisks the tone off of a sinking vowel. In fact, in a tone language where the derivational constraint seems to generally hold, what we find is that vowel assimilation rules such as (35) copy all vowel features up to, but *not* including, tone features.

(35)   $V \rightarrow \begin{bmatrix} \alpha \text{ High} \\ \beta \text{ Back} \\ \gamma \text{ Round} \\ \delta \text{ ATR} \\ \cdots \end{bmatrix} / - \begin{bmatrix} \alpha \text{ High} \\ \beta \text{ Back} \\ \gamma \text{ Round} \\ \delta \text{ ATR} \\ \cdots \end{bmatrix}$

A rule like (35) certainly exists in Igbo and Yoruba, and in Enya according to Spa [16: 47, 57]. So if two vowels come together, each with its own tone, then either one vowel is deleted and its tone is retained, as in (32), or one assimilates in quality in every regard save tone. The only empirical difference lies in the length and syllable quality of the remaining vowel(s). From the point of view of tone and its conspir-acies the same fate has come to pass. Yet the derivational constraint speaks only to the case with deletion, not the case of nearly complete assimilation: thus missing the generalization.

This is the logic of the situation. Let us look at some actual cases in more detail.

Consider two articles by Julie Lovins [11] on Lomongo, whose tonological rules, she suggests, "conspire, individually or in concert, to derive surface tone patterns on words and phrases without changing the underlying melody." Central to the analysis is what Lovins calls "tone composition," in which "the tones stay where they are when segmentals are deleted." She continues with an example, "if two vowels are juxtaposed, within a word or across word boundary, it is usual for the first vowel to be elided. Its tone remains and combines with that of the following vowel." For example,

(36)  bàlóngó bǎkáé    →   bàlóngǎkáé    'his book'
      bánà bǎmǒ        →   bánǎmǒ        'other children'
      bǒmǒ bòtámbá     →   bǒmǒtámbá     'another tree'
      bǎtswá là èmí    →   bǎtswêmí      'you who lead me away'

With a number of similar examples, Lovins concludes, "The only derived forms that occur are the ones that preserve the underlying melody . . . and the only way to get these derived forms is to posit a species of rule application that many linguists find objectionable." She is certainly correct, given the standard framework; and she is exceptional among writers on this subject in recognizing the implications for phonological theory of the type of rule she posits.

The existence of the tone melody's "stability" is our concern: how can it be that a tone refuses to be deleted when its vowel is deleted? In autosegmental formalism, this is precisely what is predicted. In any theory of generative phonology, a deletion rule deletes a *segment*. Now, if a rule – (32) for example, V-Deletion – should delete a vowel, it does not delete any of the tone segments that the vowel is associated with, since those tone segments are separate segments. The worst that can happen is that the tone segments will be left "orphaned" or free, without a vowel associated with them. That will be the interesting case to look at in detail.

The point we have just seen should be emphasized: the stability phenomenon, formerly paradoxical, is a natural consequence of the autosegmental system – not by proposing a constraint on rules, but rather by proposing in effect a new geometrical shape (in a somewhat abstract sense) for formal representations.

Let us consider in more detail the reduplication treated in Lovins's papers. Verbs are lexically marked for tone, H or L; the stem is reduplicated and an /a/ infix is added between the two copies of the stem. An L or H desinence then follows.

(37)  L-toned stem *sik* 'stop'

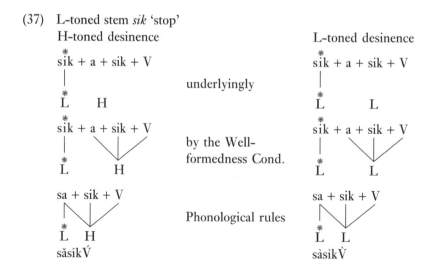

The last stage is reached by pure phonological rules: $k \rightarrow \emptyset$ and $ia \rightarrow a$.

(38)   H-toned stem *lomb* 'be shy'

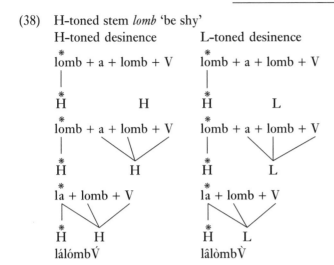

In short, from the notation we get the "conspiratorial" results automatically by keeping the syllabic and the tonal levels formally separate. It may be noted that we get the desinence tone spreading automatically,[7] as well as a formal understanding of the notion "contour tone." Furthermore, the process of total vowel assimilation – construed as, e.g., (39) – has the desired property of copying all features up to, but not including, tone features, since tone features are not features of vowels.

(39)      X . +syllabic . +syllabic . Y
     SD: 1     2        3        4 →
     SC: 1     3        3        4

The resolution of the paradox in tonal stability was derived from viewing tones as segments on an equal rank with "phonological" segments. This parallelism can be pursued; in fact, we find in general perfect formal symmetry between the two levels. The "dual," then, of vowel deletion would be tone deletion, followed by reassociation to another tone by the vowel that had been associated with the deleted tone. This in fact occurs; see the discussion of the II Main form in Igbo in [6] and Sanskrit [13].

## 3   Melody Levels

The third type of argument for autosegmental theory is motivated by the existence of "melody levels." As explained above, these are linguistically significant levels in the grammar which refer to just one or two features in the utterance. *Faute de mieux*, this has been taken sometimes to indicate tone features as "features of an entire morpheme," in some unexplained sense.

Let us begin with an example from Mende, a Mande tone language. The analysis is due to Leben [10].

On short vowels in Mende, we can find Low, High, Rising, Falling, or Rising–Falling tones. Morphemes are one to three syllables long, and if the distribution of tones over these syllables were random, we would expect to find five tonal classes of 1-syllable words, $5^2$ or 25 classes of 2-syllable words, and $5^3$ or 125 classes of 3-syllable words: 155 types in all. In fact, there are 5 classes for each, not $5^n$, and they are of a very particular sort. Leben explains this by proposing that there are only five available underlying melodies in Mende, and that the melody is mapped from left to right onto the word. The five possibilities are:

(40)   H      pɛ́lɛ́, kɔ́
         L      bɛ̀lɛ̀, kpà
         HL    kényà, mbû
         LH    nìká, nàvó, mbǎ
         LHL   nìkílì, nyàhâ, mbǎ

Such an analysis, we might note, supports the contention that contour tones are the concatenation of level tones, and that short vowels (and these in (40) are) may bear several ordered level tones.

## 3.1   Tiv verbal system

The next example is somewhat more complex and more interesting. The Tiv verbal system has been the subject of a sequence of more and more refined analyses, including Arnott's exposition [1], McCawley's reanalysis [14], and Leben's proposal [10]. The present reanalysis departs from Leben's in one particular way; I shall indicate that the inclusion of Leben's principle (which I shall call the Obligatory Contour Principle) leads to unnecessary complications, and that it should be abandoned. This leads to certain particulars that are different from their counterparts in Leben's analysis; it should be kept in mind that although I am using autosegmental notation here, the principal empirical differences between Leben's analysis and mine result from the inclusion or rejection of the "Obligatory Contour Principle," which may be stated as:

> *Obligatory Contour Principle* (Leben)
> At the melodic level of the grammar, any two adjacent tonemes must be distinct. Thus HHL is not a possible melodic pattern; it automatically simplifies to HL.

As I say, I shall argue against the inclusion of such a principle within phonological theory at the phonological or tonological level.[8] [ . . . ]

## 4   Floating Tones

Next we will consider the nature of "floating tones," a device that has proven useful in working with tone languages but whose theoretical status has always been suspect.

A floating tone is, in essence, a segment specified only for a tone which, at some point during the derivation, merges with some vowel, thus passing on its tonal specifications to that vowel. This is, in any event, the traditional view; and this traditional view, framed within the standard theory, fixes the floating tone as one of the segments, and therefore linearly ordered amongst all the other, more completely specified segments of the phonological representation.

Thus it has been suggested that certain affixes are purely tonal; Bird, for example, posits a floating L tone for the Bambara definite marker on nouns, cited in [10].

We shall say, and we shall see, that floating tones are melodic levels, much as in the previous section, that map onto the syllabic structure in a slightly more complex way than the Tiv forms. Often floating tones associate after some phonological/tonological rules have applied, though this is not always true.

Igbo presents several interesting cases of floating tones, analyzed in detail in chapter 2 of [6]. For the present, let us consider the general outlines of their behavior.

We will look at the preverbal floating H tone, a mark of subordinate clauses. We will content ourselves here with observing its behavior, leaving aside the factors conditioning its presence. If a tone "floats" when it has no vowel associated with it, let us say that the process of associating a floating tone is "docking."

We shall see four separate cases of "docking" of this preverbal H tone, four kinds of docking that are predictable on autosegmental grounds, and on no other.

To describe these effects, we must review some of the basics of the structure of Igbo. It is a Subject–Verb–Object (SVO) language; singular subject pronouns (though not plural) have two forms, noncliticizing or Strong and cliticizing or Weak. The cliticization of the subject pronoun, however, includes a syntactic movement. In certain tenses, that is, the verb stem is normally preceded by the prefix *a–* when the subject is a noun phrase (NP). This *a* is realized as *e* when the verb stem is in the 'tense' vowel harmony class. Thus, if the subject is *ányì* ('we', not a clitic) and the stem is *za*, we find (63).

(63)   ányì ázàá   àlà        za = sweep
       we   sweep floor    (stem followed by suffix -a)
       'we swept the floor'

If the subject cliticizes, the prefix *a–* disappears, because, we shall see, the cliticization puts the clitic subject into the *a*-prefix position. Thus we get (64).

(64)   ó̩ zàá àlà   'he swept he floor'   o̩ = he, she

We may formalize this operation as (65), illustrated in (66).

(65)   $\begin{bmatrix} \text{Pronoun} \\ \text{Weak} \end{bmatrix} \begin{bmatrix} \text{Verb} \\ \text{Prefix} \end{bmatrix}$   Subject Cliticization

              1              2 →
              Ø              1

(66)

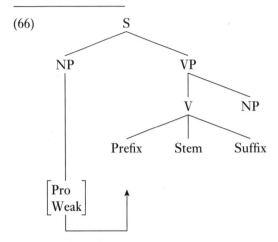

Such a rule must be a local rule, in Emonds's sense, given the general structure-preserving framework (see [3]). Therefore, if any element could appear in between the Weak subject and the prefix position, it would block this cliticization process, and thus keep the *a* prefix from disappearing.

The *na* relative-clause marker does precisely that. In a structure such as in (67), the clitic subject stays where it starts, and it co-occurs with the *a* prefix.

(67)

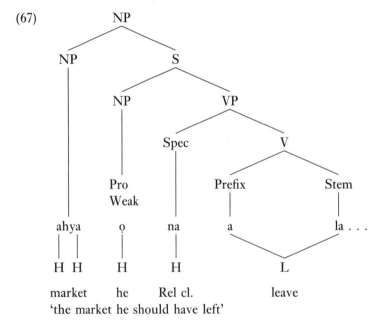

'the market he should have left'

The picture in (67) is important; around it will revolve our argument. The tone attached there with the relative-clause marker *na* is the floating tone H. We shall see that under other circumstances, that same H tone docks on other vowels, depending, we might say, on what is "closest" to it in derived structure.

We have seen first that the *na*, when present, is H-toned. The *na* may be *not* present, for two reasons: first, in a relative clause, it is optional; thus we may simply delete it and see what the derived structure is. As we observed in section 2, when we discussed tone stability, we expect the H tone to appear elsewhere. Second, and quite differently, while the *na* always marks a relative clause when it appears, the H tone appears in other subordinate clauses indicating adverbial dependency (that is, in sentences translatable as "Lest X happen, . . ."). In this second case, the H tone is not a remnant of a deleted *na*, for the *na* could not have been there in the first place.

In both cases when the subject of the clause is a normal noun (noncliticizing, that is), the final tone of the subject is raised. For example, the noun *ọ̀nụ̀* (a type of yam) shows up as *ọ̀nụ̌* in the relative clause *ọ̀nụ̌ rèré èré* 'the onu that is rotten' (*rèré èré* is a complex predicate meaning 'is rotten'). Here, as elsewhere in Igbo, the contour tone LH gener- ally simplifies to what is called a Mid tone in Igbo, but which is precisely the same as the Drop tone (D) in Tiv. Its tone is slightly lower than the first preceding High tone. But since any High tone is slightly lower than a preceding High tone if the two are separated by a Low tone, High and Mid (or Drop) are indistinguishable after a Low tone. Thus in this position, LL nouns become L + Rising or L Mid; HL nouns become H + Rising, or more commonly H + Mid, as in (68).

(68)  ázụ̌ rèré èré  'the fish that was rotten'
      ázụ̀ 'fish'

Nouns that end in a High tone do not change; see (69).

(69)  ánụ́ rèré èrú (ánụ́ 'meat')
      àkwhá rèré èrú (àkwhá 'eggs')

In all these cases, the *na* could have been present, attracted the High tone, and then these nouns would have displayed their isolation tones as cited. In the following sen- tences, the *na* may not appear, since these are not relative clauses, and the same subject tone raising occurs as noted above.

(70)  Khwàchíé úzò
      Shut the door lest . . .

| ághú | ègbùò éghú | | ághú | | |
| leopard | kill | goat | 'leopard' | | HH |
| òké | àtàà ákhú | | òké | | |
| rat | eat | palm kernels | 'rat' | | LH |
| úžè | àtàà yá | | úžè | | |
| squirrel | eat | them | 'squirrel' | | HL |
| ènwó | àtàà yá | | ènwò | | |
| monkey | eat | them | 'monkey' | | LL |

If in one of these "lest . . ." clauses, as in (70), the subject were a weak cliticizing pronoun, it would undergo the cliticization expressed in (65) and (66) above. Looking at the tree in (67), we see it would then be to the right of the H tone, in a certain sense; inasmuch as the cliticized pronoun partakes of the verb stem's L-tone just as the *a* prefix in (67), the H-tone docking rightward now will give rise to a *Falling* tone! All this is clear geometrically: see (71).

(71)

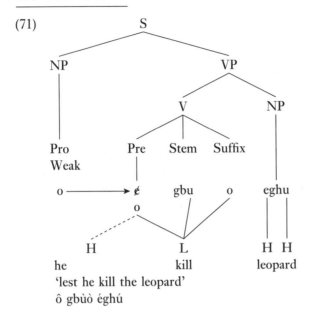

'lest he kill the leopard'
ô gbùò éghú

Lastly, when the relative clause or subordinate clause is constructed appropriately, the H tone can dock right out of its clause. Thus, if the subject is a clitic, and moves by rule (65) over the floating H (much as in (71)), the floating H may then dock leftwards onto what is to its left. If we have a relative clause where the head is coreferential with an NP in some position other than subject in the relative clause, we get a situation as in (72), and one can say either (73a), maintaining the *na*, or (73b), where the floating tone docks leftward onto the head *m̀gbè*.

(72)

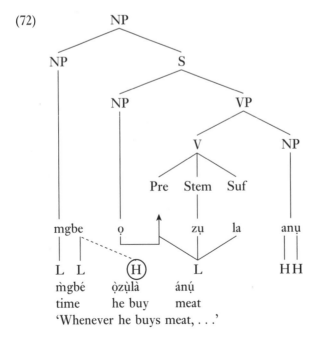

'Whenever he buys meat, . . .'

(73)   (a)   m̀gbè   ọ́náàzụ̀là ánụ́ . . .
       (b)   m̀gbè   ọ̀zùlạ̀ ánụ́ . . .

In summary, the floating H tone appearing before the verb in certain tenses in Igbo docks onto various vowels depending on the derived syntactic structure: the end of the subject of the clause it is in, or the beginning of the subject clitic pronoun of that clause, or the grammatical particle *na*, or the head of the relative clause.

## 5  Automatic Spreading

The fifth and last argument for autosegmental phonology here comes from the phenomenon of bidirectional spreading and, we would suggest, its *un*governed nature in these cases; that is, the spreading is not due to a specific phonological rule, but rather to the geometry of autosegmental representations, and its Well-formedness Condition.

It should be clear from the examples in each section how the Well-formedness Condition creates the spreading of tonemes over various syllables automatically; we have seen examples from English, Mende, and Igbo. In this section, I will look at a particularly interesting example, one in which the autosegmentalized level is not tone, but rather nasalization. The language is Guarani; the data and much of the initial arrangement of it comes from Lunt [12] and especially Rivas [15].

Let us begin by considering the forms that morphemes may take. We observe in (74) that there are basically two forms for the affixes *no*, *ro*, and *i*: each have a basically nasal form and a basically oral form.

(74)   (a)   ⁿdo + ro + haɨhu + i   (oral stem)
       (b)   nõ + r̃õ + h̃ẽⁿdú + i   (oral stem with nasal in it)
       (c)   nõ + r̃õ + nũp̃ã́ + ĩ   (nasal stem)

The prefix *nõ* thus alternates with *ⁿdo*, as does *r̃õ* with *ro*, and *ĩ* with *i*. Which alternate appears is determined by the stem, the morpheme which contains the acute accent in the examples above. In general, a vowel with an accent in Guarani is also one endowed with a nasality melody or specification. That is, if we say nasality is autosegmentalized in Guarani, we specify that the nasality melodies (essentially just Oral or Nasal) are initially associated with accented vowels, just as we saw in section 1.2 that the tone melody in English was initially associated with the accented vowel. In addition, true nasal consonants are endowed with an inherent Nasal specification on the autosegmental level (these true nasal consonants are *m*, *n*, *n*, *ŋ*, *ŋʷ*). We shall represent a stem as in (74a) by (75a); a stem as in (74b) by (75b).

(75)   (a)   haɨh*u       (b)   he D*u
                 /                   | |
                 *                   *
                 o                   NO

(For explanation of new symbols, see text.) The symbol D represents all the normal feature specifications of an *n* except for nasality – raised tongue, and so forth. When associated with a [+nasal] autosegment, the two of them *are* an *n*. The O symbolizes [−nasal]; N symbolizes [+nasal] (read "oral" and "nasal," respectively). As above, the star * indicates an accent; corresponding autosegments are accented (starred) also.

The Well-formedness Condition must apply to the forms in (75). The form in (75a) becomes all oral, as in (74a). The form in (75b) becomes the form in (76), which would be transcribed as *h̃ẽnu* in the standard theory.

(76)  heD̊u

The empirical difference between the form created by the Well-formedness Condition and the actual form is that the Condition does not create forms like ⁿ*d*, the prenasalized stops. This is not, however, a bad result; the prenasalized stop is a complex configuration, and the universal theory should not produce them automatically. Rather, the language-particular rule (77) creates the form as in (74b) from the form in (76). When we apply (77), Postoralization, to (76), we get the correct form.

(77)  Guarani Postoralization Rule:   C   V

N   O

(The reader will recall that the dotted line in an autosegmental rule indicates the addition of an autosegmental line by that rule.)

With this autosegmental interpretation of the data, let us derive the forms in (74) precisely. We note that when the Well-formedness Condition applies here, if there is an ambiguity as to whether a starred or an unstarred autosegment spreads, it is the starred element that does.

(78)   Do + ro + haihu + i       Do + ro + heD̊u + i       Do + ro + Dupa + i

N                O         N                NO         N                N   N

(78) represents the underlying forms. The Well-formedness Condition changes these to (79);[9] rule (77) Postoralization creates (80), the correct output (compare (74)).

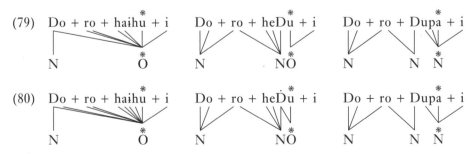

(79)   Do + ro + haihu + i       Do + ro + heD̊u + i       Do + ro + Dupa + i

N                O         N                NO         N                N   N

(80)   Do + ro + haihu + i       Do + ro + heD̊u + i       Do + ro + Dupa + i

N                O         N                NO         N                N   N

As expected, we have seen that prefixes and suffixes adopt their nasality from the stem they are attached to. These prefixes are found with the usual +morpheme boundary. Note that this bidirectionality of spreading is expressed only with additional specification if handled by a phonological rule; within autosegmental theory, the bidirectionality of the spreading is the result, in a sense, of the fact that there are prenasalized stops! That is, the existence of the prenasalized stops required the autosegmental analysis, which in turn brought with it bidirectional spreading. In summary, borrowing from Rivas [15], suffixal nasality spreading is as in (81).

(81)   $\widetilde{\text{Stem}}$ + suf → $\widetilde{\text{stem}}$ + $\widetilde{\text{suf}}$  (nasal)

   $\overline{\text{Stem}}$ + suf → $\overline{\text{stem}}$ + $\overline{\text{suf}}$ (oral)

   $\widetilde{\overline{\text{Stem}}}$ + suf → $\widetilde{\text{st}}\overline{\text{em}}$ + $\overline{\text{suf}}$ (nasal-oral)

There are also suffixes separated by word boundary (#) endowed with their own nasality specification, according to Rivas [15], as in (82).

(82)   ## Stem # Suffix ##

   ||      |      ||

   ## αNas # βNas ##

We see in (82) what has been only implicit up to this point: the universal convention that corresponding word boundaries, but not morpheme boundaries, are connected by association lines.

Another logical possibility is predicted by the notation so far: why could there not be an accented suffix – that is, one with its own nasality melody – but one which has only a morpheme boundary, not a word boundary. With a morpheme boundary, there will be no association line, and the nasality autosegments of the stem and the suffix will interact. We predict, then, the following type of suffix, one which meets the description given by Rivas for the –ré suffix.

From –ré, endowed with an oral melody on its stressed vowel, we derive ĩr̃ũré, as in (83). Autosegmental theory does not predict whether the second r is nasal or oral; when surrounded by vowels with conflicting specification as in (83), such a determination is not possible.

(83)   iru + re

   (with nasality tiers) N + O

When –re is placed on a nasal stem with a nasal consonant to the right of the accent (such as měnã) we get the correct result, as illustrated in (84), a remarkable form.

(84)   B e D a + r e      B e D a + r e

   | | |     | → | |  ＼      mé$^{\text{n}}$daré

   N N N     O   N N N      O

# 6   Conclusion

In the five general cases reviewed in the foregoing sections, we have seen that phenomena that are puzzling on the standard view of phonological representations are quite tractable and reasonable when viewed from an autosegmental perspective. We have seen, furthermore, connections between these phenomena that are not otherwise revealed. If we may draw some morals from this result, perhaps they are that advances in phonological theory may start from an interest in low-level articulatory facts; that if they are interesting, they go beyond these superficial facts to unexpected phenomena; and most importantly, that we do not begin our research with an understanding of the nature of the most elementary linguistic observables. The most astounding revelations may be those that change our conception of what we thought were the observables, either in phonology or semantics. We should not restrict our attention to constraints on rules – phonological, syntactic, or semantic – at the risk of missing the very nature of the items involved.

## Notes

This work is a revision of chapter 1 of Ref. 6. I am very grateful for the advice and encouragement of Morris Halle throughout the development of this work; Paul Kiparsky, Will Leben, and Mark Liberman have also made numerous suggestions, for which I am grateful. This work was supported by a grant from the National Institute of Health 5 TO 1 HD00111-10.

1   The requirement of "short" here is meant to avoid the possibility that a long vowel might actually be two successive short vowels, each with a level tone. This, of course, does happen frequently; it is, however, irrelevant in the present context. The situation is much the same for prenasalized stops: in some languages, these stops are clearly *one* segment, even though they have two successive feature-specifications for nasality.

2   For example, "Suprasegmental tones are by definition independent of any segments – rather than being expressed as features on segments, they are features on larger linguistic units" [10: 26].

3   One could, in this regard, accept the suggestion of Woo [17] that *all* contour tones are necessarily such concatenations. The logic of the situation would not be much changed; we would simply not need to investigate the particular language in question to come to the conclusion mentioned in the text.

4   We shall, for the sake of definiteness, assume a theory of tonal features that is defended at more length in [6]. We adopt two binary pitch features: ±Highpitch and ±Lowpitch.

$$\begin{bmatrix} +\text{Highpitch} \\ -\text{Lowpitch} \end{bmatrix} = \text{High tone (H)}$$

$$\begin{bmatrix} -\text{Highpitch} \\ +\text{Lowpitch} \end{bmatrix} = \text{Low tone (L)}$$

$$\begin{bmatrix} -\text{Highpitch} \\ -\text{Lowpitch} \end{bmatrix} = \text{Mid tone (M)}$$

The fourth possible combination

$$\begin{bmatrix} +\text{Highpitch} \\ +\text{Lowpitch} \end{bmatrix}$$

will tentatively be excluded by a universal principle. The distinction between tone and pitch is drawn in chapter 2 of [6].

5   In the present example I shall consider forms with no suffixes on the verb for simplicity of presentation. More extensive data are discussed in [6].

6   This phenomenon of stability is the subject of [5], from which this section draws heavily; further examples not mentioned here are treated there.

7   A discussion of this general type of phenomenon is the content of section 5 below.

8   In particular, I claim that it is not true at levels in the grammar where phonological and tonological rules apply. Leben's system requires there to be sequences of identically toned vowels (CV́CV́CV́) after his "tone mapping"; thus, for him, the Obligatory Contour Principle holds at the abstract levels but not at the superficial levels. In chapter 4 of [6], I argue that the opposite holds.

9   The reason why the starred autosegment has precedence in spreading in these cases, as opposed to cases like (21), is detailed in chapter 3 of [6].

# References

1   Arnott, D. 1964. Downstep in the Tiv verbal system. *African Language Studies* 5: 34–51.

2   Chomsky, N. and Halle, M. 1968. *The Sound Pattern of English*. New York: Harper and Row.

3   Emonds, J. 1970. Root and structure preserving transformations. Ph.D. dissertation, MIT.

4   Goldsmith, J. 1975. An autosegmental typology of tone. In *Papers from the Fifth Annual Meeting of the North Eastern Linguistics Society*, Harvard University.

5   Goldsmith, J. 1975. Tone melodies and the autosegment. In *Proceedings of the Sixth Conference on African Linguistics*, Ohio State University Working Papers in Linguistics no. 20.

6   Goldsmith, J. 1976. Autosegmental Phonology. Ph.D. dissertation, MIT. Published New York: Garland Press, 1979.

7   Goldsmith, J. 1981. English as a tone language. In D. Goyvaerts (ed.), *Phonology in the 1980s*, Ghent: Story Scientia, 287–308.

8   Green, M. and Igwe, G. 1963. *A Descriptive Grammar of Igbo*. Oxford: Oxford University Press.

9   Haraguchi, S. 1975. The tone pattern of Japanese. Ph.D. dissertation, MIT.

10  Leben, W. 1973. Suprasegmental phonology. Ph.D. dissertation, MIT.

11  Lovins, J. 1971. The tonology of Lomongo reduplication. *Studies in African Linguistics* 2: 257–70. See also, Melodic levels in Lomongo tonology. In *Papers from the Seventh Regional Meeting, Chicago Linguistics Society*, 1971.

12  Lunt, H. 1973. Remarks on nasality: the case of Guarani. In S. Anderson and Paul Kiparsky (eds), *A Festschrift for Morris Halle*, New York: Holt, Rinehart and Winston.

13  May, R. and Goldsmith, J. MS. Tone sandhi in Sanskrit.

14  McCawley, J. 1970. A note on tone in Tiv conjugation. *Studies in African Linguistics* 1: 123–9.

15  Rivas, A. 1975. Nasalization in Guarani. In *Papers from the Fifth Annual Meeting of the North Eastern Linguistics Society*, Harvard University.

16  Spa, J. 1973. Traits et tons en Enya, phonologie générative d'une langue Bantoue. Ph.D. dissertation, Tervuren, Belgique: Musée Royal de l'Afrique Centrale.

17  Woo, N. 1969. Prosody and phonology. Ph.D. dissertation, MIT.

# 9

# A Prosodic Theory of Nonconcatenative Morphology (1981)

## John J. McCarthy

Most structuralist accounts of morphological structure overtly or implicitly make a distinction between two formal morphological types. *Concatenative morphology*, which in the more familiar languages appears almost exclusively, involves prefixation or suffixation only. Thus, morphemes are discrete elements linearly concatenated at the right or the left end of the base of the morphological operation. Morphology of this type is subject to analysis by a relatively simple discovery procedure. Given an adequate phonological representation, concatenative morphemes can be recovered by a left-to-right (or right-to-left) parse of words searching for invariant recurrent partial strings, possibly with constant meaning or function (Hockett 1947).

The other type, *nonconcatenative morphology*, has remained rather more mysterious until now. Generally, in structuralist treatments we find only a list of the residue, those morphological operations that cannot be analyzed by the method of recurrent partials. These include reduplication, infixation, morphologically governed ablaut, and suprafixation. All of these terms are in common use except the last, which refers to, for example, the variation in tonal pattern of the stem as a mark of verbal aspect inflection in Tiv (McCawley 1970, Goldsmith 1976). Although nonconcatenative morphology as a whole has received less attention than concatenative, this is not for lack of exemplification. In a number of languages, processes like reduplication are the primary or sole morphological operations.

This residual status accorded nonconcatenative morphology in structuralist analyses extends to generative theories as well. All generative treatments known to me have relied entirely on the extremely rich transformational notation of Chomsky and Halle (1968). What is offered here instead is a new theory of nonconcatenative morphology, one which owes a great deal to Harris's (1941, 1951) notion of long components. It is a prosodic theory in the sense that it uses the devices of autosegmental phonology, which are most familiar through studies of tone and other prosody. This theory is justified extensively in this article by an analysis of the formal properties of the system of verbal derivation and aspect and voice inflection in Classical Arabic. A similar treatment of other verbal inflection and of nominal derivation and inflection can be found in McCarthy (1979).

To conclude this introduction, I will map out the overall geography of this article. Section 1 outlines the problem of the Arabic verb and its relevance to a theory of nonconcatenative morphology. Sections 2.1 and 2.2 present and partially justify much of the formal apparatus that is essential to the later analysis. Section 3 contains the analysis of the Arabic verb, with an occasional excursus into related issues in Tiberian Hebrew. Section 4 deals with the question of the form of morphological rules in this model. It also has some particular observations on reduplication and the extension of this treatment to non-Semitic languages.

## 1   Statement of the Problem

One of the classic linguistic issues is that of providing an account of the nonconcatenative morphological system prevailing in most members of the Semitic language family. Unlike the more familiar basically concatenative morphology of the Indo-European languages, Semitic morphology is pervaded by a wide variety of purely morphological alternations internal to the stem. In Arabic, for instance, there is a clear sense in which the forms in (1) are morphologically related to one another, although they do not share isolable strings of segments in concatenated morphemes:[1]

(1)   (a)   kataba 'he wrote'
      (b)   kattaba 'he caused to write'
      (c)   kaataba 'he corresponded'
      (d)   takaatabuu 'they kept up a correspondence'
      (e)   ktataba 'he wrote, copied'
      (f)   kitaabun 'book (nom.)'
      (g)   kuttaabun 'Koran school (nom.)'
      (h)   kitaabatun 'act of writing (nom.)'
      (i)   maktabun 'office (nom.)'

Even the fairly elaborate paradigm in (1) is far from exhaustive; for instance, it does not include inflectional alternations like *kutiba* 'it was written' and *makaatibu* 'offices (nom.)'.

Certain observations about this morphological system, crucial to an understanding of it, date from a very early period. It has long been known that at its basis there are roots of three or four consonants which cluster around a single semantic field, like *ktb* 'write'. Certain changes in these roots, like gemination of the middle radical in (1b), yield derivatives such as causative or agentive. Moreover, some vowel patterns seem to bear consistent meaning, like the difference in stem vocalism between active *kataba* and passive *kutiba*.

In the very earliest studies – the treatments by medieval Arabic and Hebrew grammarians, generally adopted in the work of Western Orientalists – an elaborated morphophonemic theory is complemented by only the most rudimentary analysis of paradigms like (1). This approach is usually a fairly superficial taxonomy, mediated by a notation that simply shows the citation root *fʕl* (Hebrew *pʕl*) 'do', with appropriate stem modifications. So the basic insight of these classical grammarians was to abstract away from the particular root, but with no richer understanding of the formal morphological system than this. So far as I know, there was no general treatment of relations between vowel patterns except as instantiated on a particular root.

The first modern insights into these problems appear in Harris's (1941) analysis of biblical Hebrew and Chomsky's (1951) grammar of modern Hebrew, both of which

are discussed in some detail in the appendix to this article [not repr. here]. The fundamental characteristic of Chomsky's proposal is a rule moving (or intercalating) long
component vowel patterns into triconsonantal roots ((61) in the appendix), relying crucially on transformational rule notation and integral subscripts on segments in the structural description. In view of the fact that Chomsky (1951) contains all the notational
apparatus later adopted by Chomsky and Halle (1968), it could reasonably be claimed
that transformational morphological rules, essentially similar to Chomsky's, form the
basis of the analysis of Semitic nonconcatenative morphology within the generative
tradition.

A problem closely related to the formal character of morphological rules is the formal
character of morphemes, the units that those rules manipulate. Again the standard theory
makes a fairly explicit proposal: a morpheme is a string of segments delimited by the
symbol "+" which contains no internal "+." A somewhat richer notion of the morpheme
is proposed and justified in section 2.1.

Another necessary characteristic of a morphological analysis is a theory of the structure of the lexicon and of lexical entries. The basic view, adopted by Chomsky and
Halle (1968), that the lexicon is a list of single morphemes only and that these units are
subject to lexical insertion, has been convincingly dismissed by Halle (1973), Jackendoff
(1975), and Aronoff (1976). There is no need to repeat these arguments here, so I shall
simply take it for granted that the lexicon is composed of words rather than morphemes.
Therefore, the processes described here can be seen as applying redundantly rather
than generatively, except in the case of neologisms. Nothing of significance in what
follows hinges on this assumption, however.

## 2   Formalism

### 2.1   The representation of morphemes

It is well known that a number of idiosyncratic morphological and phonological properties cluster around words like *permit*, *subsume*, and *submit*, with Latinate prefixes and
stems. In the verb form, stress invariably falls on the final syllable in spite of the possibility of further retraction. Certain special assimilation and deletion rules apply at the
boundary between the prefix and stem; compare *admit*, *assume*, *attempt*, *appear*, *accept*.
Finally, as Aronoff (1976) notes, the types of nominalizations of these forms are determined entirely by the stem morphemes: *submission*, *permission* with *mit* versus *assumption*,
*consumption* with *sume*.

This clustering of properties means that the grammar must be able to recognize
words of this type as a class composed of Latinate prefix and stem morphemes. But the
exact delineation of morphemes in the representation of these words is an empirical
question for which there are two alternative solutions.

One theory, essentially the one followed by Chomsky and Halle (1968), would
analyze *permit* as a sequence of two morphemes separated by a boundary but without
internal hierarchic or cyclic structure: *per + mit*. (It is irrelevant here whether this class
has a special boundary like "=" or not.) The boundary allows us to recognize *permit*
words as a class – they contain an internal boundary but have no other structure.

In some interesting proposals for the treatment of various junctural phenomena, Rotenberg (1978) and Selkirk (1984) present convincing arguments against the use of boundary symbols in phonological representations. They claim instead that junctural rules actually refer not to boundaries but to hierarchic morphological structure itself, structure that results from deriving one word from another. Notice that here we have an obvious problem for this theory: there is no likely internal hierarchic structure in *permit* class words, but nevertheless several rules must have access to some sort of morphological analysis of them.

There is, however, a third formal possibility. This alternative is implicit in work by Zellig Harris (1951) and essentially involves an extension of his notion of the *long component*. While the boundary solution basically says that morphemes are delimited by symbols in the segmental string, the long component theory claims that the string of segments is uninterrupted, but the morphological analysis is given by another, simultaneous level of representation. Harris's long components were designed to handle discontinuous phenomena – in particular, the Semitic roots that figure prominently in this article. But it requires very little to extend a long component analysis to include segmentally continuous morphemes like *per* or *mit*.

The formal basis of this interpretation is essentially the notation of autosegmental phonology (Goldsmith 1976). Formally, I will define a morpheme as an ordered string of $1 \times n$ feature matrices associated autosegmentally with a root node $\mu$. This is schematized in (2):

(2)

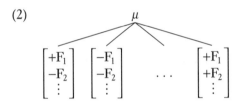

The root node $\mu$ identifies this string as a particular morpheme. Moreover, $\mu$ bears all nonphonological information associated with the morpheme, such as rule diacritics, whether it is a root or an affix, and in fact its identity as a morpheme. Note that this is not intended as a substitute for hierarchic structure where that structure is motivated. It does, however, replace all delimitation of morphemes by boundary symbols like "+." A similar proposal, though not cast in autosegmental terms, was made by Pyle (1972).

Any basically concatenative morphological system, like ordinary English morphology, has a very simple translation into this notation. For any $1 \times n$ feature matrix dominated by $\mu$, $n$ equals the cardinality of the set of all phonological features, and the daughters of any $\mu$ form a continuous segmental string. So, for example, *permit* will be represented as in (3):

(3)  $\mu$  $\mu$

[per mit]$_{N,V}$

This sort of representation achieves the desired end. The grammar can refer to *per* and *mit* as separate morphemes with special phonological and morphological properties, without reference to boundary symbols. Because separate nodes μ dominate *per* and *mit*, they are necessarily interpreted as distinct morphemes. Clearly, this proposal will trivially extend to the rest of English morphology as well.

A number of arguments can be developed in support of this position. The first type consists essentially of formal arguments, presented in some detail by Pyle (1972). The second type, given here, consists of actual cases where the μ-notation is richer than the boundary notation in ways that are essential to the expression of linguistic generalizations.

What is perhaps the most compelling argument for this characterization of the morpheme is the basic organization of the Arabic (and Semitic) lexicon around the consonantal root. All verb forms of Arabic can be partitioned into 15 derivational classes, which I will refer to by the Hebrew term *binyāním* (singular *binyắn*). I will deal with the formal properties of the binyanim in detail below. What we will be concerned with here is the derivational source of the various binyanim – what other forms in the language they appear to be most closely related to and derived from. This question is very difficult to answer for the first Arabic binyan. It is probably never derived from a verb of some other binyan, but it is usually impossible to say whether some nouns are derived from this binyan or this binyan from the nouns. Consequently, I will not discuss the source of the first binyan further in this section.

However, there is often clear evidence of a particular derivational source for a given verb of some other binyan. This sort of evidence includes the absence of any other binyanim (including the first) formed on a particular root, as well as specific semantic relationships to related nouns or verbs. It is this sort of evidence that is uncontroversially reflected in the following generalizations.

The forms in most binyanim, except the first, are derived from other binyanim of the same root or from nouns of the same root. For instance, some representative derivational relationships are exemplified in (4):

(4)   | | *Derived form* | *Derivational source* |
|---|---|---|---|
| (a) | Second binyan | First binyan |
| | ʕallam 'teach' | ʕalim 'know' |
| | kaððab 'consider a liar' | kaðab 'lie' |
| | | Noun |
| | marraḍ 'nurse' | mariiḍ 'sick' |
| | kabbar 'say battle-cry' | ʔalaahu ʔakbar 'Allah is great' |
| (b) | Third binyan | First binyan |
| | kaatab 'correspond' | katab 'write' |
| | | Fourth binyan |
| | raasal 'correspond' | ʔarsal 'dispatch' |
| | | Noun |
| | saafar 'travel' | safar 'a journey' |
| (c) | Fourth binyan | First binyan |
| | ʔajlas 'seat' | jalas 'sit' |
| | ʔaʔkal 'feed' | ʔakal 'eat' |
| | | Noun |
| | ʔašʔam 'go to Syria' | šaʔm 'Syria' |

(d)  Tenth binyan       First binyan
  stawjab 'consider necessary for oneself' wajab 'be necessary'
              Fourth binyan
  staslam 'surrender oneself'   ʔaslam 'surrender'
              Noun
  stawzar 'appoint as vizier'   waziir 'vizier'

Several interesting properties of the binyanim emerge from (4). First, it is clear that these four derived binyanim allow both nominal and verbal derivational sources for the forms of different roots. In the examples given, the first and fourth binyanim both occur as derivational sources, as do a number of different noun patterns. The second property is that there is no relationship between the form of the source and the form of the output except for the root consonants. Therefore, a fourth binyan verb could come from a first binyan verb *CaCaC* or from a noun of the pattern, say, *CaCC*. Every property of the source except its root is ignored in the form of the derived binyan. This striking fact is perhaps the most interesting characteristic of the distinctive Semitic root and pattern morphology.

Formally, this means that whatever sort of rule relates a derived verb to its source, that rule will have to ignore the formal characteristics of the source except for the root. It will have to be able to isolate the root from the vowel quality and from the canonical distribution of consonants and vowels. Under the theory proposed here, the solution to this problem is almost trivial: the root can be isolated by any rule as the morpheme marked $\mu$. Without this notation in the theory, the derivational relationships like those

  [root]

in (4) which are richly attested throughout the language would be entirely incoherent.

Another argument which supports the notion that the root consonantism is a single unit at some level of representation comes from a language game of Bedouin Hijazi Arabic, a fairly conservative modern Arabic dialect described by al-Mozainy (1981). In this game, the consonants of the root may be freely permuted into any order, though nonroot consonants and the canonical pattern of the form remain unchanged. Vowel quality, which is subject to regular phonological effects under the influence of neighboring consonants, varies correspondingly. For example, the possible permutations of *difaʕna* 'we pushed' from the root *dfʕ* appear in (5):

(5) (a) daʕafna
  (b) fidaʕna
  (c) ʕadafna
  (d) faʕadna
  (e) ʕafadna

These permutations can apparently be performed and decoded with some fluency. They clearly demand that the grammar treat the discontinuous string of root consonants as a unit, as is ensured by the $\mu$-notation.

Still another consideration lies in the realm of morpheme structure constraints. The Semitic root is subject to a number of rules governing the co-occurrence of consonants within it, a fact originally noted by the classical grammarians. For instance, Greenberg (1978) observes that, with a single exception, no root of a verb contains both ʕ and *ḥ*, the voiced and voiceless pharyngeal glides, respectively. Similar distributions hold for other points of articulation, though no such constraints apply to consonants outside the root. The conclusion must be that morpheme structure in Arabic refers to the root specific-ally, despite the fact that it is a discontinuous morpheme. Similarly, the vocalism – what I call the *vowel melody* – is not freely distributed among the vowels. For example, it is a fact that no Classical Arabic word (with the possible exception of some loans) has the vocalism *i–u*, nor does any verb have a melody that begins with *i*. Generalizations of this sort cannot be expressed without access to a notation like $\mu$ in the formulation of the morpheme structure constraints of Arabic.

There is another class of data that is richly attested in Arabic and other Semitic languages. In the standard phonological theory, phonological rules that are restricted to some morpheme or morpheme class must refer to + −boundary and perhaps also to some set of morphological diacritic features. In a nonconcatenative system, + −boundary is clearly unavailable, so such rules could not be formulated. I present three cases of this sort below in support of the $\mu$-notation. These rules must, however, be taken as pre-liminary, since they would necessarily be rewritten in the light of the more elaborated analysis of Arabic (and Semitic) morphology in subsequent sections of this article. This consideration does not affect the argument.

The first case is an assimilation rule peculiar to the eighth binyan of the Arabic verb. One characteristic of this derivational class is a *t*-infix between the first and second consonants of the root: /frq/ → *ftaraq* 'to part', /ʕrd̞/ → *ʕtarad̞* 'to place something before one'. But in verbs whose first root consonant is *w* or *y*, the high glides, we find initial geminate *t* in the eighth binyan: /wʕd/ → *ttaʕad* 'to receive a promise', /ysr/ → *ttasar* 'to play with a dreydl'. This assimilation process is demonstrably unique to precisely this set of morphological circumstances. A root-initial high glide does not assimilate to a following *t* which is part of the same root rather than the eighth binyan infix: /wtd/ → *ʔawtaad* 'tent pegs', /ytm/ → *yaytim* 'to be an orphan'. Assimilation also fails to apply in roots whose third consonant is *w* or *y* when followed by an agreement desinence such as *ta*: /ǧzw/ → *ǧazawta* 'you (m. sg.) made a raid', /rmy/ → *ramayta* 'you (m. sg.) threw'.

The upshot of these facts is that, to apply the assimilation rule correctly, the grammar must be able to identify the *t*-infix of the eighth binyan exclusively. Under a boundary-based theory, though, there is no way to locate an infix as distinct from the unit that contains it. Infixes are not delimited by + −boundary – this is an incoherent and ad hoc suggestion that would lead to such absurdities as a morpheme apparently composed solely of the first root consonant, preceding the infix: + *w* + *t* + *aʕad*.

With the $\mu$-notation, this rule can be formulated as (6), where the *t*-infix is charac-terized as a reflexive morpheme:

$$(6) \quad \begin{bmatrix} -\text{cons} \\ -\text{syll} \\ +\text{high} \end{bmatrix} \rightarrow t \; / \; \underline{\quad} \; \begin{matrix} t \\ | \\ \mu \end{matrix}$$
$$\text{[reflexive]}$$

There is, then, no logical or empirical problem with this particular case of morpheme discontinuity, even though this rule could not be expressed in a boundary-based theory.

Another interesting illustration of the necessity of the μ-notation arises in the Akkadian reflex of this binyan, as well as in the Hebrew one. Akkadian also has a *t*-infix in the so-called Gt and Gtn (passive and iterative) verbal classes: /mḫs/ → *mitḫas* 'to be struck (Gt)', *mitaḫḫas* 'to strike repeatedly (Gtn)'. But in forms where the first root consonant is a coronal spirant, we find that the spirant and the *t* exchange positions by a metathesis rule: /ṣbt/ → *ṣitbutum* → *tiṣbutum* 'to seize one another', /zqr/ → *zitqurum* → *tizqurum* 'to be elevated'. This metathesis proceeds only across an intervening vowel; thus, *iṣtabbat* 'he will seize' remains unchanged.

Again, it can be shown that this rule is restricted to a particular conjunction of morphological circumstances that require us to be able to identify the *t*-infix. In the notation proposed here, this rule is formulated as (7):

$$(7) \quad \begin{matrix} C & V & t \\ \begin{bmatrix} +\text{cor} \\ -\text{son} \\ +\text{cont} \end{bmatrix} & & \mid \\ & & \mu \\ & \begin{bmatrix} \left\{ \begin{matrix} \text{passive} \\ \text{iterative} \end{matrix} \right\} \end{bmatrix} \\ 1 & 2 & 3 \quad \rightarrow \quad 3\,2\,1 \end{matrix}$$

Another rule of Akkadian also provides support for recognizing the root as a discontinuous constituent. The nominal prefix *ma* is dissimilated to *na* in any form containing a labial root consonant: *napḫar* 'totality', *neereb* 'entrance', *narkabt* 'chariot'. Only elements of the consonantal root suffice to trigger this dissimilation; it fails before a labial stem vowel (*mazuukt* 'mortar') or a labial desinential consonant (*meriit–um* 'pasture'). Therefore, this rule must refer directly to the nonconcatenative root morphemes of Akkadian:

$$(8) \quad \text{ma} \rightarrow \text{na} / \underline{\quad} X[+\text{labial}]$$

$$\begin{matrix} \bigvee & & \mid \\ \mu & & \mu \\ & & [\text{root}] \end{matrix}$$

As in the Arabic derivational relationships, language game, and morpheme structure constraints, the grammar must have access here to the root as a string-discontinuous constituent.

In section 3, I will develop some further rules of this sort, and we will see reference to discontinuous morphemes as the basis of the analysis of Arabic word formation. The fact that it allows us to deal with these morphemes and their complex interrelations is the strongest confirmation offered for the μ-notation.

## 2.2   Theoretical framework

The foundation of the analysis presented here is the theory of autosegmental phonology as described by Clements and Ford (1979). I will assume some familiarity with this theory, and I will outline briefly only those points where it differs from the more familiar proposals of Goldsmith (1976) in ways relevant to this analysis.

The universal conventions for association are cast in terms of the mapping of melodic elements (units on an autosegmental tier) onto melody-bearing elements (units on the segmental tier). There are three such conventions, illustrated schematically by the association of lower-case melodic elements with upper-case melody-bearing elements in (9).

(i)   If there are several unassociated melodic elements and several unassociated melody-bearing elements, the former are associated one-to-one from left to right with the latter. This transforms a representation like (9a) into the one in (9b).

(ii)  If, after application of the first convention, there remain one unassociated melodic element and one or more unassociated melody-bearing elements, the former is associated with all of the latter. This transforms (9c) into (9d).

(iii) If all melodic elements are associated and if there are one or more unassociated melody-bearing elements, all of the latter are assigned the melody associated with the melody-bearing element on their immediate left if possible. This principle, which has the effect of automatic spreading, will alter (9e) to (9f).

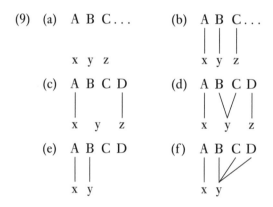

Contrary to earlier versions of this theory, however, no provision is made for automatic association of an unassociated melodic element with a melody-bearing element that already has an association. Therefore, the representation in (10) is well-formed in this new model:

(10)   A B C
       | | |
     w x y z

Only by a language-particular rule can the floating melodic element $z$ be anchored to a melody-bearing element. If $z$ remains unassociated throughout the derivation, then it receives no phonetic realization or, equivalently, is deleted in the surface representation.

The ordinary case in nontonal autosegmental systems like the one to be developed for Arabic is that floating melodic elements like $z$ in (10) are never anchored. I will refer to this characteristic informally as the *prohibition against many-to-one associations*. It is thereby ensured that segments with multiple specifications for point and manner of articulation features do not arise in the usual course of derivations.

In a few other respects, however, I will go beyond the theoretical apparatus in the cited literature. The chief difference lies in the somewhat richer notion of *autosegmental tier* presupposed here. It has been assumed that the autosegmentalization of some feature or bundle of features defines a single tier on which all and only those features are represented. I will claim instead that each language has the option of restricting every tier to autosegments which are members of a particular morpheme or morpheme class. Since a morpheme, as we have seen, is a set of feature matrices dominated by a single node $\mu$, we can say that a morphologically defined tier contains all and only the feature bundles that are daughters of a single $\mu$. In this way, as we will see, consonantal roots and vocalic melodies in Arabic, although they contain bundles of the same distinctive features, can nevertheless be represented on separate autosegmental tiers. This ensures that the association conventions for melodies can operate independently on these two tiers. Association of autosegments from different tiers to the same segments will be subject to the natural restriction that no segment receive multiple associations for the same nontonal feature. This is, in a sense, a generalization of the prohibition against many-to-one associations.

It should be noted that the original definition of an autosegmental tier is not supplanted in this model. Only one set of phonological features can appear in any column of a particular tier. Moreover, different tiers cannot contain the same features unless those tiers represent different morphemes, and then only if a particular grammar stipulates that the tiers are morphologically determined. Finally, as in the familiar version of autosegmental theory, each autosegmental tier will designate a natural class on the segmental tier as its set of tone-bearing elements, the units with which it is to be associated.

The other addition to autosegmental theory followed here is a revised version of Leben's (1973) *Obligatory Contour Principle*. Leben's principle says that no tonal melody can contain adjacent identical elements. Thus, a melody HHL is automatically simplified to HL, but HLH remains unchanged. The revisions of this principle involve two points. First, in the light of autosegmental representation of melodies, I will state it as a constraint on contiguous elements in any autosegmental tier rather than on the tonal melodies of Leben's theory. Second, in view of Goldsmith's (1976) demonstration that such a constraint alone is too strong for some aspects of Tiv conjugation, I will make the weaker claim that it operates as part of the evaluation metric rather than as an absolute universal principle. This seems to accord with the facts of Arabic, as we shall see, since the Obligatory Contour Principle is observed in all forms except for a few loan nouns.

Since we will have occasion to refer to this principle later, let us formulate it now:

(11)   *Obligatory Contour Principle* (revised)
       A grammar is less highly valued to the extent that it contains representations in which there are adjacent identical elements on any autosegmental tier.

This completes the summary of the theoretical apparatus needed in this analysis.


# 3   The Classical Arabic Verb System

## 3.1   Outline

The verb system of the triliteral root is based on 15 derivational categories and that of the quadriliteral root on four – these are the binyanim mentioned above. Although the

Arabists' nomenclature refers to them as conjugations, they are in no way similar to the more familiar conjugational types of Latin or Greek. In fact, each binyan is inflected in almost the same way as all the other binyanim. What they differ in is the arrangement of root consonantism with respect to characteristic affixes and vowel positions.

The first binyan is a possible category for nearly all roots that can appear as verbs. It is relatively unmarked morphologically, at least in the finite forms, and it has no special semantic properties. This is roughly true as well for the first quadriliteral binyan, QI. But the others, the derived binyanim, generally involve some special modification of the meaning of a related noun or verb or of the basic meaning of the root. So, for instance, the third triliteral binyan is usually reciprocal, while the sixth is usually the reflexive or effective of the reciprocal. It is, in general, an idiosyncratic property of any root whether it can appear in a particular binyan. Nevertheless, neologisms abound, loan words are easily incorporated into the system, and speakers of Modern Standard Arabic report a reasonable facility in extending a root to other binyanim and interpreting the result.

Subject to these lexical idiosyncrasies the binyanim cross-classify the roots morphologically and semantically, where the root supplies the basic meaning and the binyan (except for the first binyan) supplies some modification of this meaning or of the verbal diathesis. The meaning of any verb is not a composition of the meaning of root and binyan, but there is a reasonable amount of predictability. For instance, the root *ktb* expresses a notion like 'write'. This root occurs in eight binyanim, reflected by the following uninflected forms of the perfective active:

(12)  *Binyan*

| | | |
|---|---|---|
| I | katab | 'write' |
| II | kattab | 'cause to write' |
| III | kaatab | 'correspond' |
| IV | ʔaktab | 'cause to write' |
| VI | takaatab | 'write to each other' |
| VII | nkatab | 'subscribe' |
| VIII | ktatab | 'write, be registered' |
| X | staktab | 'write, make write' |

The characteristic morphology of these forms – permutations of vowels and consonants and so on – will emerge shortly.

Besides the binyanim, this analysis will attempt to account for several other properties of the Arabic verb system. There is a basic division into two aspects, perfective and imperfective. Voice is active or passive, with slightly different morphology for voice in the two aspects. For reasons of brevity, no account will be given here of verbal agreement, nor of mood or verbal clitics. (A full discussion of agreement can be found in McCarthy 1979.) In all other respects, though, this analysis strives for a complete account of the formal characteristics of Arabic verbal morphology.[2]

Table 9.1, which will serve as the basis for much of the analysis, displays the citation triliteral root *ktb* in all 15 triliteral binyanim and the root *dhrj* 'roll' in the four quadriliteral binyanim, organized as in any traditional grammar. Here and later, each triliteral binyan is referred to by the appropriate Roman numeral of the Orientalists' system, while the quadriliterals have a prefixed Q. The major aspect and voice inflections of the finite and

Table 9.1

| | Perfective | | Imperfective | | Participle | |
|---|---|---|---|---|---|---|
| | Active | Passive | Active | Passive | Active | Passive |
| **Triliteral Roots** | | | | | | |
| I | katab | kutib | aktub | uktab | kaatib | maktuub |
| II | kattab | kuttib | ukattib | ukattab | mukattib | mukattab |
| III | kaatab | kuutib | ukaatib | ukaatab | mukaatib | mukaatab |
| IV | ʔaktab | ʔuktib | uʔaktib | uʔaktab | muʔaktib | muʔaktab |
| V | takattab | tukuttib | atakattab | utakattab | mutakattib | mutakattab |
| VI | takaatab | tukuutib | atakaatab | utakaatab | mutakaatib | mutakaatab |
| VII | nkatab | nkutib | ankatib | unkatab | munkatib | munkatab |
| VIII | ktatab | ktutib | aktatib | uktatab | muktatib | muktatab |
| IX | ktabab | | aktabib | | muktabib | |
| X | staktab | stuktib | astaktib | ustaktab | mustaktib | mustaktab |
| XI | ktaabab | | aktaabib | | muktaabib | |
| XII | ktawtab | | aktawtib | | muktawtib | |
| XIII | ktawwab | | aktawwib | | muktawwib | |
| XIV | ktanbab | | aktanbib | | muktanbib | |
| XV | ktanbay | | aktanbiy | | muktanbiy | |
| **Quadriliteral Roots** | | | | | | |
| QI | daḥraj | duḥrij | udaḥrij | udaḥraj | mudaḥrij | mudaḥraj |
| QII | tadaḥraj | tuduḥrij | atadaḥraj | utadaḥraj | mutadaḥrij | mutadaḥraj |
| QIII | dḥanraj | dḥunrij | adḥanrij | udḥanraj | mudḥanrij | mudḥanraj |
| QIV | dḥarjaj | dḥurjij | adḥarjij | udḥarjaj | mudḥarjij | mudḥarjaj |

nonfinite verb forms head the columns. Gaps in the passive inflections indicate binyanim that are regularly intransitive and stative, and therefore not susceptible of passivization for nonmorphological reasons.

## 3.2   Consonantism

Let us consider the differences among the various binyanim in just the perfective active, where the vowel characteristics are most muted. As a kind of minimal, barely adequate account of these differences, we would have to answer the following questions:

(A)   How are the consonants arranged with respect to the vowels – what is the canonical syllable pattern of the form?

(B)   How are prefixes and infixes like *t* or *n* arranged among the root consonants?

(C)   How are the root consonants arranged with respect to each other? That is, where do clusters or geminates occur?

(D)   How is one binyan related to or derived from another?

   This last question, which would take us rather far from the purely formal issues here into the function of the various binyanim, is dealt with in McCarthy (1979).

On the other hand, a preliminary answer to the entirely formal question (A) is much easier to get. The inventory of canonical patterns in the perfective of the triliteral binyanim is listed in (13), where C denotes any [−syll] segment, including consonants and glides:

(13) (a)  CVCVC          (e)  CVCVVCVC
     (b)  CVCCVC         (f)  CCVCVC
     (c)  CVVCVC         (g)  CCVCCVC
     (d)  CVCVCCVC       (h)  CCVVCVC

Certain obvious regularities appear in (13) which the grammar ought to take account of. First, the stems of all binyanim invariably end in closed syllables (CVC). Second, there is no binyan with a sequence of two light syllables like CVCVCVC. Third, no binyan contains a light syllable after a heavy syllable like CVCCVCVC. Fourth, no binyan which begins with a consonant cluster is three or more syllables long overall.

To minimally express these regularities, the grammar should contain some sort of rules regulating the canonical distribution of consonants and vowels in the binyanim. The template (14a) generates all and only the observed canonical patterns of the binyanim in (13), provided that we exclude sequences of two light syllables by the rule (14b):[3]

(14) (a)  $[(\left\{\begin{matrix} C \\ CV \end{matrix}\right\})CV([+\text{seg}])CVC]$

     (b)  $V \rightarrow \phi \,/\, [CVC \underline{\quad} CVC]$

The notation [+seg] indicates an element that may be either a consonant or a vowel, depending on the binyan. The first expansion of the curly brackets in the template allows all and only the patterns in the first column of (13), and the second expansion allows all the patterns in the second column of (13), plus the illicit [CVCVCVC]. The rule (14b), which eliminates this last possibility, can be thought of as applying redundantly to the set of templates generated by (14a). We will, however, see evidence of alternations supporting (14b) in section 3.4.

Since it specifies the overall prosody, or syllable pattern, of a form, I will refer to the schema in (14a) as a *prosodic template*, although the term *CV-skeleton* adopted by Halle and Vergnaud (1980) may be more evocative. Prosodic templates are composed solely of the features [segmental] and [syllabic], the appropriate values of these features being abbreviated by C and V. Each binyan characteristically stipulates one expansion of this schema, choosing optional elements and consonantal or vocalic values for those units marked only as [+seg]. Therefore, we can say that one aspect of the specification of any given binyan in the grammar is an indication of the prosodic template of that binyan chosen from the set abbreviated by (14a). The stem patterns of Arabic verbs must be selected from this restricted group of possibilities and no others.

It is proposed here that the prosodic template corresponds to the segmental level in more familiar autosegmental analyses. Thus, the segmental level will contain only the features [segmental] and [syllabic], and all other features will be autosegmental. This leads to a straightforward analysis of the problem in (B) and (C) of arranging root and affixal consonantism with respect to the C-slots of the prosodic template.

Let us assume that the Arabic triliteral root is represented formally as a melody on a single, morphologically defined autosegmental tier which takes as its melody-bearing elements the [−syllabic] positions of the prosodic template. This melody contains three melodic elements composed of all features except [segmental] and [syllabic]. In this way, the root tier will provide all the information needed to distinguish consonants from one another by point and manner of articulation. Rather than list all these features, I will informally abbreviate them as *ktb* and so on, although strictly speaking *k*, *t*, and *b* in this sense are not ordinary segments but rather archisegments unspecified for [segmental] and [syllabic]. Similarly, affixes like *n* or *t* will appear on separate autosegmental tiers. These affixal tiers involve the same distinctive features as the root tier, but they are distinct because the tiers are morphologically defined, as described in section 2.2. The significance of this move will emerge shortly.

The problem now is to account for the mode of association between the melody-bearing [−syllabic] slots of the prosodic template and the autosegments of the various consonantal tiers. We will begin by considering some cases in detail.

For the templates (13a) and (13c), the problem of association is trivial. A triconsonantal root will, by the first universal convention in section 2.2, associate from left to right, resulting in a simple one-to-one association with the three C-slots of the template. This result appears in (15):

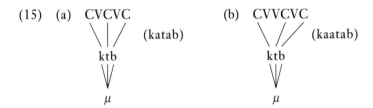

Consequently, these two cases involve no complications in root-to-prosodic template association.

Now let us examine the forms that have an affix – a consonant which is demon-strably not part of the root – mapped onto one of the slots in (13). Each of the binyanim IV, V, and VI has additional morphological material, either ʔ or *t*. For these binyanim, it suffices to associate this affixal material with the initial consonant in the template, yielding the outputs in (16):

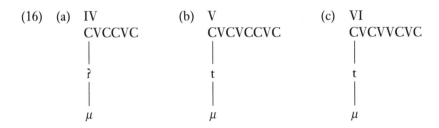

At this stage, the remaining C-slots in (16a) and (16c) can be unambiguously associated with the elements on the root tier from left to right. [ . . . ]

Another empirical consequence of this theory lies in the treatment of so-called geminate roots in Arabic. There is quite a number of roots (perhaps 200) whose second and third radicals are apparently identical: *smm*, *ḥll*, *mdd*, etc. Greenberg's (1978) statistical study of native vocabulary also found about 20 verb roots with identical first and third radicals: *qlq*, *ndn*. There is also a large number of roots restricted to nouns with identical first and third radicals: *θalaaθ* 'three'. But certainly in Arabic, and reasonably confidently in the other major Semitic languages, there are no verbal or nominal roots with identical first and second radicals, except for the unique Arabic noun *dadan*, a nursery word for 'plaything'. The grammars also note a unique Arabic root *yyy*, which means 'to write the letter *y*'.

This asymmetry in distributional restrictions between first and second root position versus other positions has not yet received a satisfactory explanation. Consider two representative roots with identical radicals in the permitted positions, like *qlq* and *smm*. The first, *qlq*, is unremarkable in the autosegmental treatment, and is formally indistinguishable from entirely regular roots like *ktb*. But the second, *smm*, as well as all other geminate roots, must be represented formally as a biliteral root *sm* according to the revised Obligatory Contour Principle presented in section 2.2, in the most highly valued grammar. This holds for each morpheme separately or, strictly speaking, for each morphologically defined autosegmental tier. Consequently, it does not apply to heteromorphemic sequences of adjacent identical units. If there were a (traditional) root of the nonoccurring type designated as *ssm*, this root would be formally identical to *smm* because of the operation of the Obligatory Contour Principle. Given this apparatus, the convention of left-to-right association can explain the absence of verbs or nouns like *sasam* versus the existence of *samam*.

Now consider the mapping of the biliteral root onto the prosodic template of the first binyan perfective:

(33)   CVCVC

    (samam)

    sm

    μ

Because mapping is from left to right, only the second radical is geminated by automatic spreading. This gemination has nothing to do with the morphology of any binyan – it depends only on filling up the available slots. Given left-to-right association, though, there is no way, short of additional unmotivated rules, to induce gemination of the first radical, so we will never end up with first binyan verbs like *\*sasam*. This is, in fact, exactly the right result, and it clearly accounts for this tremendous skewing of the Arabic (and Semitic) lexicon.[4]

In brief, Arabic allows roots of two, three, and four consonants, all of them subject to the Obligatory Contour Principle. Biconsonantal roots are realized on the surface with gemination of the second consonant as a direct consequence of the universal left-to-right association convention. Note also that the Obligatory Contour Principle excludes quadriliteral roots with adjacent identical autosegments, like hypothetical *\*ddrj* or *\*drrj*. In fact, this is the right result; there are no QI verbs of the type *\*dadraj*.

This theory also predicts the occurrence of doubly reduplicated root consonants. The only limitation on such reduplication is the difference between the number of root consonants and the number of empty consonantal slots in the template. Arabic routinely shows double reduplication in the second and fifth binyanim with roots like *sm*: *sammam, tasammam*. These are represented formally as follows:

(34)   (a)   CVCCVC   (b)

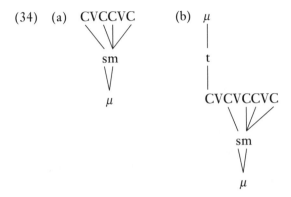

The representations in (34) are subject to the Erasure rule, but its effect is automatically reversed by the application of the third universal association convention in section 2.2. So (34) does, in fact, give the output form of the consonantism.

There is a further result of this analysis of biconsonantal verbal roots. Because of the autosegmental treatment, there is a particular formal characteristic shared by biliteral roots and those triliteral and quadriliteral roots that appear in binyanim with characteristic gemination. In every case, gemination is represented formally as a one-to-many association from the root tier to the prosodic template. This representation does not hold, however, of adjacent identical consonants that come from different morphemes and consequently from different autosegmental tiers, such as root and affix. This makes a difference in the conditioning of a phonological rule of some generality. [ . . . ]

### 3.3   Vocalism

As I have already noted, certain verbal categories such as aspect and voice are marked on the various binyanim not by the disarrangement of consonantism but rather by altering the quality of the vowels of the stem in a systematic way. This is untrue of the first triliteral binyan, so my subsequent remarks in this section are restricted to the other binyanim, and I will return to the problem of the first binyan later in section 3.4.

Let us examine the nature of this systematic variation in vowel quality. In the first column of table 9.1 above, the stem contains from two to four vocalic morae, all of which are *a*. In the second column, the last vowel is *i*, but the other one to three vowels are *u*. We will skip the third column for the moment, proceeding in the same way with the remaining columns. The net result is the following set of vowel patterns associated with verbal categories:

(39)   Perfective active        $a_2^4$
　　　 Perfective passive       $u_1^3$ i
　　　 Imperfective passive     u a$_2^4$
　　　 Active participle        u a$_1^3$ i
　　　 Passive participle       u a$_2^4$

Each of these verbal vowel patterns serves for all binyanim but I. Each pattern has one vowel that spreads to fill up all the spaces in the stem except those that are occupied by other vowels fixed at either end of the stem.

　　We now have two generalizations to account for:

(A)   The categories in (39) do not alter the canonical shape of the stem.
(B)   The categories in (39) do alter vowel quality.

The one exception to the first of these generalizations is that the imperfective prefixes V and the participles prefix mV to the stems of the binyanim. Actually, both the imperfective and the participles prefix the prosodic template affix [CV]. The melody associated with V depends on the categories in (39), while the one associated with C is invariably *m* in the participle and varies with subject agreement in the imperfective. This phenomenon, which is discussed at greater length in McCarthy 1979, shows that we can have affixes composed solely of prosodic template material, like the prefix [CV].

　　Apart from this, it is apparent that the difference in the categories of (39) lies solely in the quality of the vowels. Consequently, we can isolate melodies from each of the vowel patterns in (39). These melodies are the morphemes that mark the indicated categories, and they all appear on a morphologically defined tier which takes [+syllabic] positions of the prosodic template as its set of tone-bearing elements:[5]

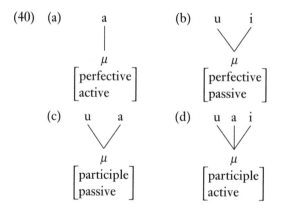

(40)   (a)        a          (b)    u    i
(c)    u    a                (d)    u    a    i

The universal conventions alone are not sufficient to ensure the correct association of these melodies with the V-slots of the prosodic template. We must first apply rule (41), which takes precedence over all the universal conventions:

(41)   *Vowel Association*

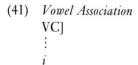

This rule says that the melodic element *i* of the perfective passive and active participle must be associated with the final vowel of the stem. The remainder of the association is accomplished by the first and third universal conventions, left-to-right association and spreading from the left. [ . . . ]

## 3.4   The first binyan

We will now turn to the issues presented by the somewhat more varied finite forms of the first triliteral binyan. (Discussion of the participles, which involve further complications, can be found in McCarthy 1979.) The first binyan is unique in that the canonical pattern of the perfective stem [CVCVC] differs other than in prefixation of [CV] from the canonical pattern of the imperfective [CVCCVC]. We can account for this alternation by rule (14b), which transforms an underlying [CVCVCVC] prosodic template to a derived [CVCCVC] one. Thus, the first binyan regularly receives the usual [CV] prefix in the imperfective and is then subject to elision of the middle vowel.[6] A conventional segmental rule with similar effect is formulated by Brame (1970).

A further peculiarity of the first binyan, and a much more complicated one, lies in the vocalism. We have isolated a single perfective and a single imperfective melody for the active of all other binyanim, but this result does not carry over to the active voice of the first triliteral binyan. First of all, in this binyan the vowel of the initial syllable is invariably *a* in both aspects. We will record this observation with a special rule inserting this vowel, associated with the first vowel of the stem:

(44)   $\begin{bmatrix} \text{First Binyan} \\ \text{Active} \end{bmatrix}$ [C V
                                          ⋮
                                          a

Separate generalizations hold for the second syllable. It is subject to alternations in a complex set of ablaut classes, which are exemplified in (45):

(45)

| | *Perfective* | *Imperfective* | *Examples* |
|---|---|---|---|
| (a) | a | i | ḍarab, yaḍrib 'beat' |
| (b) | a | u | katab, yaktub 'write' |
| (c) | i | a | ʕalim, yaʕlam 'know' |
| (d) | u | u | ḥasun, yaḥsun 'be beautiful' |

Some of these ablaut patterns are associated with verbs of a particular semantic class, though not strictly. Ordinarily, the first binyan form of a particular root is restricted to just one of these ablaut classes, but some slippage appears. There are also rate cases of anomalous ablaut, exhausting almost all the possibilities.

It is obvious that we can give only a lexical account of assignment of any given root to an ablaut class. It is further clear that there is no unambiguous ablaut function from perfective to imperfective or vice versa. That is, given any vowel in one aspect, we cannot uniquely determine its quality in the other aspect. Nevertheless, it is possible to relate imperfective to perfective if we exclude class (45d), which also has the regular semantic property of stativity. The ablaut redundancy rule (46), which reflects essentially the same observation as its counterpart in Chomsky and Halle 1968, invokes a polarity shift between aspects on the first binyan melody:

(46)  *Ablaut*

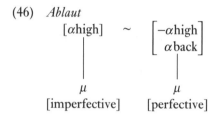

Unlike the formulation given by Chomsky and Halle, rule (46) is a generalization over the perfective and imperfective melodies, rather than the actual vowel segments of the stem. This has a few extremely interesting consequences for some facts we have already discussed.

[ ... ]

## 4  Conclusions

What has emerged in the above discussion is a partial grammar of Arabic verbal morphology that captures a number of significant but otherwise inexpressible generalizations with a simple and elegant set of language-particular rules and representations and with the mostly independently motivated universal apparatus of autosegmental phonology. This analysis and its concomitant theoretical principles constitute, without elaboration, a contribution to the problem of nonconcatenative morphology as instantiated in a Semitic language.

We can, however, delineate more sharply some of the results for linguistic theory that follow from these considerations. Two main points are discussed below: the appropriate formal power of morphological rules, and ways of extending this prosodic theory of morphology to the treatment of nonconcatenative phenomena, particularly reduplication, in languages other than Arabic. Some further results, concerned with reduplication ordering paradoxes and with the internal structure of the lexicon in a largely nonconcatenative morphological system, can be found in McCarthy 1979.

### 4.1  Formal properties of morphological rules

We have seen that, just at the level of surface phenomena, Arabic exhibits a wide variety of nonconcatenative morphology: ablaut processes, apparent movements of segments to restructure canonical patterns, reduplication, and infixation. One result of the prosodic theory is that all of this manipulation can be accomplished without recourse to transformational formalism. In generative studies of nonconcatenative morphological systems, the only means of describing phenomena like reduplication and infixation has been the use of transformational notation – ordinarily reserved for phonological rules of metathesis and coalescence – to copy or move segments. In the analysis presented here, however, it is sufficient to capture all the relevant generalizations if the theory provides morphemes on autosegmental tiers, morphological rules of the form A → B/X, and the universal and partly language-particular apparatus of autosegmental phonology. No need was demonstrated for the richer transformational formalism, in spite of the complexity of the phenomena and the depth of the analysis.

In the light of these observations, I propose the following universal principle:

(50)   *Morphological Rule Constraint (MRC)*
       All morphological rules are of the form A → B/X, where A is a single element or zero and B and X are (possibly null) strings of elements.

That is, morphological rules must be context-sensitive rewrite rules affecting no more than one segment at a time, and no richer type of rule is permitted in the morphology. It is to be assumed that the MRC applies to rules which have already been put in their most highly valued form according to the familiar procedure for minimization of features in Chomsky and Halle 1968. This is to eliminate the possibility of subverting the MRC by translating some morphological transformations into complex conjunctions of non-transformational morphological rules.

It is obvious that a theory that incorporates the MRC strongly generates a smaller class of grammars than a theory without this constraint. Morphological transformations potentially allow any arbitrary operation on a segmental string. For example, transformational morphological rules can freely move particular segments an unbounded distance within the word, copy all and only the vowels in a word, or reverse strings of finite length. If the segmental representation is further enriched by permitting integral indexing of segments, as in Chomsky's (1951) analysis of modern Hebrew intercalation described in the appendix [to this paper, not repr. here], then morphological transformations can perform their arbitrary operations on only the prime or factor-of-twelve numbered segments in the word with no further enrichment of the formalism.

These examples, although bizarre, are not facetious. It is a fact that a morphological theory without the MRC allows all of these types and in some cases values them more highly than morphological rules that actually occur in some language. A theory with the MRC is therefore significantly more explanatory than one without it.

Of course, one could object that although the MRC delimits a theory with lessened strong generative capacity, it has no corresponding effect on weak generative capacity. It is fine to eliminate morphological transformations, so the argument goes, but isn't it possible to encode the same effects into the phonological rules, which do allow transformational formalism?

The defect in this argument is that it takes no cognizance of the theory of phonological rule naturalness which, although only imperfectly understood at this point, nevertheless must be a part of linguistic theory as a whole. To see how this works, let us examine the archetypical phonological rules that must be formulated transformationally: rules of metathesis. It has been observed both traditionally and in more recent studies (Ultan 1971) that only a very limited set of possible metathesis rule types exists, depending on phonetic properties of the affected segments. One type is vowel–liquid metathesis, represented, for example, by the Maltese rule of Brame (1972). This apparently reflects a more general type of metathesis between neighboring continuants of unequal sonority, as the Latvian vowel–glide metathesis of Halle and Zeps (1966) shows. Another sort is stop–spirant metathesis, like the Akkadian rule of section 2.1. An apparently distinct type, involving identical consonants separated by a vowel, is attested in the Classical Arabic rule of section 3.2.

It is fairly clear from these brief observations, as well as others by Ultan (1971), that there exists a quite limited set of possible metathesis rules, which we could characterize as a preliminary theory of natural metathesis. Although linguistic theory allows full transformational formalism in phonological rules, it is nevertheless subject to this sort of substantive constraint. Therefore only a small subset of the formally possible metathesis rules will actually occur, since many possibilities will be excluded on phonetic grounds. Notice, however, that it is impossible to place any such constraints on the phonetic naturalness of morphological rules. It follows directly from *l'arbitraire du signe* that phonetically determined considerations of naturalness have no place in morphological rules. Therefore, any constraint on the morphology must be an essentially formal one, like the MRC.

I conclude, then, that a linguistic theory that incorporates the MRC is more constrained than and consequently superior to a theory that does not, all other things being equal. The most striking confirmation for the empirical validity of this restriction on linguistic theory is the grammar of the Classical Arabic verb developed above. Despite morphological phenomena that appear to invite analysis by morphological transformations, a revealing analysis was constructed that relies entirely on the universal apparatus of a version of autosegmental phonology and language-particular context-sensitive rewrite rules.

## Notes

This article is a revised version of portions of chapter 4 of McCarthy (1979). Some of the material in section 3.3 was originally presented at the Fifth North American Conference on Afro-Asiatic Linguistics in 1976. I am grateful for the assistance of Lee Baker, Nick Clements, Morris Halle, Jay Keyser, Paul Kiparsky, Alan Prince, Ellen Woolford, and an anonymous reviewer for *Linguistic Inquiry*.

The system for transcribing Arabic used here has its familiar values, with the following exceptions. ʕ and ħ are the voiced and voiceless pharyngeal glides, respectively. ǧ is the voiced velar spirant, and *j* is the voiced alveopalatal affricate. A subscripted dot in *ṭ, ḍ, ṣ*, and *ḏ* indicates pharyngealization, also known as emphasis. Vowel length is represented bimoraically as VV.

1   Here and subsequently I abstract away from certain generally accepted phonological processes. Forms with initial clusters, if not preceded by a vowel in the same phonological phrase, receive epenthetic ʔV. Intervocalic glottal stop and a following vowel are deleted in some forms. Some other rules apply only with roots of particular phonological types. Except in a few cases I will have nothing to say about these rules below, and I assume that they are formulated essentially as in Brame 1970, perhaps with some occasional notational adjustments for the analysis developed here.

2   Since the forms in table 9.1 involve a considerable degree of abstraction, a little caution is in order. First, the roots *ktb* and *dhrj* may happen not to occur in particular binyanim, although formally equivalent roots do. Thus, V *takattab* is not a real verb, although V *takassab* 'to earn' is one. In the first binyan, different roots belonging to different ablaut classes, treated in section 3.4, yield different vocalism from that of *ktb* in the perfective and imperfective active. Finally, the forms in table 9.1 are all stems, so they do not show mood, agreement, or case, gender, or number marking, which are not dealt with in this article.

3   The template schema in (14a) could conceivably be analyzed further. There is some evidence for a [CV] template prefix in V *takattab* and VI *takaatab*, which are fairly regularly derived from II *kattab* and III *kaatab*. A fuller treatment of this observation would necessarily take us rather far afield into the interrelationships of the various binyanim, however.

   I am indebted to Morris Halle and Alan Prince for their suggestions about the proper formulation of (14).

4   This analysis of biliteral roots is further confirmed by data from the Bedouin Hijazi Arabic language game described in section 2.1. Under this game, a form with a biliteral root like *ḥall* 'he solved' can be transformed only to *laḥḥ* and not to \**lalḥ* or \**laḥl*. This is exactly what we would expect if the game permutes a biliteral root *ḥl*, and then this root is mapped onto a [CVCC] template by the association conventions.

   I should note that this synchronic analysis is neutral with respect to the diachronic question of whether proto-Semitic had biliteral forms. This historical problem refers to actual surface representations, not to representations on an abstract autosegmental level.

5   Here, as in the preceding section, I represent melodic elements as the conventional segments *a*, *i*, and *u*. These are intended only as convenient abbreviations for the feature bundles of archisegments unspecified for [syllabic] and [segmental].

6   The information about hierarchic structure encoded into (14b) by means of square brackets ensures that, although (14b) demonstrably applies in the template of first binyan imperfectives, it fails to apply in fifth and sixth binyan imperfectives *yatakattab* and *yatakaatab*.

# References

al-Mozainy, H. 1981. Vowel Alternations in a Bedouin Hijazi Dialect: Abstract Stress and Stress. Ph.D. dissertation, University of Texas, Austin.

Aronoff, M. 1976. *Word Formation in Generative Grammar*, Linguistic Inquiry Monograph 1. Cambridge, Mass.: MIT Press.

Brame, M. 1970. Arabic Phonology: Implications for Phonological Theory and Historical Semitic. Ph.D. dissertation, MIT.

Brame, M. 1972. On the Abstractness of Phonology: Maltese í. In M. Brame (ed.), *Contributions to Generative Phonology*, Austin, Tex.: University of Texas Press.

Chomsky, N. 1951. Morphophonemics of Modern Hebrew. Master's thesis, University of Pennsylvania.

Chomsky, N. and M. Halle. 1968. *The Sound Pattern of English*. New York: Harper and Row.

Clements, G. N. and K. Ford. 1979. Kikuyu Tone Shift and its Synchronic Consequences. *Linguistic Inquiry* 10, 179–210.

Goldsmith, J. 1976. Autosegmental Phonology. Ph.D. dissertation, MIT.

Greenberg, J. 1978. The Patterning of Root Morphemes in Semitic. In S. Al-Ani (ed.), *Readings in Arabic Linguistics*, Bloomington, Ind.: Indiana University Linguistics Club.

Halle, M. 1973. Prolegomena to a Theory of Word Formation. *Linguistic Inquiry* 4, 3–16.

Halle, M. and J.-R. Vergnaud. 1980. Three Dimensional Phonology. *Journal of Linguistic Research* 1, 83–105.

Halle, M. and V. Zeps. 1966. A Survey of Latvian Morphophonemics. *Quarterly Progress Report of the Research Laboratory of Electronics* 83, 105–13.

Harris, Z. 1941. Linguistic Structure of Hebrew. *Journal of the American Oriental Society* 62, 143–67.

Harris, Z. 1951. *Methods in Structural Linguistics*. Chicago: University of Chicago Press.

Hockett, C. 1947. Problems of Morphemic Analysis. *Language* 23, 321–43.

Jackendoff, R. 1975. Morphological and Semantic Regularities in the Lexicon. *Language* 51, 639–71.

Leben, W. 1973. Suprasegmental Phonology. Ph.D. dissertation, MIT.

McCarthy, J. 1979. Formal Problems in Semitic Phonology and Morphology. Ph.D. dissertation, MIT.

McCawley, J. 1970. A Note on Tone in Tiv Conjugation. *African Linguistics* 1, 123–9.

Pyle, C. 1972. On Eliminating BM's. In P. Peranteau, J. Levi, and G. Phares (eds), *Papers from the Eighth Regional Meeting of the Chicago Linguistic Society*, Chicago: Chicago Linguistic Society.

Rotenberg, J. 1978. The Syntax of Phonology. Ph.D. dissertation, MIT.

Selkirk, E. 1984. *Phonology and Syntax: The Relation between Sound and Structure*, Cambridge, Mass.: MIT Press.

Ultan, R. 1971. A Typological View of Metathesis. *Working Papers on Language Universals* 7, 1–44.

# 10

## From *CV Phonology: A Generative Theory of the Syllable* (1983)

### G. N. Clements and S. J. Keyser

### Chapter 1: Overview

Until very recently, generative phonology was premised on the notion that phonological representation consists of linear strings of segments with no hierarchical organization other than that provided by syntactic phrase structure. In particular, the notion syllable was thought to play no role in phonological organization. However, there has been increasing evidence that the exclusion of the syllable is a serious omission in generative phonology and that many phonological rules only receive appropriate formulation in terms of this notion. As a consequence, some generative phonologists have proposed to integrate the syllable into revised versions of phonological theory.

What considerations have motivated the renewed interest in the syllable in current generative phonology? In our view, innovations in scientific theories involve two factors. The first is the identification of serious empirical inadequacies in the current research paradigm. The second is the perhaps independent development of new models which offer the possibility of treating well-known problems from a new perspective. In fact, both of these conditions have been fulfilled in the recent history of phonology.

One of the first examples of the empirical inadequacies of linear systems of generative phonology stemmed from the need to recognize a distinction between "weak" and "strong" clusters in the system of English stress (Chomsky and Halle 1968). In terms of the standard model of phonology, this distinction could not be derived directly from properties of formal phonological representation. Hence, Chomsky and Halle provided an informal, "unofficial" characterization of this distinction, defining it in terms of certain sets of substrings particular to English. In terms of this approach, the distinction between "weak" and "strong" clusters was an arbitrary property of English phonology.[1] Moreover, this distinction could not be related to the configurations which were involved in other rules of English phonology. For example, one would have to define different and equally arbitrary configurations to characterize the environment of such rules as flap formation, glottalization, *r*-deletion, and the like (see Kahn 1976). It is apparent that such an approach, if extended to other languages, would give an overly generous margin of freedom to the phonologist attempting to discover the significant generalizations governing the language under investigation.

With regard to the second point, work by Williams (1976), Goldsmith (1974, 1976), Liberman (1975), Liberman and Prince (1977), and others in entirely independent areas of phonology led to the development of models in which certain properties of utterances, such as tone and stress, were represented in terms of features or feature configurations extracted from the linear string of phonemes and arrayed on independent levels of representation. Given the ability of such approaches to provide satisfactory solutions to problems that had previously proven intractable, it was natural and appropriate that phonologists should consider the possibility of extending these approaches to new problem areas.

Under the stimulus of such work, several phonologists have offered compelling arguments for recognizing the syllable as a hierarchical unit in phonological representation. Important recent contributions include those of Kahn (1976), Selkirk (1978), McCarthy (1979b), Kiparsky (1979), Halle and Vergnaud (1979), and Leben (1980), among others. Despite widespread agreement on the basic approach, however, there is considerable divergence of opinion as to the nature of the hierarchical structure required. Fundamental questions that remain to be answered include the following. How many tiers or levels of representation are involved between the root node of the syllable and the terminal segments that it dominates? Is there a fixed number of such tiers or are they in principle unbounded? Are syllable trees binary branching or *n*-ary branching? Are the nodes of hierarchical trees labeled? If so, what are the appropriate categories? How are entities of the several tiers related to one another? Along what parameters may languages vary in their selection of alternative syllable structures?

Our point of departure in the present work is the hierarchical theory of the syllable introduced by Kahn in his influential thesis "Syllable-based Generalizations in English Phonology" (1976). In this study Kahn proposed to extend the notion of phonological representation assumed in such works as Chomsky and Halle's *The Sound Pattern of English* (1968) by introducing a new tier of representation involving strings of the symbol *S*, representing the node "syllable". These nodes are linked to segments (single column feature matrices) by association lines of the type proposed in autosegmental phonology. Each maximal sequence of segments dominated by a single node *S* constitutes a syllable, as shown in the following representation of the word *Jennifer*:

(1)

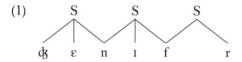

Certain properties can be extracted from this mode of representation. First, by counting the number of *S*'s on the upper tier, we see that the word *Jennifer* consists of three syllables. Moreover, we know that the three syllables in question consist of the sequences *ʤɛn*, *nɪf*, and *fr*. A further feature of Kahn's representations is the fact that certain segments may be *ambisyllabic* in the sense that they are dominated by two elements of the upper tier. Thus, in *Jennifer* the *n* and the *f* are both characterized as ambisyllabic.

Kahn's work provided a convincing demonstration of the theoretical advantages of recognizing the syllable as a hierarchical unit. In particular, he showed that a number of productive, low-level processes in English phonology interact with each other in intricate ways that resolved themselves into a small number of simple statements. He clearly demonstrated that linear alternatives were inherently incapable of giving equally satisfactory results.

Not unexpectedly, there were a number of issues which remained unresolved in this ground-breaking thesis. For example, Kahn's specification of the English syllable failed to provide a characterization of the notions "possible initial cluster" and "possible final cluster". Kahn's assumption that the set of syllable-initial clusters was coextensive with the set of word-initial clusters was incorrect as a universal claim. Further, his theory did not specify the point in phonological derivations where syllable-building rules first apply. Recent research, moreover, has suggested that there is need not only to build syllables but also to rebuild them at later points in a derivation, following the operation of certain kinds of rules such as vowel deletion and vowel epenthesis; Kahn, of course, had no occasion to consider resyllabification since the phenomena he examined did not motivate such processes. Finally, Kahn's hierarchical mode of representation was in-sufficiently rich in that it did not distinguish syllable peaks from marginal elements. For example, consider a syllable consisting of the sequence /rl/, a possible representation of the English word *earl*. In Kahn's mode of representation, these two segments are dominated by a single node S. It is impossible to tell from the tree configuration alone that it is the *r* rather than the *l* that constitutes the syllable peak. In order to make such distinctions, Kahn assigned the feature [+syllabic] to one terminal element of each syl-lable and the feature [−syllabic] to the others. However, as a number of phoneticians have pointed out, syllabicity is not an intrinsic characteristic of segments but rather involves the relationship between a segment and its neighbors on either side. In accord with this fact, it might be proposed that the syllabicity or non-syllabicity of a segment is more aptly characterized in terms of its position in a syllable tree.

One point on which there has been a convergence of opinion in the more recent literature is that in a more highly enriched theory of the syllable, syllable trees are binary branching. Earlier we raised the question of the number of levels that intervene between the segment and the root node. The binary branching theory holds that there is no upper limit on the number of such levels. Rather, the depth of branching is deter-mined by the number of terminal elements in the syllable. [ . . . ]

Another problem arises when we consider how the distinction between "heavy" and "light" syllables should be characterized in terms of binary branching trees. It has long been noted that in many languages, prosodic rules treat alike syllables containing the following sequences: V (long vowel), VG (diphthong), VC (short vowel plus consonant). Such heavy syllables contrast with light syllables, which end in single short vowels (cf. Kuryłowicz 1948). In systems of this type, for example, the hypothetical syllable [pa:] would be prosodically equivalent to the syllable [pam]. In order to express this equival-ence a binary branching theory might propose the following representations:[2]

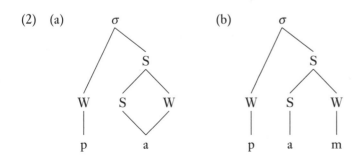

The equivalence of these two syllable types is expressed at the level of hierarchical structure where, in each case, the *S* dominated by the root node dominates the sequence *SW*.
Given this identity, one would expect the relevant terminal sequences in (2) to behave
alike with respect to phonological rules sensitive to syllable weight, a prediction which
is, in fact, correct, as noted above.

But consider now longer syllables, similar to those above but with a consonant added
to the right:

(3)   (a)                                    (b)

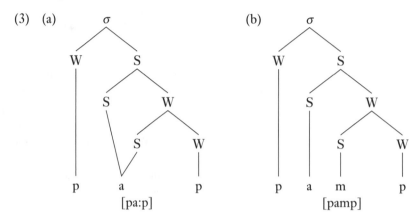

Here, too, the tree captures the structural equivalence of the terminal substrings [a:p] and
[amp]: both are exhaustively dominated by an *S* which is immediately dominated by the
root node *σ* and which immediately dominates *SW*. However, notice that there is a
difference between the long vowel in (3a) and that in (2a). In (2a), the long vowel [a:] is
a single constituent immediately dominated by the sequence *SW*. Consequently, it is
described as a single unit that occupies successively strong and weak positions in syllable
structure. In (3), on the other hand, the long vowel [a:] is no longer a constituent and is
immediately dominated by the sequence *SS*, rather than *SW*. Thus, the same terminal
sequence is treated as having two distinct structures depending upon whether or not
it is final in the syllable. A theory characterizing long vowels as in (2a) and (3a) claims
that such vowels might exhibit phonologically different behavior purely by virtue of
their different hierarchical structure. To the best of our knowledge no examples of such
a distinction exist. Similarly, we know of no evidence that the terminal strings [am] of
(2b) and (3b) behave differently by virtue of their different hierarchical structure. This
suggests that an adequate phonological theory should provide a *uniform* characterization
of the notions "heavy" and "light" syllable.

In this study we wish to explore a new approach to the syllable. In this theory, which
minimally extends the framework of Kahn (1976), we introduce a third tier in syllable
representation which mediates between the syllable tier and the segmental tier and
which we call the CV-tier. In this approach *Jennifer* will be represented as follows:

(4)

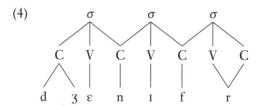

The elements of the CV-tier distinguish between syllable peaks and syllable non-peaks (or syllable margins). Specifically, any segment dominated by V is interpreted as a syllable peak, and any segment dominated only by C is interpreted as a non-peak. Thus in (4), the terminal elements [ɛ, ɪ, r] constitute syllable peaks; the remaining elements are non-peaks. Given this account of syllabicity, the old feature [+syllabic] can be dispensed with.[3] Since the major thrust of the present work is to motivate the CV-tier in phonological theory, we leave more detailed discussion of its character until later. Here, however, we note that the branching relationships between adjacent levels in this theory may not only be one-to-many, but also many-to-one, as shown in (4).

The notion of the CV-tier is not a new one in phonology. In traditional and structuralist theories, canonic constraints on the structure of certain units were frequently formulated in terms of strings of the abstract units C and V; for an early statement see Hockett (1947). Similarly, the conception of the syllable developed in Abercrombie (1967) draws heavily upon statements involving these units. What is different about the status of C and V units in the present theory is that they are regarded not as variables belonging exclusively to the vocabulary of phonological description, but as entities of formal phonological representation separate from consonants and vowels and arrayed on independent lines or tiers as shown in (4). The usefulness of such units in phonological representation was first suggested in work by Thráinsson (1978) on Icelandic preaspiration and Menn (1977, 1978) on child language acquisition. However, it was in the quite independent work of McCarthy on Semitic word formation (1979a, 1981, 1983) that the place of these units in linguistic theory was most thoroughly established. Our work, as will be apparent, is greatly indebted to McCarthy's careful and persuasive studies, which have been complemented by the work of Halle and Vergnaud (1980), Harris (1980), and others.

However, our use of the units C and V differs from McCarthy's conception in one important respect. McCarthy recognized the independent status of the CV-tier in Classical Arabic in large part on the basis of the fact that certain CV-sequences function as independent morphemes in this language. McCarthy termed such morphemes *prosodic templates*. Indeed, this evidence provided some of the most striking support for McCarthy's analyses and forms the basis of his theory of nonconcatenative morphology.

In this study we turn to evidence from quite a different area, that of syllable phonology. We provide evidence for the view that the CV-tier is a component of syllable representation regardless of its functioning in the word-formation component. Although much recent research has already demonstrated the value of pursuing this view, we believe that the full range of evidence supporting the recognition of the CV-tier in phonological representation has not yet been brought to light, and that the consequences of the CV-tier for syllable theory have not been fully appreciated. In this study we offer a unified framework which draws upon and receives motivation from phonological as well as morphological evidence.

In the view we present below, the CV-tier is not only, or even primarily, a constituent of morphological analysis, but serves in phonological representation to distinguish functional positions within the syllable. In McCarthy's model the distinction between "C" and "V" was, strictly speaking, redundant, since this distinction could be independently determined from the hierarchical syllable structure (involving binary branching and S/W labeling) imposed on the CV-tier. In the present theory the distinction between "C" and "V" is no longer redundant since the units of the CV-tier themselves define functional positions (peak versus non-peak) within the syllable. In this respect the

CV-tier can be seen as subsuming the function of the earlier feature category [syllabic]. However, the elements of the CV-tier are not merely analogues of the features [+syllabic] and [−syllabic], but serve the additional and equally important function of defining the primitive units of timing at the sub-syllabic level of phonological representation. In particular, it appears as if the useful but ill-defined notion of "phonological segment" can best be reconstructed at this level. Thus, we will show that what are normally regarded as single segments (both simple and complex) correspond to single instances of C or V on the CV-tier while geminate or bimoric sequences correspond to two units of the CV-tier. Where the correspondence between traditional usage and CV-representation is not exact, as in the case of "long" vowels and consonants (often treated as single segments), it seems that the representations offered by the present theory provide the more useful basis for phonological description. We return to a closer examination of these matters in the following chapters [not all repr. here].

Let us turn now to the set of questions raised earlier, and ask, in particular, whether a three-tiered model of the syllable is sufficiently rich to provide for a complete characterization of all statements and processes referring to the syllable and its constituents, or whether further hierarchical structure should be recognized. Many writers of the past (Trubetzkoy 1958, Pike and Pike 1947, Haugen 1956) and present (Selkirk 1978, Halle and Vergnaud 1980) have proposed a further set of constituents smaller than the syllable, taking consonant and vowel segments as their members. These constituents may be termed the onset, nucleus, and coda. Under such proposals, the word *stout* might be represented, in part, as follows:

(5)

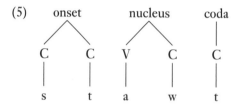

There is a certain amount of evidence suggesting that the category "nucleus" plays a role in phonological organization. This evidence consists of its role in defining the distinction between heavy and light syllables mentioned earlier. We observed that a heavy syllable ends in a long vowel, a diphthong, or else a short vowel followed by a consonant, while a light syllable ends in a single short vowel. Let us assume that long vowels are universally represented by means of the multi-attachment of a single vowel matrix to two positions on the CV-tier, as follows:

(6)

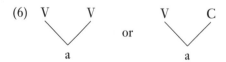

As this figure shows, the units dominating the V matrix may consist of the sequence VV or the sequence VC. The choice between these two depends upon language-specific considerations that will be elaborated upon in chapters 3 [only part of which is repr. here] and 5 [not repr. here].

The notions *light syllable* and *heavy syllable* may be formally defined in terms of the category "nucleus", where we take the nucleus to be a prosodic category consisting of any and all tautosyllabic sequences of the form V(X), where V is not preceded by tautosyllabic V, and X ranges over single occurrences of C and V. Light syllables are those containing a simple (non-branching) nucleus, that is V, while heavy syllables are those containing a complex (branching) nucleus, that is VV or VC.[4]

(7)  light syllable:

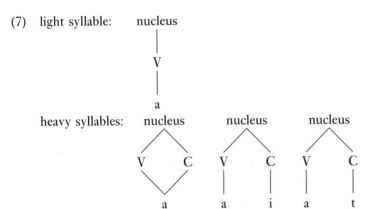

We may now return to the commonly observed fact that the phonological systems of many languages are sensitive to the distinction between heavy and light syllables. As one example, recall that the stress rules of English distinguish between what have been termed "weak" and "strong" clusters, as shown in the bracketed portions of the following words:

(8)  weak cluster:  Amer[ĭc]a
     strong clusters:  Wisc[ŏns]in
                       Ariz[ōn]a

A "weak cluster" in Chomsky and Halle's account consisted of a single short vowel followed by no more than one consonant (or else by one of certain clusters such as /pl/, /tr/, /kw/, etc.). A "strong cluster" consisted of a short vowel followed by two or more consonants (not including the set of clusters just mentioned), or else of a long (tense) vowel plus zero or more consonants. In terms of syllable representations, we may reformulate this distinction as one between heavy and light syllables (as indicated in brackets):

(9)  light syllable:

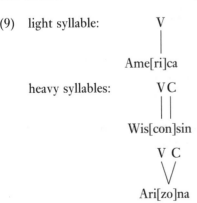

The rules for assigning regular stress in English words are sensitive to this distinction, as well as to the distinction between short and long vowels. Thus, the familiar rule for assigning main stress to nouns of three syllables or more, illustrated in the above examples, places stress on the rightmost syllable that is not a final short-vowel syllable or a penultimate light syllable. [ . . . ]

## 3.2   Evidence for the CV-tier

We now turn to a consideration of the evidence for incorporating a CV-tier into a general theory of the syllable. To begin with, we shall state our general assumptions. We propose, following Clements (1978, 1982) and McCarthy (1981), that the relation between the terminal and preterminal elements of syllable trees is analogous to the relation between adjacent tiers in other autosegmental systems such as tone and vowel harmony systems. In particular, this relationship is governed by the same set of conventions in all cases. Slightly different versions of these conventions are given in Clements and Ford (1979), Clements (1981), and McCarthy (1981). As we know of no evidence bearing upon the choice of these alternatives, which vary only slightly with regard to their empirical implications, we give the simplest version of them here in accordance with Clements (1981).

A minimal autosegmental representation consists of two tiers. Each of these tiers has assigned to it certain designated classes of features. One tier consists of a sequence of segments termed *autosegments*. The other consists of a sequence of segments which include what we term *anchors*; that is, designated classes of segments to which autosegments are linked under the Association Conventions to be stated below. An autosegment linked to an anchor will be termed the *associate* of that anchor and, conversely, an anchor linked to an autosegment will be termed the associate of that autosegment. We propose that the class of anchors in a given autosegmental system is partly determinable on universal grounds in terms of the following statements:

(10)   (a)   *tonal* autosegments are anchored to V-elements or σ-elements of syllable structure;

     (b)   *vowel harmony* autosegments are anchored to vowels (i.e. nonconsonantal segments dominated by V);

     (c)   *nonconsonants* are anchored to V-elements of syllable structure;

     (d)   *consonants* are anchored to C-elements of syllable structure.

These statements define the classes of segments that are linked to each other under the universal Association Conventions. Further classes of segments may be linked to each other either lexically or by rule in individual languages. For example, in Zulu "depressor consonants" are associated with low tones by a rule of the phonology; see Laughren (in press) for discussion. Thus, the class of anchors defined in (10) designates the class of segments subject to the Association Conventions, not the larger class of segments that may be linked to autosegments by language-specific rules or other principles.

We state the Association Conventions as follows:

(11) (a) Link free (unassociated) autosegments with free anchors pairwise from left to right until either no further autosegments or no further anchors remain:

(b) Given a string of free anchors remaining after the operation of (11a), associate each anchor with the nearest available autosegment, giving precedence to the autosegment on the left.

These conventions are principles of universal grammar, characterizing the "unmarked" pattern of association between autosegmental tiers, and apply automatically whenever they are defined in a phonological derivation.

Let us consider now a range of evidence demonstrating the empirical justification for the CV-tier.

## 3.3 Mapping

The first argument for the CV-tier that we shall cite here is drawn from McCarthy's extensive discussion of word-formation processes in Classical Arabic (1981). A representative sample of stems constructed from the root *ktb* 'write' is given below:

(12)
| *Binyan* | *Perfective* | | *Imperfective* | |
| --- | --- | --- | --- | --- |
| | *Active* | *Passive* | *Active* | *Passive* |
| I | katab | kutib | aktub | uktab |
| II | kattab | kuttib | ukattib | ukattab |
| III | kaatab | kuutib | ukaatib | ukaatab |
| IV | ʔaktab | ʔuktib | uʔaktib | uʔaktab |

Each binyan represents a different derivational category. This small sample of forms is sufficient to suggest a number of generalizations. First, each form contains the discontinuous root sequence /k ... t ... b/. Second, each column is characterized by its own special vowel sequence. Thus the first-column forms are characterized by the vowel *a*; the second-column forms by the vowel sequence *ui*; the third-column forms (discounting the first binyan form) by the vowel sequence *uai*; and the fourth-column forms by the vowel sequence *ua*. A third generalization is that each binyan selects one among a small set of possible canonical syllable patterns. Thus, binyan I selects the (underlying) pattern CVCVC; binyan II selects the pattern CVCCVC; binyan III selects CVVCVC; and binyan IV selects CVCCVC.[5]

McCarthy has shown that the word-formation processes in Classical Arabic illustrated in (12) can best be characterized if we recognize the CV-tier (in McCarthy's terminology, the prosodic template) as an independent element of phonological representation.

In McCarthy's account, a word is minimally constructed from three morphemes: a sequence of consonants, a sequence of vowels, and a sequence of CV-elements. Each is arrayed on a separate tier. Mapping proceeds according to the Association Conventions (11), supplemented by a small number of language-particular rules. Under this account, for example, the word *ktaabab* (binyan XI, perfective active) is represented in underlying form as follows:

(13)

```
                a
    C   C   V   V   C   V   C
        k       t       b
```

Application of convention (11a) yields the solid lines and application of (11b) the dashed lines in the following:

(14)

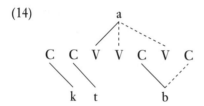

The recognition of the prosodic template as a separate tier of representation is motivated by the fact that its identity remains constant for different lexical roots as well as for different inflectional categories (aspect, as well as voice).

## 3.4   Unassociated CV-elements

A second type of argument for the CV-tier comes from languages which offer evidence of C-elements or V-elements which are unassociated with vowels and consonants in underlying representations. Such unassociated elements induce the automatic spreading of accessible consonants and vowels on the segmental tier. It can also be shown that they condition certain phonological rules.

### 3.4.1   Turkish

As a first example we return to Turkish.[6] Consider, to begin with, the suffix alternations illustrated in the following forms:

(15)

|     |       | *nom.* | *nom. pl.* | *dat.* | *3sg. poss.* | *2pl. poss.* |
|-----|-------|--------|------------|--------|--------------|--------------|
| (a) | room  | oda    | odalar     | odaya  | odası        | odanız       |
|     | river | dere   | dereler    | dereye | deresi       | dereniz      |
|     | bee   | arı    | arılar     | arıya  | arısı        | arınız       |
| (b) | cap   | kep    | kepler     | kepe   | kepi         | kepiniz      |
|     | stalk | sap    | saplar     | sapa   | sapı         | sapınız      |
|     | Ahmed | ahmet  | ahmetler   | ahmede | ahmedi       | ahmediniz    |

(15a) and (15b) represent the regular treatment of vowel-final and consonant-final stems, respectively. Here we shall abstract from the vowel quality alternations due to vowel harmony, and concentrate upon the number of segments in alternating suffixes. The suffixes of interest are therefore those of the final three columns. We see that after the vowel-final stems of (15a), these three suffixes have the shape /-yE, -sI, -nIz/, respectively, while after the consonant-final stems of (15b), the same suffixes have the shape /-E, -I, -InIz/. (We use capital letters to represent vowels which alternate regularly under vowel harmony.) The underlying form of these suffixes must be assumed to be /-yE, -sI, -nInz/, respectively. The forms of (15) thus show that Turkish has rules of suffix allomorphy which, among other things, delete suffix-initial consonants after stem-final consonants and suffix-initial vowels after stem-final vowels.[7]

There is a set of stems ending in long vowels that does not conform to the above generalizations. Consider the following representative examples:

(16)  mountain   da:   da:lar   daa   daï   dainïz
      avalanche  cï:   cï:lar   cïa   cïï   cïïnïz
      dew        ci:   ci:ler   cie   cii   ciini

We see that the suffixes here show the same alternants that they showed after the consonant-final stems of (15b); in other words, these stems are treated phonologically as though they were consonant-final.[8] We could easily predict these alternants if we could postulate a final consonant in the underlying representations of the stems. However, such a consonant never appears on the surface. Moreover, no phonological rule of Turkish gives us any indication of what the identity of such an "abstract" consonant might be: the phonological rules of Turkish would operate equally well whether we take this hypothetical consonant to be /γ/, or /θ/, or /β/, for example. For this reason such an analysis seems undesirably arbitrary.

On the other hand, it also seems inadequate simply to consider these forms as underlyingly vowel-final, and to mark them with a diacritic feature (say, [+X]). Such a feature is no less "abstract" than the hypothetical consonant of the alternative just considered, since it has no phonological manifestation. Moreover, while we could extend the rules we have motivated so far to account for these cases by allowing them to refer to the presence (or absence) of the feature [+X], such an analysis would fail to explain the fact that all the stems in this class behave uniformly as if they were consonant-final with regard to several formally independent rules of the grammar.

In short, neither the "abstract" nor the "concrete" approaches are fully satisfactory in accounting for the behavior of the stems in (16). A final proposal can be similarly eliminated: we cannot formulate the rules of suffix allomorphy in such a way as to class all long vowel stems together with consonant stems in opposition to short vowel stems, since there is a further class of long vowel stems that behave in parallel to the short vowel stems of (15); some examples follow:

(17)  la (musical note)  la:     la:lar    la:ya     la:si    la:nïz
      spelling           imla:   imla:lar  imla:ya   imla:sï  imla:nïz
      building           bina:   bina:lar  bina:ya   bina:si  bina:nïz

Intuitively, we would like to be able to represent the forms in (16) as somehow having a final consonant in their underlying representation, without committing ourselves as to what, exactly, that final consonant might be. In the autosegmental framework developed here, this can be done quite simply by postulating a free C-element in these forms which does not dominate a phonetic feature matrix on the segmental tier. Thus, the long vowels in (16) will correspond to the sequence VC on the CV-tier, while those of (17) correspond to the sequence VV. Following this proposal, the underlying representations of "mountain" and "la" are as follows:

(18)

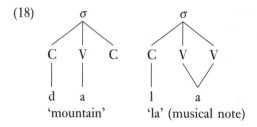

'mountain'   'la' (musical note)

The application of the rules of suffix allomorphy will be sensitive to whether the stem ends in a C or a V. However, the identify of the specific consonants and vowels on the segmental tier is irrelevant to the operation of the rules under discussion; thus, stems ending in C-elements that dominate no segmental material will behave just the same as stems whose final C-elements dominate segmental material. Returning to the example under discussion, then, since 'mountain' ends in a C-element, it triggers the rule deleting the initial consonant of the dative morpheme. The output of this rule then undergoes resyllabification (cf. (24), chapter 2 [not repr. here]). The derivation proceeds as follows:

(19)

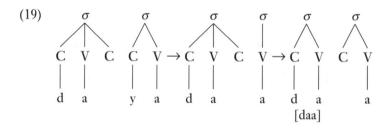

[daa]

In cases where the free C-element cannot be resyllabified by the core syllable rules of Turkish, it undergoes a rule affiliating it to the preceding vowel. We formulate this rule as follows:

(20)

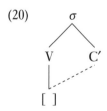

This rule accounts for the nominative singular and plural forms of (10) as follows:

(21)   (a)                     (b)

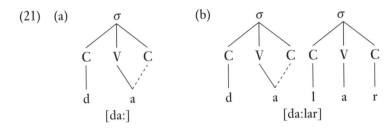

It can easily be seen that the present analysis does not incorporate the disadvantages of the "abstract" and "concrete" approaches considered earlier. First, it is a non-abstract solution in the sense that all elements postulated in underlying representation appear on the surface as well. Specifically, the free C-elements attributed to the stems of type (16) survive either as (unpronounced) onsets of syllables, as in the final three columns, or as the second mora of the long vowels, as in the remaining forms. Secondly, unlike the diacritic solution, it accounts for the uniform behavior of the stems of (16) with respect to the rules of suffix allomorphy: these stems behave "as if" they were consonant-final precisely because they are consonant-final in all respects relevant to the operation of the rules.

There are, moreover, two further advantages of the present analysis. First, it will be seen that the stem vowel in the forms of (16) alternates between long and short values, the short variants occurring before vowel-initial suffixes. These length alternations are automatically accounted for under the present analysis, as a glance at (19) and (21) will show. In (19), illustrating the dative form, the root vowel is short because the "empty" C-element is no longer tautosyllabic with it after resyllabification, and thus fails to trigger rule (20). Only in the nominative forms (21) (and other forms involving consonant-initial suffixes) is the environment of this rule met. Thus, the process of prevocalic vowel shortening is not a separate rule of Turkish grammar, but a concomitant effect of resyllabification.

A second advantage concerns a phonetic observation not yet commented on. It will be seen that both the dative and nominative forms of 'mountain' in (16) are transcribed as having long vowels, but with a difference: the long vowel of the dative is transcribed [aa], and that of the nominative [a:]. To this difference in transcription corresponds a difference in phonetics: the vowel of the dative is perceptibly longer than that of the nominative and involves a type of phonation sometimes termed "vowel rearticulation": a mode of production in which the vowel is uttered with two intensity peaks. These phonetic differences are consequences of the analysis given so far. The phonological representation assigned to the nominative characterizes this form as a monosyllable, with three units along the CV-tier (see (21a)), while the dative is represented as a bisyllabic form with four units along the CV-tier (see (19)). Given our assumption that units of the CV-tier represent timing units at the sub-syllabic level, the relative length of the two forms is predicted, while the "rearticulation" of the long vowel of the dative follows from the fact that it forms the peak of two successive syllables.

In summary, then, Turkish offers strong support for the recognition of the CV-tier as a central level of prosodic organization in phonological representation. Furthermore, it presents crucial evidence for the distinction between C-elements and V-elements on this tier as it is this distinction that permits a straightforward account of the contrast between two phonologically distinct types of long vowels in this language.[9] [ ... ]

## 3.6   The mora

Our fourth argument for the CV-tier is based upon the linguistic category "mora". We understand the mora as a unit involved in the determination of syllable weight, such that light syllables count as one mora and heavy syllables count as two. As remarked earlier in chapter 1, the distinction between light and heavy syllables plays an important role in many languages. For example, in English this distinction is crucial in predicting the placement of stress within a word.

Recall that in chapter 1, we defined heavy and light syllables in terms of units of the CV-tier. A heavy syllable is one containing a complex (branching) nucleus; and a light syllable is one containing a simple (non-branching) nucleus. The concept "mora" may be characterized in terms of this distinction as follows:[10]

(22)   A mora is any element of the CV-tier dominated by the node "Nucleus" in the Nucleus display.

[ . . . ]

## Notes

1   This problem was noted by Chomsky and Halle (1968) themselves. They commented on it as follows: "We recall that we were forced to include the 'weak cluster' option not only in the Main Stress Rule and Tensing Rules, but also in the Auxiliary Reduction Rule . . . As noted, this repetition indicates that we have failed to capture important properties of strong and weak clusters and thus points to a defect in our theory that merits further attention" (p. 241, n. 3).

2   Such representations are discussed in Kiparsky (1981) and in Ingria (1980). We know of no alternative proposals for providing unitary characterizations of heavy syllables in universal phonology. See, however, Selkirk (1980) for a somewhat different proposal for English and Harris (1983) for an alternative proposal for Spanish.

3   Notice that once we have eliminated the feature [+syllabic], vowels and glides are distinguished only by whether they are dominated by C or V on the CV-tier. For further treatment of this matter see chapter 4, and especially section 4.3.5 [not repr. here].

Obviously the elimination of the feature [+syllabic] will have important consequences for feature theory. In particular, it will impinge upon familiar accounts of French consonant truncation and liaison which have been cited as evidence for the feature [+syllabic] (cf. Chomsky and Halle 1968: 353–5). We return to this in chapter 3, section 8.

4   Note that this definition precludes language-particular restrictions on the membership of the nucleus. In all languages, any and all tautosyllabic sequences of the form VV or VC, regardless of the nature of the segmental matrices they dominate, constitute nuclei in our sense of this term.

5   Two comments are in order. First, vowel sequences in the first binyan alternate in a complex set of ablaut patterns which deviate from the patterns regularly found elsewhere, explaining the apparently anomalous vowel sequence of *aktub*. Second, the imperfective forms are characterized by a prefixed CV-sequence of which only the V-element is represented in (12); the identity of the prefixed consonant is determined by subject agreement. The apparently irregular canonic shape of the imperfective forms of the first binyan is determined by a rule which reduces underlying CVCVCVC patterns to CVCCVC patterns by elision of the medial V-element. These and other points are discussed at length in McCarthy (1981), where extensive justification is given for the analysis briefly summarized here.

6  We are again indebted to Engin Sezer for valuable discussion. For a historical perspective on the forms discussed below, see Sezer (1982).

7  The class of suffixes which undergo these rules is partly arbitrary. See, for further examples, Lewis 1967.

8  Historically the nouns in question ended in the voiced velar fricative known as *yumusak ge* (orthographically, *ğ*), which has been entirely lost in standard Turkish, although reflexes of these consonants survive as velar glides in some non-standard dialects.

9  For additional evidence motivating the distinction between two types of long vowels in Turkish, see Kornfilt 1982.

10  In some usages, the term "mora" is confined to languages in which the mora bears tone or pitch accent. We may restrict our definition to reflect this usage by adding the qualification "that functions as a tone bearing unit" to the definition in (22). The broader definition of the term "mora" as characterized in (22) will be assumed in the present discussion.

# References

Abercrombie, D. 1967. *Elements of General Phonetics*. Chicago: Aldine and Atherton.

Chomsky, N. and M. Halle. 1968. *The Sound Pattern of English*. New York: Harper and Row.

Clements, G. N. 1978. Syllable and mora in luganda. Unpublished paper, Harvard University.

Clements, G. N. 1981. Akan vowel harmony: a nonlinear analysis. *Harvard Studies in Phonology* 2: 108–77.

Clements, G. N. 1982. Compensatory lengthening and consonant gemination in Luganda. Mini-festival on Compensatory Lengthening, Harvard University. Later published as Clements 1986.

Clements, G. N. 1986. Compensatory lengthening and consonant gemination in Luganda. In *Studies in Compensatory Lengthening*, ed. L. Wetzels and E. Sezer. Dordrecht: Foris.

Clements, G. N. and K. C. Ford. 1979. Kikuyu tone shift and its synchronic consequences. *Linguistic Inquiry* 10: 179–210.

Goldsmith, J. 1974. An autosegmental typology of tone: and how Japanese fits in. In *Proceedings from the Fifth Regional Meeting of the North East Linguistic Society* (*NELS 5*), ed. E. Kaisse and J. Hankamer, Cambridge, Mass.: Harvard University Linguistics Department, 172–82.

Goldsmith, J. 1976. Autosegmental Phonology. Ph.D. dissertation, MIT. New York: Garland Press, 1979.

Halle, M. and J.-R. Vergnaud. 1979. Metrical Phonology [a fragment of a draft]. Cambridge, Mass.: MIT.

Halle, M. and J.-R. Vergnaud. 1980. Three-dimensional phonology. *Journal of Linguistic Research* 1: 83–105.

Harris, J. 1980. Nonconcatenative morphology and Spanish plurals. *Journal of Linguistic Research* 1: 15–31.

Harris, J. 1983. *Syllable Structure and Stress in Spanish: A Nonlinear Analysis*. Cambridge, Mass.: MIT Press.

Haugen, E. 1956. The syllable in linguistic description. In *Festschrift For Roman Jakobson*. The Hague: Mouton.

Hockett, C. F. 1947. Problems of morphemic analysis. *Language* 23: 321–43.

Kahn, D. 1976. Syllable-based Generalizations in English Phonology. Ph.D. dissertation, MIT. New York: Garland Press, 1980.

Kiparsky, P. 1979. Metrical structure assignment is cyclic. *Linguistic Inquiry* 10: 421–41.

Leben, W. 1980. A metrical analysis of length. *Linguistic Inquiry* 11(3): 497–509.

Lewis, G. L. 1967. *Turkish Grammar*. London: Oxford University Press.

Liberman, M. 1975. The Intonational System of English. Ph.D. dissertation, MIT. Distributed by the Indiana University Linguistics Club.

Liberman, M. and A. Prince. 1977. On stress and linguistic rhythm. *Linguistic Inquiry* 8: 249–336.

McCarthy, J. 1979a. Formal Problems in Semitic Phonology and Morphology. Ph.D. dissertation, MIT. New York: Garland Press, 1985.

McCarthy, J. 1979b. On stress and syllabification. *Linguistic Inquiry* 10: 443–66.

McCarthy, J. 1981. A prosodic theory of nonconcatenative morphology. *Linguistic Inquiry* 12: 373–418.

McCarthy, J. 1983. A prosodic account of Arabic broken plurals. In *Current Trends in African Linguistics*, ed. I. Dihoff. Dordrecht: Foris, 1: 289–320.

Menn, L. 1977. An autosegmental approach to child phonology: first explorations. In *Harvard Studies in Phonology*, ed. G. N. Clements, Cambridge, Mass.: Department of Linguistics, Harvard University, 1: 315–33.

Menn, L. 1978. Phonological units in beginning speech. In *Syllables and Segments*, ed. A. Bell and J. B. Hooper, Amsterdam: North-Holland, 157–71.

Pike, K. and E. Pike. 1947 Immediate constituents of Mazatec syllables. *International Journal of American Linguistics* 13: 78–91.

Selkirk, E. O. 1978. On prosodic structure and its relation to syntactic structure. Paper read at Conference on Mental Representation in Phonology.

Selkirk, E. 1980. The role of prosodic categories in English word stress. *Linguistic Inquiry* 11: 563–605.

Thráinsson, H. 1978. On the phonology of Icelandic preaspiration. *Nordic Journal of Linguistics* 1: 3–54.

Trubetzkoy, N. 1939. *Grundzüge der Phonologie*. Göttingen: Vandenhoeck und Ruprecht.

Williams, E. 1976. Underlying tone in Margi and Igbo. *Linguistic Inquiry* 7: 463–84.

# 11

## The Geometry of Phonological Features (1985)

### G. N. Clements

### 1 On the Notion 'Feature Bundle'

The study of the phonological aspect of human speech has advanced greatly over the past decades as a result of one of the fundamental discoveries of modern linguistics – the fact that phonological segments, or phonemes, are not the ultimate constituents of phonological analysis, but factor into smaller, simultaneous properties or *features*. The apparently vast number of speech sounds found in the languages of the world turn out to be surface-level realizations of a limited number of combinations of a very small set of such features – some twenty or so, in current analyses. This conclusion is strongly supported by the similar patterning of speech sounds in language after language, and by many extragrammatical features of language use, such as patterns of acquisition, language disablement and language change.

What is less clear is the manner in which these ultimate constituents of speech are organized. Bloomfield's well-known characterization of phonemes as 'bundles of features' suggests inherent disorganization and lack of structure. One might make this view more explicit by proposing that feature bundles have no internal organization at all, but that any two features characterizing a phoneme are as closely (or as distantly) related as any two others. It is exactly this conception that is incorporated into the familiar view of phonemes as 'feature columns', that is, single-column feature matrices. The attractiveness and wide acceptance of this view owes much to the fact that it provides phonological representations with a simple mathematical structure easily susceptible to analytical and computational manipulation, and permits an extremely elegant formalization of phonological rules (see Chomsky and Halle 1968, as well as Hertz 1982 for an application to speech synthesis).

It is less apparent, but nevertheless true, that the feature-matrix formalism incorporates certain implications for feature organization that do not follow from the vaguer notion of 'bundle'. For example, a strict interpretation of the matrix formalism excludes the possibility that features may overlap at a pre-phonetic level of description, or that feature specifications (matrix entries) might have an internal hierarchical organization of some sort. The very success of the matrix model in providing a simple, explicit view of feature representation has lent tacit support to the view that phonological features are simultaneous and unstructured at the phonological level, and that all instances of surface-level feature overlap must be analysed as an effect of phonetic implementation.

Exactly why this should be so will be clear if we consider the normal interpretation of a two-dimensional feature matrix such as the following:

(1)
|            | p | i | n |
|------------|---|---|---|
| syllabic   | − | + | − |
| sonorant   | − | + | + |
| continuant | − | + | − |
| high       | − | − | − |
| back       | − | − | − |
| voiced     | − | + | + |

Each phoneme in this matrix is defined by the set of feature values occurring in its column. More exactly, in the conception of Chomsky and Halle (1968: 164–5), a feature column is a function assigning a certain entity, a phoneme, to a set of phonetic categories which determine its physical properties. We see clearly that the notion of 'feature overlap' makes no sense within such a view; features are not entities, with the ability to expand or contract along a given row, but categories to which entities are assigned. Thus it makes no sense, for example, to ask whether the phonemes /p/ and /i/ in (1) share the same instance of the feature [−high], or two different instances of it.

Much work in recent years has suggested that some sort of hierarchical organization must be attributed to feature representation. Such organization is required in two senses: that of the *sequential* ordering of features into higher-level units, as proposed in autosegmental and metrical phonology, and that of the *simultaneous* grouping of features into functionally independent sets, shown by the more recent results of autosegmental and dependency phonology. These two observations are interdependent in a very interesting way. As several writers have shown, most explicitly Thráinsson (1978), Goldsmith (1981), Mohanan (1983) and Mascaró (1983, 1986), the study of the interaction among various sets of features, as observed (for example) in the study of assimilation rules, provides prime evidence for the nature of simultaneous feature groupings. If we find that certain sets of features consistently behave as a unit with respect to certain types of rules of assimilation or resequencing, we have good reason to suppose that they constitute a unit in phonological representation, independently of the actual operation of the rules themselves. There is a useful analogy here to syntax: many of the most enduring results of syntactic analysis have been made possible by the recognition that word-groups functioning as single units with respect to syntactic rules form hierarchical constituents in phrase-structure analysis.

A natural way of expressing these relationships in phonology is in terms of multi-tiered representations, in which individual features and groups of features are assigned to separate tiers. As we know from the study of tone, vowel harmony, nasality and the like, rules may affect segments on one tier without affecting segments on other tiers. By grouping together entire sets of features on single tiers, we in effect make it possible for them to behave as a functional unit with regard to rules of deletion, assimilation and so forth. Multi-tiered representation, as proposed in autosegmental phonology (Goldsmith 1976), provides a solution to the conceptual problems raised by feature asynchrony within a matrix formalism. If we regard features not as matrix entries but as independent units or segments in their own right, defined by specific sets of gestures and acoustic effects, then it is quite natural to suppose that they may display the behaviour of real entities, and engage in such processes as extension, contraction, deletion and insertion.

The theory developed in this paper is an extension of the work cited above, and develops an approach to the representation of co-occurrent feature hierarchy based upon the evidence provided by sequential feature hierarchy. We attempt to determine the hierarchical structure of a feature representation by examining processes that reveal the independence of certain features with respect to others. To the extent that our observations prove consistent across languages, they converge on a quite specific model of feature organization, and (as we shall see) provide us with a new criterion for phonological analysis.

## 2   Two Models of Feature Organization

To clarify our ideas, it would be useful to contrast two possible models of multi-tiered feature representation, representing opposed views of hierarchical organization. According to the first of these, phonological representations involve multi-tiered structures in which all features are assigned to their own tiers, and are linked to a common core or 'skeleton'. Such a view can be schematized as in (2):

(2)

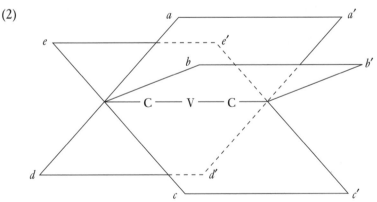

$aa' =$ sonorant tier, $bb' =$ continuant tier, $cc' =$ high tier,
$dd' =$ back tier, $ee' =$ voiced tier

In such a conception, a phonological representation resembles an open book, suspended horizontally from its ends and spread open so that its pages flop freely around its spine. The outer edge of each page defines a *tier*; the page itself defines a *plane*, and the spine corresponds to the *skeleton*. Imagine that the feature specifications '+' and '–' are sequenced along the outer edge of each page, and connected to points on the spine (C, V, C) by lines. Such *association lines* define sets of simultaneous features. If the first of these points is associated with all the features of [p] (each on its corresponding tier), the second with all the features of [i], and the third with all the features of [n], we have a representation of [pin].

(2) offers us several of the advantages of autosegmental representation by providing for processes that affect features on one tier while not affecting features on the others. Yet (2), just like (1), fails to impose any organization on the features, and is therefore equally inadequate. Given a model like (2) we have no way of expressing the fact that certain sets of features consistently behave like functional units, while other imaginable sets do not. Just as significantly, representations like (2) fail to characterize the phoneme as a unit in its own right. It has long been recognized that phonological representations are to a large extent segmentable into phonemes that behave as single units with respect to rules; indeed, this is one of the primary motivations for recognizing the phoneme as a category of linguistic theory. Rules must have access to phoneme-sized units in auto-segmental theory as well. For example, they must be able to delete consonants and vowels, or spread all the features of a consonant or vowel on to a neighbouring position in the skeleton, as in the case of compensatory lengthening processes. However, rules affecting phonemes as a unit will have a highly marked status within theories postulating rep-resentations like (2), since they have to refer to features arrayed on more than one tier. There is a very real sense in which phonemes, although analysable into individual, auto-nomous features, are integral units in their own right, and an adequate model of feature representation must be consistent with this observation.

Let us consider, as an alternative, a model developing recent proposals of Mascaró (1983, 1986) and Mohanan (1983). In this conception, individual features are organized under hierarchically superordinate nodes, which I will term CLASS NODES. The class nodes themselves are dominated by a yet higher-level class node, which (following Mohanan) I will term the ROOT NODE. The root node, in turn, is directly linked to the CV tier. Under this conception, the phonetic content of a segment is arrayed on two different types of tiers, the feature tiers and the class tiers (including the root tier). As a preliminary proposal, suppose we take the view that the class tiers are exactly the following: the root tier, the laryngeal tier, the supralaryngeal tier, the 'place' tier and the 'manner' tier (a further tier, the tonal tier, will not figure in the present discussion). These are organized as in (3):

(3)

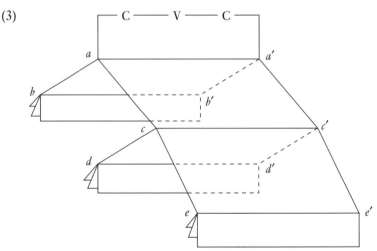

$aa'$ = root tier, $bb'$ = laryngeal tier, $cc'$ = supralaryngeal tier, $dd'$ = manner tier, $ee'$ = place tier

This conception resembles a construction of cut and glued paper, such that each fold is a class tier (labelled $aa'$, etc.), the lower edges are feature tiers, and the upper edge is the CV tier. Imagine now that each element of the CV tier is individually linked by an association line to a corresponding node on the root tier, and that the first such node is linked to all the features of [p], the second to all the features of [i], and the third to all the features of [n], all placed on the appropriate tiers. We then have a representation of the word [pin].

A model of this sort corresponds to a fundamental observation regarding the structure of the human speech-producing apparatus. The essential characteristic of speech production is that it is COMPONENTIAL in nature, involving the co-ordination of simultaneous and partly overlapping gestures (cf. Halle and Clements 1983). These gestures show varying degrees of mutual independence. For example, one can maintain a certain oral tract configuration constant, say the one appropriate for producing the vowel [a], while varying the type of laryngeal configuration, or the position of the velum. Or one can hold the laryngeal configuration constant while varying the internal geometry of the oral tract. Following this line of thought, we can identify at least the following articulatory parameters, each of which shows a high degree of independence from the others:

(4)  (a)  laryngeal configuration
     (b)  degree of nasal cavity stricture (open/closed)
     (c)  degree and type of oral cavity stricture
     (d)  a pairing of an active and a passive articulator

Within each of these categories, on the other hand, it is difficult, and sometimes impossible, to maintain one gesture while varying another freely. For example, it is relatively difficult (though not impossible) to combine a spread glottal configuration with voicing; these two features of category (4a) tend to be interdependent in most classes of sounds in most languages. The various categories of (4) are not equally independent of each other, however. While the category of laryngeal configuration is quite freely variable with respect to the other three categories, the latter three show some degree of mutual independence. For example, nasality is not contrastive in pharyngeal sounds, lateral release is not contrastive in labial sounds, low front tongue body position is limited to vowels, and so forth.

The model in (3) embodies this view of speech production. It claims that the varying degrees of independence among phonetic features can be expressed by a hierarchical grouping such that higher-branching categories tend to be more independent than lower-branching categories. More exactly, the relative independence of any two features or feature classes is correlated with the number of nodes that separate them. The geometry of (3) reflects the classification of (4) quite closely, postulating the highest degree of independence between the laryngeal features and all others, and the next highest between the manner and place features. The model in (3) differs from the classification in (4) in one respect, however, in not recognizing a hierarchical distinction between nasality and the other manner features. Since such a distinction might be expected on the basis of articulatory and acoustic considerations, one might ask whether such criteria should play a greater role in our formal model.

The ultimate justification for a model of phonological features must be drawn from the study of phonological and phonetic processes, and not from a priori considerations of vocal tract anatomy or the like. In this respect we follow the general principle that the justification for the categories and principles proposed for any linguistic level must be supported entirely by evidence pertaining to that level (cf. the 'separation of levels' in structuralist linguistics, or the 'autonomy of syntax' in current formal linguistics). Following this principle, each level seeks its own principles of analysis, and the categories appropriate to any one level may prove to be partly distinct from those appropriate to another level. Accordingly our justification for the structure of (3) will be sought entirely in the study of cross-linguistic generalizations concerning common types of phonological and phonetic processes. From this perspective, the model in (3) appears to represent a correct reflection of the types and degrees of *phonological* independence found among phonetic features. For example, it is well known that phonological processes may involve laryngeal features without affecting supralaryngeal features: relevant examples include rules of voicing assimilation, aspiration and deaspiration. Similarly (though less frequently commented on), processes may affect supralaryngeal features while not affecting laryngeal features. The lower-level branching into 'place' and 'manner' features has a similar cross-linguistic justification, deriving from processes that affect categories of one type while not affecting those of the other. Examples justifying these statements will be given below.

More specific evidence bearing upon models such as (3) can be drawn from the study of assimilation processes. It has been suggested by a number of writers (Halle and Vergnaud 1980, Goldsmith 1981, Steriade 1982, McCarthy 1984) that assimilation can be described as the spreading of an element of one tier to a new position on an adjacent tier. In this view, assimilation has the following schematic character, where A is the spreading feature:

(5)   X   Y      X   Y
      |   |   →
      A   B      A

In the output structure, A is associated with two positions on the related tier, and B has been eliminated from the representation. Now as Mohanan (1983) has pointed out, the view of assimilation characterized in (5) combined with a fairly straightforward criterion of simplicity leads us to the view that there should be three common types of assimilation processes in the world's languages: TOTAL assimilation processes in which the spreading element A is a root node, PARTIAL assimilation processes in which A is a class node, and SINGLE-FEATURE assimilation processes in which A is a single feature. More complex types of assimilation, in which more than one node spreads at once, can be described by this model, but at greater cost.

Such a view of assimilation is strongly supported by many recent studies of assimilation processes. Let us consider total assimilation first. As first pointed out by Kenstowicz (1970), long segments characteristically show the property of behaving like one unit as far as quality-sensitive rules are concerned, and like two units as far as quantity-sensitive rules are concerned. This property extends to long segments derived by rules of total assimilation as well. For example, in Luganda all geminate consonants, whether underlying or derived through a rule of total assimilation, behave as single units with respect to such quality-sensitive rules as palatalization, and as two units with respect to such quantity-sensitive rules as tone assignment. This result can be explained under the assumption that geminate consonants of both types are represented as single-feature columns (in the present theory, root nodes) linked to two positions on the CV tier (see Clements 1986 for detailed discussion). A further characteristic of geminate consonants in many languages is that they fail to be broken up by otherwise applicable epenthesis processes (Guerssel 1978). More exactly, geminate consonants appear to be impervious to epenthesis rules if they are tautomorphemic, or created by assimilation rules. This disjunction of properties can be explained under the same assumption as was made above: if underlying tautomorphemic geminates, as well as geminates created by assimilation rules, are single segments linked to two timing tier positions, then epenthesis rules will be unable to insert a vowel between them as a result of the universal prohibition against crossing association lines (see Schein 1981, Kenstowicz 1982, Steriade 1982, McCarthy 1986 for examination of cases and further discussion).

There is also considerable evidence that rules of partial assimilation create linked structure, as predicted by our theory. A closer examination of constraints on epenthesis rules shows that not only geminate consonants, but also consonant clusters that have undergone partial assimilation, are impervious to epenthesis. Thus Steriade (1982) shows that in Kolami, a Dravidian language, consonant clusters are normally broken up by an epenthetic vowel when occurring before another consonant or word-finally, with two exceptions: the rule does not apply between the two members of a geminate consonant, or between a nasal–stop sequence in which the nasal has undergone a rule assimilating it to the place features of the following stop. As Steriade points out, we can explain this pattern of exceptions on the assumption that rules of partial assimilation create partly linked structure; we thus account for the failure of epenthesis to break up geminates and assimilated nasal–stop sequences in a uniform way in terms of the universal prohibition against crossing association lines. Further evidence for such a treatment of partial assimilation from constraints on epenthesis rules can be found in Tamil (Christdas to appear) and Tangale (Kidda 1984). Evidence of a different sort has been presented by Hayes, on the basis of phonological alternations in Toba Batak, an Austronesian language (Hayes 1986). In this language, partially and totally assimilated consonant clusters pattern together with underlying tautomorphemic geminate consonants in failing to undergo an otherwise applicable rule of glottal stop formation, having the general effect $C \rightarrow ?/\!\!-\!\!C$. All other consonant clusters undergo this rule. Hayes shows that this pattern of exceptionality can be explained by general principles, on the assumption that assimilation rules create linked structures. Similar explanations for the exceptional behaviour of partially assimilated clusters have been offered by Steriade (1982) for the Sanskrit *visarga* rule and by Harris (1984) for a rule of spirantization in Havana Spanish.

Turning finally to single-feature assimilation, we have strong evidence for the spreading nature of assimilation rules in certain tone languages, whose rules distinguish single instances of H tones spread over several vowels from multiple instances of H tones linked individually to each vowel (Odden 1986; Leung 1985; Clark 1990). Evidence relevant to the analysis of nontonal features is not yet as clear, although spreading analyses have been offered for such features as voicing (Hayes 1984) and continuance (Harris 1984).

In sum, evidence for the spreading account of assimilation rules seems quite strong, and argues in favour of the multi-tiered view of feature representation proposed here. Other views of assimilation have been suggested in the literature, in particular the view that harmony and assimilation processes involve a combination of autosegmental and metrical formalisms (see Halle and Vergnaud 1981). This view represents a weakening of the present hypothesis, since while it does not exclude the possibility of treating some types of assimilation in terms of spreading rules, it provides other ways of describing assimilation as well. It is possible that such a weakening may be called for, and that assimilation by spreading may turn out to be no more than the unmarked case. In the absence of clear evidence forcing us to such a position, however, it would be desirable to maintain a single, unified formalism for the statement of all assimilation processes. A major goal of the present study is to provide a theory of representation in which all such processes can be stated in the manner shown in (5).

## 3   The Functional Unity of the Class Tiers

A major claim of the structure in (3) is that rules may affect the supralaryngeal features as a unit without affecting the laryngeal features. This claim receives some of its first and strongest motivation in the observations of Lass (1976) regarding the reductions of full consonants to the glottal consonants [ʔ] and [h], occurring commonly throughout the history of English. In Lass's analysis, such reductions are analysed as involving the deletion of the full set of 'oral tract' features, leaving behind the laryngeal features alone which constitute phonetic [ʔ] and [h].

In work drawing upon a similar view of feature organization, Thráinsson (1978) presents an analysis of the Icelandic preaspiration rule according to which the underlying geminate stops /pʰpʰ, tʰtʰ, kʰkʰ/ are realized as [hp, ht, hk], respectively. Proposing that the laryngeal features and the supralaryngeal features are assigned to separate tiers, Thráinsson argues that preaspiration is most insightfully described in terms of a rule deleting the set of supralaryngeal features of the first member of the geminate, leaving the laryngeal features behind. Thráinsson states the rule as in (6):

(6)   laryngeal tier:

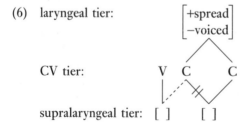

This rule applies to a CC sequence sharing the laryngeal features [+spread, −voiced] just in case they also share all supralaryngeal tier features; thus it applies to a geminate voiceless aspirated stop. The structural change indicated by the double-crossed line delinks the set of supralaryngeal tier features associated with the first C-element of the geminate, which thus retains only its laryngeal tier specification. The structural change indicated by the dashed line spreads the supralaryngeal tier features of the preceding vowel on to this element, creating an aspirated segment sharing all supralaryngeal features with the preceding vowel: in other words, an [h].

Our analysis is similar to Thráinsson's, except that under the model in (3) the laryngeal and supralaryngeal features will link to the root tier, rather than the CV tier. We must therefore replace the CV tier with the root tier in our statement of this rule, as shown in (7). In other respects, the two formulations are essentially identical:

(7)   laryngeal tier:

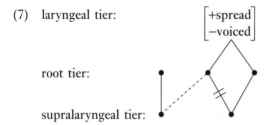

In our rules and representations, class nodes are normally represented as single points, since their feature content is entirely determined by the features which they dominate. In rule statements, however, we allow the further option that nodes may be represented by feature sets. These sets are understood as imposing a condition upon the class node they are assigned to, requiring it to dominate the features in question. Thus, the occurrence of the feature set [+spread, −voiced] on the laryngeal tier node in (7) requires that a laryngeal tier node otherwise satisfying this rule must also dominate the features [+spread, −voiced]. As a result of this condition, only voiceless aspirates will undergo the rule. (A fuller account of the formalism assumed in this theory is given in the Appendix.)

In Klamath, there is a set of phonological processes having the following effect (Barker 1964):

(8)   nl  → ll
      nl̥ → lh
      nl' → lʔ
      ll̥  → lh
      ll' → lʔ

([l̥] is a voiceless [l]; [l'] is a glottalized [l]). If we take the voiceless [l̥] to be an aspirated sound, which is motivated by the phonemic patterning of this language (all obstruent and sonorant consonants then fall into three series: plain, glottalized and aspirated), the rules listed in (8) can all be described in terms of two processes, the first spreading the supralaryngeal features of [l] backward on to [n, l], and the second dissociating the supralaryngeal features of [l̥, l']. These are stated below:

(9)   (a)   root tier:

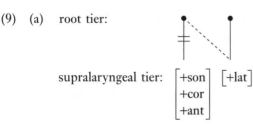

(b)   laryngeal tier:

root tier:

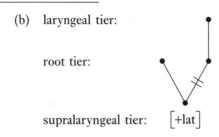

supralaryngeal tier:   $\left[+\text{lat}\right]$

I assume that only the 'marked' values of the laryngeal features, [+spread glottis] and [+constricted glottis], occur in underlying representations in Klamath. The unmarked values of these feature categories are inserted at the end of the derivation, as they play no active role in the phonology. Since all class nodes meet the condition that they dominate actual phonetic features (see Appendix), (9b) can only be satisfied by a pair of adjacent root nodes, of which the second dominates one of the marked features on the laryngeal tier. Rules (9a, b) apply in succession to provide the derivations in (8).

   A second, related (but logically independent) claim entailed by the model in (3) is that laryngeal features may operate as a unit independently of supralaryngeal features. In accordance with this view, we find that laryngeal features undergo rules specific to them in a number of unrelated languages. In Thai, for example, voiced stops, voiceless aspirated stops and voiceless unaspirated stops contrast in syllable-initial position; this contrast is suppressed finally, where only unreleased voiceless stops appear (Noss 1964). In Klamath, a three-way contrast among voiced, voiceless and glottalized obstruents is neutralized immediately preceding another stop, leading in this case to morpheme alternation (Barker 1964). In Proto-Indo-Iranian, a rule of devoicing/deaspiration affected all members of pre-pausal obstruent sequences, while a mirror image rule of voicing aspiration (Bartholomae's Law) applied to non-aspirated obstruents adjacent to a voiced aspirate (Schindler 1976); these rules, again, are motivated by alternations. All these rules apply to several members of the set of laryngeal features without affecting any supralaryngeal features.

   Let us now consider the independence of the place tier *vis-à-vis* the manner tier. I will examine here some assimilation phenomena in English. Suppose we assume the following partial distinctive feature characterization of English coronal sounds:

(10)            t, d, n, s, z   θ, ð   š, ž   r

| | t, d, n, s, z | θ, ð | š, ž | r |
|---|---|---|---|---|
| coronal | + | + | + | + |
| anterior | + | + | − | − |
| distributed | − | + | + | − |

This analysis should be uncontroversial; the characterization of [t, d, n] as [−distributed] is in accord with Gimson (1970) and my own dialect, although Ladefoged (1982) suggests some variation. The three stops [t, d, n] assimilate to the point of articulation of a following coronal consonant, so that [t, d, n] are interdental before [θ], postalveolar before [š, ž], and retroflex before [r]:

(11)

| | [t] | [d] | [n] |
|---|---|---|---|
| —θ | eighth | hundredth | tenth, enthuse |
| —š, ž | each, cheer | edge, gem | inch, hinge, insure, enjoy |
| —r | tree | dream | enrol |

Examples in the third column show that this rule applies across syllable boundaries. This rule is distinct from the rule of nasal assimilation, which applies to the prefix *in-* (*impossible*) but not to the prefix *un-* (*unpublished*); the rule under discussion here applies after *un-* as well (*unthankful, unsure, unruly*). [l] participates in this assimilation only in part, assimilating to [θ] (*health*) but not, at least not fully, to [č, ǰ] (*filch, bilge*). Note finally that this rule applies not only within words, as in the examples above, but also across word boundaries, especially in informal speech; thus the final consonants of *eight, ten, hundred* assimilate to the initial consonants of *thistles, shoes, cheeses, gems, roses*.

If we ignore the slight complication presented by [l], the rule in question may be expressed as follows:

(12)   manner tier:

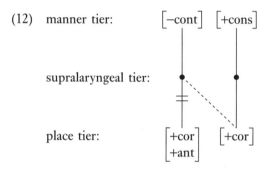

supralaryngeal tier:

place tier:

(12) applies to a form just in case the supralaryngeal tier node characterizing the first segment dominates a manner tier node characterized by the feature [−cont] and a place tier node characterized by the features [+cor, +ant], and the supralaryngeal tier node of the second dominates a manner tier node characterized by the feature [+cons] and a place tier node characterized by the feature [+cor]. If this condition is satisfied, an association is entered between the supralaryngeal tier node of the first segment and the place tier node of the second, as shown by the dashed line.

To aid the reader to see how (12) applies to a representation, I add the following figure, based upon (3):

(13)

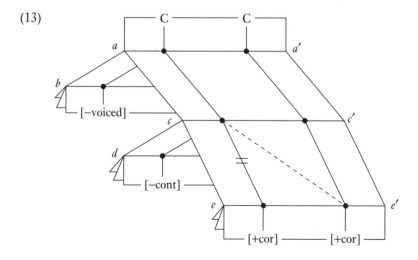

This figure is a partial representation of (for example) the segment sequence [t̪θ]. Tiers are organized as in (3), but now association lines are added to show how the lowest tiers (i.e. the feature tiers) are linked to higher-level structure. Since rule (12) is satisfied, it erases the original association line between the leftmost node of the supralaryngeal tier *cc′* and the leftmost node of the place tier *ee′*, as shown by the double-crossed line, and introduces an association between the leftmost node on the supralaryngeal tier and the rightmost node on the place tier, as shown by the dashed line. Henceforth, all dissociated features are phonetically unrealized (I assume that they are deleted by convention), while all features dominated by the rightmost node on the place tier now characterize both nodes on the supralaryngeal tier, and hence both of the C-elements on the CV tier.

It is instructive to compare the formulation in (12) with 'standard theory' statements of a rule of this sort such as the following:

$$(14) \quad \begin{bmatrix} +\text{cor} \\ +\text{ant} \\ -\text{cont} \end{bmatrix} \rightarrow \begin{bmatrix} \alpha\text{ant} \\ \beta\text{distr} \end{bmatrix} / \!-\! \begin{bmatrix} +\text{cor} \\ \alpha\text{ant} \\ \beta\text{distr} \end{bmatrix}$$

(14) is not just a renotation of (12); as is usually the case, the different notation implies an entirely different set of theoretical assumptions. The theory implied by (14) does not recognize any hierarchical organization within phonological features, and thus does not provide any principled way of characterizing a notion such as 'place of articulation'. For this reason it is unable to characterize rules of assimilation to place of articulation as a favoured rule type in grammars. From the point of view of a non-hierarchical theory of features, (14) is no more and no less ordinary than an equally 'simple' rule in which both occurrences of '[αant]' are replaced with '[αnas]', for example; but we know that rules of the latter type are extremely rare, if not unprecedented. In terms of the framework proposed here, this is explained by the fact that the features '[ant]' and '[distr]' are grouped together under the place tier, while '[nas]' falls under the manner tier. Under the assumption that only single nodes are affected by ordinary types of assimilation rules, the features [nas] and [distr] could not be affected by such a rule unless *all* the features characterizing the supralaryngeal tier were also affected.

We have so far offered evidence demonstrating the phonological independence of each of the class tiers of (3) except for the manner tier. While the individual members of this set of features, particularly [+nasal] and [+continuant], are relatively independent of the features of the other class tiers, there is very little evidence to suggest that the manner tier itself functions as a unit. If this generalization continues to be sustained, we will have to regard the manner tier as superfluous, and suppose that the so-called manner features link directly to the supralaryngeal tier node. As this issue cannot be resolved for the present, I will leave it for further research.

As a final example bearing upon the organization of features proposed in (3), let us consider some phonological rules of Sierra Popoluca, a Zoquean language of Veracruz State, Mexico, which has been described by Elson (1947, 1956) and Foster and Foster (1948). In this language, consonant clusters are restricted (with a handful of exceptions) to syllable-final position, where we find the following types: CC, represented by *ps, ks,* ʔ*C (C =* any consonant), and CCC, represented by ʔ*ps* and ʔ*ks*. The consonant inventory is /p t tʲ k b d dʲ g c č s š m n ɲ ŋ l r w j h ʔ/. Of these, /b d dʲ g l r/ do not occur in syllable-final position.

There is some reason to think that Sierra Popoluca has a rule merging sequences of identical place nodes. Evidence for this comes from a rule described by Elson as follows: 'when followed by a nasal of the same point of articulation (and not preceded by a glottal stop), voiceless stops p, t, and tʸ become a voiceless counterpart of the nasal' (Elson 1947: 15). Some examples are:

(15)   caM.'mɛ·j.miʔ      /cap.'mɛ·j.mi/      'the ocean'
       pɛN.'nɛʔ           /pɛt.'nɛʔ/          'it is swept'
       wiÑ.'ñɛʔ           /witʲ.'ñɛʔ/         'he has walked'

(capital letters designate voiceless nasals, lowered dots syllable divisions, and raised dots length). The fact that this rule applies only to consonant sequences sharing the same point of articulation suggests that identical place nodes are merged by a principle having an analogous effect to rules merging identical tones, in tonal phonology (cf. Leben 1978). The rule of nasalization can thus be stated as follows:

(16)   root tier:                [−constr] [−voiced]

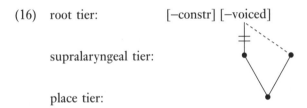

       supralaryngeal tier:

       place tier:

Comparing this rule with those of (7) and (9), we see that we are on familiar territory. The supralaryngeal tier features characterizing the segment on the right spread *en masse* on to the root tier node linked to the supralaryngeal tier node to its left, provided it dominates the feature [−voiced] and is preceded by the feature [−constr], while the leftmost supralaryngeal tier node itself is delinked. The fact that the two supralaryngeal tier nodes must be linked to a single set of place tier features is sufficient to guarantee that the rule will not apply to hetero-organic clusters, and the specification [−voiced] prevents the rule from applying to sequences like /dn/, etc.

Consider now the rule governing transitions between consonants. As Elson states it: 'Both open and closed transition occur between syllables. Open transition has the following forms: (1) the aspiration of voiceless stops when not followed by a consonant phoneme of the same point of articulation . . . and (2) the development of a lenis schwa vowel between nasals and certain other sounds. The two members of the cluster are at different points of articulation' (1947: 16). 'Close transition' is described as the lack of development of any type of aspiration or schwa vowel between the two consonants, and characterizes the remaining consonant sequences. Examples:

(17)   'kɛkʰ.paʔ           /'kɛk.pa/           'it flies'
       'miñ°.paʔ           /'miñ.pa/           'he comes'
       cf.
       kɛk.'gakʰ.paʔ       /kɛk.'gak.pa/       'it flies again'
       'ʔaŋ.kiʔ                                'yard'

It is clear from Elson's description that the feature of aspiration and the feature of lenis vocalic release are in complementary distribution, the first occurring after voiceless stops and the second after nasal stops. Since these features appear in otherwise identical environments, it would be desirable to consider the 'open transition' phenomenon to be a single feature, whose variant phonetic realizations are determined by features of the immediately preceding context. Notice first of all that what these two realizations share is the property of oral release of the airflow; we may plausibly assume that when the airflow is not characterized by glottal vibration it will be perceived as aspiration, regardless of whether the glottis is in fact in spread or neutral position, and that if it is accompanied by glottal vibration it will be perceived as a short schwa-like vowel. Let us say, then, that what we are dealing with is a single feature of oral release. Notice second, that such a feature only contrasts with *absence* of oral release when occurring between two stop sounds; in all other circumstances one of the adjacent sounds will be characterized by oral airflow, making a contrast between oral release and its absence impossible.

Given these observations, we may consider the release feature to be simply a 'floating' occurrence of the feature [+continuant], inserted between two stops by the following rule:

(18)  ø → [+cont]/[−cont] — [−cont]

By the operation of this rule, we have the surface forms [kɛk[+cont]paʔ], [miñ[+cont]paʔ], etc., where the specific implementation of the feature [+cont] is determined by speech physiology rather than language-specific rules.

(18) is as yet inadequate, however, since we have not accounted for the condition on its application that the two stops in question should *not* be homorganic. Normally, negative conditions of this type are highly marked in phonology; what is more, this condition is simply the complement to the homorganicity condition involved in the nasalization rule (16). It is reasonable to think that the formal account we gave of the homorganicity condition in (16) also plays a role in the explanation of the non-homorganicity condition in (18).

The answer is quite simple, if we adopt a proposal by Steriade (1982), called the Shared Features Convention. According to this convention, when the output of a rule creates a configuration in which some feature matrix is shared between two adjacent segments, then all remaining identical features undergo merger. I will here take the liberty of reformulating the convention as in (19), in accordance with the theory of feature geometry assumed in this study:

(19)  *Shared Features Convention* (adapted from Steriade 1982)
      Given a representation satisfying (b) resulting from a representation satisfying (a) as the result of a rule, where F, G are single features and the dots designate root tier nodes, (b) is converted into (c):

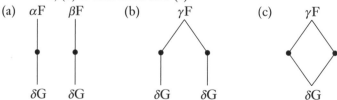

Informally paraphrased, this convention states that if two root nodes should come to dominate a single feature as the result of a rule, then any other identical features that they dominate are immediately merged into one. Let us also assume that when any two class tier nodes come to share all features as a result of (19), they are also merged. Now this convention applies to the output of the rule of Sierra Popoluca merging identical place nodes. As this rule creates partially linked structure, linking of identical features is maximized by the Shared Features Convention. In particular, two adjacent stops sharing the same point of articulation will merge the identical feature sequence [−cont] [−cont] into a single, multi-attached feature. Let us compare the representations of the sequences [kp] and [kg], as they result from the operation of this convention:

(20)   [cont] tier:

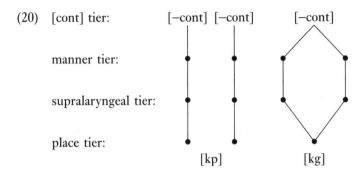

It is now apparent why the rule inserting the release feature, (18), applies to sequences like [kp] but not to sequences like [kg]: in the first, the structural description of the rule is satisfied, while in the second it is not.


## 4   The Phonetic Content of the Class Tiers

We have so far said nothing about the phonetic content of the various class tiers, and we turn to this topic now. I assume a standard set of features for the purposes of the present discussion, though with no crucial consequence for the main lines of the discussion.

The class of laryngeal features comprises the set [spread], [constricted] and [voiced]. I assume that tone features are distinct from other laryngeal features, though we find a limited degree of interdependence in some languages, such as Thai (Yip 1982) and Zulu (Laughren 1984).

The manner features are traditionally those concerned with the degree and manner of constriction in the oral tract (regardless of the location of the constriction), and therefore include such features as [consonantal], [sonorant], [continuant], [lateral] and [strident]. The feature [nasal] will be tentatively assigned to the manner tier as well. While it does not fall together with the other members of this set in terms of its aerodynamic properties, this consideration is irrelevant to our analysis, which (as remarked earlier) depends upon phonological, rather than physiological, criteria. We will therefore regard the above analysis as provisionally correct, postponing a detailed classification to the time when more decisive evidence becomes available.

Let us turn now to a consideration of the place features. In the classification of Chomsky and Halle (1968), there is a set of features that typically distinguishes place of articulation in consonants but not in vowels, which we will call set P (mnemonic for 'primary'), and a set of features that typically distinguishes place of articulation in vowels, but not consonants, which we will call set S (for 'secondary'). The members of set P include [coronal], [anterior] and [distributed], and the members of set S include [high], [back] and [rounded]. These feature sets are not entirely disjoint, since retroflex vowels take the 'marked' values [+coronal, −distributed] from set P, and consonants with secondary articulation take 'marked' values from set S, such as [+rounded] for rounded consonants, or [+high, −back] for palatalized consonants. I assume that both set P and set S features are members of the class of place features, and leave open the question of whether they form two new class nodes of their own, or directly link to the place tier.

The analysis presented so far, which treats consonants and vowels as largely identical in their feature composition, fails to account for a number of striking asymmetries in the rule-governed behaviour of consonants and vowels.

First, when we consider phonological rules of place assimilation, we find that rules of vowel-to-vowel assimilation frequently include mention of the variable '$C_0$', indicating that the assimilation process takes place regardless of the nature or number of intervening consonants. For example, a traditional statement of a rule fronting a vowel before a front vowel in the next syllable would be: V → [−back]/—$C_0$ [−back]. On the other hand, rarely if ever do we find any well-justified use of the variable '$V_0$' in rules of consonant-to-consonant assimilation: consonants tend to assimilate to adjacent consonants only. I am unaware, for example, of any language in which a nasal becomes homorganic to a consonant across an intervening vowel. This asymmetry between the behaviour of consonants and vowels, which was originally brought to my attention by Morris Halle, calls for an explanation which the present theory does not so far provide.

A further asymmetry involves sequences of the form CV or VC, where the C is a 'plain' consonant, i.e. one having no secondary articulation. We commonly find rules in which the C assimilates to set S features of the V (palatalization, velarization, rounding), but rarely if ever do we find rules in which the V assimilates to set S features of the C (e.g. acquiring the features [−high], [−back], [−round], etc.).

We may begin to find our way to an explanation if we consider more closely the way in which redundant place features are assigned to consonants and vowels. In the case of 'plain' consonants (those without secondary articulations), the assignment of redundant class S features is largely context-dependent, depending on the nature of adjacent vowels. Thus consonants are typically rounded before rounded vowels, velarized before back vowels, and so forth. In the case of vowels, however, the assignment of redundant class P features is context-free: thus vowels are normally [−anterior], regardless of the consonantal context.

Given this observation, the consonant/vowel asymmetries noted above can be explained within representational systems that allow three-way distinctions between segments characterized by [+F], [−F] and [øF] (or absence of F), for one or more features F. In the context of autosegmental analyses, we frequently find motivation for recognizing such underlying three-way distinctions, such as that between high-toned, low-toned and toneless vowels. Under theories requiring all segments to be fully characterized for all features, there is no straightforward way of representing such a three-way opposition.

In autosegmental phonology, which is not subject to such a constraint, such distinctions can be easily captured on the assumption that some segments are 'incompletely characterized' by certain features – that is, not linked to any occurrence of such features on the relevant autosegmental tier.

We may now account for the second of the consonant/vowel asymmetries noted above, the fact that vowels do not assimilate to set S features of (plain) consonants, by assuming that set S features are underlyingly unspecified in such consonants. Only in case of phonemically contrastive 'secondary articulations' will a consonant have an inherent specification for a given class S feature. Vowels, on the other hand, are always specified for set S features, and hence consonants may readily assimilate to these features.

We may easily see that this analysis accounts for the first of the asymmetries noted above as well, the non-occurrence of '$V_0$' in rules of place assimilation involving consonants. Such rules may not ignore intervening vowels since vowels are *opaque* with respect to features of set P. I assume that these features are assigned by the following rule, which applies in the unmarked case:

(21)
$$\begin{bmatrix} -\text{cons} \\ \alpha\text{back} \end{bmatrix} \rightarrow \begin{bmatrix} -\text{ant} \\ -\alpha\text{cor} \\ +\text{distr} \end{bmatrix}$$

But rules of place assimilation in vowels may ignore intervening consonants, since these elements are normally *transparent* with respect to features of set S, which determine place in vowels. Under this analysis, only consonants bearing secondary articulations (set S features) will have the ability to 'block' vowel-to-vowel assimilation. This is exactly what we observe in Turkish, for example, where the consonants /k, g, l/ block backness (velar) harmony just in case they are opaquely specified for the feature category [back] (Clements and Sezer 1982).

The analysis presented here might appear problematical in the light of the fact that the feature categories [back] and [high] have often been used, in the literature, to characterize place of articulation in consonants. However, these features are not required in a four-place consonant system having the consonants /p t c k/, as (22) shows:

(22)

|          | p | t | c | k |
|----------|---|---|---|---|
| labial   | + | − | − | − |
| coronal  | − | + | + | − |
| anterior | + | + | − | − |

Further distinctions are made available by the feature categories [distributed] and [strident]. Only in the case of languages having consonants with secondary articulations, such as Turkish or Russian, or in the case of languages contrasting two or more consonants in the velar/uvular/pharyngeal region, do the feature categories [back] and [high] have a contrastive value. In other languages, we may consider these features to be either contextually determined through assimilation, or else to have the status of 'enhancement' features, in the sense of Stevens et al. 1986.

The distinction between, for example, plain [l], palatalized [ʎ] and 'dark' [ɫ] may now be characterized in the following manner:

(23)

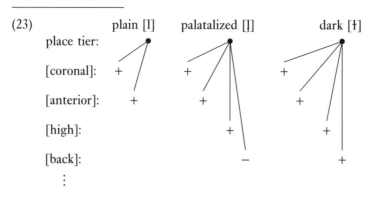

place tier:    plain [l]  palatalized [ļ]   dark [ł]

[coronal]:  +    +      +

[anterior]:  +    +      +

[high]:        +      +

[back]:        −      +

⋮

It is clear that the principle leading to 'undercharacterized' representations such as the first of those in (23) is of broad application. For example, we may represent [h ʔ] as segments uncharacterized for any place features, acquiring their place features by assimilation to adjacent vowels, as noted by Lass and Thráinsson. Similarly, in many languages we find nasal formatives which always occur adjacent to a consonant, and which always assimilate to the point of articulation of that consonant. We may assume that such nasal elements are characterized only for laryngeal and manner features, acquiring place features by assimilation. In the limit case, all class nodes are absent, in which case we have the so-called empty or ghost consonants and vowels of the CV tier. While segment types such as these were anomalous under previous theories of phonological representation, the present framework provides a principled account of them, relating their apparently 'exotic' characteristics to more familiar phenomena. [ . . . ]

## 6 Summary and Conclusions

This paper has explored some of the possibilities made available by recent developments in nonlinear phonology, suggesting that feature representation does not involve two-dimensional matrices in the sense of classical Jakobsonian and generative phonology, but rather multi-tiered, hierarchical structures of the type shown in (3). Such a theory of phonological representation offers a constrained theory of assimilation processes, according to which all assimilation rules involve the spreading of a single node: the root node, a class node or a feature node. The study of consonant–vowel asymmetries reveals that the features responsible for distinctions in the location of the primary constriction ('place' features) are subdivided into two sets, of which one is universally present in consonants and vowels, and the other is normally absent in consonants. This theory generalizes to the treatment of other 'underspecified' segments, suggesting that class nodes may be absent in certain segment types, such as the laryngeal glides, which lack supralaryngeal features, or the 'always-homorganic' nasals, which lack the place features.

An interesting consequence of this model of feature representation is that many prosodic phenomena that have appeared in the past to require 'autosegmentalized' or 'projected' features, extracted from feature matrices and represented on special tiers, may be treated as cases of ordinary assimilation. For example, it is not necessary to suppose that certain vowel features are placed on special tiers in order to account for vowel harmony phenomena in Turkish (cf. Clements and Sezer 1982); all we need assume is that some formatives (suffixes) are systematically uncharacterized for certain place features in vowels, namely [back] and [round], and that harmony effects result from spreading rules blocked only by segments which are opaquely characterized for the spreading feature. Similarly, the treatment of spirantization in Spanish proposed by Mascaró (1984) does not require a special tier for the feature [continuant], since we need do no more than assume that certain segment types, in this case voiced non-strident obstruents, are systematically uncharacterized by continuancy.

If these remarks are on the right track, then what distinguishes languages with long-distance assimilation phenomena may be no more than the fact that they systematically omit certain feature specifications that are normally present in other languages. The strongest version of this hypothesis would be the view that there are no special feature tiers or projections at all, and that all cases of harmony and assimilation can be handled within the restrictive theory of representation proposed here, limiting parametric variation to the set of features that can be systematically uncharacterized. Intransigent cases remain, however, and the development of these ideas must await further study.

## Appendix

The hierarchical organization of a segment has the formal structure of a tree diagram rooted in one or more elements of the CV tier, whose terminal symbols are the feature specifications '+' and '−'. Consider the following partial representation of [s]:

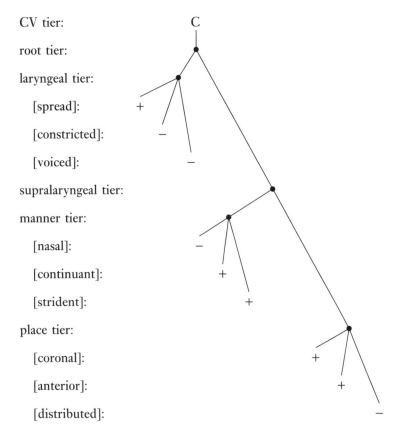

CV tier:    C

root tier:

laryngeal tier:

  [spread]:        +

  [constricted]:   −

  [voiced]:        −

supralaryngeal tier:

manner tier:

  [nasal]:         −

  [continuant]:    +

  [strident]:      +

place tier:

  [coronal]:       +

  [anterior]:      +

  [distributed]:   −

This partial representation consists of fifteen nodes, each arrayed on its own tier. The class nodes are the root tier node, the laryngeal tier node, the supralaryngeal tier node, the manner node and the place node. Given any two nodes M, N such that M lies on the path between N and the root of the tree, M is said to DOMINATE N; if no node intervenes between M and N, M IMMEDIATELY DOMINATES N. Each feature CHARACTERIZES every node that dominates it; thus the place node in the diagram above is characterized by the features [+coronal, +anterior, −distributed], and both the root node and the C node are characterized by all the features of the representation. We may define a PHONETIC SEGMENT as any element of the CV tier together with all the features characterizing it: thus the diagram above is a representation of the phonetic segment [s].

Nodes of the same class or feature category are ordered under the relation of CONCATENATION and define a TIER. Each tier is one member of an ordered pair of tiers ⟨P, Q⟩ such that nodes arrayed on P immediately dominate nodes arrayed on Q. Given two tiers forming the ordered pair ⟨P, Q⟩, tier P is said to (IMMEDIATELY) DOMINATE tier Q, and P, Q are ADJACENT tiers, and define a PLANE. As the relation of domination is transitive, if tier P dominates Q and Q dominates R, P also dominates R. The relation of adjacency, on the other hand, is non-transitive, symmetrical and irreflexive. Thus if tier R is adjacent to S and S is adjacent to T, R is not adjacent to T; if R is adjacent to S, S is adjacent to R; and no R is adjacent to itself.

Let us designate a node on tier P as n(P), a node on tier Q as n(Q), etc. Branches link nodes only on adjacent tiers. A branch linking n(P) and n(Q) is termed an ASSOCIATION LINE. Representations consisting of several phonetic segments in succession are governed by the well-formedness conventions of autosegmental phonology, which apply individually to each plane. In particular, association lines may intersect only at tiers; i.e. no association lines cross.

Given a pair of ordered tiers ⟨P, Q⟩, the nodes n(P) are ANCHORS for the nodes n(Q), in the sense of Clements and Keyser (1983). These conventions allow one-to-many and many-to-one associations between nodes of adjacent tiers. It follows from these conventions that representations may contain features that are not dominated by class nodes, and class nodes that are not dominated by other class nodes, but will not contain class nodes that do not dominate features, except in the hypothetical case where a class node does not lie in the domain of a feature (i.e. where there is no accessible feature to link to the class node).

Rule formalism assumed in this work is the same as that assumed elsewhere in autosegmental phonology. For example, just as in the statement of autosegmental tone rules, tier P of the ordered pair ⟨P, Q⟩ may be written above or below tier Q, indifferently; thus statements (i) and (ii) below are equivalent:

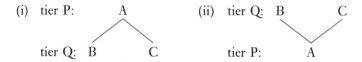

(i)   tier P:        A

      tier Q:   B        C

(ii)  tier Q:  B           C

      tier P:        A

In this work, however, a further abbreviatory convention is adopted. Given a configuration of type (iii) occurring as a subpart of a phonological representation K, where S is a class tier, T is any tier adjacent to S, and the *n* are nodes of any appropriate type,

(iii) satisfies (iv), a subpart of some structural description SD of a rule R, only if node n(S) in (iii) dominates $[\alpha F]$ in K (where $\alpha = +$ or $-$):

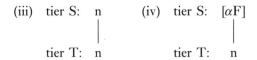

(iii)   tier S:   n          (iv)   tier S:   $[\alpha F]$

tier T:   n                  tier T:   n

Under this convention, '$[\alpha F]$' in (iv) designates a class tier node n(S), not a feature $[\alpha F]$, and is to be understood as a condition placed upon the node n(S) in (iii) being tested as a possible match for n(S) in (iv), requiring it to dominate the feature $[\alpha F]$ in K. Accordingly, a class tier node n(S) in K 'matches' n(S) in (iv) just in case it dominates the feature $[\alpha F]$, and is associated with a node n(T). As an example, rule R below (containing (iv) as a subpart) is applicable to representation (v), since all nodes of R are matched by corresponding nodes of (v), and derives (vi):

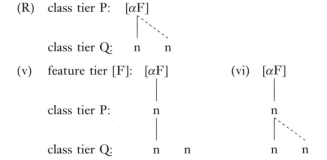

(R)   class tier P:   $[\alpha F]$

class tier Q:   n   n

(v)   feature tier [F]:   $[\alpha F]$          (vi)   $[\alpha F]$

class tier P:   n                         n

class tier Q:   n   n                     n   n

This convention gives us the effect of feature percolation.

## Note

In preparing this paper I have benefited from discussion with Joan Mascaró, S. J. Keyser, Patricia Keating and Prathima Christdas. Thanks are also due to Kenstowicz and Kisseberth (1979) for problem 2, chapter 2.

## References

Aronoff, M. and R. T. Oehrle (eds). 1984. *Language Sound Structure*. Cambridge, Mass.: MIT Press.
Barker, M. A. R. 1964. *Klamath Grammar*. Berkeley: University of California Press.
Chomsky, N. and M. Halle. 1968. *The Sound Pattern of English*. New York: Harper and Row.
Christdas, P. 1988. Tamil phonology and morphology. Ph.D. dissertation, Cornell University.
Clark, M. M. 1990. *The Tonal System of Igbo*. Dordrecht: Foris.
Clements, G. N. 1986. Consonant gemination and compensatory lengthening in Luganda. In Sezer and Wetzels: 37–77.
Clements, C. N. and S. J. Keyser. 1983. *CV Phonology: A Generative Theory of the Syllable*. Cambridge, Mass.: MIT Press.

Clements, G. N. and E. Sezer. 1982. Vowel and consonant disharmony in Turkish. In H. van der Hulst and N. Smith (eds), *The Structure of Phonological Representations*, vol. 2, Dordrecht: Foris, 213–55.

Elson, B. 1947. Sierra Popoluca syllable structure. *International Journal of American Linguistics* 13: 13–17.

Elson, B. 1956. Sierra Popoluca morphology. Ph.D. dissertation, Cornell University.

Foster, M. L. and G. M. Foster. 1948. Sierra Popoluca speech. Washington, D.C.: U.S. Government Printing Office, Smithsonian Institution, Institute of Social Anthropology.

Gimson, A. C. 1970. *An Introduction to the Pronunciation of English*, 2nd edn. London: Edward Arnold.

Goldsmith, J. 1976. *Autosegmental Phonology*. Ph.D. dissertation, MIT. Published New York: Garland, 1979.

Goldsmith, J. 1981. Subsegmentals in Spanish phonology: an autosegmental approach. In W. W. Cressey and D. J. Napoli (eds) *Linguistic Symposium on Romance Languages*, 9, Washington, D.C.: Georgetown University Press, 1–16.

Guerssel, M. 1978. A condition on assimilation rules. *Linguistic Analysis* 4: 225–54.

Halle, M. and G. N. Clements. 1983. *Problem Book in Phonology*. Cambridge, Mass.: MIT Press/ Bradford Books.

Halle, M. and J.-R. Vergnaud. 1980. Three dimensional phonology. *Journal of Linguistic Research* 1: 83–105.

Halle, M. and J.-R. Vergnaud. 1981. Harmony processes. In W. Klein and W. Levelt (eds), *Crossing the Boundaries in Linguistics*, Dordrecht: Reidel, 1–22.

Harris, J. 1984. La espirantización en castellano y la representación fonológica autosegmental. In Publications del Department de Filologia Hispànica de la Universitat Autònoma de Barcelona, Estudis Gramaticals 1, *Sèrie Lingüística*. Barcelona.

Hayes, B. 1984. The phonetics and phonology of Russian voicing assimilation. In Aronoff and Oehrle (1984), 318–28.

Hayes, B. 1986. Assimilation as spreading in Toba Batak. *Linguistic Inquiry* 17: 467–99.

Hertz, S. 1982. From text to speech with SRS. *Journal of the Acoustic Society of America* 72: 1155–70.

Kenstowicz, M. 1970. On the notation of vowel length in Lithuanian. *Papers in Linguistics* 3: 73–114.

Kenstowicz, M. 1982. Gemination and spirantization in Tigrinya. *Studies in the Linguistic Sciences* 12: 103–22.

Kenstowicz, M. and C. W. Kisseberth. 1979. *Generative Phonology*. New York: Academic Press.

Kidda, M. 1984. Morpheme alternation in Tangale: a syllable structure approach. Paper presented at the 15th Annual Conference on African Linguistics, UCLA.

Ladefoged, P. 1982. *A Course in Phonetics*, 2nd edn. New York: Harcourt Brace Jovanovich.

Lass, R. 1976. *English Phonology and Phonological Theory*. Cambridge: Cambridge University Press.

Laughren, M. 1984. Tone in Zulu nouns. In G. N. Clements and J. Goldsmith (eds), *Autosegmental Studies in Bantu Tone*, Dordrecht: Foris, 183–234.

Leben, W. R. 1978. The representation of tone. In V. Fromkin (ed.), *Tone: A Linguistic Survey*, New York: Academic Press, 177–219.

Leung, E. 1985. Verb tones in Llogoori. Paper presented at the 16th Annual Conference on African Linguistics, Yale University.

McCarthy, J. 1984. Theoretical consequences of Montañes vowel harmony. *Linguistic Inquiry* 15: 291–318.

McCarthy, J. 1986. OCP effects: gemination and antigemination. *Linguistic Inquiry* 17: 207–63.

Mascaró, J. 1983. Phonological levels and assimilatory processes. MS, Universitat Autònoma de Barcelona.

Mascaró, J. 1984. Continuant spreading in Basque, Catalan, and Spanish. In Aronoff and Oehrle (1984), 287–98.

Mascaró, J. 1986. Compensatory diphthongization in Majorcan Catalan. In Sezer and Wetzels, 133–46.

Mohanan, K. P. 1983. The structure of the melody. MS, MIT and National University of Singapore.

Noss, R. B. 1964. *Thai Reference Grammar*. Washington, D.C.: Foreign Service Institute.

Odden, D. 1986. On the role of the Obligatory Contour Principle in Phonological Theory. *Language* 62: 669–73.

Schein, B. 1981. Spirantization in Tigrinya. *MIT Working Papers in Linguistics* 3: 32–42.

Schindler, J. 1976. Diachronic and synchronic remarks on Bartholomae's and Grassman's Laws. *Linguistic Inquiry* 7: 622–37.

Sezer, E. and L. Wetzels (eds). 1986. *Studies in Compensatory Lengthening*. Dordrecht: Foris.

Steriade, D. 1982. Greek Prosodies and the Nature of Syllabification. Ph.D. dissertation, MIT.

Stevens, K. N., S. J. Keyser and H. Kawasaki. 1986. Toward a phonetic and phonological theory of redundant features. In J. Perkell and D. H. Klatt (eds) *Invariance and Variability of Speech Processes*, Hillsdale, N.J., London: Lawrence Erlbaum Associates, 493–509.

Thráinsson, H. 1978. On the phonology of Icelandic preaspiration. *Nordic Journal of Linguistics* 1: 3–54.

Yip, M. 1982. Against a segmental analysis of Zahao and Thai. *Linguistic Analysis* 9: 79–94.

# 12

## Inalterability in CV Phonology (1986)

### Bruce Hayes

Geminate consonants and long vowels frequently resist the application of rules that would a priori be expected to apply to them; i.e., they are frequently 'inalterable'. This article argues that, by invoking the theory of CV Phonology, it is often possible to predict which phonological rules are unable to affect long segments. The prediction follows from rather minimal assumptions about how rules apply to forms.

A long tradition of phonological research has shown that geminate consonants and long vowels behave exceptionally. Within generative phonology, the work of Kenstowicz (1970), Pyle (1970), Fidelholtz (1971), Guerssel (1977, 1978), Leben (1980), Steriade (1982), and others has uncovered at least three exceptional properties of these long segments:

(1)  (a)  *Ambiguity*: Long segments act in some contexts as if they were two segments, in others as if they were one.

      (b)  *Integrity*: Insofar as they constitute two segments, long segments cannot be split by rules of epenthesis.

      (c)  *Inalterability*: Long segments often resist the application of rules that a priori would be expected to apply to them.

The theory of CV Phonology, as applied to length (cf. Leben 1980, McCarthy 1981a, Steriade 1982, Clements and Keyser 1983), has provided convincing theoretical accounts of the first two properties mentioned above, Ambiguity and Integrity. However, the problem of Inalterability has, in my opinion, not yet been adequately dealt with.

Consider a specific instance, to be discussed in greater detail below. In Persian (cf. Cowan and Yarmohammadi 1978), a rule I will call /v/-Weakening converts /v/ to /w/ whenever it occurs in, roughly speaking, syllable-final position (2a). Unexpectedly, /v/-Weakening fails to affect syllable-final /v/ whenever it forms the first half of a geminate, as (2b) shows:

(2)  (a)  /nov-ru:z/ → *nowru:z* 'New Year' (lit. 'new day')
           (cf. *novi:n* 'new kind')
          /jæv/ → *jæw* (→ *jow*) 'barley'
           (cf. *jævi:n* 'made of barley')

      (b)  *ævvæl* 'first'
          *morovvæt* 'generosity'
          *qolovv* 'exaggeration'

In this instance, the long segment /vv/ is clearly inalterable. Now, it is certainly possible to write a version of /v/-Weakening that respects Inalterability by appropriately complicating the structural description. However, as I will show below, the phenomenon is quite widespread; this suggests that it would be wrong to write Inalterability into individual rules. Rather, we should seek a general principle that predicts cases of Inalterability automatically.

To locate such a principle is not trivial, because not all rules respect Inalterability. An example of a rule that does not may be found in Feinstein's 1979 phonological analysis of Sinhala, an Indo-European language of Sri Lanka. He proposes a rule of Cluster Simplification, which freely applies to geminates:

(3)  Sinhala Cluster Simplification

$C \rightarrow \emptyset \: / \: C$___$]_{syl}$

*kand.da* → *kanda* 'hill-SG.DEF'

Thus an adequate account of Inalterability should be able to predict which rules cannot affect long segments and which rules can. Ideally, the principle that makes this prediction should not be an arbitrary stipulation, but should follow naturally from general principles. This article is an attempt to provide such an account.

The exposition is organized as follows. I begin with a review of CV Phonology, showing how the properties of Ambiguity and Integrity are consequences of it. In §2, I propose a CV account of Inalterability, and defend it with examples from a number of languages. In §3 [not repr. here], I discuss alternative proposals; the results are summarized in §4.

1. *CV Phonology* is an outgrowth of autosegmental phonology, as developed in Goldsmith 1976 and other works. The basic tenet of CV Phonology is that the property of syllabicity is represented on a separate autosegmental tier from the strictly segmental features. The tier specifying syllabicity, or 'CV tier', is linked to that specifying the remaining features, or 'melodic tier', with association lines in standard autosegmental fashion. As is normal in autosegmental phonology, the theory allows for one-to-many and many-to-one associations. Some of these principles are illustrated in figure 12.1 by a CV representation of the English word *junior*, phonetically [ǰuːnyr̩]. In particular, observe that the symbols *i* and *u* suffice for both glides and vowels, with the CV tier determining which they stand for. Many-to-one associations between tiers may be found in affricates, short diphthongs, and prenasalized stops; one-to-many associations occur in long vowels and geminate consonants.

The literature is now replete with evidence supporting the CV view of phonological structure. McCarthy (1979, 1981b) originally motivated the independent existence of the two tiers by showing that, in Semitic languages, morphemes may be defined on either one. Later work has shown the applicability of the CV framework in solving problems in reduplication (Marantz 1982); compensatory lengthening (Steriade 1982, Clements 1985, 1986), secret language games (Yip 1982, Odden MS); global rule application (Clements and Keyser 1983); phonotactics (Prince 1984); and speech error analysis (Stemberger 1984).

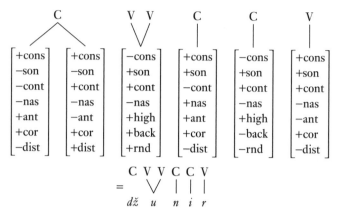

Figure 12.1

A number of general principles governing CV representation are generally or partially agreed upon in the literature. Three of them will be important below:

*The Obligatory Contour Principle* (Leben 1973, McCarthy 1986), devised originally by
Leben (1973) for tonal phonology, forbids sequences of identical segments where a single
multiply linked segment could replace them. Hence a long vowel must be represented
as (4a), not (4b):

(4)  (a)  V V          (b)  V V
          \\/               | |
           a                a  a

I assume that the Obligatory Contour Principle is a statement of markedness, assigning
greater value to the structure of (4a). This structure is thus selected by the language
learner in the absence of evidence to the contrary. By the same token, languages sometimes contain rules of 'melodic degemination', converting input structures like (4b) to
(4a). That (4a) should be more highly valued is plausible, given that it represents the
same phonetic substance as (4b) less redundantly.

*Prohibition on crossing association lines*   Configurations like (5) are universally ill-formed,
and rules are blocked when such configurations would be derived:

(5)  *C V
      ╳
      a  t

*Assimilation as spreading*   Halle and Vergnaud (1980), as well as others, argue that total
assimilation rules do not actually change a segment into something more like its neighbor,
but rather involve spreading of the trigger segment's melody onto the target segment's
CV position, in the same fashion that tonal autosegments spread. Thus a rule assimilating
/t/ totally to /k/ carries out the following operation:

(6)

To show some of the effects of these principles, I will first discuss how they solve the problems of Ambiguity and Integrity. The results obtained in these areas will be directly relevant to my proposal concerning Inalterability.[1]

1.1  *Ambiguity*  The phonological framework of *SPE* (Chomsky and Halle 1968) provides two ways of describing long segments: they can be single segments bearing the feature value [+long], or they can be sequences of two short segments bearing identical feature specifications. Generative phonologists working in the post-*SPE* period rapidly found that neither description could account for the way phonological rules treat long segments (see Kenstowicz 1970, Pyle 1970, Fidelholtz 1971, Sampson 1973, Barkaï 1974, Malone 1976, 1978). For some rules, only the sequence description allowed for an adequate account; but other rules required that long segments be counted as units, necessitating the feature description. Kenstowicz (1970) tentatively suggested letting long segments start out as sequences, applying all rules that demand this representation – then converting the sequences to [+long] units, and applying the rules that demand the feature representation. However, this proposal proved to be untenable: Fidelholtz showed that the independently needed rule-orderings of Micmac are inconsistent with it; and Kenstowicz (1970) demolished his own scheme by pointing out a rule of Lithuanian that demands both representations at the same time.

Although the post-*SPE* research failed to solve the problem of Ambiguity, it did identify the difficulties much more precisely. In addition, Kenstowicz (1970) uncovered a generalization that will be important here: for the most part, the rules that demanded a sequence representation were 'prosodic rules', which affect stress, tone, and length itself. The rules requiring the feature [+long] were mostly rules affecting segment quality. However, as Fidelholtz pointed out, nothing in the theoretical framework of the time provided any formal account of the intuitive distinction between prosodic and qualitative rules.

Consider now how Ambiguity can be dealt with in CV phonology. The theory represents most long segments as single melodic segments linked to two C or V positions, in accordance with the Obligatory Contour Principle:

(7)  (a)  (b)

These representations largely solve the problems uncovered in earlier research: the long segments form single units on the tier responsible for representing quality, and two-segment sequences on that responsible for representing quantity.

Consider two examples, which appear to be quite typical. In Hausa (Klingenheben 1928), diphthongs and long vowels may not occur in closed syllables. When such configurations arise through morphological combination, they are resolved by shortening long vowels and deleting the second halves of diphthongs:

(8)  (a)  *á:-n-kà*        → *ɗánkà* 'your son'
         son-of-2m.sg.
      (b)  *kái-n-kà*       → *kánkà* 'your (m.sg.) head'
         head-of-2m.sg.
      (c)  *kyáù-n-fúskà:* → *kyánfúskà:* 'beauty of face'
         beauty-of-face

This situation clearly requires that long vowels be represented as sequences; if they were represented as [+long], then the shortening of long vowels could not be collapsed with the structurally similar simplification of diphthongs. CV Phonology can account for the facts straightforwardly. To shorten long vowels, the rule must delete a V position:

(9)   Hausa Shortening
      $V \rightarrow \emptyset / V \_\_\_ C]_{syl}$
      (a)   C V V C . C V → C V C . C V

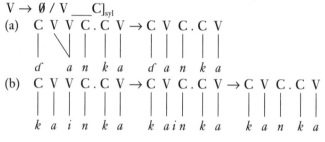

      (b)   C V V C . C V → C V C . C V → C V C . C V

In (9b), *kánkà*, the melodic segment /i/ is stranded by vowel deletion; such stranded segments are deleted by convention (McCarthy 1981b: 382, 399).
      Consider now a purely qualitative rule. In Lithuanian (Kenstowicz 1970), the vowels /e e:/ are backed to /o o:/ before the vowel /u/ and the glide /w/. Such a rule must treat long vowels as units; otherwise it would convert /eeu/, for example, to *[eou] rather than [oou]. In CV phonology, the rule is expressed on the melodic tier, where vowel quality is represented:

(10)   Lithuanian Backing

$$\begin{bmatrix} -\text{cons} \\ -\text{high} \end{bmatrix} \rightarrow [+\text{back}] / \_\_\_ \begin{bmatrix} -\text{cons} \\ +\text{back} \\ +\text{high} \end{bmatrix}$$

Such a rule can affect both long and short vowels:

(11)   (a)   V V V → V V V          (b)   V V → V V

                *e   u        o   u                   *e   u        o   u
              (= [o:u])                    (= [ou])

   The significance of these examples is that neither the feature representation nor the sequence representation of length can alone account for both cases. The Hausa example requires the sequence representation in order to capture the parallel behavior of long vowels and diphthongs; the Lithuanian example requires the feature representation to generalize over long and short vowels. CV Phonology makes both representations available, and correctly predicts which one will be relevant from whether the rule affects quantity or quality. It will be seen shortly that Kenstowicz's generalization about quantity and quality also plays an important role in Inalterability.

1.2  *Integrity*  In languages with both long segments and rules of epenthesis, it has been consistently found that epenthetic segments cannot be inserted between the halves of long segments. Abu-Salim (1980) describes an interesting case from Palestinian Arabic. Omitting some irrelevant details, epenthesis in this language works as follows:

(12)  Palestinian Epenthesis

$$\emptyset \rightarrow V \;/\; C\underline{\quad}C \;\;\begin{Bmatrix} C \\ \# \end{Bmatrix}\;\; \text{(applies iteratively, right-to-left)}$$
$$\phantom{\emptyset \rightarrow V \;/\;} |$$
$$\phantom{\emptyset \rightarrow V \;/\;} i$$

Here are some examples:

(13)  (a)  /ʔakl/  →  ʔakil  'food'
      (b)  /ʔakl-kum/  →  ʔakilkum  'your food'
      (c)  /jisr  kbiir/  →  jisrikbiir  'a big bridge'
           bridge big
      (d)  /l-ʔakl  l-mniiḥ/  →  lʔakllimniiḥ  →  lʔakillimniiḥ
           DEF-food DEF-good  'the good food'

The statement of Epenthesis under (12) is inadequate in one respect: it fails to state that the rule is blocked when it would insert /i/ in the middle of a geminate:

(14)  (a)  ʔimn  (*ʔimim) 'mother'
      (b)  sitt-na (*sititna) 'our grandmother'

Steriade, following a suggestion by Jonathan Kaye, argues that this effect results automatically from principles of CV Phonology. Observe that an epenthesis rule must insert both a V position and the melody associated with it. If long segments normally have the structure given in (15), with multiple association, then it is impossible to split them without violating the universal constraint against crossing association lines:

(15)  (a)  C V C C → *C V C V C
           | | V     | | X
           ʔ i  m    ʔ i  i  m

      (b)  C V C C → *C V C V C
           | | V     | |  X
           ʔ i  m    ʔ i  m  i

Thus the theory automatically predicts that Epenthesis should not be able to split geminates.

    Some further facts support this analysis. Note that the structure for geminates under (15) would be expected to arise only within morphemes, where the Obligatory Contour

Principle enforces it. Where a geminate arises through morpheme concatenation, each morpheme must provide a melodic segment from its lexical entry, giving the structure under (16a). For convenience I will refer to these accidental geminates as *fake*, while the doubly linked variety found within morphemes will be called *true* geminates:

(16)　(a)　Fake geminates　　(b)　True geminates

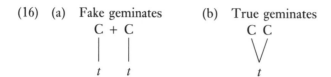

Unlike true geminates, fake geminates should be freely splittable by epenthesis, since no association lines would cross. As Abu-Salim points out, this is indeed true in Palestinian Arabic:

(17)

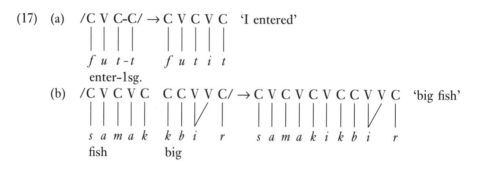

(a)　/C V C-C/ → C V C V C　'I entered'

　　　　*f u t - t*　　*f u t i t*
　　　　enter–1sg.

(b)　/C V C V C　C C V V C/ → C V C V C V C C V V C　'big fish'

　　　*s a m a k*　*k b i*　*r*　　*s a m a k i k b i*　*r*
　　　fish　　　big

One additional fact provides even stronger support for the theory: a heteromorphemic geminate WILL resist epenthesis, provided it derives from a rule of total assimilation. This again follows from standard assumptions. In CV Phonology, total assimilation is expressed as the autosegmental spreading of the melody to an adjacent C slot, creating a true geminate as the output. This is illustrated in figure 12.2 with the Palestinian rule that assimilates the definite article /l/ to coronal segments.

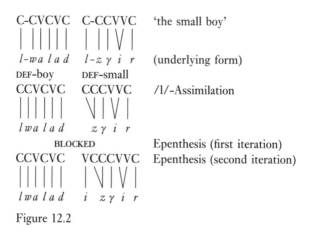

| C-CVCVC | C-CCVVC | 'the small boy' |
| *l-wa l a d* | *l-z γ i r* | (underlying form) |
| DEF-boy | DEF-small | |
| CCVCVC | CCCVVC | /l/-Assimilation |
| *l wa l a d* | *z γ i r* | |
| | BLOCKED | Epenthesis (first iteration) |
| CCVCVC | VCCCVVC | Epenthesis (second iteration) |
| *l wa l a d* | *i z γ i r* | |

Figure 12.2

Here the /zz/ that results from /l/-Assimilation forms a true geminate. This blocks Epenthesis on its first iteration, producing [lwaladizzɣi:r] instead of the expected [lwaladizzɣi:r].

The predictions of CV theory concerning Integrity extend to other languages and rule types. Thus epenthesis is also unable to split true geminates in Berber (Saib 1976, Guerssel 1977, 1978), Moroccan Arabic (Guerssel 1978), Amharic (McCarthy 1986), and Tiberian Hebrew (McCarthy 1986). Metathesis rules (e.g., of the form CCV → CVC) are clearly also subject to the predictions of the theory; cases in which metathesis fails to split geminates may be found in Berber (Guerssel 1978), Tunisian Arabic (Kenstowicz and Pyle 1973), and Classical Arabic (McCarthy 1981b: 398–9). Finally, CV theory predicts that epenthesis rules which insert consonants to break up vowel clusters should not be able to split up long vowels. This is indeed true in Kíhehe (Bantu, Tanzania; Odden and Odden 1985) and in Sinhala (Feinstein 1979).

2. *Inalterability*  The summary above suggests that the phenomenon of Integrity follows from independently motivated principles of CV Phonology: (a) the Obligatory Contour Principle, (b) the ban on crossing association lines, and (c) the statement of assimilation as spreading. Together, these determine the geminates subject to Integrity: monomorphemic geminates, and heteromorphemic geminates derived by assimilation. Obviously, this set would not be a natural class a priori. The predictions of CV Phonology concerning Integrity thus constitute a rare instance of a successful (albeit elementary) 'theorem' in phonology.[2] I will now consider whether the same kind of theorem can be derived for the phenomenon of Inalterability.

2.1  *The role of CV theory*  To start, I will show that merely adopting CV representations does not, of itself, solve the Inalterability problem; but it does provide a different perspective. To demonstrate this, I will discuss in greater detail the Persian rule of /v/-Weakening mentioned earlier.

In Modern Persian, [w] is a distributional variant of underlying /v/: roughly speaking, [w] occurs when it follows a short vowel and is not syllable-initial (cf. Cowan and Yarmohammadi). An additional rule of /æ/-Backing takes /æ/ to /o/ whenever it precedes /w/. The rules of /v/-Weakening and /æ/-Backing result in alternations like these:

(18)  (a)  *mi:-ræv-æm*          'I am going'
           PRES-go-1sg.
      (b)  *bo-row* (< /bo-ræv/)   'go!'
           IMP-go

(19)  (a)  *nov-i:n*             'new kind'
           new-SUFF
      (b)  *now-ru:z* (< /nov-ru:z/)  'New Year'
           new-day

20   (a)  *mi:-dæv-i:d*          'you are running'
           PRES-run-2pl.
      (b)  *pa:-dow* (< /pa:-dæv/)   'gofer'
           foot-run(ner)

The /v/-Weakening rule is also supported simply by the surface complementary distribution of [v] and [w]:

(21) (a)  *pa:ltow*  'overcoat'      *mow*      'vine'
         *četowr*   'how'           *dowre*    'era'
    (b)  *væli:*    'but'           *voǰu:d*   'existence'
         *kešvær*   'country'       *omi:dva:r* 'hopeful'
         *ga:v*     'bull'          *hi:vdæh*  'seventeen'
         *ǰozv*     'except'        *særv*     'cypress'

As the data make clear, /v/-Weakening should be stated as applying to a /v/ that occurs in the same syllable as a preceding short vowel. I state the rule as follows, using Kahn's (1976) formalism for syllable membership:

(22)  Persian /v/-Weakening

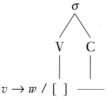

The rule says: 'Convert /v/ to /w/ when its associated C position shares the same syllable with a short vowel.' The rule applies to underlying /šenæv/ as in figure 12.3.

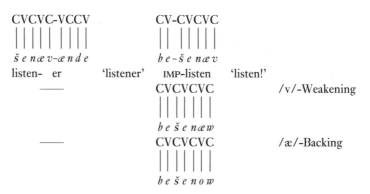

Figure 12.3

We now can consider how /v/-Weakening might be expected to affect a true geminate /vv/ in CV theory. Plausibly, the derivation would be as follows:

(23)  V C C → V C C
       | \/   | \/
       æ  v   æ  w

Since /v/ is linked to a C position following a short vowel, it should undergo the rule. This is the wrong result, since /vv/ is in fact inalterable; cf. numerous examples like *ævvæl* 'first', *morovvæt* 'generosity', *qolovv* 'exaggeration'.

Note that derivations similar to (23) actually occur for Lithuanian Backing, as in (10)–(11). It is not immediately clear why Persian /v/-Weakening should behave differently.

The point of this is that CV Phonology does not by itself solve the Inalterability problem; it merely makes different wrong predictions: phonological rules will wrongly affect entire geminates, rather than halves of geminates. But with a minor revision, CV theory CAN account for Inalterability, correctly distinguishing the Persian and Lithuanian cases. I will now show how this can be done.

2.2   *An account of inalterability*   A survey of the cases known to me reveals the following generalization: roughly speaking, the rules subject to Inalterability are those which mention both the CV tier and the melodic tier (cf. rule 22); but those rules which escape Inalterability are formulated on just one tier (cf. Hausa Shortening, rule 9; Sinhala Cluster Simplification, rule 3; and Lithuanian Backing, rule 10). While the correlation is not perfect, I believe it forms the basis of an adequate account. To make this account rigorous, it is necessary to make explicit the criteria by which one may determine when a rule must mention a particular tier. My criteria are as follows:

(a)   Any rule mentioning distinctive features other than [syllabic] must obviously mention the melodic tier; e.g., a rule that refers to the natural class of glides and vowels must mention the melodic tier in order to include [–consonantal].
(b)   Any rule that appeals to the class of consonants or to the class of vowels must mention the CV tier, where syllabicity is represented.
(c)   Any rule that refers to position within the syllable (e.g., 'syllable-initial') must refer to the CV tier. Here I follow Clements and Keyser in assuming that it is the CV tier which is incorporated into syllables. This is a plausible assumption, given that elements of the melodic tier are often spread over more than one syllable, which would result in improper bracketings if the melodic tier were syllabified.

These three criteria normally suffice to identify the tiers that a rule must mention. Thus Persian /v/-Weakening (22) must mention the melodic tier to identify /v/, and the CV tier to ensure that the /v/ is tautosyllabic with the preceding vowel.

The next step is to show that the proposed dependence of Inalterability on the number of tiers mentioned is not to be stipulated, but follows naturally from independent principles. What is special about two-tier rules, I would argue, is not that they mention two tiers, but that they include association lines in their structural descriptions. Such rules are ambiguous in a way that has not yet been clearly resolved. To clarify this ambiguity, I will refer to the schematic example (24), below.

Suppose that some phonological rule P contains in its structural description autosegments $\alpha$ and $\beta$, linked by an association line, as in (24a). Suppose further a representation R, which contains the autosegments A and B. A is an autosegment analyzable by $\alpha$ (e.g., if $\alpha$ is [+coronal], A could be the melodic autosegment /t/); and B is an autosegment analyzable by $\beta$. The crucial question is: What association lines should be present in representation R in order for rule P to apply to it? Two logical possibilities exist.

(a) First, we might suppose that P is applicable to R if A is linked *at least* to B, where A and B may also be linked to other autosegments. Under this interpretation, P may apply to any of the candidates for R under (24c):

(24)  (a)   Rule P contains $\alpha$.

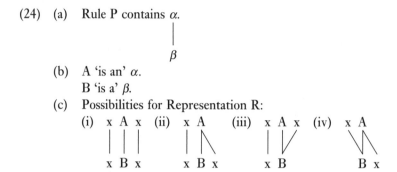

                    $\beta$

(b)   A 'is an' $\alpha$.
      B 'is a' $\beta$.

(c)   Possibilities for Representation R:

This interpretation was tacitly adhered to in the derivation of (23).

(b) The other possible interpretation is that rule P applies to R only if A is *uniquely* linked to B, and vice versa. If this is true, P would apply only to representation (24ci).

These two interpretations seem about equally plausible a priori; only data can determine the right choice. I will show here that, if the second option is taken, then the Inalterability problem is solved directly. For clarity, I will give a name to my interpretation of association lines:

(25)  *Linking Constraint*   Association lines in structural descriptions are interpreted as exhaustive.

This formulation is intended to cover structural descriptions in which an autosegment is multiply linked: an autosegment bearing *n* linkages in a structural description must be matched to an autosegment bearing exactly *n* linkages in the actual form, as seems natural.

Note that the Linking Constraint will be relevant only if the $\alpha$ and $\beta$ in the structural description actually have association lines attached to them. If an autosegment appears in a structural description with no lines attached, this should be interpreted as allowing any number of association lines, including zero. Thus a bare autosegment in a structural description does not mean that it is necessarily 'floating'. Rather, I assume (following standard practice) that a 'necessarily floating' autosegment must be marked as such by circling it. The meaning of the Linking Constraint is summarized below, where $\alpha$ is an autosegment appearing in a rule:

(26)  (a)   $\alpha$ = $\alpha$ linked to any number of autosegments.
      (b)   @ = $\alpha$ linked to no autosegments.
      (c)   $\alpha$ = $\alpha$ linked to exactly one autosegment.
          |

      (d)   $\alpha$ = $\alpha$ linked to exactly two autosegments (etc.)
          $\wedge$

[ . . . ]

4 *Conclusions* The theory I have presented can be thought of as an amplification of Kenstowicz's (1970) typology of how phonological rules refer to length. He contended that rules can be roughly divided into two kinds: quality rules, which treat long segments as units; and quantity rules, which treat long segments as sequences. CV Phonology provides an explicit formal implementation of Kenstowicz's suggestion, thus overcoming Fidelholtz's objection that Kenstowicz's claim had no theoretical expression. In addition, the theory I have proposed here suggests that there is a third category of rules, which refer both to quantity (in our terms, to positions on the CV tier) and to quality (to melodic segments). It is this third category that respects Inalterability. The existence of 'quantity/quality' rules, and the fact that such rules show a very special property, provides a further argument that CV Phonology is the correct formal expression of Kenstowicz's original idea.

The other part of my proposal, which is clearly more speculative, was to try to derive the Inalterability of quantity/quality rules more or less as a theorem. The assumption that was required, i.e. the Linking Constraint, seems a plausible candidate for a universal principle, simply because it is primitive in character and involves no arbitrary stipulations. To my knowledge, it is the most general solution available that fits the data.

## Notes

I would like to thank Diana Archangeli, G. N. Clements, B. Elan Dresher, Wilson Gray, Morris Halle, Patricia Keating, Phil LeSourd, Joseph Malone, John McCarthy, Brian McHugh, David Odden, Russell Schuh, Donca Steriade, and Charles Ulrich, among others, for their very helpful advice and comments on the research reported here. None of them should be held responsible for shortcomings.

An early version of this article was presented as Hayes 1984.

1 Two further issues within CV Phonology are not strictly relevant to the proposal I will make below. I mention them here for rigor's sake:

(a) In some versions of CV Phonology, the symbols C and V are replaced by the single unit X, with consonants distinguished from vowels by virtue of their location within a hierarchical syllable structure: vowels are X's included within the syllable Nucleus, while consonants are extranuclear X's (cf. Kaye and Lowenstamm 1986, Prince 1984, Levin 1982). As far as I can tell, everything I say below can be expressed equally well in either version of the theory. I use C's and V's for expository simplicity.

(b) The CV representations originally posited by McCarthy (1979, 1981b) for morphology involve placing each melodic morpheme on a separate tier. As Steriade (1982: 103–7) points out, these multi-tiered representations sometimes lead to problems when put to phonological use; phonology apparently requires a single tier for all melodic segments. McCarthy (1986), citing unpublished work by R. Gutmann Younes, suggests a straightforward procedure that collapses multi-tiered morphological representations into just two tiers before the phonological rules apply. I assume that this procedure is correct, and that all the phonological rules described here apply to its output.

2 A caveat: These results appear to hold only for 'local' autosegmental linkings, such as those found in geminate consonants and long vowels. Autosegmental phonologists have also posited long-distance linkings, extending over several syllables, to handle phenomena such as tonal spreading and vowel harmony. Such linkings sometimes fail to respect Integrity; cf. examples from Hungarian in Clements 1976 and from Pasiego Spanish in McCarthy 1984. Moreover, long-distance linkings suffer from a serious Ambiguity problem of their own. For example, a sequence of high-pitched syllables is sometimes best analyzed as a single, multiply linked high tone, and sometimes as a sequence of high tones. This can happen even in a single language; thus in Shona (Odden 1980,

1984), a high-toned sequence must be analyzed as a series of high tones for the verbal morphology; as a single, multiply linked high tone for the nominal morphology; and again as a tone sequence for the phrasal phonology.

Given that long-distance linking leads to problems in Ambiguity and Integrity, it is not surprising that it should yield counterexamples to my proposal below concerning Inalterability. The Venda rules of Pre-Penult Simplification and Final Simplification (Cassimjee 1983) are two particularly compelling cases; both arise because of long-distance linking. It is clear that distinguishing the behavior of long-distance vs. local linking is a major problem which goes beyond the scope of this article. In what follows, the discussion will therefore be confined to local linking.

# References

Abu-Salim, Issam M. 1980. Epenthesis and geminate consonants in Palestinian Arabic. *Studies in the Linguistic Sciences* (University of Illinois, Urbana) 10/2: 1–11.

Barkaï, Malachi. 1974. On duration and spirantization in Biblical Hebrew. *Linguistic Inquiry* 5: 456–9.

Cassimjee, Farida. 1983. An autosegmental analysis of Venda nominal tonology. *Studies in the Linguistic Sciences* (University of Illinois, Urbana) 13/1: 43–72.

Chomsky, Noam, and Morris Halle. 1968. *The Sound Pattern of English*. New York: Harper and Row.

Clements, George N. 1976. Neutral vowels in Hungarian vowel harmony: an autosegmental interpretation. NELS 7: 49–64.

Clements, George N. 1985. The geometry of phonological features. In *Phonology Yearbook*, 2: 225–52. Repr. in part here as ch. 11.

Clements, George N. 1986. Compensatory lengthening and consonant gemination in Luganda. In Sezer and Wetzels 1986: 37–77.

Clements, George N. and S. Jay Keyser. 1983. *CV Phonology: A Generative Theory of the Syllable*. Cambridge, Mass.: MIT Press.

Cowan, J. Ronayne, and Lotfollah Yarmohammadi. 1978. The Persian verb reconsidered. *Archív Orientální* 46: 46–60.

Feinstein, Mark. 1979. Prenasalization and syllable structure. *Linguistic Inquiry* 10: 245–78.

Fidelholtz, James L. 1971. On the indeterminacy of the representation of vowel length. *Papers in Linguistics* 4: 577–94.

Goldsmith, John. 1976. Autosegmental Phonology. Ph.D. dissertation, MIT. Published, New York: Garland, 1979.

Guerssel, Mohamed. 1977. Constraints on phonological rules. *Linguistic Analysis* 3: 267–305.

Guerssel, Mohamed. 1978. A condition on assimilation rules. *Linguistic Analysis* 4: 225–54.

Halle, Morris, and Jean-Roger Vergnaud. 1980. Three-dimensional phonology. *Journal of Linguistic Research* 1: 83–105.

Hayes, Bruce. 1984. Inalterability in CV Phonology. Paper presented at the 15th meeting of NELS, Brown University.

Kahn, Daniel. 1976. Syllable-based generalizations in English phonology. Ph.D. dissertation, MIT. Published, New York: Garland, 1979.

Kaye, Jonathan, and Jean Lowenstamm. 1986. Compensatory lengthening in Tiberian Hebrew: theoretical implications. In Sezer and Wetzels 1986: 97–132.

Kenstowicz, Michael J. 1970. On the notation of vowel length in Lithuanian. *Papers in Linguistics* 3: 73–113.

Kenstowicz, Michael J. and Charles Pyle. 1973. On the phonological integrity of geminate clusters. In M. J. Kenstowicz and Charles Kisseberth (eds), *Issues in Phonological Theory*, The Hague: Mouton, 27–43.

Klingenheben, August. 1928. Die Silbenauslautsgesetze des Hausa. *Zeitschrift für Eingeborenen Sprachen* 18: 272–97.

Leben, William. 1973. Suprasegmental Phonology. Ph.D. dissertation, MIT. Published, New York: Garland, 1979.

Leben, William. 1980. A metrical analysis of length. *Linguistic Inquiry* 11: 497–509.

Levin, Juliette. 1982. Reduplication and prosodic structure. MS, Dept. of Linguistics, MIT.

McCarthy, John J. 1979. Formal Problems in Semitic Phonology and Morphology. Ph.D. dissertation, MIT. Published, New York: Garland, 1985.

McCarthy, John J. 1981a. The representation of consonant length in Hebrew. *Linguistic Inquiry* 12: 322–7.

McCarthy, John J. 1981b. A prosodic theory of non-concatenative morphology. *Linguistic Inquiry* 12: 373–418.

McCarthy, John J. 1984. Theoretical consequences of Montañés vowel harmony. *Linguistic Inquiry* 15: 291–318.

McCarthy, John J. 1986. OCP effects: gemination and antigemination. *Linguistic Inquiry* 17: 207–63.

Malone, Joseph. 1976. Messrs Sampson, Chomsky and Halle, and Hebrew phonology. *Foundations of Language* 14: 251–6.

Malone, Joseph. 1978. Heavy segments vs. the paradoxes of segment length: the evidence Tiberian Hebrew. *Linguistics*, special issue, 119–58.

Marantz, Alec. 1982. Rereduplication. *Linguistic Inquiry* 13: 435–82.

Odden, David. 1980. Associative tone in Shona. *Journal of Linguistic Research* 2: 37–51.

Odden, David. 1984. Stem tone assignment in Shona. In George N. Clements and John Goldsmith (eds), *Autosegmental Studies in Bantu Tone*. Dordrecht: Foris, 255–80.

Odden, David. MS. A non-linear approach to vowel length in Kimatuumbi. Yale University.

Odden, David and Mary Odden. 1985. Ordered reduplication in Kíhehe. *Linguistic Inquiry* 16: 497–503.

Prince, Alan S. 1984. Phonology with tiers. In Mark Aronoff and Richard T. Oehrle (eds), *Language Sound Structure*. Cambridge, Mass.: MIT Press, 234–45.

Pyle, Charles. 1970. West Greenlandic Eskimo and the representation of vowel length. *Papers in Linguistics* 3: 115–46.

Saib, Jilali. 1976. A Phonological Study of Tamazight Berber: Dialect of Ayt Ndhin. Ph.D. dissertation, UCLA.

Sampson, Geoffrey. 1973. Duration in Hebrew consonants. *Linguistic Inquiry* 4: 101–4.

Sezer, Engin, and Leo Wetzels. MS (eds). 1986. *Studies in Compensatory Lengthening*. Dordrecht: Foris.

Stemberger, Joseph Paul. 1984. Length as a suprasegmental. *Language* 60: 895–913.

Steriade, Donca. 1982. Greek prosodies and the nature of syllabification. Ph.D. dissertation, MIT.

Yip, Moira. 1982. Reduplication and C-V skeleta in Chinese secret languages. *Linguistic Inquiry* 13: 637–61.

# 13

# Prosodic Morphology (1986)

## John J. McCarthy and Alan S. Prince

This work has circulated in manuscript form since October 1986. Its basic contents were first presented at the third West Coast Conference on Formal Linguistics in the spring of 1986. It has been cited variously as McCarthy and Prince 1986; McCarthy and Prince, forthcoming, and even (optimistically) as McCarthy and Prince, in press.

Many of the proposals made here have been revised, generalized, or superseded in subsequent work (see the bibliography), including a book manuscript of nearly the same title by the same authors. Junko Itô and Armin Mester suggested to us that it might still be useful to make the 1986 manuscript available in a somewhat more official way, and in 1996 we did that, issuing it as Rutgers Center for Cognitive Science Technical Report 32, with an updated bibliography, with outright errors noted and corrected, and with some added commentary (set off with horizontal lines above and below).

The material reprinted here is excerpted from that 1996 Technical Report. Cross-references to sections not included here are signalled by a dagger (†). The full text of the Technical Report may be purchased from the Center for Cognitive Science, Rutgers University, New Brunswick, NJ 08903, USA. It is also available at no cost over the Internet at http://ruccs.rutgers.edu/tech_rpt/pm86all.pdf.

Readers interested in learning about more recent developments in this area may want to examine some of the offerings of the Rutgers Optimality Archive (http://ruccs.rutgers.edu/roa.html), including the following works:

McCarthy, John and Alan Prince. 1995. Faithfulness and reduplicative identity. In Jill Beckman, Laura Walsh Dickey, and Suzanne Urbanczyk (eds), *University of Massachusetts Occasional Papers in Linguistics 18: Papers in Optimality Theory*, Amherst, Mass.: Graduate Linguistic Student Association, 249–384. [Rutgers Optimality Archive #60.]

McCarthy, John and Alan Prince. In press. Faithfulness and identity in Prosodic Morphology. In René Kager, Harry van der Hulst, and Wim Zonneveld (eds), *The Prosody Morphology Interface*. Cambridge: Cambridge University Press. [Rutgers Optimality Archive #216.]

# 1   Introduction

## 1.1   Templatic morphology within Prosodic Theory

A central strategy for deriving words requires that a base accommodate to a target frame: the invariant that identifies a morpheme lies in its overall shape rather than in its phonemic composition. The reduplicative perfect prefix of Indo-European is always (C)V; its content is borrowed from the root. The causative/factitive 'measure II' of the Classical Arabic verb conforms to the pattern CVCCVC. Such descriptive observations lie at the heart of recent studies of reduplicative and root-and-pattern morphologies. Here we will inquire into the nature of the targets used in such systems: we will show that they must be defined in terms of the categories and rules of prosody, as provided by the theory of syllabification, stress, and accent. Our immediate goal is to provide a basis for nonconcatenative morphology; our broader goal is to circumscribe the modes of reference to structural information in phonology and to characterize the class of structures that are authentically essential to phonological representation.

Basic findings in prosody place strong conditions of adequacy on template theory. It is worth examining the chief interactions, since we can immediately rule out many plausible-seeming approaches while establishing the general constraints within which template theory must work.

Consider first the role of **counting** in grammar. How long may a count run? General considerations of locality, now the common currency in all areas of linguistic thought, suggest that the answer is probably 'up to two': a rule may fix on one specified element and examine a structurally adjacent element and no other. For example, the 'End Rule' of Prince (1983) focuses on one edge of a domain and selects the element adjacent to that edge for some specified operation; similar cases can easily be multiplied.

What elements may be counted? It is a commonplace of phonology that rules count moras ($\mu$), syllables ($\sigma$), or feet (F) but never segments. Many languages place a two-mora bound on the minimum size of major-category words; this follows from the prosodic hierarchy, if prosodic words must contain feet and feet can be no smaller than $2\ \mu$. Exactly this state of affairs is demonstrated for Estonian in Prince 1980; an interesting side-effect is that the rule of apocope apparent in the nominative singular is blocked when its output violates this condition:[1]

(1)   Estonian Word Minimality
   (a)   /kana/     kana     *kan     'chicken, nom.sg.'
   (b)   /konna/    kon:n             'pig, nom.sg.'
   (c)   /tänava/   tänav             'street, nom.sg.'

Final consonants are provably extrametrical, so that no form like *kan* is admissible as a noun. In Kyoto (Kansai) Japanese, where the one allowed final consonant (N) is fully moraic, content words shaped CV are excluded: all historically monomoraic items have been lengthened (CV > CV:) to conform to the $2\ \mu$ limit. A typical variation is reported for Caughnawaga Mohawk in Michelson 1981: verbs must be disyllabic, and undersized collocations of morphemes are expanded by epenthesis.

(2)   Mohawk Word Minimality
    (a)   /k + tats + s/        *i*ktats       'I offer'
    (b)   /hs + ya?ks + s/    *i*hsya?ks  'you are cutting'

Crucially, Mohawk prosody is insensitive to the light/heavy distinction, so that F is minimally $[\sigma\sigma]$.[2]

Counting restrictions often determine nonphonological allomorphy as well. In Dyirbal (Dixon 1972), by a kind of compensation, the ergative suffix is bimoraic *-ŋgu* with minimal (disyllabic) bases but monomoraic *-gu* with longer ones.

(3)   Dyirbal Size-based Allomorphy
    (a)   /yaṛa/        yaṛa-ŋgu     'man'
    (b)   /yamani/     yamani-gu    'rainbow'

A short word contains a single F; a long word, something more.[3] In English, comparative *-er* and superlative *-est* are pretty much restricted to minimal (monopod) words:

(4)   English Size-based Allomorphy
    (a)   redder        stupider      noblest
    (b)   yellower     *obtuser     *augustest

Outside the realm of morphology proper, we find that the *to*-dative alternation in English is essentially limited to one-foot verbs (Grimshaw 1985): thus, 'give/offer the men the ball', but *'donate the men the ball'.

---

Counting Allomorphy
An analysis of syllable/mora-counting allomorphy in terms of prosodic circumscription is offered in McCarthy and Prince (hereafter M&P) 1990a. A different account, based on prosodic subcategorization, is put forward in M&P 1993a: ch. 7. Other recent work includes Mester 1995 and Kager 1996a, b.

---

No language process, however, is known to depend on the raw number of **segments** in a form: a robust finding, given the frequency and pervasiveness of counting restrictions. It should come as no surprise that templatic morphology can't count segments either. If a reduplicative prefix target could be XXX – three segments, unadorned with prosodic structure – the following impossible type of system should be common:

(5)   Hypothetical XXX Reduplication
    (a)   badupi   →   BAD badupi
    (b)   bladupi  →   BLA bladupi
    (c)   adupi   →   ADU adupi

What's prosodically incoherent here is the segmental equation of monomoraic BLA with bimoraic BAD and ADU.

It is striking, then, that current theories of template form are essentially segmental, allowing prosodic annotation as an option or alternative to be called on when necessary. The CV-theory of McCarthy (1981), taken up in Marantz 1982, has been generalized to the syllable-point theory of Lowenstamm and Kaye (1986) and the X-theory of Levin (1983), most extensively explored in Levin 1985. In the syllable-point theory, uncharacterized segmental skeletal nodes are seen as dependents of syllables. In the X-theory, in its various instantiations, a level of segmental structure, unmarked for the C/V distinction, is distinguished by higher-level prosodic structure. Although studies conducted within these theories have vastly increased our knowledge and understanding of templatic systems, their basic representational assumptions cannot stand. Templates by their nature count elements: CV- or X-theories must count segments, and must count many of them. Consider the template-of-templates that generates the various forms of the Classical Arabic verb:

(6)   Segmental Skeleton for the Arabic Verb
    (a)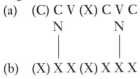

    (b)   (X) X X (X) X X X

By this, seven segments must be counted. Our proposal (in section 2.4) will be that the template is [σ σ], the familiar count to two, with extrametricality allowing for the extra initial position. Within X-theory, the simplest and therefore most highly valued templates are purely segmental: indeed Levin (1985) proposes that the (impossible) template XXX is attested in Mokilese: below, we show that the actual template is $\sigma_{\mu\mu}$, a heavy syllable. The descriptive success of XXX is an artifact of the restricted syllable structure of this language.

---

The XXX Template

In fact, what Levin (1985) proposes is that the Mokilese template is [XXX]$_\sigma$, not bare XXX. (The erroneous attribution in the text is a result of consulting a low-quality photocopy of Levin 1985.) The point still holds, though. In segmentalism, XXX is the simplest and therefore most highly valued template, yet it is factually impossible. Moreover, even with a syllabic appurtenance, as in [XXX]$_\sigma$, it still characterizes a factually impossible situation of segment counting, in which there is an equivalence among the prosodically disjoint set CCV, CVV, CVC, and VCC.

---

Alone among students of the template, Hyman (1985) has rejected a segmental level of representation in favor of a weight structure that is essentially moraic. Our results, although largely complementary to his, bear significant resemblances to his work.

    The fundamental goal of a template representation system must be to characterize the shape-invariant that unites the various allomorphs. Here prosody diverges notably from segmentalism. If we say that the template is [σ], then all segmental sequences comprising a licit syllable of the language are in the equivalence class: {V, CV, CVC, CCVC}, for example, would be a typical set of realizations. Since no single segmental string is conserved, segmentalism must supplement the representational theory with principles that serve to equate strings in the set. Following Marantz (1982), segmental theories spell out the template as the longest observed realization (or even the union of the observed realizations, if distinct from the longest); when an insufficiency of melody leaves template slots empty, they are discarded. The distinction between the two approaches can be made clear with an example. In the Philippine language Ilokano, the progressive is formed by reduplicative prefixation, as shown below:

(7)   Reduplication in Ilokano
      (a)   /basa/        ag – BAS – basa        'be reading'
      (b)   /adal/        ag – AD – adal         'be studying'
      (c)   /takder/      ag – TAK – takder      'be standing'
      (d)   /trabaho/     ag – TRAB – trabaho    'be working'

Segmentalism must analyze the prefix as CCVC, explicitly counting out the maximal monosyllable.[4] We propose that the target is simply $\sigma$; given a copy of the bare melody, it satisfies itself to the fullest extent allowed by the usual rules of the language.

(8)   $\sigma$  +  $\sigma\sigma\sigma$

      trabaho trabaho

Notice that stem syllabification is inhibited by the usual onset priority considerations, hence [tra][ba] . . . ; the prefix $\sigma$ faces no such competition, hence [trab].

As example (7) illustrates, segmentalism is typically faced with an excess of underlying slots. There are well-known ways in which unfilled slots influence phonology and morphology (Selkirk 1981, Clements and Keyser 1983, Marlett and Stemberger 1983, Lowenstamm and Kaye 1986). It is a remarkable fact that empty templatic slots have never been convincingly detected outside their endo-theoretic role in melody association.[5] We conclude that they do not exist.

In essence, segmentalism must hold that all template elements are optional until proven otherwise. It is thus in principle incapable of specifying, in the representation, that certain elements are obligatory, a common situation. We show below that the reduplicative prefix in Ponapean is a heavy syllable: segmentally, this means CVX, with the X required and the C optional. The additional conditions follow immediately from the syllabic characterization, since onsets are optional initially in the language, and heavy syllables must of course have a postnuclear element. Nothing in the segmental theory guarantees this result.

One final observation seals the case against excess elements in templates. It is a stable empirical finding that templates imitate – up to extrametricality – the prosodic structure of the language at hand. There is no Arabic template CVCCCVC; correlatively, the syllabification of the language disallows triconsonantal clusters. Segmental theory, however, cannot derive this result. Since excess or stray elements are erased, they are free to occur, and indeed must occur in other circumstances. Were they present, even fleetingly, they could perturb melody association in easily discoverable ways. For example, the Arabic template CVCCVC, with which *CVCCCVC would be neutralized, requires special conditions to override left-to-right association; these could be stated to make a phony distinction between CC and *CCC, introducing an otherwise inexpressible contrast into the language. In this way a pseudo-contrast in the CV-domain, protected from surfacing by stray erasure, can be projected into the melodic domain, where it would survive to visibility. Section 2.4 contains further discussion of the Arabic case.

Within prosodic theory, where the actual shape-invariant can be identified, it is possible to assume a natural condition on template interpretation:

(9)   Satisfaction Condition
      All elements in a template are obligatorily satisfied.[6]

All three of the problems stemming from segmental shape specification are resolved:

(i)   Under the Satisfaction Condition no excess material is ever present in the representation, giving us the easiest and least stipulative explanation for its unresponsiveness to phonological probing: nonexistence.

(ii)  Patterns of obligatoriness and optionality will follow in general from independent characterization of the prosodic units, both universally and language-specifically. (This is merely a somewhat tardy extension of reasoning well-established in phonology, where such optionality-stipulating notations as '( )' and zero-subscript have faded in the face of accurate representation of prosody.)

(iii) The fact that the templates are bounded by a language's prosody follows from their being literally built from that prosody.

The actual shape-invariant defining a templatic morpheme must be prosodic, then, rather than segmental. Even at this descriptive level it becomes clear when languages with moderately complex prosody are examined that prosodic categories must be admitted into template theory. 'CVC' seems a plausible enough prefix; but when the next language over (e.g. Ilokano instead of Agta), shows 'CCVC', correlated with the appearance of two-consonant onsets, it becomes harder to avoid the correct generalization. The Classical Arabic templates appear relatively simple (though, as noted above, spelled segmentally they violate counting norms); turn to modern Hebrew, with a rich range of syllable-initial clusters to include, and the stipulative character of segmental spell-out becomes apparent (McCarthy 1984b; section 2.4 below). Nash (1980: 139) identifies the Warlpiri verbal reduplicative element as a foot, indeed as the ordinary stress-foot of that language, because it equates a single long-voweled syllable to two short-voweled syllables. In fact, the literature demonstrating the need for reference to prosodic structure in characterizing morphological structure is quite substantial; in addition to the works just cited, it includes Archangeli (1983, 1984), Lowenstamm and Kaye (1986), Yip (1982, 1983), Steriade (1985), Levin (1983, 1985), and Marantz (1982). What these works share is a concern with showing the necessity for prosody in the template; but they also share the recognition of a segmental level of skeletal representation.

Template theory therefore includes prosody; considerations reviewed here from counting theory and from the expression of shape invariance show that it must include nothing else. The rest of this document constitutes a *demonstratio* (in the sense that brought Galileo before the Inquisition) of this result.

## 1.2   Outline of the theory

Here we sketch the system of available categories and the principles of mapping that accommodate a base to a prosodically specified template.

### 1.2.1   The prosodic categories

The following units of structure will be called on:

(10)   The Prosodic Categories
    Wd   'prosodic word'
    F   'foot'
    $\sigma$   'syllable'
    $\sigma_\mu$   'light (monomoraic) syllable'
    $\sigma_{\mu\mu}$   'heavy (bimoraic) syllable'
    $\sigma_c$   'core syllable'

These elements are well-established outside of morphology. The theory of phonology uncontroversially recognizes the categories 'prosodic word' (Wd) and 'syllable' ($\sigma$). Stress theory provides the categories 'foot' (F), 'light syllable', and 'heavy syllable'. We adopt the traditional moraic terminology: light syllables ($\sigma_\mu$) contain one mora, heavy syllables ($\sigma_{\mu\mu}$) two (see Hyman (1985), Prince (1983) for recent discussion). Studies of syllabification proper have long recognized the centrality of the syllable CV, the 'core syllable' ($\sigma_c$). We interpret $\sigma_c$ to include $\sigma = V$ in languages which allow optionality of onsets.[7] The prosodic units are arranged hierarchically (see Selkirk (1980a, b) for the most explicit discussion of this point).

    Special status is often accorded to the **minimal** version of a category; we therefore recognize as part of morphology a minimizing predicate 'min'. In general, if $X^n$ is a level-n prosodic category expanding into several categories $X^{n-1}$, then $\min(X^n) = [X^{n-1}]_{X^n}$. For example, a prosodic word is typically a sequence of feet; so $\min(\text{Wd}) = [F]_{\text{Wd}}$. Appropriate technical development, which we postpone, would simplify the descriptive vocabulary in favor of a more restricted set of categories interacting with the 'min' operator: $\sigma_c$ can be identified as min $\sigma$, and perhaps $\sigma_{\mu\mu}$ as min F.

---

Minimal Word
Further formal development is found in M&P (1990a, 1991a, b). One refinement that emerges in this work is the "loose" minimal word, which contains a foot plus an unfootable syllable, in a loose interpretation of the prosodic hierarchy (cf. M&P 1993a: Appendix; 1995a; Itô and Mester 1992; Hewitt 1992).

---

    The category min Wd is particularly central; indeed, the many appearances of the category word in reduplicative and templatic systems all have the minimality requirement attached. There's an interesting variation in interpretation of min Wd which shows that the min-operator can be composed with itself at least once: in section 2.4.1 below, we show that min Wd may be any licit foot of the language, as in the Yup'ik proximal vocative, or it may be the minimal Foot which can yet be a word, that is to say a single syllable, as in the English hypocoristic: min min Wd.

---

More on the Minimal Word

The notion 'minimal word' builds on earlier work by Prince 1980 and Broselow 1982. Subsequent literature on the minimal word in phonology includes Akinlabi 1995; Buller et al. 1993; Dunlap 1991; Golston 1991; Hayes 1991, 1995; Itô and Hankamer 1989; Kager 1993b, 1996a; Kiparsky 1992; McDonough 1990; Mester 1994; Myers 1987; Orgun and Inkelas 1992; Piggott 1992; Prince and Smolensky 1993; Wilkinson 1986. Work on the minimal word in morphology includes Cho 1991; Cole 1990; Crowhurst 1991a, b; Itô 1991; Itô et al. 1992; Itô and Mester 1992; M&P 1991a, b; Mester 1990, 1995; Ola 1995; Spring 1990a, b; Tateishi 1985 [1989]; Weeda 1992; Yip 1991. In M&P 1994a, b, we argue that the minimal word has no actual status as a primitive template – instead, it is just the most harmonic form of PrWd under the metrical constraints PARSE-SYLL and ALL-FEET-RIGHT/LEFT.

---

A final point. Nothing in our proposals hinges on any conception of the mora as a unit of intrasyllabic constituency beyond its essential role in measuring weight. Thus, although we adopt the notational expedient of adjoining, for example, the onset to the first mora of each syllable, this in no way bears on our results. Instead, the issue of appropriate intrasyllabic constituency is addressed on its own terms in section 3.1[†].

## 1.2.2   Foot typology

The repertory of feet that we require will differ somewhat from that made familiar in the work of Halle and Vergnaud (1978) and Hayes (1980); in particular, we will need to recognize the foot $[\mu\ \mu]$. We will therefore propose and justify a modified universal typology, which is closer to the practice of McCarthy (1979) and Prince (1980), and which reflects the findings of Hayes (1985).

Our first assumption is that feet are maximally binary; 'unbounded feet' are non-primitive, as demonstrated in Prince (1985). We distinguish between two fundamental foot-types on the basis of the quantitative relation between the two members: the balanced foot [u u] and the asymmetrical foot [v w] where v < w (in practice, $[\sigma_\mu\ \sigma_{\mu\mu}]$). In his (1985) study of alternating patterns, Hayes found that in quantity-sensitive (QS) systems heavy syllables are always foot-final; he points to the psychology of grouping temporal sequences as the cause. The asymmetrical foot must therefore be quantitatively iambic.

A second important finding of Hayes's is that quantity-insensitive (QI) feet are overwhelmingly trochaic in labeling. Here again he points to the psychology of grouping: a sequence of objectively even pulses is typically parsed as trochaic (cf. 2/4 and 4/4 time). We therefore assume two prominence principles responsive to quantitative relations.

(A)   **Quantity/Prominence Homology**: for a,b ∈ F, if a > b quantitatively then a > b stresswise.

(B)   **Trochaic Default**: for a,b ∈ F, if a = b quantitatively then F = [s w].

In languages which do not recognize distinctions of quantity, only rule (B) applies; feet being of the balanced variety, they are necessarily trochaic. In languages distinguishing heavy and light syllables, the bracketing is as we predict: feet are $[\sigma_\mu\ \sigma_{\mu\mu}]$, $[\mu\ \mu]$, and when permitted $[\mu]$. The assignment of prominence shows some interesting variations. If (A) and (B) were the only principles involved, we would expect that quantity-sensitive systems would have both iambic and trochaic feet in them: iambic on the asymmetrical feet, trochaic on the balanced feet. Such systems are in fact attested: Cairene Arabic (McCarthy 1979) has exactly this pattern. But the most commonly encountered system has [w s] prominence on all feet, regardless of their quantitative make-up. We propose that this is due to a requirement of uniformity which has more to do with the integrity of the system than with its phonetic bases. If a quantity-sensitive language is to have a single labeling rule, it must be [w s], since Quantity/Prominence homology cannot be systematically denied. A third type of system enforces uniformity of labeling only within individual words: the example is Yidiɲ (Hayes 1985). Words are bracketed into bisyllabic feet from left to right; then quantity sensitivity is invoked: long vowels are shortened in foot-initial position, leaving only legitimate balanced or asymmetrical feet. Any word containing an asymmetrical foot has iambic rhythm throughout; words with only balanced feet are trochaic. We can express this typology of quantity sensitivity in this way:

(C)  **Uniformity Parameter**

A language may require that all feet have the same labeling (i) everywhere (ii) within the word.

The three principles (A), (B), and (C) have somewhat different status. Principle (A) 'Quantity/Prominence Homology' is dominant: the familiar QS systems all observe it. Principle (C) 'Uniformity' is parasitic upon (A), and as a parameter of description, it may be turned off, as in Cairene. Principle (B) 'Trochaic Default' is typically a true default rule, subject to overrule by 'Uniformity'.

The range of possible prosodic systems is generated by the various possible combinations of foot-types and prominence rules. There's only one QI system, with the balanced foot $[\sigma\ \sigma]$, necessarily trochaic. Three major QS systems emerge:

[I]   using both feet $[\sigma_\mu\ \sigma_{\mu\mu}]$ and $[\mu\ \mu]$,
[II]  using only $[\sigma_\mu\ \sigma_{\mu\mu}]$,
[III] using only $[\mu\ \mu]$.

System [I] is of course the usual QS alternating pattern, with a (possibly dominant) iambic component. System [II] is the 'unbounded foot' type and may be supplemented by the placement of a (balanced) foot at word-edge (Prince 1985). System [III] is found in Japanese (see Poser 1985 [1990] and below) and may also be attested in Southern Paiute (Sapir 1930) and Weri (Boxwell and Boxwell 1966, Hayes 1980).

The Southern Paiute case deserves some discussion. The language is remarkable in having a stress rule that can evidently divide long vowels between feet. According to Sapir's description, the stress pattern is generated by applying feet $[\mu\ \mu]$ left-to-right, where $\mu = V$ and long vowels are VV. In such word-shapes as CV-CVV-CV . . . , this results in syllable-splitting, giving [CV-CV][V-CV]. Although this is unusual, the truly odd thing from the present point of view is that the feet are iambic.

A further datum bears on the matter: Harms (1966) and K. Hale (p.c.) report that there is a surface difference between true long vowels and underlyingly heterosyllabic VV sequences (<*VGV): whereas the sequences may surface iambically stressed, the true long vowels always have phonetic stress on their initial mora. We take this to be the result of a rule erasing syllable-internal foot structure and assigning prosodic status to $\sigma$, which allows the normal prominence structure of the syllable to assert itself. In certain environments, such a rule will derive feet [$\sigma_\mu \; \sigma_{\mu\mu}$]. Consider the crucial example [CV-CV][V-CV]: adjusting $\sigma$-internal F-structure gives [CV-CVV][CV]. If this is right, the Southern Paiute system does indeed contain the crucially iambic foot [$\sigma_\mu \; \sigma_{\mu\mu}$]. At prominence assignment, uniformity may be invoked to guarantee iambic labeling.

An important consequence of this system is that iambic rhythm is crucially dependent upon the appearance of heavy syllables in a language. (Curiously, this does not follow from previous theories even if iambicity is directly linked to QS. For QS, as a property of rules rather than representations, can be defined in such a way that a given language has no candidates for heavy syllables: for example, suppose the quantity distinction is set at V/VV in a language without long vowels.) Iambic rhythm is phonetically proper only to asymmetrical feet; uniformity spreads it to balanced feet.

The revised typology argued for here provides exactly the feet we shall encounter in templatic systems: QI [$\sigma \; \sigma$] and QS [$\sigma_\mu \; \sigma_{\mu\mu}$] and [$\mu \; \mu$].

---

Foot Theory
A similar foot theory was independently proposed by Hayes 1987. Subsequent developments of this theory include Prince 1991; Hayes 1991, 1995; Hewitt 1992; Kager 1992, 1993a, c; and Mester 1995.

---

### 1.2.3   Mapping principles

Accommodation to a template is essentially the prosodic reparsing of a copy of the base. Under this rubric there are many variations consistent with the general prosodic hypothesis that we wish to establish: here we sketch one approach, deferring detailed discussion of alternatives (in part until section 4[†]) on the grounds that choice between them, though of great empirical interest, is largely orthogonal to the main issue. In order to highlight the main line of argument – the prosodic character of template structures – we will for now refrain from radical revision of the mapping process.

We'll assume with Marantz (1982) that the entire segmental melody of the reduplication domain is copied; with Broselow and McCarthy (1983–4), that it is copied onto a new plane, although we will not carefully represent this where noncrucial.

We also assume that mapping of the segmental material into the template is directional: LR for prefixes, RL for suffixes, free choice for root-and-pattern systems. For reduplicative affixation, this presumably boils down to the fact that the affix occurs at an edge: prefixes reprosodize at the beginning, suffixes at the end of the domain (-copy). Call this edge-in reprosodization; we return to it below.

Current views require emendation, under any conception of template form, in their handling of template/melody mismatch. Free loss of melodic material under phoneme-driving leads to false predictions. Consider the prefix σ, commonly treated as CVC in languages where that is the maximal syllable. What happens when it attaches to a word of the form CV.VC? The Ilokano progressive provides an example:

(11)   "No-Skipping" in Ilokano Reduplication
       /dait/      ag-DA-da.it     'sew/ be sewing'

When /i/ fails to map, persistence in the LR sweep should extend the search to the final /t/, predicting *ag-DAT-da.it, a pattern of loss that appears to be impossible. The same effect is met with in the other direction – see the discussion of Manam in section 4[†]. The doctrine of persistence is motivated by actual losses observed in CV (that is, $\sigma_c$) reduplication. For example, Sanskrit *druv-* > *DU-druv-* 'run' shows that failure of a C (here, *r*) to map does not prevent association from continuing until the target is satisfied. The persistence doctrine vastly overgeneralizes from this one pattern. Aside from mapping to $\sigma_c$, there are no other cases where nonadjacent melody elements are rendered adjacent by directional mapping to template: loss occurs freely only when the mapping process is finished and the continuous substring left over disappears, as in *ag-TAK(der)-takder, ag-DA(it)-dait*, etc. Stem-template systems are similar, when they allow any loss from the root, e.g. Arabic quinqueliterals (McCarthy 1981).

A plausible account of this finding is that mapping must always be continuous, except that under compulsion the head of a constituent such as onset can be taken for the whole thing. We will put off explicit technical development, however, since competing theories offer no advantage in dealing with the problem, and simply assume that skipping of melody elements is impossible outside accomodation to $\sigma_c$. It is not implausible that the mapping operation actually defines $\sigma_c$: if the core syllable is removed from the vocabulary of prosodic constituents, it can be derived from the light syllable ($\sigma_\mu$) by this idiosyncratic mode of mapping. As before, we postpone technical development of this possible simplification.[8]

A related issue also emerges from our results. The otherwise reduplication-specific principle of phoneme-driven association (Marantz 1982) turns out to be superfluous. With a prosodic theory of the skeleton, association is effectively skeletally driven[9] – it is edge-in reprosodization of the copied melody by the affixal skeleton. We develop this consequence of our theory explicitly in section 4[†].

Finally, we will follow Broselow and McCarthy (1983–4) in assuming that the domain of affixation may be delimited prosodically as well as morphologically. In particular, the notion min Wd may be called on to pick out a subsequence of the stem which can serve as a kind of pseudo-stem for purposes of affixation and associated processes. This notion of domain is important not only in certain types of infixing reduplication but in peripheral reduplication as well.

## 2   Elaboration and Exemplification

In this section, we look at three types of reduplication, prefixation, suffixation, and infixation, and then turn to nonreduplicative templatic morphology.

## 2.1  Prefixation

### 2.1.1  The simple syllable as prefix target

A common form of reduplication prefixes to the base as much of its initial substring as can be put into a syllable of the language. The Ilokano progressive, cited above, provides a clear example (Bernabe et al. 1971):

(12)  Ilokano Progressive Reduplication
| | BASE | $ag + \sigma + $ BASE | |
|---|---|---|---|
| (a) | /basa/ | ag - BAS - basa | 'be reading' |
| (b) | /dait/ | ag - DA - da.it | 'be studying' |
| (c) | /adal/ | ag - AD - adal | 'be studying' |
| (d) | /takder/ | ag - TAK - takder | 'be standing' |
| (e) | /trabaho/ | ag - TRAB - trabaho | 'be working' |

It has been emphasized in the literature that reduplication does not in general **copy** a prosodic constituent of the base (Moravcsik 1978); forms such as *ag.BAS.ba.sa* confirm the observation. What's copied is the base's segmental melody, as in Marantz 1982;[10] the prefix $\sigma$ then draws its content from that melody according to the syllabification rules of the language.

(13)

The difference between the prefix syllable *bas* and the stem-initial syllable *ba* is explained by the different prosodic requirements placed on the two domains. Since the stem must be through-syllabified, its syllable *ba* is limited by competition from the following syllable, which maximizes its own onset; the prefix syllable *bas*, being alone in its domain, is free to develop to the greatest extent allowed.

---

Ilokano Reduplication
The form of reduplication in Ilokano is in fact a **heavy** syllable, not a simple syllable. Hence, /dait/ reduplicates as *da:-da.?it* or, in some dialects, *dad-da.?it*. See Hayes and Abad 1989.

---

In Orokaiva (Healey et al. 1969), repetitive prefixation interacts in an interesting and typical way with syllabification constraints. These are the relevant data:

(14)  Orokaiva Verbal Reduplication
| | | | |
|---|---|---|---|
| (a) | waeke | WA–waeke | 'shut' |
| (b) | hirike | HI–hirike | 'open' |
| (c) | tiuke | TI–tiuke | 'cut' |
| (d) | uhuke | U.H–uhuke | 'blow' |

Healey et al. describe reduplication as copying the "first CV or VC of stems." The language only allows syllables V, CV, and CVN; the N is homorganic to a following C and disappears word-finally in favor of vowel nasality. Codas, then, must be nasal and can only *share* place-of-articulation specification – they must be 'linked' in the sense of Steriade (1982); word-finally a nasal may be extrasyllabic. We interpret the coda requirement in the manner of Itô (1986) as a filter on syllable-final elements:

(15)   Coda Condition

$$\ast \quad \sigma$$
$$|$$
$$c$$
$$\text{Place}$$

Condition (15) asserts that syllable-final consonants may not have a place of articulation (whence the fact that hypothetical word-final nasals are expressed only by vowel nasality); since the Geminate Constraint (Schein and Steriade 1986, Hayes 1986) will prevent it from analyzing a doubly linked place-matrix, blocking its application, it follows that an admissible syllable-final consonant will be place-linked to a following consonant.

The Coda Condition will rule out ever taking the prefix $\sigma$ to include CVN, since the N will never be linked to the stem-initial consonant, which follows it syllabically.

The behavior of the $\sigma$-prefix establishes that the principles of lexical syllabification hold in the prefix + stem domain. An immediate consequence is the special treatment accorded to vowel-initial stems: in the LR sweep mapping phonemes into prosody, the first C of the copied melody finds a place as the onset of the stem-initial syllable.

(16)   $\sigma$     $\sigma\,\sigma\,\sigma$

uhuke uhuke

As is perhaps universal in lexical syllabification, a syllable will take an onset whenever it can.

The Orokaiva CV/VC pattern might suggest to the unwary that the prefix is XX, the long-sought-for example of segmental reduplication. As with the XXX affix discussed above, any descriptive success of XX is no more than a freak of the limited prosody at hand. The putative bisegmental affix can hardly be expected to make its appearance in a language where #CC and #VV are found. The $\sigma$-affix, on the other hand, is entirely free to occur, with its realizational variants determined by independent considerations. This particular realization – in which an application of the Onset Rule has resulted in apparent 'extra' copying – we will see to be of fundamental importance as we look at other languages. It characterizes not only the distribution of XX and its congeners, but also the otherwise inexpressible notion 'maximal intersyllabic cluster' and the typology of reduplicative suffixes.

Orokaiva Reduplication
The analysis of Orokaiva reduplication given in the text is unlikely to be correct. The theoretical point – that the template need not be coextensive with the observed reduplicant – is made equally well by the Oykangand example, immediately below, and the Mokilese *and-andip* pattern, on p. 255 below. But in examples like *uhuhuke*, it is almost certainly the case that the reduplicant is **infixed**, after an initial onsetless syllable: *u-HU-huke*. This pattern of infixation is also seen in Uradhi, Timugon Murut, as on p. 36[†], as well as Sanskrit (p. 254 below) and many other languages. (The question then arises as to how an Oykangand-type analysis of Orokaiva is to be ruled out on principled grounds!) Optimality Theory sheds some light on this infixing pattern; see M&P 1993a, b, 1994a, b, and the remark on p. 40[†]. On phenomena in Arrernte ["Aranda"] that are similar to those of Oykangand, involving an apparent "VC" unit, see Breen 1990, Henderson (to appear), Turner and Breen 1984, and Wilkins 1984, 1989.

Strikingly similar facts, which bear on the realization issue, are reported for Oykangand in Sommer 1981:[11]

(17)   Reduplication in Oykangand
    (a)   /eder/    ED-eder    'rain'
    (b)   /algal/    ALG-algal    'straight'
    (c)   /igu-/    IG-igun    'go'

Here the $\sigma$-affix creates a somewhat richer array of patterns because final consonants are allowed more freely:

(18)   $\sigma$   $\sigma$ $\sigma$

    algal algal

Oykangand words may not begin with consonants. Sommer has taken this to mean that Oykangand **syllables** must – *contra naturam* – be similarly restricted, at least underlyingly; he cites reduplication as presumptive evidence for the claim, proposing that it copies a 'syllable', i.e. VC*. Since such an operation is in all likelihood impossible, rather than merely unusual (as Sommer himself suggests), the reduplication evidence cannot support the syllabic claim. The present theory resolves the issue, providing an analysis which depends only on the universally expected (and phonetically observable) syllabification of the language.

The evidence reviewed here shows that the ultimate shape of a reduplicated sequence is sensitive in subtle ways to the character of syllabification in a language. When syllabification across the prefix–stem boundary is permitted, as in Orokaiva and Oykangand, an extra consonant will be taken to fill an empty onset position. In Ilokano, by contrast, stem and prefixes form separate syllabification domains, and empty onsets are filled with epenthetic glottal stop: from /ag+$\sigma$+adal/, we get [a.gad.ʔadal]. Consequently no $\sigma$C-pattern is found. A like pattern, pervading all prefixes, reduplicative and non-reduplicative, is observed in Sundanese (Robins 1959).

ONSET, Templates, and Alignment
The constraint ONSET is fundamental to OT syllable typology (Prince and Smolensky 1993).
Through domination of constraints on the form of the reduplicant (i.e. templatic constraints),
it leads to the kind of "extra" copying seen in Oykangand and other examples below (Mokilese,
p. 255 below, Tzeltal, p. 32[†], and Chamorro, p. 44[†]). The templatic constraints involved here
are those that pertain to the *alignment* of its edges – for instance, in Oykangand, the right edge
of the reduplicant is misaligned with a syllable-edge, in *AL.G-algal*. See M&P 1993a: ch. 7;
1994a, b; 1995a.

## 2.1.2   The core syllable as prefix target

The most familiar and well-studied instances of core syllable ($\sigma_c$) reduplication are provided by Sanskrit and Greek (Steriade 1982, 1985), but the phenomenon is by no means
restricted to Indo-European. Tagalog uses it to mark several morphological categories
(Bowen 1969), for example, the Recent Perfective:

(19)   Core Syllable Reduplication in Tagalog
   (a)   ka-TA-trabaho     'just finished working'
   (b)   ka-I-ipon         'just saved'
   (c)   ka-GA-galit       'just got mad'
   (d)   ka-BO-bloaut      'just gave a special treat'

Characteristic is the reduction of initial clusters to one element, a result that comes
through mapping to $\sigma_c$, which tolerates no more than one onset consonant. The normal
selection of the first consonant in a cluster, as we have noted, engages the notion of
phoneme-driving and the theory of what elements may be skipped.

(20)     $\sigma_c$ +     $\sigma$ $\sigma$ $\sigma$

         trabaho trabaho

The Core Syllable
Steriade (1988), expanding on the claims of the present work, proposes that the simple onset
of the core syllable template is to be related to a syllable-markedness parameter, and she
implements this idea with a truncation rule applying to the copied material. In M&P 1993a,
1994a, b, 1995a, universal constraints on syllable structure interact, under Optimality Theory,
with constraints on exactness of copying, to produce the core syllable phenomenon as well as
other possible unmarked properties of the reduplicant, exactly paralleling the way syllable
restrictions are imposed in ordinary (nonreduplicative) phonology. On this 'Generalized Template'
theory of prosodic morphology, see also Gafos 1995; Rosenthall, to appear, Urbanczyk 1996a,
b, to appear.

The Sanskrit verb reduplicates in five of its forms, four according to the pattern $\sigma_c$:
the present, the aorist, the perfect, and the desiderative. In every case the simplification

of the initial cluster proceeds in the same way: the least sonorous member is preserved. Steriade (1982) is able to derive this with LR mapping on the assumption that onsets are of strictly rising sonority; if copying takes only syllabified material, then extrasyllabic elements such as initial /s/ in s-obstruent clusters will not appear on the prefix: thus *tsar* > *TA-tsar*, but *sthaa* > *TA-sthaa*.[12] Choice of vocalism in the prefix varies from category to category and involves considerable phonological complexity irrelevant to present concerns (see Steriade 1985 for discussion). However, the behavior of vowel-initial roots is of some interest. They appear to be poorly represented in all categories except the perfect, where the following rules hold (Whitney 1889: section 783):

(21) Perfect Reduplication in Sanskrit V-initial Roots

    (a) $\sigma_c + \sqrt{a}C$  →  a+aC > a:C

    (b) $\sigma_c + \sqrt{i}C$  →  i+iC > i:C                                     (weak   grade)

                      →  i+aiC > iyaiC   ⇒  iye:C   (strong grade)

    (c) $\sigma_c + \sqrt{u}C$  →  u+uC > u:C                                   (weak   grade)

                      →  u+auC > uvauC  ⇒  uvo:C   (strong grade)

    (d) $\sqrt{V}CC$, $\sqrt{V}VC$ do not usually form reduplicated perfects.

Since the postvocalic C is not taken as an onset, as it is in Orokaiva and Oykangand, we must conclude that syllabification is not allowed across the prefix–root boundary, at least at the relevant level of the lexical phonology. Evidence that this is true comes from the behavior of the high-vowel roots (21b, c). Steriade (1985) points out that "the general rule of Glide Formation fails to apply to such forms: intermediate *u-áuca* does not become *váuca*, surface *\*voca*." She offers an account in terms of rule ordering and the Strict Cycle. But if Glide Formation is a process of filling an empty onset, then it cannot apply across a boundary that is a barrier to onset formation. The surface forms are derived as in Steriade's analysis, by the application of postcyclic Glide Insertion and vowel fusion (Whitney 1889: section 126).

Most of the relatively small number of vowel-initial forms attested from outside the categories (21a, b, c) show a remarkable variation on the normal pattern:

(22) Other V-initial Forms in Sanskrit

    (a) $\sqrt{\text{iir}}$         iir-IR-é             (pf.)

    (b) $\sqrt{\text{am}}$       aam-AM-at[13]      (aor.)

    (c) $\sqrt{\text{aap}}$      aap-IP-an        (aor.)

    (d) $\sqrt{\text{arp}}$       arp-IP-am        (aor.)

    (e) $\sqrt{\text{edh}}$      ed-IDH-isa       (des.)

    (f) $\sqrt{\text{aç}}$        aç-Iç-isa         (des.)

Although the form *aamamat* (a+am+am+at) suggests syllabification into the prefix, the other forms are inconsistent with this. The vocalism in (22c, d, f), with /a/ reduplicating as /i/, is normal for aorist and desiderative; cf. aor. *a+ti-tras+am*, des. *bi-badh+isa* (Whitney 1889: sections 858, 1029). Furthermore, it is always the second instance of the root which is segmentally reduced, as in *arp-IP+am*. What additional data is available from grammatical sources follows this pattern without exception:

(23)   V-initial Aorist and Desiderative Forms
   (a)   Aorists:
       √arc       aarc-IC+am
       √ubj       aaubj-IJ+am[14]
       √arh       aarj-IH+am
       √rdh       aard-IDH+am
       √iiks      aaic-IKS+am.
   (b)   Desideratives:
       √arh       arj-IH+isa
       √und       und-ID+isa
       √rdh       ard-IDH+isa

We conclude that vowel-initial roots do indeed use suffixation. In addition, the pattern of losses indicates that the suffix can only be $\sigma_c$, with cross-boundary syllabifications.

---

Sanskrit Vowel-initial Reduplication
As noted in Kiparsky 1986, the pattern in the aorist is *infixation*, not suffixation, as incorrectly claimed here. E.g. *ar-PI-pam*, not *arp-IP-am*. In M&P 1993a, the various reduplicative peculiarities of Sanskrit vowel-initial roots result from the force of the constraint ONSET. This relates aspects of Sanskrit reduplication to Orokaiva above (p. 249) and Timugon Murut etc. below (p. 36[†]).

---

Melody copying and association are incoherent with a $\sigma_c$ suffix; see sections 2.2[†] and 4[†] for discussion. The suffix is therefore satisfied by spreading, as in Steriade's (1982) analysis of Greek. Consider the linking process that creates *arpipam*:

(24)   $\sigma + \sigma_c + \sigma$

       arp      am

If copying were involved rather than spreading, the vowel could be copied as *a* and turned into *i* by a rule associated with reduplication of aorist, desiderative, and (sometimes) present. The desiderative *undidisa* from √und permits no such account, since *u* never reduplicates an *i*; such forms are explicable only if the suffix's vowel has been fixed at *i*. The aorist *aaubijIJam* (/a+ubj+$\sigma_c$+am/) from √ubj is a similar case.[15] The vowel *i* is therefore inserted, evidently by default specification, and the filling of then open syllabic positions comes about through spreading rather than copying, in much the same way as Steriade (1982) has proposed for Greek prefixing reduplication.
   Roots with final clusters of falling sonority behave in the same way:

(25)   $\sigma + \sigma_c + \sigma\sigma$

       und      isa

The one case where *infixing* occurs (*aaikIKSam* from √iiks) follows smoothly, given Steriade's theory of Sanskrit syllabification by which the rising sonority of *ks*- suffices to license it as an onset:

(26)   $\sigma + \sigma_c + \sigma$

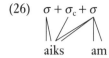

The proposed analysis depends crucially on the assumption that the final suffix (the one after the reduplicant $\sigma_c$) begins with a vowel, opening up an onset position. This is in fact the case for both aorist and desiderative.

The reduplicating aorist shows an interesting divergence from the simple $\sigma_c$ form: it 'aims always at establishing a diversity between the reduplicating and radical syllables, making the one heavy and the other light (Whitney 1889: section 858b)'. There are three general rules:

(27)   Prefix/Stem Complementarity
    (a)   If the root is light (CVC, since all aorist suffixes are vowel initial), the prefix vowel is lengthened; thus √ris gives *a+RII-ri.s+am*.
    (b)   If the root begins with a cluster, the prefix is already heavy and nothing happens: √krudh gives *a+KU-k.ru.dh+am*.
    (c)   If the root is heavy, the prefix remains light: √diks gives *a+DI-dik.s+am*.

Evidently there is a rule making the prefix syllable heavy – inserting a mora – before a light stem syllable.[16] The rule cannot apply if the stem syllable already has the full complement of two moras. By familiar processes (Ingria 1980), the prefix vowel spreads automatically to fill the empty mora position. Notice that the designation $\sigma_c$ governs only the initial mapping process, creating a $\sigma$ which is as liable to phonological manipulation as any other.[17]

### 2.1.3   The heavy syllable as prefix target

#### 2.1.3.1   Mokilese

Mokilese reduplication has been insightfully analyzed by Levin (1983, 1985) within the segmental framework. We argue here that the affix shape invariant must be construed prosodically.

The progressive aspect of the Mokilese verb is formed by prefixation of a heavy syllable target, as can be seen from the following data provided by Harrison and Albert (1976), who explicitly note the generalization:

(28)   Reduplication in Mokilese, /CVC . . . / Stems
| | | |
|---|---|---|
| pɔdok | pɔd-pɔdok | 'plant' |
| mʷiŋe | mʷiŋ-mʷiŋe | 'eat' |
| kasɔ | kas-kasɔ | 'throw' |
| wadek | wad-wadek | 'read' |
| pilɔd | pil-pilɔd | 'pick breadfruit' |
| dɔpʷɔ | dɔpʷ-dɔpʷɔ | 'pull' |
| poki | pok-poki | 'beat' |

(29)   Reduplication in Mokilese, /CV/ and /CV.V . . . / Stems
    pa         paa–pa        'weave'
    wi.a       wii–wi.a      'do'
    di.ar      dii–di.ar     'find'

(30)   Reduplication in Mokilese, /CV: . . . / Stems
    kookɔ      koo–kookɔ     'grind coconut'
    sɔɔrɔk     sɔɔ–sɔɔrɔk    'tear'
    čaak       čaa–čaak      'bend'

The examples in (28) show the target $\sigma_{\mu\mu}$ being satisfied by an initial substring of melodic elements.

In (29) association from the copy must fail to satisfy the target. Examples like /pa/ simply lack the stuff to fill out a heavy syllable by 1:1 mapping; and since the vowel sequences of the other two examples are always heterosyllabic, a form like *di.ar* can only link *di*, never *dia*, to a syllabic prefix. (As noted above, the mapping must stop with the failure of *a* to link, so that *dir-di.ar* is not a possible outcome.) The single successfully linked vowel must therefore be spread to fill the second mora position.

The examples of (30) show that a long vowel is copied as long – a phenomenon dubbed 'transfer' in Clements 1985, which obviously requires some refinement of the mapping procedure. We consider techniques for dealing with it in section 4.3[†].

Quantitative Transfer
This phenomenon and its significance were first noted by Levin 1983. An account of it is given in M&P 1988. Other relevant work includes Hammond 1988, Steriade 1988, and Selkirk 1988. For recent work on Mokilese reduplication, see Blevins 1996.

A search of the dictionary reveals that superheavy CVVC syllables are found only at word-end, presumably because of the availability of consonant extrametricality there. The two-mora requirement imposed by the prefix is therefore satisfied maximally by CVV: whence *sɔɔ-sɔɔrok*, never *\*sɔɔr-sɔɔrok*.

A third pattern generating long vowels is observed in (31), where CVG-initial stems give a CVV prefix.

(31)   Reduplication in Mokilese, Diphthongal Stems
    pou.ce     poo–pouce     'connect'
    dau.li     daa–dauli     'pass by'
    au.do      aa–audo       'fill'

Mokilese has a general rule of diphthong formation, summarized as follows by Harrison and Albert: "a high vowel becomes a glide after a lower vowel and before a consonant or at the end of a word." (This is not fully accurate – their own example is *ka+onopda* → *kɔwnopda* 'cause + prepared = to prepare'.) All instances of [y] are derivable; [w] is arguable phonemic in only a few words (p. 32[†]). This suggests an analysis in which the basic syllabification is *po.u.ce, da.u.li, a.u.do*, paralleling *wi.a, di.ar* in (29), giving rise to exactly the same pattern of association. Interestingly, some speakers allow CVG reduplication, with *audo* > *au-audo*, showing that for them diphthongal nuclei are at least possible in the basic syllabification.

The behavior of the CV.V-initial stems in (29) and (31) demonstrates clearly that the prefix cannot be XXX, pure segmentalia, but includes the information that the result in these cases must be a licit single syllable of the language.

Of particular interest – as usual – is the behavior of vowel-initial stems.

(32)   Reduplication in Mokilese, V-initial Stems
   (a)   ir          ir-r-ir         'string'
   (b)   onop        on-n-op         'prepare'
   (c)   idip        id-d-idip
   (d)   alu         al-l-alu        'walk'
   (e)   uruur       ur-r-uruur      'laugh'
   (f)   andip       an-d-andip      'spit'

Form (32f) shows the syllabification effect we've seen before: both the prefix $\sigma_{\mu\mu}$ and the stem-initial onset are satisfied from the copied melody:[18]

(33)   $\sigma_{\mu\mu}$   $+\sigma$   $\sigma$

andip   andip

In cases where there is no separate consonant for the stem onset, the moraic consonant spreads to fill it. This can be best understood in relation to a process Harrison and Albert call 'Boundary Lengthening'. Before 'loosely bound' suffixes the following changes take place:

(34)   Boundary Lengthening
   (a)   Before a V-initial suffix, a single final consonant is geminated:
            did # e → didde              'this wall'
            puk # ɔr → pukkɔr            'only books'
   (b)   Before a C-initial suffix, final vowels are lengthened.
            indi # la → indiila          'go-down and away'
            si # pas → siipas            'a bone'
            pina # ki # di → pinaakiidi   'cover with'

This class of suffixes adds a mora to a preceding syllable, as is clear from (34b). Associated with the process is a rule spreading the stem-final C (construed melodically) into the empty onset position of V-initial (ditto) suffixes, which we display in (35):

(35)   Onset Filling

$\sigma$   $\sigma$

c   v

This is, of course, exactly the rule evidenced in the reduplicated prefixes (32a–e).

A further generalization is possible. If the reduplicative prefix is included in the class of 'loosely bound' affixes, it is no longer necessary to specify that the prefix is bimoraic: this follows from the general pattern of boundary lengthening. The prefix, then, is plausibly interpreted as a kind of clitic, prefixation as a kind of (near-) compounding. The actual progressive prefix then reduces to the familiar σ, with its prosodic properties following from its morphological affinities.

### 2.1.3.2   Ponapean: heavy and light σ as prefixes

Ponapean, a Micronesian language closely related to Mokilese, uses a richly varied pattern of reduplications to mark the durative in verbs. It has been analyzed in Rehg and Sohl 1981, the source of all data, in Levin 1985 from the segmentalist point of view, and in McCarthy 1984a, where fundamental elements of prosodic conditioning in the system are recognized and treated. We examine it afresh not only because it provides instances of $\sigma_{\mu\mu}$ and $\sigma_\mu$ as prefix targets, but also because it illustrates how higher-order categories, F in particular, can determine affixal prosody.

---

More on Ponapean
More recent work on Ponapean phonology and morphology includes Goodman 1995, Itô 1989, M&P 1991a, b.

---

As elsewhere, the empty onset provokes special treatment; we will focus first on the more perspicuous behavior of C-initial stems.

#### 2.1.3.2.1   Ponapean I: consonant-initial stems

With monosyllables, the reduplicative prefix takes the form $\sigma_\mu$ or $\sigma_{\mu\mu}$ in quantitative complementarity with the base:

(36)   Light base – $\sigma_{\mu\mu}$ prefix

|     |      |                |                |
| --- | ---- | -------------- | -------------- |
| (a) | pa   | PAA-pa         | 'weave'        |
| (b) | mi   | MII-mi         | 'exist'        |
| (c) | pu   | PUU-pu         | 'bent, crooked' |
| (d) | lo   | LOO-lo         | 'be caught'    |
| (e) | lal  | LAL-lal        | 'make a sound' |
| (f) | rer  | RER-rer        | 'tremble'      |
| (g) | mem  | MEM-mem        | 'sweet'        |
| (h) | kaŋ  | KAŋ-kaŋ        | 'eat'          |
| (i) | pap  | PAM-pap        | 'swim'         |
| (j) | dod  | DON-dod        | 'frequent'     |
| (k) | dil  | DIN-dil        | 'penetrate'    |
| (l) | kik  | Kiŋ-kik        | 'kick'         |
| (m) | pʷil | PʷIL-i-pʷil    | 'flow'         |
| (n) | par  | PAR-a-par      | 'to cut'       |
| (o) | tep  | TEP-e-tep      | 'kick'         |
| (p) | tep  | TEP-i-tep      | 'begin'        |

Some phonology is visible here. At the surface, nonfinal syllables can close only on gemin-ates or assimilated nasals. A variety of assimilation rules at various strata of the grammar respond to this restriction; see Rehg and Sohl (1981: 56–64), McCarthy (1984a), Itô (1986) for discussion. When there is no assimilation, impermissible clusters such as those in (m–p) are broken up with vowels. It is important to note that the process of cluster break-up is not limited (as some assimilations are) to reduplicated structures.[19] We there-fore abstract away from the Epenthesis process in identifying the prefix as syllabic.

(37)  Heavy base – $\sigma_\mu$ prefix
  (a)  duup        DU-duup        'dive'
  (b)  miik        MI-miik        'suck'
  (c)  m$^w$aaw    M$^w$A-m$^w$aaw 'good'
  (d)  laud        LA-laud        'big, old'
  (e)  reid        RE-reid        'stain'
  (f)  pou         PO-pou         'cold'
  (g)  pei         PE-pei         'fight'
  (h)  mand        MA-mand        'tame'
  (i)  leŋk        LE-leŋk        'acrophobic'
  (j)  kens        KE-kens        'ulcerate'

The light base is CVC; the heavy base CVV, CVCC, or CVVC. This contrast is reconciled with the familiar light/heavy distinction (CV vs. CVX) if final consonants are extrametrical. McCarthy (1984a) adduces independent evidence in support of this claim. Nouns are subject to a min Wd requirement demanding two moras at the surface. When they are underlyingly CV or CVC, they are vowel-lengthened to CVV and CVVC (respectively). Forms CVV, CVCC, and CVVC are untouched. Extrametricality puts the CVC forms in the monomoraic class and further predicts that only the (intrametrical) vowel is available for satisfying the obligatory second mora.

Jane Grimshaw suggests that quantitative complementarity be viewed as the con-sequence of a requirement on higher-order structure to the effect that a reduplicated monosyllable contain no more than a single foot. Although the stress system of Ponapean is not discussed in Rehg and Sohl (1981), it is fair to assume that any quantity-sensitive prosody will tolerate at most one heavy syllable per foot. We further assume that F is minimally bimoraic: this allows us to interpret the Noun min Wd requirement in the usual way as min Wd = F. We can take the prefix to be $\sigma$, unspecified for weight, which will satisfy itself maximally up to the foot limitation, recorded here:

(38)  *Monosyllable/Monostress Rule* (Grimshaw)
      Reduplicated monosyllables contain one and only one F.

If feet are strictly iambic, then a form like *mem* meets (38) by containing one F and one loose syllable: *[mem]me(m)*. If asymmetrical trochaic feet can be derived, then it ends up as a single tidy foot. Stems like *mand*, of course, reduplicate as perfect iambs: *maman(d)*.

Polysyllables also choose between $\sigma_\mu$ and $\sigma_{\mu\mu}$, but the grounds for choice are, on the face of things, remarkable. First, the mundane: when the initial syllable is light, the prefix is $\sigma_{\mu\mu}$:

(39)  Polysyllabic Stem – light initial syllable
  (a) rere   RER-rere    'to skin or peel'
  (b) dune   DUN-dune   'attach in a sequence'
  (c) deyed   DEY-deyed   'eat breakfast'
  (d) dilip   DIN-dilip   'mend thatch'
  (e) pepe   PEM-pepe   'swim to'
  (f) sarek   SAN-sarek   'uproot'
  (g) siped   SIP-i-siped   'shake out'
  (h) taman   TAM-a-taman  'remember'
  (i) tepek   TEP-e-tepek   'kick'
  (j) lɔŋe   Lɔŋ-(i)-lɔŋe   'pass across'
  (k) katoore  KAT-(i)-katoore  'subtract'
  (l) li.aan   LII-li.aan    'outgoing'
  (m) ri.aala  RII-ri.aala   'be cursed'
  (n) lu.ak   LUU-lu.ak   'jealous'
  (o) lu.et   LUU-lu.et   'weak'

Phonological notes: Forms (d–f) show the typical assimilations. Forms (g–k) show insertion into unassimilable clusters: those in (j, k) are optional and characteristic of casual speech; those in (g–i) are obligatory and copy the *following* vowel, as can be seen by application of the rule elsewhere.[20] As above, we abstract away from predictable epentheses to reveal the uniformly syllabic character of the prefix. Forms (l–o) show automatic spreading of the vowel to fill the required second mora. Since vowel sequences like *i.a* and *u.a* are necessarily heterosyllabic, they can't be mapped into the prefix σ, and the mapping must stop with the stem's first vowel melodeme. (As we have seen before, it is universally impossible to skip over the unassociated vowel to seize on a following consonant: *lin-liaan.*)

 Complementarity makes its appearance when the first syllable is heavy,[21] but surprisingly does not respond to the first syllable at all: the **second** syllable's weight determines the weight of the prefix.

(40)  $\sigma_\mu$ with Heavy second syllable
  (a) luumʷuumʷ  LU-luumʷuumʷ  'be sick'
  (b) maasaas   MA-maasaas   'cleared of vegetation'
  (c) tooroor   TO-tooroor   'be independent'
  (d) waantuuke  WA-waantuuke  'count'

(41)  $\sigma_{\mu\mu}$ with Light second syllable[22]
  (a) duupek   DUU-duupek   'starved'
  (b) meelel   MEE-meelel   'true'
  (c) nOOrok   NOO-nOOrok   'greedy'
  (d) peese   PEE-peese   'be acquainted'

Viewed in terms of the sequential structure of the syllable string, the rule of complementarity is mysterious indeed: not only is it nonlocal, but it skips over an entity ($\sigma_{\mu\mu}$) of exactly the same type that it's looking for.

The prosodic effect is, however, uniform and simple: the output contains exactly two feet. We therefore adopt for polysyllables a foot-condition analogous to that imposed on monosyllables:

(42)  *Polysyllable/Two-Stress Rule*
      Reduplicated polysyllables must have exactly two feet.

If there are two heavy syllables in the stem, as in (40), the prefix must shrink to $\sigma_\mu$ to avoid running over the 2F limit: thus *[maa][saas]* → *[mamaa][saas]*. With only one heavy syllable in the stem, as in (41), the prefix $\sigma$ is free to expand maximally, indeed must do so: whence *[duupek]* → *[duu][duupek]*.

Notice that the Polysyllable Rule applies equally well to the forms of (39); all are monopod bases, so that the FF target can only be achieved via $\sigma_{\mu\mu}$-prefixation: thus from *[dune]* we get *[dun][dune]*.

What we have here is a kind of templatic morphology superimposed on the reduplication process. The prefix is always $\sigma$, but monosyllable stems satisfy a template F, polysyllables a template FF. The templates impose weight requirements on the prefix and mediate the transmission of just that kind of nonlocal information which affects the foot structure of the word.

There is one final class of C-initial polysyllables to consider: those beginning with a syllabic nasal. They reduplicate exactly as expected, given the associated phonology. (Syllabic nasals capitalized in the examples.)

(43)  Syllabic Nasals
      (a)  M.med          M.m-i-m.med              'full'
      (b)  ŋ.ŋar          N.ŋ-i-ŋ.ŋar              'see'
      (c)  Mʷ.mʷus        Mʷ.mʷ-u-mʷ.mʷus          'vomit'
      (d)  M.pek          M.p-i-m.pek              'search for lice'
      (e)  N.da           N.d-i-n.da               'say'
      (f)  Mʷ.pʷul        Mʷ.pʷ-u-mʷ.pʷul          'to flame'

Syllabic nasals are only allowed word-initially, preceding a consonant to which they are homorganic. Even there they are liable to degemination in forms like (a–c) (p. 36[†]) and in forms like (d–f) they show optional prothesis of /i/ or /u/, the latter appearing with rounded initial consonants or when the vowel of the first syllable is round (p. 56[†]). Rendered word-internal by morphology, the nasals must desyllabify: for example, *ka+mned* 'cause to be full' emerges as bisyllabic *kam.med*. Epenthesis of *i/u* is therefore internally obligatory.

Putting all this together, we see that a form like *M.pek* reduplicates like e.g. *dune* (39b). As a polysyllable, it must satisfy a template FF; therefore $\sigma$ expands as $\sigma_{\mu\mu}$, *Mp*. The derived form *Mp–M.pek* undergoes the general rule of epenthesis, emerging as *M.pim.pek*.[23]

### 2.1.3.2.2   Ponapean II: vowel-initial stems
The single essential peculiarity of vowel-initial stems is that a vocalic element of one sort or another appears between the expected $\sigma$-satisfying prefix and the stem:

(44)   Reduplication of Vowel-initial Stems
    (a)   el              el-*e*-el         'rub, massage'
    (b)   uk            uk-*u*-uk       'fast'
    (c)   it              it-*i*-it         'stuffed'
    (d)   aan          a-*y*-aan      'be accustomed to'
    (e)   oon         o-*y*-oon      'hung over'
    (f)   eed          e-*y*-eed      'strip off'
    (g)   iik          i-*y*-iik       'inhale'
    (h)   uuk         u-*y*-uuk     'lead'
    (i)   uutoor     uu-*y*-uutoor  'independent'
    (j)   alu         al-*i*-alu      'walk'
    (k)   inen       in-*i*-inen    'straight'
    (l)   urak       ur-*u*-urak    'wade'

Except for (44i) *uu-y-uutoor*, which should parallel (40c) *to-tooroor*, the general rules for choosing between $\sigma_\mu$ and $\sigma_{\mu\mu}$ are clearly in effect: the heavy monosyllables of (d–h) get the $\sigma_\mu$ prefix; the others, $\sigma_{\mu\mu}$.

    Mokilese resolves the empty onset problem by spreading the syllable-final C: Mok. *alu* 'walk' becomes *al-l-alu*. Ponapean responds to the structural pressure in a different way: the empty stem-initial onset is filled, we propose, with a glide /y/. Intervocalically, as in (d–i), that is exactly what we see. But glides are disallowed postconsonantally. Therefore they vocalize, presumably via a rule which adjoins the preceding consonant, whereupon they will assimilate in quality to any following high vowel and to any vowel in monosyllables.[24] By this account, Ponapean *alu* goes to *al-y-alu*, surfacing as *a.li.a.lu*, while *el* 'rub' goes to *el-y-el*, surfacing as *e.leel*.

    There is some variation in the high-vowel class of heavy monosyllables: *iik* may reduplicate as *ik-iik*, *uuk* as *uk-uuk*. Rehg and Sohl note a possible source in analogy with *uk* (b) and *it* (c). Formally, we can get this by exceptionally blocking glide insertion and allowing the stem-initial onset to pick the copy's final consonant, as in Orokaiva and others above. Another reported variant is *uwuuk* for *uyuuk*, presumably due to allowing the language's general glide insertion process to operate in the reduplication environment.

    One small class remains, which lies outside the general pattern discussed here: glide-initial light monosyllables, which reduplicate with a fixed prefix G*e*-.

(45)   Reduplication of Glide-initial Stems
    (a)   wa        we-wa      'carry'
    (b)   was      we-was    'obnoxious'
    (c)   yang    ye-yang    'accompany'

It's possible to imagine a story assimilating these to the vowel-initial class, whereby the inserted *y* vocalizes and dissimilates to *e* – so that *ua > u-y-ua > u-e-ua*. But it hardly seems worth it,[25] especially since the pattern is being lost from the language in favor of treating the forms as consonant-initial.

### 2.1.3.2.3   Ponapean III: conclusion
Ponapean demonstrates quite unambiguously the fully prosodic character of reduplication. The categories foot, syllable, and mora interact to characterize the reduplicating

prefix in a quite general way. Even the (typically quirky) onsetless stems fit into the core system with a minimum of special handling.

#### 2.1.3.2.4   Ponapean IV: proleptic and historical note

The survival of the 'base vowel' in the reduplication of a small class of (currently) monosyllablic stems indicates that the process was originally one of foot reduplication, where $F = \mu\,\mu$, subsequently subject to a variety of reductions particular to the reduplication structure. (A similar remark can be made for Mokilese.) It is clearly possible to mount a synchronic description based on this premiss. We resist the temptation on the grounds that the bulk of the reductions follow immediately from specifying the prefix target as $\sigma\,(\sigma_\mu,\ \sigma_{\mu\mu})$. Independent rules of the language defining syllable and mora tell us what to take and when to amplify by insertion. Furthermore, the principles (38) and (42) assigning foot templates to mono- and polysyllabic bases determine the form of the prefix $\sigma$ in an entirely straightforward way, resolving the otherwise inscrutable issue of quantitative complementarity – if we take the prefix to be $\sigma$. These considerations suggest strongly that the system has in fact been reanalyzed along the lines suggested here.

### 2.1.4   Minimal word/foot as prefix

A particularly clear illustration of the interaction between reduplication and prosodic constituency is provided by the Australian language Diyari, described by Austin (1981). We will discuss below another Australian system, which involves interesting variations on the same pattern.

Diyari has both CV and CVC syllables, with no vowel-length contrast. Consonants are prohibited at the end of a phonological word. Within a root, stress is assigned to each odd–numbered nonfinal syllable, counting from the left (this is a typical pattern in Australian languages);[26] thus, the foot is of the trochaic, non–quantity-sensitive type which must branch (whence the absence of stress on final syllables). All phonological words of Diyari contain at least two syllables.[27] It follows, then, that the minimal phonological word of Diyari is just a single foot, which we know independently to be disyllabic. Diyari prosody is indifferent to the subsyllabic moraic structure (that is, $\sigma$ *is a* $\mu$).

Diyari reduplication is of the type most commonly found in Australia, a prefixed copy of CV(C)CV:

(46)   Diyari Reduplication

| | | |
|---|---|---|
| wiḻa | wiḻa-wiḻa | 'woman' |
| kanku | kanku-kanku | 'boy' |
| kuḻkuŋa | kuḻku-kuḻkuŋa | 'to jump' |
| tʲilparku | tʲilpa-tʲilparku | 'bird sp.' |
| ŋankaṇṭi | ŋanka-ŋankaṇṭi | 'catfish' |

Consider what we must explain about this pattern of reduplication. The reduplicated sequence is exactly two syllables, of which the first may be CV or CVC, while the second is CV. From our observations about Diyari prosody, we conclude that the reduplicative affix in this language is just the minimal phonological word, $W_{min}$. Everything follows from this. We must reduplicate two syllables, because the minimal phonological word is a trochaic foot. The second syllable of the reduplication must be open, because it immediately precedes a phonological word juncture.

In effect what we are saying is that reduplicated forms in Diyari are word-level compounds of an F (= Wd$_{min}$) template with a normal word. This is confirmed by Austin's (1981) careful arguments demonstrating that the reduplicated string forms a separate phonological word from the base. Each portion of a reduplicated string takes a separate main word stress (*dúnkadúnka* 'to emerge'), and the vocalic allophony in the stressed syllable of the reduplication as well as the prestopping of intervocalic nasals after the stress confirm this. It follows, then, that the reduplicative affix in Diyari is the minimal free base for word-level compounding.

---

Diyari Reduplication
The original proposal that Diyari reduplication is foot-based is due to Poser (1982). The analysis was subsequently revised and published as Poser 1989. In the text, we argue that the Diyari reduplicative template is to be identified as the **minimal word** of the language. In M&P 1994a we show that the special status of the *minimal* word as template follows, under Optimality Theory, from its being the most harmonic prosodic word possible with respect to constraints on metrical parsing. Background for this claim includes Spring 1990a, where the general PrWd is argued to play a templatic function, and Itô and Mester 1992, where differing notions of minimality are derived by placing branching constraints on PrWd; see Itô et al. 1996 for development of these in terms of Alignment.

In M&P 1994b the argument is taken one step further: we argue that PrWd itself enters as the canonical prosodic realization of the *morphological* category **stem**. Diyari reduplication is therefore stem-compounding, and the behavior of the Diyari reduplicant follows from the identification of its lexical status as *stem*. No prosodic template is required. This then leads to the Generalized Prosodic Morphology Hypothesis: that templatic conditions are the reflection of canonical prosodic restrictions on the morphological category that an item (such as a reduplicative morpheme) belongs to, categories like *stem* and *affix*. These restrictions are imposed by the standard constraints on prosodic structure and morphology–prosody alignment, universal under OT, which dominate the faithfulness constraints relevant to the item's realization. There are no reduplication-specific structural constraints – 'templates'. This seems like the minimal theory one could hold, since morphemes must be assigned to some category (affix, stem, . . . ).

---

A similar example, but one in which the evidence for minimum word size is of an even more striking character, is provided by the Australian language Lardil. All information on Lardil comes from Hale 1973, Klokeid 1976, and Hale's unpublished field notes and dictionary. Our discussion of Lardil closely follows the insightful treatment of Lardil phonology in Wilkinson 1986.

---

Lardil Phonology
Wilkinson 1986 was published, in revised and truncated form, as Wilkinson 1988. Prince and Smolensky 1993: ch. 7, show how (the bulk of) Lardil nominal phonology follows from the interaction of constraints, almost all of which are clearly universal in character.

---

Lardil syllables are of the form CV(V)(C), but there are quite rigid restrictions on final consonants. Only apicals and palatoalveolars are licensed syllable-finally.[28] As is characteristic of Australian languages, only vowels count as moras, and stress is assigned by a trochaic foot.

Lardil actively enforces a minimum word-size requirement of two morae (that is, one foot). Words containing only one mora must be augmented by the suffixation of a morphologically empty *a*:

(47)    Augmentation in Lardil

|     | Underlying | Uninflected | Accusative |           |
| --- | --- | --- | --- | --- |
| (a) | /peer/ | peer | peerin | 'ti-tree sp.' |
|     | /maan/ | maan | maanin | 'spear gen.' |
| (b) | /parŋa/ | parŋa | parŋan | 'stone' |
|     | /kela/ | kela | kelan | 'beach' |
| (c) | /wik/ | wika | wikin | 'shade' |
|     | /wun/ | wunta | wunin | 'rain' |

The nouns in (47a) are monosyllabic but bimoraic, while those in (47b) are disyllabic and bimoraic. In these two types, no augmentation occurs in the uninflected form. The nouns in (47c) are underlyingly monomoraic, since they contain only a single short vowel. In the uninflected form, they must undergo augmentation to meet the minimum word-size requirement of two morae.

This requirement functions in another way as well. Words that are three or more morae long undergo truncation of any final vowel:

(48)    Truncation in Lardil

| /yiliyili/ | yiliyil | yiliyilin | 'oyster' |
| --- | --- | --- | --- |
| /yukarpa/ | yukar | yukarpan | 'husband' |

The fact that shorter nouns like those in (47a) do not undergo this truncation follows directly from the minimum word-size requirement – no truncation is possible without reducing such nouns below the minimum size. (See the Estonian parallel in section 1.)

Lardil has at least two types of reduplication, nominal and verbal. Nominal reduplication, as in many cognate languages, is frozen but nevertheless clearly discernible as reduplication. It generally copies two morae: /muŋkumuŋku/ 'wooden axe', /karikari/ 'butterfish'. Verbal reduplication, a phenomenon whose existence and properties were first noted by Wilkinson, is a more productive morphological process with a discernible iterative meaning:

(49)    Reduplication in Lardil

|           | Simple | Reduplicated |           |
| --- | --- | --- | --- |
| /keleth/ | kele | kelekele | 'cut' |
| /kelith/ | keli | kelikeli | 'jump' |
| /parelith/ | pareli | parelpareli | 'gather' |
| /lath/ | latha | laala | 'spear' |
| /neth/ | netha | neene | 'strike' |
| /ŋaalith/ | ŋaali | ŋaalŋaali | 'thirst' |

The underlying forms of all verb roots end in the verb marker *-th*. This marker protects the final vowel of long verbs from truncation (as in *pareli*) and appears overtly in the simple form of short verbs (like *petha*) preceding the augment *a*.

It is apparent that verbal reduplication is foot- or minimal word-sized as well, and it exhibits several properties that we have met with and will again as we treat reduplication phenomena from other languages. In cases like *kelekele*, the consequences of foot reduplication are obvious. Less apparent, but equally straightforward, is the fact that a long vowel, although a single syllable, contains two moras and thus satisfies the foot/ minimal word template, as in *yaalŋaali*.[29] Furthermore, the copying of a final consonant in this case and in *parelpareli* is explained by the independent syllabic well-formedness conditions of the language – only apicals and palatoalveolars are copied finally, because only they are permitted in syllable-final position.[30]

Examples like *laala* exhibit the strict shape invariance called for by the Satisfaction Condition. Here we find a short vowel copied as long, thereby satisfying the requirement that the reduplicative affix contain two moras. Such requirements are immutable – since there is no erasure of unassociated skeletal positions, all prosodically characterized positions in the affix must be filled in accordance with the requirements of the language. Since no way to fill a mora other than a vowel is permitted in Lardil, what we find is spreading of the vowel to this slot, as in the diagram in (50):

(50)

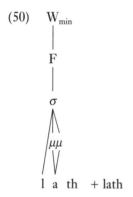

The final *th* is not associated because it is not a licit syllable- (and therefore foot-) final consonant of the language.[31]

The situation in yet another Australian language, Yidiɲ (Dixon 1977; Nash 1979–80), is somewhat different. The relevant data are as follows:

(51)   Reduplication in Yidiɲ

| mulari | mulamulari | 'initiated man' |
| kintalpa | kintalkintalpa | 'lizard sp.' |
| kalamparaa | kalakalamparaa | 'March fly' |

In Yidiɲ, the foot is disyllabic, QI (at the point when stress is assigned – cf. section 1), and so stress is assigned to every odd-numbered syllable from the left. It is clear from Dixon's discussion that the phonology systematically treats Yidiɲ reduplicated words as compounds, just as Diyari does.

We analyze Yidiɲ reduplication as F (= W$_{min}$), the disyllabic foot, as do Nash (1979–80) and Hayes (1985). The problem is obviously one of accounting for whether or not the reduplicative affix contains a final consonant. In Diyari, this determination is made solely by word-level prosody – no word-final consonants are licensed, so none appear in the compound reduplicative affix. In Lardil, the same determination is made by syllable-level prosody – only apicals and palatoalveolars are permitted syllable-finally, so only they associate with the right edge of the copy. Yidiɲ exhibits a different situation.

Nash (1979–80) proposes that only the phonemic melody elements of the first foot in the base are available for reduplicative association. This crucially distinguishes the *r* of *mulari*, which is not in the foot, from the *l* of *kintalpa*, which is. In our terms, this is stated somewhat differently: reduplication is prefixation of the minimal word to the minimal word. Thus, Yidiɲ reduplication comes under the parameter of our theory (and of Broselow and McCarthy's (1983–4)) in which a designated prosodic constituent is the base for reduplicative affixation, rather than a morphological constituent. This situation is obvious and essential in the analysis of certain types of infixing reduplication in section 2.3[†]. In the Yidiɲ case, the prosodic constituent base is initial, and it receives a prefix, so positionally the affix appears to be simply prefixed. But the behavior of final consonants reveals the true nature of the process.

Affixation to a prosodic constituent has essentially the same formal properties as affixation to a morphological one. The affix is placed relative to the designated constituent, and only the phonemic melody elements associated with that constituent are copied and available for association. We can now turn to the details of Yidiɲ.

Nash (1979–80) argues that clusters like *lp* and *mp* are systematically distinguished in Yidiɲ phonology; the latter are prenasalized stops (therefore tautosyllabic), while the former are heterosyllabic. Several factors support this view. First, the only major type of triconsonantal cluster in the language is CNC, where NC is a putative prenasalized stop. Second, various phonological alternations support this interpretation. Third, slow speech pronunciations show the expected loss of prenasalization (which does not occur word-initially), but do not affect true clusters. We will therefore write the prenasalized stops as a single melodic element, *B*.[32]

The examples in (51) would then be prosodized as follows:

(52)   (a)   F          (b)   F          (c)   F  F

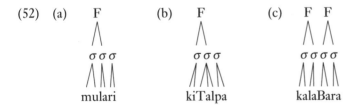

mulari          kiTalpa          kalaBara

Under our account, affixation to the minimal word (F) means that only the phonemic melody elements associated with this constituent are copied and available for association. This produces exactly the desired result: the only consonant that can associate with the end of the reduplicative skeleton is one that itself is part of the prosodically characterized base of reduplication – the initial foot of the word. There is no notion of 'foot-copying' here; rather, the Yidiɲ paradigm follows from the interaction of the minimal-word base and the minimal-word reduplicative affix.

It is strong evidence in support of this approach that combining independently needed properties of the theory in this way yields results that are otherwise inexplic-able. Moreover, we now have a closely parametrized account of the minimal distinction between Lardil *parel-pareli* and Yidiɲ *mula-mulari*: the former characterizes the base of reduplicative affixation in purely morphological terms (the stem), while the latter opts for a phonological characterization (the minimal word). The distinction is not capturable in segmental skeleton terms without invoking mechanisms that have the same effect as those we need in any case; it does no good to say that Yidiɲ reduplicates CVCCV because of *kintal-kintalpa*.

---

Reduplication in Yidiɲ and Lardil
This contrast is analyzed in terms of prosodic circumscription in M&P 1990a.

---

This account of Yidiɲ suggests an analysis of certain recalcitrant cases in Austronesian languages. We focus on Makassarese. According to Aronoff (1985),[33] reduplication in Makassarese displays a peculiar kind of phonological and morphological sensitivity:

(53)   Reduplication in Makassarese
    (a)   Disyllabic Words
        ballak        ballak-ballak    'house'
        golla         golla-golla     'sugar'
        tau           tau-tau         'person'
        tauŋ         tauŋ-tauŋ      'year'
    (b)   Longer Words
        kaluarak    kaluk-kaluarak   'ant'
        manara      manak-manara    'tower'
        balao       balak-balao     'rat'
        baine       baik-baine     'woman'

The consonant *k* is evidently in complementary distribution with *ʔ*; we may therefore regard the *k* appearing at the right edge of the copy in (53b) as an inserted *ʔ*.

The reduplicative affix in Makassarese is obviously disyllabic (the vowel sequences are all heterosyllabic); since the language has penultimate stress and appears to lack monosyllables, this too is an instance of $W_{min} = F$ reduplication. Aronoff states the generalization underlying these two patterns of reduplication – one without and one with final *ʔ* – as follows. If the boundary of the second syllable copied does not coincide with a morphological boundary, then insert *ʔ* at the end of the second syllable. Otherwise copy the syllable-final consonant if there is one.

Our interpretation of this regularity is the following. In Yidiɲ, the minimal word that is the base of reduplication actually coincides with a foot already present in the form, since stress is assigned from the left. In Makassarese, though, stress is assigned from the right, so the minimal word base must result from a prosodic reparsing of the original from the left. This reparsing simply selects the first two syllables as a minimal word. Copying of the phonemes of this minimal word and association with the affixal minimal word yield the pattern in (53a). The pattern in (53b) (and its near parallel in Tagalog)

involves a situation where the minimal word derived by reparsing – the phonologically characterized base – does not exhaust a morpheme. It is precisely in this conflict
between morphology and phonology that Makassarese develops the intrusive $k$.

---

Makassarese Reduplication
The analysis given in the text is incorrect; it cannot account for additional data that were not
available at the time. For the evidence, and a different analysis, see Aronoff et al. 1987, M&P
1990a offers an account of Makassarese based on prosodic circumscription. M&P 1994a
develops a complete treatment within Optimality Theory.

---

Yidiɲ and similar Australian languages, with stress assigned from the left, have no
such reparsing, deriving the minimal word base from simple inspection of the foot structure; consequently they can have no such rule. Makassarese and like-minded languages
must reparse; they may then compensate for the difference between phonological and
morphological edges. The formal characterization of this process in Makassarese remains
obscure; but the context is not. Our theory independently requires a minimal word
base, derived by reparsing, to achieve the surface pattern of copying in this language.
The rule of ʔ insertion records the success of this reparsing as a measure of morphological integrity. The otherwise inexplicable condition on ʔ insertion follows from this
conception of the phonological base

---

Prosodic Reparsing
The notion of prosodic reparsing is developed within circumscription theory in M&P 1995a.

---

## 2.4 Templatic morphology

The first arguments for morphological skeleta came from consideration of a purely
templatic system, the derivational categories of the Arabic verb. Such systems are characterized by nearly complete independence of melody from skeleton throughout the
morphology. In addition to this pure templatic morphology, there are at least two other
types of templates which typically occur in languages without pervasive reliance on this
mode of word formation. Templatic truncation phenomena involve massive reductions
in word size under specific morphological requirements. In another class of cases,
morphemes of a particular type are required to meet a templatic shape, even though no
direct support from alternations supports active enforcement of this requirement.

### 2.4.1 Truncation

What we are calling here truncation is not that; it is specification of a template to which
the melody (possibly enhanced with some prosodic structure along the lines developed
in section 4[†]) is directly associated. Words are not being chopped to fit by leaving off
prosodic units. Instead, starting at some designated point, the melodic elements of
a word are associated with a template, providing a nearly universal analogue to the
morphological resources of Semitic.

Most commonly in systems of vocative or nickname formation, but occasionally elsewhere, languages enforce a foot/minimal word template, resulting in systematic patterns of shortening input words:

(77)   Truncation
       Yapese (Jensen 1977: 101, 114) $W_{min}$

| Full Noun | Vocative |
|---|---|
| luʔag | luʔ |
| bayaad | bay |
| maŋɛɛfɛɛl | maŋ |

Central Alaskan Yup'ik Eskimo (Woodbury 1985) F (= $W_{min}$?)

| Full Noun | Proximal Vocative |
|---|---|
| Aŋukaɣnaq | Aŋ ~ Aŋuk |
| Nupiɣak | Nup ~ Nupix/Nupik |
| Cupǝl:aq | Cup ~ Cupǝl |
| Aŋivɣan | Aŋif |
| Kalixtuq | Kal ~ Kalik |
| qǝtunɣaq | Qǝt ~ Qǝtun |
| Maɣ$^w$luq | MaX$^w$ |
| Aɣnaɣayaq | Aɣǝn |
| NǝŋqǝXalɣia | Nǝŋǝq |
| Qakfaɣalɣia | Qak ~ Qakǝf |
| Akiuɣalɣia | Akiuk |

Afar (Bliese 1981: 97, 267) $\sigma + am$ (= $W_{min}$?)

| Frequentative | Gloss |
|---|---|
| tokam tokmeeni | 'you (pl.) ate' |
| yuʕam yuʕrufeh | 'he rested' |
| aram argaʕuk | 'he cut' |
| tifam tifiʕ | 'it dripped' |
| tubam tubleeni | 'you (pl.) saw' |
| yamam yamaateeni | 'they come' |

Japanese (Poser 1984a; 1984b: 42ff; Itô, p.c.) F(F)
(a)   Hypocoristics

| Name | Hypocoristic |
|---|---|
| midori | mii+tyaN |
| | mit+tyaN |
| | mido+tyaN |
| siNzaburoo | siN+tyaN |
| | siNzabu+tyaN |
| wasaburoo | waa+tyaN |
| | wasa+tyaN |
| | sabu+tyaN |
| | wasaburo+tyaN |

(b) ICU Student Argot

| | |
|---|---|
| iN kuri | 'Introduction to Christianity' |
| zyene edo | 'General Education' |
| iN liN | 'Introduction to Linguistics' |
| fure maN | 'freshman' |
| iN toro | 'introduction' |

(c) Abbreviations

| | |
|---|---|
| paasonaru koNpyuutaa | paso koN |
| waado purosessaa | waa puro |
| imeezyi tyenzyi | ime tyeN |
| paNtii sutokkiNgu | paN suto |
| konekusyon | kone |
| sutoraiki | suto |
| zeminaaru | zemi |
| irasutoreesyon | irasuto |

We have presented a rich variety of examples because this type of templatic morphology has been insufficiently recognized in the literature. Let us take each case in turn.

---

**More on Truncation**

The literature on truncation is much more extensive now than it was in 1986. It includes a comprehensive survey by Weeda 1992, new theoretical developments in Benua 1995, and treatments of particular languages, including (and this is only a sample) Arabic (M&P 1990b), Swedish (Morris 1989), French (Plénat 1984, Steriade 1988, Scullen 1993), Spanish (de Reuse n.d., Crowhurst 1992), Nootka (Stonham 1990), Choctaw (Martin 1989, Lombardi and McCarthy 1991), Papago (Hill and Zepeda 1992), Catalan (Cabré and Kenstowicz 1995), Rotuman (McCarthy 1996), and Japanese (Tateishi 1985 [1989], Mester 1990, Poser 1985 [1990], Itô 1991, Itô and Mester 1992, Perlmutter 1992, Itô et al. 1996).

---

In Yapese, the smallest licit independent word is a CVC syllable, and this clearly corresponds to the output of vocative truncation. The monosyllabism requirement is not surprising, but the demand that the word be consonant-final is. Since the language tolerates long vowels, it is somewhat surprising that CVV monosyllables are not permitted. We have already seen – for instance, in the case of Kamaiurá – that languages may place special requirements on word-final consonants. Such requirements, in our theory, are expressed purely melodically, via the mechanisms of association. That is, a nonvocalic melody element must be linked to the final mora in the minimal (bimoraic syllable) word. We show in section 2.4.3.1[†] that similar rules of association are needed even in a theory that has C/V skeleta and that ours is in fact a superior theory of their properties. Yapese extracts the entire melody, then associates with the $\sigma$ template from left to right.

The Yup'ik case, which is closely analyzed in prosodic terms by Woodbury (1985), is a clear (and unique) example in which the morphology must make reference to a quantity-sensitive iambic foot. The patterns assumed by proximal vocatives correspond exactly to the complex requirements that the Yup'ik stress system must in any case place on this foot-type – it is monosyllabic or disyllabic, it contains at least two moras, it must end in a consonant, and bimoraic syllables are permissible only on the right. In contrast with the complete generality of the template, the mode of association is somewhat idiosyncratic. Normally, association begins at the left edge, but occasionally it starts inside the word. Pairs like *Cup/Cupəl* show that both types of iambic quantity-sensitive feet can be associated with a single melody. The form *Akiuk* exhibits a compressed (that is, monomoraic) diphthong. This compression also fulfills the requirements of the language – full diphthongs are impossible in closed syllables.

In Afar, a minimal word (monosyllabic like Yapese) template is associated with the base melody from the left. The gerundial suffix *am* is attached to this truncated form, and the result is used as an independent word in a paronomastic construction. This is not reduplication of the usual sort, since it is evidently postsyntactic, but is rather a mechanism for creating cognate gerunds. (Afar also has the option of using an untruncated form in the same way.)

Finally, the case of Japanese is the richest we have yet seen. Poser (1982) carefully demonstrates that the bases of hypocoristics with suffixed *tyaN* are composed of one or two bimoraic units. As in Eskimo, the mode of association is somewhat idiosyncratic, with most speakers confining their choices to one of the options reported. Nevertheless, it is clear that the requirement of bimoraicity can be fulfilled in several different ways without regard to syllabic structure.

Poser reports impressionistic evidence of a bimoraic rhythmic unit in Japanese which he calls the 'foot'. The other data from this language, coming from two sorts of abbreviations, confirm this result. With very few exceptions, such abbreviations are also constructed from one or two bimoraic units. Even more compelling evidence for this conclusion emerges in a secret language of entertainers described by Tateishi (1985 [1989]). This secret language performs the following permutations:

(78)   Japanese Secret Language

| Base Form | Secret Form | |
|-----------|-------------|--|
| maneezyaa | zyaamane | 'manager' |
| koohii | hiikoo | 'coffee' |
| ippatu | patuiti | 'a shot' |
| oNna | naaoN | 'woman' |
| mesi | siimee | 'meal' |
| hi | iihii | 'fire' |

As Tateishi observes, the secret language forms are all composed of exactly two bimoraic feet, regardless of the mora count of the original.[34] The skeleton of the disguised form, then, is simply FF, while the mode of association is obviously one of great complexity.

---

*Zuuja-go*
A comprehensive analysis of this secret language, with significant theoretical development, is presented in Itô et al. 1996.

---

The English truncated words are a type of templatic morphology based on the composition of minimality: min(min(Wd)). The minimal phonological word of English is the foot; it functions in the formation of echo words, as we show below. In truncated words, the template is the minimal foot: $\min(F) = \min(\min(Wd)) = \sigma$. English and Yup'ik truncations provide a nice contrast: the former is $\min(\min(Wd))$, therefore $\sigma$, the latter is $\min(Wd)$, therefore F.

English has a large number of truncated words, which Jespersen (1928– ) calls 'stump-words', that may appear alone or with an affix like -er(s), -ie, -y, or -o. A few examples of the many hundreds of these appear in (79):

(79)   English 'stump-words'

| | |
|---|---|
| rugby | rugger |
| pregnant | preggers |
| Bolshevik | Bolshy |
| Jonathan | Jono |

Similar data, although without a regular morphological relationship, are found in English affective verbs in -er, like *patter, quaver, flicker, glister*.

The base of the truncated form, minus any affix, is invariably a single stressed syllable $(= \min(\min(Wd)))$.[35] In no case does the truncated form contain more than one syllable (modulo the affixes), nor does it ever retain any consonants which could not be assigned to a minimal word template. Thus, *rugby* or *pregnant* cannot form the phonotactically permissible but morphologically ungrammatical affectives *\*rugber* or *\*pregners*. Furthermore, the assignment of melodic material to the $\sigma\ (= W_{min})$ template is indifferent to the syllabification of the base, so the affective is *Bolshy* in spite of the fact that *Bolsh* does not constitute a syllable of *Bolshevik*.[36] In other words, the formation of stump-words is not an operation of truncation, but rather of assignment of melody to template. This is true cross-linguistically: truncation the phenomenon is not truncation the operation, but rather is association with a specified template. Finally, we note that the affixes appearing on these affective words are all stress-neutral, as we would expect of a morphological pattern that requires a form in the shape of a phonological word.

The mere volume of the forms and the ease with which they are coined suggests that this process is quite productive in English. Nevertheless, there are a few idiosyncrasies. Nicknames, but not other affective words, are subject to various neotenous segmental changes, like *Bobbie* from *Robert*. Association of the melody is normally from the left edge in, as we would expect from unmarked left-to-right association, but in a very few forms association begins at the stressed syllable: *tater* (< *potato*), *tec* (< *detective*).

A few instances of truncation invoke a prosodic constituent demonstrably different from the foot or minimal word. Both known cases involve taking reduction of the weakly stressed member of a compound to its limiting case: truncation.

Truncation in Zuni (Newman 1965) applies to the left branches of all compounds (80a) and to stems before certain suffixes (80b). The result of truncation retains only the initial (that is, stressed) consonant and vowel of the original:

(80)   Zuni Truncation

| | | | |
|---|---|---|---|
| (a) | tukni | tu-mokʷkʷ'anne | 'toe-shoe = stocking' |
| | melika | me-kʷ'iššo | 'Non-Indian-negro = black man' |
| | melika | me-ʔoše | 'Non-Indian-be:hungry = hobo' |
| | paču | pa-lokk'a-akʷe | 'Navajo-be:gray = Ramah Navajo' |

(b)                    *Familiar*
          kʷʼalasi     kʷʼa-mme             'Crow'
          suski        su-mme               'coyote'
          kuku         ku-mme               'father's sister'

It is evident that the truncation process is based on a monomoraic syllable template with LR association of the entire melody.[37] Can this template be derived from some higher-level unit of the language? Since words invariably have initial stress, there is no appeal to foot here. Nonfunction words appear to always be at least bimoraic, so the minimal word is also not in play. The Zuni monomoraic or core syllable does, however, correspond to the minimal root, and this seems a plausible constraint to place on the members of compounds or suffixed words.

Like Zuni, Madurese (Stevens 1968; Weeda 1986 [1987]) also displays truncation in connection with compounding, and also like Zuni, Madurese truncation is anchored on the stressed syllable, in this case final. Truncation applies to the left branch of certain compounds (81a), to the left branch of one type of root reduplication (81b), and spontaneously in certain words (81c):

(81)   Madurese Truncation
       (a)   usap            sap-lati              'handkerchief' ('wipe' + 'lip')
             uriŋ            riŋ-tua              'parents' ('person' + 'old')
             tuzhuʔ          zhuʔ-ənpul           'pinky' ('finger' + 'pinky')
             pasar           sar-suri              'afternoon market'
                                                   ('market' + 'afternoon')
       (b)   bit             bit-abit             'finally'
             buwaʔ-an        waʔ-buwaʔ-an         'fruits'
             maen-an         en-maen-an           'toys'
             ŋastan-e        tan-ŋastan-e         'to hold'
             estre           tre-estre            'wives'
             chapphluk-an    phluk-chapphluk-an   'a noise'
       (c)   settoŋ          toŋ                  'one'
             duwaʔ           waʔ                  'two'
             enghi           ghi                  'yes'
             uriŋ            riŋ                  'person'

The template here is a simple syllable σ. As Weeda (1986 [1987]) notes, the introduction of tautosyllabic clusters into Madurese ('wives' and 'a noise' in (81b)) is paralleled by a comparable development in the truncated forms. The σ template explains this; a segmental skeleton cannot. As in the other cases, the operation is not true truncation. Rather, association to the σ template begins with the left edge of the root-final syllable and proceeds until the phonemic melody is filled or the independently characterized positions in σ are exhausted.

The only roots of Madurese shorter than two syllables are function words (Stevens 1968: 51), so neither minimal root nor *a fortiori* minimal word can be appealed to. The template here, then, is independent of higher-level prosodic units, and so rests directly on the syllable.

## 2.4.2   Templatic well-formedness requirements

Languages frequently place templatic requirements on morphemes or derived forms of a particular class. These requirements are not actively enforced in the sense of generating alternations the way truncation does, but they exist passively in that all members of the class must conform to them. The by now familiar minimal word or root is a clear instance of this type, but in most cases the template is unmodified by the minimality predicate. For example, Indo-European root monosyllabism is expressed by a $\sigma$ template which demands that all roots be exactly one syllable long, neither more nor less. A substantial subset of the English affective vocabulary involves a similar rule.

English echo words involve total reduplication of a (typically) nonoccurring base with some unsystematic changes in vocalism or consonantism: *jingle-jangle*, *helter-skelter*. Although this is not a regular or orderly domain of English morphology, it is nevertheless a very common and possibly productive one; Jespersen (1928– ) observes that it is quite frequent, and Thun (1963) has collected over 4,000 different examples from throughout the history of the language.

Inspection of these extensive data yields the following observations, which hold virtually without exception. An English echo word may be a word-level compound of two stressed syllables (*hob-nob*), of two disyllabic words of the form stressed-unstressed (*fiddle-faddle*), or of two trisyllabic words stressed-unstressed-unstressed (*higgledy-piggledy*). Occasionally the two halves of the compound differ in canonical pattern, but always within this range of possibilities: *plug-ugly*, *pitter-pat*, *kitty-cat*.

In sum, an echo word must be a compound of exactly two metrical feet, each of which constitutes a separate phonological word. This is equivalent to regarding them as compounds of two minimal words $W_{min}$. English metrical feet are composed of a stressed syllable followed by zero, one, or two unstressed syllables (the last derived by syllabic extrametricality at both junctural positions in the compound), which corresponds to the distribution of reduplicated echo words.

This formal requirement not only generates the occurring types but, naturally enough, excludes many nonoccurring ones. Echo words are impossible with an unstressed syllable preceding the foot (*\*banana-cabana*) or with more than one foot (*\*phalarope-kalatrope*).

Another example of this sort is provided by a class of Jamaican Creole affective words called iteratives. According to DeCamp (1974; see also McCarthy 1983), iteratives are reduplicated words built on a monosyllabic template, to which is optionally added an unspecified (and therefore harmonizing) core syllable to indicate greater intensity or a specified *i* to mark jocosity:

(82)   Jamaican Iteratives
| | |
|---|---|
| mak-mak | 'muddy' |
| graŋ-graŋ | 'firewood' |
| maka-maka | 'muddy (intensive)' |
| priti-priti | 'very pretty' |

Potential iteratives not conforming to the monosyllabic pattern are excluded (e.g. *kyerfl-kyerfl*). DeCamp not only collected a very large set of actual iteratives, but also went so

far as to experimentally confirm the boundaries of the phenomenon by testing hypothetical iteratives with five informants. Thus, the generalization about canonical pattern
is confirmed by quite careful scrutiny.

## 2.4.3   True templatic morphology

The final case is represented by the classic templatic systems, those in which the template directly expresses the morphological possibilities of the language. We discuss here
Semitic and the templatic formation of the habilitative in Cupeño.

### 2.4.3.1   Semitic

Proposals to reduce the Classical Arabic templatic system to prosodic structure have
been pursued before (Levin 1983, Lowenstamm and Kaye 1986, Yip 1983), but always
with a skeletal tier of segment-sized units. We will show that the segmental skeleton is
entirely superfluous, and we will develop several novel arguments for a prosodic characterization of this system, considering fully the consequences of our moves.

The basic data, presented in the CV-notation, are contained in (83):

(83)   Arabic Templates
    (a)   Verbal Templates
        CVCVC        CVCCVC
        CVVCVC      CCVCVC
        CCVCCVC    CCVVCVC
    (b)   Nominal Templates
        CCVC          CVCC
        CVCVC        CVVCVC
        CCVVC        CVCVVC
        CVCCVC      CVVCVC
        CVCCVVC    CCVCCVVC
        CVVCVVC    CCVCVVC
        CCVVCVVC

These skeletal patterns exhaust those assumed by canonical, unaffixed nouns and verbs.
There also exist noncanonical nouns – these generally fail to participate in Arabic root-
and-pattern morphology or behave somewhat idiosyncratically when they do.

---

More on Semitic Morphology
An account of Arabic nominal and verbal template forms that aims at thoroughness is presented in M&P 1990b. It is further refined in Prince 1991, McCarthy 1993, and M&P 1991b.
(The account of Arabic plural templates in M&P 1990a should also be mentioned.) Other
relevant literature on the morphology of various Afro-Asiatic languages includes Bat-El 1989,
1992; Dell and Elmedlaoui 1992; Gafos 1996; Guerssel and Lowenstamm 1994; Hayward
1988; Hoberman 1988; Inkelas 1990; Lowenstamm and Kaye 1986; Moore 1989; Prince
1991; Sharvit 1994; Yip 1988.

---

All indications in Arabic point toward a split between monomoraic CV syllables and bimoraic CVC and CVV syllables. The stress system divides up light and heavy syllables along these lines, and a corresponding distinction is made in the otherwise unrelated system for scanning verse.

We must also recognize a place for peripheral unsyllabifiable consonants. Such consonants are a consequence of peripheral extraprosodic syllables in the skeleton. These syllables, we stipulate, have exactly one consonant melody associated with them; they will develop vocalism only when they cease to be peripheral and therefore extraprosodic (or, ultimately, in the postlexical phonology). This vocalism is supplied either by affixes or ultimately by epenthesis. We will say a bit more about these syllables below.

A syllabic characterization of the Arabic skeleta, using the moraic distinction between light and heavy syllables and extraprosodicity defined in this way, is as follows:

(84) Arabic Skeleta Prosodically

| Syllabic Skeleton | Corresponding CV-skeleton |
|---|---|
| $\sigma \, (\sigma)$ | CVCC |
| $(\sigma) \, \sigma$ | CCVC |
| $(\sigma) \, \sigma \, (\sigma)$ | CCVVC |
| $\sigma_\mu \, \sigma$ | CVCVC |
| $\sigma_{\mu\mu} \, \sigma$ | CVVCVC, CVCCVC |
| $\sigma_\mu \, \sigma \, (\sigma)$ | CVCVVC |
| $\sigma_{\mu\mu} \, \sigma \, (\sigma)$ | CVVCVVC, CVCCVVC |
| $(\sigma) \, \sigma_\mu \, \sigma$ | CCVCVC |
| $(\sigma) \, \sigma_{\mu\mu} \, \sigma$ | CCVCCVC, CCVVCVC |
| $(\sigma) \, \sigma_{\mu\mu} \, \sigma \, (\sigma)$ | CCVCCVVC, CCVVCVVC |
| $(\sigma) \, \sigma_\mu \, \sigma \, (\sigma)$ | CCVCVVC |

It should be noted that the weight (mora count) of the last metrical syllable in each skeleton is unmarked because these syllables are invariably heavy. We will bring this up again below.

There are many results that follow from this reanalysis of the Arabic skeletal system.

1   This approach permits us to require that Arabic skeleta in general are subject to a minimum size of one metrical syllable and a maximum size of two metrical syllables. The former is not somehow independently necessary – there are a few noncanonical nouns with no syllables, like *bn*. The latter follows from general conditions of locality imposed on counting rules, as described in section 1. Verbs are subject to more stringent constraints: they are minimally and maximally disyllabic.
2   We can extract out the generalization, already noted, that the last metrical syllable is always bimoraic. That is, $\sigma \rightarrow \mu\mu \, / \_\_\_ \, ]$.
3   Unsyllabifiable sequences are limited to peripheral position, a consequence of the usual constraints on the distribution of extraprosodicity. The corollary to this is that, modulo the extraprosodic elements, Arabic skeleta are well-formed sequences of syllables. This is not a trivial result; since Classical Arabic and most dialects have epenthesis rules that would regularize even template-internal unsyllabifiable strings, the underlying well-formedness of the template demands an explanation. Moreover,

as we noted in section 1, medial unsyllabifiable segments could be used to cook the results of left-to-right association.

4   Subject to these other three requirements, the occurring skeleta are a result of the free concatenation of the representational vocabulary (heavy and light syllables, extraprosodicity). There are no gaps: all and only the elementary patterns generated by free concatenation function in the morphological system.

5   There is no true skeletal contrast between CVC and CVV syllables; the apparent differences are accounted for by melody-to-skeleton association rules of great generality. To prove this, we distinguish two cases. The last metrical syllable, always heavy, is also always CVC if it is truly the last syllable. If it is followed by an extraprosodic syllable, it is CVV except when it is also initial (that is, in the template [σ (σ)]). The language simply displays no contrast in these cases; the nouns that would require such a contrast (*gaaz* 'gas', *ʔusquff* 'bishop') are transparent loans, extraordinarily rare, and thoroughly noncanonical. Thus, it is a simple matter to describe the contexts in which a CVC syllable occurs; these contexts trigger a rule of root-to-skeleton association, linking the rightmost root consonant with some unit of the skeleton.

Likewise, there is no CVC/CVV contrast in other syllables (those marked as bimoraic in (84)). The distinction between CVV and CVC syllables internally is accounted for by rules of somewhat lesser generality. In particular, the verbal skeleton CVCCVC is not freely available – it is the result of an association rule deriving medial gemination (*kattab*) that any analysis requires, or it arises under the force of the requirement that all root consonants be associated with some prosodic element (as in the quadriliteral verb *daHraj*).[38]

6   As we noted in section 1, the apparent restrictions on Arabic skeleta that would follow from segment counting actually follow from syllable counting and the relatively simple independently motivated syllable structure of this language. The proof of this claim is the evidence adduced in McCarthy (1984b) from modern Hebrew. The richer syllable structure of modern Hebrew is reflected in the richer possibilities for disyllabic templatic verbs: *ʔišknez* 'make Ashkenazic', *šlimper* 'make sloppy', *stingref* 'take shorthand'. There is no difference between the cognate templates in Classical Arabic and modern Hebrew; the sole difference lies in the licensing of tautosyllabic consonant clusters in the latter.

7   Arabic consonants linked to extraprosodic syllables do not have the same properties as truly unsyllabified consonants. In Cairene Arabic, triconsonantal clusters are normally resolved by epenthesis after the second consonant: VCC*i*CV. As expected, initial clusters in loans are split in the equivalent way, so that the epenthetic vowel also lodges in an open syllable: *sibirtu* 'spirit', *bilastik* 'plastic'. But initial clusters of words formed on templates (that is, all words except loans) undergo epenthesis in a way otherwise unprecedented in the language: *ʔijtama* 'he met'. The posited linking to an initial extraprosodic syllable distinguishes this sort of epenthesis from the more general phenomenon observed in loans and other clusters.

These arguments lead to a single conclusion: all vestiges of segmental structure, cast as C/V, X, or whatever, must be removed from the Arabic skeleton. The maximum generality and regularity of skeletal form is achieved by limiting the descriptive vocabulary to syllables, moraic annotations, and extraprosodicity.

# Notes

Preparation of this document was supported by the National Science Foundation (grant SBR-9420424) and Rutgers University. We owe a large debt to John Alderete and Jill Beckman, whose assistance was indispensable.

1   A similar point is made about apocope in Lardil by Wilkinson (1986).
2   We might say $\mu = \sigma$ in such cases.
3   Word-length distinctions are made on similar grounds in biblical Hebrew (Dresher 1983), Japanese (M. Liberman, reported in Poser (1984b)), and Ponapean (see section 2.1). Other cases of counting allomorphy abound – Spanish (Harris 1979), Pukapukan (Chung 1978), Maaori (Biggs 1961) – all referring to syllables or moras.
4   Notice that syllable theory proper doesn't even do this kind of extensive counting: most syllable length restrictions follow from pairwise sonority transition requirements; the rest from hierarchy. Discussion appears in section 3.1[†].

    G. N. Clements has suggested to us (April 1985, p.c.) that a descriptor C* could be used to refer to consonant sequences of unspecified length. The development of prosodic theory has eliminated such devices from phonological rules proper; it seems worthwhile to us to extend the result generally.
5   The one argument in the literature which crucially relies on unfilled template slots is Everett and Seki (1985); we deal with it below in section 2.2[†].
6   Condition (9) is probably a special case of the general principle for interpreting structural descriptions throughout phonology. As the notion of strict adjacency at the appropriate level (tier, grid stratum) replaces string specification devices, it becomes likely that no language-specific stipulation of optionality is allowed in rules.
7   There are various ways to guarantee this interpretation. In essentially the terms of Steriade (1982), one can say that the primary act of syllabification is to adjoin at most one C to a following V – the Onset Rule. This is Hyman's (1985) conception of the creation of the elementary mora. This is distinct from, say, Kahn's conception in which the primary move is to associate $\sigma$ to V. Then $\sigma_c$ indicates an application of this primary adjunction, which may fail to create CV if there's no C to take.
8   It is possible, for example, that the mapping observed in $\sigma_c$ is related to the notion 'minimal affix'.
9   Davis (1986) proposes skeletally driven association only for infixes; we regard it as universal.
10   Refinements on melody copying are explored in section 4.3[†].
11   Sommer cites a pattern of internal reduplication for some polysyllabic stems:

    (a)   /iyalme-/      iy-ALM-almey    'play'
    (b)   /anaŋumi-/   anaŋ-UM-umin   'peek'

    Without a more extensive account of Oykangand phonology and morphology, it is not entirely clear what to make of these examples. They do suggest, however, that prefixation might actually be to the minimal word rather than to the word proper: this would cover all the cases. See below, section 2.3[†]. Sommer also cites the pair /oyelm/ 'back again' and *OYEL-oyelm* 'straight back again', which he notes is limited to this one word.
12   Alternative accounts are made possible by the present theory. Suppose, for example, that mapping is not really LR but rather head-to-head on prosodic constituents. Then the head – least sonorous member – of the onset cluster would be chosen, regardless of the extrasyllabicity situation. An account along these lines must assume that the representation analyzed by the prefix contains prosodic information.
13   Lengthening of the initial vowel is due to the 'temporal augment' /a+/.
14   The long initial diphthong *aau* is a regular consequence of adding the augment *a-* to vowel-initial roots (Whitney 1889: section 136a) and has nothing to do with the peculiarities of the reduplicating subclass of aorists.

15  The aorist evidence is less clearcut since the syllabic incorporation of the augment a- into the erstwhile root syllable provides a source for i, if it can be copied (this being a rather familiar way that syllabification muddles morpheme boundaries).

16  The same rule applies in the intensive (section 1002.III.f) in the older language. Discussion of the poorly attested intensive, which involves a number of interesting descriptive problems (see Steriade 1985), will be postponed to a later work.

17  Quantitative complementarity should probably be understood in terms of higher-order prosodic structuring. Suppose that the actual rule is to impose an asymmetrical (iambic) foot LR. This is always possible, because the aorist prefix a- necessarily forms a light syllable. If the root syllable is heavy, a clash would result: this typically blocks the process. Interestingly, there are cases where the root syllable is lightened (section 861) to accommodate the iambic pattern; thus √raadh gives a-RAA-radham, √krand gives a-CIk.rad.am. This equivocation is familiar from other clash-driven processes: when there are several solutions, variability is likely. Quantitative complementarity also shows up in Ponapean (see below) and in most cases of counting allomorphy rules (section 1), with strong indications of a similar but not identical prosodic basis.

18  Harrison and Albert claim that this effect is only observed with NC clusters, but they cite no evidence to support the restriction. The alternative we would conceivably find in other clusters is *appapta* from hypothetical *apta*.

19  Rehg and Sohl distinguish four types of vowel insertion.

 1  Prothesis of *i/u*, providing a vocalic nucleus to supplant a syllabic nasal. Thus, *m.pe* 'beside it' may be pronounced *im.pe*. Choice between *i* and *u* is phonetically predictable. (pp. 55–6)

 2  Copying of the following vowel, whereby *ak+dei* → *ak-e-dei*, *ak+tantat* → *ak-a-tantat*. Various conditions obtain (pp. 92–4).

 3  General Epenthesis of i/u, with choice determined as in <1>, to break up any impermissible cluster not otherwise dealt with. "In slow, careful speech they are less likely to be employed than in rapid, less careful speech" (p. 94).

 4  Appearance of 'base vowel' (pp. 87–91). Of great interest to the present argument is the preservation of some etymological final vowels in suffixation and in reduplication of mono-syllabic roots. With the verbalizing suffix -niki 'to have the thing characterized by the base', we find, for example:

   (i)   kiil    'skin'    kil-i-niki
   (ii)  ŋiil    'voice'   ŋil-e-niki
   (iii) diip    'sin'     dip-a-niki

According to Rehg and Sohl, it is the base vowel that breaks up the cluster in (36l–o), accounting for the phonologically inexplicable difference between *tep-e-tep* 'kick' and *tep-i-tep* 'begin' – cf. transitives *tepek* 'kick' and *tapi* 'begin'. Given the plethora of insertions in the language, it's not at all clear that the cited data unambiguously establish the claim. Supposing, however, that it is correct, are we driven to the etymologizing conclusion that reduplication is bisyllabic (= F), with various subsequent reductions? We think not. With McCarthy (1984a) we propose that the 'base vowel' is a kind of floating affixal melodeme associated with certain roots, which is allowed to surface when a free vowel slot presents itself. In support of this, we note that there are only three types of base vowel /i a e/, out of a seven-vowel system, a typical grammaticalization of opaque phonology. The reader is referred to Harris (1985) for discussion of a rather similar phenomenon in Spanish, and to Itô (1986) for analysis of the assimilation/epenthesis system in Ponapean.

20  Rehg and Sohl cite the following paradigm:

   (i)   /ak+dei/      ak*e*dei
   (ii)  /ak+pʷuŋ/     ak*u*pʷuŋ
   (iii) /ak+tantat/   ak*a*tantat

For discussion of conditions under which a copy vowel appears, see Rehg and Sohl 1981: 92–4.

21  Rehg and Sohl say more particularly that the first syllable must contain a long vowel, but they cite no evidence to support a distinction between CVV and CVC.

22  Note here the transfer of vowel length. See below, section 4† for discussion. The $\sigma_{\mu\mu}$ prefix cannot extend itself all the way to CVVC (*duup-duupek) because superheavy syllables are allowed only word-finally. Compounds, of course, consist of two words: e.g. (40d) waantuuke 'count'.

23  Another possible line of analysis would be to hold that syllabic nasals arise by optional dropping of initial i/u. Then impek exactly resembles Mokilese andip.

24  Rehg and Sohl report some optionality in what appears to be the nonhigh vowel class: thus amas reduplicates as either amiamas or amaamas, ewetik as either ewiewetik or eweewetik.

25  Notice that among other peculiarities ua would have to be treated as a heavy monosyllable to get the $\sigma_{\mu}$ prefix.

26  For discussion of some irrelevant complications in Diyari stress assignment, see Poser 1986.

27  All grammatical words of Diyari also contain at least two syllables, except for the particle ya 'and'.

28  As Itô (1986) shows, the interaction of syllabic well-formedness conditions with constraints on the analyzability of geminates in Lardil and other languages permits the homorganic nasal-stop clusters as well.

29  This example also exhibits the phenomenon of transfer, which we take up below in section 4.3†.

30  In Wilkinson's analysis, even derived palatoalveolars count for this purpose. Lardil has a rule converting all consonants to the corresponding palatoalveolar before a labial: /pit+puri/ pitʸpuri 'smell (source)', /wik+puri/ witʸpuri 'shade (source)'. This rule applies to the verb marker th in reduplications of labial-initial roots, as in the example patitʸpati already cited, or in pethal/peetʸpe 'bite'. Given the extensive alternations among apicals and nonapicals in the language, it is likely that this analysis is reconstructible without the notion 'derived palatoalveolar'.

31  There is an additional complication in Lardil reduplication. We find reduplications like thaltii/thaltiithaltii 'stand up', where base-final length appears in original and copy. Against this are forms like patii/patitʸpati 'sit with legs outstretched', where length is lost, and noun-to-verb reduplications like ŋarnda/ŋarndaŋarndaa 'crotch/spread the legs apart', in which length appears only in the original and not the copy. It appears that these length alternations have a great deal to do with a poorly understood rule of final vowel lengthening marking intransitives.

32  There is an alternative account of clusters like mp that is equally compatible with our theory. If they are regarded as true heterosyllabic clusters, rather than single melodic units, then all facts about their surface distribution will equally well follow from Itô's (1986) licensing theory, presented above in connection with the analysis of Orokaiva. Only homorganic nasal-stop clusters will have the crucial branching structure at the articulator tier, thereby exempting them from various aspects of syllabic well-formedness. The pattern of reduplication in kalakalamparaa (*kalam-kalamparaa) then follows from the Geminate Constraint as well: the putative minimal word kalam would contain only half of a structure that branches at the articulator tier – therefore only kala is copied and available for association.

33  Reporting on joint work with Ellen Broselow.

34  There is one exception to this: trimoraic trisyllabic words like piyano become yanopi. Although there is no reason to doubt the accuracy of this observation, it is interesting that Osamu Fujimura, a native speaker of Japanese but not of this secret language, strongly felt that this must be a mistake.

35  The syllabic character of stump-words has been independently noted by David Nash and Jane Simpson in unpublished work.

36  Those with strong intuitions of ambisyllabicity may wish to contemplate examples with a different stress pattern. For example, Altoona would necessarily truncate as Altie, *Allie.

37  Newman (1965) has initial clusters in his analysis of Zuni, but these are restricted to Cʔ. This idea has little merit and causes many problems, so I have reinterpreted these as glottalized consonants.

38  A comparable point has been made by Levin (1983) and Broselow (1984).

# References

Akinlabi, Akinbiyi. 1995. Prosodic truncation and template satisfaction in Ibibio verbs. In Kola Owolabi (ed.), *Language in Nigeria: A Festschrift for Ayo Bamgbose*, Ibadan: Group Publishers, 75–90.

Archangeli, Diana. 1983. The root CV-template as a property of the affix: evidence from Yawelmani. *Natural Language & Linguistic Theory* 1, 348–84.

Archangeli, Diana. 1984. Underspecification in Yawelmani Phonology and Morphology. Ph.D. dissertation, MIT.

Aronoff, Mark. 1985. Talk on Makassarese reduplication presented at University of Massachusetts, Amherst.

Aronoff, Mark, Azhar Arsyad, Hassan Basri, and Ellen Broselow. 1987. Tier configuration in Makassarese reduplication. In Anna Bosch, Barbara Need and Eric Schiller (eds), *Papers from the 23rd Annual Regional Meeting of the Chicago Linguistic Society, Part Two: Parasession on Autosegmental and Metrical Phonology*, Chicago: Chicago Linguistic Society, 1–15.

Austin, Peter. 1981. *A Grammar of Diyari, South Australia*. Cambridge: Cambridge University Press.

Bat-El, Outi. 1989. Phonology and Word Structure in Modern Hebrew. Ph.D. dissertation, UCLA.

Bat-El, Outi. 1992. Stem modification and cluster transfer in modern Hebrew. MS, Tel-Aviv University.

Benua, Laura. 1995. Identity effects in morphological truncation. ROA-74. Rutgers Optimality Archive, http://ruccs.rutgers.edu/roa.html. In Jill Beckman, Laura Walsh Dickey, and Suzanne Urbanczyk (eds), *University of Massachusetts Occasional Papers in Linguistics 18: Papers in Optimality Theory*, Amherst, Mass.: Graduate Linguistic Student Association, 77–136.

Bernabe, Emma J. Fonacier, Virginia Lapid, and Bonifacio Sibayan. 1971. *Ilokano Lessons*. Honolulu: University of Hawaii Press.

Biggs, Bruce. 1961. The structure of New Zealand Maori. *Anthropological Linguistics* 3, 1–54.

Blevins, Juliette. 1996. Mokilese reduplication. *Linguistic Inquiry* 27/3, 523–30.

Bliese, Loren F. 1981. *A Generative Grammar of Afar*. The Summer Institute of Linguistics, University of Texas at Arlington.

Bowen, J. Donald (ed.). 1969. *Beginning Tagalog: A Course for Speakers of English*. Berkeley: University of California Press.

Boxwell, H. and M. Boxwell. 1966. Weri phonemes. *Papers in New Guinea Linguistics* 5, 77–93.

Breen, Gavan. 1990. The syllable in Arrernte phonology. MS, School of Australian Linguistics and IAD (Institute for Aboriginal Development).

Broselow, Ellen. 1982. On the interaction of stress and epenthesis. *Glossa* 16, 115–32.

Broselow, Ellen. 1984. Default consonants in Amharic morphology. In M. Speas and R. Sproat (eds), *Papers from the January 1984 MIT Workshop in Morphology*, Cambridge, Mass.: MIT Dept. of Linguistics, 15–32.

Broselow, Ellen and John McCarthy. 1983–4. A theory of internal reduplication. *Linguistic Review* 3, 25–88.

Buller, Barbara, Ernest Buller, and Daniel Everett. 1993. Stress placement, syllable structure, and minimality in Banawa. *International Journal of American Linguistics* 59/3, 280–93.

Cabré, Teresa and Michael Kenstowicz. 1995. Prosodic trapping in Catalan. ROA-32, Rutgers Optimality Archive, http://ruccs.rutgers.edu/roa.html. *Linguistic Inquiry* 26/4, 694–705.

Cho, Young-mee Yu. 1991. A phonological constraint on the attachment of particles in Korean. In S. Kuno et al. (eds), *Harvard Studies in Korean Linguistics* 4, 37–46.

Chung, Sandra. 1978. *Case Marking and Grammatical Relation in Polynesian*. Austin: University of Texas Press.

Clements, G. N. 1985. The problem of transfer in nonlinear morphology. *Cornell Working Papers in Linguistics* 7, 38–73.

Clements, G. N. and S. J. Keyser. 1983. *CV Phonology*. Cambridge, Mass.: MIT Press.

Cole, Jennifer Fitzpatrick. 1990. The minimal word in Bengali. In Aaron Halpern (ed.), *The Proceedings of the Ninth West Coast Conference on Formal Linguistics*, Stanford, Calif.: Stanford Linguistics Association, 157–70.

Crowhurst, Megan. 1991a. Minimality and Foot Structure in Metrical Phonology and Prosodic Morphology. Ph.D. dissertation, University of Arizona, Tucson.

Crowhurst, Megan. 1991b. Demorafication in Tübatulabal: evidence from initial reduplication and stress. In Tim Sherer (ed.), *Proceedings of North East Linguistic Society 21*, Amherst, Mass.: Graduate Linguistic Student Association, University of Massachusetts, 49–64.

Crowhurst, Megan. 1992. Diminutives and augmentatives in Mexican Spanish: a prosodic analysis. *Phonology* 9, 221–53.

Davis, Stuart. 1986. Published as Davis 1988.

Davis, Stuart. 1988. On the nature of internal reduplication. In Michael Hammond and Michael Noonan (eds), *Theoretical Morphology: Approaches in Modern Linguistics*, San Diego, Calif.: Academic Press, 305–23.

de Reuse, Willem J. n.d. The derivation of Spanish hypocoristics in a nonconcatenative theory of morphology. MS, University of Texas, Austin.

Dell, François and Mohamed Elmedlaoui. 1992. Quantitative transfer in the nonconcatenative morphology of Imdlawn Tashlhiyt Berber. *Journal of Afroasiatic Languages* 3, 89–125.

DeCamp, David. 1974. Neutralizations, iteratives, and ideophones: the locus of language in Jamaica. In David DeCamp and Ian Hancock (eds), *Pidgins and Creoles: Current Trends and Prospects*, Washington, D.C.: Georgetown University Press, 46–50.

Dixon, R. M. W. 1972. *The Dyirbal Language of North Queensland*. Cambridge: Cambridge University Press.

Dixon, R. M. W. 1977. *A Grammary of Yidiɲ*. Cambridge: Cambridge University Press.

Dresher, B. Elan. 1983. Postlexical phonology in Tiberian Hebrew. In M. Barlow, D. Flickinger and M. Wescoat (eds), *Proceedings of WCCFL 2*, Stanford, Calif.: Stanford Linguistics Association, 67–78.

Dunlap, Elaine. 1991. Issues in the Moraic Structure of Spanish. Ph.D. dissertation, University of Massachusetts, Amherst.

Everett, Dan and Lucy Seki. 1985. Reduplication and CV skeleta in Kamaiurá. *Linguistic Inquiry* 16, 326–30.

Gafos, Adamantios. 1995. On the proper characterization of 'nonconcatenative' languages. MS, Johns Hopkins University. ROA-106, Rutgers Optimality Archive, http://ruccs.rutgers.edu/roa.html.

Gafos, Adamantios. 1996. The Articulatory Basis of Locality in Phonology. Ph.D. dissertation, The Johns Hopkins University.

Golston, Chris. 1991. Minimal word, minimal affix. In Tim Sherer (ed.), *Proceedings of the North East Linguistic Society 21*, Amherst, Mass.: Graduate Linguistic Student Association, University of Massachusetts, 95–110.

Goodman, Beverley. 1995. Features in Ponapean Phonology. Ph.D. dissertation, Cornell University, Ithaca, N.Y.

Grimshaw, Jane. 1985. [On dative verbs]. MS, Brandeis University.

Guerssel, Mohamed and Jean Lowenstamm. 1994. Talk presented at Second Colloquium on Afro-Asiatic Linguistics, Sophia Antipolis, France.

Hale, Kenneth. 1973. Deep-surface canonical disparities in relation to analysis and change: an Australian example. *Current Trends in Linguistics* 11, 401–58.

Halle, Morris and Jean-Roger Vergnaud. 1978. Metrical structures in phonology. MS, MIT.

Hammond, Michael. 1988. Templatic transfer in Arabic broken plurals. *Natural Language & Linguistic Theory* 6, 247–70.

Harms, Robert T. 1966. The measurement of phonological economy. *Language* 42, 602–11.

Harris, James. 1979. Some observations on "Substantive principles in Natural Phonology." In Daniel Dinnsen (ed.), *Current Approaches to Phonological Theory*, Bloomington: Indiana University Press, 281–93.

Harris, James. 1985. Spanish word markers. In F. H. Nuessel, Jr (ed.), *Current Issues in Spanish Phonology and Morphology*. Bloomington: Indiana University Linguistics Club.

Harrison, Sheldon and Salich Y. Albert. 1976. *Mokilese–English Dictionary*. Honolulu: University Press of Hawaii.

Hayes, Bruce. 1980. A Metrical Theory of Stress Rules. Ph.D. dissertation, MIT. Distributed by the Indiana University Linguistics Club. Pub. New York: Garland, 1985.

Hayes, Bruce. 1985. Iambic and trochaic rhythm in stress rules. In M. Niepokuj et al. (eds), *Proceedings of the Thirteenth Meeting of the Berkeley Linguistics Society*, Berkeley: Berkeley Linguistics Society, 428–46.

Hayes, Bruce. 1986. Inalterability in CV phonology. *Language* 62, 321–51. [Repr. in part as ch. 12]

Hayes, Bruce. 1987. A revised parametric metrical theory. In J. McDonough and B. Plunkett (eds), *Proceedings of NELS 17*, Amherst, Mass.: Graduate Linguistic Student Association, University of Massachusetts, 274–89.

Hayes, Bruce. 1991. Published in expanded form as Hayes 1995.

Hayes, Bruce. 1995. *Metrical Stress Theory: Principles and Case Studies*. Chicago: University of Chicago Press.

Hayes, Bruce and May Abad. 1989. Reduplication and syllabification in Ilokano. *Lingua* 77, 331–74.

Hayward, R. J. 1988. In defence of the skeletal tier. *Studies in African Linguistics* 19, 131–72.

Healey, Alan, Ambrose Isoroembo, and Martin Chittleborough. 1969. Preliminary notes on Orokaiva grammar. *Papers in New Guinea Linguistics* 9, 33–64.

Henderson, John. forthcoming. Number-marking in Arrernte verbs. MS, University of Western Australia. Paper presented at Australian Linguistic Society Annual Conference, Macquarie University, North Ryde, 1990.

Hewitt, Mark. 1992. Vertical Maximization and Metrical Theory. Ph.D. dissertation, Brandeis University.

Hill, Jane and Ofelia Zepeda. 1992. Derived words in Tohono O'odham. *International Journal of American Linguistics* 58, 355–404.

Hoberman, Robert. 1988. Local and long-distance spreading in Semitic morphology. *Natural Language & Linguistic Theory* 6, 541–50.

Hyman, Larry. 1985. *A Theory of Phonological Weight*. Dordrecht: Foris.

Ingria, Robert. 1980. Compensatory lengthening as a metrical phenomenon. *Linguistic Inquiry* 11, 465–95.

Inkelas, Sharon. 1990. Prosodic replacement in modern Hebrew. In Michael Ziolkowski et al. (eds), *Papers from the 26th Regional Meeting of the Chicago Linguistic Society. Part Two: The Parasession on the Syllable in Phonetics and Phonology*, Chicago: Chicago Linguistic Society, 197–212.

Itô, Junko. 1986. Syllable Theory in Prosodic Phonology. Ph.D. dissertation, University of Massachusetts, Amherst.

Itô, Junko. 1989. A prosodic theory of epenthesis. *Natural Language & Linguistic Theory* 7, 217–60.

Itô, Junko. 1991. Prosodic minimality in Japanese. In Karen Deaton, Manuela Noske, and Michael Ziolkowski (eds), *CLS 26-II: Papers from the Parasession on the Syllable in Phonetics and Phonology*, Chicago: Chicago Linguistic Society, 213–40.

Itô, Junko and Jorge Hankamer. 1989. Notes on monosyllabism in Turkish. *Phonology at Santa Cruz* 1, 61–70.

Itô, Junko, Yoshihisa Kitagawa, and R. Armin Mester. 1992. Prosodic type preservation in Japanese: evidence from *zuuja-go*. SRC-92-05, Syntax Research Center, UC Santa Cruz. ROA-99, Rutgers Optimality Archive, http://ruccs.rutgers.edu/roa.html. Published in revised form as Itô et al. 1996.

Itô, Junko, Yoshihisa Kitagawa, and R. Armin Mester. 1996. Prosodic faithfulness and correspondence: evidence from a Japanese argot. ROA-146, Rutgers Optimality Archive, http://ruccs.rutgers.edu/roa.html. *Journal of East Asian Linguistics* 5, 217–94.

Itô, Junko and Ralf-Armin Mester. 1992. Weak layering and word binarity. MS, University of California, Santa Cruz.

Jensen, John T. 1977. *Yapese Reference Grammar*. Honolulu: University Press of Hawaii.

Jespersen, Otto. 1928– . *A Modern English Grammar on Historical Principles*. London: G. Allen & Unwin.

Kager, René. 1992. Are there any truly quantity-insensitive systems? In Laura Buszard-Welcher, Lionell Wee, and William Weigel (eds), *Proceedings of BLS 18*, Berkeley: Berkeley Linguistics Society, 123–32.

Kager, René. 1993a. Alternatives to the iambic-trochaic law. *Natural Language & Linguistic Theory* 11: 381–432.

Kager, René. 1993b. Consequences of Catalexis. In H. van der Hulst and J. van de Weijer (eds), *Leiden in Last*, HIL Phonology Papers, 1 (The Hague: HIGL), 269–98.

Kager, René. 1993c. Shapes of the generalized trochee. In Jonathan Mead (ed.), *Proceedings of WCCFL II*, Stanford, Calif.: Stanford Linguistics Association, 298–312.

Kager, René. 1996a. Stem disyllabicity in Guugu Yimidhirr. OTS-WP-TL-96-008. ROA-70, Rutgers Optimality Archive, http://ruccs.rutgers.edu/roa.html. In M. Nespor and N. Smith (eds), *HIL Phonology Papers II*, The Hague: 59–101.

Kager, René. 1996b. On affix allomorphy and syllable counting. OTS-WP-TL-96-006. ROA-88, Rutgers Optimality Archive, http://ruccs.rutgers.edu/roa.html. In U. Kleinhenz (ed.), *Interfaces in Phonology*, Stadia Grammatica 41, Berlin: Akademie Verlag, 155–71.

Kiparsky, Paul. 1986. The phonology of reduplication. MS, Stanford University.

Kiparsky, Paul. 1992. Catalexis. MS, Stanford University.

Klokeid, Terry. 1976. Topics in Lardil Grammar. Ph.D. dissertation, MIT.

Levin, Juliette. 1983. Reduplication and prosodic structure. MS, MIT.

Levin, Juliette. 1985. A Metrical Theory of Syllabicity. Ph.D. dissertation, MIT.

Lombardi, Linda and John McCarthy. 1991. Prosodic circumscription in Choctaw morphology. *Phonology* 8, 37–71.

Lowenstamm, Jean and Jonathan Kaye. 1986. Compensatory lengthening in Tiberian Hebrew. In L. Wetzels and E. Sezer (eds), *Studies in Compensatory Lengthening*, Dordrecht: Foris, 97–132.

Marantz, Alec. 1982. Re reduplication. *Linguistic Inquiry* 13, 435–82.

Marlett, Stephen and Joseph Stemberger. 1983. Empty consonants in Seri. *Linguistic Inquiry* 5, 617–39.

Martin, Jack. 1989. Infixation and extrametricality in prosodic morphology: three rules from Greek. MS, University of North Texas.

McCarthy, John. 1979. Formal Problems in Semitic Phonology and Morphology. Ph.D. dissertation, MIT.

McCarthy, John. 1981. A prosodic theory of nonconcatentive morphology. *Linguistic Inquiry* 12, 373–418.

McCarthy, John. 1983. Morpheme form and phonological representation. Paper presented at Sloan Conference on Hierarchy and Constituency in Phonology, University of Massachusetts, Amherst.

McCarthy, John. 1984a. Ponapean reduplication. MS, University of Texas, Austin.

McCarthy, John. 1984b. Prosodic organization in morphology. In M. Aronoff and R. Oehrle (eds), *Language Sound Structure*, Cambridge, Mass.: MIT Press, 299–317.

McCarthy, John. 1993. Template form in prosodic morphology. In Laurel Smith Stvan et al. (eds), *FLSM III: Papers from the Third Annual Meeting of the Formal Linguistics Society of Midamerica*, Bloomington: Indiana University Linguistics Club, 187–218.

McCarthy, John. 1996. Extensions of faithfulness: Rotuman revisited. MS, University of Massachusetts, Amherst. ROA-110, Rutgers Optimality Archive, http://ruccs.rutgers.edu/roa.html.

McCarthy, John and Alan Prince. 1988. Quantitative transfer in reduplicative and templatic morphology. In Linguistic Society of Korea (ed.), *Linguistics in the Morning Calm* 2, Seoul: Hanshin Publishing Co., 3–35.

McCarthy, John and Alan Prince. 1990a. Foot and word in prosodic morphology: the Arabic broken plurals. *Natural Language & Linguistic Theory* 8, 209–82.

McCarthy, John and Alan Prince. 1990b. Prosodic morphology and templatic morphology. In M. Eid and J. McCarthy (eds), *Perspectives on Arabic Linguistics: Papers from the Second Symposium*, Amsterdam: Benjamins, 1–54.

McCarthy, John and Alan Prince. 1991a. Prosodic minimality. Paper presented at University of Illinois Conference *The Organization of Phonology*.

McCarthy, John and Alan Prince. 1991b. Linguistics 240: Prosodic Morphology. Lectures and handouts from 1991 LSA Linguistic Institute Course, University of California, Santa Cruz.

McCarthy, John and Alan Prince. 1993a. Prosodic morphology I: Constraint interaction and satisfaction. MS, University of Massachusetts, Amherst, and Rutgers University.

McCarthy, John and Alan Prince. 1993b. Generalized alignment. In Geert Booij and Jaap van Marle (eds), *Yearbook of Morphology 1993*, Dordrecht: Kluwer, 79–153.

McCarthy, John and Alan Prince. 1994a. The emergence of the unmarked: optimality in Prosodic Morphology. ROA-13. Rutgers Optimality Archive, http://ruccs.rutgers.edu/roa.html. In Mercè Gonzàlez (ed.), *Proceedings of the North East Linguistics Society 24*, Amherst, Mass.: Graduate Linguistic Student Association, 333–79.

McCarthy, John and Alan Prince. 1994b. Two Lectures on Prosodic Morphology. The Utrecht Workshop on Prosodic Morphology. ROA-59, Rutgers Optimality Archive, http://ruccs.rutgers.edu/roa.html.

McCarthy, John and Alan Prince. 1995a. Prosodic Morphology. In John Goldsmith (ed.), *A Handbook of Phonological Theory*, Oxford: Basil Blackwell, 318–66.

McCarthy, John and Alan Prince. 1995b. Faithfulness and reduplicative identity. ROA-60, Rutgers Optimality Archive, http://ruccs.rutgers.edu/roa.html. In Jill Beckman, Suzanne Urbanczyk, and Laura Walsh (eds), *University of Massachusetts Occasional Papers in Linguistics 18: Papers in Optimality Theory*, Amherst, Mass.: Graduate Linguistic Student Association, 249–384.

McDonough, Joyce. 1990. Topics in the Phonology and Morphology of Navajo. Ph.D. dissertation, University of Massachusetts, Amherst.

Mester, Ralf-Armin. 1990. Patterns of truncation. *Linguistic Inquiry* 21, 478–85.

Mester, Ralf-Armin. 1995. The quantitative trochee in Latin. *Natural Language & Linguistic Theory* 12, 1–61.

Michelson, Karin. 1981. Stress, epenthesis, and syllable structure in Mohawk. In G. N. Clements (ed.), *Harvard Studies in Phonology II*, Bloomington: Indiana University Linguistics Club.

Moore, John. 1989. Doubled verbs in Modern Standard Arabic. *Phonology at Santa Cruz* 1, 93–124.

Moravcsik, Edith. 1978. Reduplicative constructions. In Joseph Greenberg, Charles Ferguson, and Edith Moravcsik (eds), *Universals of Human Language 3: Word Structure*, Stanford, Calif.: Stanford University Press, 297–334.

Morris, Mitzi. 1989. Swedish nickname formation. *Phonology at Santa Cruz* 1, 125–71.

Myers, Scott. 1987. Tone and the Structure of Words in Shona. Ph.D. dissertation, University of Massachusetts, Amherst.

Nash, David. 1979–80. Yidiny stress: a metrical account. *Cunyforum* 7/8, 112–30.

Nash, David. 1980. Topics in Warlpiri Grammar. Ph.D. dissertation, MIT. Pub. New York: Garland, 1986.

Newman, Stanley. 1965. *Zuni Grammar*. Albuquerque: University of New Mexico Press.

Ola, Olanike Olajumoke. 1995. Optimality in Benue-Congo Prosodic Phonology and Morphology. Ph.D. dissertation, University of British Columbia, Vancouver.

Orgun, C. Orhan and Sharon Inkelas. 1992. Turkish prosodic minimality. Paper presented at 6th International Conference on Turkish Linguistics, Anadolu University, Eskişehir, Turkey, August 1992.

Perlmutter, David. 1992. Pervasive word formation patterns in a grammar. Paper presented at BLS.

Piggott, Glyne. 1992. Satisfying the minimal word. MS, McGill University, Montréal.

Plénat, Marc. 1984. Toto, fanfa, totor et même guiguitte sont des anars. In François Dell et al. (eds), *Forme sonore du langage*, Paris: Hermann, 161–82.

Poser, William. 1982. Why cases of syllable reduplication are so hard to find. MS, MIT.

Poser, William. 1984a. Hypocoristic formation in Japanese. In Mark Cobler et al. (eds), *Proceedings of the Third West Coast Conference on Formal Linguistics*, Stanford, Calif.: Stanford Linguistics Association, 218–29.

Poser, William. 1984b. The Phonetics and Phonology of Tone and Intonation in Japanese, Ph.D. dissertation, MIT.

Poser, William. 1986. Diyari stress, metrical structure assignment, and the nature of metrical representation. In M. Dalrymple et al. (eds), *Proceedings of the West Coast Conference on Formal Linguistics 5*, Stanford, Calif.: Stanford Linguistics Association, 178–91.

Poser, William. 1989. The metrical foot in Diyari. *Phonology* 6, 117–48.

Poser, William. 1985 [1990]. Evidence for foot structure in Japanese. *Language* 66, 78–105.

Prince, Alan. 1980. A metrical theory for Estonian quantity. *Linguistic Inquiry* 11, 511–62.

Prince, Alan. 1983. Relating to the grid. *Linguistic Inquiry* 14, 19–100. [Repr. in part as ch. 21.]

Prince, Alan. 1985. Improving tree theory. *Proceedings of the Berkeley Linguistics Society* 11, 471–90.

Prince, Alan. 1991. Quantitative consequences of rhythmic organization. In Karen Deaton, Manuela Noske, and Michael Ziolkowski (eds), *CLS 26-II: Papers from the Parasession on the Syllable in Phonetics and Phonology*, Chicago: Chicago Linguistic Society, 355–98.

Prince, Alan and Paul Smolensky. 1993. Optimality Theory: constraint interaction in generative grammar. MS, Rutgers University, New Brunswick, and University of Colorado, Boulder.

Rehg, Kenneth L. and Damien G. Sohl. 1981. *Ponapean Reference Grammar*. Honolulu: University of Hawaii Press.

Robins, R. H. 1959. Nominal and verbal derivation in Sundanese. *Lingua* 8, 337–69.

Rosenthall, Samuel (to appear) The prosodic base of the Hausa plural. In René Kager, Harry van der Hulst, and Wim Zonneveld (eds), *The Prosody–Morphology Interface* (Cambridge: Cambridge University Press).

Sapir, Edward. 1930. Southern Paiute, a Shoshonean language. *Proceedings of the American Academy of Arts and Sciences* 65/1–3.

Schein, Barry and Donca Steriade. 1986. On geminates. *Linguistic Inquiry* 17, 691–744.

Scullen, Mary Ellen. 1993. The Prosodic Morphology of French. Ph.D. dissertation, Indiana University, Bloomington.

Selkirk, Elisabeth. 1980a. Prosodic domains in phonology: Sanskrit revisited. In Mark Aronoff and Mary-Louise Kean (eds), *Juncture*, Saratoga, Calif.: Anma Libri, 107–29.

Selkirk, Elisabeth. 1980b. The role of prosodic categories in English word stress. *Linguistic Inquiry* 11, 563–605.

Selkirk, Elisabeth. 1981. Epenthesis and degenerate syllables in Cairene Arabic. In H. Borer and J. Aoun (eds), *Theoretical Issues in the Grammar of the Semitic Languages*, Cambridge, Mass.: MIT Press, 209–32.

Selkirk, Elisabeth. 1988. A two-root theory of length. MS, University of Massachusetts, Amherst.

Sharvit, Yael. 1994. Issues in the Phonology and Morphology of the Modern Hebrew Verbal System: Alignment Constraints in Verb Formation. ROA-23, Rutgers Optimality Archive, http://ruccs.rutgers.edu/roa.html.

Sommer, Bruce. 1981. The shape of Kunjen syllables. In D. L. Goyvaerts (ed.), *Phonology in the 1980s*, Ghent: E. Story-Scientia, 231–44.

Spring, Cari. 1990a. Implications of Axininca Campa for Prosodic Morphology and Reduplication. Ph.D. dissertation, University of Arizona, Tucson.

Spring, Cari. 1990b. How many feet per language? In Aaron Halpern (ed.), *The Proceedings of the Ninth West Coast Conference on Formal Linguistics*, Stanford, Calif.: Stanford Linguistics Association, 493–508.

Steriade, Donca. 1982. Greek Prosodies and the Nature of Syllabification. Ph.D. dissertation, MIT.

Steriade, Donca. 1985. Reduplication, ablaut, and syllabicity in Sanskrit. MS, MIT.

Steriade, Donca. 1988. Reduplication and syllable transfer in Sanskrit and elsewhere. *Phonology* 5, 73–155.

Stevens, Alan. 1968. *Madurese Phonology and Morphology*. New Haven: American Oriental Society.

Stonham, John. 1990. Current Issues in Morphological Theory. Ph.D. dissertation, Stanford University.

Tateishi, Koichi. 1985 [1989]. Theoretical implications of the Japanese musician's language. In E. Jane Fee and Katherine Hunt (eds), *Proceedings of the Eighth West Coast Conference on Formal Linguistics*, Stanford, Calif.: Stanford Linguistics Association, 384–98.

Thun, Nils. 1963. Reduplicative Words in English; a study of formations of the types tick-tick, hurly-burly, and shilly-shally. Thesis, Uppsala.

Turner, Margaret Mary and Gavan Breen. 1984. Akarre rabbit talk. *Language in Central Australia* 1, 10–13. [NB: Breen identifies the languages as Eastern Arrernte rather than Akarre, p.c.]

Urbanczyk, Suzanne (to appear) Double reduplications in parallel. In René Kager, Harry van der Hulst, and Wim Zonneveld (eds), *The Prosody–Morphology Interface* (Cambridge: Cambridge University Press).

Urbanczyk, Suzanne. 1996a. Morphological templates in reduplication. In *Proceedings of NELS 26*, Amherst, Mass.: GLSA.

Urbanczyk, Suzanne. 1996b. Patterns of Reduplication in Lushootseed. Ph.D. dissertation, University of Massachusetts, Amherst.

Weeda, Donald. 1986 [1987]. Formal properties of Madurese final syllable reduplication. In Anna Bosch et al. (eds), *Papers from the 23rd Annual Regional Meeting of the Chicago Linguistic Society, Part Two: Parasession on Autosegmental and Metrical Phonology*, Chicago: Chicago Linguistic Society, 403–17.

Weeda, Donald. 1992. Word Truncation in Prosodic Phonology. Ph.D. dissertation, University of Texas, Austin.

Whitney, W. D. 1889. *Sanskrit Grammar*. Cambridge, Mass.: Harvard University Press.

Wilkins, David. 1984. Nominal reduplication in Mparntwe Arrernte. *Language in Central Australia* 1, 16–22.

Wilkins, David. 1989. Mparntwe Arrernte (Aranda): Studies in the Structure and Semantics of Grammar, Ph.D. dissertation, Australian National University, Canberra.

Wilkinson, Karina. 1986. Syllable structure and Lardil phonology. MS, University of Massachusetts, Amherst.

Wilkinson, Karina. 1988. Prosodic structure and Lardil phonology. *Linguistic Inquiry* 19, 325–34.

Woodbury, Anthony. 1985. Meaningful phonological processes: a consideration of Central Alaskan Yupik Eskimo prosody. MS, University of Texas, Austin.

Yip, Moira. 1982. Reduplication and CV-skeleta in Chinese secret languages. *Linguistic Inquiry* 13, 637–62.

Yip, Moira. 1983. Redundancy and the CV-skeleton. MS, Brandeis University.

Yip, Moira. 1988. Template morphology and the direction of association. *Natural Language & Linguistic Theory* 6, 551–77.

Yip, Moira. 1991. Prosodic morphology of four Chinese dialects. *Journal of East Asian Linguistics*, 1/1.

# 14

# On the Role of the Obligatory Contour Principle in Phonological Theory (1986)

## David Odden

In autosegmental phonology, a sequence of adjacent identical tones can be represented (a) as a single tone mapped onto multiple vowels, (b) as a one-to-one
mapping between multiple tones and vowels, or (c) as a combination of these
extremes. The Obligatory Contour Principle (OCP) has been proposed as a constraint which restricts tonal representations to a one-to-many mapping between
tones and vowels. It is argued here that the strongest form of the OCP is falsified
by a number of languages which distinguish single vs. multiple tones associated
with a sequence of vowels. The language-particular violations of the OCP constitute a strong argument for the full power of autosegmental phonology.

1   *Overview*   The literature on tone from the past decade makes it clear that no
coherent picture is possible if tonal features are represented as an indistinguishable part
of the phonetic matrix of the elements (typically vowels) which bear them. Segmental
theories of tone fail to explain why vowels can be deleted and still leave their tones
behind – or why tonal morphemes can be added to stems, with no segmental material to
support the tonal feature. But if we assume, as in the theory of autosegmental phonology, that tonal features are formally separate from the elements which bear them – and
are connected to these elements with 'association lines' – then we can explain the partial
independence of tonal features and the segments which bear them.

The autosegmental theory of tone yields highly insightful and elegant analyses of
tonal grammars in which no analysis at all is possible under a segmental view. Perhaps
a better metric of the success of autosegmental phonology is the fact that we can test
empirical hypotheses regarding formal properties of tonal grammars (e.g. the Well-
Formedness Conditions of Goldsmith 1976, Haraguchi 1977, and Clements and Ford
1979). The success of the theory can in part be attributed to the fact that, although it is
more enriched than the segmental theory, the facts of language demand the use of this
extra power.

The victory of autosegmental phonology might have been rendered hollow if the
theory had merely encompassed the entire segmental approach, adding its own descriptive devices on top: phonological theory would be greatly complicated in some areas,
with no compensatory simplification elsewhere. There is no question that the general
sense of coherence which autosegmental phonology has brought to the study of tone is
the primary justification for accepting that theory, regardless of any question of more

vs. less powerful theories. However, certain of the more powerful descriptive devices of an autosegmental approach also render pointless various complex and ad hoc segmental descriptions (cf. Leben 1978, Goldsmith 1976). Moreover, attempts have been made, within the framework of autosegmental phonology, to restrict its power. This paper discusses the status of one such restriction, the Obligatory Contour Principle (OCP).

One of the outstanding problems in constraining autosegmental phonology is that its machinery allows multiple surface analyses of identical phonetic strings. Within a totally unconstrained version of the theory, a string of four consecutive H-tones could be given any of the eight analyses seen in (1).[1]

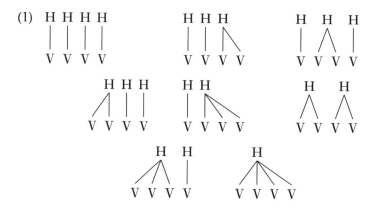

(1)

It then appears that autosegmental phonology entails a less determinate set of principles governing the acquisition of tone. Clearly, some principle is needed to resolve this dilemma.

A constraint first discussed by Leben (1973), and named the OCP by Goldsmith, disallows many of these analyses. As first set forth by Leben, the principle states that, when two identical tones are associated with adjacent vowels, the rightmost tone is deleted (and the leftmost is associated with the freed vowels). In Leben's 1978 version, both underlying and derived tonal representations are subject to the OCP. This principle goes far toward constraining the power of autosegmental phonology: only the last representation in (1) is well-formed. Since theories with greater generative power are less desirable than ones with less power, the OCP intrinsically increases the attractiveness of autosegmental phonology. Interestingly, counter-examples to the OCP, in which at least some of the distinctions in (1) are needed, constitute an even stronger kind of argument for an autosegmental theory of tone – since, if it turns out that such distinctions are needed (as I shall argue here), then only an autosegmental theory of tone can make any sense of them.

Desirable as it may be to restrict autosegmental phonology so as to disallow the multiple analyses of (1), many participants in the debate have argued that the OCP is too strong. Goldsmith presents analyses of various languages – including Tiv (Bantoid, Nigeria) and Etung (Benue-Congo, Nigeria) – in which floating tonal *melodies* are mapped onto vowels – but violate the OCP, in that the melodies contain multiple adjacent identical tones. As Goldsmith points out, rejection of the OCP is one fundamental difference between his view of tonal structure and that advocated by Leben (1973). For example,

Goldsmith analyses the Recent Past B and Subjunctive tenses in Tiv as having the tonal melody $HH\{B_{2\Sigma}/L_{2\Sigma}\}$;[2] he also argues that some classes of lexical items in Etung have the tonal melody HHL vs. HL, or LLH vs. LH.[3]

Given the potential benefits of the OCP, it would be unwise to reject hastily such attempts to restrict the theory; a more conservative approach would be to weaken the OCP only where necessary. This then raises the question whether the counter-examples to the OCP might fit into a well-defined class. It turns out that many of the claimed counter-examples, as in Etung, need not be so classified if one allows tones to be associated with vowels in the lexicon, following an approach like that of Pulleyblank. Since Goldsmith eschews associating tones with vowels in the lexicon, he has to accept an analysis in which Etung words are characterized by contrasting melodies such as HHL vs. HL. But if lexical associations of tones and vowels are allowed, then the melodies of Etung are fewer: HHL and HL are the same melody, differing only in the position within the word where their tones are associated, as in (2).

(2)   H L          H   L
      /\ |          |   /\
    *ngare* 'pepper'  *akpuga* 'money'

Such an analysis is plausible since, in Etung, the putative HHL melodies do not 'migrate' to the right or left when prefixes or suffixes are added to the stem. Thus there is a significant theoretical trade-off between allowing lexical associations of tone, on the one hand, and violating the OCP, on the other. This suggests the possibility that a number of the putative exceptions to the OCP might be false counter-examples, depending crucially on the unmotivated assumption that tones are not lexically linked with vowels.

The number of genuine counter-examples to the OCP is perhaps smaller than Goldsmith suggests; but they do exist. It turns out that most such counter-examples can be reduced to cases of identical floating tones in a grammatical tonal melody (as in the Tiv tone melody proposed by Goldsmith), or else are invoked merely to eliminate lexical tone associations. In the following sections [only the first of these is repr. here], I will consider three Bantu languages – Shona of Zimbabwe, and Kishambaa and Kipare, both of Tanzania – with the hope of shedding some light on the precise nature of the OCP. I argue that the essential insight of the principle is already expressed by the independent scientific principle of Occam's Razor. Specifically, I claim that the OCP cannot be maintained as a universal (thus supporting Goldsmith's contention), and that it plays no role as a formal constraint on possible grammars. The phenomena which motivate the OCP, I argue, follow from a general principle of grammar selection, by which underlying representations which conform to the OCP are preferred unless explicit evidence shows that such representations are untenable. Almost paradoxically numerous counter-examples to the OCP can be found when one considers tonal representations which involve the concatenation of tones across morphemes. The lack of adherence to the OCP in derived representations follows from the fact that the principle is not universal, and is therefore not available cost-free to every language. To derive the effect of the OCP in tone sequences between morphemes, a language must explicitly include a rule to collapse adjacent identical tones. Such a grammar is more complex than one which lacks such a rule; and to the extent that languages select simpler grammars, the OCP will be violated in derived representations.

2   *Shona*   Crucial evidence bearing on the validity of the OCP as a universal can be found in Shona,[4] where we find two classes of counter-examples – plus one phenomenon which supports a weakened version of the OCP. I shall show that the underlying tonal associations of non-derived morphemes in Shona obey the OCP – but that morphologically derived tonal sequences, as well as underived floating tonal melodies, violate the OCP. I turn first to the question of derived vs. non-derived tonal sequences, as exemplified in the morphological 'associative' construction.

Shona has a number of tonal processes, discussed by Odden (1980), which apply in the so-called associative constructions. Certain prefixes – such as *-e-* or *-re-* 'of',[5] *ne-* 'with', and *se-* 'like' – are used to subordinate a following NP to another noun within a phrase, yielding structures like *bhúku ré-mwaná* 'book of child' (where *mwaná* 'child' is preceded by the associative prefix *ré-*).[6] The associative prefixes share a number of phonological, morphological, and tonal similarities. The most important of the tonal rules which applies here is Associative Lowering (AL), which lowers an H which stands after the H of an associative prefix. A strictly segmental statement of the rule would be that 'The initial string of H tones after the associative prefix is lowered':

(3)      Noun                          'with Noun'
   (a)   *hóvé*         'fish'            *né-hove*
   (b)   *mbúndúdzí*    'army worms'      *né-mbundudzi*
   (c)   *bénzíbvunzá*  'inquisitive fool'  *né-benzibvunzá*

One would hope to construct a fairly simple rule such as (4) to account for these alternations:

(4)   Associative Lowering
      $H \Rightarrow L / H \underline{\hspace{1em}}$
            [+assoc]

However, with a strictly linear account, where each vowel bears a separate tone, rule 4 cannot apply correctly. Given underlying *né-hóvé*, only the first H of the syllable *ho* stands after the associative prefix, which conditions the rule. Either right-to-left or left-to-right iterative application of (4) will yield \**né-hové*, since only the first H stands immediately after the determinant prefix – if the representations to which AL applies are purely segmental.

If AL were stated so as to apply to any H-tone in an associative construction (placing the burden on a global morphological feature, rather than a phonological property), the result would still be incorrect, since only the absolute initial sequence of H's is lowered (as shown by *né-benzibvunzá* 'inquisitive fool'). Furthermore, the actual tone of the associative prefix is crucial in determining the applicability of the lowering rule. If an associative prefix bears L-tone, it cannot trigger lowering, as shown by *va-Fárái* 'of Farai'. Additional examples showing that associative prefixes must bear H-tone in order to condition lowering are provided by forms with two or three associative prefixes, such as *né-e-hóvé* 'with-of-fish' (from underlying *né-é-hóvé*). Application of AL to the H-tone of the prefix *-é-* yields an L-tone on the prenominal prefix, thus preventing the second prefix from lowering the H-tones of the following noun. If there are three associative prefixes before a noun, the first lowers the H of the second, which prevents the second from lowering the tone of the third – which then (because of its retention of H) causes lowering of the H-tones of the noun. This left-to-right self-bleeding application is illustrated by the form *sé-ne-é-hove* 'like-with-of-fish' (from underlying *sé-né-é-hóvé*).

The paradox in applying AL to a string of H-tones evaporates completely if we reject the assumption of a one-to-one mapping between tones and vowels – i.e. if we reject the linear theory of phonology. On the assumption that one tone can be mapped onto many vowels, rule 4 is retained unmodified. It applies to the underlying autosegmental representations on the left in (5), giving the phonetic representations directly.[7]

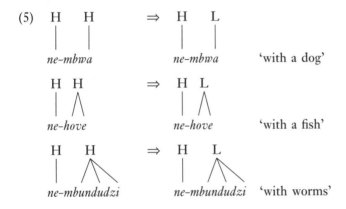

(5)   H   H      ⇒   H   L
      |   |          |   |
      ne-mbwa        ne-mbwa        'with a dog'

      H H          ⇒   H   L
      | /\             | /\
      ne-hove          ne-hove      'with a fish'

      H   H        ⇒   H   L
      | /\             | /\
      ne-mbundudzi     ne-mbundudzi  'with worms'

A crucial assumption of this analysis, which is amply justified by the data, is that what appears to be a phonetic string of adjacent H's in (3a–c) is properly represented as a single H, associated with a number of vowels. Shona thus provides data which bear on the representation of adjacent identical tones: judging from the evidence of AL, the OCP seems vindicated, since adjacent identical tones are represented as one tonal autosegment. Moreover, this constraint on representation is consistent in the lexicon.[8] Were it the case that *any* combination of H's and lines were possible, as in (1), then we would also expect non-existent alternations like those in the invented examples of (6).

(6)   H   H   H      ⇒   H   L   H
      |   |  /\            |   |  /\
      ne-hwahwahwa         *ne-hwahwahwa

      H   H  H        ⇒   H   L   H
      | /\ |              | /\  |
      ne-hwehwehwe        *ne-hwehwehwe

Thus the OCP must be a principle of phonological organization in the lexicon of Shona.[9] This principle can be imposed in one of two ways. The weaker and inherently less interesting approach is to relegate the OCP to the status of a language-specific fact underlying representations in Shona, of no greater theoretical significance than that the language has no lateral consonants. Alternatively, the OCP can be explained on universal grounds. For reasons that will become clear below, the proposed universal is not precisely the one suggested by Leben, but rather is a universal constraint on lexical representations.

Shona presents three classes of counter-examples to the OCP. I believe that the vast majority of such counter-examples fall into one of these categories:

(7)  (a)  Identical tones in the underlying form of some words, where they are parts of separate morphemes.
    (b)  A sequence of identical tones derived by application of a phonological rule to a sequence of non-identical tones.
    (c)  Floating-tone morphemes which are composed solely of tones, and which happen to have adjacent identical tones.

Absent here is any counter-example where contrasts in associated tones, such as those in (1), are needed in the lexicon. In Odden 1980, as an empirically required retreat from the strongest version of the OCP, I proposed that the principle is valid for all (underived) lexical entries.

It is clear that the OCP cannot be an 'active' principle in Shona in the sense that any violations of it (however derived) would require modification via some universal collapsing transformation, merging adjacent identical tones. If we view the OCP as having rule-like properties, as well as being a static constraint on well-formedness in the lexicon, it has many opportunities to apply within Shona derivations; yet it demonstrably never does. Thus Shona presents counter-examples of class 7a. Were the OCP to apply to H-tones concatenated across morpheme or word boundaries, we would lose the distinction between, on the one hand, one H associated with three vowels, and, on the other hand, two H's, one associated with two vowels and the other associated with one vowel. Thus the type of contrasts seen in (1) are not found in underlying representations in Shona, but they are found in derived representations.

One such case where the OCP has the opportunity to apply, but fails to, is in the derivation of stems which stand after a string of associative prefixes with underlying H-tone. AL applies to the H of the second prefix, but not to the H of the stem in underlying *né-é-hóvé* 'with-of-fish'. If the OCP were an active principle which controlled Shona derivations, then it should have created the structure of (8).

(8)      H

AL could not apply to this structure – since, at the autosegmental level where the rule applies, there is simply one H. Even if one were to concoct some version of AL which would unhook the H from all vowels but the first, and put an L in the proper place on the tonal tier, the rule would still wrongly lower both the underlying H of the second prefix -e- and the H of the stem. Additional cases of violations of the OCP because of the concatenation of H-toned morphemes are discussed by Odden (1980).

Shona also violates the OCP in cases of type 7c, where a morpheme in composed solely of an unassociated tonal melody which contains two adjacent H-tones. It is shown by Odden (1981, 1984) that verbs in subordinate clauses receive a floating tonal melody HHLB – where B is a copy tone realized as H in H-toned roots and as L in L-toned ones. The two H's of this melody are mapped onto the leftmost available vowels, which are generally the second and third stem vowels; and the tonal pair LB is mapped as far left as possible onto the 'final vowel' tense/aspect suffix.[10] In a typical L-toned verb like -rim- 'plow', we find two consecutive H-tones on the second and third stem vowels, because of application of the mapping rule: e.g. váká-rimísísiran-a 'they having made plow for each other intensively'. The tones LB are mapped onto the final syllable, where B is realized as L; in conjunction with the melodic L, this is simplified to a single L by the Twin Sister Convention. A typical H-toned verb like -pófomadz- 'blind' has the root-initial H followed by the two melodic H-tones; the 'final vowel' bears a H, which is the realization of the variable B-tone when associated with a H-toned root, e.g. váka-pófómádzisisiran-á 'they having made quite blind for each other'. The L-toned component of the LB pair is shifted by the Leftward Shift rule, and spreads further leftward by a language-specific rule.

A number of arguments can be given in support of the claim that this tonal melody contains two adjacent H-tones, and therefore constitutes a counter-example to the OCP. The most obvious is that verbs inflected with this tonal melody exhibit two H-tones. If the melody were composed of a single H, then we would expect every toneless vowel to have a H; or if that H did not spread to toneless vowels, we would expect only one surface H. We would not expect one H to surface as precisely two H-tones; since the melody contains two H-tones which cannot be derived from a single H by any independently motivated rules, the melody must contain two H-tones.

A second, more compelling, argument can be made for two independent H-tones in the HHLB melody, based on the manner in which this tonal melody is mapped onto reduplicated stems. The presence of two H's in the verbal tone melody explains why the entire melody – in particular the tonal sequence LB – is compressed onto the leftmost copy of the stem if that stem contains three or more syllables, but is distributed over both copies of the stem if the leftmost stem-copy contains fewer syllables. The leftmost stem-copy, in (9), contains the entire HHLB melody in váka-tóresá-toresa 'they having repeatedly made take', with three stem syllables. The first H is mapped onto the leftmost syllable re (9b), and the second H onto the syllable sa (9c). The tone pair LB (realized as LH) is also mapped onto the medial syllable sa (9d), since it contains the leftmost final vowel morpheme. Because of a rule of Fall Simplification, the first H-tone of the complex tone resulting from mapping is deleted (9e); and because of Leftward Shift, the L-toned component of the resulting rising tone is shifted to the preceding syllable (deleting any existing tone), giving the surface tone pattern HLH within the leftmost stem (9f).

But when the stem contains fewer than three syllables, the tone melody is distributed over the entire reduplicated stem, and is not confined to the leftmost stem-copy; this is shown by váka-tórá-tóresá 'they having made repeatedly take' in (10). Note that the

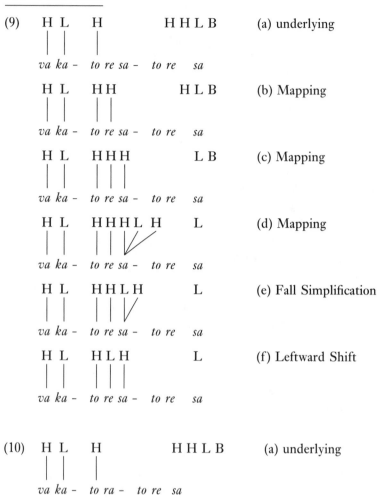

word-final syllable bears a H, which is the reflex of the LB component of the tonal melody. The two H's of the melody are mapped onto the syllables *ra* and *to* respectively (10b–c); at this point, the tonal pair LB cannot be associated with the leftmost stem's final vowel because of the association line between the second melodic H and the initial syllable of the second stem-copy. The word-final 'final vowel' receives the pair LB (realized as LH, 10d), and the L of the rising tone shifts left because of the Leftward Shift rule (10c).

The relationship of the number of syllables in the first stem-copy to whether the melody is distributed over both copies, or only the rightmost one, follows automatically from the analysis provided in Odden 1984 – but only if the tone melody contains two H's and therefore violates the OCP. Thus a model where adjacent identical tones automatically collapse into one tone is untenable in its strongest form. [ . . . ]

5   *Discussion*   In summary, our investigation into the OCP [not all repr. here] has the following results. On the negative side, we have encountered a number of cases where the OCP fails to hold. Quite generally, it does not collapse identical tones in separate morphemes (e.g. in Shona or Kishambaa); nor does it constrain segmentless floating-tone melodies (such as the HHLB melody of Shona). It does not constrain floating-tone sequences in stems (Kikuyu), nor the combination of identical associated and floating tones (Yala Ikom). It does not constrain identical tones separated by a vowel but no tone (Yoruba), nor does it constrain associated tone sequences (Kishambaa, Temne, and one dialect of Shona). In short, as a universal constraint, the OCP appears to be solidly counter-exemplified. On the positive side, we have seen that lexical representations in another dialect of Shona – and in Etsako, Igbo, Supyire (Gur, Mali: Carlson 1983), and Venda, *inter alia* – must obey the OCP; and we have seen that adjacent identical tones in separate morphemes must be collapsed into one multi-attached tone in Kipare, Akan, Isoko, Kikuyu, and Tangale. Therefore, the OCP – the spirit, if not the letter of the constraint – does some work for us.

What, then, is the OCP? It is clear that it cannot be a universal principle, never violated by any language. But this does not mean that it is of no interest, or that it was a well-intentioned but false hypothesis. Another possibility is that obedience to the OCP is a binary parameter: either a language obeys it, or not. This possibility is refuted by the fact that Shona observes the OCP in the lexicon, but not in the rule component. A third possibility is that the OCP is a parameter which is determined for each component: a language may obey it in the rule component, or in the lexicon, or in both. But even this view of the OCP is falsified for two reasons. First, we have seen that Tangale has a derivational version of the OCP for tonal phonology, but not for segmental phonology (although Tangale does have an underlying segmental OCP); thus, whatever the OCP is, it is not a unified general principle. Second, while OCP effects are found in the grammar of Kipare, the OCP cannot be maintained as a global condition on all parts of the rule component. Rather, it appears to hold for certain later parts of the grammar (where Final Lowering and Leftward Spreading apply – but not earlier, where Leftward Shift applies). Thus the OCP appears to be ordered among the rules of the grammar; let us therefore call it an 'ordered principle'. Such a principle would be a condition which must be satisfied by rules or representations of a grammar, and which would hold true not at all stages of the grammar, but beginning only at some arbitrary point, to be specified ad hoc for each language containing the principle. However, it strikes me as peculiar to speak of 'ordered' principles. Just as feasible is the possibility that the OCP is a rule, when it in fact exists, of the following form (e.g. in Kipare):

(11)   $\alpha T \Rightarrow \emptyset / \alpha T$ __

One possibly significant difference between a rule and an 'ordered principle' is that a rule can apply only once per cycle, while an 'ordered principle' could (and should) apply wherever it has the opportunity to apply in the same cycle. A situation such as the following could exist: Suppose that the OCP were a principle ordered in the grammar of L after rule W and before rule X, which applies to 'OCP-obedient' representations. Assume a rule Y, ordered after X, which changes L to H in some environment. (Cases where L is deleted and H spreads by the W[ell-] F[ormedness] C[onditions] would be irrelevant.) Further assume a rule Z, ordered after Y, which changes H to L in some environment. Now assume a string HLH which satisfies (or will satisfy) the structural descriptions of rules Y and Z. When Y applies, the string HHH will result. If the OCP is an 'ordered principle' of the grammar, then it could 'apply' again to this output, yielding one H-tone (associated with many vowels). Rule Z could then lower the H-tone on each of these vowels. If the OCP is a grammatical rule, then it cannot 'persist', and Z will lower only one of the H-tones. If one could discover a language where this were the case, then one would have incontrovertible proof that the OCP exists as some sort of 'principle' which governs large parts of derivations, and cannot be treated as an ordered rule. But until such examples are attested in the literature, we must reject the view that the OCP is a 'principle', rather than a rule.

Let us now consider the reason for the existence of the OCP (be it a morpheme structure condition, as in Shona, or an ordered rule, as in Kipare). Recall that it strives to eliminate some of the analytic indeterminacy which results from allowing the same phonetic sequence to be represented in numerous ways (i.e. the eight tonal representations of four H-tones seen in (1)). The reasoning behind this concern is that, since we do not want to present children with too many alternatives when presented with four H-tones in a row, we need a principle. But of course, if they are presented with data like those of Kishambaa, where one vs. two H-tones in sequence have different phonetic realizations – or where they undergo morphophonemic rules differently, as in the non-Karanga dialects of Shona – then they will have no difficulty in reaching the appropriate underlying representations. It would be quite perverse to assume that children prefer to construct non-universal hypotheses which fly in the face of available data. The problem arises where there is absolutely no evidence which would force children to analyze a string of identical tones in one way vs. the other. In such a case, they will presumably have to appeal to some general principle for organizing tonal grammars, to choose between competing hypotheses. It is also reasonable to assume that the theoretically preferred analysis could occasionally be selected over a less-preferred and, from the viewpoint of the adult grammar, more accurate analysis; a language which violates the OCP is not fated to flout that principle for all time.

What form of Occam's Razor do children use, then, to reduce the number of choices to be made? And why does this particular principle, rather than some other, resolve their problem? Let us consider the eight representations in (1) as possible candidates.

Most of the eight (those with two or three H-tones, and their various association lines) can be ruled out as not governed by any recognizable principle. The two serious possibilities are, by process of elimination, the following:

(12)   (a)   Assume that a string of adjacent identical tones is represented as one tone associated with each of the vowels of the sequence.

      (b)   Assume that a string of adjacent identical tones is represented as a string of identical tones, each associated with one vowel of the sequence.

The question is whether there is any reason (perhaps following from some higher principle of grammar or science) to prefer (12a) over (12b). My suggestion is that the choice is motivated by two general principles. The implication of (12b) is that one needs extra evidence to postulate representations where a tone is associated with more than one vowel; by contrast, (12a) implies that a tone associated with more than one vowel is the normal case. But (12b) is an essential component of the linear theory of tone, which assumes that tones and vowels are in a one-to-one relation (as well as being inextricably bound to each other). Principle 12b is in direct conflict with the WFC which states that any vowels which bear no tones are associated with available tones. That condition necessarily gives rise to violations of (12b). So the very existence of autosegmental phonology (the framework within which it makes sense to talk about the difference between single and multiple association of tone in the first place) would tend to select principle (12a) over (12b). Logically, one could maintain a theory of tone which prefers one-to-many mappings of tones to vowels in derived representations, via the application of a WFC, but which also prefers one-to-one mappings of tones to vowels in underlying representations; however, a more homogeneous, consequently preferable theory results if we avoid such direct conflicts.

Another principle which selects (12a) over (12b) is formal simplicity. Given these two representations (which are, by hypothesis, both consistent with the data of the language), all other things are indeed equal; therefore the grammar with fewer tones specified in the lexicon will be selected. But that is the grammar which obeys (12a), i.e. the OCP. The appeal to simplicity also helps to explain why many of the counter-examples to the OCP, as a principle which governs underlying forms, are from instances of floating-tone sequences. The simplest representation of two H-tones in a language with lexically linked tones will be one tone with multiple links; but the simplest representation of two unlinked H-tones will be two separate H-tones. The latter conclusion follows from the very nature of the alternative to specifying two H-tones in the lexical melody, namely the stipulation of a special rule of spreading – or some ad hoc pre-linking rule which overrides the one-to-one, left-to-right nature of the WFC's.

My suggestion, then, is that the OCP deserves no special theoretical status in phonological theory: It is not formally different from rules such as one which spreads H rightward, or deletes the second part of a rising tone. The fact that languages repeatedly exhibit some effects of the OCP is to be attributed to the fact that children learning a language must make some principled decision regarding the correct representation of adjacent identical tones. But they can deduce the relevant principle by selecting one which is simple and not in conflict with the WFC's, i.e. that adjacent identical tones should be represented as single tones with multiple associations.[11] The view that the OCP simply is the characterization of the optimal lexical representation has two interesting empirical consequences. First, it predicts that most languages will obey the OCP in the lexicon (this is a consequence of the stronger principle that, when a language has no evidence to the contrary, it must obey the OCP in the lexicon). This seems to be true, since counter-examples of the type found in Kishambaa, Temne, and non-Karanga dialects of Shona are not common.[12] Second, this view also predicts that identical tones separated by morpheme boundary will not tend to collapse into a single tone – since such a collapsing does not occur by any universal convention, but requires the addition of a language-specific rule. Thus my view also correctly explains why languages with identical tone-collapsing rules of derivation are not as common as languages which lack such rules.

One conclusion which has been reached here is that the OCP plays absolutely no role as a formal constraint on phonological representations, and that all its work can better be accomplished via the simplicity metric. Another more general and more significant conclusion can be reached as to whether multiple association of tones with vowels is something to be avoided. I believe that a highly revealing view of tonal processes can result if one exploits one of the resources of autosegmental phonology, namely the distinction between one-to-one and many-to-one associations between tones and vowels. Although a theory which allows such a distinction appears to be descriptively more powerful than one which does not, the facts of language are simply not so restricted that the number of tonal autosegments can be rigorously determined by the number of vowels in an utterance. Such distinctions are absolutely necessary, and can in fact lead to simpler analyses (including the elimination of unbounded input strings). Since certain types of ad hoc theoretical devices are obviated by employing multiple associations between vowels and tones, a trade-off in generative power is entailed by accepting a theory with both one-to-many and many-to-many associations between vowels and tones. As a concrete example of this trade-off, Clark (1985) argues for a more constrained theory of phonetic representations in disallowing floating tones as downstep operators; however, her theory depends on a distinction between multi-attached and singly attached tones. It may well be that other apparent problems in tonal phonology have their resolution in the judicious exploitation of such distinctions. To invoke contrasts like those in (1) is perhaps not ad hoc, but revealing.

## Notes

I would like to thank Sam Bayer, Hazel Carter, Mary Clark, Nick Clements, John Goldsmith, Bruce Hayes, Mike Kenstowicz, Will Leben, and Douglas Pulleyblank – as well as audiences at the University of Texas, UCLA, Queens College (CUNY), OSU, and Yale University – for valuable data, comments, and criticisms on earlier drafts of this paper. I would also like to thank the Provost of Yale University for support.

1   Even more analyses are possible (an infinite number), if one is allowed the distinction between a vowel associated with one H-tone and a vowel associated with two H-tones. Such analyses can be ruled out by the Twin Sister Convention – a special case of the OCP as discussed by Clements and Keyser (1983) – whereby adjacent identical tones, associated with the same tone-bearing unit, simplify to one tone. However, McHugh (1984) presents a possible counter-example to this convention from Kichaga (Bantu, Tanzania).

2 Pulleyblank (1983) argues for a different model of Tiv tonology, which eliminates Goldsmith's complex disjunction of B and L tones within the melody; but two H's, not simplified by the OCP, are still required in H-toned stems (though only via concatenation of a stem H and a melodic H). Thus Goldsmith's general point is still supported by Tiv.

3 Thus HHL stems such as *éfô* 'cloth' or *ńgárè* 'pepper' contrast with HL stems such as *ègòm* 'jaundice' and *ákpùgà* 'money'.

4 The dialect of Shona discussed here is that of Karanga, but the same facts and analysis can be found in some other dialects; e.g. the same arguments can be made for the Zezuru dialect discussed by Fortune (1980). The importance of this caveat will be clear in §3 below, in which I discuss a dialect of Shona for which the argument does not hold.

5 The morphological form of the possessive prefix varies according to the class of the noun by which the possessed NP is preceded. Nouns fall into 19 morphological classes, each of which induces a specific pattern of agreement on the possessive prefix.

6 Following tradition, H-tone will be marked with an acute accent, and L-tone with no accent.

7 Interestingly, a similar argument is given by Leben (1978) from Etsako (Edo, Nigeria), which is only remotely related to Shona. In Etsako, L is raised to H before the associative morpheme; and since that L may be associated with multiple vowels, the phonetic realization of this rule is that a number of vowels are simultaneously raised: hence *àmè* ASSOC *èθà* becomes *ámé* ASSOC *èθà* 'father's water'. A similar argument has been presented for Venda (Bantu, South Africa) by Cassimjee (1983) – who points out that the lowering of a string of H-tones requires lexical representations like those found for Shona, with a single H associated with multiple vowels. Cassimjee does not mention whether the lowering rule applies only to a string of H's within a single morpheme, or whether the string of tones which are lowered may be distributed over several morphemes. This point, as we will see, is crucial.

8 Here and elsewhere, when I refer to tonal representations 'in the lexicon', I mean specifically 'in single non-derived formatives, prior to the application of phonological rules'. It should thus be clear that 'in the lexicon' is not used here with the meaning which it has in lexical phonology.

9 As indicated in §1, there is often a trade-off between violating the OCP and regarding the tones of words as pre-associated in the lexicon. Shona provides empirical evidence that the two issues are independent. It contrasts HHL with HLL (i.e. *hákáta* 'diviner's bones' vs. *séndere* 'place forbidden for farming'); both of these undergo AL in the same fashion, lowering their initial strings of H-tones (*né-hakata*, *né-sendere*). But the approach which Goldsmith employs for Etung – postulating the contrasting MELODIES HHL vs. HL – is impossible in Shona; such an approach would incorrectly predict that only the first H in *hákáta* should lower. It follows that tones in Shona must also be lexically associated, since the melody HL appears as HHL in one case but as HLL in another: Shona needs both the OCP and lexical tone associations. Singler (1980) argues that, if we dispense with the OCP, we can eliminate lexical associations between tones and vowels in Mende and other languages; and a similar argument is presented for Mende by Conteh et al. (1983). In neither analysis, however, is it clear why violating the OCP is assumed to be more highly valued than lexical association of tone – other things being equal. Given the facts of Shona, it is impossible to reject on theoretical grounds an analysis of Mende based on lexical associations of tones to vowels. There is no need to postulate a contrast between lexically associated tones and floating tones within morphemes in Shona.

10 Verb stems are composed of a root; a number of suffixes for causative, passive, and reciprocal (*inter alia*); and a final vowel -*a*, -*e*, or -*i*, determined by the tense of the verb, which is the final morpheme in a verb stem. Thus the -*a* in *váká-rimísísiran-a* 'they having made plow for each other intensively' is the 'final vowel'. Since the entire stem can be reduplicated, a reduplicated verb has two 'final vowels': *váká-rimísísiran-a-rimisisiran-a*.

11 A similar sentiment is expressed by Goldsmith (1976: 135), who states that "the Obligatory Contour Principle is a condition not on possible underlying forms, but on simply-learnable grammars; not all grammars, however, need be simple." What, then, is the difference between the evaluative view of the OCP set forth by Goldsmith and the 'selection principle' view

espoused here? In the present view, if an OCP-obedient lexical representation for a language is consistent with the primary data, then children must select the OCP-obedient representation. But in the 'simplicity' view, they may select a representation which violates the OCP, albeit at extra 'cost'. Of course, if the grammars are otherwise evaluated identically, children will be forced by the evaluation metric to select the simpler grammar (i.e. the one which obeys the OCP). The 'simplicity' view of the OCP will therefore yield the same result as the 'selection principle' view, through the added step of assigning 'extra cost' to grammars which needlessly deviate from the OCP.

12   Examples of the Shona/Venda/Etsako/Igbo/Supyire type, where the OCP demonstrably holds in the lexicon, are not frequent either. What is common is that languages tend to have no evidence at all which uniquely selects among conflicting underlying representations.

# References

Carlson, Robert. 1983. Downstep in Supyire. *Studies in African Linguistics* 14: 35–45.

Cassimjee, Farida. 1983. An autosegmental analysis of Venda nominal tonology. *Studies in the Linguistic Sciences* (Urbana) 13/1: 45–72.

Clark, Mary. 1985. Downsteps without floating tones. University of New Hampshire.

Clements, George N. and Kevin C. Ford. 1979. Kikuyu tone shift and its synchronic consequences. *Linguistic Inquiry* 10: 95–108.

Clements, George N. and Samuel J. Keyser. 1983. *CV Phonology*. Cambridge, Mass.: MIT Press.

Conteh, Patrick et al. 1983. A reanalysis of tone in Mende. In *Current Approaches to African Linguistics*, vol. 2, ed. Jonathan Kaye et al., Dordrecht: Foris, 127–37.

Fortune, George. 1980. Shona grammatical constructions. Harare: Mercury Press.

Goldsmith, John. 1976. Autosegmental Phonology. Ph.D. dissertation, MIT. Published, New York: Garland, 1979.

Haraguchi, Shosuke. 1977. *The Tone Pattern of Japanese: An Autosegmental Theory of Tonology*. Tokyo: Kaitakusha.

Leben, William. 1973. Suprasegmental phonology. Ph.D. dissertation, MIT. New York: Garland, 1979.

Leben, William. 1978. The representation of tone. In Victoria Fromkin (ed.), *Tone: A Linguistic Survey*, New York: Academic Press, 177–90.

McHugh, Brian, 1984. Phrasal tone rules in Kirua (Vunjo) Chaga. Master's thesis, UCLA.

Odden, David. 1980. Associative tone in Shona. *Journal of Linguistic Research* (Bloomington) 1/2: 37–51.

Odden, David. 1981. Problems in Tone Assignment in Shona. Ph.D. dissertation, University of Illinois, Urbana.

Odden, David. 1984. Stem tone assignment in Shona. In G. N. Clements and John Goldsmith (eds), *Autosegmental Studies in Bantu Tonology*, Dordrecht: Foris, 255–80.

Pulleyblank, Douglas. 1983. Tone in Lexical Phonology. Ph.D. dissertation, MIT.

Singler, John. 1980. The status of lexical associations and the Obligatory Contour Principle in the analysis of tone languages. BLS 6: 442–56.

# 15

# Phonology with Tiers (1984)

## Alan S. Prince

*Tiers, tiers and tiers. Rounds.*
J. Joyce

## 1  Types of Tiers

### 1.1  Phone and terminal

The theory of compensatory lengthening put forth in Prince (1975) and Ingria (1980) requires a distinction between the phonetic segment and the syllabic slot that it fits into. The idea is that a segment may be deleted in such a way as to leave behind the slot it occupied; adjacent phonetic material will then fill up the empty slot through the familiar process of autosegmental spreading. Thus, ancient Greek [e:mi] 'I am' derives from /es + mi/ like this:

(1)

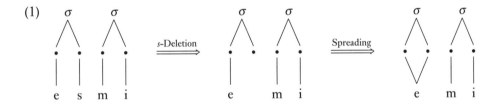

Similarly for Hebrew *ha:ʕi:r* 'the city', which derives from *haʕʕi:r* via a general degemination of laryngeal-pharyngeal glides such as ʕ.

A second notion, derived from McCarthy (1979, 1981), is that the relation between the segmental string and the syllabic terminal nodes is governed by some version of the Obligatory Contour Principle (Leben 1973), so that "long vowel" means $\overset{\bullet\ \ \bullet}{\underset{\vee}{}}$ at all levels of description. Thus, the representation of [e:mi] on the far right-hand side of (1) is not a freak of derivation, but merely the normal structure that any long vowel always has. The Obligatory Contour Principle entails a parallel treatment of "long" or geminate consonants. In Finnish, for example, a word like *luussa* 'bone, iness. sg.' must have this representation (details of syllabic hierarchy omitted for clarity):

(2)

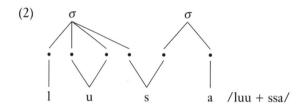

l          u          s          a      /luu + ssa/

The basic idea is that there is a level, or "tier," where the purely qualitative phonetic properties are represented, under the Obligatory Contour Principle, and a distinct tier of syllabic terminal nodes that determines quantitative structure. (I assume of course that this is universal and that there is no such feature as [±long].) I will call the segment string the *P tier* (*P* for *phone*) and the tier of syllabic terminals the *ST tier*.

This notion is interesting inasmuch as there are things to say about P and ST that cannot be said or said easily of the usual homogeneous phonological string. McCarthy (1979, revised as 1981) provides excellent evidence for the distinction in his analysis of Semitic morphology. He shows that the Semitic *root* is defined at P, whereas the word-forms associated with various morphological categories (e.g., "intensive verb") are defined at ST. (He calls ST the level of *prosodic templates*, which he spells out as sequences of C and V.)[1] Thus, the D-stem ("intensive") of the verb has the prosodic template CVCCVC. A typical root is *ktb*, pure P-level information. The perfective aspect is realized by the morpheme /a/. Putting all these together gives *kattab*:

(3)

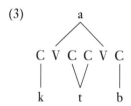

(A special restriction rules out *katbab*; see McCarthy 1979, 1981 for details.)

It might be thought that all of this apparatus is special to Semitic. In fact, what is peculiar to (and about) Semitic is not the P/ST distinction, but the use of it to define different systems of morphemes – root vs. stem-pattern – and further, the splitting of P-level morphemes into two types, a vowel class (e.g. /a/) and a consonant class (*ktb*). The effect of the latter is to put vowels and consonants into different tiers, since each tier has morphological integrity. The result is spreading patterns as in (3), where /a/ spreads "across" *t*, in an apparent (but only apparent) violation of the fundamental maxim of trans-tier association: no crossing. In the ordinary case, a P sequence will consist of only one tier and thereby retain an obvious linearity. Thus, for example, /lusa/ could be *lusa, lu:sa, lus:a, lu:s:a, lusa:*, etc., but never *lusua, slusa, lusla*.

(4)

l  u  s      a = lusla

We needn't look far to find languages where at least some morphology makes use of the ST tier, or "prosodic templates." Harris (1980) has demonstrated their importance in Spanish. Also consider English, whose few inflections are remarkably similar in form /z/ for 3rd sg. pres., /z/ for noun plural, /z/ for possessive NP, /d/ for past tense. Clearly, all regular inflection is built on the template C and on the melody "voiced alveolar obstruent," with a single featural choice open to distinguish categories: [±continuant]. Finnish inflections, though more elaborate, display a similarly narrow range of structural and melodic variation. Consider the following subset of the case endings:

(5) (a) C     -t        nominative plural
             -n        genitive
    (b) CV    -tA       partitive
             -nA       essive
    (c) CCV   -ssA      inessive
             -llA      adessive
             -stA      elative
             -ltA      ablative

(The vowel *A* emerges harmoniously as *a* or *ä*.) Notable is the use of limited melodic material: just one vowel and consonants *n*, *t*, *s*, *l*, the non-*r* coronals of the language. Even if we analyze inessive and adessive as *s* + *nA* and *l* + *na* (the regressive assimilation of *n* being independently motivated), we are still left with a morpheme template CV, to which *n* or *t* may attach, and a template C, which connects with the full range of permissible consonants (5a, 5c). The verbal paradigm has within it an even more striking use of the melody/template distinction. The first and second person endings (used in all tenses and moods) are the following:

(6)       Singular    Plural
    1st   -n            -mme
    2nd   -t           -tte

It is immediately clear that there is a singular template C and a plural template CC*e*. Given that Finnish phonology must independently turn *m* to *n* word-finally (cf. *puhelin* 'telephone, nom. sg.' vs. *puhelimet* 'nom. pl.'), it emerges that the first person morpheme is /m/, the second person /t/ – P-level information that is shared by the structurally distinct singular and plural endings C and CC*e*.

    Compensatory lengthening shows that an ST node can persist when its P content is removed. Work following McCarthy's lead has shown that the P/ST distinction is necessary for a fully general definition of "morpheme" in a number of languages – including, it seems, English. In what follows, I will explore yet a third line of evidence, showing that various phonological generalizations in Modern Standard Finnish depend crucially on the tiering of representations into P and ST. The facts discussed will be rather typical typologically, so that universality of the P/ST distinction will be the invited inference.

## 1.2  Length as sequence

As a preparatory step, let us establish that "long" vowels and consonants are indeed represented as sequences in Finnish. In an important sense, it is probably unnecessary to cite language-particular evidence, since Universal Grammar presumably dictates that all "long" elements are sequential in the sense proposed here: they take up two units at ST. However, since Finnish is exactly the kind of language that contains the classical arguments for regarding length as gemination, it will do no harm to cite a few of them.

For vowels, at least three considerations point to the desired conclusion. (1) Long vowels and diphthongs are equated in the law which says that they can only appear underlyingly in the *first* syllable of a stem. Given sequential representation, we can say that noninitial stem syllables are maximally CVC, a straightforward, purely structural restriction. (2) Long vowels can arise from morphological combination of short vowels. Thus, *talo:n* 'house, ill. sg.' comes from *talo + hen* via assimilation of the suffix vowel (*talo + hon*) and deletion of *h* (*taloon*) – cf. *luuhun* 'bone, ill. sg.', from stem *luu*, where the *h* remains. The null hypothesis is that there is no difference between these derived long vowels and the others, and that no special rule exists to treat these epiphenomenal nuclei. (Notice that resyllabification of derived *lo.on* into surface *loon* follows from reassertion of the most basic principle of syllabification, minimization of the number of syllables with null onsets.) (3) There is a rule that deletes single vowels and shortens "long" vowels before the past tense marker + *i* +. Thus, *matkusta + i + n* 'I traveled' becomes *matkustin*. Similarly, *voi + i + n* 'I was able' surfaces as *voin*, with loss of stem-final *i*. And, crucially, the past tense of a long-vowel stem like [jä:] 'remain' is *jäin*, from *jää + i + n*. Only geminate representation allows the evident identity of the shortening and deletion processes to be expressed.

For consonants, there are three similar considerations. (1) In syllable structure, long consonants behave like heterogeneous clusters, closing one syllable and beginning the next. No syllable can begin C:V. Thus, long consonants must occupy positions in both syllables, just what we expect if they are sequences. Using a feature like "long" on a single segment will obviously require special moves to make the syllable structure come out right. As evidence for the factual claim, we can adduce (a) unshakeable native speaker certainty, (b) equivalence of geminate-closed and cluster-closed syllables in the assignment of secondary stress (see Carlson 1979), and (c) a similar equivalence with respect to the rule of consonant gradation (see below for some details). Thus, consider the grading of *p* to *v* in *kylpy* 'bath' in both inessive (-*ssä*) and elative (-*stä*) cases: *kylvyssä*, *kylvystä*. (2) Long consonants can arise from morphemic concatenation that happens to bring together two identical segments: for example, *airut* 'herald, nom. sg.' but *airut:a* 'part. sg.' from *airut + ta*. (For the partitive suffix, cf. *luuta* 'bone, part. sg.'.) As with vowels, we wish to be able to embrace the null hypothesis: that there is nothing to say. (3) A rule reducing clusters deletes a consonant before a sequence of two Cs and before (what would be) a long consonant. Thus, *laps + ta* 'child, part. sg.' becomes *lasta* (*pst* ⇒ *st*), and *tuhant + ta* 'thousand, part. sg.' becomes *tuhat:a* (*nt:* ⇒ *t:*). Clearly, we want C → $\phi$/____CC, basically,[2] without the long/double disjunction.

Let there be no more colons.

## 2   Consonant Sequencing

The basic constraints on consonant clustering in Finnish follow from the definition of "possible syllable" in the language.[3] In the native vocabulary, the onset consists of at most one unit; the rime of at most three. Within the rime, sonority must decline strictly, so that there can be no clusters of tautorimal obstruents or of tautorimal sonorant consonants; *art, ant, aat, aar, aut* would then be acceptable rimes; **ast*, **ats*, **alm*, **arn* would not. (Notice that the sonority of vocalic segments can vary with position in a way that sonority of consonants cannot.) *A fortiori*, there are no tautosyllabic geminates.

From syllable structure it follows that consonant clusters can be maximally three units long – two ending a rime plus one from the following onset. For example: *korkki* 'cork', *kynttilä* 'candle', *helppo* 'easy', *salskea* 'slender', *konsti* 'trick', *poltta* 'burn', etc. However, not all possible combinations of consonants are allowed, even across syllable boundary. Thus, although *tt, tk, st, ts, pp, ps, kk, ks, sk* are permitted, no nongeminate obstruent cluster may end in *p*: **tp*, **kp*, **sp*,[4] **hp*. (Nasal or liquid plus *p* is fine: *mp, lp, rp*.) How can this be stated formally? In standard nontiered phonology *$C_p$ will not do, because it would wrongly outlaw the case where C = *p*. We could add the condition C ≠ *p* as an arbitrary complication of the statement, simply conceding the observation. But the tier theory offers a simple explanation for the exceptional behavior of geminate clusters. The sequencing constraint *[−son]*p* concerns only P-tier matters (place of articulation of obstruents); therefore, in the Leibniz–Chomsky "best of all possible worlds," the constraint should be stated on the P tier alone uncluttered by cross-tier conditions. Thus, it cannot hold of geminates, since by the Obligatory Contour Principle they are not represented in P.

The P/ST tiering theory predicts that geminates should be systematically excluded from sequencing constraints based on changes of phonetic quality (place, manner, voicing, etc.). Finnish bears out this prediction quite well. Two further constraints on obstruent clustering are worth noticing, and each displays the expected lack of interest in geminates.

(i) CC clusters beginning with a noncoronal obstruent – *p, k* – are either geminate or *s*-final: only *pp, kk, ps, ks* are native, giving **pt*, **kt*, **pk*. In the P tier, this boils down to *[−son][−cont]. The fact that *pp, kk* end on stops is irrelevant to P constraints.

(ii) The middle C of CCC clusters must be *s*: *pyrstö* 'fish- or bird-tail', but **pyrtsö*, **pyrtkö*, etc. This requirement can be expressed equivalently as a filter *[+cons][−cont] [+cons] or as a positive template [+cons]s[+cons]; but in either case geminates do not fall under the proscription (or description). Forms like *helppo* 'easy', *poltta* 'burn', *tarkka* 'exact', *pulssi* 'pulse', *kanssa* 'with' are in no way abnormal. Once again, P-level constraints appear to be concerned only with transitions of quality, as expected.

## 3   Vowel Sequencing

Finnish has eight vowel qualities: *a, e, i, o, u, ä, ö, ü* (spelled *y*). Combination of vowels in words (and, therefore, morphemes) is governed by a rule of front–back harmony, in which *i*, *e* are neutral. Within a *syllable*, additional constraints hold on VV sequences. Only *i*, *u*, *ü* may form the second element of a diphthong.[5] And, of course, any vowel may be geminate (long). From a "standard theory" perspective, this requires a clumsy disjunction: in tautosyllabic $V_1 V_2$, $V_2 = [+high]$ *or* $V_1 = V_2$. The question is, naturally, why it is gemination (equality) that plays the disjunctive role, and not some other arbitrary relation. The answer is obvious in P/ST theory: the constraint on diphthongs pertains (intrinsically) to the P tier, where there is no gemination and consequently no second term ($V_1 = V_2$) in the constraint. As with consonants, letting the P tier be governed by the Obligatory Contour Principle results in certain predictable differences between geminates and other sequences, while allowing for the correct treatment of geminates as sequences (on the ST tier).

## 4   Environment of Consonant Gradation

An onset consonant *p*, *t*, *k* of a short, closed, noninitial syllable weakens in various ways: voicing, spirantizing, assimilating, or disappearing altogether, depending on environment and on the consonant itself. Thus, geminates simplify ($pp \rightarrow p\phi$, etc.), homorganic sonorant-stop clusters turn to geminate sonorants (e.g., $mp \rightarrow mm$), *k* deletes, *p* becomes *v*, *t* becomes *d*. The exact formulation of the changes will not concern us here, though it is of obvious interest; rather, we will concentrate on the environment in which they take place.[6]

It is clear that there are both ST-tier and P-tier restrictions on the process. The affected consonant must be an onset and must be in a closed syllable. Yet not every onset is affected – only the obstruent stops. The ST restriction, taken at face value, can be given as follows:

(7)   ST:   [C   V   C   σ]
           ↓
           "weak"

Further consideration of Finnish structure suggests that the traditional description "short closed syllable," which is encoded in (7), may be unduly concrete. Underlyingly, and at the level at which Gradation Weakening applies, there may be no long vowels or diphthongs outside the first syllable of a word; this is certainly true within stems. Therefore, any heavy syllable must be "short and closed"; the prosodic environment of weakening is then simply "onset of a heavy syllable," as suggested in Prince (1980). However, due to uncertainties about derivational suffixes, I will follow the course of prudence and keep (7) for present purposes.

P-level constraints on weakening include not only identification of the affected onset as *p*, *t*, *k*, but also some limitation on the preceding segmental environment. This is evident in the fact that obstruent clusters do not suffer weakening: *st*, *sk*, *tk* (the only relevant clusters) are immune to gradation (cf. *matka/matkan* 'trip, nom./gen.' vs. *halpa/halvan* 'cheap, nom./gen.'). The weakening obstruent must appear in the environment [+son] ___. And here again, the tierless theory encounters the by now familiar inadequacy: for geminates do not count as obstruent clusters in this law (cf. *hattu/hatun* 'hat, nom./gen.'). The initial *t* of *tt* does not block gradation (*tt* ⇒ *tɸ*); the initial *t* of *tk* does. In P/ST theory, this apparent peculiarity is, of course, an expected consequence of the fact that constraints on phonetic quality hold over the tier where phonetic quality is represented. The final statement of the rule environment is as in (8):

(8)  *Gradation Weakening*

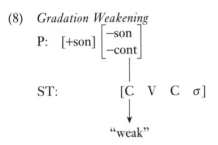

For purposes of comparison, the representations of /matka + n/ and /hattu + n/ are given in (9):

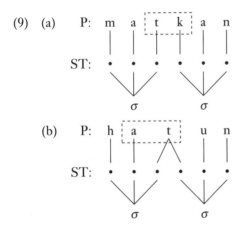

The relevant sequences on the P tier are boxed. What then is "weak"? Suppose, for concreteness, that it is [+voiced]: rule (8), Gradation Weakening, applies this feature to the onset slot of the affected syllable, to the ST-tier element – not to the P-tier element, which would cause voicing of the entire geminate. Thus, the result is (10):

(10)  ∵
⌣
    hatun → hatdun

(Clearly, some technical development is required here, to clarify tier-internal structuring, to govern the amalgamation and severing of association lines. Since my focus is on the environment of the rule, rather than the change it performs, I will not broach these further issues here.) A subsequent rule would delete such *d*s, removing the syllable-initial slot, to yield surface *hatun*.

The argument from gradation for distinguishing P-tier and ST-tier conditions in phonological rules rests on the integrity of the gradation process itself. It has often been noted in recent discussions of the phenomenon that of all the changes that fall under the name of gradation, only degemination remains productive in the modern language. If the rule simply degeminates *p*, *t*, *k*, no special postsonorant condition need be imposed – geminates always follow sonorants as a consequence of the syllable structure limitations mentioned earlier. However, the argument does not require that rule (8) survive for long periods in the language; only that it be wholly present at some given stage, during which it represents the authentic circumstances of a unified process.

# 5   Concluding Remarks

The distinction between syllabic terminal nodes and the qualitative phonetic content that they carry is diversely motivated. The main burden of this paper has been to indicate how the P-tier/ST-tier distinction can be used as the basis for a theory of sequencing that goes beyond the usual view that co-occurrence of segments is interestingly constrained only syllable-internally. Finnish is sufficiently rich to illuminate the details of such a theory and, concomitantly, to somewhat obscure the main lines and root predictions. Consider a language that has only CV syllables – the simplest type allowed by universal syllable theory. Here there can be no question of sequencing constraints. A minimal complication of the ST tier adds CVC syllables to the basic repertory, giving rise to consonant sequences and associated (trans-syllabic) constraints on transitions of phonetic quality. The simplest such constraint would prohibit the P tier from containing any consonant-quality sequences at all, essentially preserving the qualitative structure of CV languages. Thus, we expect to find many languages that allow closed syllables only when the syllable-closing consonant begins a geminate cluster; this ought to represent the next step in complication after the strict CV languages. My impression is that this prediction is near to correct, with the proviso that sequences of homorganic nasal + consonant are typically also allowed. Notice that such NC clusters are very near to geminate, suggesting that the feature of nasality should be segregated from the others, allowing us to directly specify that place of articulation may not change – that is, there cannot be two place specifications in a row. Languages that take this form are (for example) Southern Paiute and Japanese. Italian represents an interesting further development: syllables may end on liquids, fricatives, and stops of both oral and nasal varieties, but a syllable-final stop must either be the starting point of a geminate or a nasal homorganic to what follows. Here again we want to put nasality on a separate subtier (and perhaps voicing as well) so we can say that in a P tier there is simply no sequencing of stops. Finnish then takes its place further down the scale of complexity, permitting P-tier sequences, but only under various restrictions.

Finally, notice that to have long vowels is to admit two V slots into the ST tier; yet the presence of long vowels in a language does not imply that every diphthong that combines two short vowels is also to be found. Quite the contrary: it seems to be quite normal to have long vowels and no diphthongs at all, or a very restricted set of them, as in Finnish. The theory advocated here makes it quite easy to eliminate diphthongs (or classes of diphthongs) while maintaining the quantitative structure at ST that supports long vowels: the simplest constraint on vowel sequences is of course to disallow them altogether (*[+voc][+voc]), which leaves only spreading to fill the available ST slots.

## Notes

1 There is a live issue here about the nature of the units I am calling *syllabic terminals*. McCarthy shows clearly that syllabic terminals must be characterized to the extent that C and V can be distinguished from one another; that is, they cannot just be pure locations. Yip (1982) makes use of G, for "glide," in addition to C and V. One might wish to spell out such distinctions in terms of constraints on the higher-order constituent structure of the syllable, in order to avoid directly characterizing the syllabic terminal nodes as C, V, etc. However, it seems clear that the syllabic nonterminals provide the wrong kind of descriptive vocabulary for dealing with many CV matters. They enforce, for example, a distinction between *onset* consonant and *rime* (or *coda*) consonant that is never called on in the association patterns of consonantal morphemes; furthermore, they allow for, even suggest as the most natural case, the construction of inappropriate constituency-based templates. Imagine a form in which all consonants had to be in onsets – easy enough to spell out as ONON . . . (N = nucleus) – or a form in which none could be in onsets (RRR . . . ); but of course such template conditions are quite unheard of. Recall also the use of the CV tier in Marantz (1982), which responds directly to Edith Moravcsik's (1978) fundamental insight that reduplication is by and large not based on syllabic constituency. A different line of conjecture would have sonority information accessible at the level of syllabic terminals; C, V, G then refer in a skeletal way to the elementary distinctions of sonority, which induce syllable structure. However, there is evidence that a notion of pure position, unconstrained by C/V content, can be called on, as Prince (1975) and Ingria (1980) have assumed. Consider the Hebrew definite article prefix *ha-*. It causes gemination of a following consonant: *ha-* + *da:ba:r* = *hadda:ba:r*. Yet when that consonant is a "guttural" and degeminates by general rule, the vowel of the article compensatorily lengthens, filling the now empty *consonant* slot: *ha-* + *ʕr* = *ha:ʕi:r*. We want to say that the article is /haX/, where X is just a slot. In some dialects of Yupik (Reed et al. 1977), syllables CV̆ are strengthened when they are stressed and precede a stressed syllable. If the conditioning syllable is CVV – containing a long vowel or diphthong – then a simple gemination of its initial consonant takes place: CVCVV → CVC$_i$C$_i$VV. More interesting is the case where the conditioning syllable is closed: here lengthening of the vowels /a i u/ takes place, CVCVC → CVVCVC, but schwa induces gemination of C, CəCVC → CəCCVC. The apparently aberrant behavior of schwa has a straightforward explanation: schwa can never be long (geminated) or, more generally, part of a diphthong, either in the lexicon or as a result of phonological rule. Thus, we want to say that stressed CV acquires a postvocalic *position* before another stressed syllable: the position is filled in with neighboring material, vowel or consonant according to the strictures of the language. Compare also the treatment of Italian vowel-lengthening and *raddoppiamento* in Chierchia (1982).

2 The rule is subject to various other constraints that do not affect the outcome of the present argument and will therefore be left unexplained.

3 The phonotactic constraints discussed here and in the next section are derived from the work of Karttunen (1970). Of course, she should not be held responsible for the way I have chosen to formulate them.

4 The cluster *sp* does show up in recent loans, e.g. *aspirin*.

5 I take it that *ie* and *uo* (*üö*) may be omitted from consideration, since they derive from *ee* and *oo* (*öö*). However, even if they are not so derived, the descriptive complication they would induce does not bear on the essentials of this argument.

6 There is some morphological interference with the conditioning of the rule in the modern language, but not enough to render the basic phonology obscure or problematic. Lehtinen (1962) provides a useful survey of the details of gradation. The treatment given here abstracts away from morphological expansions and contractions of the fundamental phonological environment.

# References

Carlson, L. 1979. Word stress in Finnish. Unpublished paper, MIT.

Chierchia, G. 1982. An autosegmental theory of Raddoppiamento. In J. Pustejovsky and P. Sells (eds), *Proceedings of NELS XII*, Amherst, Mass.: Graduate Linguistic Student Association, 49–62.

Harris, J. W. 1980. Nonconcatenative morphology and Spanish plurals. *Journal of Linguistic Research* 1, 15–31.

Ingria, Robert. 1980. Compensatory lengthening as a metrical phenomenon. *Linguistic Inquiry* 11, 465–97.

Karttunen, Frances. 1970. Problems in Finnish Phonology. Ph.D. dissertation, Indiana University.

Leben, Will. 1973. Suprasegmental Phonology. Ph.D. dissertation, MIT.

Lehtinen, M. 1962. *Basic Course in Finnish*. Indiana University Publications, 47, Ural and Altaic Series. Bloomington: Indiana University Press.

Marantz, Alec. 1982. Re: reduplication. *Linguistic Inquiry* 13, 433–82.

McCarthy, John. 1979. Formal Problems in Semitic Phonology and Morphology. Ph.D. dissertation, MIT.

McCarthy, John. 1981. A prosodic theory of nonconcatenative morphology. *Linguistic Inquiry* 12, 373–418. [Repr. here in part as ch. 9]

Moravcsik, E. 1978. Reduplicative constructions. In J. H. Greenberg (ed.), *Universals of Human Language*, Vol. 3: *Word Structure* (Stanford, Calif.: Stanford University Press), 297–334.

Prince, Alan. 1975. The Phonology and Morphology of Tiberian Hebrew. Ph.D. dissertation, MIT.

Prince, Alan. 1980. A metrical theory of Estonian quantity. *Linguistic Inquiry* 11, 511–62.

Reed, I., O. Miyaoka, S. Jacobson, P. Afcan, and M. Krauss. 1977. *Yup'ik Eskimo Grammar*. Alaska Native Language Center and Yup'ik Language Workshop, University of Alaska, Fairbanks.

Yip, Moira. 1982. Reduplication and C-V skeleta in Chinese secret languages. *Linguistic Inquiry* 13, 637–61.

# 16

## Immediate Constituents of Mazateco Syllables (1947)

### Kenneth L. Pike and Eunice Victoria Pike

## 1  Orientation

It is well known that sentences have an internal structure which can be analyzed in terms of successive layers of immediate constituents.[1] Thus, the sentence *Poor John ran away* divides first into *Poor John* and *ran away*, then *Poor John* divides into *Poor* and *John*, while *ran away* divides into *ran* and *away*, and so on.

It is convenient to describe syllables of Mazateco[2] in a similar fashion. The structure of these syllables does not consist of a series of sounds equally related, like beads on a string, but is rather like an overlapping series of layers of bricks. The different layers in the syllable tend to have different phonetic and grammatical characteristics.

## 2  First Division: Margins versus Nuclei

The majority of Mazateco syllables consist of a single chest pulse, as in hma[2] (in which the number following a syllable gives its tone; 1 is high level, 4 is low level, and so on) *black*. Some syllables, however, begin with a nasal consonant followed by two consonants – the second a glottal stop – before the vowel. In these syllables a weak chest pulse for the nasal precedes a strong chest pulse for the vowel; the weak and strong chest pulses fuse into a single functioning syllable. For this type of syllable note the words ntʔe[1] *good* or *industrious*, nčʔa̧[1] *cold*, and nkʔa[3] *tall*.

The releasing[3] – i.e. trigger – segments in the syllable comprise its marginal elements. One, two, or three consonants may enter a syllable margin, as in the following illustrations: to[3] *fruit*; čʔa[1–3] *a load*; hnko[3] *one*.

The main part of syllable pulse itself – the nucleus of the syllable – is carried by the vowels. One, two, or three vowels may enter a syllable nucleus, as follows: sa[1–1] *moon*; čao[3–4] *dust*; koai[3] *he will go*. Two vowels juxtaposed, as in the second of the preceding illustrations, do not make two syllables; the two vowels are pronounced together very rapidly, so that the timing seems to be about the same as that for a single vowel. The nucleus of the syllable takes about the same length of time – within the limits of perception – regardless of the number of vowels it contains, whether one or two or three.

The syllable must be divided into margin and nucleus for other reasons than their relation to the chest pulse, however.

Mazateco is tonal, with significant lexical or grammatical pitch on each of its syllables. Many words differ in meaning with concomitant differences of pitch, but such pitch contrasts are limited exclusively to the segments here called the vowels, and the vowels are limited to the nuclei. Now of the margins many of the consonants – especially the nasals – have noticeable pitch characteristics; there is a sharp functional difference, however, between the pitch on the consonants and the pitch on the vowels: The pitches on the items called consonants never form contrasts in such a way as to carry different meanings. The contrastive tone in the language is a characteristic of the nucleus of the syllable; this constitutes one of the major reasons for separating the margin from the nucleus of the syllable on the first division of the syllable into its immediate constituents.

One other minor reason may be given for the breaking of constituents between the margin and nucleus: a nucleus may contain a nasalized vowel. Now if such a vowel occurs in the nucleus, every other vowel in that nucleus is also nasalized; the nasalization covers the entire nucleus. However, the nasalization does not pass over to the margin, even when the segment immediately preceding the nucleus is very similar to a vowel in its phonetic characteristics. A rapid vowel i at the beginning of a nucleus is quite similar to the consonant y just preceding a nucleus. Nevertheless, the vowel i would be nasalized, but the y would not be nasalized, by a preceding nasalized vowel, as in the following illustration: si$^1$tį$^2$ya$^3$ *he shakes*, or *stirs (something)*.

## 3   Second and Third Divisions: Principal versus Subordinate Consonants, of Margins

Turning now specifically to the margins, one finds the following alphabetical list of single consonants which may precede the nucleus in a syllable: b, c, č, ç̌, d, g, h, k, l, m, n, ñ, p, r, r̃, s, š, t, v, y, ʔ.

The unaspirated stops t and k become voiced after nasals, unless followed by h: ti$^{3-4}$ *boy*, ki$^3$šo$^{1-3}$ *landslide*, na$^3$nta$^{1-3}$ *water*, nka$^4$hao$^4$ *a water hole*. An extremely small number of loans containing t from Spanish do not follow this rule, and words containing them are marked with an asterisk to show that they are not completely assimilated; in them, stops remain voiceless: *sie$^2$nto$^4$ *hundred*.

The voiceless unaspirated stop p occurs only in loan words, as does also the voiced stop b and the voiced fricatives d and g: bo$^1$r̃o$^{1-3}$ *burro*, mba$^{3-4}$ *godfather* (Spanish compadre), šo$^3$mbe$^{3-4}$ *hat* (Spanish sombrero), se$^2$da$^4$ *silk* (Spanish seda), *ga$^2$nčo$^4$ *crochet hook* (Spanish gancho).

The glottal stop ʔ at times is actualized as a complete stop, and at other times optionally as a laryngealization (or 'glottalization') of the following vowel. When ʔ is the second member of a consonant cluster, a vowel which follows it phonemically may phonetically have a slight pre-articulation before the ʔ, but such a sequence with light pre-articulation contrasts phonemically with a sequence of consonant, full vowel, glottal stop, and full vowel: nʔąį$^{4-3}$ *father*, na$^4$ʔi$^4$-vi$^4$ *a mother (who is) here*; čʔo$^4$ *bud*, čo$^4$ʔo$^1$ *hiccough*; note also nʔo$^1$ya$^{1-3}$ *class of potato*, no$^2$ʔya$^2$ *we (incl.) hear*; sʔoia$^1$ *we (incl.) grind*; šo$^1$ʔya$^{1-3}$ *rose*.

The affricates act like the stops in becoming voiced following nasals unless the combination of nasal plus affricate is in turn followed by h. Three affricates occur: alveolar c [ts], alveo-palatal č, and a retroflexed alveo-palatal ç̌: coa⁴ *he will hold*, čoa⁴ *sign*, ç̌oa⁴ *plate*; nca⁴ *my hand*, ya¹nčhị¹⁻³ *women*, ya¹nčhị⁴ *meat hook, clothes tree*, nča⁴ *horn*, nčao̧³ *tomorrow*, ncha³ *his hand*.

These phonetically complex units must be considered single phonemes because they act like simple consonant phonemes in their entrance into consonant clusters. Occasional unassimilated loan words contain č unvoiced after nasals and are marked with an asterisk: *ga²nčo⁴ *crochet hook* (Spanish gancho).

Of nasals, there are m, n, and ñ; the alveolar n becomes velar before velar stops: ha⁴ma⁴ *a root*, ni³sa³⁻⁴ *water jug*, ño³ *four*, to³nka³⁻⁴ *small gourd*.

The sibilant s has no marked variants; alveo-palatal š has considerable retroflexion before vowels, but less before consonants: sa¹⁻³ *moon*, ša¹⁻³ *work*, ška¹⁻³ *trousers*.

The phoneme h takes many forms: before vowels or y, it assumes their shape; before nasals, it becomes a voiceless nasal fricative: ha⁴ *hawk*, li⁴hi⁴ *grass*, hnti¹ *dirty*, hma² *black*.

The phoneme v is a bilabial fricative with flat (i.e. not markedly rounded) lips; before h it becomes voiceless: va³-na³ *I am sad*, vha³ti²-na³ *I am thirsty*.

The alveo-palatal voiced glide y has no marked variants. It differs from i in that it does not carry contrastive tone, is not nasalized by contiguous nasalized vowels, and may begin the syllable. The y always goes with the chest pulse of the nucleus which it precedes, whereas the i often enters a syllable pulse with a vowel which it follows; the break between syllables is different in the following words, occurring before y in the first illustration, but after i in the second: sʔa⁴-yʔa³na³ *he is going to carry for me*, sʔai⁴ ʔa³na³ *I will not be busy in the afternoon*. The y is not nasalized in the following word: si¹kị²ya³ *he lends*.

Of the three remaining consonant phonemes, the voiced lateral l is the most frequent; r (a light, voiced flap) is very rare (in only three morphemes of native origin in the data at hand); r̃ (a trill) occurs only in Spanish loans: la⁴hao⁴ *stone*, to¹ro¹hčo¹⁻³ *lizard*, ko²r̃e⁴ *godmother* (Spanish comadre).

The consonants which have been listed are found in various combinations. These combinations present a definite structure. In the structure of the clusters certain of the consonants may be considered the principal ones, and others subordinate.

In the great majority of clusters of two consonants, (43 out of the 47 recorded), one of the two must be h, n, or ʔ. In the remaining clusters, s or š must be present. The h, n, ʔ, s, or š may well be considered a subordinate element in the cluster, whereas the other consonant – chosen from a much larger list – may be considered the principal member, (1) because the articulation of the subordinate one tends to be secondary,⁴ tertiary, or subprimary in relation to the primary articulations of the other members of the clusters, and (2) because of the drastic limitation in the number of clusters which the restricted number of subordinate elements imposes.

The subordinate member of the two-consonant cluster may come first or second. Note the following specific clusters:

With subordinate h as first member: ht, hk; hc, hč, hç̌; hv, hy; hm, hn (varying to nhn in the word hne⁴ *tepexilote* – a certain palm nut), hñ; hti⁴ *fish*, hka³⁻⁴ *stubble*; hce¹⁻³ *a sore*, hči⁴ *small*, ha⁴hčo³ *in the opening of*; hva⁴⁻³ *watery*, hyo³-na³ *I want*; hma² *black*, hno⁴ *corn*, hña¹⁻³ *woods*.

With subordinate n as first member: nt, nk; nc, nč, nç̣; nta⁴⁻³ *good*, nka⁴hao⁴ *water hole*; nca⁴ *my hand*, nči²ʔe³ *bent*, nça⁴ti¹⁻³ *comb*.

With subordinate ʔ as first member: ʔv, ʔy; ʔm, ʔn, ʔñ; ʔva⁴ *hook*, ʔya⁴ *rainbow*; šo¹ʔma¹⁻³ *earthen jar*, na⁴ʔni¹⁻³ *brier*, ni³ʔña³⁻⁴ *writing pen*.

With subordinate h as second member: th, kh; ch, čh, çh; vh; mh, nh; sh, šh; tha⁴ *light in weight*, kha̧³ *bad smelling*; che⁴⁻³ *clean*, čha⁴ *brother-in-law (brother of husband)*, čhoa⁴ *skin*; vhi² *he goes*; vʔa³mhȩ⁴⁻³ *I walk*, nhȩ³-na³ *it is gained by me*; sha³ *bitter*, šhao³ *dew*.

    Clusters with a stop or affricate as the first member and h as the second member cannot be considered as single complex aspirated consonant phonemes, (1) because of the pressure of the pattern from parallel clusters with the h as the first member (th, ht; kh, hk; ch, hc; čh, hč; çh, hç̣); (2) because of the presence of clusters with h as the second member but nasal or sibilant as the first member (mh, nh, sh, šh); and (3) because of the parallel types with ʔ as the first or second member of the cluster (ʔv, ʔm, tʔ; mʔ, sʔ, lʔ, etc.).

With subordinate ʔ as second member: tʔ, kʔ; cʔ, čʔ; çʔ; vʔ, yʔ; mʔ, nʔ, ñʔ; sʔ, šʔ; lʔ; tʔi̧³ *go* (imperative), kʔia⁴ *then*; ¢ʔe² *lazy*, čʔoa¹⁻³ *parrot*; çʔoa¹⁻³-le⁴ *pieces left over*; vʔe⁴⁻³ *I hit*, yʔa³ *I carry*; mʔȩ⁴⁻³ *he is sick*, nʔo̧¹⁻³ *rope*, ñʔa̧i³ *difficult*; sʔoi¹⁻³ *fiesta*, šʔi̧⁴ *man*; lʔi¹⁻³ *fire*.

    Clusters with a stop or affricate as the first member and ʔ as the second member cannot be considered as single complex glottalized consonant phonemes, (1) because of the parallel with the clusters with ʔ as the first member (ʔv, ʔm, etc.); (2) because of the presence of the clusters with ʔ as the second member but a nasal, sibilant, lateral, or voiced fricative as the first member (mʔ, sʔ, lʔ, vʔ, etc.); (3) because of the parallels with h; (4) because there is usually a very slight open transition between the stop and the ʔ in the same syllable, so that the stops are not phonetically glottalized – i.e. they are not made with egressive pharynx air; and (5) this phonetic gap between the stop and the ʔ in clusters is often further accentuated in that ʔ may be actualized as the laryngealization of the following vowel rather than as a separate complete stop, while often there is a slight pre-articulation of the vowel before the ʔ (but after the oral stop in the sequence of oral plus glottal stop).

With subordinate s as first member: sk; ska¹ *crazy*.

With subordinate š as first member: št, šk; šn (rare – only in the illustration given); šti³⁻⁴ *children*, ška¹⁻³ *trousers*; nka³šni³⁻⁴ *Chiquihuitlan*.

    In certain of the clusters just listed, it may be observed that both members of the cluster may occur elsewhere as the subordinate member. This effects the clusters hn, ʔn, nh, nʔ, sh, šh, sʔ, and šʔ, and šn. Apart from this list, the consonants h and ʔ never occur as the principal member of a cluster; for this reason it is convenient to consider them the subordinate members here also. Thus, they occur before the principal member in hn, ʔn, but after the principal member in nh, nʔ, sh, šh, sʔ, and šʔ. Supporting this conclusion are the following facts; s and š are rarely subordinate members, and are best considered principal ones in sh, šh, sʔ, and šʔ; there are no parallels for n subordinate but second in the cluster, so in hn, ʔn, and šn the n is best considered the principal member.

Clusters of three consonants also occur. In them, two consonants of each cluster are always found to be chosen from the list of subordinate consonants already listed.

The two subordinate consonants in a cluster of three consonants may be distributed in one of two ways: either the two subordinate consonants may precede the principal one, or one of the subordinate consonants may precede but the other follow the principal consonant. Note the following lists of clusters:

With the subordinate consonants ʔn before the principal member of the cluster: ʔnt, ʔnk; ʔnc, ʔnč, ʔnč̣; ʔnto³ *rotten*, ʔnki⁴⁻³ *he hoes*; li⁴ʔnci²⁻³ *brown hawk*, ʔnči⁴ *wet*, či³ʔnc̣o³ *blackberry*.

With the subordinate consonants hn before the principal member of the cluster: hnt, hnk; hnč, hnč̣; hnti¹ *dirty*, hnka³ *wing*; vi³hnči⁴⁻³ *you (sing.) look for*, hnča³ *salty*.

With the subordinate consonant n preceding the principal member of the cluster but with ʔ following the main member: ntʔ, nkʔ; ncʔ, nčʔ, nč̣ʔ; ntʔe¹ *industrious*, nkʔa³ *tall*; ncʔe⁴ *his brother*, nčʔa̧¹ *cold*, nc̣ʔoe¹ *he hears*.

With the subordinate consonant n preceding the principal member of the cluster but with h following the main member: nth, nkh; nch, nčh, nč̣h; nthao⁴ *wind*, nkhi̧² *many*; nchao¹⁻³ *rust*, nča¹ *fat*, ya¹nč̣hi̧⁴ *meat hook, clothes tree*.

With the subordinate consonant h preceding the principal member of the cluster but with ʔ following the main member: hcʔ, hčʔ; hcʔe¹⁻³ *sprout*, ʔnti¹hčʔa⁴ *orphan*. These clusters are rare, and tend to vary to cʔ and čʔ.

With the subordinate consonants s or š preceding the principal member of the cluster, but with ʔ following the main member: skʔ; štʔ; škʔ; skʔao¹ *it will break*; ha⁴štʔa⁴⁻³-la²nka¹ *goodbye*, škʔȩ¹ *thin*.

When two consonants comprise a consonant cluster, its immediate constituents are the two consonants, respectively, with one of them the principal constituent and the other the subordinate constituent. When three consonants comprise the cluster, it is best to consider that the first consonant comprises the first constituent, and the next two consonants the second constituent, (1) since the first consonant tends to be phonetically very weak when the syllable comes at the beginning of utterances and (2) since that consonant occasionally syllabifies partially with the preceding syllable in the middle of utterances. Thus the immediate constituents of the cluster hnt are h and nt, and then the constituents of nt are n and t.

The layers of immediate constituents of the syllable ncʔoai³⁻⁴ *our (excl.) stomachs*, in so far as has been analyzed in the preceding paragraphs, can be symbolized as follows: ([n][c/ʔ])(oai³⁻⁴); subdivisions of the nucleus will be given in following sections.

## 4  Second Division: Vowels versus Tones, of Nuclei

Turning to the nuclei, one must conclude that the entire sequence of vowels in a single syllable constitute the first immediate constituent of the nucleus, and that the entire sequence of (contrastive) tones on that nucleus constitutes its second immediate constituent. It will not do to attempt to correlate each vowel with one and only one tone, or each tone with one and only one vowel.[5]

The reasons for this analysis of the constituents are the following: (1) Each nucleus is of approximately the same length, as has already been pointed out, but since the nuclei may contain from one to three vowels in this length of time, the vowels do not constitute units of length coincident with the length of the nuclei of the syllables; similarly, since the nuclei may contain from one to three tones in approximately the same length of time, neither do the tones constitute units of length coincident with the length of nuclei. (2) If the nucleus has three vowels and but one tone, that one tone is spread over the three vowels; if the nucleus has one vowel but two tones, those two tones are both pronounced on the single vowel, forming a rapid glide. In summary, the number of vowels is independent of the number of tones, and the number of tones is independent of the number of vowels, while the length of the nucleus remains – within perceptual limits – nearly constant.

In the following illustrations, notice that the first syllable has a single vowel and single tone; the second, two vowels but one tone; the third, three vowels but one tone; the fourth, one vowel but two tones; the fifth, two vowels but two tones; the sixth, three vowels but two tones; the last syllable of the seventh, two vowels but three tones. All of these nuclei should be pronounced with approximately the same speed: (1) ki$^3$ *he went*, (2) skai$^4$ *you will fall*, (3) koai$^4$ *he will go*, (4) se$^{4-3}$ *he sings*, (5) čai$^{2-3}$ *you (sing.) dance*, (6) nčoai$^{2-3}$ *you (sing.) come*, (7) va$^{4-3}$ntia$^{4-2-3}$ *I travel*.

The first layer of immediate constituents of the nucleus of the syllable may now be added to the formula previously given, as follows: ([n][c/ʔ])([oai][$^{3-4}$]).

The vocalic constituent may be considered the principal one, and the tonal constituent subordinate, (1) because the articulations for the vowels are primary[6] but for tone are tertiary, and (2) because the first part of the vocalic element seems to be morphologically slightly more stable than the first part of the tonal element, though the second part of each is likely to change in the morphology.

## 5   Third and Fourth Divisions:
## Principal versus Subordinate Vowels

There are four nonnasalized vowels: i, e, a, o, and their corresponding nasalized types: i̧, ȩ, a̧, o̧. The vowel a varies freely toward [ʌ]; e tends to be phonetically [ɛ]; i has no prominent variants; o varies freely over a considerable range from [o] to [u]. Following nasals – but not preceding them – the oral vowels tend to become slightly, though nonphonemically, nasalized. Note the following illustrations for the vowels: khi$^3$ *it appears*, khi̧$^2$ *far*, cře$^4$ *his*, cřȩ$^4$ *bad*; ša$^{1-3}$ *work*, ša̧$^{1-3}$ *liquor*; čho$^3$ *you (pl.) write*, čho̧$^{4-2}$ *woman*.

The vowels occur in various combinations. Oral vowels may occur in sequence within a nucleus, and nasalized vowels may do likewise, as in hkoe$^3$ *rough*, or to̧a̧$^2$ *fierce*. No sequence is found of an oral vowel followed by a nasalized vowel, or of a nasalized vowel followed by an oral vowel, in the same nucleus – nor are mixed sequences found between syllables, since every nucleus is preceded by its consonantal margin.

When the nucleus of a syllable contains but one vowel, any of the vowels may be found: ti$^{3-4}$ *boy*, te$^3$ *ten*, ša$^{1-3}$ *work*, to$^3$ *fruit*; ya$^1$si̧$^3$ *his neck*, thȩ$^3$ *his forehead*, sa̧$^3$ *sour*, nti$^4$to̧$^4$ *immediately*.

When the nucleus of a syllable contains two vowels, any vowel may occur as the second of the two, but only a, i, or o may occur as the first; e does not appear in a vowel cluster as the first of two. When a stem vowel e has some other vowel fused to it in the morphology, the following changes occur: ei > ai, ea > e, eo > ao: vře$^1$te$^{4-3}$ *he chases* + -i$^3$ *dependent pronoun of second person singular* > vře$^2$tai$^{4-3}$ *you (sing.) chase*; vře$^1$te$^{4-3}$ *he chases* + -a$^3$ *dependent pronoun of first person singular* > vře$^{4-3}$te$^{4-3}$ *I chase*; vře$^1$te$^{4-3}$ *he chases* + -o$^3$ *dependent pronoun of second person plural* > vře$^2$tao$^{4-3}$ *you (pl.) chase.*

For two reasons the second vowel of two may be considered the principal one: (1) Usually the second is phonetically the more prominent, since in the rapid pronunciation of the two-vowel nucleus the first tends to be reduced very sharply while the second remains the stronger and seems to carry the larger share of the tonal glide if one is present. (2) In two-vowel clusters the second position may have the more diverse types of vowels, since the vowel e may occur there but not in the first position. Morphological divisions do not help to establish the principal and subordinate positions in clusters of two vowels, since many clusters which contain a morphemes boundary between their vowels may have homophonous clusters with no such barrier and with no difference of phonological juncture. Note the following words; in the first word of each pair the vowel cluster will be part of the stem, but in the second word there will be a morpheme division between the vowels: cřoi$^{1-3}$ *sun*, ni$^2$choi$^{2-3}$ *you (sing.) toast*, nkia$^{1-3}$ *shade*, vře$^{4-3}$-hia$^{4-3}$ *I put in.*

The vowel e occurs in clusters only when the entire cluster is part of the stem; it never occurs in a vowel cluster as a morpheme distinct from the stem even though fused to it; all other vowel clusters can be found either as part of a stem or with morpheme division between them, as in the preceding illustrations.

Note the following specific clusters of two vowels in single-syllable nuclei:

With subordinate i as first member: ie (rare, only one sample, and tending to vary to e), ia, io; si$^1$khie$^2$ *he uses up*, si$^{4-3}$křia$^{4-3}$ *I paint*, ni$^2$křio$^{4-3}$ *you (pl.) paint.*

With subordinate a as first member: ai, ao; nřai$^{4-3}$ *father*, čhao$^{4-2}$ *an egg.*

With subordinate o as first member: oi, oe, oa; vi$^2$thoi$^4$ *you (sing.) go out*, shoe$^2$ *hot*, khoa$^4$soa$^{4-3}$ *shame.*

Nasalized vowels occur with the same distribution in clusters as do the oral vowels:

With subordinate į, ą, or ǫ as first member: įe (rare, and tending to vary to ę), įa, įǫ; ąi, ąǫ; ǫi, ǫe, ǫa; křįe$^3$ *dead*, ki$^3$cįa$^{4-3}$ *I was born*, ki$^3$cįǫ$^{4-3}$ *you (pl.) were born*; hą$^3$řąį$^{1-3}$ *name*, čąǫ$^{1-3}$ *earthquake*; křǫį$^{1-3}$ *you (sing.) will go*, škǫę$^1$ *not ripe*, tǫą$^2$ *fierce.*

Clusters of three vowels also occur in single syllables. The first two vowels of the clusters are limited to the groups ia, oi, oa; the third vowel of the cluster is limited to i, a, or o. The vowel e does not occur in any position in a cluster of three. [ . . . ]

The first break in the immediate constituents of a three-vowel cluster comes between the second and third vowels (indicating greater unity between the first two than between the second and third), (1) because the third, if i or o, appears to be slightly less prominent than the second (but the third may be approximately equal or even stronger if it is the vowel a), and (2) because there is without exception a morphological barrier between the second and third vowels since a third vowel is always part of a fused pronominal element. The vowel e never occurs as the third of a cluster.

The formula for the immediate constituents of nc?oai$^{3-4}$ *our (excl.) stomachs* can be made more specific on the basis of the data just given: $([n][c/?])([\{o/a\}\{i\}][^{3-4}])$.

Inasmuch as all of the clusters of vowels listed above, (1) contain either i or o, and many of them contain both, and (2) since it has been stated that the first element of such a cluster tends to become phonetically weak, it is expedient to present the reasons why these items are vowels and are not the consonants y and w (or v) respectively.

The following evidence indicates that none of the segments written as o in the vowel clusters – whether first, second, or third – must be interpreted to be the consonant w or v:

(1)   No consonant w exists in the language, either at the beginning of utterances or in the middle of them.

(2)   The consonant v is phonetically very different from the sound represented by the symbol o in the clusters; v is fricative, with lips approximately parallel, even when the second element of a consonant cluster, whereas o represents a frictionless sound with rounded lips wherever it occurs in the cluster: hao$^2$ *two*, va$^3$-li$^2$ *it is grievous to you*, soa$^{4-3}$-li$^2$ *it is shameful to you*.

(3)   The contrastive tone is spread over all vowels in a cluster, including any o, but not over v: ti$^1$ve$^3$ *he knows*, toi$^{4-2}$ *slowly*.

(4)   Various kinds of contrasts can be demonstrated between v and o (in the following samples, C represents some consonant and V some vowel): between V.vV and VoV (with difference of syllable division indicated by a lowered dot): ci$^4$.-vi$^4$ *yours here*, nchi̱o̱i̱$^3$ *you let go*, ci̱$^2$.-vi$^4$ *none here*; between V.v?V and Vo.?V: ka$^2$.v?a$^3$ *he carried*, kao$^4$.-?a̱$^{3-4}$ *with me*; between an o and contiguous v, as in Co.vV: čo$^3$.va$^2$ *we (incl.) talk*, (contrast čoa$^4$ *sign or symbol*); between ?vV and ?oV: ?va$^4$ *hook*, -?o̱a̱$^{3-2}$ *we are five*; co$^2$?va$^3$ *he walks*, nčha$^2$?o̱a̱$^3$ *I scold*; ?vi$^{4-3}$ *he drinks*, s?oi$^4$ *fiesta*; similarly with h: hva$^{4-3}$ *watery*, -ho̱a̱$^3$ *on the surface of (with first person subject)*; hva$^{4-3}$ *watery*, -hoa$^2$ *we are two*; between CV.?vV and C?oV: co$^2$.?va$^3$ *he walks*, c?oa$^3$ *his mouth*.

(5)   Pattern analogy shows that both o and i in oi are vowels: In the cluster io, the more prominent is o, which is undoubtedly vocalic; similarly, the i is undoubtedly vocalic in oi. Both of these parallel the a of ia. On the other hand, a is certainly vocalic in ai and ao, even though it is less prominent than the i and the o, since there is no consonant with which it could be confused. Once vowels such as the a are found to carry but little prominence while preceding another vowel, the pattern allows both i and o in ia and oa to be vocalic even though they also have little prominence and precede another vowel. In other words, assuming a to be always vocalic, even when the first of a cluster of two vowels, the pattern pressure on o and i can be expressed in a proportionate formula:

a : ao :: i : ia;      a : ai :: o : oa;

a : oa :: i : ai;      a : oa :: o : ao.

Similar evidence shows o and i to be vocalic when they occur as the third vowel of a cluster; compare the last vowels of the clusters ioa, ioi, iao, oia, oao.

(6)   Following ʔ as the second consonant of a cluster, o is laryngealized; v is not laryngealized after ʔ: nʔo$^{1-3}$ *rope*, ʔva$^4$ *hook*. In the pattern VʔV the second vowel is not laryngealized, but in vʔV the vowel is so affected: thǫ$^2$ʔa$^3$ *talkative*, vʔa$^3$ *he carries*, ti$^1$vʔa$^3$ *he is carrying*, thio$^1$ʔa$^3$ *they are not busy*.

   Preceding h, v is unvoiced, but o is not affected: ka$^2$vhe$^3$ *it is done*, kao$^4$-he$^{2-3}$ *with him*, nto$^4$ho$^4$ *soap*, ya$^4$-vhi$^2$ *there he goes*, li$^2$-yao$^3$-hį$^2$ *it is not sharp*.

(7)   All vowels of a cluster are nasalized, if one of them is nasalized, but v is not nasalized next to nasalized vowels: ni$^2$tǫ$\text{a}$į$^{2-3}$ *you (sing.) fight*, va$^3$sę$^1$va$^3$sę$^3$ *he puts in the middle*.

(8)   The changing of o to v would give nonpermitted types of consonant clusters: No consonant cluster contains more than three consonants, but four would result in the following: šo$^4$nthoa$^4$ *door*. No consonant clusters have v as the second element unless they begin with h or ʔ, but others would result: čoa$^4$ *plate*, cʔoi$^{1-3}$ *sun*, and many others. No consonants occur finally in isolated syllables, nor at the end of words, but v would then so occur: vʔe$^2$cʔoao$^3$ *you (pl.) beg*, vʔe$^2$škiao$^{4-3}$ *you (pl.) read*.

(9)   In a three-vowel cluster, the changing of a medial o to v would make an error by forcing one syllable of three vowels to appear as two syllables of one vowel each: contrast vʔe$^2$nʔiǫį$^{1-3}$ *you (sing.) braid*, ʔi$^4$-vi$^4$ *here*, nʔį$^3$-vi$^4$ *man here*.

(10)   The changing of o to v when it is the first member of a vowel cluster would complicate the statement of morphology, necessitating morphophonemic statements to cover the instances in which a stem vowel is followed by a fused pronominal vowel: vi$^3$tho$^3$ *he goes out*, but vi$^2$thoa$^4$ *I go out*. This would be further complicated by the fact that not all vowels would so change under these circumstances, since the a would remain a: ka$^{4-3}$ *he falls*, kai$^{4-3}$ *you (sing.) fall*.

   Much of the evidence just given indicates at the same time that segments written as v in the present material must not be written as o. These evidences include its phonetic character and conditioned variants, existing contrasts, and so on:

(11)   The changing of v to o would eliminate from the writing many of the contrasts actually existing phonetically; it would prevent the use of symbols which could be defined so as to represent at all times the different phonetic variants of o and v. It would symbolize some groups of two syllables as single syllables, since groups of two or three vowels form single syllables whereas two vowels separated by v form two syllables. It would create apparent clusters of five or more vowels, in sequences such as ti$^1$vʔe$^1$cao$^3$va$^3$-vi$^4$ *he is scattering (something) here*, whereas three vowels are the most allowed in a cluster. It would destroy much of the symmetry of the pattern of consonant clusters by eliminating many of those with v. It would appear to change one syllable into two in sequences such

as vʔa³ *he carries.* It would have vowels-initial in utterances, which actually do not occur thus, in syllables such as va³-na³ *it is grievous to me.*

Once it is amply demonstrated that the segment o as the first of a vowel cluster is actually a vowel and not a consonant, it follows by analogy that i may be the first vowel of a cluster and does not have to be y. The evidence for such a segment functioning as a vowel rather than a consonant is almost as strong, however, as for o. The chief difference is that y and i are phonetically much more similar in Mazateco than are the o and v. In the vast majority of instances, however, there is no doubt; i is a vowel whether it occurs as the first, second, or third of those segments written here as clusters of vowels. The evidence for i as a vowel largely parallels that already given for o; the same numbering will be maintained as for o, for ready reference:

(1)   Though w was lacking to parallel o, y is present to parallel i; no evidence here either way.

(2)   y and weak i as first of a vowel cluster are quite similar; no evidence.

(3)   Contrastive tone on i but not on y, but difficult to hear its beginning on rapid forms; evidence weak.

(4)   Strong evidence from contrastive words, to separate y and i: V.yV and ViV: ko³.ya³ *he waits,* khoia¹⁻³ *I will go,* khǫ³.ya³ *he sews;* between V.yʔV and Vi.ʔV: sʔa⁴.-yʔa³-na³ *soon he will carry for me,* sʔai⁴.ʔa³-na³ *I will not be busy in the afternoon;* between i and contiguous y as in Ci.yV: vi³nti³.ya² *it is arched* (contrast ntia⁴⁻² *road*); between ʔyV and CʔiV: ʔya⁴ *rainbow,* ntʔia³⁻⁴ *house;* ni³ʔya³⁻⁴ *home,* nʔįa² *we (incl.) make,* cį²ʔya³ *no one,* nka³cʔia³⁻² *all (incl.);* similarly with h: hyo³-na³ *I am willing,* -hįǫ²⁻³ *not you (pl.).*

(5)   Strong evidence from pattern analogy, already presented above, to show i as a vowel whether first, second, or third in the cluster: a : ao :: i : ia; a : oa :: i : ai; etc.

(6)   i but not y laryngealized after a consonant plus ʔ : čʔi⁴ *drunk,* ʔya⁴ *rainbow,* ntʔia³⁻⁴ *house,* li²ʔya³ *no one.*

(7)   i but not y nasalized in a cluster with a nasal vowel: čįa³ *near,* si¹kį²ya³ *he lends.*

(8)   i changed to y would give nonpermitted consonant clusters in the following illustrations: si¹hao²ya³ *he divides,* nhįǫ²yao³⁻⁴ *meat tamale.*

(9)   In the middle of a three-vowel cluster, i changed to y would upset the syllabification: khoia¹⁻³ *I will go;* compare ko³ya³ *I wait.*

(10)   i changed to y as the first of a cluster would complicate the morphological state-ment: khi⁴⁻³ *he writes,* khia⁴⁻³ *I write;* compare vʔe¹ʔma³ *he hides,* vʔe²ʔmao³ *you (pl.) hide.*

(11)   The additional statements about the changing of v to o can all be applied to the changing of y to i, and need not be repeated here.

Clusters of two or three vowels cannot be considered single complex phonemes, because of the contrastive but analogous pairs such as io and oi, ia and ai, ao and oa, oai and iao, ioa and oia, oao and iai. Supporting this conclusion is the fact that many of the clusters of two vowels and all of the clusters of three vowels are interrupted grammatically though not phonetically by a morpheme barrier: si$^1$choa$^3$ *he makes happy* + -i$^3$ *sec. per. sing. dep. subj. pronoun* > ni$^2$choai$^3$ *you make happy*, and so on.

Every full word in isolation or in context contains a stress on its last syllable. Certain dependent morphemes may follow words and be rhythmically grouped with them but left unstressed; these enclitics are indicated by a hyphen between them and the words which they follow: ni$^3$ʔya$^{3-4}$-na$^4$ *my home*. A different set of stressless morphemes may precede words and be proclicized to them; these are indicated by an en-dash between them and the words to which they are proclicized: ʔa$^3$–ʔnti$^1$-ni$^1$ *is it small?* Proclitics receive stress when joined directly to enclitics, in which case a hyphen is terained between them: ya$^4$-ve$^4$ *there*.

Vowels or vowel clusters which are stressed take a bit longer for their pronunciation than do unstressed vowels or clusters of vowels: In the following pairs of words, the vowel or vowel cluster in the final syllable or before hyphen is given more prominence and is longer than the other vowels: ntia$^4$ʔya$^{1-3}$ *bull thistle*, khoa$^4$soa$^{4-3}$ *shame*, si$^1$khao$^2$ʔa$^3$ *he advises*, ti$^4$hnta$^1$-lai$^4$ *sing it!*

Some restriction exist in the relationship between permitted margins and permitted vowels of the nuclei:

The vowel o may not be preceded by the consonant v or clusters with v.

The vowel e may not be preceded by the consonant š.

The vowel i may not be preceded by the consonant ñ or clusters with ñ.

The nasalized vowels have the same limitations, and in addition may not be preceded by v, y, l, r, or their clusters, nor by m, n, and ñ.

The combinations oV and iV may follow Cʔ but not ʔ or Vʔ; this restriction does not apply to oạ or iạ, etc., nor to simple o and i. Thus one finds cʔoa$^3$ *his mouth*, ntʔia$^{3-4}$ *house*, -ʔoạ$^{3-2}$ *we are five*, to$^3$nco$^2$ʔo$^{3-4}$ *spider*, ʔi$^4$-vi$^4$ *here*, but not *ʔoa or *ʔia.

Certain other combinations are very rare: m + o, ti$^2$moa$^3$ *I am mowing*; č or its clusters, + e, čhe$^1$ʔę$^{1-3}$ *rooster's comb* (alternate čhi$^1$ʔę$^{1-3}$); ñ + e, ti$^2$vʔe$^{4-3}$ñe$^{4-3}$ *I am burying*; č, or its clusters, + e, nče$^{4-2}$ *cooked whole corn*; y + e, ye$^4$ *snake*; y, or its clusters, + i, nka$^3$yi$^3$he$^{3-4}$ *all*; č, or its clusters, + i, ti$^1$čhi$^{4-3}$ *festered*, ya$^1$nčhi$^4$ *meat hook, clothes tree*.

## 6  Third and Fourth Divisions: Principal versus Subordinate Tones

The basic tones of Mazateco are four. Each of these tones is phonetically level, within the limits of perception. The only difference between them is their relative height; the relative height of the tone of any syllable is proportionate to the height of the tone of other syllables in the immediate context. The specific number of vibrations per second is immaterial to the tone; the momentary differences or contrasts within specific contexts are pertinent to the tonal system. Thus, a tone which is significantly – phonemically, contrastively – high at one moment, is high in that context because it contrasts with certain other lower tones; if a moment later the pitch of the entire utterance is lowered, the 'high' tone remains high since it still is higher than the other syllables, even though it may now actually be lower in pitch than any of the syllables were in the previous pronunciation of the same sentence. Compare the following illustrations (the highest tone is written with the numeral 1, the lowest with 4): c$\check{r}$e$^1$ ?nti$^{1-3}$ *small pheasant*, c$\check{r}$e$^1$ he$^{3-4}$ *big pheasant*, c$\check{r}$e$^1$ c$\check{r}$e$^{2-3}$ *lazy pheasant*, c$\check{r}$e$^3$ ?nti$^{1-3}$ *small membrane (such as of an orange section)*, c$\check{r}$e$^1$ c$\check{r}$e$^4$-ni$^1$ *it is his pheasant*.

The distance between the four contrastive pitches seems, to English speakers, to be very slight. The tones appear to be much closer together than the three contrastive level tones of Mixteco,[7] for example. The pitch gap between the tones has not yet been measured; the range of deviation for each of the tones must await instrumental analysis.

The tones have no striking subphonemic variants which occur either freely or conditioned by particular kinds of contexts.

When two different level tones are juxtaposed on a single syllable nucleus, they fuse to form a glide. The glide itself is not significant, but must be analyzed phonemically in terms of its beginning point and ending point. The glide is very rapid, since the total length of the nucleus is but little affected by the presence of two tones. Three tones may similarly coalesce into a two-direction glide – a rising–falling one. [ . . . ]

Clusters of two tones must be analyzed as sequences of two- or three-tone phonemes, rather than single but phonetically complex gliding tone phonemes, for the following reasons: (1) The beginning and ending points of the glides can be phonetically equated with the level tones of the system, while (2) the combination of tones form an analogous but contrastive pattern in groups such as 2–4 versus 4–2, 3–4 versus 4–3, 2–3 versus 3–2; and (3) none of the sequences are completely unique in structure, but are paralleled by others which are the same except for the substitution of the precise tone under consideration. Furthermore, (4) morphological barriers come in the middle of most of the glides, while those glides which do not have morphological junctures in the middle of them are paralleled by tone glides in which such morphological breaks do so occur.

In a cluster of two tones, the first is best considered the principal one, and the second subordinate, for the following reasons: (1) There is greater diversity of permitted occurrence of tones as the first of the cluster, since any of the four may be first, but tone 1 may not be second. (2) The first tone is usually the more prominent of the two (occasionally – especially with rising glides – the second may be of equal prominence, however). (3) The second element is very frequently a subordinate grammatical element fused to the stem tone represented by the first tonal element.

In a cluster of three tones, the third is best considered subordinate to the cluster of the first two, for the following reasons: (1) The third tone is likely to be phonetically weak. (2) The permitted tones in the third position in the cluster are limited to tones 3 and 4. (3) The third tone is always a part of a subordinate morpheme fused to a stem which contains a tonal cluster.

The immediate constituents of a tonal cluster, then, break first between the second and third tones, and then between the first and second tones. In the syllable -ntiao$^{4-2-3}$ (from ntia$^{4-2}$ *road*) of khoa$^1$-ntiao$^{4-2-3}$ *you (pl.) will travel*, the immediate constituents may be symbolized thus: (n/t)([{i/a}{o}]-[{⁴/²}{³}]). Compare also the constituents of ncʔoai³⁻⁴ *our (excl.) stomachs*: ([n][c/ʔ])([{o/a}{i}][³/⁴]); the constituents of -nčʔoai¹⁻³ (from nčʔoe¹ *he hears*) in ni²khi³nčʔoai¹⁻³ *you (sing.) notify* are similar.

## Summary

The isolated Mazateco syllable may be composed of a nucleus of from one to three vowels, with from one to three tones superimposed upon the nucleus as a whole (but without one-to-one correlation with the vowels of that nucleus), and of a margin of from one to three consonants.

When the margin is composed of two consonants, one of them is the principal one and the other is subordinate to it; the subordinate consonant may precede or follow the principal one. When the margin is composed of three consonants, two of them are subordinate to the third, and they may both occur before the principal consonant, or one after and the other before it. In a cluster of three consonants, the first break of immediate constituents occurs following the first subordinate consonant.

The nucleus has a break between its vowels and tones for its first layer of immediate constituents.

When two vowels are contained in the nucleus, the second is the principal one. If three vowels are present, the immediate constituents break between the second and third.

When two tones are contained in the nucleus, the first is the principal one. If three tones are present, the immediate constituents break between the second and third.

The layers of immediate constituents in the syllable may be indicated by the following sample formulas: (č)(o/⁴) *animal*, (t/h)(o/⁴) *gun*, ([ʔ][n/t])(o/³) *rotten*, (y)([a/o][³]) *sharp*, (k)([{o/a}{i}][⁴]) *he will go*, (s)([o][⁴/³]) *warm*, (s/ʔ)([o/i][¹/³]) *you will grind*, (k/h)([{o/i}{a}][¹/³]) *I will go*, ([n/t])([{i/a}{i}][{⁴/²}{⁴}]) – the morpheme ntia⁴⁻² *road* in khoa¹ntiai⁴⁻²⁻⁴ *we (excl.) will travel*.

The preceding formulas indicate the successive layers of immediate constituents. In order to symbolize the subordination of one constituent to another, however, a different symbolism is necessary. In the following diagram, subordinate constituents will be raised higher than the principal ones to which they are subordinated; vertical lines separate the layers of immediate constituents:

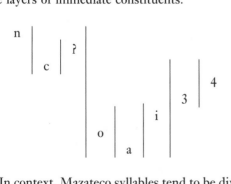

In context, Mazateco syllables tend to be divided as they would be in isolation. In the middle of utterances of normal or rapid speech, however, the first consonant of a cluster at the beginning of one syllable may pass partially to the preceding syllable. The foreigner in speaking the language, however, is much more likely to err by transferring too much rather than too little of the consonant to the preceding syllable.

# 8  Application

One may now inquire, "What is the significance of this approach, for languages other than Mazateco?" The answer: It may ultimately explain various problems in which phonetic sequences of sound appear to have simultaneously both phonemic unity and phonemic complexity. In English, for example, [aⁱ], [aᵘ], [ɔⁱ] are phonetically complex. Because of their contrasts with each other, and for other reasons,[8] it seems best to consider them sequences of phonemes, i.e. /ai/, /ai/, /ɔi/. On the other hand, they act in distribution much like [eⁱ], [oᵘ], [iᵛⁱ], [uᵛᵘ], which may best be analyzed as single phonemes,[9] i.e. /e/, /o/, /i/, /u/. The explanation of this apparent dilemma appears to be that the phonemic sequences /ai/, /au/, /ɔi/ constitute vocalic nuclei; these phonemically complex nuclear elements have a distribution which is similar to that for the phonemically simple nuclei /e/, /o/, /i/, /u/.

Similarly, in Totonaco, a sequence of vowel plus glottal stop may best be interpreted as a nuclear inner layer comprised of a sequence of two phonemes, i.e. /Vʔ/, rather than a single laryngealized ('glottalized') vowel.[10]

These three instances, Mazateco, English, and Totonaco, lead us to postulate the following: *Sounds in syllables (or morphemes) may occur in structural layers, or in series of 'immediate constituents'; an inner core comprised of a sequence of phonemes may, in larger structural sequences, on a higher layer of distribution, act as a single unit.*

We need further criteria before such immediate constituents – or those of syntax – can be analyzed independently and uniformly by various workers. This difficulty, should not, however, prevent us from recognizing the existence of some such structural layering.

## Notes

1   See e.g., Bloomfield 1933; Pike 1943b, with diagram p. 70. For intonational analysis, see Pike 1945a.
2   A language of Oaxaca, Mexico. The data for this paper was gathered under the auspices of the Summer Institute of Linguistics in annual field trips by one of the authors (E.V.P.) from 1936 to 1945, and in 1936 and 1938 by the other author (K.L.P.). The latter was able to make further investigation and contribute toward the preparation of this manuscript in 1945, as part of the work undertaken as Lloyd Post-Doctoral Fellow of the University of Michigan.
3   For instrumental studies of the releasing and arresting action of consonants in the syllable, see Stetson 1928. For discussion of the relation of the syllable pulse to the phoneme, see Stetson 1945.
4   Articulations in the mouth are primary, those in the nose secondary, those in the throat tertiary; if two articulations occur simultaneously in the mouth, the one with the least degree of closure becomes subprimary (Pike 1943a: 131–3).
5   This constitutes one of the fundamental differences between the tonal systems of Mixteco and Mazateco. In Mixteco such a positive correlation of one tone to one vowel and vice versa constitutes a key to its tonal structure. Compare Pike 1944, 1945b.

6   See n. 4.

7   The four contrastive tones of Mazateco seem even closer together than the four contrastive end points of the intonations of American English. The organization of the pitch contrasts is likewise different: in Mazateco the pitches are largely lexical, basic to specific morphemes, and contributing to lexical meanings, whereas in English the pitches are superimposed upon the sequences of consonants and vowels of the sentence in such a way as to carry adventitious meanings, or 'shades of meaning'. For reference to Mixteco and English, see nn. 5 and 1.

8   Presented in part in an article by Pike (1947), on English vowels.

9   See n. 8.

10  See Aschmann 1946; much of Aschmann's phonetic data has been checked with his informant by K.L.P.

## References

Aschmann, Herman P. 1946. Totonaco phonemics. *International Journal of American Linguistics* 12: 34–43.

Bloomfield, Leonard. 1933. *Language*. Chicago: University of Chicago Press.

Pike, Kenneth L. 1943a. *Phonetics: A Critical Analysis of Phonetic Theory and a Technic for the Practical Description of Sounds*. University of Michigan Publications in Language and Literature, 21. Ann Arbor: University of Michigan Press.

Pike, Kenneth L. 1943b. Taxemes and immediate constituents. *Language* 19: 65–82.

Pike, Kenneth L. 1944. Analysis of a Mixteco text. *International Journal of American Linguistics* 10: 113–38.

Pike, Kenneth L. 1945a. *Intonation of American English*. Ann Arbor: University of Michigan Press.

Pike, Kenneth L. 1945b. Tone puns in Mixteco. *International Journal of American Linguistics* 11: 129–39.

Pike, Kenneth L. 1947. On the phonemic status of English diphthongs. *Language* 23: 151–9.

Stetson, R. H. 1928. A study of Speech Movements in action. *Arch. Néer. Phon. Expér.*, vol. 3. The Hague.

Stetson, R. H. 1945. *Bases of Phonology*. Oberlin.

# 17

# The Syllable (1982)

## Elisabeth O. Selkirk

English provides a particularly good illustration of the proposition that the syllable is a linguistically significant unit which must have its place in phonological theory. The reasons generally given in support of the syllable as a theoretical construct are three-fold, and English provides pertinent evidence in each of these areas. First of all, it can be argued that the most general and explanatory statement of phonotactic constraints in a language can be made only by reference to the syllabic structure of an utterance. Second, it can be argued that only via the syllable can one give the proper characterization of the domain of application of a wide range of rules of segmental phonology. And third, it can be argued that an adequate treatment of suprasegmental phenomena such as stress and tone requires that segments be grouped into units which are the size of the syllable. The same three reasons leading to the postulation of the syllable can be shown to motivate the existence of privileged groupings of segments within the syllable which must be thought of as constituent-like linguistic units themselves.[1] The notion of the syllable that will emerge from this examination of English is therefore one of a hierarchical unit; an internally structured tree quite analogous to a tree representing syntactic structure.

## 1　The Representation of the Syllable

*1.1*　In what follows, special attention will be given to the question of the representation of the syllable and especially to the hypothesis that the syllable is an element of a hierarchically organized prosodic structure. One of the main sources of support for this hypothesis comes from the demonstration that the syllable has internal structure, and for this reason we will dwell at some length on questions of syllable constituency. The other main source of support for the hypothesis is the demonstration that there exists a higher-order hierarchical prosodic structure of which syllables must be seen as building blocks.[2] Being structured within and forming an integral part of a larger structure without, how can the syllable be anything but a structural, suprasegmental, prosodic unit itself?

In our view, the phonological representation of an English monosyllabic word like *flounce* is structured as in (1)

(1)

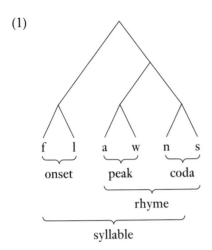

(where the letters should be taken as standing for the corresponding distinctive feature matrices). There is a first major bipartite division of the syllable – into *onset* (the initial consonant cluster) and *rhyme* (the rest). The rhyme in turn divides into two parts – the *peak* (containing the syllabic nucleus) and the *coda* (the final consonant cluster).[3] Of course not all syllables in English are so rich in internal structure: *cow* [kaw] has only a simple (non-branching) onset, a complex peak, and no coda at all; *fat* [fæt] has a simple onset, a simple peak and a simple coda; *aye* [aj] has a complex peak, but no onset and no coda.

Before moving to a defense of this particular analysis of English, it will be useful to address the question of syllable-internal structure in somewhat more general fashion. Pike (1967) has argued that it is a universal of syllable composition that a constituent structure break exists between a syllable nucleus (our 'peak') and its margins (our 'onset' and 'coda'). The argument for constituency is based, in part, on distributional or phonotactic considerations:

> The possibility of substitution of one phoneme for another in a particular slot in the margin, for example, is likely to be more dependent upon the particular phonemes manifesting other slots in that margin than it is by the particular phonemes manifesting the nucleus of such syllables. I.e., if a formula CCV is manifested by /s/ in the first consonant slot, and the nucleus slot is filled by the phoneme /a/, the list of phonemes which fill the second consonant slot are more likely to be controlled by the presence of the /s/ than they are by the presence of the /a/ – e.g., they may be limited to voiceless consonants after the voiceless /s/, etc. Such considerations indicate that a closer relationship exists between the two consonants than exists between either consonant and the vowel. (Pike 1967: 386–7)

The claim thus is that the likelihood of the existence of phonotactic constraints between the position slots in the syllable (as well as the strength or inviolability of those constraints, one might add) is a reflection of the immediate constituent (IC) structure relation between the two slots: the more closely related structurally (in the obvious sense), the more subject to phonotactic constraints two position slots are. We will call this the IC principle of phonotactics. According to this principle, therefore, onset, peak, and coda are units within which the tightest phonotactic constraints obtain.

The grouping of peak and coda into a constituent is advocated as a universal of syllable composition by Kuryłowicz (1948), one reason for this being similar to Pike's. The claim made is that co-occurrence restrictions between peak and coda are always more likely to exist (and indeed are quite common) than are restrictions between either peak or coda and the onset. The explanation offered is that the former two comprise a constituent.

As any detailed analysis of the phonotactics of the English syllable shows,[4] it is within the onset, peak, and coda that the strongest collocational restrictions obtain. By contrast, there are no phonotactic restrictions at all for the language which involve onset and peak, for example. The existence of this array of restrictions follows from a single principle, the IC principle of phonotactics, if one assumes an IC analysis of the syllable.

A theory giving an IC analysis of the syllable, and incorporating this principle, is clearly superior to one where syllable structure is defined merely in terms of a sequence of segments (which is the approach of Hooper 1976, for example), for it allows for quite a restrictive characterization of the notion 'possible phonotactic constraint of language L'. A purely linear representation of the syllable *flounce* might look like (2):

(2) $ $f_1$ $l_2$ $a_3$ $w_4$ $n_5$ $s_6$ $

The fact that strong phonotactic constraints existed between positions 1 and 2, 3 and 4, or 5 and 6, but not between other pairs, would be given no significance by the linear syllable theory, unless explicit provisions were incorporated to the effect that "syllable-initial consonant clusters, the sonorant elements of syllable centers, and syllable-final consonant clusters tend to exhibit phonotactic constraints among themselves." But, still, the statements remain ad hoc, for they follow from no more general principle of grammar. The IC approach to the syllable, on the other hand, permits a single eminently simple statement that will cover the same facts. We conclude from this that phonotactic considerations do indeed support an IC analysis of the syllable.

More telling even than these phonotactic arguments for internal structure in the syllable are those provided by phonological rules, for phonological rules must 'look at', i.e. operate in terms of, the properties of phonological representation. In this sense, phonological rules are analogous to transformations of the syntactic component, whose operations on syntactic representation are dependent on, and therefore may provide arguments for, the particulars of syntactic constituent structure. One would of course hypothesize that the constituency of the syllable in phonological representation that is revealed by the operation of phonological rules would be the same as that motivated by phonotactic considerations. And, indeed, if it can be shown that there is a systematic coincidence of the constituent units required by rules of the phonology and those required for phonotactics, then in the absence of direct evidence from phonological rules, the investigator would be justified in relying on phonotactics alone in assigning an internal analysis of the syllable.

The arguments of Pike and Kuryłowicz in favor of a hierarchical conception of the syllable have not been limited to phonotactics. They have shown that an internal structural analysis makes available a superior treatment of phonological processes in languages. For example, Pike (1947: 142) argues for the nucleus (= peak) on the grounds that it serves as a unit with respect to suprasegmental phenomena such as pitch and stress. Pike and Pike (1947) adduce evidence from numerous phonological rules, suprasegmental and segmental, for a particular IC analysis of the syllable in Mazateco. In addition, as a point in favor of the rhyme constituent, Kuryłowicz (1948), Pike (1967: 391) and Newman (1972: 303) have observed that it makes possible a unified treatment of the heavy–light syllable distinction which plays such an important part in stress systems. The light syllable CV can be characterized as one whose rhyme is simple, non-branching, while the heavy syllable, be it CVC or CVV (a long vowel) is one with a complex, or branching, rhyme. Other phonological, or shall we say phonetic, phenomena such as duration and closeness of transition between segments might also be taken as revealing of the immediate constituent structure of the syllable.[5] We touch on some of these phenomena below.

There is one additional general question for the theory of the representation of the syllable that we wish to pose. We have argued thus far that the syllable has immediate constituent structure. The next logical question is whether the nodes of this constituent structure are labeled. Or, to put the question in broader terms, is there anything to be said about the nature of syllable-internal constituents aside from the fact that they may branch? We are inclined to believe that the answer is yes, and specifically, that a case can be made for associating two distinct types of information with the nodes, i.e. the constituents as a whole. The considerations giving support for including each of these will be reviewed in turn.

One might first want to ask whether the labels syllable, onset, rhyme, peak, and coda, which we have so far used merely as descriptive terms, should be assigned to their respective nodes in a representation. That is, should the representation (1) be recast as (3)?

(3)

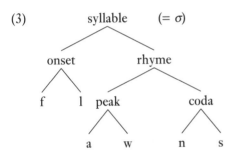

The preliminary answer we have to offer is that while the prosodic category label 'syllable' is required in representations, support for naming its internal constituents in this way is currently lacking. The evidence pointing to the need for the 'syllable' label emerges in the examination of higher-order prosodic structure. See Selkirk (1980), for example, where it is shown that the label is necessary in order to identify the syllable as a unit distinct from any other branching structure (be it 'larger' or 'smaller' than the syllable).

A second suggestion is that the nodes be characterized as a complex of distinctive features, i.e. that selected distinctive features may be assigned to a node or syllable structure, with the interpretation of this being that any segment or constituent dominated by a node labeled [+F] is characterized as [+F]. This suggestion may be thought of as a particular implementation of the theory of Vergnaud (1976) according to which adjacent segments bearing the same specification $\alpha$ for some feature $F_i$ are to be represented as being dominated by a tree labeled $\alpha F_i$. In general, it seems reasonable to entertain the possibility that, by convention, any features shared by the segments or constituents immediately dominated by some node be assigned to that node itself. (McCarthy (1977) hints at a convention of this sort in assigning the node dominating a coronal cluster like *st* in English the feature [+coronal].) Following this convention, the representation (1) would be recast as (4):

(4)

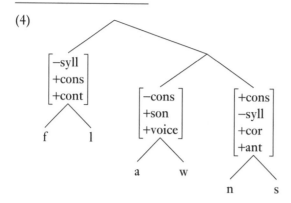

Such a representation allows for the possibility that some phonological rules may operate in terms of the features of constituent nodes. (This, in essence, is Vergnaud's suggestion.) For example, it would permit an elegant characterization of the fact that in Arabic and Berber the domain of so-called emphasis (i.e. pharyngealization) is the syllable;[6] the rule pharyngealizing the syllable when it contains a pharyngeal phoneme can simply be seen as assigning the feature [+Constricted Pharynx] to the syllable node.

Similarly, vowel nasalization in French can be conceived of as the attribution of the features of nasality to the constituent (VN), with consequent replacement of the consonantal segment by the features of the vowel. The result is a compensatorily lengthened nasal vowel: ($\widetilde{VV}$). These two examples are simply indicative of the importance of representing the features borne in common by a sequence of segments for the characterization of phonological rules.

A final suggestion concerning node labeling within the syllable will be entertained. It builds on the observation that in a binary branching constituent of the syllable, one member tends always to be 'weaker' than the other. Pike and Pike (1947) described this relation as the 'subordination' of one to the other. Extending the theory of hierarchical prosodic structure of Liberman (1975) and Liberman and Prince (1977) to the syllable, this relation can be given a formal representation, by labeling the 'subordinate' node *w* and the other *s*.[7] With nodes labeled in this fashion, the representation (1) would take on the shape of (5) (ignoring the other two types of node-related information just discussed):

(5)

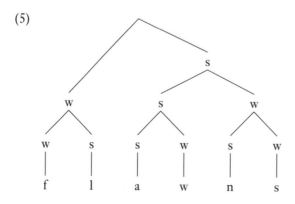

The peak is of course strong ($s$), i.e. more sonorous, than the onset. And within each of the other constituents, the $s$ has been assigned to the more sonorant element. This approach incorporates the suggestion made by Pike (1967: 387ff) and McCarthy (1977) that the assignment of $w$ (= 'subordinate' status) vs. $s$ can be made, at least partly, on the basis of the relative ranking of the two segments (or constituents) on a universally defined sonority hierarchy.[8]

It has been claimed, by Hooper (1976: 15) for example, that syllable-final position (the coda) is universally "weak." According to the $s/w$ node labeling theory, this need not be stipulated at all: it immediately follows from the $s/w$ theory, on the assumption that syllables always branch into onset and rhyme, and rhyme into peak and coda. The coda is weak (with respect to its sister peak), and is lower in the tree than the onset (which is weak with respect to the rhyme). The strength hierarchy which can be assigned to these constituents, according to the Liberman and Prince algorithm (1977: 259) is thus peak, onset, coda.

Note that not all constituents are composed of members of differing sonority, in which case a language-particular specification of the $s/w$ relation may have to be made. Consider, for example, a hypothetical peak composed of the vowels $i$ and $u$, which have the same rank on the sonority hierarchy. The constituent could be either (i̇ u̇) or (i̇ u̇). In the first case, one would expect the phonetic outcome to resemble [iw] (a falling diphthong) and in the second [yu] (a rising diphthong). Thus, whether a language has diphthongs that are falling or rising can be seen as resulting from the language-specific assignment of $sw$ vs. $ws$ to its complex peak. Note that the idea of having gliding result from the $s/w$ relation allows one to consider the possibility that a distinctive feature such as [±syllabic] is not necessary to the capturing of the glide–vowel distinction. (Indeed, one should ask whether such a feature as [±syllabic] is at all required, once the notion of syllable is introduced into phonological theory.)

It should be noted that the three separate suggestions for the characterization of nodes in syllable structure that have been reviewed here, the first of which will be adopted only with respect to the label 'syllable', are mutually compatible. They are not different, conflicting theories about how nodes should be labeled. Rather, they are theories which touch on different aspects of the representation, which all require some treatment in the phonology. Because the graphic representation of these three types of information, alone or all together, is extremely ungainly, we will make the practice in what follows of leaving this information out of syllable structure representation, unless it is crucial for the discussion.

Now it must be recognized that the question of what the syllable looks like in phonological representation is a distinct one, logically, from the question of how the grammar of a language is to give expression to the notion 'possible syllable of L', and, specifically, to the notions possible onset, peak, coda, and rhyme. That is, individual representations of syllables do not state generalizations about syllable structure any more than individual noun phrases in a syntactic representation state generalizations concerning the notion 'possible noun phrase' in a language. A grammar must therefore provide for some statement of the notion 'possible syllable of L', this statement being distinct from any phonological representation of the language. Let us suppose that for each language this statement is in the form of a template and an accompanying set of phonotactic constraints somewhat in the spirit of Fudge (1969) and Hooper (1976), but with differences that will become apparent. These together specify all the possible syllable types of the language, and can be thought of as serving as well-formedness conditions on the syllabic structure of the phonological representations of a language. They are, in essence, tree-checking devices.

Suppose, for example, that the syllable template for English looks something like (6):

(6)

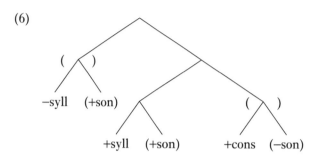

The function of the template is to encode the gross characteristics of syllable structure: (i) the composition of the syllable in terms of segment types identified by the major class features [±syllabic], [±sonorant] [±consonantal], (ii) the order of these segment types within the syllable,[9] (iii) the structural relations between the segment types (defined in IC terms), and (iv) the optionality of segments or groups of segments (= constituents) within the syllable. The role of the template in the grammar will be discussed in later sections of this paper. Suffice it to say here that it contributes to defining the well-formedness of the syllable structure of particular phonological representations. A necessary condition for the well-formedness of a representation is that, within a syntactic domain specified for the language, the syllabic structure of the representation be *non-distinct* from the template. Roughly speaking, a syllable tree of a phonological representation is said to be non-distinct from the template if its branching matches the branching of the template, and the distinctive feature matrices of its segments are not distinct from the corresponding feature matrices of the template.[10] It is easy to see that the representation of *flounce* given in (1) is non-distinct from the template (6). Note, furthermore, than the template includes provisions for optionality. Thus, the entire onset is optional (cf. *as, aye, in*, etc.) and, if present, may contain just one consonant (cf. *pie, fate, so*, etc.), the second being optional. Clearly, if a syllable in phonological representation contains only the non-optional member of a pair within a constituent, it is not to be considered to be distinct from the template.

The template on its own does not give a characterization of English syllable structure that is sufficiently restrictive, though. Formulated as in (6), it allows for more types than are ever evidenced in English. For example, in the onset, if the first consonant is a labial, then it may not be followed by *w*, or if it is an *s*, it may not be followed by *r*. And in the peak, for example, only a limited variety of diphthongs are available: *j* is not possible after any back vowel except *ɔ* and *a*. These further restrictions do not find a natural expression in a template like (6). Following Fudge (1969), we acknowledge that another type of formal device is required in the grammar to express such phonotactic constraints. Fudge calls them 'collocational restrictions', and gives them the form of an implication on the order of "if a second position in onset is *w*, then first position is not [+labial]." (Alternatively, one could think of them as filters on the output of an "overgenerating or overly permissive template."[11] They might have the form *[+labial]*w*. We will take no firm position on this matter here.) Clearly, then, a second condition on the well-formedness of the syllabic structure of a representation is that it not be ruled out by the collocational restrictions of the language.

*1.2* An examination of English reveals evidence that supports the approach to the representation of syllable structure that has been outlined here. Motivation for internal constituency on the basis of phonotactics is particularly strong (following the IC principle), and while the operation of phonological rules and their relation to syllable constituency in English has not received much attention in the framework of generative grammar, some very suggestive work pointing to internal constituency has been carried out by phoneticians and will be referred to.

Let us first look at the onset constituent. According to template (6), any consonant in the phoneme repertory of English may serve alone as the onset. This is correct, except for *ž* and *ŋ* which will have to be excluded in a separate statement. The template also says that the onset contains at most two consonants, and that if it does contain two, the second must be a sonorant.[12] One could consider not specifying that the second place consonant has to be a sonorant, and change the onset in (6) to –*syll* (–*syll*). But since the more restrictive –*syll* (+*son*) of (6) does not exclude any possible onsets, and removes the need for mentioning an additional collocational restriction in the grammar, we retain it. Note that the template does not state a further restriction on onsets that must find expression in the grammar: that when there is a second sonorant consonant in the onset, the first consonant must be a non-sonorant. This information could conceivably be incorporated into the template itself, by modifying the onset portion to look like the following: (–*son*) (+*son*). But it seems undesirable to make this modification: first, because, with it, the template no longer says in direct fashion that *any* consonant (i.e. [–syll]) can be the sole element of the onset, and second, because the fact that the first must be a non-sonorant when there is a sonorant that follows should quite likely be seen as following from some universals of syllable structure and therefore not require direct expression in the grammar.[13] So we propose instead that the grammar of English contain a collocational restriction associated with the template to the effect that if there is a second consonant in the onset, the first must be an obstruent.

A fair number of additional collocational restrictions on possible onset combinations must be stated. These must express the fact that (i) only stops and voiceless fricatives appear as the first member, (ii) that *j* never appears as a second member, (iii) that only *s* may appear with *m* or *n*, (iv) that *w* never appears after labial consonants, or *š* or *st*, (v) that *r* never appears after *s* or *h*, and (vi) that *l* never appears after *t*, *d*, *š*, *h*, or *sk*.[14] Given the IC principle espoused by Pike and Kuryłowicz and adopted by us, the existence of these constraints between first and second consonants, and the absence of any between these consonant positions and the vowels that follow, indicate a grouping of the consonants into a constituent.

Looking now at clusters with initial *s*, we see that they provide the sole instances of onsets where the second consonant may be an obstruent (e.g. *stay*, *spite*, *sky*, *sphere*)[15] and of onsets with three consonants instead of two or one (cf. *split*, *spry*, *stray*, *scream*, *square*). Should the statement about possible onsets in English, which we have expressed in the template (6), be modified so as to include an additional place for *s*? The answer is no, for to do so would fail to give recognition to the fact that clusters of *s* plus obstruent form a unit that may occupy a single obstruent slot, wherever that slot may appear in the syllable. In the coda as well, as we shall see, *s* plus obstruent clusters may appear where otherwise only a single obstruent would be allowed. To include a provision for an extra *s* in both onset and coda would be to deny that they are really the same fact.[16] What we propose to account for the special status of these *s* clusters is what we will call an *auxiliary* template, a sort of corollary to the general template in (6). It would be formulated as (7), and says, essentially, that *s* plus obstruent may qualify as a single obstruent in English.

(7)

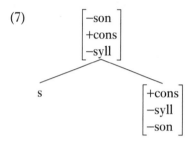

A phonological representation of English is ruled well-formed, if it is non-distinct from the general template (6), taken in conjunction with the auxiliary template (7) (and obeys the appropriate restrictions). For example, the representation of the word *splint* (8) is ruled well-formed because the circled segments and nodes are non-distinct from the general template (6), while the remaining (squared) segments, unaccounted for by (6), are allowed by the auxiliary template:

(8)

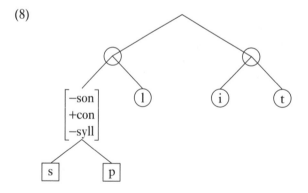

Turning next to the peak, we see that it must contain a single syllabic element, be it a single vowel (cf. *pat, kiss, hex*, etc.) or a syllabic sonorant (cf. *stir* [str̩], *muddle* [mʌdl̩], *chasm* [kæzm̩], etc.). Making use of the additional [+son] place, one finds the diphtongs *aj, aw,* and *ɔj* (cf. *kite, cow, toy*). One might also wish to contend that the offglides *j* and *w* of the diphthongized tense vowels in English (e.g. *beat, boat, boot*, etc.) occupy that second sonorant position in the peak, though it is not obvious that they do so in underlying representation, i.e. if the glide is introduced by a phonological rule.[17] We will also be claiming that the other sonorant consonants *r*, *l*, and the archiphoneme *N* may occupy second position in the peak, under certain circumstances. This claim will be defended in the context of our discussion of the coda.

There are strong restrictions on what segments may cohabit the peak. Thus, if the second element is *j*, the only preceding back vowels allowable are *ɔ* and *a*. The restrictions being discussed are restrictions on *underlying* segment combinations. Consequently, if the glides of the diphthongized tense vowels *ij* and *ej* are derived by rule, then it is correct to say that the *a* and *ɔ* are the only vowels permitted to precede *j* in the peak. And similarly, the glide *w* may be said to follow no vowel but *a*, if the diphthongized *uw* and *ow* are derived by rule. Otherwise, the restriction would have to state that *w* could follow no vowel but *a*, *o*, *u*. Again, such restrictions as these can be taken as giving an indication of a close structural tie between the two elements. By contrast, no such restrictions obtain between a vowel and a following obstruent, which we claim to belong to the coda constituent.

As for the coda, the template (6) states (i) that it is optional (cf. *cow*, *bee*, *aye*, etc.), (ii) that it may contain any single consonant (cf. *cat*, *dog*, *seem*, *ease*, *off*, *feel*, *wane*, etc.), (iii) that it contains at most two consonants, and (iv) that if there are two consonants in the coda, the second must be an obstruent (cf. *wax*, *waft*, *adze*, *glimpse*, (= ms), *fifth*, *apt*, *James*, etc.). There is a limited class of apparent exceptions to the third claim about the general template, but these are explainable in terms of the auxiliary template (7). Consider, in particular, a word like *next*, with three post-peak obstruents. Its structure is that of (9):

(9)

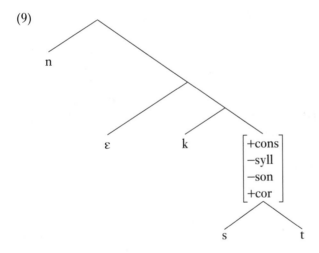

The *st* combination is able to qualify as a single obstruent, however, according to (7), so that this monosyllable does indeed conform to the general syllable template (6).[18]

One extremely important collocational restriction on the coda in English is this:

(10)   The second consonant of the coda must be a coronal.

It is this restriction which describes the absence in English of words such as *rifk* (vs. *rift*), *sipf* (vs. *six*), etc. Again, apparent counterexamples to (10) like *wasp* and *ask* can be explained in terms of the auxiliary template (7). According to (7), *s* plus obstruent groups can qualify as single consonants; because of this, *wasp* and *ask* will not be ruled out by (10).

Reconsidering the representation (9) in view of restriction (10), it is to be noted that here the convention that the features shared by the segments of a constituent become associated with the immediately dominating node plays a crucial role. It is this convention that induces the feature [+cor] on the node dominating *st*, thereby allowing the representation (9) to conform to the [+cor] requirement on consonants occupying second place in the coda. Accordingly, we predict (correctly) that *sk* and *sp*, which do not share the common specification for coronality, will not be permitted as second and third consonants in a coda cluster (cf. *\*eksp*, *\*ipsk*, etc.).

The templates (6) and (7), in conjunction with (10), would in principle permit the existence of complex codes with *s* groups in first position. But these do not seem to be possible (cf. *\*nespt*, *\*lisks*, etc.), unless the final coronal is interpreted as an inflectional element, and it will be argued immediately below that such elements do not "count" in determining the well-formedness of syllables in English. Appeal must therefore be made to an additional collocational restriction, which will explicitly rule out *s* groups as first members of a two-consonant coda.

In sum, the claim being made by the conjunction of the templates (6) and (7), and the collocational restrictions alluded to, is that the only bi-consonantal codas permitted in English are those with coronal second elements, that the only tri-consonantal codas are those with *st* (or *sθ*) in second or third place, and that codas of more than three are absolutely excluded.

What then of words like *acts* (*kts*), *texts* (*ksts*) or *sixths* (*ksθs*)? The first has a tri-consonantal coda of a type that is not allowed, and the second and third contain quadri-consonantal codas, impermissible according to our analysis. Should the template (6) be modified so as to allow for yet another [+cons] position? (Note that the consonants extending the codas beyond the predicted limits are always [+cor]). Fudge's (1969) answer to this question is in the affirmative. The position of Fujimura and Lovins (1978) and that of McCarthy (1977) is that an unlimited number of [+cor] positions should in principle be allowed in the coda. But the correct answer, we claim, is no. The analysis should remain as it stands. Observe first of all that the only forms seeming to require an extension of the template's coda include inflectional endings. To extend the template would be to predict, incorrectly, we believe, that monomorphemic forms in English could appear with the codas, e.g. *kts* and *ksθs*. Furthermore, general considerations having to do with the syntactic domain of the template in English, i.e. the domain over which well-formed syllable structure is defined, would require that, in underlying representation, the inflectional suffixes *not* be taken into consideration. Inflectional affixes are *word* affixes, and as such are outside the basic domain of syllabification, which is the word-initial category *root*. (On the root–word distinction, see Selkirk 1982a, b.[19]) And finally, even if *phonetically* a word with an inflectional ending is sometimes indistinguishable from a monomorphemic word (cf. *find* vs. *fined*), the operation of certain phonological rules, such as voicing assimilation, suggests that at a more abstract level the endings do not have the same relation to preceding segments of the syllable as do consonants contained within the coda (compare, for example, *width*, with regressive voicing assimilation ([wɪtθ] < /wɪdθ/) to *kits* [kɪts] and *lids* [lɪdz], with progressive assimilation).

We conclude that the inflectional endings are outside the domain of syllabification, and therefore that they require no modification of the template. (These points will be developed at greater length in the last section of the chapter.)

There are a number of quite strong additional collocational restrictions affecting the coda, and these can be taken as further support for a coda constituent. To cite just one: if there is a second consonant in the coda, the first may not be *b, g, v, č, ǰ, š,* or *ž*.

Turning now to the rhyme as a whole, we must discuss first the question of the place of post-vocalic sonorants in syllable structure. As was mentioned above, the template (6) states that the sonorant liquids *l, r* and nasals, *n, m,* and *ŋ* may cohabit the peak with a vowel. However, this cohabitation is possible only if the vowel is simple, i.e. occupying only the first position in the peak. When a vowel is complex, as in the case of diphthongs, and as we shall see, the tense diphthongized vowels, post-vocalic nasals and liquids must be analyzed as part of the coda (which they can be, in their capacity as consonants). So, for example, the words *while* [wajl], *wire* [wajr], and *wine* [wajn] consist of a complex peak *aj* and a coda consonant *l, r,* or *n*. But the words *Paul* [pɔl], *pour* [pɔr], and *pawn* [pɔn] with simple vowels may be given two analyses – as containing a complex peak and no coda, or as containing a simple peak and a coda consonant. With this in mind, we can now see that the template, combined with restriction (10), makes the following interesting prediction: that within the same syllable, the sequence simple vowel plus sonorant may be followed by *any* consonant, whereas the sequence complex vowel plus sonorant can be followed only by a coronal consonant. (These restrictions are pointed out by Fudge 1969.) The former array of possibilities, exemplified partially in (11),

(11)   land   lam(b)   ban(g)                lunge   —       —
       lard   orb      —                     purge   warm    barn
       bald   —        —                     bulge   elm     kiln

       lint   lamp     ink      month        hunch   prince  —
       heart  harp     lark     hearth       arch    purse   wharf
       hilt   help     elk      health       gulch   pulse   elf

follows from the fact that simple vowel and sonorant can act as a peak, leaving the following consonant alone in the coda, and the fact that the template puts no restrictions on single-consonant codas. The restrictions in the latter case, exemplified for nasals in (12), have their explanation in the fact that a complex vowel occupies the entire peak, requiring that a following sonorant plus consonant be treated as a complex coda, and the fact that in a complex coda the second consonant must be [+cor].

| (12) | (a) | | *nt* | *nd* | *nk* | *mp* |
|---|---|---|---|---|---|---|
| | | *aj* | pint | find | * | * |
| | | *aw* | mount | mound | * | * |
| | | *ɔj* | point | — | *20 | * |
| | (b) | *ij* | — | fiend | * | * |
| | | *ej* | paint | — | * | * |
| | | *uw* | — | wound | * | * |
| | | *ow* | (won't) | — | * | * |

(12a) shows examples of the "real" diphthongs with various finals, and supports our claim. (12b) is instructive as well. Here we see that the tense vowels place the same restrictions on the following coda that the real diphthongs do. These facts can be taken as evidence that in the underlying representation, where the template is applicable, the tense vowels are either long, i.e. geminate (VV) and therefore complex, or diphthongal. As for clusters with *l* or *r* plus coronal following a complex peak, they are far less common, but those that are attested are compatible with our claim: *wild, whilst, field, Gould, old, weird, pierce.*

The fact that sonorants must form part of the peak when followed by non-coronals indicates that the collocational restriction which must be stated to exclude syllable-final combinations of *n* (or *m*) plus *v* or *f*, for example, cannot be stated as restrictions on possible *codas*; rather, they are restrictions on possible *rhymes*. Moreover, because combinations including the liquids *l, r* plus *z* are permitted as possible peak-plus-coda combinations, the collocational restriction excluding them must be stated at the level of the rhyme. Here, then, are instances of phonotactic constraints on peak plus coda. Since none are attested on peak and onset, we would conclude, following the IC principle, that it is correct to join peak and coda in the rhyme constituent.

This concludes our review of the phonotactics of English syllables. Basing ourselves on facts concerning phonotactics, i.e. the distribution of segment types, we have been led to draw conclusions concerning the nature of the phonological representation, in particular concerning units internal to the syllable. In adopting this approach, we follow in the footsteps of numerous scholars who have argued for the larger unit syllable as a part of phonological representation on the grounds that the notion of possible "word" or morpheme in a language is definable, in large part, on the basis of syllables: a possible "word" is simply a sequence of possible syllables. (The term *word* is placed in quotation marks at this point since we do not intend to imply that the domain of syllabification in English is the word (cf. Selkirk 1982). At present, we employ it to indicate, vaguely, the notion of a domain over which syllable structure is defined.) For example, to use an example from Kahn (1976: 57ff), *atktin* is not a possible "word" of English. Assuming a syllabic analysis of "word" in English, the non-existence of *atktin* is predicted simply from the fact that it cannot be "parsed" as a sequence of well-formed English syllables. (*tk* cannot close a syllable, nor can *kt* begin one.) The matter is not so simple in a theory not making use of the syllable, as Kahn demonstrates: the statements required to rule out such a form are cumbersome, and fail to express the appropriate generalizations. A theory incorporating the syllable is therefore preferable, the argument goes, for it allows for a natural and explanatory statement of the phonotactics of words. Our argument, which has drawn heavily on the insights of Fudge (1969), within a framework roughly corresponding to that of Pike and Pike (1947) and Pike (1967), has been that the phonotactics of the syllable itself lead to the postulation of units of representation within the syllable, that the syllable has an internal immediate constituent structure with labeled nodes.

It would be reasonable to ask that phonological, rule-related evidence be adduced for this particular hypothesis concerning the internal structure of syllables, before it is adopted with any degree of certainty. We are unfortunately not in a position here to answer in full to that demand, but will point out in the course of our examination of English which areas seem to offer promising leads in the search for confirming evidence.

One of these areas is the phonetic study of duration in relation to the hierarchical organization of the utterance.[21] For example, work on the duration of English vowel–glide combinations, which in our analysis together comprise the peak of the syllable, seems to show that they function as a unit on a par with simple vowels, which in our theory are also peaks. Lehiste and Peterson (1960) report that the length of simple vowels and complex vowels (branching peaks) is affected in the same way by the voiceless/voiced property of a following obstruent: vowel length before voiceless vs. voiced is in the ratio of 2:3 in both cases. Fujimura and Lovins (1978) report on additional very promising durational evidence suggesting that vowel and glide form a unit. Evidence such as that provided by Chen (1970), who claims that there is a constancy (approximate) in the length of vowel-plus-stop combinations, could be taken as supporting the existence of the rhyme. According to Chen, a lengthening of the vowel (as before voiced stops) coincides with a shortening of the consonant. That is, one could say that within a constituent like the rhyme the duration of one element is adjusted in function of another.[22] Other areas which bear examination in the light of syllable-internal structure are nasalization,[23] voicing assimilation, and so on.

*1.3*  The conception that we are espousing here of the syllable as a linguistic unit having internal structure and entering, moreover, into a higher-order prosodic structure is at variance with a number of other conceptions of the syllable which have had some currency in present and past work in phonology. Consider first the commonplace view that the syllable is merely that sequence of segments in a representation that is delimited by syllable boundaries or juncture elements. Advocates of the syllable boundary approach to representing the syllable may differ in their ideas about whether syllable boundaries are part of underlying phonological representation, and, if not, about just how they are assigned to the representation, but all agree that, once syllabified, the representation would look something like (13), where a selected symbol, be it "$" or ".", serves as the boundary:

(13)  $  CVC  $  CV  $    or    .  CVC  .  CV  .

This non-hierarchical conception of the syllable has been an extremely popular one in phonological works that do give a place to the syllable in phonological representation. To name just a few of the more prominent adherents of the boundary approach to the syllable, we might cite Bloch and Trager (1942), Trager and Smith (1951), Jones (1956), Hockett (1955), Haugen (1956), Pulgram (1970), Hoard (1971, 1977),[24] Venneman (1972), Hooper (1972, 1976, 1977), and Bailey (1978). This view of the representation of the syllable is perhaps the most obviously available one within the theory of phonological representation which has been prevalent in work in phonology in the last five decades and which is assumed by the above-mentioned, i.e. that phonological representation consists of a strictly linear arrangement of phonemes and boundary or juncture elements.[25] According to this theory, all information relevant to the functioning of phonological rules (or to the statement of phonotactic constraints) must be encoded in the sound segments (= phonemes) or in the boundary or juncture markers which are located between the segments.[26] Syllables are therefore defined in terms of their boundaries.

In the preceding discussion, we have already mentioned some of the drawbacks of a non-hierarchical approach to the syllable. These include its inability to provide an explanation for the sorts of phonotactic constraints on syllable composition that one typically finds in languages. In the absence of an IC analysis of the syllable, many generalizations about the phonotactics of the syllable cannot be given descriptively adequate expression. And the same goes for generalizations concerning phonological processes. The notion 'heavy syllable' cannot be given a unitary characterization along the lines suggested by Pike, Kuryłowicz, and Newman. A general hypothesis concerning the relation between durational constancy and linguistic units longer than, smaller than, or equal to the size of the syllable, such as that advocated by Lehiste (1971), could not even be entertained. No straightforward way of representing the syllable or its subparts as units over which "suprasegmental" features such as emphasis, nasalization, backness, etc. could be predicated could be made available. There would be no means of representing that special relation of relative strength (s vs. w) which one might reasonably claim to obtain between pairs of segments or groups of segments. And finally, no means is afforded of fitting the syllable into a conception of a higher-order hierarchical organization of the utterance which has been shown to be necessary for the proper treatment of such phenomena as stress and rhythm. These reasons in and of themselves are sufficient to justify the rejection of the boundary approach to the representation of the syllable in favor of a hierarchical approach. There is one additional, rather important, reason which *could*, in principle, be adduced, and it involves the phenomenon of ambisyllabicity.

The term *ambisyllabic* or some comparable term such as *interlude* has been employed by phoneticians and phonologists alike[27] to describe consonants which are considered to belong to both a preceding and a following syllable at the same time, as in words like *happy*, *butter*, *coming*, *college*, etc. It has been observed, first of all, that no clear break between the syllables is perceptible in these cases, and, secondly, that the consonants in this context seem to display a special sort of phonological behavior (to be reviewed below). These peculiarities are best explained, the claim goes, by considering the consonants to be ambisyllabic – neither just syllable-initial nor just syllable-final, but both at the same time. Clearly, ambisyllabicity, if it exists, would provide a further argument against the boundary approach to the syllable: a syllable boundary cannot be simultaneously before and after some segment of the string.[28] Were ambisyllabicity not to exist, another, superior, explanation having been found for the special behavior of the consonants in the examples cited, the syllable boundary theory would not be much better off, however, for there still are too many other reasons for rejecting it.

The issue of whether or not these consonants are indeed ambisyllabic is important not just because it may make available yet another argument against syllable boundaries. It is important for the theory of the representation of the syllable that we are developing here and for the theory of hierarchical prosodic structure as a whole, for ambisyllabicity would constitute the sole instance we know of where the tree structures of phonological representation are not well-formed, in the formal sense that a node of the tree (in this case, a terminal element) is immediately dominated by two separate nodes, giving overlapping constituents. We believe that ambisyllabicity does not exist, however, and that the phenomena claimed to result from ambisyllabicity can be expressed eminently well in other terms. (See section 2.)

The most important set of arguments in favor of ambisyllabicity and its role with respect to phonological rules has been put forth by Kahn (1976), and we will examine his analysis as well as the theory of the representation of the syllable within which it is couched. Kahn develops an approach to the syllable which is suprasegmental in the sense that the syllable is a linguistic unit on a level of the phonological representation distinct from the segmental level, and an association between syllable and segments must be defined. But this theory of the syllable is significantly different from ours. To be more precise, Kahn conceives of his as an "autosegmental" theory of the syllable which is quite analogous to the "autosegmental" theory of tone eleborated by Goldsmith (1976) and others. (In Goldsmith's theory, tones are represented on an autosegmental level distinct from the segmental level, and certain universal laws, as well as language-specific rules, govern the association of these tones with the segmental level.) Given Kahn's theory, the representation of *flounce* would be (14):

(14)

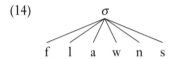

As for the representation of *study*, which is claimed to contain an ambisyllabic conson-ant, it would be converted from the basic (15a) into (15b), where the medial consonant is associated with two syllables.

(15)   (a)

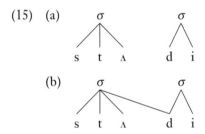

        (b)

But this autosegmental theory of the syllable suffers from the same shortcoming as the boundary theory of the syllable, and so must be rejected.[29] In an autosegmental framework, it is impossible to view the syllable as a structural unit of a fully ramified prosodic structure. There is no sense in which autosegmental entities like tones (or syllables) are arranged in a hierarchy with respect to each other. Thus, the syllable could not be viewed as having an internal structure; nor could it be represented as part of a higher-order prosodic tree. Given this, the same criticisms that were levied against the boundary approach can be levied against Kahn's.[30]

To sum up, we have argued in this section that the syllable has a structure that is to be represented as a well-formed bracketing, in the way described. In the following section we treat the issue of how syllable structure is assigned in the language, and in treating the issue of resyllabification, we present arguments against the notion of ambisyllabicity.

## 2  The Principles of Syllabification

The questions we wish to address in this section are these: How does syllable structure become associated with the phonological representations of a language? What is the nature of the principles of syllabification? In answering them, we must make a distinction between principles of *basic syllable composition* (BSC) and principles of *resyllabification*. The principles of BSC take the form of a template and an accompanying set of collocational restrictions, as discussed and exemplified in sections 1.1 and 1.2. We will not assume that the principles of BSC "apply," in the sense that they participate in a phonological derivation, converting a phonological representation consisting of a sequence of segments into a syllabified phonological representation. Rather, we think of them as well-formedness conditions on underlying phonological representation, which thus is to be thought of as having syllabic structure. As for the principles of resyllabification, which we present below, they may be thought of as participating in a derivation, in the sense that they perform operations on the (already syllabified) phonological representation, modifying it in particular ways.

*2.1*   Recall that in the grammar of English, there is a general template (repeated here as (16)), which specifies the gross features of BSC in the language, an auxiliary template (repeated here as (17)), which permits combinations of *s* plus obstruent to function like a single obstruent with respect to the general template, and a rather detailed set of collocational restrictions, which enumerate the particular co-occurrence restrictions that are not expressible in template form.

(16)

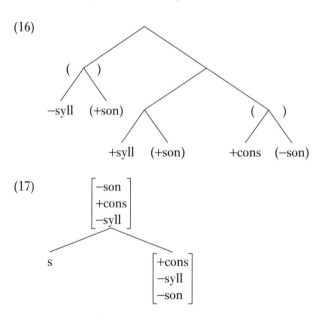

(17)

Taken all together, these define the basic syllable composition of the language. As we suggested in 1.1, a phonological representation will be ruled well-formed if it is non-distinct from the template(s) and does not violate the collocational restrictions. To put it another way, one could say that the grammar rules a phonological representation well-formed if its syllable structure can be *parsed* according to the templates and also satisfies the collocational restrictions.

Consider, for example, the well-formed English monosyllables of (18), in contrast to their un-well-formed counterparts of (19).

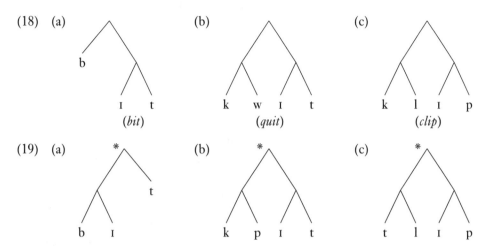

(18) (a) b ɪ t (*bit*)  (b) k w ɪ t (*quit*)  (c) k l ɪ p (*clip*)

(19) (a) * b ɪ t  (b) * k p ɪ t  (c) * t l ɪ p

(19a) is ruled out because of incorrect branching: a [+syll] element may form a constituent only with a consonant that follows, according to template (16). (19b) is out on the grounds that in a bi-consonantal onset, the second consonant must be [+son], unless it is a combination of *s* plus obstruent, following templates (16) and (17). Finally, (19c) is ruled out because there is a collocational restriction which states that in the onset an *l* may not follow a [+cor] consonant.

Turning next to a consideration of polysyllables, it will become clear that several additional conditions must be imposed in defining the well-formedness of the syllabic structure of an utterance. Parsability with respect to the templates and satisfaction of the collocational restrictions are not enough. First, consider the simple case of a word like *allow*. There are two syllable structure analyses of the word that are consistent with the principles of BSC: ʌ.*law* or ʌl.*aw* . (Note that here we adopt the convenience of employing the period to indicate the limits of syllables, since the internal bracketing is irrelevant to our present point.) But only the first is correct (as can be seen from the fact that *l* is pronounced with its light, syllable-initial version). To cite a few additional examples, the syllabifications *pro.strate, ac.tress, ar.cane* are clearly the only correct ones, though *pros.trate, prost.rate, act.ress* and *arc.ane* would all be permissible, given the principles of BSC in English. In general, when a medial consonant or consonant cluster may be analyzed as either a coda or an onset according to BSC, it is the onset analysis which prevails. A number of scholars have proposed that in syllabification (in our terms, the determination of the well-formedness of some syllabic structure) the following universal principle be respected:

(20) *Maximal Syllable Onset Principle*
In the syllable structure of an utterance, the onsets of syllables are maximized, in conformance with the principles of basic syllable composition of the language.[31]

And we concur in considering this principle to be part of linguistic theory.

The (near) minimal pair *pattern* [pæDr̩n] from /pætrn/ vs. *patron* [pejtr̩n] offered by Bloomfield (1933: 122), would seem to suggest that, internal to the syllable, the principle of onset maximalization is not at play. If one assumes that the syllabicity of sonorants comes about as a result of their being accorded the status of peak in the syllable, then we see that in the first case the underlying *trn* is analyzed as (21a), and in the second as (21b):

(21)   (a)                              (b)

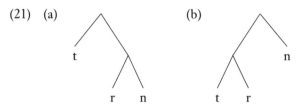

If this interpretation of these facts is correct, then the principle stated in (20) is to be interpreted as one promoting the maximalization of an onset only *with respect to the coda of the preceding syllable.*

Another issue which arises when considering polysyllables, though not in the case of English, has to do with the fact that BSC principles may differ according to the place a syllable happens to occupy in the word. In French, for example, a greater range of onset types is available for word-initial syllables than for syllables placed elsewhere in the word. So, while *sl* or *ps* are permissible onsets in *slave* or *psychologie*, within the word they must belong to separate syllables: *Is.lande, cap.sule.* We will not have anything more to say on the subject here, confining ourselves to the observation that in a general theory of the syllable and syllabification, the principles of BSC may not be identical for all parts of the word.

Finally, a consideration of polysyllables in English brings to the fore the question of the syntactic (i.e. morphological) domain of syllabification. We wish only to point out here that this domain may vary from one language to another, and will therefore have to be specified for each language. In English, this domain is smaller than the word, as is shown by such pairs as *incline* [ɪn.kʰlajn] vs. *inklike* [ɪŋk.lajk]. As we shall see in 2.3 [not repr. here], the aspiration of *k* and voicelessness of *l* in the former case testify to the syllabification that we would expect according to the principles outlined above. *Inklike*, however, does not obey principle (20): the *k* is syllable-final (and therefore non-aspirated), and the *l* is voiced (hence syllable-initial). The limits of the syllables correspond to the limits of the suffix *-like* and the preceding stem. The generalization, we claim, is that the limits of the highest root or, equivalently, the lowest word always coincide with the limits of a syllable, and that the limits of word affixes always coincide with a syllable limit as well (cf. Selkirk 1984). Note, furthermore, that from this it follows that word limits always coincide with syllable limits.

To sum up, we conceive of the principles of basic syllable composition of a language as consisting of a template (with auxiliary templates possible in addition) and a set of collocational restrictions. To be defined as well-formed, the syllable structure of an underlying phonological representation must of necessity satisfy these basic principles. It must moreover satisfy the (universal) principle favoring maximal onsets. And, of central interest to us, it is required to satisfy these principles only within the limits of certain syntactically or morphologically specified domains. [ . . . ]

# Notes

This article was written in 1978, and has been circulated informally since then. It was intended that it should form part of my book *Phonology and Syntax: The Relation between Sound and Structure* [published as Selkirk 1984]. I have decided to publish it separately now, unrevised, for it will not now fit in the book. My views on the nature of syllable structure have changed somewhat since 1978, as have the views of other scholars, but I feel that there is enough of value in the present piece to merit its publication at this time.

1   We are certainly not alone in ascribing internal constituent structure to the syllable. See Pike (1967), Lehiste (1971), Fudge (1969), Fujimura and Lovins (1978), McCarthy (1977) on English syllable structure, and especially Pike and Pike (1947), Newman (1972), Fudge (1969) and McCarthy (1977) on other languages as well.

2   The primary sources of the notion of hierarchical structure within the tradition of generative grammar are Liberman (1975) and Liberman and Prince (1977). See also Lehiste (1970) and Pike (1967).

3   The terms *onset*, *peak*, and *coda* are due originally to Hockett (1955). In employing rhyme to name the constituent including peak and coda, we are following Fudge (1969).

4   See e.g. Bloomfield (1933); Whorf (1940); O'Connor and Trim (1953); Fudge (1969).

5   For some interesting remarks concerning the relation between close transition and syllable constituency in Estonian, see McCarthy (1977).

6   See e.g. Lehn (1973) and Broselow (1976) on Cairo Arabic, and Saib (1978) on Berber.

7   The idea for labeling syllable-internal structure in this way has been attributed to P. Kiparsky.

8   Pike (1967), drawing on E. V. Pike (1954), suggests the ranking according to sonority:

p   t   k
    ç   č
b   d   g
m   n
f   s   x   h
    i   u
        a

The liquids *r*, *l* should presumably find their place somewhere near the vowels. Hierarchies such as these have received quite a bit of attention in recent work on the syllable in phonological theory. (See Hankamer and Aissen (1974), Hooper (1976), among others), for the observation has been made that sounds nearer the extremities of the syllable tend to be less sonorous, according to some such hierarchy, than sounds nearer the center of the syllable. For some discussion of how this observation can be built into a theory of the internally structured and *s/w*-labeled syllable, see McCarthy (1977).

9   Some of the ordering may be predictable according to a universal sonority hierarchy, stipulating that the more sonorous segment types are closer to the center of the syllable, but not all, cf. Hooper (1976).

10   On the distinctness and non-distinctness of feature matrices, see Chomsky and Halle 1968 (henceforth *SPE*), n. 7.

11   Cf. Chomsky and Lasnik (1977) on the notion 'filter'.

12   Below we shall see that *sp, st, sk, sf, spl, str*, etc., apparent counterexamples to these claims about the template, must be accounted for by a special provision, an auxiliary template which does not form part of the general template (6).

13   Fudge (1969) also argues against (−son) (+son) on the grounds that a sonorant which is the sole consonant in an onset does not exhibit the same kinds of restrictions with respect to the composition of the rhyme that a second-position sonorant does. For example, he points out that

syllables with *l* in second position of the onset resist having an *l* inside the rhyme, e.g. **flilt* (but *flint, flit, flirt*), whereas an *l* alone in the onset can occur with a later *l*, e.g. *lilt, loll*. Fudge is quite correct in observing that if such constraints were to be viewed as restrictions on what can co-occur in the various "slots" of the syllable template, no principled distinction between the status of the two *l*'s can be made if the onset of the template is of the form (–son) (+son).

14  We consider *sclerosis, schlitz*, and others to be non-representative.

15  The orthographic *sv*, occurring just once in the English language (*svelte*) is pronounced [sf] and is therefore to be treated as /sf/ phonologically. Note that /sf/ is itself of limited use in the language: it is found in only four or five roots, all of Greek origin.

16  We are indebted to Fudge (1969) and McCarthy (1977) for signaling the importance of this fact.

17  For discussion of the much disputed matter of the phonemic, i.e. phonological, representation of tense vowels *i, u, e, o* in English, see Bloomfield (1933), Trager and Bloch (1941), Swadesh (1947), Pike (1947), and *SPE*, among others.

18  Note that the existence of the [ksθ] coda in *sixth* (the sole one of its kind) requires us to consider that the auxiliary template allows for *sθ* clusters to occupy a single consonant slot. The fact that *sθ* never appears initially would therefore have to be considered as merely accidental. The situation with *sθ* is in a sense the converse of that with *sf*. Initial *sf* clusters are allowed only because of the auxiliary template, just like *sp, st*, and *sk*. But *sf* does not appear in codas. Again, this must be considered to be accidental.

19  These points are developed at greater length in Selkirk (1984: ch. 3).

20  There is one form, the onomatopoetic *oink*, which includes a complex non-coronal coda preceded by a complex peak. We do not consider it to be representative.

21  See, especially, the work of Lehiste (1971).

22  Cf. Chen (1970) and discussion in Fujimura and Lovins (1978).

23  Cf. Malecot (1960), Raphael et al. (1975), Fujimura and Lovins (1978).

24  In earlier work, however, Hoard (1971) seems to advocate a view of the syllable closer in spirit to that of Pike (1967), whereby the syllable forms part of the hierarchical organization of the utterance.

25  This is the theory put forth in generative phonology, see especially *SPE*, with the difference that generative phonology also considers the syntactic-labeled bracketing of a sentence to form part of its phonological representation. Note that *SPE* gives no place to the syllable in phonological theory.

26  In a radical critique of this theory of phonological representation, some members of the London school of prosodic analysis, inspired by Firth (1948), have rejected the segment entirely as a unit of representation, replacing it with the syllable, of which such feature as place and manner of articulation are predicted. See e.g. Henderson (1949). In their recent work on the syllable, Fujimura and Lovins (1978) again pose the question of whether the segment need find a representation, once the syllable is given a place in linguistic theory. Their approach is to reject the segment, but to still allow for a sequential ordering of feature specifications within the syllable.

27  See e.g. Bloch and Trager (1942), Jones (1956), Pike (1967), Hockett (1955), Rischel (1964).

28  Any suggestions that the boundary be placed in the "middle" of the segment in such cases (as has been advanced by Hyman 1977, e.g.) is incoherent, given the theory of phonological representation in which it is concluded, and vitiates the whole boundary approach.

29  Note that the autosegmental theory of the syllable is by no means merely a notational variant of the syllable boundary theory, as Hooper (1976) declares. One major difference is the possibility of representing ambisyllabicity.

30  The syllable theory of Anderson and Jones (1974) and Jones (1976) can be taken to be similar in some respects to that of Kahn, insofar as the syllable is viewed as a suprasegmental entity and non-well-formed trees are allowed. In their system, medial consonant sequences are systematically ambisyllabic: as long as a consonant sequence is a permissible syllable-initial sequence as well as a permissible syllable-final sequence, it is always treated as ambisyllabic. There are some serious drawbacks to this approach, as Vogel (1977) and Hoard (1971) have pointed out.

31  In some form or other the principle is assumed, or explicitly stated, by Hoard (1971), Hooper (1976), Kahn (1976), among others.

# References

Anderson, J. M. and C. Jones. 1974. *Phonological Structure and the History of English*. Amsterdam: North-Holland Publishing Company.

Bailey, C. J. 1977. The syllable: syllabization and markedness. Paper presented at the Symposium on Syllable and Segment Organization, University of Colorado at Boulder, October 1977.

Bell, A. and J. Bybee Hooper (eds). 1978. *Syllables and Segments*. Amsterdam: North-Holland Publishing Co.

Bloch, B. and G. L. Trager. 1942. *Outline of Linguistic Analysis*. Linguistic Society of America Special Publication. Baltimore: Waverly Press.

Bloomfield, Leonard. 1933. *Language*. New York: Holt. Repr., Chicago: University of Chicago Press.

Broselow, Ellen. 1976. The Phonology of Egyptian Arabic. Ph.D. dissertation, University of Massachusetts, Amherst.

Chen, M. 1970. Vowel length variation as a function of the voicing of the consonant environment. *Phonetica* 22, 129–59.

Chomsky, Noam, and Morris Halle. 1968. *The Sound Pattern of English*. New York: Harper and Row.

Chomsky, Noam and Howard Lasnik. 1977. Filters and control. *Linguistic Inquiry* 8, 425–504.

Firth, J. R. 1948. Sounds and prosodies. *Transactions of the Philological Society*, 127–52. Repr. in F. R. Palmer (ed.), *Prosodic Analysis* (London: Oxford University Press, 1970), 1–26.

Fudge, E. C. 1969. Syllables. *Journal of Linguistics* 3, 253–86. [Repr. here in part as ch. 19]

Fujimura, Osamu and J. Lovins. 1978. Syllables as concatenative phonetic units. In Bell and Hooper 1978: 107–20.

Goldsmith, John. 1976. Autosegmental Phonology. Ph.D. dissertation, MIT.

Hankamer, Jorge and Judith Aissen. 1974. The sonority hierarchy. In A. Bruck, R. A. Fox, and M. W. Lagaly (eds), *Papers from the Parasession on Natural Phonology of the Chicago Linguistic Society*, 131–45.

Haugen, Einar. 1956. The syllable in linguistic description. In M. Halle et al. (eds), *For Roman Jakobson*, The Hague: Mouton, 213–21.

Henderson, E. J. 1949. Prosodies in Siamese. *Asia Minor*, NS i, 189–215. Repr. in F. R. Palmer (ed.), *Prosodic Analysis* (London: Oxford University Press, 1970).

Hoard, James. 1971. Aspiration, tenseness and syllabicization in English. *Language* 47, 133–40.

Hockett, Charles. 1955. *A Manual of Phonology*. Indiana University Publications in Anthropology and Linguistics, 11 *International Journal of American Linguistics* 21/4: part 1.

Hooper, Joan Bybee. 1972. The syllable in phonological theory. *Language* 48, 525–40.

Hooper, Joan Bybee. 1976. *An Introduction to Natural Generative Phonology*. New York: Academic Press.

Hyman, L. 1977. On the nature of linguistic stress. In L. Hyman (ed.), *Studies in Stress and Accent*, Los Angeles: University of Southern California Press, 37–82.

Jones, C. 1976. Some constraints on medial consonant clusters. *Language* 52, 121–30.

Jones, D. 1956. The hyphen as a phonetic sign – a contribution to the theory of syllable division and juncture. *Zeitschrift für Phonetik und Allgemeine Sprachwissenschaft* 9/2, 99–107.

Kahn, Daniel. 1976. Syllable-based Generalizations in English Phonology. Ph.D. dissertation, MIT.

Kuryłowicz, J. 1948. Contribution à la théorie de la syllabe. *Biuletin Poskiego Towarszistwa Jezyko-Znawaczego* 8, 80–113.

Lehiste, Ilse. 1971. Temporal organization of spoken language. In L. L. Hammereich, R. Jakobson, and E. Zwirner (eds), *Form and Substance: Phonetic and Linguistic Papers Presented to Eli Fischer-Jørgensen*, Copenhagen: Akademisk Forlag, 159–69.

Lehiste, Ilse and G. Peterson. 1960. Duration of syllable nuclei in English. *Journal of the Acoustical Society of America* 32, 693–703.

Lehn, W. 1973. Emphasis in Cairo Arabic. *Language* 39, 29–39.

Liberman, Mark. 1975. The Intonational System of English. Ph.D. dissertation, MIT.

Liberman, Mark and Alan Prince 1977. On stress and linguistic rhythm. *Linguistic Inquiry* 8, 249–336.

Malecot, A. 1960. Vowel nasality as a distinctive feature in American English. *Language* 36, 222–9.

McCarthy, John. 1977. On hierarchic structure within syllables. Unpublished MS, MIT.

Newman, Paul. 1972. Syllable weight as a phonological variable: the nature and function of the contrast between "heavy" and "light" syllables. *Studies in African Linguistics* 3, 301–23.

O'Connor, J. D. and J. L. M. Trim. 1953. Vowel, consonant, syllable – a phonological definition. *Word* 9, 103–22.

Pike, E. V. 1954. Phonetic rank and subordination in consonant patterning and historical change. *Miscellanea Phonetica* 2, 25–41.

Pike, Kenneth. 1947. Grammatical prerequisites to phonemic analysis. *Word* 3, 155–72.

Pike, Kenneth. 1967. *Language in Relation to a Unified Theory of the Structure of Human Behavior*. The Hague: Mouton.

Pike, Kenneth and E. V. Pike. 1947. Immediate constituents of Mazateco syllables. *International Journal of American Linguistics* 13, 78–91.

Pulgram, E. 1970. *Syllable, Word, Nexus, Cursus*. The Hague: Mouton.

Raphael, L. J., M. F. Dorman, F. Freeman, and C. Tobin. 1975. Vowel and nasal duration as cues to voicing in word-final stop consonants: spectrographic and perceptual studies. *Journal of Speech and Hearing Research* 18, 389–400.

Rischel, J. 1964. Stress, juncture and syllabification in phonemic description. In *The Proceedings of the Ninth International Congress of Linguists, Cambridge, Massachusetts 1962*, The Hague: Mouton, 85–93.

Saib, J. 1978. Segment organization and the syllable in Tamazight Berber. In Bell and Hooper 1978: 93–106.

Selkirk, Elisabeth. 1980. The role of prosodic categories in English word stress. *Linguistic Inquiry* 11/1.

Selkirk, Elisabeth. 1982. *The Syntax of Words*. Linguistic Inquiry Monograph Series. Cambridge, Mass.: MIT Press.

Selkirk, Elisabeth 1984: *Phonology and Syntax: The Relation between Sound and Structure*. Cambridge, Mass.: MIT Press.

Swadesh, Morris. 1947. On the analysis of English syllabics. *Language* 23, 137–50.

Trager, G. L. and Bernard Bloch. 1941. The syllabic phonemes of English. *Language* 17, 223–46.

Trager, G. L. and H. D. Smith. 1951. *An Outline of English Structure*. Studies in Linguistics, Occasional Papers, 3. Normal, Okla. Battenberg Press.

Vennemann, T. 1972. On the theory of syllabic phonology. *Linguistische Berichte* 18, 1–18.

Vergnaud, J.-R. 1976. Formal properties of phonological rules. In J. Butts and J. Hintikka (eds), *Basic Problems in Methodology and Linguistics*, Dordrecht: Reidel, 299–318.

Vogel, Irene. 1977. The Syllable in Phonological Theory with Special Reference to Italian. Ph.D. dissertation, Stanford University.

Whorf, B. L. 1940. Linguistics as an exact science. In J. B. Carroll (ed.) *Language, Thought and Reality*, Cambridge, Mass.: MIT Press, 220–32.

# 18

# Compensatory Lengthening in Moraic Phonology (1989)

## Bruce Hayes

## 1 Introduction: The Prosodic Tier

The structure of the CV tier and its formal descendants has been a matter of much debate in phonological theory. The original CV tier proposed by McCarthy (1979) has been retained to the present by some researchers, but has also been challenged by other theories of prosodic tier structure. Levin (1985) and Lowenstamm and Kaye (1986) have proposed to replace the symbols C and V with a uniform sequence of elements, represented here as Xs. The elements of this "X tier" are distinguished from each other by their organization into a fairly rich syllable structure, which includes a nucleus node:

(1)  (a)  *CV Theory*

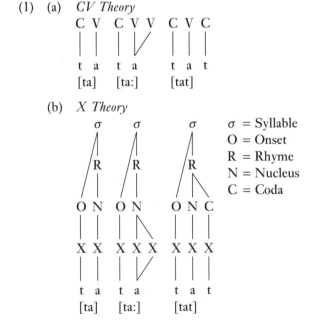

(b)  *X Theory*

σ = Syllable
O = Onset
R = Rhyme
N = Nucleus
C = Coda

Both CV theory and X theory can be characterized as *segmental* theories of the prosodic tier: the number of prosodic elements in an utterance corresponds intuitively to the number of segments it contains.

Hyman (1984, 1985) and McCarthy and Prince (1986) have suggested a more radical proposal. The prosodic tier they favor has just one kind of unit, as in X theory, but instead of representing a segment, this unit represents the traditional notion of *mora*. The mora has a dual role in this theory. First, it represents the well-known contrast between light and heavy syllables: a light syllable has one mora, a heavy syllable two. Second, the mora counts as a phonological position: just as in earlier theories, a long segment is normally represented as being doubly linked. In the version of moraic theory I adopt here, the schematic syllables under (1) would be represented as in (2), where $\mu$ = mora:

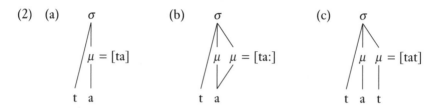

(2)  (a)   $\sigma$          (b)   $\sigma$          (c)   $\sigma$

$\mu$ = [ta]        $\mu$ $\mu$ = [ta:]        $\mu$ $\mu$ = [tat]

t  a              t  a              t  a  t

Moraic theory is not a segmental theory, as there is no level at which segment count is depicted. McCarthy and Prince take this as an advantage of the theory, in that there are no known phonological processes that count segments, although many processes count moras or syllables.

In this article I argue that the proposals of Hyman, McCarthy, and Prince for a moraic theory of segment structure are supported by typological observations about compensatory lengthening. I will make three basic points.

First, compensatory lengthening (hereafter CL) is subject to prosodic constraints: segments that undergo deletion yield CL only if they occupy particular positions within the syllable. Moreover, the choice of the nearby segment that lengthens to compensate for deletion is also limited. Such constraints show that CL is guided by a *prosodic frame* encompassing the relevant segments; the structure of the prosodic frame determines which segments may trigger CL when deleted and which segments may lengthen compensatorily.

Second, moraic theory is well suited for the formal description of the prosodic frame, but segmental prosodic theories (X theory and CV theory) are not. In fact, when such theories are beefed up sufficiently to handle the full range of CL types, they reduce to something like the claim that any segment can lengthen to compensate for the loss of any other segment. This claim goes against a large body of evidence.

Third, as de Chene and Anderson (1979) originally suggested, the prosodic frame that governs CL is partly *language-specific*. In particular, only languages that have a syllable weight distinction allow CL. This fact also distinguishes the various theories: moraic theory posits partly language-specific prosodic structures, which vary according to a language's criterion of syllable weight. In contrast, segmental prosodic theories assign the same structure to the same sequence (for the relevant purposes) in all languages. The moraic theory thus captures a cross-linguistic distinction missed by segmental prosodic theories.

This article is organized as follows. I first outline a specific version of moraic theory. Next, I show how simple cases of CL are accounted for by moraic and by segmental prosodic theories. I then discuss more unusual cases of CL and point out the expansions that they require in the power of segmental prosodic theories. This somewhat detailed section is crucial to the argument: the aspects of CL that I propose to explain through the notion of prosodic frame might also be explained by limiting the possible melody-to-skeleton associations permitted in segmental prosodic theories. What I will show is that no such limitations are tenable.

With this done, I give the central argument: the typology of CL demonstrates that it takes place within a prosodic frame of the kind provided in moraic theory, and the segmental prosodic theories are unable to account for the same facts. Further, I show that the segmental prosodic theories are unable to account for the correlation of CL with language-specific criteria of syllable weight.

In the remaining sections I discuss some additional issues in moraic theory, examine earlier work, and summarize the results.

For convenience, in what follows I will use X theory as the representative of all segmental prosodic theories. The arguments against X theory can be translated into arguments against CV theory without difficulty.


## 2   Moraic Phonology


An important aspect of both Hyman's (1985) and McCarthy and Prince's (1986) work is the claim that the moraic structure of languages can vary. For instance, in some languages (such as Latin) CVV and CVC syllables count as heavy and CV as light; whereas in others (such as Lardil) only CVV is heavy, and both CVC and CV are light. The claim of moraic theory is that these languages differ in their rules for assigning moraic structure; CVC is assigned two moras in Latin and one mora in Lardil.

Languages that exhibit a syllable weight distinction typically also have a vowel length distinction, and vice versa. This is to be expected in a moraic theory, since the same formal configuration, bimoraic syllables, is used to represent both. We would not expect the correlation to be absolute, however: a few languages allow heavy syllables but do not permit a vowel to occupy two moras (see below); and a language could in principle have long vowels but happen to lack phonological rules that diagnose a syllable weight distinction.

The existence of language-particular moraic structure is an important part of the theory: it predicts that in the absence of additional adjustment rules, the same criterion of syllable weight will be relevant throughout the phonology of a single language (Hyman (1985: 12)). Thus, in Latin (Allen 1973) CVC counts as heavy for multiple rules and constraints (for instance, stress, metrics, and Iambic Shortening). In contrast, in Lardil several rules (truncation, augmentation, reduplication) count CVC as light (Hale 1973, Wilkinson 1988).

Although isolated problems exist, the idea of language-particular moraic structure seems well motivated. Contrary to the (implicit) prediction of *SPE* (Chomsky and Halle 1968), a typical phonology is not a random collection of possible rules but an integrated system. By factoring out moraic structure as an overall property of a language's phonology, we come closer to a theory that describes phonological systems rather than just rule collections. As we will see, the matter of language-particular phonological structure becomes particularly clear in reference to CL.

## 2.1    Underlying forms and rules

An explicit moraic theory must characterize the ways in which individual languages assign moraic structure and, where possible, also develop principles that are invariant across languages.

Languages differ in the extent to which moraic structure is phonologically contrastive. Below I discuss the moraic structures that must occur in underlying forms for at least some languages, noting that in other languages the same structures may be derivable by rule. My account follows in certain respects the proposals of van der Hulst 1984: 68–73).

In languages with contrastive vowel length, long vowels have two moras, short vowels one. I assume that this is reflected directly in underlying forms:

(3)    (a)    $\mu\ \mu$    (b)    $\mu$

$$ = \text{/i:/} \qquad\qquad = \text{/i/} $$

i    i

It is often assumed that syllabicity is not represented on the segmental tier. If this is the case, we must face the fact that there are languages in which glides and short vowels contrast (see Guerssel 1986 for Berber, Harris 1987 for Spanish, and Hayes and Abad 1989 for Ilokano). This contrast can be represented if we adapt an idea of Guerssel's and assign no mora at all to an underlying glide, as in (4):

(4)    =    /y/

i

The basic principle assumed is that segments receive the same number of moras underlyingly that, in the absence of additional rules, they will bear on the surface.

This principle can be extended to consonants. Ordinary short consonants are represented as underlyingly moraless, giving them the same underlying structure as glides:

(5)    =    /n/

n

The claim is that short consonants will not bear a mora unless assigned one by rule (see below).

Geminates almost always bear a mora; for example, a sequence like [anna] has three moras, versus two for [ana]. To distinguish geminates from single consonants, I assign them a single mora underlyingly:

(6)  μ

   |  = /nn/

   n

The surface double linking of a geminate is derived by the rules of syllabification outlined below and is not present in underlying forms, as in segmental prosodic theories.
   The remaining case is a consonant linked underlyingly to two moras:

(7)  μ  μ

   n

This configuration is rare, but it does appear in Kimatuumbi (Odden 1981), which permits long syllabic [m̩m̩,n̩n̩,ŋ̩ŋ̩], and in Gokana (Hyman 1985: 42), which has [m̩m̩].
   The structures outlined in (3)–(7) receive their explicit interpretation when they
are grouped into syllables by a syllabification algorithm. Syllabification has attracted
sophisticated theoretical attention (see, for example, Steriade 1982, Dell and Elmedlaoui
1985, and Itô 1986), and the following is intended only as a cursory account. I suggest
that syllabification consists of the following: (a) selection of certain sonorous moraic
segments, on a language-specific basis, for domination by a syllable node; (b) adjunction
of onset consonants to the syllable node, and of coda consonants to the preceding mora.
Adjunction is subject to language-specific conditions on syllable well-formedness and
the division of intervocalic clusters. The following schematic derivations illustrate the
procedure:

(8)  (a)

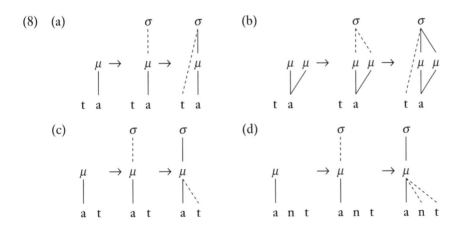

I assume that an underlying geminate (one mora) or long syllabic consonant (two moras)
has its consonant melody "flopped" onto a following vowel-initial syllable. This creates
an onset (hence a preferred syllable structure) without disrupting moraic value:

(9)   (a)

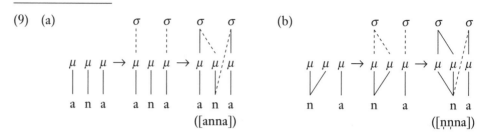

It can be seen that the proposed underlying form for a geminate is not so abstract as it might first seem, since the underlying form depicts the surface moraic value. The general principle is that contrastive mora count, not length *per se*, is represented underlyingly.

Moraic consonants sometimes occur without an adjacent vowel, as in the case of syllabic nasals (for instance, [n̩ta]). Such moraic consonants can have the same underlying representation as geminates, the difference being that the flopping process of (9) is inapplicable, so that the consonant bears only one link on the surface and serves as the nucleus of a separate syllable. The existence of the flopping process described under (9) is supported by the patterning of syllabic nasals in Gokana (Hyman 1985: 41), where it accounts for actual alternations such as [m̩] 'inside' ~ [m̩mĩ] 'inside this', from /m̩-í/.

The next ingredient of the analysis is the set of language-specific rules that supply "weight by position" – in other words, render closed syllables heavy in certain languages. The basic idea is that certain coda consonants are given a mora when they are adjoined to the syllable, by the following rule schema:

(10)   *Weight by Position*

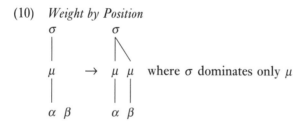

where $\sigma$ dominates only $\mu$

Following earlier work, I assume that prevocalic consonants must be parsed as nonmoraic onset elements, and thus can never receive weight by position. The Weight by Position rule is illustrated in (11) with schematic forms for a language in which all closed syllables count as heavy.

The scheme just outlined is the most typical case for languages in which CVC counts as heavy. We must also account for languages like Lardil, where CVC is light. I assume that such languages have no Weight by Position rule, so that the final consonant is made a daughter of the final mora. Hyman (1985: 8) points out that in some languages only a subset of the consonants make their syllable heavy when they occur in coda position. This can be described by placing restrictions on $\beta$ in the language-particular version of the Weight by Position rule.

(11)

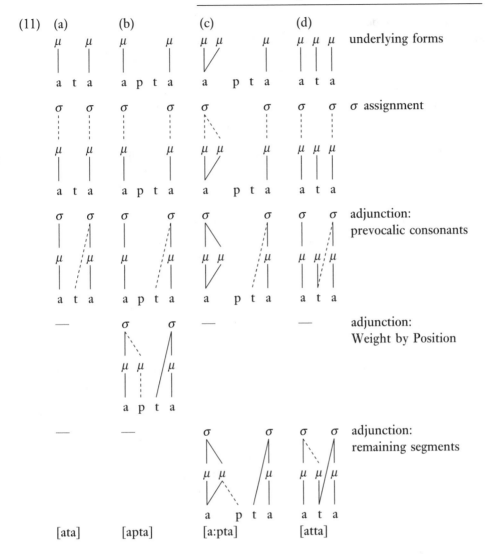

Weight by Position is formulated to produce syllables with a maximum of two moras. This is a strong claim; it says that distinctions of syllable weight are at most binary. The claim is probably too strong, and I will return to this issue later in the article [not repr. here].

This completes the set of rules for assigning moraic structure. Note that the full variety of underlying forms is relevant only for languages that employ moraic structure contrastively; in fact, many languages need not include moras in underlying forms at all. If (a) the distribution of high vowels and glides is predictable, (b) there is no vowel length contrast, and (c) there are no geminates, then underlying forms may consist simply of segmental strings, with all moras inserted by rule.

My proposal differs somewhat from those of Hyman and of McCarthy and Prince. The main argument for my analysis is that it provides the simplest description of possible contrasts in mora count. The three-way contrast in the vocoid series /y/–/i/–/i:/ is represented as the distinction between zero, one, and two moras, which is the same as the surface mora count of these segments. The three-way contrast among consonants shown in (5)–(7) is also represented as a zero–one–two contrast in mora count, again reflecting surface form. By adopting these underlying forms, I believe that most of the criticisms of moraic phonology made by Odden (1986b) can be answered satisfactorily.

My proposal is also to be preferred, I believe, to accounts that place actual syllable structure (rather than just moraic structure) in underlying forms. The reason is that there are apparently no cases in which the division of consonants into syllables is underlyingly contrastive, as for example in /a.bla/ versus /ab.la/. A theory that includes full syllable structures in underlying forms predicts that these could exist. My claim is that there is no such thing as contrastive syllabification, only contrastive mora structure.

To summarize so far, I assume that moras appear in underlying representation, to represent length and syllabicity contrasts. Moras can also be created by language-specific versions of the Weight by Position rule. Other than that, nonmoraic segments are simply adjoined to the appropriate position: the mora for syllable-final consonants and the syllable for syllable-initial consonants. The representations that result appear to be adequate for the two tasks that moraic theory must carry out: representation of segment length and of syllable weight.[1]

## 3   Compensatory Lengthening in X Theory and Moraic Theory

Compensatory lengthening can be defined as the lengthening of a segment triggered by the deletion or shortening of a nearby segment. Here is a simple example, taken from Ingria 1980. In Latin the segment /s/ was deleted before anterior sonorants (it apparently went through an intermediate stage of [z]; I ignore this and other complications). When the deleted /s/ followed a vowel, the vowel became long, as shown in (12):

(12)   (a)   s → Ø / ___ $\begin{bmatrix} +son \\ +ant \end{bmatrix}$

      (b)   *kasnus   →   ka:nus   'gray'
           *kosmis   →   ko:mis   'courteous'
           *fideslia   →   fide:lia   'pot'

A strictly linear theory of phonology, such as that proposed in *SPE*, has difficulties in describing this change. The /kasnus/ → [ka:nus] case can be described using trans-formational notation, as in (13):

(13)   (a)   V s $\begin{bmatrix} +son \\ +ant \end{bmatrix}$
        1 2  3   → 1 1 3
     (b)   /kasnus/ → kaanus = [ka:nus]

However, this rule turns out not to cover all the relevant cases, because *word-initial* /s/ also deleted before anterior sonorants:

(14)  *smereo:     →   mereo:      'deserve-1 sg.-pres.'
      *snurus      →   nurus       'daughter-in-law'
      *slu:brikus  →   lu:brikus   'slippery'

Rule (13a) fails to predict this. The problem that a linear phonological theory faces is to formulate a rule that deletes /s/, compensatorily lengthens a preceding vowel, yet is also able to delete /s/ when no vowel precedes it. There is no clear solution to the problem in linear theory.[2]

Both X theory and moraic theory are able to overcome this difficulty.

## 3.1   X theory

In X theory, the central insight is that the deletion of /s/ must take place on the segmental tier only. This leaves an empty X slot on the prosodic tier. If we then assume a rule that spreads a vowel melody onto a following tautosyllabic empty X position, we derive a long vowel. Note that in the derivation of (15c), I have suppressed the Rhyme node, a practice I will follow throughout to save space.

(15)  (a)   /s/ Deletion
            $s \rightarrow \emptyset$ / ____  $\begin{bmatrix} +son \\ +ant \end{bmatrix}$     (segmental tier only)

      (b)   Compensatory Lengthening
            X X']$_{syl}$   where X' is an unaffiliated prosodic position

            $\alpha$

      (c)   Example: *kasnus → ka:nus

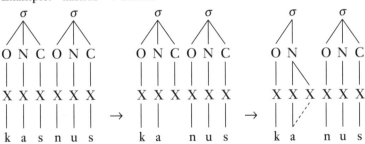

In (15c) the output form has undergone readjustment of its syllable structure, so that the newly created long vowel is syllabified as a long nucleus rather than as a nucleus + coda sequence. The assumption behind this, following McCarthy (1979) and others, is that syllabification applies throughout the derivation to adjust the ill-formed outputs of rules. This assumption will be important in what follows.

For the cases in Latin where /s/ deletes initially, I assume a convention that is widely supported in the literature: stray elements that are not filled by rule are deleted. This allows /s/ to disappear word-initially without a phonetic trace:

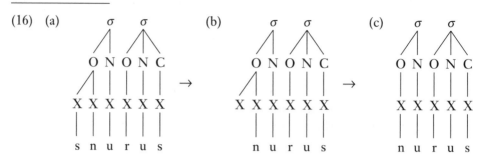

This argument for X theory is due to Ingria (1980). He expresses it in a different notation, which I have translated for consistency.

## 3.2  Moraic theory

The moraic account of the Latin facts would be essentially the same as in X theory: the /s/ deletes only on the segmental tier, as in (17a). If a mora is stranded, it is filled by spreading from an immediately preceding vowel by the rule stated in (17b).

(17)  (a)  */s/ Deletion*

$$s \rightarrow \emptyset / \underline{\hspace{1em}} \begin{bmatrix} +son \\ +ant \end{bmatrix} \qquad \text{(segmental tier only)}$$

(b)  *Compensatory Lengthening*

$\mu \quad \mu'$     where $\mu'$ is a segmentally unaffiliated mora

$\alpha$

(c)

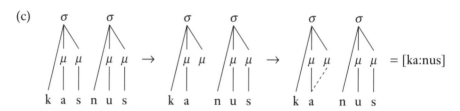

The assignment of a mora to the coda consonant /s/ is well motivate: CVC syllables in Latin behave as heavy for purposes of stress, metrics, and other phenomena.

If the /s/ is word-initial, it has no moraic value. Because of this, /s/ Deletion word-initially does not strand anything, and nothing further happens.

(18)

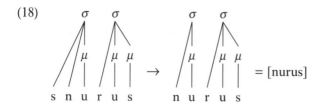

Note that moraic theory provides a somewhat neater account of the CL process. We need not stipulate that vowel melodies spread only onto syllable-final empty positions, because it is only in syllable-final position that an empty position is created – this is independently motivated by the fact that only syllable-final consonants make their syllable heavy. This point will be made in more forceful terms later on.

To summarize: both X theory and moraic theory can provide an adequate account of Latin CL, as well as a large number of parallel cases. Thus both are a clear improvement over a linear model of phonology. The crucial principle common to both theories, which will be important later, is the following: for CL to occur, deletion must create an empty prosodic position (X or $\mu$).

## 3.3   On the status of compensatory lengthening conventions

In both (15b) and (17b) the CL process is stated as though it were a language-specific phonological rule. This is unsatisfactory, as one would like to make CL an automatic consequence of the deletion. For this reason, Ingria (1980), Steriade (1982), and others have suggested universal conventions that yield CL as an automatic result.

The difficulty with this is that some languages (for instance, Finnish) lack CL entirely, even though long vowels are possible and the relevant deletion processes exist. Further, certain other languages (for instance, Lesbian and Thessalian Greek (Steriade 1982, Wetzels 1986) fill an empty syllable-final position not by lengthening the vowel but by spreading the following consonant leftward to create a geminate. In Tiberian Hebrew (Lowenstamm and Kaye 1986) the situation is more complex: empty coda positions are filled by gemination in the normal case, but by vowel lengthening when the following consonant belongs to the class of gutturals, which do not permit gemination.

On the other hand, there are facts suggesting that it would be wrong to characterize CL as a language-particular phonological rule, ordered among the other rules. The reason is that in a number of languages (for instance, Ancient Greek (Steriade 1982, Wetzels 1986), Turkish (Sezer 1986), and Latin (Bichakjian 1986)) several distinct deletion rules lead to CL. If CL is a rule, and if we are to analyze the system without loss of generality, then CL must be ordered after all the deletion rules that trigger it. But this implies that empty elements persist through much of the derivation (from the first deletion rule up to the CL rule), a claim that is unsupported by the evidence and leads to considerable excess descriptive power (Dresher 1985). The more reasonable assumption, then, is that CL occurs immediately following every deletion rule. This implies that CL cannot be an ordinary, linearly ordered phonological rule.

The correct view, I believe, is that CL rules such as (17b) form part of the *syllabification principles* of individual languages. That is, the way in which empty prosodic positions are provided with segmental content forms part of syllabification. The syllable-forming rules for an individual language may specify that empty prosodic positions are syllabified by spreading from the preceding vowel (as in Latin and most dialects of Ancient Greek), or from the following consonant (as in Lesbian and Thessalian Greek), or not at all (as in Finnish), or even variably, depending on whether the following consonant is allowed as a geminate, as in Tiberian Hebrew.

Attributing CL to syllabification provides a plausible account of two facts. First, as McCarthy (1979) has argued, syllabification rules apply whenever their structural description is met. Second, syllabification rules are language-specific, within certain universally determined limits. These two properties are what we want to attribute to CL: typically, it is pervasive within an individual language, but the mechanism that yields it is not universal.

It may be asked why a spreading operation should be included in the syllabification mechanisms. A plausible account of this is provided by Itô's (1986) notion of Prosodic Licensing: phonological material must be incorporated into the next higher level of prosodic structure; otherwise, it is deleted by Stray Erasure (Steriade 1982, Harris 1983). A natural extension of this principle would state that higher-level phonological elements, such as moras, are also subject to Stray Erasure if they fail to dominate any lower-level element. The spreading operations embodied in language-specific CL conventions form part of the syllabification algorithm because they have the effect of licensing empty moras.

A final note: even in a language whose syllabification principles include a CL convention, CL is *not* the inevitable result of consonant loss in the environment of vowels, even in languages that have phonemic vowel length. For example, Sezer (1986) shows that some, but not all, of the consonant deletion rules of Turkish lead to CL. An adequate theory of CL must allow for the phenomenon, but not require it. This is in fact straightforward in multitiered theories, because rules of deletion can be stated in more than one way. If consonant loss is expressed as deletion of an entire segment complex, including the associated element on the prosodic tier (X or $\mu$), then there will be no CL, because there will be no stranded element. In what follows I will focus on rules in which deletion takes place on the segmental tier only, so that CL is possible. However, it should be kept in mind that the occurrence of CL is not a necessary prediction of the theory. [ . . . ]

## 9   Conclusions

The central claim I have argued for is that CL is not a random collection of temporal compensations for segment loss. Rather, it operates in lawful fashion, respecting prosodic structure in a way that is correctly characterized by moraic theory. There are two crucial phenomena: (a) CL does not compensate for segments lost from onset position. Since onset consonants do not make weight, they are not assigned prosodic positions in moraic theory, and thus do not induce temporal compensation when they are lost. (b) CL is confined to languages that have a syllable weight contrast. Moraic theory explains this by making prosodic structure partly language-specific: only languages with a syllable weight distinction have bimoraic syllables; hence, only such languages can have CL.

X theory (as well as its variants) is singularly unsuited to describing these patterns. It assigns the same prosodic structure to identical sequences across languages, irrespective of the presence or absence of a syllable weight contrast. Thus it is unable to explain why CL occurs only when there is a preexisting syllable weight distinction. Moreover, X theory assigns every segment in the string its own prosodic position, including onset segments. It thus fails to explain why onset segments do not induce temporal compensation when they are lost. One might attempt to recover the missing prediction by placing constraints on what segments may associate with what positions in the syllable.

As I have tried to show, however, when X theory is applied to the more exotic types of CL, such constraints prove to be untenable; the situation comes close to one in which anything can link to anything. Once this is admitted, the claim of X theory is essentially that any segment can lengthen to compensate for the disappearance of any other segment. This is clearly the wrong prediction to make.

I have also discussed a less well studied type of CL, in which the loss of a vowel leads to CL in the preceding syllable. The proposed mechanism for this is Parasitic Delinking, whereby vowel loss induces loss of syllable structure, rendering a stray mora accessible to the preceding syllable. This mechanism makes a general prediction: when a stranded mora moves to a different syllable on the surface, such movement must always be to the left, since rightward movement would violate the ban on crossed association lines. All the cases of trans-syllabic movement I have found so far (the vowel loss cases, Ilokano, and *Managerial* Lengthening) involve movement to the left.

Finally, I have suggested that a number of phenomena support the existence of trimoraic syllables. In the best-studied case, Estonian, it appears that a trimoraic account offers substantial advantages over the alternative metrical analysis.

## Appendix: Further Issues in Moraic Theory

The main body of this article focuses on issues of CL. However, moraic theory has many consequences elsewhere in phonology, and a fair comparison of theories requires us to consider whether there are any significant results that can be obtained under segmental prosodic theories that cannot be obtained under moraic theory. My own view is that this is not the case, and I will try to support this view in the following discussion.

### A1   Onsets and rhymes

The version of moraic theory I have adopted posits that the syllable contains no onset or rhyme constituents, and it must therefore provide an alternative account of the evidence that has been presented in the literature in favor of onsets and rhymes. I believe that although this evidence involves genuine and significant cross-linguistic generalizations, it is not necessarily best interpreted as requiring onset/rhyme constituency. The three most significant arguments are as follows.

First, the rhyme is supported by its ability to express syllable weight distinctions, as branching versus nonbranching. This clearly does not distinguish between theories, as moraic theory can express the same distinction with mora count.

A second argument is discussed by Harris (1983) and Steriade (1988): many phonological rules (such as English /r/ Dropping, Cuban Spanish /n/ Velarization) are difficult to characterize in linear terms or with a structureless syllable but can be straightforwardly described as applying to segments within the rhyme. The observation seems valid, but as Donca Steriade (personal communication) has suggested to me, the relevant distinctions can be reconstructed in moraic theory. If we assume that onset consonants depend directly from the syllable node (McCarthy and Prince 1986), rather than from the first mora (Hyman 1985), then the notion of "rhyme-internal segment" can be reformulated as "segment dominated by $\mu$." Steriade points out that this offers an additional theory-internal advantage: we can state that in the unmarked case association of moras and segments is one-to-one.

A third argument for onsets and rhymes is based on the fact that co-occurrence restrictions on segments within the syllable are typically confined to onset-internal sequences and rhyme-internal sequences; that is, in the normal case a well-formed onset plus a well-formed rhyme equals a well-formed syllable. Though this is not a universal, it is defended as a strong tendency by Fudge (1987).

This generalization can also be characterized without the use of the rhyme: such constraints characteristically are constraints on total syllable weight, and thus are aptly stated moraically. For example, in Hausa and many other languages the possible syllables are CV, CVV, and CVC; *CVVC and *CVCC are excluded. This could be described as involving an upper limit on rhyme length of two segments. But it could equally be characterized as a limit of two moras per syllable and one segment per mora. Similarly, the well-known English constraint that allows /paynt/, but not */paymp/ and */payŋk/ (Fudge 1987: 369), can also be stated moraically: the upper limit on moras is two, and only coronals may occur after the second segment of a mora.

It remains to be seen whether there is a true asymmetry in vowel-onset versus vowel-coda dependencies, not based on weight, which would motivate onset and rhyme constituents.

McCarthy and Prince (1986) discuss these and other issues, such as language games said to involve movement of the onset. In no case does there appear to be compelling evidence for onset/rhyme constituency. I differ from McCarthy and Prince only in explicitly rejecting the possibility of grouping consonants under onset or coda nodes. Such nodes could in principle count as prosodic positions, which, as I have shown, must be avoided.

## A2   Contour segments

Affricates and other contour segments are sequential in featural content but phonologically monosegmental. Segmental prosodic theories represent them as segment sequences linked to a single slot. For example, Clements and Keyser (1983: 35) represent the distinction between Polish /či/ 'whether' and /tši/ 'three' as in (86):

(86)   (a)   /či/:   C   V        (b)   /tši/:   C   C   V

　　　　　　　　　　 t  š  i　　　　　　　　　　t  š  i

Since moraic theory posits no prosodic slots for onset segments, it is incompatible with this account.

However, as McCarthy and Prince (1986) point out, moraic theory is compatible with an alternative representation for affricates proposed by Sagey (1986: 49–52): an affricate involves sequential branching for the feature [continuant], within a tree model of segment structure of the kind proposed in Clements 1985. Sagey and McCarthy and Prince argue that such a representation is to be preferred on independent grounds to the representation of (86a). I will not repeat their discussion here.

## A3 /yi/ and /wu/

Under normal assumptions, syllables beginning with /yi/ and /wu/ are not easy to represent under the version of moraic theory I am proposing. Although such syllables are missing from many languages (Kawasaki 1982), they are not so rare as to be exotic. The most obvious way of representing such syllables in moraic theory would be as in (87):

(87) (a)

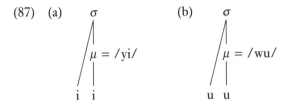

But the representations of (87) violate the Obligatory Contour Principle (OCP), a principle that, although controversial (Odden 1986a, 1988), does a great deal of work in nonlinear phonology; see McCarthy (1986) and much other work.

Another possibility, suggested by McCarthy and Prince (1986), is as in (88):

(88) (a)

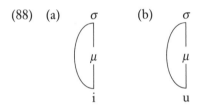

The difficulty with this proposal, as Janeway (1987) has pointed out, is that it necessitates placing actual syllable structure in underlying forms, to distinguish /yi/ from /i/ and /wu/ from /u/. As noted earlier, there is good reason to place only moraic structure, not syllable structure, in underlying forms, in order to derive the cross-linguistic generalization that syllable division is always predictable. Adopting (88) would destroy this prediction.

The best answer, I believe, is to adopt Hyman's (1985) suggestion that, at least in some languages, glides differ from vowels in being [+consonantal] rather than [−consonantal]. Such a featural difference would allow us to represent /yi/ and /wu/ without violating the OCP:

(89) (a)

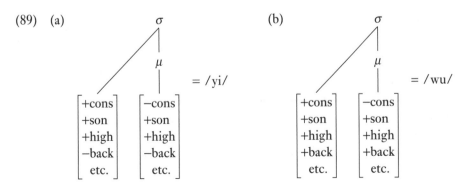

The (rather numerous) languages in which /yi/ and /wu/ are ill-formed represent /y/ and /w/ as [−consonantal], thus ruling out /yi/ and /wu/ by the OCP.

Phonetic observation, at least of English, supports Hyman's suggestion. In the pronunciations of English *ye* and *woo* I have observed, /y/ and /w/ have considerably greater constriction than the following vowel, suggesting they are phonologically less sonorous.

In Central Alaskan Yupik glides actually contrast with vowels when they occur in coda position, as in surface minimal pairs such as (90) (Woodbury 1987: 687):

(90)   (a)   [áŋyalí:yulú:ni] 'he was excellent at making boats'
       (b)   [áŋyalíyyulú:ni] 'he was EXCELLENT at making boats'

Coda consonants in this language are arguably mora-bearing; hence the contrast can be depicted only if glides and high vowels are featurally distinct:

(91)   (a)

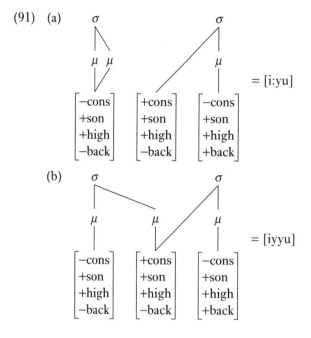

As Hyman (1985) points out, in Semitic languages glides may appear in consonantal roots, most dramatically in the root /y/ *yayay* 'to write the letter *y*' (McCarthy 1981: 396). Representing Semitic glides as [+consonantal] can solve the long-standing problem of how to indicate that they are to be mapped onto syllable-peripheral rather than nuclear positions.

To conclude: there is evidence that at least some glides are not the same thing as nonsyllabic high vowels, being featurally distinct from them. A prediction of the moraic theory adopted here is that the /y/ and /w/ of /yi/ and /wu/ will normally pattern as featurally distinct from /i/ and /u/, and not as nonsyllabic vowel segments.

## A4 Syllable-initial geminates

The theory of moraic phonology provides no straightforward way to represent a syllable-initial geminate. This is arguably the right prediction to make on a typological basis; the great majority of geminates across languages are divided between syllables. For the remaining cases, there are a number of possible accounts. In many instances one can argue that the first half of the geminate is actually a separate syllable, as in (92):

(92)  σ σ

$\mu\, /\mu$  = [m̩ma]

m  a

This appears to be the correct representation for Luganda, where the first half of a geminate (even an obstruent) is tone-bearing (Clements 1986). It also appears to be correct for Ponapean (McCarthy and Prince 1986).

Another possibility is that syllable-initial geminates have two segmental positions, as in (93):

(93)       σ

           μ

v  v  a

This is a plausible account for Russian, where such geminates arise through the deletion of jer vowels. In some dialects of Russian (Jones and Ward 1969) syllable-initial [š,š̠,] arises by simplification of /šč/, which would yield the same structure.

This account violates the OCP, but this seems less reason to reject it than for (87). The reason is that the OCP violations are derived by morpheme concatenation or by phonological rule, and are not underlying. The evidence in favor of the OCP seems considerably stronger for underlying representations than for derived forms.

A third possibility is to allow a stray mora to occur extrasyllabically, as in (94):

(94)        σ

$\mu\quad /\mu$  = [mma]

m  a

Such a configuration would be expected to occur only word-initially, as word-peripheral position is characteristic of extrasyllabic elements (Steriade 1982, Itô 1986). Restriction to word-initial position does appear to be a typical property of syllable-initial geminates cross-linguistically.

The upshot is that moraic theory provides straightforward representations for geminates in their usual, intervocalic position. The locations where the theory forces us to consider more marked analytical alternatives are precisely the locations where geminates are uncommon across languages.

Both syllable-initial geminates and the case of /yi/ and /wu/ raise a general question about the evaluation of theories. In describing these configurations, moraic theory faces some awkwardness in comparison to segmental prosodic theories. Yet these configurations are demonstrably marked, being avoided in numerous languages. The compensation for the descriptive awkwardness of moraic theory is that it can be interpreted as directly reflecting the markedness of the relevant configurations. In contrast, segmental prosodic theory says nothing about why so many languages should avoid /yi/, /wu/, and syllable-initial geminates. I believe that the ability of moraic theory to account for widespread patterns of markedness should be given more weight in assessing the evidence than any particular awkwardness in the analysis of individual languages.

## Notes

Many people have provided me with helpful comments on earlier versions of this work. In particular, I would like to thank G. N. Clements, A. Cohn, M. Hammond, H. Hock, L. Hyman, P. Keating, M. Kenstowicz, A. Lahiri, I. Lehiste, B. Levergood, J. McCarthy, A. Mester, K. Michelson, D. Minkova, D. Perlmutter, A. Prince, D. Steriade, L. Wetzels, and two anonymous reviewers for *Linguistic Inquiry*.

1   Discussion of further issues in moraic phonology not directly related to CL appears in the Appendix.
2   A diehard linearist might write two rules: one lengthening vowels before /s/ + [+ant, +son] clusters and another deleting /s/ before [+ant, +son]. This is clearly undesirable, because (a) vowels typically do not lengthen before clusters, (b) the appearance of the same /s/ + [+ant, + son] cluster in both rules is highly suspicious, and (c) the lengthening is not depicted as compensatory (that is, the lengthened vowel does not take up the time vacated by the /s/). Those not convinced by these problems should consult Odden 1981, where it is shown that the same two-rule strategy applied to Kimatuumbi would fail on empirical grounds.

## References

Allen, W. S. 1973. *Accent and Rhythm*. Cambridge: Cambridge University Press.
Bichakjian, B. 1986. When Do Lengthened Vowels Become Long? Evidence from Latin and French. In Wetzels and Sezer 1986: 11–36.
Chomsky, N. and M. Halle. 1968. *The Sound Pattern of English*. New York: Harper and Row.
Clements, G. N. 1985. The Geometry of Phonological Features. *Phonology Yearbook* 2, 225–52.
Clements, G. N. 1986. Compensatory Lengthening and Consonant Gemination in Luganda. In Wetzels and Sezer 1986: 37–77.
Clements, G. N. and S. J. Keyser. 1983. *CV Phonology*. Cambridge, Mass.: MIT Press.
de Chene, E. B. and S. R. Anderson. 1979. Compensatory Lengthening. *Language* 55, 505–35.
Dell, F. and M. Elmedlaoui. 1985. Syllabic Consonants and Syllabification in Imdlawn Tashlhiyt Berber. *Journal of African Languages and Linguistics* 7, 105–30.

Dresher, E. 1985. Constraints on Empty Positions in Tiered Phonology. MS, Department of Linguistics, University of Toronto.

Fudge, E. C. 1987. Branching Structure within the Syllable. *Journal of Linguistics* 23, 359–77.

Guerssel, M. 1986. Glides in Berber and Syllabicity. *Linguistic Inquiry* 17, 1–12.

Hale, K. 1973. Deep-Surface Canonical Disparities in Relation to Analysis and Change. In T. Sebeok (ed.), *Current Trends in Linguistics*, vol. 11, The Hague: Mouton, 401–58.

Harris, J. 1983. *Syllable Structure and Stress in Spanish*. Cambridge, Mass.: MIT Press.

Harris, J. 1987. Sonority and Syllabification in Spanish. MS, Department of Linguistics and Philosophy, MIT.

Hayes, B. and M. Abad. 1989. Reduplication and Syllabification in Ilokano. *Lingua* 77, 331–74.

Hyman, L. 1984. On the Weightlessness of Syllable Onsets. In C. Brugman and M. Macaulay (eds), *Proceedings of the Tenth Annual Meeting of the Berkeley Linguistics Society*, University of California, Berkeley, 1–14.

Hyman, L. 1985. *A Theory of Phonological Weight*. Dordrecht: Foris.

Ingria, R. 1980. Compensatory Lengthening as a Metrical Phenomenon. *Linguistic Inquiry* 11, 465–95.

Itô, J. 1986. Syllable Theory in Prosodic Phonology, Ph.D. dissertation, University of Massachusetts, Amherst.

Janeway, R. 1987. Luganda in Moraic Theory. MS, Department of Linguistics, UCLA.

Jones, D. and D. Ward. 1969. *The Phonetics of Russian*. Cambridge: Cambridge University Press.

Kawasaki, H. 1982. An Acoustical Basis for Universal Constraints on Sound Sequences, Ph.D. dissertation, University of California, Berkeley.

Levin, J. 1985. A Metrical Theory of Syllabicity. Ph.D. dissertation, MIT.

Lowenstamm, J. and J. Kaye. 1986. Compensatory Lengthening in Tiberian Hebrew. In Wetzels and Sezer 1986: 97–146.

McCarthy, J. 1979. Formal Problems in Semitic Phonology and Morphology. Ph.D. dissertation, MIT. (Available from Indiana University Linguistics Club, Bloomington.)

McCarthy, J. 1981. A Prosodic Theory of Nonconcatenative Morphology. *Linguistic Inquiry* 12, 373–418.

McCarthy, J. 1986. OCP Effects: Gemination and Antigemination. *Linguistic Inquiry* 17, 207–63.

McCarthy, J. and A. Prince. 1986. Prosodic Morphology. MS, University of Massachusetts, Amherst, and Brandeis University, Waltham, Mass.

Odden, D. 1981. A Nonlinear Approach to Vowel Length in Kimatuumbi. MS, Ohio State University, Columbus.

Odden, D. 1986a. On the Role of the Obligatory Contour Principle in Phonological Theory. *Language* 62, 353–83.

Odden, D. 1986b. Review of Hyman (1985), *Language* 62, 669–73.

Odden, D. 1988. Anti Antigemination and the OCP. *Linguistic Inquiry* 19, 451–75.

Sagey, E. 1986. The Representation of Features and Relations in Nonlinear Phonology. Ph.D. dissertation, MIT.

Sezer, E. 1986. An Autosegmental Analysis of Compensatory Lengthening in Turkish. In Wetzels and Sezer 1986: 227–50.

Steriade, D. 1982. Greek Prosodies and the Nature of Syllabification. Ph.D. dissertation, MIT.

Steriade, D. 1988. Review Article: Clements and Keyser, *CV Phonology*. *Language* 64, 118–29.

van der Hulst, H. 1984. *Syllable Structure and Stress in Dutch*. Dordrecht: Foris.

Wetzels, L. 1986. Phonological Timing in Ancient Greek. In Wetzels and Sezer 1986: 279–344.

Wetzels, L. and E. Sezer (eds). 1986. *Studies in Compensatory Lengthening*. Dordrecht: Foris.

Wilkinson, K. 1988. Prosodic Structure and Lardil Phonology. *Linguistic Inquiry* 19, 325–34.

Woodbury, A. 1987. Meaningful Phonological Processes: A Consideration of Central Alaskan Yupik Eskimo Prosody. *Language* 63, 685–740.

# 19

# Syllables (1969)

## E. C. Fudge

## 1  Introduction

Kohler (1966a, 1966b: 346–8) asks whether the syllable is a phonological universal, and concludes negatively.[1] The way to support such a conclusion is not difficult to imagine: the sort of specific objections to the syllable which Kohler raises would, if well-founded, be sufficient to prove his case.

I would wish to maintain the opposite point of view: I would like to state my firm belief that the syllable is a phonological universal. Like any other act of faith, this involves at least three parts: (i) close study of a set of hypotheses, (ii) selection of one of these as being more likely to be true than the others, and (iii) a willingness to face up to counter-claims against the selected hypothesis and also to put it to the test oneself. Kohler's counter-claims are, I think, sufficiently answered by Anderson (1969) (the arguments of Haugen (1967: 806–8) are also germane), and I will not discuss them systematically in this article (though on occasion I will indicate the relevance of the point I am making to a specific counter-claim). Other such counter-claims I will face, and I hope answer, as they are made.

In the meantime it is clearly incumbent upon me to test my selected hypothesis, first by making it explicit (see §2 below), and then by attempting to relate it to the facts of as many languages as possible (§§3–5 below [not all repr. here]): one complete failure will, of course, be sufficient to destroy it as a universally applicable hypothesis. On the other hand, any facts in a particular language which I am able to handle particularly neatly by using the syllable could provide me with genuine ammunition against those of my opponents who go further than saying that the syllable is not a phonological universal. Kohler, for example, makes the very strong claim that it is universally possible to do without the syllable: '. . . it can be demonstrated that the syllable is either an *unnecessary* concept, because the division of the speech chain into such units is known for other reasons, or an *impossible* one, as any division would be arbitrary, or even a *harmful* one, because it clashes with grammatical formatives' (1966a: 207; 1966b: 346). In such cases, opponents will have to show how a phonology without syllables would cope with the relevant facts.

## 2 Theoretical Preliminaries

2.1 The function of the syllable is twofold:

(a) To provide a basis for distinctive prosodic features: 'Les particularités prosodiques n'appartiennent pas aux voyelles en tant que telles, mais aux *syllabes*' (Trubetzkoy 1949: 196). Even where tone- or stress-elements are not directly attributable to syllables, their domains (morae, etc.) will be related to the syllable: 'L'unité pros-odique phonologique n'est pas à vrai dire simplement identique à la "syllabe" (au sens phonétique), mais elle a toujours un rapport avec la syllabe, étant donné qu'elle est, selon les langues, une partie déterminée de la syllabe ou toute une suite de syllabes' (ibid. 99; also examples, 202–3).

(b) To account for constraints on possible phoneme sequences (Pike 1947: 180–1): this will be our main concern in this paper. Some of these constraints are accounted for by setting up a syllable structure (Firth 1957b: 17) and then postulating differ-ent systems at different places in the structure (Allen 1957: 72; Cheng 1966: 139); in other cases, the choice of a particular element at one place affects the range of choice at another place (Allen 1957: 72–4; Hill 1966: 217–20).

2.2 With what strata or levels of description will our syllable be associated? And what will be the status of its component parts?

It appears likely that at least two different types of syllable will have to be postulated. These will correspond roughly to the traditional phonetic syllables and phonemic or phonological syllables (Rosetti 1963 and works cited there): 'On peut définir la syllabe phonologique et l'opposer à la syllabe phonétique' (ibid. 21). Our phonological syl-lable will be defined as an element of the systematic phonemic level (in the abstract sense of Fudge 1967: 3–8), and our phonetic syllable as an element of the systematic phonetic level (Chomsky 1964: 68) (more specifically, of the extrinsic allophonic type – Ladefoged 1967; Fudge 1969). The first type will not necessarily bear any close relation to actual pronunciation. Such syllables will consist of bundles of systematic phonemic features (preferably labelled in non-phonetic terms); it is hoped that they will provide a common basis for the description of mutually comprehensible dialects, even when these are phonetically very different from each other. The second type will represent the norm of pronunciation of a particular dialect or variety, and such syllables might consist of bundles of articulatory features (Ladefoged 1967: 49–50) or some representation of the neurophysiological basis of the relevant articulations (Fromkin 1966; Tatham and Morton 1968).

There is no necessary one–one relation between the phonemic syllables underlying an utterance and the phonetic syllables underlying it. This lack of isomorphism charac-terizes our syllables in both of their functions (§2.1):

(a) 'If the nuclei of phonetic syllables do not coincide with such units of tone or stress placement it is frequently helpful to postulate for descriptive purposes phonemic syllables which are structural units, related to phonetic syllables, but whose nuclei do so coincide' (Pike 1947: 145).

(b) 'For particular languages the student must be prepared to find that the phonetic syllable does not correspond with the most pertinent structural grouping of segments. Just as segments must be analyzed into the structural phonemes, so phonetic syllables must be analyzed into the structural phonemic syllables' (ibid. 90).

Thus in French we have the well-known 'mute *e*', which although normally realized as zero, yet must be taken into consideration at a phonemic level: on any other basis, various morphological facts are more difficult to state, while the rules of French metrics cannot be stated at all. As an example of such morphological facts we will consider how masculine and feminine forms of adjectives are related. Phonetically we have the forms shown in table 19.1: each form is monosyllabic. The rules for stating the relations are impossibly complex if we take the masculine as basic; with the feminine form as our starting point we have:

Table 19.1

|        | *masc.* | *fem.* |            | *masc.* | *fem.* |
|--------|---------|--------|------------|---------|--------|
| 'high' | o | ot | 'yellow' | ʒon | ʒon |
| 'ugly' | lɛ | lɛd | 'fine' | fɛ̃ | fin |
| 'large' | gro | gros | 'healthy' | sɛ̃ | sɛn |
| 'grey' | gri | griz | 'holy' | sɛ̃ | sɛt |
| 'red' | ruʒ | ruʒ | 'good' | bõ | bɔn |

| | |
|---|---|
| -ʒ, -on | remain unchanged |
| -in, -ɛn → | -ɛ̃ |
| -ɔn → | -õ |
| -t, -d, -s, -z → | zero |

Table 19.2 shows a less phonetically based approach incorporating ə as a phoneme (the approach of Togeby (1951) is rather similar to this); all the feminines are now disyllabic, and so are the masculine forms of 'red' and 'yellow'. The masculine is now the best choice for the base form, and the rules are as follows:

Table 19.2

|        | *masc.* | *fem.* |            | *masc.* | *fem.* |
|--------|---------|--------|------------|---------|--------|
| 'high' | hot | ho-tə | 'yellow' | ʒo-nə | ʒo-nə |
| 'ugly' | lɛd | lɛ-də | 'fine' | fin | fi-nə |
| 'large' | gros | gro-sə | 'healthy' | sɛn | sɛ-nə |
| 'grey' | griz | gri-zə | 'holy' | sɛNt | sɛN-tə |
| 'red' | ru-ʒə | ru-ʒə | 'good' | bɔn | bɔ-nə |

*Morphological rule*

Adj. → Adj. +ə (subject to the general constraint that two instances of ə
  fem.      masc.      cannot be adjacent in the same word – thus ru-ʒə and ʒo-nə
                         do not add another ə)

*Phonological rules* (of relevance throughout the language)

$$\begin{bmatrix} i \\ \varepsilon \\ \mathfrak{o} \end{bmatrix} + \begin{Bmatrix} n \\ N \end{Bmatrix} \rightarrow \begin{bmatrix} \tilde{æ} \\ \tilde{æ} \\ \tilde{o} \end{bmatrix}$$ when not separated by syllable boundary

t, d, s, z, ə → zero   word-finally

As a further example consider the English 'long u' vowel. Its phonetic realization as [ju:] gives rise to the possibility of initial (phonetic) clusters consisting of [Consonant] + [j] parallel to [Consonant] + [w], [l] or [r] which realize phonemic clusters. Phonetic syllable structure would thus differ from phonemic under two heads:

(a) The inventory of elements capable of acting as the second member of initial clusters will differ (three terms at the phonemic level, four at the phonetic); the fact that only the [u:] vowel normally follows a [j]-cluster does not affect the issue. Actually there are a few words with initial [CjV] where [V] is not [u:], the outstanding example being *piano*. For those who pronounce [piˈænou] this is obviously trisyllabic phonetically and phonemically, and it could be a phonemic trisyllable /pĭ – æ̆ – nou/ even for those who pronounce [ˈpjænou]. It could be treated as a loanword, but is perhaps well enough established to indicate one type of structural innovation which might spread in English in the future.

(b) The inventory of elements capable of acting as the first member of initial clusters will differ (stops and voiceless fricatives, except palatals, at the phonemic level; all consonants except palatals and [w], [r] and [l] at the phonetic).

2.3 The relation of phonetic syllables to chest-pulses (Stetson 1945: 6) or puffs of air (Rosetti 1963) or voicing (Hála 1961) will not be discussed. Systematic elements are not defined in terms of their physical manifestations – in fact they are not so much *defined* as *postulated* as elements of the abstract calculus in terms of which the underlying system may be described. Only after they are postulated (as a system characterized by certain relations) are these abstract elements linked up by realization rules with observable phenomena; these last *characterize* rather than *define* the abstract elements. The justification for postulating one system of elements and realization rules rather than another is a twofold 'renewal of connection' (Firth 1957b: 1): (i) that they enable one to predict what types of phonetic events are likely to occur (cf. Chomsky's 'observational adequacy', 1964: 29–30), (ii) that they agree with the intuitions of native speakers about their language (cf. Chomsky's 'descriptive adequacy', ibid. 29–30). If in addition there is independent phonetic justification for postulating some element, then this will provide further confirmation of the correctness of so doing. For instance, the great difference in acoustic status between vowels and consonants (consonants being acoustically modifications of vowels rather than elements in their own right – Hockett 1955: 206–8) would tend to confirm the appropriateness of a syllable which is basically CVC in nature.

There is also the point that some aphasics are incapable of pronouncing certain words, but remember and reproduce the number of syllables and the position of word-stress (Jakobson 1968: 64).

The glossematic use of the term 'definition' with its insistence on distributional criteria alone (cf. Togeby 1951: 80–7) can be just as misleading as uses which imply definition in terms of intrinsic properties. Again we may say that a systematic element is *characterized* rather than *defined* by its distribution: thus the fact that Danish p and k have identical distributions does not matter – they are first postulated as distinct elements, and may then be said to be characterized by identical distribution (cf. Bazell 1953: 16). Hjelmslev's circular[2] 'definition' of 'syllable' and 'accent' (each in terms of the other) (1939: 266–8) is not circular if it is understood as a characterization of syllable and accent, which are both in fact postulated as primitives. The same could be said of A. A. Hill's 'definition' of vowel and consonant (1958: 68–9).

For an approach to the morpheme which is analogous to our own approach to phonemic elements, see Koutsoudas 1963: 'The morpheme is that unit of grammar the arrangement of which is specified by the syntax and the resulting sequences of which are used to predict the physical form of utterances' (169).

It should be remembered that the procedures by which we set up the syllable in a particular language (or by which we decide where to place syllable-boundaries in words of that language) are no part of its definition as a theoretical unit, either in general or in that language. This is not to say that such procedures are not important in the 'discovery' phase of linguistic work, but is an affirmation that this phase is to be carefully distinguished from the 'presentation' phase, and it is this latter which is theoretically basic – discovery procedures are essentially 'trial-and-error' in nature, and must be evaluated in terms of whether their results accord with the system best fitted for the description of the language. Chomsky's denial of the theoretical status of complementary distribution (1964: 93) is presumably to be understood in this light.

2.4   One important problem which any theory of the syllable must face is the relationship of syllable and morpheme. The adoption of a generative framework poses this problem in an acute form: at what point and in what way can a syllable-based phonology (such as Saporta and Contreras, 1962) be 'fitted into' a morpheme-and-formative-based grammar (such as Halle 1959)? Kohler in effect cuts the Gordian knot, saying that because there is no simple answer to this question, a syllable-based grammar is just unthinkable: '. . . it can be demonstrated that the syllable is either an *unnecessary* concept, . . . or an *impossible* one, . . . or even a *harmful* one, because it clashes with grammatical formatives' (1966a: 207; 1966b: 346). In fact, explicit recognition of this lack of isomorphism has not prevented other scholars from seeing the need for both types of unit: 'Morph patterns may be entirely linked to syllabic pattern, as in Chinese; strongly linked to syllabic pattern, as in the Bantu dialects; feebly linked to syllabic pattern, as in Turkish or English; or independent of syllabic pattern, as in the Semitic dialects' (Bazell 1953: 62).

2.5   The manner of the tie-up between syllable and morpheme cannot be understood unless a clear distinction is made between the *morpheme* (a functional, grammar-oriented unit, not decomposable into phonemes) and the *morph* (an overt, phonology-oriented unit, consisting in general of a sequence of phonemes), the relation between the two being one of representation: thus English *sank* consists of one morph (four phonemes in length) representing two morphemes. For this distinction see Bazell 1953: 51–60.

2.6   The phonological element *word* consists from one point of view of a string of morphs which as individual morphs have no necessary relation to syllables (cf. the quotation from Bazell above), and consists from the other point of view of a sequence of an integral number of syllables – thus the string of morphs is related to the syllable, but only indirectly, via the word. If a morpheme or a string of morphemes forming a constructional unit happens to be represented by a single word, we shall treat this as purely coincidental: in other words *grammatical word* is not an element with systematic status. On the grammatical level morphemes will be combined into *constructs*, whose limits will not necessarily coincide with word-boundaries at all: thus morphemes of tense are best regarded as being in construction grammatically with a complete predicate, although morphs representing such morphemes are very frequently bound to the verb stem (cf. Harris 1951: 278–9, 1957: 325).

The extreme case is exemplified by the interrogative particle *-ne* in Latin: grammatically the construction is Q + Nucleus not Q + first word, while phonologically we have the CV syllable *-ne* appearing as the last syllable of the first (phonological) word (N.B. not 'attached to' that word – in any particular instance when *-ne* is present, I feel it is more appropriate to say that the morph or morph-sequence to which it is attached does not form a word, irrespective of the fact that it does in cases when *-ne* is not present: thus in *Caesar veniet* 'Caesar will come' *Caesar* is a word, while in *Caesarne veniet* 'will Caesar come?' *Caesar* is not a word).

Only slightly less extreme are cases like the Chinese *-de* which, when attached to the last of a string of syllables representing a phrase or a clause, enables that phrase or clause to function as a noun-modifier. Grammatically, the construction is, say, Clause + Adjectivalizer, while phonologically, it is Last syllable of phrase + *-de*, irrespective of the grammatical status of that syllable – the pitch of the *-de* is entirely dependent on the tone of the syllable to which it is attached (Hockett 1947: 257).

Very similar, again, is the English *'s* problem: in *the King of England's hat*, is *-'s* a word? If not, how can it be in construction with a phrase (*the King of England*)? But if it is, how is it that it never occurs as a free form? The solution is to recognize that phonological constructions may not correspond with grammatical ones: grammatically we have Noun phrase + Possessive, while phonologically we have *the* + *King* + *of* + *England's* + *hat. England's* is a word, while *England* (in this particular instance) is not.

Thus the grammatical hierarchy ought to be strictly distinguished from the phonological hierarchy (see figure 19.1) (see Pike 1967: ch. 9, esp. 409–10). There will be close correspondence or even identity between elements in certain particular cases (cf. Bazell's statement of the relation between syllable and morph quoted in §2.4 above): the dotted lines in figure 19.1 show some of these possible correspondences. Morphs form the bridge between the two hierarchies: the relation between morphemes and morphs, and the morphic composition of words (this latter area is, I think, as near as one gets to 'grammatical words') together comprise the domain of morphology (which ought to be kept distinct from phonology, and not included within it as seems increasingly to be the fashion nowadays). The link between morphs and the structures generated by the phonological hierarchy might be effected by an algorithm which takes in order the

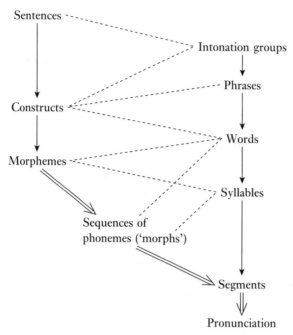

Figure 19.1

phonemes composing the morphs and assigns them to appropriate segments in syllable- and word-structure. This would provide a means of adjusting the syllabic position of phonemes belonging to a morph according to the morphic context of the latter – the /v/ of *drive* is syllable-final, whereas it is more natural to take the /v/ of *driving* as syllable-initial (cf. Kuryłowicz 1948: 82–3).

Chomsky and Halle's 'phonological phrases' (1968: 9–10) correspond to our intonation groups (being the 'maximal domains for phonological processes'): the rules for inserting phonological phrase boundaries are part of the rules for converting 'syntactic surface structure' (the output of the syntactic component) into 'phonological surface structure' (the input to the phonological component) (pp. 10, 13). This framework suffers from the disadvantage of introducing necessary phonological elements in an *ad hoc* manner, rather than systematically, stating relations between the various elements. These relations are in fact comparatively simple: each element consists of a string of an integral number of instances of the element next below it – a phrase consists of one or more words, a word of one or more syllables. The only more complex structure is the syllable, in which branching structures, as opposed to strings, are relevant (see the following section).

2.7   Obviously the morphs and the structures generated by the phonological hierarchy must be compatible with one another. The question arises, which type of structure has logical priority? In other words, are the sequences of phonemes of which morphs consist subject to the constraints embodied in the syllable-structure rules, or is the converse the case? In the latter case, without syllable-structure rules, the rules for morph-structure can only be of the 'finite-state' type (as Šaumjan (1962) claims); this leads to such problems as the difficulty in treating VC syllables as special cases of CVC syllables, which in turn leads to unnecessarily complicated descriptions such as Roceric-Alexandrescu 1967. Syllable-structure rules with the possibility of zeros in some places enable us to use 'phrase-structure' type rules (cf. again Šaumjan 1962), which greatly reduce the number of distinct syllable-types (e.g. in Roceric-Alexandrescu's case, from 20 to 4 or less).

Moreover, morph-structure rules will either not apply to morphs without vowels (e.g. English s/z plural, t/d past, and perhaps stress-shift denoting nominalization), or need to be made more complex to account for such cases; with a properly constituted set of syllable-structure rules, on the other hand, this problem does not arise (see below, §5). Incidentally, one wonders how Kohler would treat a bi-morphic word like *goes* – would he violate his third objection (i.e. that syllable-division and morph-division sometimes clash) by accepting it as a monosyllable? His only alternative would be to call it a disyllable, which seems rather unsatisfactory and unnecessary.

Halle's 'morpheme-structure rules' (1959: 39, 58–61) appear to be (finite-state) morph-structure rules pure and simple: syllables play no explicit part in the phonology. In a recent article Stanley (1967) proposes that Halle's notion of an ordered set of morpheme-structure rules on a par with other types of phonological rule should be replaced by an unordered set of 'morpheme-structure conditions' different in form from the phonological rules proper, and to be kept separate from them. It is important to note Stanley's claim (p. 432) that morpheme-structure conditions of a certain type ('positive conditions') are required for the purpose of 'stating restrictions on syllable-structure, that is, in stating restrictions involving the features Consonantal, Vocalic and perhaps Obstruent'. While it is true that these proposals represent a step forward, they still suffer from two important drawbacks:

(a) Their 'finite-state' character remains unchanged;
(b) They only work really well for languages of the special type in which morph and syllable correlate very closely: the example given in the text (p. 427) is an extreme case of this type. The typical situation in a Semitic language is very different: morphs are of three distinct types:
   (i) Roots, most frequently of the form CCC,
   (ii) Infixes, usually of the form VV (with zero as a possible choice for either V),
   (iii) Particles, Prefixes and Suffixes, usually (C)V(C).

Types (i) and (ii) are discontinuous and 'interweave', yielding sequences over which the usual type of syllabic constraints operate, and for which syllable-structure rules must therefore be set up as completely distinct from the morph-structure rules for the major word-classes.

To talk in terms of syllables is then necessary; however, it is not sufficient. Chomsky and Halle (1968) continually invoke syllables, monosyllables, disyllables, etc. in their less formal discussions (in the text frequently, but sometimes also within the systems of rules proposed), and even postulate a feature Syllabic 'which would characterize all segments constituting a syllabic peak' (p. 354). Unfortunately, none of these terms are made explicit in the text or in the rules; we are left to infer that a monosyllable is probably a formative with only one vowel ('In monosyllables, the vowel receives primary stress' (p. 16)), and perhaps also that a syllable is a sequence of phonemes containing one and only one vowel ('$\overset{1}{\Sigma}$ [is] a stressed syllable, that is, a string of the form $C_0 \overset{1}{V} C_0$' (p. 35)). The term 'syllable' does not even figure in the index of Chomsky and Halle 1968.

In fact, we may state that it is not satisfactory to deal with the structure of one element in terms of statements designed to deal with the structure of an essentially different and only indirectly related element. If we want to state syllable-structure, we must explicitly introduce the element 'syllable' into our linguistic description, and state its relations to the other elements of the phonological hierarchy; it is precisely this which Chomsky and Halle fail to do. [ . . . ]

# 4  Example II

4.1   Before proceeding to a thorough investigation of the structure of English syllables (§5 below), we will set the scene by briefly considering syllable-structure in Chinese (chiefly Mandarin) with special reference to certain questions of internal structure which will be more generally relevant (and which, in particular, will be relevant to English).

It is, of course, impossible to say whether syllable-structure formulae for Chinese are syllable-relevant or morph-relevant (since these two units are indistinguishable in Chinese – see §2.4). This was pointed out by Hockett: 'Hartman's "syllable" = our "monosyllabic microsegment"; Hartman, like his predecessors, does not discover disyllabic microsegments, and does not examine too closely the problem of establishing syllables as phonologically relevant units to start with' (1947: n. 27). Accordingly, we must be prepared to find that some of the constraints on phoneme-combinations in English, or any other language, are morph-relevant or word-relevant rather than syllable-relevant (here I would emphasize that the syllable is a *necessary* unit, not an *all-sufficient* one). This does not, however, imply that we must justify syllables *in advance* (as Hockett appears to demand here): as stated earlier (§2.3), we postulate them, and hope to justify this by the applicability of our description to the facts of the language.

4.2   There is no dearth of studies on Chinese syllable-structure (e.g. Firth and Rogers 1937; Hockett 1947; Scott 1947, 1956; Halliday, 1959 (appendix A); Cheng 1966): the large number presumably reflects the fact that Chinese dialects in general demand such a treatment. The four-place structure proposed by Hockett (1947: 258–9; Joos 1957: 221) and Cheng (1966: 142, cf. 146) for Mandarin appears to be useful for the description of many other Chinese dialects; we will adopt it here in preference to other structures. Like Cheng (1966: 135–6) we will exclude 'morphophonemically derived' syllables from the set of syllables to be considered. Figure 19.2 shows the various systems operating at each place. We have adopted Hockett's three-vowel system (1947: 259; Joos 1957: 221), replacing # by I, rather than the five-vowel system proposed by Cheng (1966: 140–2), in which the distinction i – u – ü appears (redundantly) at two places in the structure. In this particular case, no attempt has been made to equate elements of one system with elements of another (cf. Allen 1957: 75); this does not imply that it will never be possible to do this (cf. §5.1 below).

The setting-up of syllable-structure clearly accounts in an appropriate way for the majority of the systematic restrictions on sound-sequences: the remainder of these may be stated in terms of the co-occurrence of particular elements of one system with

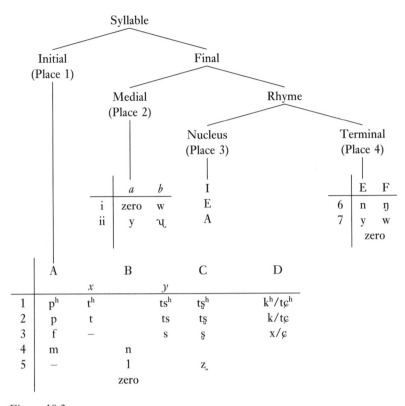

Figure 19.2

particular elements of another – adapting Firth's terminology (1957b: 11–14) to the phonological level, we might call these 'collocational restrictions' as opposed to the 'colligational restrictions' summarized in figure 19.2.

4.3   As stated by Hockett (1947: 259) (and equivalently by Cheng (1966: 145)), /w/ does not occur at place 2 and place 4 in the same syllable, and the same is true of /y/, except for /yAy/ which is 'rare and perhaps only literary' (Hockett 1947: 259, and cf. n. 16). These facts may be stated as follows:

Rule 1: 2(*b*) $\Rightarrow$ ~4(F7)

Rule 2: 2(ii) $\Rightarrow$ ~4(E7) *except*: /.yAy²/, /kʰyAy³/

(where superscript numerals represent tones and . represents the selection of zero). Rule 1 may be paraphrased as follows: 'If phonemic element *b* occurs at place 2, then phonemic element F7 cannot occur at place 4.' The exceptional syllables could be called 'deviant syllables' (extending the terminology of Chomsky (1961: 233–5) to a phonological context), or 'semi-syllables' (extending Katz 1964 similarly); the latter has the disadvantage of suggesting something which is half a syllable in length, and we shall therefore adopt the former term. Rule 1 will be called a 'non-violable constraint', while rule 2 (which permits exceptions) will be called a 'violable constraint' (though see the note in parentheses under 'Rules linking places 1 and 4' (§5.8)).

# 5   Example III

5.1   Figure 19.3 shows the scheme for English syllable structure as it will be set up for the purposes of this study. In partial justification for this scheme we will consider certain alternative possibilities and explain why we have rejected them (§§5.2–5.7 below [not all repr. here]).

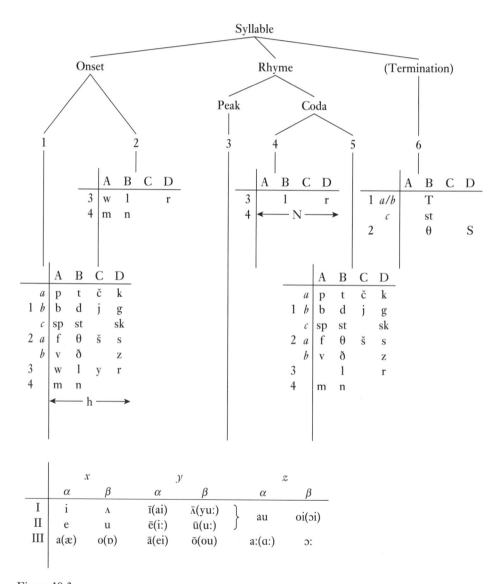

Figure 19.3

Place 6 is used in word-final syllables only, and may be occupied by one of the members of the system operating there, or by a string of two (exceptionally three) of these members. Thus *boxes* is represented as /b.o.kSS/ (one phonological syllable although two phonetic syllables), and *sixths* as /s.i.kS$\theta$S/, where the symbol . indicates the selection of zero. Realization rules for B1*a/b*, D2 at place 6 are as follows:

$$/D2/ \rightarrow \begin{cases} \text{[iS] in the context } (\left\{\begin{matrix} C \\ D2 \end{matrix}\right\})(\underline{\quad\quad}) \\ \text{[S] elsewhere} \end{cases}$$

$$/B1a/b/ \rightarrow \begin{cases} \text{[iT] in the context } (B1)(\underline{\quad\quad}) \\ \text{[T] elsewhere} \end{cases}$$
(where parentheses enclose single segments)

The voicing feature is then added to the extrinsic allophones [S], [T], according to its value in the preceding allophone. If place 6 is non-zero, this usually implies there is a morph-boundary immediately before it, though /S/, /T/ and /st/ occasionally occur without a boundary: *next* /n.e.kst/, *James* /j.ā.mS/, *apt* /..a.pT/, *glimpse* /gliNpS/, etc. Where a monomorphemic word can be accounted for either by selecting places 4 and 5 or by selecting places 5 and 6 (e.g. *hand*), the former will be preferred.

The distinction between m and n at place 5 is not generally made in syllables which are not word-final: thus *rumble* is represented as /r.ʌN - b.e.l./ (hyphens denote syllable-boundaries, while vertical lines will be used when it is desired to show morph-boundaries). There are a few exceptions to this rule in which /m/ must be fully specified, e.g. *gremlin*, *clumsy*.

For the counter-phonetic position of s, z, and r within the consonant-system see my earlier paper (Fudge 1967: 20–1). Notice that we are implying here that, e.g., r in place 4 is comparable, if not precisely equatable, with r in place 1, and moreover nearly all the consonants occurring at place 5 may be precisely equated with their opposite numbers in place 1. This is in direct contrast with the Chinese case of §4, as well as differing from the normal Firthian teaching on the subject (Allen 1957: 74–5). Unless we do this, there is no way of allowing the same phoneme to occupy different syllabic positions in different forms of the same lexeme: thus (cf. the example of §2.6 above) *drive* is /drī.v./, while *driving* is /drī.. - v .iNg./; *bind* is /b.īNd./, while *binding* is /b.ī.N - d.iNg./.

The inclusion of post-vocalic r (places 4 and 5) must not be taken as implying that the scheme does not apply to 'r-less' dialects: $D_3$ is an abstract element which in some dialects (notably RP) may often have no realization of its own, but which will, so to speak, contribute to the realization of the preceding vowel. For RP we have the realization rules shown in table 19.3. There is syncretism between /ir/, /er/, and /ʌr/ in positions 1 and 3 (though some Scots dialects maintain the distinctions at the realization level – Grant 1914: 50, 55–6, 62). There is also syncretism between /or/ and /ōr/ in the same positions (though again some Scots dialects maintain a distinction between *horse* [hɔrs] and *hoarse* [hors] (ibid. 58–9) – phonemically perhaps /h.ors./ versus /h.ōrs./). On the other hand, the distinction must be maintained when certain derivational affixes follow: *abhor* must be /..a.b - h.o.r./ because of *abhorrent* /..a.b - h.o.. - r|.eNt./, while *store* must be /st.ō.r./ because of *storage* /st.ō.. - r|.ā.j./; it is, however, conceivable that this is again a question of different subsystems of the vocabulary.

Table 19.3

|  | Position 1 | Position 2 | Position 3 |
|---|---|---|---|
| /ir/ | ə:r (*stirring*) | ir (*stirrup*) | ə: (*stir*) |
| /er/ | ə:r (*deterring*) | er (*ferry, deterrent*) | ə: (*deter*) |
| /ʌr/ | ə:r (*furry*) | ʌr (*hurry, recurrent*) | ə: (*fur, hurt*) |
| /ar/ | a:r (*starry*) | ær (*marry, comparative*) | a: (*star, cart*) |
| /or/ | ɔ:r (*abhorring*) | ɔr (*lorry, abhorrent*) | ɔ:/ɔə (*abhor, port*) |
| /īr/ | ai(ə)r (*firing, iris*) | | aiə (*fire*) |
| /ēr/ | iər (*fearing, hero*) | | iə (*fear, fierce*) |
| /ᴧ̄r/ | juər (*furious, during*) | | juə (*pure*) |
| /ūr/ | uər (*touring*) | | uə (*tour*) |
| /ār/ | ɛər (*bearing, fairy*) | | ɛə (*bear, scarce*) |
| /ōr/ | ɔ:r (*storing, storage, story*) | | ɔ:/ɔə (*store*) |
| /aur/ | auər (*flowering*) | | auə (*flower*) |

Position 1: before a vowel morph-finally, when followed by an inflexional affix or an affix like adjectivalizing -*y*
Position 2: before a vowel otherwise
Position 3: elsewhere

Another important syncretism is that of /ᴧ̄/ and /ū/ which in RP occurs:

(i)   for all speakers, after /w/, /r/, /l/ and palatals, i.e. all consonants in the same row or column as /y/. The pivotal position of /y/ in this group ties in very nicely with the relation

Realization of /ᴧ̄/ = Realization of /y/ + Realization of /ū/;

(ii)  for most speakers, after /s/ and /z/;
(iii) for some speakers, after /θ/.

Other varieties of English (including many American types) lose the contrast after any alveolar consonant.

Phonetically identical pairs of words may sometimes have differing representations: *find* /f.īNd./ and *fined* /f.ī.n | T/, *board* /b.ord./ and *bored* /b.ō.r | T/. Although *tide* /t.ī.d./ and *tied* /t.ī.. | T/ are pronounced identically in RP, this does not hold in Scots, where they are [tʌid] and [taed] respectively (cf. Grant 1914: 63); admittedly, though, this could be regarded purely as due to the morph-final position of /ī/ in the second case.

These considerations indicate that the scheme proposed has interesting possibilities as the basis for a diasystem, though there will be distinctions in some dialects that it cannot handle, e.g. the contrast in certain Northern Irish dialects between *lie* 'tell lies' and *lie* 'recline'.

Some of the phonemic elements are more firmly established in the system than others: the *z* vowels are the most marginal among the vowels while the θ/ð opposition is perhaps the most questionable consonant distinction ([ð] occurring intervocalically, and initially in demonstratives, etc.; [θ] in other positions[3]). The vowel zIIIα (phonetically [aː]) is particularly marginal, as nearly all of its occurrences can be regarded as realizations of other, well-established, phonemic elements or sequences. Thus (for RP):

1   /ar/  →    [aː]  in Position 3 (see figure 19.3)

2   /al/  →    [aː]  in the context: (———) $\left(A\begin{Bmatrix}2a\\4\end{Bmatrix}\right)$

     (i.e. before f and m)

3   /a/  →     [aː]  in the following contexts:
 (i)   (———) (D3) in Position 1 (see figure 19.3)
      (i.e. before r)

 (ii)   (———) $\left(\begin{Bmatrix}A\\B\\D\end{Bmatrix}\begin{Bmatrix}1c\\2a\end{Bmatrix}\right)$ (i.e. before voiceless fricatives except š)

     except in Position 2, thus: *pass, passing,* but *passage, tassel* with [æ]; *telegraph(ing)* but *telegraphic, traffic* with [æ].

 (iii)   (———) (4) $\left(\begin{Bmatrix}B1\\C1\\D2\end{Bmatrix}a\right)$ (i.e. before -nt, -nč, -ns)

     except in Position 2, thus: *plant, planted,* but *plantation, canter* with [æ]; *dance, dancing,* but *fancy* with [æ].
and possibly (iv) word-finally in a non-reduced syllable: *grandma.*

There are many exceptions to these rules: thus the context for rule 2 could be extended to 'before f, v, or m' to handle *halve,* but there would then be difficulties with *valve* and (in some dialects) *salve.* Other exceptions:

(a)   [æ] instead of expected [aː]: (rule 3(ii)) *ass, crass, gas, lass, mass: gaff, (riff-)raff: asp:* (rule 3(iii)) *ant, cant* 'hypocrisy', *pant, rant; stance.*
(b)   [aː] instead of expected [æ]: (rule 3(ii)) *master, basket, rascal; father, rather;* (rule 3(iii)) *command, demand, slander.*
(c)   either pronunciation: *drastic, lather* ([dræstik], but [laːðə] in my speech).

Indications are that exceptions are increasing rather than decreasing, i.e. phoneme zIIIα is gaining ground: the introduction of abbreviations (*caff, maths, Staffs*) takes place without the rule being applied.
 The occurrences of [ɔː] can to some extent be accounted for in an analogous fashion:

1   /or/  →    [ɔː] in Position 3
2   /al/  →    [ɔː] in the context: (———) (Dl *a*) (i.e. before k)

2a   /a/  →    [ɔː] in contexts: (———)(B3)$\left(\begin{Bmatrix}\#\\B1\\D2\end{Bmatrix}\right)$

     (i.e. before -lt, -ld, -ls and word-final l)

and (for some older dialects)

3   /o/   →   [ɔː] in the following contexts:

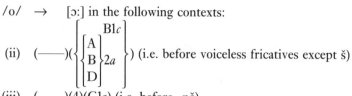

(ii)   (——)({$\begin{Bmatrix}\begin{bmatrix}A\\B\\D\end{bmatrix}_{2a}\\ B1c\end{Bmatrix}$}) (i.e. before voiceless fricatives except š)

(iii)   (——)(4)(C1a) (i.e. before -nč)

5.2   First we will attempt to justify the particular branching structure postulated for the English syllable. Other possible schemes include those of figures 19.4, 19.5 and 19.6.

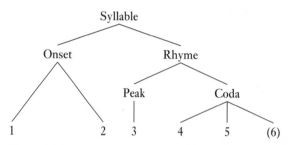

Figure 19.4

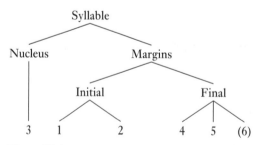

Figure 19.5

Figure 19.6

We have preferred figure 19.3 for the following reasons:

(a)   Figure 19.4 implies that there are two types of Coda (non-word-final, in which place 6 is not used, and word-final); it also links the normally morphological place 6 too closely to the Coda – we shall want to ignore place 6 when we come on to study co-occurrence restrictions within the syllable (§5.8 below; also Fudge 1970: §3.2).

(b)   Figure 19.5 implies that the relationship between Peak and Coda is no closer than that between Peak and Onset. For English this is by no means true – more important in this case than the facts adduced by Kuryłowicz (1948: 104) in support of the branching structure shown in figures 19.3 and 19.4 is the fact that certain Peaks do not co-occur with certain Codas (only *x*-vowels with /-Np/, /-Nk/ and /-Ng/, etc.), while there is no such constraint between Onset and Peak (cf. T. Hill 1966: 209).

(c)    The last fact mentioned under (b) is also one reason why we reject the scheme of figure 19.6 (for which see Togeby 1951: 55). Furthermore, transformational rules would be needed for this approach – for reasons against this, see §5.6 below.

5.3    The next alternative to figure 19.3 is the scheme of figure 19.7, in which [sp], [st], and [sk] are regarded as realizations of clusters of two phonemes. The chief advantage of the preferred scheme (for which I am indebted to Kohler (1967b: 151); something like it was also proposed by Firth (1936: 543; 1957a: 73), though Firth also appears to have advocated that *str-* etc. should also be taken as indivisible units) is that it avoids the necessity of postulating an extra place in the syllable structure (place 0) at which a system of only one element operates, and which must be filled by zero except when place 1 contains p, t, k, m, n, and perhaps f, v; other advantages include the avoidance of an arbitrary decision on whether to identify the stop portion of [sp] with the stop of series *a* (i.e. [p]) or that of series *b* (i.e. [b]) (though admittedly this could be achieved by postulating that the *a/b* distinction does not operate in phonemes of series 1 when they are preceded by s), and the possibility of separating 'the inherent structures /sp, st, sk/ from the alien ones /sf, sv/' (Kohler 1967b: 151).

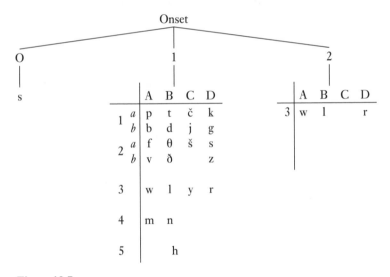

Figure 19.7

5.4    Figure 19.8 shows what appears to be a simpler set of systems for the Onset places – in figure 19.3 the occurrence of w, l, r, m, and n is redundant, since no combinations occur in which both elements are members of this set; in figure 19.8 this redundancy is eliminated by the exclusion of series 3 and 4 from place 1. Figure 19.3 is preferred at this point because in our later study of constraints within the syllable (§5.8 below) it becomes apparent that the collocational restrictions for l, r, m, n in initial clusters are more stringent than for l, r, m, n standing alone in initial position. There is the

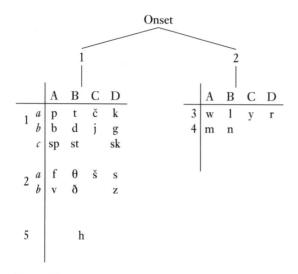

Figure 19.8

additional advantage that the scheme of figure 19.3 establishes place 1 as presupposed with respect to place 2: in other words, if place 1 is empty, then place 2 must also be empty. [ . . . ]

5.7   As for places 1 and 2 (§5.4 above), a slightly smaller inventory could be obtained by deleting r from place 5, but again this would obscure the difference between the collocational restrictions which operate on final r (alone) and those which affect r in final clusters. We can eliminate m and n from place 5 only if we are willing to make words like *elm*, *kiln* deviant, while l must be retained because of the fairly large group *girl*, *curl*, etc. Thus, unlike the case of §5.4, although the inventory is reduced, the system remains just as complex (no rows or columns can be removed).

5.8   We will now proceed to a statement of collocational restrictions, using rules like those formulated for Chinese (§4.3 above). First we will list the non–violable constraints:

General rules:

| | |
|---|---|
| 1(zero) $\Rightarrow$ 2(zero) | (These rules establish places 1 and 5 as the heads of |
| 5(zero) $\Rightarrow$ 4(zero) | Onset and Coda respectively) |

Rules governing initial clusters:

$$2(\text{non-zero}) \Rightarrow 1(\left\{\begin{matrix} A \\ B \\ D \end{matrix}\right\}\left\{\begin{matrix} 1 \\ 2a \end{matrix}\right\})$$
(Only stops and voiceless fricatives (but not those of series C) can stand first in initial clusters)

| | | |
|---|---|---|
| 2(4) | $\Rightarrow$ 1(D2a) | (Only s can form initial clusters with m and n) |
| 2(A3) | $\Rightarrow$ ~1(A) | (No pw-, bw-, spw-, fw- except in loan-words) |
| 2(B3) | $\Rightarrow$ ~1(B) | (No tl-, dl-, stl-, θl-) |

Rules governing final clusters (excluding place 6):

$$4(4) \quad \Rightarrow 5(\left\{\begin{matrix}1a\\1b\\2a\end{matrix}\right\})$$    (Nasals form final clusters with plosives and voiceless fricatives only)

$$4(B3) \Rightarrow 5(\left\{\begin{matrix}1a\\1b\\2a\\A2b\\4\end{matrix}\right\})$$    (l forms final clusters with plosives, voiceless fricatives, v and nasals only)

$$4(D3) \Rightarrow \sim5(\left\{\begin{matrix}A1c\\D1c\\B2b\\D3\end{matrix}\right\})$$    (r forms final clusters with any consonant except sp, sk, ð, r; the place-name *Thirsk* would have to be treated as exceptional)

Rules dealing with constraints between places 3 and 4:

$4(4) \quad \Rightarrow 3(x)$   unless $5(D2)$ or $5(B1)$     (Note that D2 and B1 are the alveolars:
$4(B3) \Rightarrow 3(x)$   unless $5(B1b)$         unmarked again?)
$4(D3) \Rightarrow 3(x)$   unless $5(D2a)$ or $5(B1b)$

Rules dealing with constraints between places 2 and 4:

$2(B4) \Rightarrow \sim4(B3)$   (No syllable begins with sn- and ends with an l-cluster)
$2(4) \quad \Rightarrow \sim4(4)$
$2(B3) \Rightarrow \sim4(B3)$   (The same element cannot be selected in both place 2 and place 4)
$2(D3) \Rightarrow \sim4(D3)$

It is at this point that we can justify the inclusion of w, l, r, m, and n at place 1 as well as place 2 (§5.4 above): the rule $1(B3) \Rightarrow \sim4(B3)$ is violated by the word *lilt*, $2(B3) \Rightarrow \sim5(B3)$ by *flail* (see below). The constraint $1(B3) \Rightarrow \sim5(B3)$ is hardly worth stating: of the sixteen possible words of the form /l.V.l./, at least four actually occur (*lull, loll, lall, lisle*, and perhaps *loyal*) – a fairly high proportion. Twaddell (1939, 1941) notices the very low incidence of lVl and rVr in German, but cannot make the distinction between, for example, ClVlC and l.V.l, for the very reason that he has not postulated a syllabic framework, but works entirely in 'finite-state' terms.

Rules dealing with constraints between places 3 and 5:

$5(zero) \Rightarrow \sim3(x)$   word-finally

This rule could be extended to all syllables if single-consonant interludes following *x*-vowels (Hockett 1955: 52) were treated as belonging phonemically to both the preceding syllable and the following syllable: thus *butter* would be /b.ʌ.t - t.e.r./, and there would need to be a rule stating that geminated consonants within a word were realized as single consonants. The words *is, was, has, does, says, had, did, said, could, should, would* are exceptions if we treat their final consonants as S or T (rather than z or d) as indicated by the grammar. Alternatively, we could omit this rule altogether and permit *x*-vowels to occur word-finally, with the proviso that they were realized like their *y*- or *z*-vowel counterparts (cf. rule 3(iv) above (§5.1); also Chomsky and Halle 1968: 74–5): this is made more complex by vowel reduction.

Rules dealing with constraints between places 1 and 5:
     1(1c) ⇒ ~5(1c)   (syllables do not both begin and end with s + stop except where 'stop' is T in place 6)

     We will now list some of the violable constraints, together with the deviant words which violate them (for the asterisks see below, §5.10):

Rules linking places 2 and 4:
     2(B3) ⇒ ~4(D3)   blurb, blurt, *clerk, flirt, slurp, splurge
     2(D3) ⇒ ~4(B3)   *grilse
     2(4)  ⇒ ~4(3)    smarm, *smart, *smelt (the verb *to smelt*), smirch, smirk, snarl, snort

(Note that *blurred*, *thrilled*, *snored*, etc. are /blʌ.rT/, /θri.lT/, /sno.rT/ respectively, and hence do not violate these rules.)

Rules linking places 1 and 4:
     1(B3) ⇒ ~4(B3)       lilt
     1(D3) ⇒ ~4(D3)       (No examples: the rule is included here rather than as non-violable because of its similarity to the preceding rule. This means a slight modification to our earlier definitions: by our present criterion both Rule 1 and Rule 2 of §4.3 would be counted as violable)
     1(A4) and 5(A) ⇒ ~4(4)   mumps
     1(B4) ⇒ ~(4)         *(a)noint, *nymph (*ninth* is /n.ĩ.n|θ/)

Rules linking places 2 and 5:
     2(4)  ⇒ ~5(4)        smarm
     2(A4) ⇒ ~5(A)        smarm
     2(B4) ⇒ ~5(B)        *snail, snide, *?snood, snoot, snort, snot, snout (Rather a lot of exceptions tolerated – unmarked alveolars again)
     2(B3) ⇒ ~5(B3)       *flail
     2(D3) ⇒ ~5(D3)       drear, and perhaps *briar, *friar (*prayer and *drawer fit the pattern, but probably include morph-boundaries)

[ . . . ]

5.10   Further violable constraints could be formulated, but it is noticeable that the number of deviant words becomes large. However, some of the lists of deviant words are interesting from a semantic point of view – consider the following rules involving syllables ending in clusters of Nasal + Consonant:

4(4) and 5(A)  ⇒ ~1(A)     blimp, bump, frump, mumps, pimp, plump, pomp, primp, *pump, vamp

4(4) and 5(D1) ⇒ ~1(D1)    clang, clank, cling, clink, clonk, clung, clunk, conk, crank, *gang, gink, gong, gunk, *king, kink, skunk.

The lists of deviant words contain a very high proportion of words which could very loosely be described as 'expressive' (this notion will be made more explicit in Fudge 1970; we will content ourselves here with pointing out the large number of onomatopoeic and pejorative words). Words not falling into this category have been asterisked in the lists here and in §5.8 above. Analogous to the two rules just given are the following (but note the rather different character of the deviant-word lists):

4(4) and 5(B) ⇒ ~1(B)     daunt, *dent, *dint, *don't, *(re)dound, *land, *lend, *lent, *lint, *(a)noint, *stand, *(in)stant, *stint, (a)stound, *strand, stunt, *(re)straint, taint, taunt, *tend, *tent, *tint, *trend, *(ro)tund, also *(ek)stend, *(ek)stent

4(4) and 5(C) ⇒ ~1(C)     *change

In the first case there are twenty-six exceptions, of which all but five are asterisked; in the second there is only one exception, and that is asterisked.

We will interpret this situation as indicating that column B is unmarked relative to A, C, and D: this is reminiscent of the 'unmarked alveolar' hypothesis again, except that B does not correspond completely with the alveolar place of articulation. In fact, however, when D is divided into D1 (velars) and D2/3 (alveolars) we see that the latter behave very much more like the other alveolars than like D1 (see table 19.4). This strongly suggests that it is allophonic features (notably place of articulation) rather than phonemic features which are operative at this level. The figures for labials (A) and velars (D1) show con-clusively that these two places are marked in relation to the alveolars (B and D2/3) for syllables of the type under consideration. The figures for palatals (C) are so small as to preclude the drawing of reliable inferences (cf. Twaddell 1939: 197–9).

Table 19.4   Deviant words containing syllables of the form C(L)VNC, summarized according to place of articulation of the C's at places 1 and 5. The first figure of each pair gives the number of deviant words, the second gives the number of these which have the semantic feature 'expressive'.

|          |      | Place 5: | | | | |
|----------|------|------|------|------|------|------|
|          |      | A    | B    | C    | D1   | D2/3 |
|          | A    | 11/9 | 67/2 | 23/10| 34/15| 18/6 |
|          | B    | 14/6 | 26/5 | 11/5 | 33/9 | 9/2  |
| Place 1: | C    | 4/2  | 5/2  | 1/0  | 4/2  | 1/0  |
|          | D1   | 13/7 | 19/6 | 9/5  | 17/14| 4/1  |
|          | D2/3 | 7/2  | 17/2 | 5/2  | 26/6 | 3/0  |

The facts that have been touched on in this last section will be treated at greater length in a study (Fudge 1970) which supports the hypothesis that there is a statistical connection between syllabic structure and the semantic feature of 'expressiveness'.

## Notes

1   I would like to put on record my appreciation of the many discussions I have had with Klaus Kohler on the topic of this paper – although not productive of agreement, they have always been cordial and constructive. I am grateful to several others for suggestions, notably John Wells and David Crystal.
2   Alleged to be circular by Togeby (1951: 75), though Hjelmslev claims explicitly to be avoiding circularity (Hjelmslev 1939: 267).
3   Exceptions to this rule are not lacking: *bathe, loathe* (neither of which I would regard as including an intervocalic [ð]), *ether* (with intervocalic [θ]). This does not detract from the value of stating the rule – even an '80% rule' is well worth stating, provided that the exceptions to it are indicated.

## References

Allen, W. S. 1957. Aspiration in the Hārautī nominal. In *Studies in Linguistic Analysis*, Oxford: Blackwell, 68–86.

Anderson, J. M. 1969. Syllabic and non-syllabic phonology. *Journal of Linguistics* 5: 136–42.

Bazell, C. E. 1953. *Linguistic Form*. Istanbul: Istanbul Press.

Cheng, R. L. 1966. Mandarin phonological structure. *Journal of Linguistics* 2: 135–59.

Chomsky, N. 1961. Some methodological remarks on generative grammar. *Word* 17: 219–39.

Chomsky, N. 1964. *Current Issues in Linguistic Theory*. Janua Linguarum, Series Minor, 38. The Hague: Mouton.

Chomsky, N. and Halle, M. 1968. *The Sound Pattern of English*. New York: Harper and Row.

Firth, J. R. 1936. Alphabets and phonology in India and Burma. *Bulletin of the School of Oriental Studies* 8: 517–46. Also in Firth 1957a: 54–75.

Firth, J. R. 1957a. *Papers in Linguistics, 1934–1951*. London: Oxford University Press.

Firth, J. R. 1957b. A synopsis of linguistic theory, 1930–1955. In *Studies in Linguistic Analysis*, Oxford: Blackwell, 1–32.

Firth, J. R. and Rogers, B. B. 1937. The structure of the Chinese monosyllable in a Hunanese dialect (Changsha). *Bulletin of the School of Oriental Studies* 8: 1055–74. Also in Firth 1957a: 76–91.

Fromkin, V. A. 1966. Neuro-muscular specification of linguistic units. *Language and Speech* 9: 170–99.

Fudge, E. C. 1967. The nature of phonological primes. *Journal of Linguistics* 3: 1–36.

Fudge, E. C. 1969. Mutation rules and ordering in phonology. *Journal of Linguistics* 5: 23–38.

Fudge, E. C. 1970. Phonological structure and 'expressiveness'. *Journal of Linguistics* 46: 161–88.

Grant, W. 1914. *The Pronunciation of English in Scotland*, 2nd edn. Cambridge: Cambridge University Press.

Hála, B. 1961. La syllabe, sa nature, son origine et ses transformations. *Orbis* 10: 69–143.

Halle, M. 1959. *The Sound Pattern of Russian*. The Hague: Mouton.

Halliday, M. A. K. 1959. *The Language of the Chinese 'Secret History of the Mongols'*. Publications of the Philological Society, 17. Oxford: Blackwell.

Harris, Z. S. 1951. *Methods in Structural Linguistics*. Chicago: University of Chicago Press.

Harris, Z. S. 1957. Co-occurrence and transformation in linguistic structure. *Language* 33: 283–340.

Haugen, E. 1967. Review of B. Sigurd, *Phonotactic Structures in Swedish*. *Language* 43: 803–9.

Hill, A. A. 1958. *Introduction to Linguistic Structures*. New York: Harcourt Brace.

Hill, T. 1966. The technique of prosodic analysis. In C. E. Bazell et al. (eds), *In Memory of J. R. Firth*, London: Longmans, 198–226.

Hjelmslev, L. 1939. The syllable as a structural unit. In *Proceedings of the Third International Congress of Phonetic Sciences*, Ghent: Laboratory of Phonetics of the University, 266–72.

Hockett, C. F. 1947. Peiping phonology. *JOAS* 67: 253–67. Also in Joos 1957: 217–28.

Hockett, C. F. 1955. *A Manual of Phonology*. International Journal of American Linguistics Memoir 11. Bloomington, Ind.

Jakobson, R. 1968. *Child Language, Aphasia and Phonological Universals*. Janua Linguarum, 72. The Hague: Mouton.

Joos, M. (ed.) 1957. *Readings in Linguistics*. New York: American Council of Learned Societies and Chicago: University of Chicago Press.

Katz, J. J. 1964. Semi-sentences. In J. A. Fodor and J. J. Katz (eds), *The Structure of Language*, Englewood Cliffs, N.J.: Prentice-Hall, 400–16.

Kohler, K. J. 1966a. Is the syllable a phonological universal? *Journal of Linguistics* 2: 207–8.

Kohler, K. J. 1966b. Towards a phonological theory. *Lingua* 16: 337–51.

Kohler, K. J. 1967b. Modern English phonology. *Lingua* 19: 145–76.

Koutsoudas, A. 1963. The morpheme reconsidered. *International Journal of American Linguistics* 29: 160–70.

Kuryłowicz, J. 1948. Contribution à la théorie de la syllabe. *Bulletin de la Société Polonaise de Linguistique* 8: 80–114. Also in *Esquisses Linguistiques* (1962).

Ladefoged, P. 1967. *Linguistic Phonetics*. Working Papers in Phonetics 6. Los Angeles: UCLA.

Pike, K. L. 1947. *Phonemics*. Ann Arbor: University of Michigan Press.

Pike, K. L. 1967. *Language in Relation to a Unified Theory of Human Behavior*. The Hague: Mouton.

Roceric-Alexandrescu, A. 1967. Entropy and syllable-structure in Rumanian. In J. Hamm (ed.), *Phonologie der Gegenwart*, Graz, Vienna, and Cologne: *WSIJb* Ergänzungsband 6, 189–94.

Rosetti, A. 1963. *Sur la théorie de la syllabe*, 2nd edn. Janua Linguarum, Series Minor, 9. The Hague: Mouton.

Saporta, S. and Contreras, H. 1962. *A Phonological Grammar of Spanish*. Seattle: University of Washington Press.

Šaumjan, S. K. 1962. Problemy Teoretičeskoj Fonologii. Moscow. Trans. into English by A. L. Vanek, rev. S. K. Šaumjan and P. M. Wasziuk, as *Problems of Theoretical Phonology*, Janua Linguarum, Series Minor, 41. The Hague and Paris: Mouton, 1968 [1969].

Scott, N. C. 1947. The monosyllable in Szechuanese. *Bulletin of the School of Oriental and African Studies* 12: 197–213.

Scott, N. C. 1956. A phonological analysis of the Szechuanese monosyllable. *Bulletin of the School of Oriental and African Studies* 18: 556–60.

Stanley, R. 1967. Redundancy rules in phonology. *Language* 43: 393–436.

Stetson, R. H. 1945. *Bases of Phonology*. Oberlin, Oh.: Oberlin College.

Tatham, M. A. A. and Morton, K. 1968. Some electromyography data towards a model of speech production. University of Essex Language Centre Occasional Papers.

Togeby, K. 1951. *Structure Immanente de la Langue Française*. TCLC 6. Copenhagen: Nordisk Sprog- og Kulturforlag.

Trubetzkoy, N. S. 1949. *Principes de Phonologie*, tr. J. Centineau. Paris: Klincksieck.

Twaddell, W. F. 1939, 1941. Combinations of consonants in stressed syllables in German. *AL* 1: 189–99; 2: 31–50.

# 20

# On Stress and Linguistic Rhythm (1977)

## Mark Liberman and Alan Prince

## 0  Prospectus

In this essay a new theory of stress and linguistic rhythm will be elaborated, based on the proposals of Liberman (1975).[1] It will be argued that certain features of prosodic systems like that of English, in particular the phenomenon of "stress subordination," are not to be referred primarily to the properties of individual segments (or syllables), but rather reflect a hierarchical rhythmic structuring that organizes the syllables, words, and syntactic phrases of a sentence. The character of this structuring, properly understood, will give fresh insight into phenomena that have been apprehended in terms of the phonological cycle, the stress-subordination convention, the theory of disjunctive ordering, and the use of crucial variables in phonological rules.

Our theory will employ two basic ideas about the representation of traditional prosodic concepts: first, we represent the notion *relative prominence* in terms of a relation defined on constituent structure; and second, we represent certain aspects of the notion *linguistic rhythm* in terms of the alignment of linguistic material with a "metrical grid."

The perceived "stressing" of an utterance, we think, reflects the combined influence of a constituent-structure pattern and its grid alignment. This pattern–grid combination is reminiscent of the traditional picture of verse scansion, so that the theory as a whole deserves the name "metrical." We will also use the expression "metrical theory" as a convenient term for that portion of the theory which deals with the assignment of relative prominence in terms of a relation defined on constituent structure.

Section 1 [not repr. here] will apply the metrical theory of stress-pattern assignment to the system of English phrasal stress, arguing this theory's value in rationalizing otherwise arbitrary characteristics of stress features and stress rules. Section 2 [not all repr. here] will extend this treatment to the domain of English word stress, adopting a somewhat traditional view of the assignment of the feature [+stress], but explaining the generation of word-level patterns of stress in terms of the metrical theory developed to treat the phrasal domain. Section 3 [not repr. here] will introduce the concept of alignment with a *metrical grid* – fundamentally a formalization of the traditional idea of "stress-timing." We will argue that this concept is central to a satisfactory account of the so-called rhythm rule, and also gives a realistic picture of relative stress at the syllabic level.

### 0.1  A note on the data

For the most part, this article will advance its case in terms of a reanalysis of old observations, rather than a flourish of new ones. The body of descriptive data we propose to reinterpret has been common (differences of detail aside) to the linguistic tradition that includes the American structuralists as well as Generative Phonology; it includes the distribution of stressed and unstressed syllables in English words, the location of main word stress, the differential treatment of lexical and supralexical constituents, the preservation of relative prominence under embedding, and so forth.

Over the years, some fundamental characteristics of this description have been called into question on one basis or another. For example, it has been proposed (most notably by Bolinger) that it is incorrect to extend the notion *stress* beyond the word level, *sentence stress* being merely a matter of pitch-accent placement. This same point of view holds that word stress itself is no more than a guide to the word-level location of those (phrasal) pitch accents that the speaker chooses to impose.

Although it is not our purpose here to argue the point, we feel that the structuralists (and their generative heirs) were closer to the truth. English is a stress language, not a tone or pitch-accent language; English stress patterns, within and among words, have phonetic reality as rhythmic patterns entirely independent of their role in orchestrating the placement of intonation contours.

This much should not be difficult to establish experimentally. One promising line of inquiry relies on the fact that it is possible to mimic an arbitrary English utterance while substituting reiteration of a single syllable (e.g. *ma*) for each syllable of the original. Such "reiterant speech" shows stable durational patterns, which depend on the stress pattern and constituent structure of the utterance,[2] just as durational patterns in natural speech do. It has been shown[3] that listeners are able to extract stress and constituent-structure information from reiterant speech, and that (under the conditions of the cited experiment) duration is the dominant cue in both cases.

In perception experiments, the use of reiterant speech guarantees that stress-pattern perceptions cannot be derived from the hearer's knowledge of the words involved; control of $F_0$, possible by using analysis–resynthesis techniques, can be used to separate out the role of "pitch accent" (a role that is perhaps less central to stress-pattern perception than is generally believed). In analysis of production data, the reiterant speech technique permits the study of prosodic influences on duration (as well as amplitude, etc.) in an environment free from segmental influences.

In both production and perception, it is not hard to show the *existence* of stress patterns in English as a descriptive category independent of intonation contour. It remains to be seen whether the particulars of traditional descriptions of stress, or for that matter our reanalysis of them, will provide an adequate framework for phonetic research in this area. We feel, in any case, that both phonologists and phoneticians stand to learn a great deal from the attempt to find out. [ . . . ]

## 2   Words

Hierarchical stress subordination is as characteristic of words as it is of phrases and compounds. The perceived array of prominence in words like *éxecùte* and *cógnàte* closely resembles that of compounds like *làbor únion*, *dòg dáys*; phrases like *rèd ców*, *glòbed péonie* are similar to such words as *pontóon*, *arránge*; the pattern of *ùnion fínance commìttee* is echoed in words like *execútion*, *pòlyprópylène*, *etcétera*.

In terms of the theory being explored here, this can only mean that words have an internal metrical structure in which syllables and groups of syllables are weighed against each other. For words, as for phrases, the pattern of subordinations is known to be essentially lawful, and we must expect to find a rule to distribute node labels below the phrasal level, just as we found a metrical version of the NSR (Nuclear Stress Rule) and CSR (Compound Stress Rule).

However, in dealing with words, as opposed to phrases, we cannot appeal to a syntax of syllables that would design the trees for us, independent of prosodic considerations. We must therefore discover the relevant principles of construction.

## 2.1   Word trees

Consider first the simple situation in which a stressed syllable is weighed against unstressed syllables. It accords quite directly with the intuition behind metrical comparison to regard the stressed syllable as *strong*, its unstressed compeers as *weak*. This, taken with the restriction to binary branching, dictates tree shape and labeling for words like *labor, caprice, Pamela*:

(15)

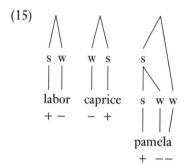

The (+,−) marks indicate the value of the segmental feature [±stress] for the vowels they are written under. Although in the examples cited *s* dominates only (+) and *w* only (−), this perfect correlation cannot be maintained in general, since a [+stress] vowel may well be metrically weak, as words like *gymnast, raccoon* show:

(16)   (a)          (b)

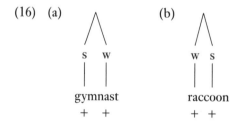

The submetrical distinction in prominence made available by the contrast between *w*/+ and *w*/− shows itself when we compare *modest* with *gymnast* or *balloon* with *raccoon*.

(17)   (a)          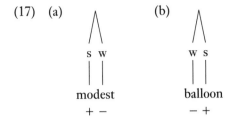          (b)

Metrically, *modest* and *gymnast*, *balloon* and *raccoon*, can only be identical, because the members of each pair have identical patterns of *relative* prominence. Examples like these show that the familiar segmental (or syllabic) distinction marked by the feature [±stress] must be maintained within metrical theory.

We hypothesize, then, that the correlation between $(s,w)$ and $[(+,-)$ stress] is given by the following implication:

(18)   If a vowel is $s$, then it is [+stress].

By contraposition, (18) tells us that if a vowel is [−stress], it must be $w$. Principle (18) will be regarded as a well-formedness condition on metrical structures, functioning to disallow the output configuration (19):

(19)        *s
            |
            V
        [−stress]

Principle (18) may be paraphrased by saying that only a stressed syllable may be the *strong* element of a metrical foot.

Observe that the condition (18) gives only one parsing for *Pamela*, eliminating the logically possible (20b, c):

(20)   (a)          (b)          (c)

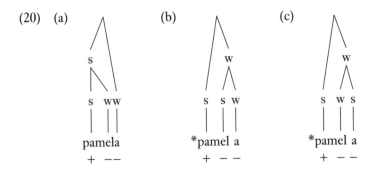

When we turn to words in which a stressed vowel is flanked on both sides by stress-less vowels, we find ambiguities of analysis.

(21)   (a)                    (b)

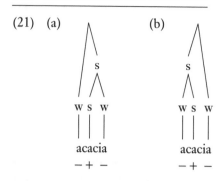

Our principles determine the labels, but allow both rhythmic divisions equally. Although it is possible that such multiplicity could exist and function, we submit that only (21a) is correct, and that English metrical structure is well-defined, in accord with the following description:

(22)   (a)   Every sequence of syllables +−, +−−, +−−−, etc. forms a metrical tree. Because of the condition limiting [−stress] to weak positions, and because of the bivalent (binary-branching) character of metrical trees, the structure and labeling of the sequences is uniquely determined. We have, necessarily, left-branching trees, looking like this:

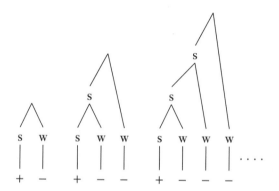

(b)   The syllable-dominating trees of provision (a) are organized into a right-branching tree whose root is associated with the syntactic node immediately dominating the entire word. The arrangement will look like this:

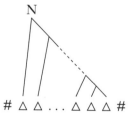

(This description will be modified slightly in 2.4 below [not repr. here], when certain more complex cases are considered.)

Imposing these patterns on *acacia* decides in favor of (21a), [[<sub>w</sub>a][<sub>s</sub>cacia]]; similar results are guaranteed for the parsing of *America*:

(23)   (a)                      (b)

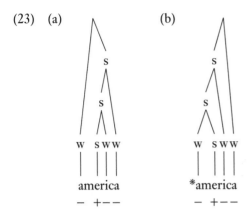

A straightforward method of developing the patterns described in (22a, b) is to start at the end of the word and work leftward, stopping at each [+stress] to build up as much of the tree as possible. In a word like *reconciliation*, for example, the first stop is at *-at-*, and a trochaic foot is erected:

(24)

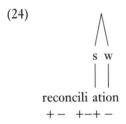

The next stop is *-cil-*, and here again a trochee will be called for; but further arborization is also possible, and the two trochees will be joined into a higher-level unit:

(25)

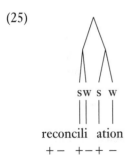

A final calculation at the first syllable completes the tree:

(26)

S W   SW S W

reconcili ation
+ −   +−+ −

Observe that in a word like *execute*, the first stop – at the stressed syllable *-ute-* – will not result in the creation of metrical structure; the next stop will arborize the (+,−) sequence *exec-* and join it to the remaining *-ute*, generating the structure (27):

(27)

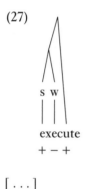

S W

execute
+ − +

[ . . . ]

## 2.7  Remark on the cycle

There is a striking difference in kind between the evidence for the phonological cycle within words and the evidence for the cyclicity of phrasal stress rules. The motive and the cue for the phrasal cycle has been the fact that, in languages like English, patterns of relative prominence are largely determined by syntactic constituent structure and are quite generally preserved under embedding. Within words, however, such motivation from the character of prominence phenomena is entirely lacking. Morphology, the analogue of syntax, falls far short of providing a constituent structure of syllables that is adequate to metrical labeling. On the one hand, many polysyllables are monomorphemic (e.g. *Tatamagouchi*), so that morphology has nothing to say about their internal organization; on the other hand, when morphology does provide structure, it is typically irrelevant to metrical grouping. Consider, for example, the word *compensation*: morphology will analyze it as [[compensat] ion], while phonology must see the principal significant division as [[compen][sation]]; the two parsings are grossly incompatible.

In addition, morphological embedding freely disrupts the pattern of relative prominence. In *compensate*, the first syllable predominates over the third; in *compensation*, the relationship is reversed; in *compensatory*, these two prominences are utterly reduced, and the weakest syllable of the inner constituent (-*pen*-) becomes the strongest syllable of the entire word. The prosodic constituent structure varies correspondingly, changing from word to word, regardless of the constants of morphological relatedness.

(83)

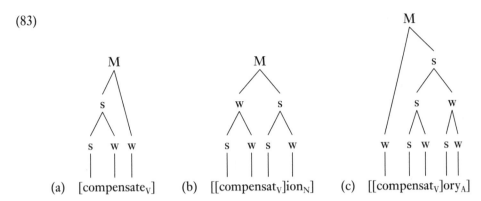

(a)  [compensate_V]   (b)  [[compensat_V]ion_N]   (c)  [[compensat_V]ory_A]

The primary evidence for the subword cycle comes from the persistence of the segmental mark [+stress], unmoored from any syntagmatic relations it may enter into. Consider the following array of facts:

(84)

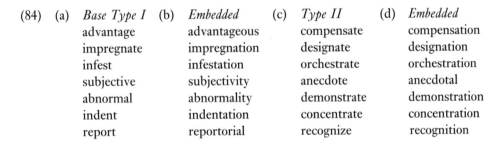

|  | (a) *Base Type I* | (b) *Embedded* | (c) *Type II* | (d) *Embedded* |
|---|---|---|---|---|
|  | advantage | advantageous | compensate | compensation |
|  | impregnate | impregnation | designate | designation |
|  | infest | infestation | orchestrate | orchestration |
|  | subjective | subjectivity | anecdote | anecdotal |
|  | abnormal | abnormality | demonstrate | demonstration |
|  | indent | indentation | concentrate | concentration |
|  | report | reportorial | recognize | recognition |

The interesting action takes place in the second syllable. In column (84b), the second-syllable vowels are all nonreduced [æ, ɛ, ɔ]; in column (84d), which contains words of similar make-up, in terms of segments and prominence, the analogous vowels are uniformly reduced; they are schwa (with perhaps some environmental coloration). Whether the vowel reduces or not in the complex word correlates perfectly with its status in the base forms listed in columns (84a) and (84c). If it is unstressed in the base, as in column (84c), it is unstressed when embedded; if stressed as in (84a), it shows stress when embedded, and does not, therefore, admit of reduction to schwa. (Notice, too, a clearly perceptible rhythmic difference between the words of columns (84b) and (84d), a consequence, presumably, of their different (±) stress patterns.)

This kind of phonological dependency between complex words and the simpler words they contain is widespread in the lexicon of English and generally quite regular. Exceptionality involving Type II words is, we believe, unknown; there are apparently no alternations of the hypothetical form *concntrate* ~ *concɛntration*. Among Type I words, a certain amount of unexpected reduction is found, but it appears to lie within a phonetically circumscribed domain: metrically weak nonlow vowels occasionally collapse with following tautosyllabic sonorants, even when they should bear a protecting stress. We find such examples as *commṇtary* (*commɛnt*), *consḷtation* (*consʌlt*), *transfṛmation* (*transfɔrm*), and, optionally, *sentimṇtality* (*sentimɛntal*). Note that there are nonreduced instances of all these: as in *indɛntation, confɔrmation, exʌltation*. Perfectly regular, though unstressed, is the second syllable of *confirmation*; as noted above, the vowel [r̩] of *confirm* is always stressless when metrically weak in medial position. In fact, *all* syllabic liquids and nasals (*m̩ n̩ l̩ r̩*) are stressless when medially weak, and we can conclude that what is unusual about words like *transformation* is the coalescence of the vowel with the sonorant /r/; after that, the reduction of the resulting *r*-colored vowel (or syllabic *r*) is completely normal.

A second, very similar type of translexical redundancy involves the location of (secondary) stresses in long, morphologically complex words. Consider the following examples:

(85)  (a)  recíprocal          (b)  recíprŏcality       (c)  Tátămăgóuchi
          corpóreal                corpórĕálity            Pássămăquóddy
          artifícial               artifícĭálity           cátămărán
          original                 orígĭnálity             hétĕrŏdýne
          munícipal                munícĭpálity            Wínnĕpĕsáukee
          relígious                relígĭósity             Kálămăzóo
          volúminous               volúmĭnósity            ánthrŏpŏmórphic

The marked vowels of column (85a) are all short underlyingly (for the last, cf. *volŭme*), and they are stressed by the ordinary operation of the ESR (English Stress Rule). The interesting contrast is between (85b) and (85c): words in (85c) have a second stress as far back from their endmost stress as is possible; the words in (85b), which have a syllable structure identical in the relevant respects to that of the words in (85c), show a second stress that falls one syllable short of its greatest possibilities (e.g. *\*orígĭnálity*). This shortfall means that the derived word will have a stress just where its base has one. As with the reduction cases, we regularly find a stressed syllable where we could as easily find a stressless one if the rules operated freely or randomly.

Paradigms like these show conclusively that the (±) stress pattern of a complex word depends on the (±) stress pattern that its morphological constituents assume in isolation. The most elegant and restrictive device proposed to represent this kind of pervasive "transderivational" relationship, and the one we shall accept, is the phonological cycle. By means of it, aspects of the derivation of subconstituents become, literally, part of the derivation of the whole. In *SPE* and Halle and Keyser (1971), the marked stresses on such words as *reláxation, originality* necessitated cyclic application in a direct, "observational" way; for without it, no stress would be placed on those syllables by the posited rule system, which differs from ours in not having an iterative stress rule. Theories of this sort depend on derivations of the following form:

(86)  *Noniterative Derivation Type*

$$[[[\text{origin}_N]\text{al}_A]\text{ity}_N]$$

| | |
|---|---|
| First Cycle, Stress | + _____ |
| Second Cycle, Stress | + _____ |
| Third Cycle, Stress |     + |
| Other Rules | − _____ |
| Output | oríginálity |

Under the present analysis, of course, no such straightforward argument for the cycle, based on the mere presence of [+stress], is available. The iterative rule we have postulated – and we have been careful to illustrate its operation at every step with non-complex words – has the capacity to place stress appropriately in *relaxation, originality*, etc. We need simply mark such words for weak retraction. To do so, however, would be to abandon the generalization that such stress positioning correlates with morphological composition. Even if it could be argued that weak retraction is the "unmarked" mode for complex words, and therefore need only be stipulated once for the entire class, the argument from lost generalization still has force; with a cycle to transmit to the whole word the features that its parts earn on their own, the fact that suffixes like *-al, -ous, -ive, -age*, etc. induce weak retraction when stressed follows directly from the fact that the ESR treats them quite normally when they end a constituent; no lexical stipulation is required, general or specific, to guide the stressing of such suffixes and the words they belong to.

To accommodate this generalization within our analysis, we must slightly modify the ESR and our conception of its effects. The ESR takes on the following shape:

(87)   *ESR* (Cyclic Version)

$$V \rightarrow [\text{+stress}] \, / \, \underline{\quad} \, C_0 \left( \begin{array}{c} V \\ \begin{bmatrix} -\text{long} \\ -\text{stress} \end{bmatrix} \end{array} (C) \right)_a \left( \begin{array}{c} V \\ [\langle -\text{long} \rangle_d] \end{array} C_0 \right)_b (\acute{V} \, X)_{c \, \alpha}]$$

Conditions: $\sim$c $\supset$ d, $\alpha = $ N, A, V

The rule has been changed to measure from the end of a constituent rather than from the end of a word; and the term *a* has been further restricted so that it can only correspond to stressless syllables. This will prevent it from skipping over the cyclically assigned stress of *originality, religiosity*, etc. Term *b* must, however, on our account, be able to analyze a stressed syllable, in order to correctly derive words like *compensatory*.

What of the metrical constituent structure entailed by the ESR? The first thing we determined about morphological embedding was that it fails to preserve relative prominence relations and (hence) the prosodic structures that represent those relations. Any trees erected by the ESR on a cycle below the word level simply do not influence further processing. They do not, apparently, survive the passage to the next cycle. We need, therefore, to amend our theory of tree building with a clause that ensures what might be called "deforestation" at the beginning of each cycle.

(88)   *Deforestation*

Before applying any rules on a cycle, erase all prosodic structure in the domain of that cycle.

This will leave the ESR with a slate that is clean except for the residue of [+stress] marks deposited by applications on earlier cycles.

Derivations like (89) will result:

(89)

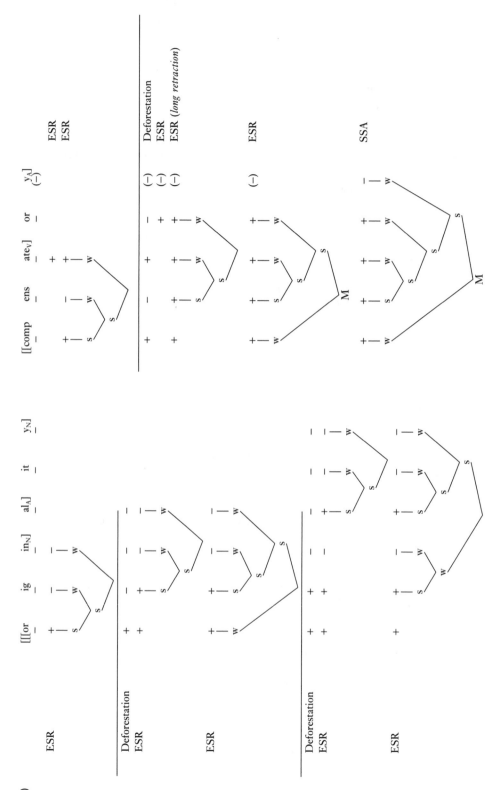

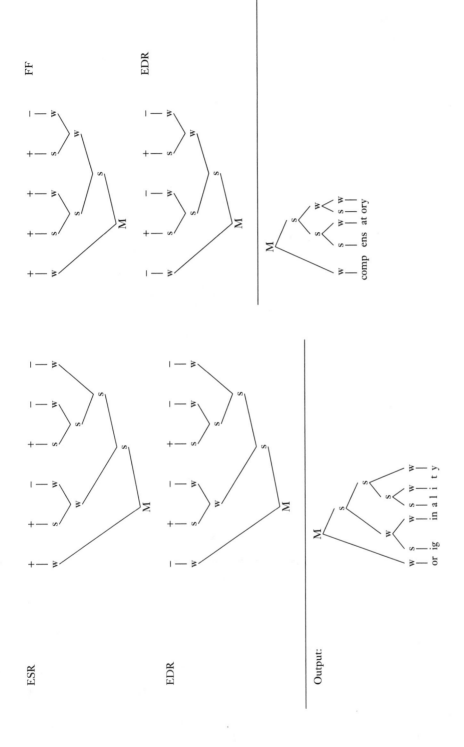

Metrical stress theory is thus brought into consistency with cyclic application of rules like the ESR. (Note that the Destressing Rule (70) [not repr. here] remains word-level.) Because the subword cycle is not defined on metrically relevant bracketing the way the phrasal cycle is, the present theory does not illuminate the structure-dependence of (±)-stress rules. As in former theories, this is a special property that does not follow from independent assumptions about the nature of the grammar.

Given cyclicity, then, and our understanding of the arboreal consequences of applying stress, a principle is required to adjudicate among the conflicting structural claims of various cyclic applications of the ESR; we offer (88), Deforestation, which rules in favor of the last cycle on which the rule operates, the one that encompasses the whole word. Further evidence is of course needed to establish (88) as the correct interpretation of the phenomenon, in the face of the many imaginable technical and conceptual alternatives. It is interesting to note that the other well-known mode of phonological organization, grouping of segments into syllables, also changes under morphological embedding: compare the second syllable of *ex-plain* with that of *ex-pla-na-tion*; if stress rules are sensitive to syllable structure *per se*, as suggested above, then there must be de- (and re-) syllabification at each cycle, just as there is de- and re-forestation. Principle (88), then, which may be the metrical reflection of a more embracing theory of cyclic reorganization, allows us to present a version of the ESR (87), that can play a key role in representing the system of "translexical" regularities typified by the data discussed in this section. [ . . . ]

## Notes

We would like to thank J. B. Grimshaw, M. Halle, S. J. Keyser, R. P. V. Kiparsky, D. L. Nanni, E. O. Selkirk, and J.-R. Vergnaud for much valuable discussion of the materials presented in this article.

1   Aspects of the these proposals, or ideas similar in spirit, are to be found in Fischer-Jørgensen 1948; Rischel 1964, 1972. This previous work will be discussed at the end of sectior 3 [not repr. here].
2   Cf. Liberman and Streeter 1976.
3   By Nakatani and Schaffer 1976.

## References

Fischer-Jørgensen, E. 1948. Some remarks on the function of stress with special relation to the Germanic languages. Congr. Intern. Sc. Anthropol. and Ethnol., Comptes-Rendus, Troisième Session, Bruxelles 1948, 86–8.

Liberman, M. 1975. The intonational system of English. Unpublished doctoral dissertation, MIT, Cambridge, Mass.

Liberman, M. and L. Streeter. 1976. Use of nonsense syllable mimicry in the study of prosodic phenomena. Paper delivered at Acoustical Society of America meeting, San Diego, Nov. 1976.

Nakatani, L. and J. Schaffer. 1976. Hearing words without words: prosodic cues for word perception. Paper delivered at Acoustical Society of America meeting, San Diego, Nov. 1976.

Rischel, J. 1964. Stress, juncture and syllabification in phonemic description. Proceedings of IXth International Congress of Linguists, 1962, 85–93.

Rischel, J. 1972. Compound stress in Danish without a cycle. Annual Report of the Institute of Phonetics, University of Copenhagen (ARIPUC) 6, 211–28.

# 21

# Relating to the Grid (1983)

## Alan S. Prince

## 1 Introduction

### 1.1 The argument

Metrical theory, as originally formulated, employs two distinct hierarchical structures: the $s/w$ relational tree and the metrical grid. Relative prominence is represented abstractly as a relation between constituents in the $s/w$ trees. (I call it "abstract" because the $s/w$ relationship is not interpreted.) Mapping such trees terminal by terminal to a metrical grid provides the basis for a temporal–rhythmic interpretation. We can think of metrical theory as giving a two-stage mapping between surface structures and the grid: first, a translation into (binary-branching) $s/w$ trees; second, an interpretation of the $s/w$ relations thus derived in terms of alignment with the grid.

(1)  Surface Structure $\xrightarrow{T_b}$ $s/w$ Trees $\xrightarrow{P_{s/w}}$ Grid

As the theory has developed, almost all of the research has concentrated on $T_b$ and the grid has receded into oblivion. For example, Selkirk has enriched $T_b$ to include the assignment of prosodic *categories* (foot, word, phrase, etc.) to the nodes in phonological trees (Selkirk 1980). Many theorists have sought in constraints on tree form and tree labeling an explanation for the character of lexical stress patterns in the world's languages. (See, for example, Halle and Vergnaud (1978), McCarthy (1979), Hayes (1980, 1981), and the references therein.) One might reasonably surmise that the grid, if it even exists, lies outside linguistic theory; that it is a matter of phonetic realization and not a properly linguistic level at all.

In this article, I will pursue the opposite tack. I will show that surface structure (words and phrases) should be related directly to the grid, without the intervention of a level where calculations with $s$ and $w$ take place on trees. The essentials of the alignment are to be accomplished by a single, one-parameter rule: strengthen the leftmost (rightmost) element in a domain (= word, phrase). This will be supplemented by a "rhythm rule" that operates locally on the grid to rearrange certain awkward or disfavored configurations. Where no independently definable domains are relevant, as inside a word or stem, alignment with a rhythmically optimal grid will be argued to be the principal determinant of stress pattern. On the negative side, then, the argument will show that much of the apparatus of metrical theory is inessential to its fundamental goals – for example, binary branching trees, *s/w* labeling rules, branchingness conditions. More positively, a full theory of stress patterns will emerge, significantly simpler than its current rivals, yet still well within the thematic premises of the hierarchical program initiated by Liberman.

## 1.2   The grid: a heuristic introduction

The metrical grid comes out of the description of musical rhythm (cf. Liberman 1975; Jackendoff and Lerdahl 1981; Lerdahl and Jackendoff 1983). Imagine a sequence of even pulses: x x x x x x x x x x. . . . A time signature, such as 2/4, imposes a kind of implicit metric on the pulse train, distinguishing certain pulses or positions as intrinsically stronger than others.

(2)   $\frac{2}{4}$ ♩♩ | ♩♩ | ♩♩ | ♩♩ |
      x   x   x   x

     x x   x x   x x   x x . . .

The new strength distinction adds a level to the grid. The stronger grid positions are those that have entries at the higher level. Further differentiation occurs when the beat itself is split into subunits. It is a fact of musical life that when a beat (or subbeat – any grid position) is divided in two, the first half is felt to be naturally stronger than the second half.

(3)   (a)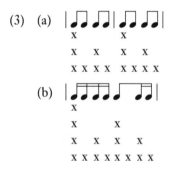
         x       x

         x   x   x   x

         x x x x   x x x x

(b)
         x

         x       x

         x   x   x   x

         x x x x x x x x

The typical 2/4 pattern – a stronger first and a weaker second beat – is represented in the cited grids as a relation between the highest and next-highest levels. Examples (3a, b) show finer detail in the medial strata. Notice that the *absolute* height of a grid column has no meaning; the layering of the grid expresses a network of relations.

    The grid can also be thought of as a "hierarchy of intersecting periodicities" (to use Liberman's plangent phrase). Each level then represents a certain period, or rate of repetition, the frequency diminishing as altitude increases. In example (3b), level-1 elements occur eight times per measure, level-2 elements four times, level-3 elements twice, and top-level elements just once per measure, marking the strong first downbeat. The strength of a grid position is determined by the number of periodicities that coincide there. In the musical examples, the frequency goes down by half for each transition to a higher level; this reflects a binary subdivision of measure and beat. Nothing in the idea of the grid demands strict binarity, of course, and other ratios of musical subdivision may well exist: an empirical question.

In its linguistic incarnation, the grid is responsive to the relative strength of syllables, words, phrases, etc., as they are disposed by the rules and freedoms of the language. Consequently, it will not typically assume the immaculately alternating, evenly sub-divided form that is felt behind, for example, 2/4 time.

(4)
```
                        x
     x                  x
     x   x              x
     x   x   x  x  x    x
```
Jim saw her in the park.

The linguistic grid, however, does aspire to the state of music, and this rhythmicity provides a fundamental motivation for the construct. When infelicities in grid form appear in the normal course of linguistic concatenation, it is often the case that various steps are taken to remedy them. A clear example is the Rhythm Rule of English, which readjusts certain otherwise expected patterns of prominence when they would result in a nonalternating or "clashing" grid.

(5)   (a)       x          (b)   x
```
             x   x               x   x
             fourteen            women
```

(c)
```
                                        x
                                  x     x
                              x   x     x   x
             fourteen + women ≠ fourteen women
```

(d)                 x
```
             x      x
             x   x  x   x
             = fourteen women
```

The grid of (5c), obtained by merely juxtaposing the words and supplying the final word with unmarked phrase stress, contains a *clash*, a too-great proximity of elements at the same level. In this case English allows a readjustment, represented in (5d).

The explicit hierarchization of prominence in the grid allows a direct account of the notion "stress clash" in terms of level structure and proximity of grid elements. More generally, the notion of *eurhythmicity* (or preferred grid configuration) will be found to play a central role in determining patterns of prominence in both phrases and words.

## 1.3   Projecting grids from metrical trees

In Liberman and Prince (1977) two methods of interpreting prominence from *s/w* trees are discussed, but only one is recommended. Since the trees contain (in one form or another) all the information that is generated by the *Stress Subordination Convention* of Chomsky and Halle (1968; hereafter, *SPE*), it is possible to extract it and derive a prominence pattern that exactly recapitulates the *SPE* *n*-stress numbering. To do this requires a tree-measuring calculation of the following sort:

(6)   SPE *Numbering*
   For any terminal node *a*, determine the first *w* that dominates *a*. Count the number of nodes that dominate this *w*. Add 1. This is the *SPE* stress number of *a*.

Suppose terminal node *a* is the main-stress of the phrase. Then *no w*'s dominate it. Adding 1 to this 0 gives 1: *a* is the 1-stress. To see why the technique works for the other stresses, observe that each node that dominates the-first-*w*-above-*a* corresponds to an *SPE* cycle on which *a* is *not the primary stress*: that is, a cycle on which *a* is demoted according to the Stress Subordination Convention. Adding up these demotions correctly will give the *SPE* ranking.

Rule (6) is more elegantly formalized in Carlson 1978 and in Halle and Vergnaud 1978. These authors assign a stress number to every node in the tree, not just the terminals. Elegance aside, rule (6) makes clear the rather amazing power of a cycling Stress Subordination Convention to calculate subtle *arithmetic* details of tree structure. Is there another linguistic rule that distinguishes degree-4 depth of embedding from degree-5?

There is nothing *inherent* in the relational *s/w* tree that would lead to the particular rank ordering of terminals entailed by rule (6). To impose *SPE* Numbering on metrical theory involves an auxiliary hypothesis of considerable complexity and indeed – from the metrical point of view – arbitrariness. The relational representation says simply that at a given level one subconstituent is stronger than the other.

How then are we to interpret the dictum "*s* is stronger than *w*"? Given any metrical (sub)tree, we can find its strongest terminal element – its *head* – by the following argument. We start at the root and examine its two daughters: surely the *s*-sister must dominate a terminal that is stronger (in terms of the grid) than anything in *w* (what would *s* mean if this were not true?). Therefore, we must direct our attention to the *s*-daughter of the root. If it dominates a terminal, we are done: it is the head. If not, we can simply repeat the argument: for surely this *s*'s own *s*-daughter must contain something stronger than anything in its *w*-daughter. If that *s*-daughter is terminal, we are done. If not, we continue, repeating the argument until there are no more daughters to decide between. In this fashion, we can pursue an unbroken chain of *s*'s down from the root of any subtree to arrive unambiguously at its head.

This argument is canonized as the *Relative Prominence Projection Rule* (Liberman 1975; Liberman and Prince 1977: 316).

(7)   *Relative Prominence Projection Rule*
   For any pair of sisters $\{s,w\}$, *s* must contain a node that holds a grid position stronger than any held by terminals of *w*.
   Equivalently (and more directly), we can say:
   For any pair of sisters $\{s,w\}$, $H(s) > H(w)$, where $H(N)$ = the strongest element in *N*, the head of *N*.

To see how the RPPR works out for some typical examples, consider the tree–grid associations of (8) and (9).

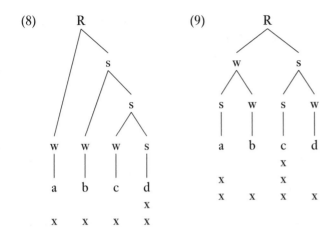

(8) (9)

In (8), the element *d* is the head of R. Appropriately, it holds the strongest position. Going up the ladder of *s*'s, we see that the RPPR is met at every level; therefore, (8) represents a satisfactory match.

In (9), *c* is H(R), head of the whole tree, so by the RPPR we have $c > a,b,d$. Because *ab* is a constituent, a further relation is induced: $a > b$. The grid of (9) conforms to these restrictions, so it is licensed by the RPPR.

Consider now the grids of (10) as candidates for matching up to the tree of (8).

(10)   (a)                    (b)       x       (c)                    (d)       x

                 x                 x    x                      x              x x

           x     x           x x    x                x    x                x x x

           x x x x           x x x x                 x x x x              x x x x

            a b c d           a b c d                 a b c d              a b c d

All of these grids respect the constraint $d > a,b,c$, which is the only information that the RPPR obtains from tree (8). This plurality of interpretations makes it clear that the RPPR establishes only a partial ordering among terminals. In particular, the RPPR never relates terminals that are immediately dominated by *w* (and, conversely, always relates terminals immediately dominated by *s*).

Of course, not every possibility admitted by the RPPR is commonly realized – or even realized at all – in the actual pronunciation of forms like (8). But this need not be a disastrous consequence. In Liberman and Prince (1977: 323) it is suggested that a "flattened out" structure like that of grid (8) corresponds more closely to speakers' actual perceptions than the highly articulated result of *SPE* Numbering.

Grid (8) is distinguished by being *minimal* in the obvious way: it has less structure than any other interpretation of the tree [w w w s]. The RPPR can be supplemented with a natural principle of minimality to pick out (8) as fundamental. Divergences from the "flattest" interpretation will arise from subtle variations of emphasis consistent with overall *s/w* structure (Pierrehumbert 1980: 37), as well as from the pressures of eurhythmicity and phrasal demarcation. For example, in a [w w w s] tree like (8), the first *w* is often felt to be more strongly stressed than the others. This fact might be recorded as a supplementary principle of prosodic realization, based on constituent structure and linear order, distinct from the primary interpretation of the stress pattern. It is not necessary to retreat to *SPE* Numbering, which arguably exceeds intuitive judgments of relative stress in its overspecification. A different, and perhaps firmer, line of evidence in favor of the RPPR is found in Pierrehumbert 1980. For accurate acoustic predictions, her theory of intonation patterns requires the kind of stress values allowed by the RPPR, and it goes distinctly astray if *SPE* Numbering is adhered to.

Finally, it may be worth noting that the RPPR is the weakest theory of tree interpretation consistent with the intuitive sense of "*s*" and "*w*." Were it any weaker, some *s/w* relations would go unenforced. The theory could be enriched in a number of ways (for example, as in *SPE* Numbering) by taking various aspects of tree geometry (and arithmetic) into account. Any enrichment would necessarily preserve the orderings-of-prominence *required* by the RPPR; it could only *add* more prominence relations to this basic set, neither contradicting nor diminishing RPPR constraints. For these conceptual reasons alone, the RPPR has a strong claim on our attention.

## 2   Direct Relatability

### 2.1   The End Rule

Let us assume, then, that the RPPR gives the basis for an accurate account of syllabic stress patterns. With this in mind, let us reconsider the descriptive problem posed by phenomena that fall under the *Nuclear Stress Rule* of *SPE*. Consider the treatment of a right-branching tree:

(11)

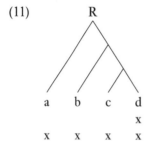

The goal is to achieve the association presented in (11). In standard metrical theory, this would be attained by labeling the tree according to the rule "All sisters stand in the relation [w s]" and then interpreting the resultant *w/s* tree in the light of the RPPR. Grid (11) is the minimal grid consistent with a [w s] labeling of tree (11).

Because the grid carries over so little of the information in the tree, there is another, more direct route to the match-up. Instead of assigning a metrical potency to every node, we can deal just with *terminals* according to a rule like this: "In any constituent C, the rightmost terminal is strongest." In tree (11), the constituents are [cd], [bcd], [abcd]. Clearly, strengthening *d* alone, as in grid (11), will satisfy the rule.

A moment's thought will bring the conviction that the stated rule will in fact capture the effect of [w s] labeling on any tree whatever, no matter how complicated or erratic its branching pattern may be. Inspection of (12) may be useful.

(12)

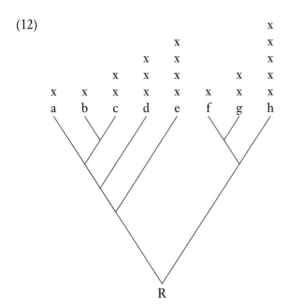

Formal proof of the equivalence between uniform [w s] labeling under the RPPR and "Rightmost terminal is strongest in every constituent" can be accomplished by an induction on the number of nodes in a tree, using the RPPR definition of "$s$ is stronger than $w$": namely, $H(s) > H(w)$. Notice that under this definition, for any constituent C labeled [w s] throughout, $H(C)$ must be the rightmost terminal of C.

It should be equally clear that uniform [s w] labeling is equivalent to the grid alignment condition "*Left*most terminal is strongest in every constituent." Now because uniform labeling plays such a central role in prosodic description, a tantalizing speculation presents itself: perhaps the theory of stress patterns ought to involve only a direct relation between surface structures and grids, without the intervention of tree-labeling and tree-interpreting operations. Perhaps, indeed, the essential burden of assigning stress to a constituent structure can be borne entirely by the *End Rule* (13).

(13)  *End Rule*
    In a constituent C, the leftmost/rightmost terminal in C is associated to a stronger grid position than any other terminal in C.

[ ... ]

## Overview

The theory presented here is built up from several independent subtheories. The theory of (what might be called) *accessibility* prescribes the calculations that can be made on the basis of structural information alone; its fundamental principle is that only a strictly peripheral entity may be accessed. The End Rule and the rule of extrametricality are the chief beneficiaries of accessibility theory. The End Rule stresses first or last syllables; selects a first or last stress as main word-stress; promotes a first or last word-stress to phrasal prominence. The hierarchy of the grid allows these operations to be understood as formally identical, because "first or last" applies not to the terminal string but to positions within a grid level. Extrametricality mitigates the rather severe character of the End Rule by allowing a single peripheral unit – segment, mora, syllable, morpheme – to have its projection at a specified level overlooked in the calculation of the next level's structure. Extrametricality itself falls under the principle of accessibility: only an accessible constituent – first or last – may be extrametrical. Accessibility also influences the mode of operation of PG, Perfect Grid Construction, since the rule typically starts from one end of a word or the other.

It seems clear that the relevance of accessibility theory extends beyond the formulation of stress patterns; as well it should, since it has nothing in particular to do with the phonetics of stress. Autosegmental mapping typically begins at the periphery, according to various authors; Clements and Ford (1979) suggest the initial syllable as a universal starting point, while Marantz (1982) uses both ends. Pitch-accent systems also display signs of the accessibility phenomenon. The Basic Accentuation Principle (BAP) of Kiparsky and Halle (1977) attaches high tone to the first accent or, in accentless words, the first syllable; this parallels exactly those stress rules that seek out the first heavy syllable and, failing heavy syllables, default to the first syllable. Presumably the analysis should be parallel as well, making crucial use of the End Rule. This indicates a limited amount of hierarchization in accent systems, whereby an accent can be considered adjacent to a domain's edge so long as no other *accent* intervenes. It is important that no arguments for constituency in pitch-accent systems have come forth along the lines of those for the foot in stress systems: arguments that aim to establish independent support for a proposed constituent, e.g. as the domain of various phonetic and phonological processes distinct from the mere distribution of accents or stresses. Lacking footlike constituency, pitch-accent systems still display accessibility phenomena attributable to the End Rule. Accessibility cannot be reduced to calculations upon tree structure; the correct generalization involves a constituent-free hierarchy like the grid, which the End Rule acts upon.

The other subtheories involved [not all of which are discussed in this excerpt] are the theory of *rhythm*, the theory of *syllable representation*, and the theory of *prosodic levels*. The theory of rhythm takes clash as a central construct; coupled with a principle of maximal rhythmic organization, the anticlash constraint derives the essentials of so-called alternating patterns. The rules associated with the theory of rhythm are Perfect Grid Construction (PG), which establishes a perfect grid, maximally organized up to a certain level and clash-free, and Move *x*, which reorganizes otherwise unavoidable clashes. Perhaps something like Remove *x* also belongs here, permitting the outright deletion of clashing elements. We have seen how the syntactic conditions that bound Move *x* may follow from considerations of clash and hierarchy, rather than being primitive, as has been assumed.

The theory of syllable representation governs the mapping of syllabic material to grid positions. The proposal made here refers to the sonority envelope of the syllable, rather than to any internal constituency. The stressedness of heavy syllables is derived from their (fundamentally) bipositional representation. Bipositionality may also explain the role played by postvocalic material in establishing the light/heavy opposition.

The theory of prosodic levels relates morphological and syntactic constituency to the grid, as well as phonological elements such as syllables. It has impinged on our discussion principally in the requirement that such and such a unit *culminate* (to use François Dell's felicitous term) in a single entry, defining a certain correlative level. Much remains to be clarified here, particularly the extent to which prosodic levels are simply derivative from morphological–syntactic constituency.

In conclusion. I offer a summary of the rule types admitted in the present theory, with an account of the parameters to which they are sensitive.

(119)  (a)  *ER(E;L;FCO)*
The End Rule, at edge E = {Initial, Final}, at level L = {$\Sigma$, Wd, P},with or without Forward Clash Override (FCO).

(b)  *PG(D;A;FCO)*
Constructs the *perfect grid*, moving in direction D = {RL, LR}, starting with altitude A = {peak, trough} with FCO option.

(c)  *e/m(E;C;L)*
Declares extrametrical the constituent C = {consonant, vowel, segment, mora, syllable, morpheme, word(?)} that is adjacent to edge E at level L = {0, $\sigma$, $\Sigma$, ...}.

(d)  *QS(Son)*
Bipositional representation of heavy syllables, with each grid position minimally sonorous at level *Son*.

(e)  *MS*
Mora Sluicing adjunct to QS, which produces monopositional representation by eliminating weak second mora position from grid.

(f)  *Move x(D;L)*
Resolves clash by moving grid entry in direction D to nearest landing site, applying up to level L.

## Note

This is a revised version of a paper expanded from a talk given in April 1981 to the Trilateral Conference on Formal Phonology, held at the University of Texas at Austin and funded by Sloan Foundation grants to the Massachusetts Institute of Technology, the University of Massachusetts, and the University of Texas. I would like to thank the participants in that conference (most especially Yasuaki Abe, Edit Doron, Morris Halle, Robert Harms, Paul Kiparsky, John McCarthy, Bill Poser, and Lisa Selkirk), as well as Mark Liberman, Gennaro Chierchia, Jane Grimshaw, and Mats Rooth, for valuable comments and discussion. Thanks to Grimshaw, Halle, McCarthy, and Liberman, and to Ray Jackendoff and an anonymous *LI* reviewer for comments that helped shape the revision. Special thanks to Jay Keyser and Jerry Allen, who make things a lot easier. The work reported here was supported in part by NSF Grant BNS 77-05682.

## References

Carlson, L. 1978. Word Stress in Finnish. MS, MIT, Cambridge, Massachusetts.

Chomsky, N. and M. Halle. 1968. *The Sound Pattern of English*. New York: Harper and Row.

Clements, G. N. and K. Ford. 1979. Kikuyu Tone Shift and Its Synchronic Consequences. *Linguistic Inquiry* 10, 179–210.

Halle, M. and J.-R. Vergnaud. 1978. Metrical Structures in Phonology. MS, MIT, Cambridge, Massachusetts.

Hayes, B. 1980. A Metrical Theory of Stress Rules. Ph.D. dissertation, MIT.

Hayes, B. 1981. A Metrical Theory of Stress Rules. Bloomington, Ind.: Indiana University Linguistics Club.

Jackendoff, R. and F. Lerdahl. 1981. On the Theory of Grouping and Meter. *Musical Quarterly* 67, 479–506.

Kiparsky, P. and M. Halle. 1977. Towards a Reconstruction of the Indo-European Accent. In L. Hyman (ed.), *Studies in Stress and Accent*, SCOPIL 4, Los Angeles. USC, 209–38.

Lerdahl, F. and R. Jackendoff. 1983. *A Generative Theory of Tonal Music*. Cambridge, Mass., MIT Press.

Liberman, M. 1975. The Intonational System of English. Ph.D. dissertation, MIT.

Liberman, M. and A. Prince. 1977. On Stress and Linguistic Rhythm. *Linguistic Inquiry* 8, 249–336. [Repr. in part here as ch. 20]

McCarthy, J. 1979. Formal Problems in Semitic Phonology and Morphology. Ph.D. dissertation, MIT.

Marantz, A. 1982. Re Reduplication. *Linguistic Inquiry* 13, 435–82.

Pierrehumbert, J. B. 1980. The Phonology and Phonetics of English Intonation. Ph.D. dissertation, MIT.

Selkirk, E. 1980. The Role of Prosodic Categories in English Word Stress. *Linguistic Inquiry* 11, 563–605.

# 22

# Extrametricality and English Stress (1982)

## Bruce Hayes

## 1 Introduction

One distinguishing trait of generative phonology is a belief in the explanatory value of notational devices: in many cases, the invention of a good notation has revealed the simplicity behind systems that initially seemed complex. A good formal device takes on a life of its own, revealing previously unseen connections and stimulating further inquiry. A successful notation also increases our understanding of how complex phonological systems can be learned by children: if children undertake language learning equipped with some mental analogue of our graphic formalisms, their task is a much easier one. In this article, I offer a small extension of our set of formal devices, the extrametricality rule, and attempt to demonstrate its explanatory value.

In the metrical theory of stress, a syllable is called *extrametrical* if it is ignored by the stress rules; that is, treated as if it were not there. This notion was first introduced in Liberman and Prince's (1977) pioneering article as a means of handling the deviant stress patterns of words like *állegòry*, *álligàtor*, and *Áristòtle*. These words are exceptional in that they have branching constituents on the right that are labeled *weak*; compare *Áristòtle* with the regular *ànecdótal*:

(1)  Áristòtle     ànecdótal

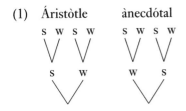

Liberman and Prince (hereafter LP) suggested that if certain cases of word-final *-y*, *-ŗ*, and *-ļ* are extrametrical, then the word trees in which they appear can be labeled by the normal rule for nouns, which makes final nonbranching constituents weak. *Aristotle* would thus be labeled in the same way as, say, *anecdote*:

(2)  ánecdòte     Áristòtļ

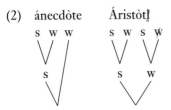

LP equivocate on the formal means by which syllables are to be designated as extra-metrical, but opt tentatively for an analysis based on Chomsky and Halle (1968, hereafter *SPE*), in which surface-final [i,r̩,l̩] are derived from underlying nonsyllabic /y,r,l/ by a rule of Sonorant Syllabification, which applies after metrical labeling:

(3)   *Sonorant Syllabification*
      [+son] → [+syl] / C __ #

In a later note, however, Nanni (1977) pointed out that essentially the same behavior that is displayed by *-i*, *-l*, and *-r* is found in words ending in the suffix *-ative* (cf. *ímitàtive*, *ínnovàtive*), where an analysis in which a final syllabic sound is derived from a nonsyllabic sonorant would be impossible. Nanni's analysis of *-ative* shows that extrametricality must be a diacritic property of at least some morphemes.

My purpose here is to extend the notion a step further, arguing that languages may contain extrametricality *rules*, which may apply to large segments of the vocabulary. The use of extrametricality rules will be shown to have explanatory value in capturing insights about the English stress system, in the treatment of word-final syllables in languages where stress is sensitive to syllable quantity, and in the construction of a universal theory of possible foot shapes.

What does an extrametricality rule look like? With a couple of doubtful exceptions, the candidates known to me all adhere to the following format.

(4)   X → [ +extrametrical] / __ ]$_D$

where X is single phonological constituent, such as rhyme, segment, consonant, or suffix; and [ . . . ]$_D$ is the domain in which the stress rules of the language apply (usually the phonological word or phrase). There are two claims embodied in (4). First, the material marked as extrametrical must always be a single, unvarying unit, so that, for example, we could not replace the familiar Latin stress rule with a rule of final stress plus an extrametricality rule of the form (5):[1]

(5)   $(C_0\bar{V}C)(VC_0)$ → [ +ex] / __ ]$_{word}$

The second claim of (4) is that extrametricality is assigned only at the right edge of stress domains. This generalization holds true of a large number of stress systems, but may not be absolute; see the discussion of Winnebago stress in Hayes (1981: 71–2). It thus may be necessary to include the mirror image of (4) in the theory as a marked option.

Let us now consider two examples of extrametricality rules. According to McCarthy (1979a, b), the stress pattern of Classical Arabic (and some of its modern descendants) is based on the distinction of light (CV), heavy (CVV and CVC), and superheavy (CVVC and CVCC) syllables. Stress falls (a) on superheavy syllables, which may occur only in phrase-final position; (b) otherwise, on the rightmost nonfinal heavy syllable; (c) otherwise, on the initial syllable. Some examples are as follows:

(6)   kaatibáat      'writer (fem. pl.)'
      yušáariku      'he participates'
      mámlakatun     'kingdom (nom. sg.)'
      kátaba         'he wrote'

One way of looking at the pattern of (6) is to say that word-final syllables are demoted one position down the hierarchy of syllable weight: superheavy syllables are treated as heavy, while heavy syllables are treated as light. We can then say that stress is placed as far to the left as possible, subject to the condition that only light syllables may be skipped over. The "demotion" of word-final syllables is accomplished straightforwardly with an extrametricality rule of the form (7):

(7)  *Final Segment Extrametricality*
     [+seg] → [ +ex] / __ ]$_{word}$

Once (7) has applied, we can proceed with the stress derivation. Following Selkirk (1980), I assume that the feature [+stress] is to be excluded from phonological representations, to be replaced by a division of the prosodic structure into a level of *feet*, dominated by a *word tree*. In Classical Arabic, we can say that at the right edge of the word, a metrical foot is constructed which is left-branching and unbounded in size, and in which all syllables dominated by right branches must be light. Adopting McCarthy's formalism, we express this by requiring that all right branches dominate nonbranching nodes on a projection consisting solely of syllable rhymes. Sister nodes of the foot are labeled *s w*:

(8)  kaatibaat    mamlakatun    yušaariku
     aa i aat     am a a un     u aa i u    rhyme projection
     aa i aaṭ     am a a uṅ     u aa i ṷ    Final Segment Extrametricality
     aa i aaṭ     am a a uṅ     u aa i ṷ    Foot Construction

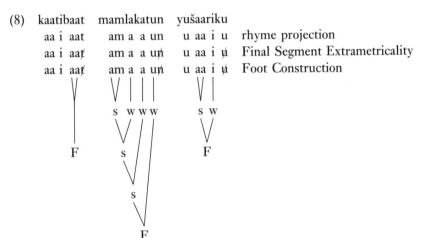

After the application of Foot Construction, a universal convention to be discussed below adjoins the final rhyme of *yušaariku* to the neighbouring foot. The complete metrical structure involves the creation of a word tree which is right-branching, with sister nodes labeled *w s*. For clarity I will represent the division between foot and word trees with a horizontal line, as follows:

(9)  kaatibáat        mámlakatun       yušáariku

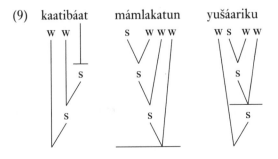

It should be clear from these derivations that an extrametricality rule can carry out just the demotion in weight of final syllables that is needed to derive the Arabic stress pattern with a maximally simple foot construction rule. Similar extrametricality rules can account for the deviant criteria for syllable weight in final position that are found in many other languages, for example, Hindi, Meadow Cheremis (Hayes 1981), Ancient Greek (Steriade 1979), Estonian (Prince 1980), and Spanish (Harris 1983).

Stress in Hopi, as discussed in Jeanne (1978), is another case in which extrametricality provides a straightforward analysis. As (10) shows, Hopi stress normally falls on the first syllable if it is heavy, and on the second syllable if the first syllable is light:

(10)  (a)  táavo        'cottontail'
           páawik$^y$a    'duck'
      (b)  $^?$ácvewa    'chair'
           léstavi       'roof beam'
      (c)  qötósompi     'headband'
           melóoni       'melon'

I hypothesize that this pattern is the result of applying the following rules:

(11)  (a)  At the left edge of a word, construct a foot on the rhyme projection, such
           that
           1   the foot contains at most two syllables;
           2   the left node of the foot, if any, dominates a nonbranching rhyme;
           3   the sister nodes are labeled w s.
      (b)  Incorporate this foot and any leftover syllables into a left-branching word
           tree, in which sister nodes are labeled s w.

Some examples of how (11) works are as follows:

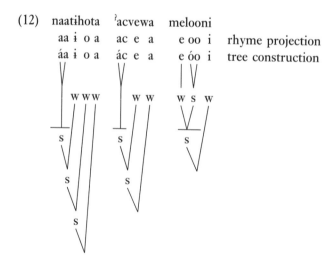

(12)  naatihota    $^?$acvewa    melooni
      aa i o a     ac e a        e oo i    rhyme projection
      áa i o a     ác e a        e óo i    tree construction

There is an additional complication in the Hopi stress rules that must be accounted for: a disyllabic word always receives initial stress, even if its first syllable is light:

cf. *kóho* 'wood', *wári* 'to run', *láho* 'bucket'. The problem can be resolved if we assume that there is an additional rule in Hopi that marks word-final syllables as extrametrical:

(13)   *Hopi Extrametricality*
       syllable → [ +ex] / __ ]$_{word}$

Rule (13) forces the Foot Construction rule to ignore the final syllable of *koho*, resulting in the construction of a nonbranching foot:

(14)   (a)   koho          (b)   qötösompi

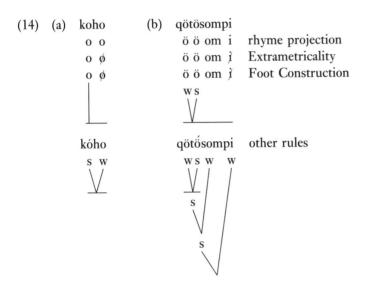

|       |       |
|-------|-------|
| o o   | ö ö om i   rhyme projection |
| o ø   | ö ö om i̧   Extrametricality |
| o ø   | ö ö om i̧   Foot Construction |

       kóho                qötösompi   other rules

The two preceding examples show that the device of rule-governed extrametricality can play a useful role in the formulation of stress rules. What I wish to argue here is that there are reasons to prefer the extrametricality analyses over other devices that seem a priori equally plausible. For example, stress in Classical Arabic is handled by McCarthy (1979a, b) under quite different assumptions. McCarthy claims that the canonical foot template for Classical Arabic is not uniformly left-branching, as I have suggested, but rather that the rightmost node of the foot is free. This allows word-final heavy syllables to be skipped over without the device of extrametricality, as in (15):

(15)   mamlakatun
       am a a un   rhyme projection

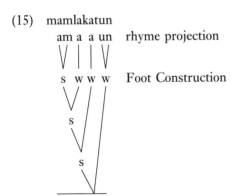

       s  w w w   Foot Construction

The word-final superheavy syllables are handled with an entirely different device, which will not be discussed here. As far as I know, there are no language-internal grounds available to decide between McCarthy's analysis of *mamlakatun* and the one proposed here. We can make an argument, however, if we address questions of stress rule typology. Following Halle and Vergnaud (1978), I assume that an adequate metrical theory of stress rules must include an inventory of possible foot types. Each foot type may be regarded as a template, usually of varying size, which is fitted to the string of syllables or rhymes. I would hypothesize that the conditions on the terminal nodes of a foot are of just two kinds: a terminal node may be free, or it must belong to one of two classes defined by some binary distinction of prominence, such as branching versus nonbranching rhymes, long versus short vowels, high versus low tone, and possibly a few others. Crucially, the same criterion of prominence must be used throughout the foot template. Here we will express templates as disembodied trees, using $X$ to designate free terminal nodes and $x$ for nodes which must dominate members of the less prominent class. Using this notation, the foot templates for my analyses of Classical Arabic and Hopi stress are as given in (16a) and (16b), respectively.[2]

(16)    (a)   X (x) (x) (x) . . .          (b)   (x) X

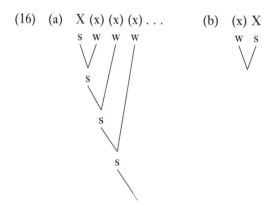

McCarthy's analysis of Classical Arabic requires a somewhat different template, as in (17):

(17)   X (x) (x) (x) . . . (X)

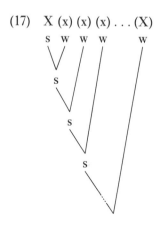

(17) is equivalent to (16a) with the addition of a free final node.

The argument here arises from the question of whether we can strengthen metrical theory by eliminating any of these templates from the universal inventory. The data in Hayes 1981 and other works indicate that the template (16a) is widespread: it is employed in all positions of the word, in numerous languages. By contrast, the template (17) appears *only in word-final position* in all well-motivated analyses of which I am aware. This is a mystery which extrametricality is well suited to clear up: languages in which feet have the surface form of (17) are to be accounted for with extrametricality rules, either rules of the form I have posited for Classical Arabic, or in the simpler cases, just rules marking final syllables as extrametrical. The restriction of such feet to word-final position follows from the more general restriction that extrametricality rules apply only at the right edge of the stress domain; (17) need not be included as a primitive foot template. We see, then, that although both of the foot templates (16a) and (17) allow for a descriptively adequate account of Classical Arabic stress, only the former is consistent with a more restrictive, explanatory theory of stress rules.

A similar argument can be made for the extrametricality account of Hopi stress. The most plausible rival analysis would be to posit a late stress fronting rule, which would apply only in disyllables:

(18)  *Stress Fronting*
$$\#\# \; X \; X \; \#\# \rightarrow \#\# \; X \; X \; \#\#$$
$$\quad\;\; \text{w} \; \text{s} \qquad\qquad\;\; \text{s} \; \text{w}$$
$$\quad\;\; \bigvee \qquad\qquad\quad\; \bigvee$$

This rule would correctly front the stress in *kóho* (< *kohó*), but would not apply to *qötösompi*, since the relevant *w s* constituent is not word-final (cf. (14b)). To decide between the rival analyses, we can appeal to universal grounds. It appears that cases similar to Hopi are fairly common; that is, languages in which stress placement is calculated from the beginning of the word, but with an overriding restriction that the final syllable must not be stressed (cf. Hayes 1981: 79). As Hyman (1977: 42) points out, however, the mirror image case is conspicuously missing: no language calculates stress from the end of a word, with an overriding restriction barring stress from the initial syllable. Once again, the theory of extrametricality offers an explanation of the phenomenon: if we use it to account for stress systems like Hopi, then the asymmetry follows from the restriction of extrametrical syllables to word-final position. This restriction is independently motivated by the role that extrametricality plays in the construction of word-final feet, as in Classical Arabic.

Another foot template that extrametricality would allow us to eliminate from the general theory is the one governing stress in Latin and a number of other languages, in which the antepenult is stressed in words of more than two syllables having a light penult; otherwise the penult. Under orthodox metrical assumptions, this would follow from a foot template of the form (19a), along with a word tree subordinating any remaining syllables in the word to the final foot. (19b) illustrates this with words from Latin:

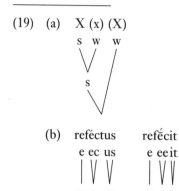

(19)   (a)   X (x) (X)

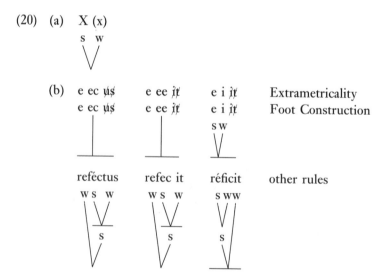

However, all the known cases of stress templates having the form (19a) appear in word-final position (see Hayes 1981: 67). This fact again suggests an extrametricality analysis, in which the extrametrical elements are word-final rhymes. The foot template would be as shown in (20a), the mirror image of Hopi:

(20)   (a)   X (x)

Again, the restriction of feet having the form (19a) to final position is a consequence of the extrametricality theory, but would go unexplained if we allowed (19a) as part of the primitive inventory of foot templates.

   A final, trivial constraint must be added to our account: in order to stress Latin mono-syllables, we must assume that extrametricality rules are blocked if their application would mark the entire stress domain as [+ex]. This condition is apparently universal, and thus should not add any cost to the grammars of particular languages.

Thus far I have left aside the question of how extrametrical elements are adjoined to the prosodic structure. I assume here that the constituent structure of syllables is present in underlying representation, so that no adjunction rule is needed for extrametrical segments; extrametricality does not mean that these segments are unattached from their syllables in any way, but simply that they are ignored for purposes of foot construction. Extrametrical syllables, by contrast, must be attached to feet by rule, if feet are to be created in phonological derivations. We may tentatively formulate a Stray Syllable Adjunction convention as follows:

(21)   *Stray Syllable Adjunction* (SSA)
       Adjoin a stray syllable as a weak member of an adjacent foot.

SSA can be identified as the missing rule completing the derivations of (8) and (20b). Notice that a convention of this sort is needed in metrical theory anyway, in order to assign a metrical interpretation to syllables that are rendered stray after the feet have been constructed, either through destressing (i.e. defooting) rules or through segmental epenthesis and vocalization processes. I assume, then, that SSA is a universal convention, which applies whenever it can after the rules of foot construction have applied. Notice that (21) is formulated ambiguously in the case of stray syllables occurring between feet. We will find evidence later to make the formulation of SSA more precise, removing this ambiguity.

In this section, I have tried to argue for the plausibility of rule-governed extrametricality on universal grounds. The theory allows us to constrain the inventory of possible foot templates; explains the restriction of certain surface foot shapes to word-final position; accounts for the fact that special "avoidance clauses" such as the one in Hopi refer to final syllables but not initial ones; and provides an account of the deviant criteria for syllable weight that are found in final position. What is needed to establish the extrametricality theory firmly, however, is to show that it can provide insights into the workings of complex but reasonably well-understood stress systems. One good example, I believe, is Harris's (1983) account of stress in Spanish, which adheres to an extrametricality framework quite close to what is proposed here. In the remainder of this article [not repr. here], the theory is applied to English stress. I will show that by using extrametricality, we can simplify the rules, capture new generalizations, and account for previously unexplained phenomena. [ . . . ]

# 3   Summary

To conclude, I will summarize the advantages that extrametricality brings to our description of English stress. The principal arguments are five in number: (a) The analysis can capture the unity of stress assignment in nouns and suffixed adjectives on one hand, and verbs and unsuffixed adjectives on the other. (b) It is no longer necessary to mark each suffix in the lexicon for one of three modes of retraction behavior; all systematic stress retraction follows from independently motivated rules. (c) The retraction behavior (actually *non*retraction behavior) of *-ation* in cyclic derivations is an automatic consequence of the rules, rather than a mystery. (d) The stress pattern of long monomorphemes exemplified by *Háckensàck ~ Àdiróndàck ~ Monádnòck* is a direct result of the system, augmented by an independently motivated destressing rule. (e) Much of what is arbitrary in the LP rules for labeling the word tree follows automatically from the extrametricality rules.

In addition, the theory has forced us to examine three areas where it initially appeared to fail. In each case, the examination led to a deeper understanding of the phenomenon in question: (a) The stress retraction pattern exemplified by *Winnepesáukee, Àpalàchicóla,* and *Mamároneck* turned out to follow neatly from the rules proposed, augmented by the independently needed rule of Poststress Destressing. (b) The stress behavior of Greek prefix–stem words followed straightforwardly from a compound analysis. (c) The supposed Long Retraction induced by $\check{V}\check{V}$ sequences turned out not to involve a stress rule at all, but rather a segmental rule of glide vocalization, which had favorable consequences elsewhere.

I believe that this represents progress, in fact, progress of just the right sort: ideally, a formal device that is motivated by its ability to capture universal generalizations about stress rules should provide clearer and more insightful accounts of complex individual stress systems. This is the case with the present analysis. We originally proposed a theory of extrametricality rules to account for three very general phenomena: the restriction of certain foot templates to final position, the frequent need for differing criteria in determining the weight of final syllables, and the asymmetry in "avoidance clauses" such as the one governing Hopi stress. Once adopted, the new device led quite directly to a more insightful account of the English stress pattern.

## Notes

Many thanks to Morris Halle, Paul Kiparsky, S. Jay Keyser, Alan Prince, and many others for their advice and help. The research reported here was supported in part by an NSF Graduate Fellowship.

1   In this respect extrametricality differs crucially from the notion of "stripping" developed in Lee (1969, 1975).

2   The templates of (16) contain information that is in fact redundant under the theory: given a (left/right) branching foot, it is in general true that the optional branches are the (right/left) ones, that only the (right/left) nodes may be restricted to the less prominent category, and that labeling will usually be (s w/w s). Justification for these claims may be found in Hayes 1981.

## References

Chomsky, N. and M. Halle. 1968. *The Sound Pattern of English*. New York: Harper and Row.

Halle, M. and J.-R. Vergnaud. 1978. Metrical Structures in Phonology. Unpublished MS, MIT.

Harris, J. 1983. *Syllable Structure and Stress in Spanish: A Nonlinear Analysis*. Cambridge, Mass.: MIT Press.

Hayes, B. 1981. A Metrical Theory of Stress Rules, Ph.D. dissertation, MIT. Revised version distributed by Indiana University Linguistics Club, Bloomington, Ind.

Hyman, L. 1977. On the Nature of Linguistic Stress. In L. Hyman (ed.), *Studies in Stress and Accent*, Southern California Occasional Papers in Linguistics 4, Los Angeles: USC.

Jeanne, L. 1978. Aspects of Hopi Grammar. Ph.D. dissertation, MIT.

Lee, G. 1969. English Word-Stress. In R. Binnick, A. Davison, G. Green, and J. Morgan (eds), *Papers from the Fifth Regional Meeting of the Chicago Linguistics Society*, Chicago: University of Chicago Press, 389–406.

Lee, G. 1975. English Word Stress and Phrase Stress. In D. Goyvaerts and G. Pullum (eds), *Essays on the Sound Pattern of English*, Ghent: Story-Scientia, 219–47.

Liberman, M. and A. Prince. 1977. On Stress and Linguistic Rhythm. *Linguistic Inquiry* 8, 249–336. [Repr. here in part as ch. 20]

McCarthy, J. 1979a. Formal Problems in Semitic Phonology and Morphology, Ph.D. dissertation, MIT.

McCarthy, J. 1979b. On Stress and Syllabification. *Linguistic Inquiry* 10, 443–66.

Nanni, D. 1977. Stressing Words in *-Ative*. *Linguistic Inquiry* 8, 752–63.

Prince, A. 1980. A Metrical Theory for Estonian Quantity. *Linguistic Inquiry* 11, 511–62.

Selkirk, E. O. 1980. The Role of Prosodic Categories in English Word Stress. *Linguistic Inquiry* 11, 563–605.

Steriade, D. 1979. Degenerate Syllables and the Accentual System of Ancient Greek. Unpublished MS, MIT.

# Index

NOTE: Page numbers in bold indicate a whole paper. Page numbers followed by *n* indicate information is to be found in a note.